25.00

W9-CMB-960

A Variorum Commentary on

the Poems of John Milton

MERRITT Y. HUGHES
General Editor

THE COMPLETE SERIES

The Latin and Greek Poems
  Douglas Bush

The Italian Poems
  J. E. Shaw and A. Bartlett Giamatti

The Minor English Poems
  A. S. P. Woodhouse and Douglas Bush

Paradise Lost
  Merritt Y. Hughes

Paradise Regained
  Walter MacKellar

Samson Agonistes
  William R. Parker and John M. Steadman

English Prosody
  Edward R. Weismiller

A Variorum Commentary on

The Poems of
John Milton

Volume One

THE LATIN AND GREEK POEMS
DOUGLAS BUSH

THE ITALIAN POEMS
J. E. SHAW *and* A. BARTLETT GIAMATTI

New York
COLUMBIA UNIVERSITY PRESS

First published 1970 by
Columbia University Press, New York
International Standard Book Number: 0 231 08879 5
Library of Congress catalog card number: 70 129962
Printed in Great Britain

Publication of this VARIORUM COMMENTARY
ON THE POEMS OF JOHN MILTON was made possible by funds granted by the Carnegie Corporation
of New York. That Corporation is not, however,
the author, owner, or proprietor of this publication,
and is not to be understood as approving by virtue
of its grant any of the statements made or views
expressed therein.

Preface

MERRITT Y. HUGHES

General Editor

This attempt to provide a variorum edition of critical commentary on the complete poems of Milton was commissioned by the interested section of the Modern Language Association of America at its meeting in December 1949, after a survey among the members by the late J. Milton French of Rutgers University. If he had not declined the honour, he would have been named the general editor. In consultation with him the original editorial board was established. Without dipping further into history, it may be said that *Samson Agonistes* was handled by the late William R. Parker of Indiana University whose work will be finished by John M. Steadman of the Huntington Library, that *Paradise Regained* is being treated by Walter MacKellar of New York University, *Paradise Lost* by the general editor, the minor English poems by the late A. S. P. Woodhouse of the University of Toronto and Douglas Bush of Harvard University, and the prosody of all the English poems by Edward R. Weismiller of George Washington University. Douglas Bush's commentary on the Latin and Greek poems, his original assignment, is the first to be published; along with it is the commentary on the Italian poems by the late James E. Shaw of the University of Toronto, whose work has been brought up to date by A. Bartlett Giamatti of Yale University. Advisory members of the board are Geoffrey Bullough of the University of London and B. A. Wright, formerly of the University of Southampton.

Publication of the projected variorum commentary was undertaken jointly by the Columbia University Press and Routledge & Kegan Paul, with the aid of a generous grant from the Carnegie Foundation. It was agreed that it was neither necessary nor feasible to include another text, that all texts should be those of the Columbia edition of Milton's works. No attempt has been made to supplement its textual notes, but we have not hesitated to discuss variant readings wherever critical questions hinge upon them.

The last variorum edition was that of H. J. Todd, which first appeared in 1801. The valuable work of Todd's predecessors is fully described in Ants Oras' *Milton's Editors and Commentators from Patrick Hume to Henry John Todd (1695–1801)* (Tartu, 1931). Editions and scholarly and critical writings of the nineteenth and twentieth centuries have been listed in several bibliographies: David H. Stevens' *Reference Guide to Milton from 1800 to the Present Day* (University of Chicago, 1930); a supplement by Professor Harris F. Fletcher, *Contributions to a Milton Bibliography, 1800–1930* (University of Illinois, 1931); and Professor Calvin Huckabay's *John Milton: A Bibliographical Supplement, 1929–1957* (Duquesne University, 1960; rev. ed. forthcoming). There are also the annual bibliographies that appear in *Publications of the Modern Language Association of America* and *Studies in Philology*, and the *Annual Bibliography* of the Modern Humanities Research Association.

The bulk of Miltonic scholarship and criticism has grown so enormously since Todd (who included only scraps of what might be called criticism) that his successors, more than a century and a half later, are beset with problems of selection and condensation. The problems of line-by-line annotation have been both eased and aggravated by a succession of modern editors, from David Masson and A. W. Verity to the present, and by the great advances in our knowledge of the seventeenth century and the traditions it inherited. While the chief end is interpretative criticism, the larger part of a variorum commentary must necessarily be given to supplying information of all kinds, from the history and meaning of words to the history and meaning of ideas. Our object in this work is to furnish a body of variorum notes and discussions uniting all available scholarly illlumination of the texts on all levels from the semantic and syntactical to those of deliberate or unconscious echoes of other works in all the languages known to Milton. In notes on the longer passages we have considered their inner rhetorical organization and involvements in the design of the poem as a whole, in the backgrounds of the literary traditions of which they themselves are outstanding developments, and in the many aspects of Milton's interests—theological, cosmological, hexameral, historical, psychological, and so on. In the headnotes to the shorter poems and in the introductions to the longer ones we have treated matters of dating and the circumstances of composition as far as sound evidence permits. And in the introductions to the longer poems we have tried to present the continuing and active discussion of the major problems of theme and artistry in conjunction with our notes on the relevant passages.

Madison, Wisconsin
16 March 1970

PREFACE TO VOLUME 1

DOUGLAS BUSH

Some procedures followed in this volume are explained at the end of the Introduction.

I am grateful to the University of Illinois Press and Professor Harris F. Fletcher for being allowed the use of proofs of his *Intellectual Development of John Milton*, vol. 2, and for the same beneficence to the Clarendon Press and the late William R. Parker with respect to his *Milton*. I am indebted to the American Council of Learned Societies and to the Harvard Graduate Society for Advanced Study for grants which have covered many miscellaneous expenses. I owe much, as in the past, to the staff of the Harvard libraries and, in the summer, to the Dartmouth College Library.

Contents

Contents

Contents

THE ITALIAN POEMS

THE LATIN AND GREEK POEMS

Introduction

※

Among the large store of Latin verse written in England from the Middle Ages up to, say, Landor, only Milton's poems, or a few of them, can be said to have remained generally known to students of English literature. They have escaped the common oblivion because of their authorship, their autobiographical value, the illustrative quality of all the poems and the intrinsic vitality of some. Without them we should have a much poorer understanding of the evolving character, sensibility, ambitions, and artistic equipment of the young poet. Further, because Milton accepted so whole-heartedly the discipline and the aims of the orthodox Renaissance scholar-poet, his saturation in the Latin language and poetic technique had its effects upon his English poetry early and late. Thus for several reasons Milton's Latin verse is a far more central part of the canon than the Latin verse of such contemporaries as George Herbert or Crashaw or Marvell (not to mention Phineas Fletcher and Cowley and others). It is also a relatively bulky portion of Milton's minor poetry; the *Poems* of 1645 contained some 195 pages of text, 120 of English (and Italian), 74 of Latin (1,650 lines), and 1½ of Greek; with the pieces added in 1673 and items not included in either edition, the total of Latin verse is just short of 1,800 lines.

Introductions to the individual poems take up unavoidable problems of dating and say something of their themes and formal character and of what they contribute to our picture of the developing poet. Here only some general comments and illustrations can be offered.

Although Milton's Latin verse has come to occupy a unique niche, he was at the start only doing, and doing better than others, what generations of college poets did before and after him. Since the writing of Latin verse was a part of formal education, and since all students were at least bilingual, Latin verse—much less often Greek—was

3

written by a multitude of young men as a natural extension of their academic exercises; few of them could have achieved respectable English verse, but Latin, like death, was a mighty leveler. Births, marriages, and deaths in the royal family, the death of national or academic personages, and public events automatically inspired poems and anthologies from the nests of singing or croaking birds in Cambridge and Oxford. Turning over Milton's earlier Latin pieces, we see that, as long as bishops and beadles were subject to mortality, the young craftsman did not lack a subject.

But the importance of Latin verse was rarely apparent in the effusions of university students. The great mass of Neo-Latin verse and prose, apart from such works as *Utopia* and some of Erasmus', has long sunk below the general and even the scholarly horizon, yet in Milton's earlier days Latin still was, in a much diminished degree, what it had been for centuries, the language of literature as well as of learning. The great age of Neo-Latin verse was the late fifteenth and the earlier sixteenth centuries, and—not to mention the lesser poets of the old and big collections—the Italian Poliziano, Pontano, Mantuan, Sannazaro, Castiglione, Vida, and others, and the Dutch Secundus and the Scottish George Buchanan, had a European reputation which remained more or less strong in the seventeenth century. In that century few Neo-Latin poets of comparable fame appeared, though Grotius—like Milton, a signal example of precocity—was one, and Casimir Sarbiewski, the 'Polish Horace' or 'Christian Horace,' was another. But while literature in the vernaculars was now crowding Latin to the wall, we remember Bacon's feeling that these modern languages would play the bankrupts with books, and Milton's account, in *The Reason of Church-Government* (1642), of his having to choose between the claims of Latin and English. One reason that bore heavily upon an ambitious English author Milton made clear in that passage and in the earlier *Epitaphium Damonis* (lines 168–78): that to write in English was to have no readers outside Britain, instead of winning the European audience craved by a poet like Milton, who was so highly conscious of being the heir of the European tradition. Apart from Buchanan, the only poets of British birth who achieved

4

continental fame were John Owen and John Barclay: and when Milton did, proudly, gain a European hearing, it was through his controversial Latin prose.

Milton decided, happily, in favor of his native language, but it was in Latin that he first learned the elements of his art; and—whatever he might have been without such training—he emerged at 21, in the *Nativity*, as an accomplished, sure-footed master of form and style in English. By the date of that poem, Christmas, 1629, he had written probably all of the *Elegiarum Liber* except *Elegy* 6 (which came within a few days after the *Nativity*) and some epigrams, and a good part of the *Sylvarum Liber*—two obituary poems, the small epic on the Gunpowder Plot, *In quintum Novembris*, and probably the two philosophical pieces akin to academic prolusions, *Naturam non pati senium* and *De Idea Platonica*. Later, probably in 1631–2, during his last year at Cambridge, Milton wrote *Ad Patrem*, telling his generous father that he must be a poet and not be encumbered by a gainful employment (the choice of Latin for such a poem was a delicate compliment to the father's humane interests and a reminder of the literary education he had provided for his son). In 1638–9, when the *Nativity* and *L'Allegro* and *Il Penseroso* and *Comus* and *Lycidas* were behind him, Milton's Italian travels and association with Italian scholars and poets evoked a group of Latin pieces, the epigrams on Leonora Baroni and the poems to Salsilli and his Neapolitan host, Manso. In the latter Milton first set forth his plan for a British epic, and this was elaborated in 1639–40 in the *Epitaphium Damonis*. A last and isolated piece—if we neglect the satirical epigrams of 1651 and 1654—was the epistolary ode to John Rouse, librarian of the Bodleian, apropos of a lost copy of Milton's *Poems*. Thus most of his Latin poems were occasional. All of them, being Milton's, have their degree of interest. The most important, as documents or poems or both, are the two intimate epistles to Diodati (*Elegies* 1 and 6), the second of which declares his high conception of the poet-priest; the epistle to his old tutor, Thomas Young (*Elegy* 4), in which, as critics have remarked, the embryo Puritan appears; the two springtime poems, *Elegies* 7 and 5, which—especially the latter—reveal the young Puritan's sensuous intensity; the small epic, 'an epyllion, a mock-epyllion,' in E. K. Rand's phrase, which in retrospect can be said to contain a first crude sketch of Satan; *Mansus*; and what has commonly been regarded as Milton's crowning achievement in Latin verse, the deeply felt elegy on Diodati; and some would add the two philosophical pieces, which show the young thinker as a modernist in the debate over the supposed decay of nature and as an ardent Platonist in the much older debate between Platonism and Aristotelianism.

For Milton's early devotion to Ovid one must quote the familiar words from the *Apology for Smectymnuus* (1642) in which he looked back upon

the smooth Elegiack Poets, whereof the Schooles are not scarce. Whom both for the pleasing sound of their numerous writing, which in imitation I found most easie; and most agreeable to natures part in me, and for their matter which what it is, there be few who know not, I was so allur'd to read, that no recreation came to me better welcome. (*Works* 3, 302.)

And although, as he went on to report, he turned away from the sensual world of the Roman elegy to the amatory idealism of the Christian Dante and Petrarch, he still applauded the art of the Romans. That continuing influence, of Ovid especially, is borne out by editorial annotations of even the later Latin poems (and there were echoes of Ovid, mainly from the *Metamorphoses*, in the late as well as the early English poetry). It is needless to add that, though his sexual susceptibility is so strongly evident (and was to be in *Paradise Lost*), Milton has nothing of the salty sensuality which, in a number of Neo-Latin poets, may have its place along with religious devotions; but his seriousness and frequent exaltation could accommodate the genial, humorous, and witty. The phrase 'most agreeable to natures part in me'—in other words, 'most attractive to my native gifts and my merely natural and human self as distinguished from the self that belongs to the world of grace'—suggests how Milton's Latin verse could express the natural boy and young man, the normal impulses and experience that are less manifest in the predominantly religious and ethical English poetry.

While he could experiment up to the last (witness the ode to Rouse), Milton did not set out, like most of the famous Neo-Latinists, to write in all the classical and neoclassical genres and in a wide variety of metres. His two divisions, *Elegiarum Liber* and *Sylvarum Liber*, fell far short of the customary range, although these groups included a number of epistles and obituary poems, some epigrams, the miniature epic, and the two philosophical disquisitions (one in serio-comic vein). Milton worked almost wholly in two metres. The *Elegiarum Liber* is of course in the elegiac metre of his early favorites, Ovid, Propertius, and Tibullus. The chief poems of the other group—*In quintum Novembris, Naturam non pati senium, Ad Patrem, Mansus*, and *Epitaphium Damonis*—are in hexameters. Although the best elegies show an assured ease, with no sign of constraint, Milton found in the hexameter, says Leicester Bradner,

a much more suitable medium for his use. In the short sentences required by couplets his great gift for the expansive poetical paragraphs was allowed no room for development. . . Furthermore, the shift in form implies a shift in models. It meant bringing up in his mind the firmer, narrative tone of the *Metamorphoses* instead of the softness of the *Amores* and *Tristia*; and above all it meant the example of Vergil. There is a new seriousness in the three poems we have just been discussing [*Ad Patrem, Mansus, Epitaphium*], a feeling that they are poetry in their own right and not youthful pastime, no matter how well done.[1]

In its very nature, and because scholarly knowledge was the only prerequisite for writing it, the huge mass of Renaissance Latin verse may seem the most artificial and conventional verse ever turned out. To moderns not historically minded, it may all look like a colossal anachronism, a Sahara from which dry neoclassical winds carried dust over into vernacular writing. Yet for Renaissance humanists—as for countless medieval writers—it was a thoroughly natural medium and, even if it was predestined to die as the modern literatures grew, it had its share, along with ancient literature, in civilizing and refining taste, and in sustaining

[1] Leicester Bradner, *Musae Anglicanae: A History of Anglo-Latin Poetry 1500–1925* (New York, 1940), 116.

the continuity and universality of European culture.[2] And, though it stood far below the higher levels of classical poetry, it reflected in part the modern world of its many writers and readers. Neo-Latin poets sought not only to imitate the ancients in subject matter, attitude, and manner, but to adapt ancient idiom to modern subjects, to write about their own world as an ancient—or a Christianized ancient—might have written. What the writer had the pleasure of restoring or remoulding, the reader had the pleasure of recognizing—antique jewels in new settings, and more or less original imitations of the antique. If most of these imitations were only paste of varying quality, and often had few virtues beyond elegance or correctness (a more rigorous standard than medieval Latin poets had set themselves), the better poets in their better moments could achieve authentic poetry or at least agreeable verse.

As a poet in English, Milton very early demonstrated his instinct for working within an established convention and his ability to transcend and re-create it. In the Latin verse, for the most part the product of his immaturity (from his eighteenth to his twenty-second year), he was somewhat more content to stay within the convention, although even his thinnest exercises may have some bold touches, some hints of the harmonious Miltonic vision, and the better poems may be real poetry. The Milton who wrote most of the Latin verse was much younger than the famous Renaissance Neo-Latinists commonly were when they produced the main body of their work. He was not more learnedly familiar

[2] Some broad surveys are: F. A. Wright and T. A. Sinclair, *A History of Later Latin Literature from the Middle of the Fourth to the End of the Seventeenth Century* (London and New York, 1931); Paul van Tieghem, *La Littérature latine de la renaissance; étude d'histoire littéraire européenne* (Paris, 1944); Frederic J. E. Raby, *A History of Secular Latin Poetry in the Middle Ages* (2 v. Oxford, 1934); F. J. E. Raby, *A History of Christian-Latin Poetry from the Beginnings to the Close of the Middle Ages* (2d ed. Oxford, 1953); Leo Spitzer, 'The Problem of Latin Renaissance Poetry,' *Studies in the Renaissance*, 2 (1955), 118–38; John Sparrow, 'Latin Verse of the High Renaissance,' *Italian Renaissance Studies*, ed. E. F. Jacob (London, 1960); James E. Phillips and Don C. Allen, *Neo-Latin Poetry of the Sixteenth & Seventeenth Centuries* (Los Angeles, 1965); W. Leonard Grant, *Neo-Latin Literature and the Pastoral* (Chapel Hill, 1965), assembling his articles of the previous decade.

For England, see Bradner (n. 1 above) and his 'Supplemental List' (*Library* 22, 1967, 93–103); and Wolfgang Mann, *Lateinische Dichtung in England vom Ausgang des Frühhumanismus bis zum Regierungsantritt Elisabeths* (Halle, 1939).

than they with ancient and modern Latin, but he was, even in youth, far more richly endowed (for that matter, more richly endowed than the ancients, with one possible exception), and his greater personality and power asserted themselves. It is a commonplace that he revealed his own feelings much more fully and intimately in his early Latin than in his early English poems; in the latter, while there was much indirect self-revelation, he seems to have held from the beginning the classical ideal of impersonal objectivity (to use 'classical' in its broad and timeless sense). In Latin, although Milton, like his famous predecessors, is conscious of the varying demands of decorum, one may hazard the impressionistic opinion that he cannot be said, like them, or in their degree, to have developed a characteristic and consistent style and tone. In most of his Latin verse he is too individual or too modern in his themes and material, too little concerned with reproducing antique or pseudo-antique attitudes and atmosphere, and too eclectic in his diction and idiom. He is not so much a sedulous ape as a young poet who happens to be expressing himself in Latin. Even his early saturation in Ovid did not make his style markedly Ovidian, except at moments. To emphasize the relative actuality and authenticity of Milton's Latin poems (if such words can embrace his sense of heaven as well as of earth and man) is doubtless to exaggerate a kind and degree of difference that needs qualification on both sides. Such virtues were not absent from other practitioners, and Milton's personal force and flavor went along with the imitation that was the *sine qua non* of Neo-Latin writing.

Critical opinion, which has naturally been preoccupied with Milton's English poetry, has always stressed the artistic skill of his best Latin verse, and in the later nineteenth and the twentieth century has shown an added awareness of rarer and more positive virtues. Dr Johnson endorsed the judgment 'that Milton was the first Englishman who, after the revival of letters, wrote Latin verses with classick elegance.'[3] Landor, while finding many faults, declared in his Landorian way that Milton's

---

[3] *Lives of the English Poets*, ed. G. B. Hill (3 v. Oxford, 1905), 1, 87. Testimonies from Johnson, Landor, Coleridge, Pattison, Masson, and E. K. Rand are quoted by MacKellar, *Latin Poems of John Milton* (New Haven, 1930), 18–19.

Latin verse had 'single sentences..., ay, single images, worth all that our island had produced before.'[4] Coleridge thought that, if the poems had come down to us as written in the age of Tiberius, they would have been considered very beautiful.[5] Leigh Hunt, in the first of several essays, said he preferred Milton's 'Latin poetry, *as poetry*, to any thing in the miscellaneous productions of Ovid, Tibullus, or any other Latin writer, except Catullus.'[6] Mark Pattison's verdict is representative of modern opinion (though other Neo-Latin poets could at times achieve 'real emotion'):

Milton's Latin verses are distinguished from most Neo-Latin verse by being a vehicle of real emotion. His technical skill is said to have been surpassed by others; but that in which he stands alone is, that in these exercises of imitative art he is able to remain himself, and to give utterance to genuine passion.[7]

We cannot here go into the training and tools supplied by Milton's formal education: these have been concretely studied by Donald L. Clark (*John Milton at St. Paul's School*, New York, 1948) and Harris F. Fletcher (*The Intellectual Development of John Milton*, Urbana, 1 and 2, 1956 and 1961); and, from a special angle, by Davis P. Harding (*Milton*

---

[4] 'Southey and Landor,' *Complete Works*, ed. T. E. Welby (12 v. London, 1927–31), 5, 332.

[5] *Table Talk* (London, 1835), 2, 270; *Coleridge's Miscellaneous Criticism*, ed. T. M. Raysor (Cambridge, Mass., 1936), 431; *Coleridge on the Seventeenth Century*, ed. R. F. Brinkley (Durham, N.C., 1955; cited hereafter as 'Brinkley'), 552.

[6] 'On the Latin Poems of Milton,' *Literary Examiner*, 30 August 1823, 130; *Leigh Hunt's Literary Criticism*, ed. L. H. and C. W. Houtchens (New York, 1956), 178.

[7] *Milton* (London and New York, 1879), 41. Some later and fuller discussions are: E. K. Rand, 'Milton in Rustication,' *SP* 19 (1922), 109–35; K. C. M. Sills, 'Milton's Latin Poems,' *Classical Journal* 32 (1936–7), 417–23; L. Bradner (see n. 1 above); W. H. Semple, 'The Latin Poems of John Milton,' *Bulletin of The John Rylands Library* 46 (1963), 217–35; D. C. Allen, 'Milton as a Latin Poet' (1965: see Phillips and Allen, n. 2 above). Important critical comment appears in J. H. Hanford, 'The Youth of Milton' (1925: see below, *El* 1, headnote, n. 7), E. M. W. Tillyard, *Milton* (London and New York, 1930), and A. S. P. Woodhouse, 'Notes on Milton's Early Development,' *UTQ* 13 (1943–4), 66–101. Two more special studies are: F. R. B. Godolphin, 'Notes on the Technique of Milton's Latin Elegies,' *MP* 37 (1939–40), 351–6, and W. R. Parker, 'Notes on the Chronology of Milton's Latin Poems' (1952: see below, *El* 1, headnote, n. 5). Parker's massive *Milton: A Biography* (2 v. Oxford, 1968), which of course includes general comments on the Latin poems and discussions of dates, etc., is cited throughout simply as 'Parker.' Milton's Latin elegies are studied in unpublished dissertations by Stanley Koehler and Virginia M. Chaney (see n. 12 below).

and the Renaissance Ovid, Urbana, 1946: cited hereafter as *Ovid*). But one question must be raised, although no real answer can be given: that is, how far, in writing his earlier Latin poems, Milton consulted or remembered any of the various phrase-books, such as those of Johannes Buchler and Ravisius Textor, which were recommended for young verse-makers and were widely used (Clark, 205). We have no way of knowing how Milton worked, and it would be quite impossible to load annotations with phrases that could have been drawn from the manuals. However, it may serve as a concrete illustration of growth in independence if we look for a minute at *Epithetorum Ioann. Ravisii Textoris Epitome* (London, 1595). Milton as a boy may have used the little book, or others like it, but it is taken here only as a representative compilation of common nouns with lists of appropriate epithets. In the 20 lines of *Carmina Elegiaca* (*Works* 1, 326), which Milton presumably wrote at school and did not print among his poems, there are twenty-two nouns that have adjectives; seventeen of these nouns are in the *Epitome*, and of these eleven or more have one of the epithets listed.[8] To take *Elegy* 6 of 1629 for random comparison, it has some eighty-nine nouns with adjectives, and seventy-four of these nouns are in Textor; but only nine times does Milton use one of Textor's epithets.[9] Even if Milton never saw the book, the difference indicates much greater originality of both phrasing and idea. Of course, as we have observed already, no Neo-Latin poet escaped, or wished to escape, the use of classical and sanctified phrases.

A related question cannot be answered either. The full editions of Textor's *Epitheta* (e.g. 1602, 1606) not only listed epithets under common and proper nouns but quoted a line from an ancient or modern poet to illustrate each. It is possible that in some instances, where

---

[8] These are: *leves somnos, tepidi tori, excubitor gallus, Flammiger Titan, nitidum iubar, rosa siluestris, fragrantes odores, vitreo rore, molli lecto, languentes somnos, tabifici morbi*. Besides, *laetum* (*laeta arva*, line 6) is listed in Textor under *Gramen*, not *Arvum*; *excultum* (*excultos modos*, 8) is listed under *Carmen*, not under *Moduli*; *imbellis* (*imbellis sopor*, 14) under *Somnus*, not *Sopor*.

[9] The nine cases are: *virides corymbos* (15), *dulcia carmina* (35), *festa chorea* (44), *tenellus Amor* (52), *puro fonte* (62), *freta longa* (72), *sanguine nigro* (75), *sacer vates* (77).

Milton seems to be combining phrases from many quarters, he had such a useful collection at hand. Yet many cases do not seem to admit of that explanation, and it may be that few if any are to be thus explained. One may reasonably assume that so ardent and so gifted a poet as Milton would acquire most of his language from poetry and not, unless at moments, from such helps. At any rate it would, again, be out of the question to indicate in the present annotations what quoted lines and phrases appear in Textor, not to mention other books of the sort.

When his earliest poems were written, Milton already knew a fair amount of Greek, and he might use Homer and Hesiod in particular, but naturally in Latin verse Greek lore appeared in the Latin costume it had long since acquired. There are two external guides to Milton's early reading in Latin and Greek, the program of authors read in school and those cited in his academic prolusions and early letters; but these do not take us very far. Whatever the aid given by the imposed tasks of pedagogical routine, by the close rhetorical analysis of the classroom, by dictionaries and thesauri of various kinds, and by the presumed stores of a private phrase-book, anyone who can get through, or even dip into, the annotations on the Latin poems must conclude that the young man had carried his studies well beyond the exacting requirements of humanistic education, that he had observed and assimilated technical minutiae, and that he had an extraordinary mass of Latin poetry in his head. If one may rely on a general impression of the bulk of probably borrowed and adapted phrases (and the nature of the case forbids anything but a guess), Milton's chief creditors are Ovid (the whole corpus), then Virgil, then Propertius, Tibullus, Horace, Catullus, and Seneca, in a bunch; but he seems to draw, in varying degrees, upon the whole range of ancient poets from Plautus through Lucretius and Persius and Juvenal and Martial to such writers of now faded lustre as Statius, Silius Italicus, Valerius Flaccus, and Claudian. Among the Neo-Latinists, a debt to Buchanan has long been recognized; it is clear in *In quintum Novembris*, less clear in the springtime and amatory elegies. A few other modern poets or poems have been occasionally cited by editors, such as Vida (whose *Christiad* Milton alluded to in *The Passion*, line 26) and Castiglione's elegy *Alcon*. Milton's apparent adaptation of a line from Sannazaro (see the note on *El* 5. 121–2 and also the note on *El* 1. 21–2) makes plausible other parallels with that poet.

Over stock phrases we do not need to linger, except to remark that the majority are found in Latin poetry at large and that some are recognizably Ovidian mannerisms. Variations on common phrases appear even in the youthful and stereotyped *Carmina Elegiaca*: such variations may be seen anywhere in Milton's Latin verse. A large number of notes have to do with phrases which, however familiar many of them might be to early readers, cannot be called commonplaces; on these too Milton works variations, often blending items from various sources in a *callida iunctura*. We need not ask whether he actually borrowed, consciously or unconsciously; it is enough for our purpose that his phrases are there and can be compared with phrases in ancient and later poets. For a simple instance, one of the most familiar Virgilian tags is the onomatopoeic *quadrupedante putrem sonitu quatit ungula campum* (*A.* 8. 596), which editors cite in connection with Milton's *Cornea pulvereum dum verberat ungula campum* (*El* 4. 119). His variation may have been suggested by the less familiar Silius Italicus 6. 217, *cornea gramineum persultans ungula campum* (and cf. Lucan 6. 83, *Ungula frondentem discussit cornea campum*).

Two examples of epic feeling and tone occur together, perhaps not without conscious hyperbole, in the most unlikely of contexts, Milton's cries of pain after his momentary sight of a girl whose beauty had set him on fire. The first is a reference to Zeus's throwing Hera's son Hephaestus out of heaven (*El* 7. 81–2):

> Sic dolet amissum proles Junonia coelum,
> Inter Lemniacos praecipitata focos.

We have here little of the elaborate picture and rhythms of the famous lines on Mulciber in *Paradise Lost* (1. 740–6), but the distich is in its way a no less serious and 'romantic' version of Homeric comedy (*Il.* 1. 590–4), especially in the phrase *amissum coelum* from a poet whose imagination is always taking flight to heaven. Then comes another example of lost light and life:

Talis & abreptum solem respexit, ad Orcum
Vectus ab attonitis Amphiaraus equis.

The story of the Greek seer's being swept below the earth by Zeus is
striking enough, and Milton by his dramatic compression improves on
Statius (*Th.* 7. 820–4), whom editors quote:

> rectos defert in Tartara currus
> respexitque cadens caelum campumque coire
> ingemuit, donec levior distantia rursus
> miscuit arva tremor lucemque exclusit Averno.

And the theme draws in other phrases, the *Amphiaraus equis* that ends
both Ovid, *P.* 3. 1. 52, and Propertius 3. 13. 58, and Ovid's glance at the
stricken Hippolytus, *ab attonitis excutiaris equis* (*Ibis* 578). Many notes
illustrate Milton's possible fusion of phrases, images, and ideas from the
most diverse quarters, his instinct for combining, compressing, expanding, and varying common allusions. On the line *Nec me (crede mihi)*
terrent Semelëia fata (*El* 5. 91) D. P. Harding remarks: '*Semelëia fata*
is the precursor of such highly condensed expressions in *Paradise Lost*
as "Atlantean shoulders," "Typhoean rage," and "Circean call"'[10]—
and one might add 'all that pain.'

The pleasure of recognizing an ancient jewel in a new setting is sometimes attended by something of a shock because of the radical and even
violent change it has undergone. One notorious instance is the last line
of *El* 3, on Bishop Andrewes: *Talia contingant somnia saepe mihi.* Warton,
Landor, and E. K. Rand are among those who have observed the young
poet's audacity in applying to his vision of the dead bishop in heaven
what Rand calls 'a wish from one of Ovid's most unblushing rhapsodies
on a golden day with Corinna': *proveniant medii sic mihi saepe dies!*
(*Am.* 1. 5. 26).[11] Milton also apparently remembered the partly similar
wish of Tibullus (1. 1. 48): *hoc mihi contingat.*

---

[10] *The Club of Hercules: Studies in the Classical Background of Paradise Lost* (Urbana, 1962),
14.
[11] T. Warton, ed., *Poems upon Several Occasions...by John Milton* (2nd ed. rev. London,
1791); Landor, *Works* 5, 325; Rand, *SP* 19 (1922), 133.

The adaptation of specifically pagan images and phrases to Christian uses and contexts had been one of the conspicuous neo-pagan features of Renaissance Ciceronianism, but the practice was universal, and was carried on in entire good faith, among poets in the vernaculars as well as in Latin; two great exemplars are Spenser and Milton. For writers of Latin verse, at least if they were classical purists in language, such a practice was a virtual necessity; but most of them were not purists, and certainly not Milton. While he utilized pagan images and phrases for Christian ideas (for a few random examples, see the notes on *El* 3. 59, *El* 4. 111, and *Mansus* 93–100), he also echoed the Bible, sometimes, apparently, the translation of Tremellius, Junius, and Beza which he later used for his theological treatise. Among all the books of the Bible probably none supplied such a proportion of images, in his English poems early and late, as Revelation, and the Latin poems also have their glimpses of the heavenly city—which may be Olympus, with a difference. The most startling example of the fusion of pagan and Christian comes at the end of the *Epitaphium Damonis*: whereas in the corresponding climactic vision of *Lycidas* (172–81) the imagery is almost entirely from Revelation, in the Latin elegy the Biblical is almost submerged in the Dionysiac revels of Zion.

The poetic technique of Milton's seven elegies has been concretely analyzed by Stanley Koehler in an unpublished dissertation,[12] and his findings may be briefly summarized. (His evidence must of course be left out, but some particular comments are cited in the notes below.)

---

[12] 'Milton and the Roman Elegists: A Study of Milton's Latin Poems in their Relation to the Latin Love Elegy', Princeton University, 1941 (208 pages): 'Produced by Microfilm-Xerography by University Microfilms, Ann Arbor, Michigan, 1967' (cited hereafter as 'Koehler').

I have also read Virginia M. Chaney, 'The Elegies of George Buchanan in relation to those of the Roman Elegists and to the Latin Elegies of John Milton', Vanderbilt University, 1961 (288 pages): 'Produced by Microfilm-Xerography by University Microfilms, Ann Arbor, Michigan, 1967.' Miss Chaney gives a descriptive account (35–96) of Buchanan's elegies, a list of parallels between them and the Roman elegies (97–152), a description of Milton's elegies, with references to the Romans (153–207), and a comparison of Buchanan and Milton (208–43). Most of her citations had been noted by commentators and all except one (see *Patrem* 105 n.) had been recorded in my notes some years before her thesis was written.

After discussing the resemblances and more obvious differences in content between the Roman poems and Milton's, Koehler examines (82–127) a sampling of the diction of the elegies, using as a basis other scholars' studies of the relative colloquialism of the Roman elegists in contrast with the elevation of the *Aeneid*. He concludes (127) that what colloquial words Milton uses 'are distributed throughout the Latin poetry, there being no marked difference in this respect between Milton's Latin elegies and poems that belong theoretically to a higher level of style.' We should not, however, necessarily assume inadequate sophistication in the young poet, since

the relative infrequency of the colloquial terms throughout the Latin poetry, and the appropriateness with which they are used when they do appear, indicate that Milton was not unaware of their nature. And in this case, if we use the word Vergilian in its broader sense, as indicating the dignified and conservative manner of epic as contrasted with the less formal, and often conversational style of the elegy, we may say that an educated Roman of the Augustan Age would, even in the seven elegies, have found Milton's Latin more Vergilian than Ovidian in tone.

This last judgment may be thought very questionable: it rests on discussion of only a small number of words and phrases, far too small to yield any general assessment of style and tone, and some of the 'Vergilian' items are not peculiar to Virgil and the epic style.

Indeed Koehler himself, in the third part of his thesis (131–201), on versification, shows that, not merely in the metrics of the elegiac couplet, but in a variety of rhetorical devices, Milton studiously follows Ovid, Propertius, and Tibullus—as of course we should expect from his avowed devotion to 'the smooth Elegiack Poets'. And, while in the substance of his elegies Milton shunned the sensual motives of the Romans and treated the erotic only in innocent ways, no moral or religious scruples cooled the devotion to 'their art' that he also avowed. Thus Milton eagerly studied and exploited the rhetorical and metrical techniques of the Romans, adapting their practice to his own instincts and preferences. He unfailingly observed two prime rules of the elegiac distich: 'no substitution of spondee for dactyl in the fifth foot of the hexameter...nor in the second half of the pentameter line, which must be wholly composed of dactyls' (Koehler, 131). F. R. B. Godolphin (see n. 7 above) showed that Milton followed Propertius and Ovid in the placing of the caesura at the fifth half-foot of the hexameter (over 90 per cent in the two Romans and Milton). He observed strictly 'the rule that the first hemistich should always coincide with the end of a word' (Koehler, 134). Milton's use of elision is more or less normal. 'In the pentameter Milton shows himself to be closely following the practice of Ovid in the use of dissyllabic endings' (ibid. 137); his pentameters have no monosyllabic endings and only one trisyllabic one (*tenebras* in *El* 6. 4). Milton was—like Buchanan—somewhat less scrupulous in his epigrams in the elegiac metre (*Apologus* and *Ad Leonoram* 1 and 2). Going on from Godolphin, Koehler (139–50) illustrates Milton's frequent and sometimes skilful use of rhyme, both at the ends of lines and within lines and groups of lines (see, e.g., the notes below on *El* 1. 23–4, 2. 19–24, 5. 66 and 100–4); in this respect Milton is much closer to Propertius than to Ovid and Tibullus. Then he achieves various special effects, quick or slow, smooth or strident, through various combinations of dactylic and spondaic feet, short or long syntactical units, balance and repetition of words and phrases, the heaping up of long or short vowels and of soft or harsh consonants (devices so greatly employed in his English poetry). His couplets, like the Romans', are normally closed. Finally—to mention a small matter apparently not noted by Koehler— Milton reproduces a number of Ovid's verbal and rhetorical mannerisms, e.g., beginning a line with *Fallor?* (see *El* 5. 5 n.) or *Forsitan* (*El* 7. 89 n.). In short, in the elegies at least, Milton naturally follows the Roman masters and, however eclectic he may be, he is surely much closer to them than to the Virgil of the *Aeneid*.[13]

[13] The following summary of Kevin J. Aylward's dissertation, 'Milton's Latin Versification: The Hexameter' (Columbia University, 1966) is taken verbatim from *Dissertation Abstracts* 27 (November 1966), 1331–1332A:

'A study of Milton's Latin versification must consider these two questions: 1) what habits and tendencies constitute Milton's Latin prosody, and 2) to what degree does he approximate the versification of such classical Latin writers as Vergil and Ovid? Since Milton obviously was not free to improvise his own Latin prosody, the extent of his conformity to classical canons inevitably becomes the more significant question. This dissertation provides a

We have observed only a few elements in Milton's Latin verse. In general, it discloses and illustrates a good many facets of the mind and character, the sensibility and technique, of the English poet. In temper and outlook he is both the Renaissance scholar-poet and the Christian humanist; his predecessors were not always, or so positively, the latter.

full and detailed survey of Milton's hexameter versification, and also documents his approximation to classical Latin versification.

Milton's Latin versification reflects the Latinity of the sixteenth and early seventeenth centuries. The doctrine of the hexameter with which Milton was familiar is reconstructed from texts as disparate as the school grammars and rhetorics, the phrase books and other aids to ambitious verse composition, and the Latin *Poetics* of Vida, Scaliger, and Pontanus. This doctrine has some disconcerting shortcomings. Donald L. Clark and Harris F. Fletcher, among modern scholars, do not take these shortcomings into account when they discuss Milton's schooling at St. Paul's. Professors Clark and Fletcher also disregard the pointed disparagement of grammar school instruction in Latin versification by some scholars and teachers of the period.

Impressive though they sometimes are, even the ambitious *Poetics* suffered from the absence of a tradition of systematic research such as modern scholarship has developed. Their authors could not use the accumulated research of two or three previous generations to buttress or modify the traditional doctrine of the hexameter, which was really very incomplete. The modern student of metrics or the writer of Latin verse composition enjoys this convenience. Milton, no doubt, supplemented the limited contemporary doctrine by such insights as he gained from judicious and perceptive readings in classical Latin authors. Even so, the inadequacies of his guides—manuals and pretentious *Poetics* alike—probably put him at a disadvantage. In any event, his versification seems to be quite eclectic. He obviously appropriates—not always discreetly—some mannerisms from Vergil or Ovid; he also overlooks or ignores characteristics which invited attention from a perceptive reader.

Several of Milton's Latin poems exhibit distinctive, even peculiar, preferences. The early *In Quintum Novembris* is conspicuously uncertain or indiscreet in several respects. The following *Naturam Non Pati Senium* shows an arbitrary preference in elision. The *Ad Patrem* is elegiac in its avoidance of elision; it also uses one word type strangely. The *Epitaphium Damonis* includes a refrain which does not manage with complete success an unusual variety of final cadence. All these texts, as well as the *Mansus*, are indifferent to a major distinction between the versification of Vergil and that of Ovid, the initial molossic word. The *Seventh Elegy* is inept in its distribution of molossic words. The *Third Elegy* twice elides iambic words, something which Ovid never does in eleven thousand elegiac hexameters. The elegies generally do not exclude rigorously enough a variety of elision and a form of *caesura* which are not elegiac. Milton apparently does not associate the iambic word form with a sense pause as often as classical practice suggested.

It may not be fair to look to Milton for Latin verse which could anticipate with complete success the conclusions and insights of modern Latin metrics. On the other hand, any serious attempt to determine his competence at the level of versification has to reckon with the evidence which I have presented in this dissertation. In this perspective, Milton does not seem to be as correct or as traditional as we have been led to expect.

And whereas his early English poems are either 'pure poetry' or, much more often, express chiefly religious and ethical attitudes and ideas, in Latin Milton reveals not only his religious and ethical but his secular interests, both private and public. That the English poet was intensely responsive to natural and feminine beauty is amply clear, but the first and most direct revelations were made in Latin. His developing consciousness of his poetical vocation is recorded more fully in Latin than in English. We have proof of intellectual independence, if not necessarily of genius, in his rebellion against his tutor and Cambridge. We see a good deal of his continuing capacity for friendship, not only in his special attachment to Diodati and the gaieties and gravities, even the sense of dependence, that went with it, but in his feelings toward Young, Salzilli, Manso, and Rouse. We learn something of his early respect for bishops, of his views of the Church and the religious situation, of his anti-Catholic sentiments, and of his philosophical and religious optimism and his allegiance to Plato. These and other details round out a portrait that modifies what could be pieced together from Milton's early English poems and that helps to explain them.

David Daiches takes account of Milton's Latin verse in discussing his 'problem in establishing himself as a native English poet on almost too solid classical foundations.'[14] In the early Latin verse the apprentice poet naturally submitted himself most fully to classical influence. In *El* 4, addressed to his old tutor, a Presbyterian divine, there is 'something engaging and slightly comic' in Milton's display of knowledge and skill and the 'riot of classical imagery.' As for the famous *El* 5, 'Though Ovidian in style almost to the point of parody, this rapturous welcome to spring nevertheless pulses with genuine feeling. At the same time, it does not contain a single image derived from observation of the English countryside. Everything is turned into classical mythology and classical literary landscape.' [Still, Milton's senses were not unaware of the nightingale, the sun and stars, dew, grass, flowers, and soothing breezes.]

[14] 'Some Aspects of Milton's Pastoral Imagery,' *More Literary Essays* (Edinburgh and London, 1968), 96–114. Daiches' comments on the *Epitaphium Damonis* are noticed under that poem.

Whether the genuine excitement 'is about spring and the new movement of life it brings to the countryside or, as seems more likely, about his own poetic virtuosity and its promise of creativity, is debatable.' Whichever motive is primary, the two are explicitly related in *Fallor?...adest?* (5–6).

'The other Latin elegies, for all their occasional moments of personal confession, are clever exercises...' Apropos of *El* 7, Daiches queries the conventional opinion 'that the young Milton expressed in Latin feelings about sex and love that he never expressed in his English poetry' [and with the Latin verse the Italian may be linked]. But Daiches does not perhaps altogether meet that point by saying that for the young Milton a poem in Latin was 'an evident artifact' and that knowledge of Latin poetry 'was proof of art, not confession of identity of point of view.'

As artist, Milton is from the beginning a learned and conscious mixture of traditionalism and forceful originality. Even in his most youthful exercises he knows what he is doing, and in the better poems he has a disciplined instinct for organizing details into a coherent whole; the welcome of spring, for example, at first sight an outpouring of formless exuberance, proves to have an almost geometrical structure. Another Miltonic characteristic appears, at appropriate moments, in sonorous rhythms, often achieved through the manipulation of proper names (see, for instance, *Mansus* 84 and the comments quoted in the note on the line). Syntactical units may be long and elaborate (though they are often short and simple), but they very rarely lack clarity. Milton frequently uses or adapts phrases that occur in Latin poets of the Silver Age (and those of the Bronze Age as well), yet he hardly ever approaches the strained, elliptical phrasing and allusiveness of some of them. If in the early poems, more than in most Neo-Latin verse, there was an excess of mythology (perhaps a mark of Propertian influence especially), that was pruned; and it contributed to what became, in Milton's English poetry, the most controlled and inspired evocation of myth in the whole Renaissance tradition. The same thing can be said, *mutatis mutandis*, of the rhetorical texture in general; periphrasis, for example, was one mode of elevation or inflation that was conspicuous in classical and still more so in modern Latin. Milton, like most poets, had his poetic measles, but he worked off that disease of youth in Latin, so that few traces of a rash appeared in English; compare the turgid personification of Tragedy in *El* 1. 37–8 with the sober one in *Il Penseroso* 97–8. But such a general remark leaves out the considerable body of more mature Latin verse that is competent, interesting, or moving poetry, from the ecstatic celebration of spring in *El* 5 to the several ecstatic visions of heaven. We might end with one line from one of these, *Aeternaeque morae stabunt immobilis aevi* (*Ad Patrem* 31), which is, as Tillyard says (*Milton*, 78), 'quite clear and quite untranslatable...mature and perfect Milton: tense, serene, and, as befits the subject, trancelike; unequalled till the description of heavenly beatitude in *Lycidas*.'

To descend from heaven to the earthly and scholarly, a word may be said about the latest edition of the Latin poems with full textual notes. In the preface to the second volume of her edition of Milton's poetical works (Oxford, 1952–5), Helen Darbishire returned thanks to her collaborator, H. W. Garrod, for his 'critical editing of the Latin Poems, a task which no editor has seriously undertaken before.' While 'editing' here means purely textual editing, this astonishing remark ignored not only the early Newton and Warton (whom Garrod cited for the majority of his notes) but the full textual apparatus—much fuller than Garrod's— in the Columbia *Works* (1, 578–98) and in H. F. Fletcher's facsimile edition (1, Urbana, 1943), both of which editions Miss Darbishire had just cited for their complete collations of the English poems. Apart from the insertion of a number of commas, Garrod's main contribution was in the way of gratuitous emendations, most of which he had put forward in the anonymous facsimile (Oxford, 1924) of the *Poems* of 1645; one very Bentleian item is dealt with below in the note on *Procan* 46. The chief puzzles (see the notes below on *El* 5. 126 and *In quintum Novembris* 150, 171) Garrod did not discuss. Since the textual data are readily accessible in the editions mentioned, and since they seldom involve a question of poetical concern, they are not ordinarily recorded in the present annotations. Readers interested in Milton's false quantities (some fifteen), and in the misprints and mispunctuation of the 1645 and 1673 editions, may turn to the compendious summary in Garrod, pp. xviii–xix. Milton, like many of his predecessors and contemporaries, used Latin as if it were a second native language, but he had not arrived at later Etonian standards of impeccable correctness.

To come to the present volume, the Columbia edition of Milton (20 v. 1931–40) is, as the general editor says in his preface, used throughout the Commentary (it is cited as *Works*).

Editors and commentators from Warton and Todd onward have pointed out echoes in Milton's Latin as well as his English verse. Such annotations were assembled and largely augmented—along with augmented miscellaneous material—in Walter MacKellar's invaluable edition (with translations) of the Latin poems (New Haven, 1930). A good deal of fresh annotation was added in Merritt Y. Hughes's editions, *Paradise Regained, the Minor Poems, and Samson Agonistes* (New York, 1937) and *Complete Poems and Major Prose* (New York, 1957); in my notes here, 'Hughes' means the earlier of these books. The Columbia Index (2 v. 1940) listed under the various authors references for parallels cited by editors. The only extensive collection of new classical parallels since MacKellar was made by G. B. A. Fletcher (*MP* 37, 1939–40, 343–50); in my notes these items are labeled 'Fletcher' (to be distinguished from Harris F. Fletcher, who is often cited in other connections). The present annotations—to speak only of parallels between Milton and other poets—incorporate the findings of MacKellar, Fletcher, and others along with those of earlier commentators, and add a good many more from both ancient and Neo-Latin poetry, from authors hitherto cited seldom or not at all as well as from the accepted ones. The new citations, like those accumulated before, include probable or possible borrowings and adaptations, but the whole exhibit is rather illustrative than argumentative. While there is always, in this sort of thing, the danger of merely multiplying proofs that Milton wrote in Latin, the full—though far from exhaustive—array of parallels may, one hopes, be justified because they help us to recognize the climate and the traditional *mystique* of Neo-Latin verse, and also the scope it gave for modern and individual utterance; to see, if we wish to look, the premises and the nature of the Neo-Latin and neoclassical poetic process. Moreover, a number of parallels for a particular phrase or idea may serve at times as a warning against a too hasty assumption of a single 'source.'

In the notes here, classical and Neo-Latin parallels are quoted, so far as space allows, when the phrasing is more or less similar to Milton's. If the sole concern is with substance, references only may be given: such matter appears, often in great abundance, in Renaissance annotations (e.g. those of Regius and Micyllus on Ovid) and in various large dictionaries, but there is little room for quoting secondary sources—especially if one feels, as I do, that Milton drew far more from poetry than from works of reference. For the sake of general convenience, almost all classical authors are quoted from the volumes in the Loeb Classical Library (for particular reasons sometimes referred to as 'L.C.L.'). In some cases, e.g. Claudian (whose titles are often long and whose poems are cited by number), ease of reference is furthered by a parenthetical citation of volume and page. So far as it was feasible or profitable, pre-Miltonic editions were consulted in regard to variant readings: thus Manilius' *Astronomica* is quoted from A. E. Housman's *editio minor* (Cambridge, 1932), but one or two variant readings are given from the edition of Joseph Scaliger (Leyden, 1600). It was usually not feasible to quote pre-Miltonic editions of classical or Neo-Latin authors because of their common lack of line numbers and of their not being commonly available. In quotations from Milton's works and from other early texts of Latin or English verse and prose, italics, ligatures, abbreviated forms of words, quantitative accents, etc., are disregarded. Abbreviated titles are used for works frequently cited: those for ancient classical writings are normally the standard ones given in modern Latin and Greek dictionaries; abbreviations for a few of these and for other and later titles are identified in the Index to this volume. The initials G.B., B.A.W., and A.S.P.W., which appear in occasional notes, indicate remarks made on an early draft of this commentary by Geoffrey

Bullough, B. A. Wright, and the late A. S. P. Woodhouse. The bare data of the Chronological Table will be amplified in the volume on the minor English poems, which will have an extended survey of the chronological facts and problems concerning poems written up to 1658, and some comment on Milton's inner development.

CHRONOLOGICAL TABLE*

I	II	III
Milton born, Bread St., Cheapside, London	9 Dec. 1608	
M. enters St Paul's School		1620? 1615?–20
Ps 114, 136	9 Dec. 1623–8 Dec. 1624	
EProl, CarEl, Asclep, RH		1624–6?
PhilReg		1624–6? 1634? 1642–5?
Mary Powell baptized	24 Jan. 1625	
M. admitted to Christ's College, Cambridge	12 Feb. 1625	
M. matriculates in University	9 April 1625	
Epigrams on Gunpowder Plot		*c.* 1625–6?
M. in London, rusticated from college?	Part of Lent term, 1626	
El 1 (written at home)	April 1626	
M. apparently in Cambridge for Easter term	19 April f.	
Procan (Gostlin d. 21 Oct. 1626)	Oct.–Nov. 1626	
El 2 (Ridding d. between 19 Sept. and 28 Nov.)	Oct.–Nov. 1626	

* Column II lists more or less certain dates, Column III some conjectures.

I	II	III
El 3 (Andrewes d. 25 Sept. 1626; funeral 11 Nov.)	Oct.–Nov. 1626	
QNov	Before 5 Nov. 1626 (early autumn and perhaps summer)	
Eli (Felton d. 5 Oct. 1626)	Oct.–Nov. 1626	
Prol 1–5		1626–9? 1631–2?
Hor		1626–9?
El 4 (to T. Young)	March–April 1627	
FInf (on niece buried 22 Jan. 1628?)		22 Jan.–9 April 1628? 1625–26?
El 7		1 May 1628 (or 1627? 1630?)
Sonn 1–6		1628–30
Naturam		June 1628?
Prol 6; *Vac*	July(?) 1628	
M. takes B.A. degree	26 March 1629	
El 5	April–May 1629	
May		1 May 1629?–31?
Idea		*c.* 1629–31?
M. buys works of G. della Casa	December 1629	
Nat	Christmas 1629	
El 6	Dec. 1629–Jan. 1630	
Epilogue appended to *El* 7		1630–45
Passion	*c.* 26–8 March 1630	

I	II	III
Shak	1630–24 March 1631	
Carrier 1, 2	Jan.–Feb. 1631	
EpWin	April–May 1631	
L'All; *IlPen*	Summer 1631 (or 1632?)	
Prol 7		1631–2?
Patrem		1631–2? (1634–7?)
Arc		1632? (1629–33?)
M. takes M.A. degree	3 July 1632	
M. at home (Hammersmith)	July 1632–35	
M. begins to record poems in Cambridge MS.		1632? 1637?
Sonn 7 (on 24th birthday)	9 Dec. 1632	
Time		Dec. 1632? (1630?)
Circum		1 Jan. 1633 (1631?)
LetFr		Jan.–Feb.?, 1633
SolMus		Feb.–Mar. 1633?
A Mask (*Comus*)	Performed 29 Sept. 1634	
Ps cxiv (Greek trans.)	Nov. 1634	
M. at home (Horton)	1635–April 1638	
Milton's mother d.	3 April 1637	
Comus pub. (ed. Lawes)	1637–March 1638	

I	II	III
Important letter to Diodati (*Works* 12, 22–9)	Dated 23 Sept. 1637 (probably should be 23 Nov.)	
Star Chamber decree on censorship	11 July 1637	
Edward King drowned	10 August 1637	
Lyc written	November 1637	
Lyc pub. (*Justa Edouardo King*)	1638	
Sir Henry Wotton's letter to M. (prefixed to *Comus*, 1645)	13 April 1638	
M. in Paris	April?–May 1638	
M. journeys through France to Nice; sails to Genoa	May–June 1638	
M. in Florence (*c.* 2 months)	July?–Aug.–Sept. 1638	
C. Diodati buried	27 Aug. 1638	
M. in Rome (*c.* 2 months)	Oct.–Nov. 1638	
Sals written	Nov.(?) 1638	
M. in Naples	December 1638	
Mansus written	Dec. 1638–Jan. 1639	
M. in Rome again (*c.* 2 months)	Jan.–Feb. 1639	
Leon 1, etc., written	1639?	
M. in Florence again (*c.* 2 months)	March–April 1639	
M. in Venice (a month)	April?–May 1639	
M. in Geneva	June 1639	

I	II	III
M. returns to England	July–Aug. 1639	
M. in lodgings in London, near Fleet Street	1639?–40 (nearly a year)	
EpDam written	Late 1639–early 1640	
EpDam privately printed		1639–45
Long Parliament meets	3 Nov. 1640	
M. living in Aldersgate Street	1640 (autumn?)–1645	
M. sets down list of subjects for tragedies		*c.* 1641
Ref pub.	May 1641	
PE pub.	June–July 1641	
Animad pub.	July (?), 1641	
RCG pub.	Jan.–Feb. 1642	
Apol pub.	April 1642	
M. marries Mary Powell	*c.* 29 May–1 June 1642 (French, *L.R.* 2, 61); 'probably early in July' (Parker, 230; cf. 862–74)	
Mrs Milton returns to parents' home	Probably 'not long before 22 Aug.' (Parker, 873, n. 21)	
Outbreak of Civil War	22 Aug. 1642	
Sonn 8	*c.* 13 Nov. 1642	
Sonn 9–10		1642–5
Parliamentary ordinance on censorship	14 June 1643	

I	II	III
Westminster Assembly convened	1 July 1643	
DDD pub.	*c.* 1 Aug. 1643	
DDD (2nd ed., revised and enlarged)	Jan.–Feb. 1644	
Educ pub.	*c.* 4–5 June 1644	
Bucer pub.	August 1644	
Areop pub.	November 1644	
Attacks on M.'s divorce tracts. Controversy on toleration	1644 f.	
Acced written?		1645?
Tetr and *Colas* pub.	*c.* 4 March 1645	
M. and wife reunited	1645 (before November)	
M. living in Barbican	Sept.–Oct. 1645– Sept. (?), 1647	
Sonn 11 and 12	1645–6	
Poems (dated 1645) pub.	On or before 2 Jan. 1646	
M. working on *HistBr* (bks. 1–4) and *DocCh*	1646–9	Parker, Shaw-cross, and Carey would include *SA*
Sonn 13 (to Lawes)	9 Feb. 1646	
Daughter Anne b.	29 July 1646	
Sonn 14 (on Mrs Thomason)	December 1646	
NewF		1646–7
Rous	23 Jan. 1647	

I	II	III
J. Milton senior d.	March 1647	
M. living in High Holborn	Aug. (?), 1647–March 1649	
Log and *HistMosc* written?		*c.* 1648? (Parker)
Ps 80–88 versified	April 1648	
Sonn 15 (Fairfax)	14 June–17 Aug. 1648	
Daughter Mary b.	25 Oct. 1648	
King Charles executed	30 Jan. 1649	
Eikon Basilike (by J. Gauden) pub.	1–9 Feb. 1649	
TKM pub.	*c.* 13 Feb. 1649	
M. appointed Secretary for Foreign Tongues to Council of State	15 March 1649 (held office till 1659; as a Latin Secretary, 1654–9)	
OAP pub.	May 1649	
Eikon (reply to *Eikon Basilike*) pub.	*c.* 6 Oct. 1649	Or *c.* 6 Nov. (Parker)
M. living in Scotland Yard	Nov. 1649–Dec. 1651	
Period of the Commonwealth	1649–53	
Def 1 pub.	24 Feb. 1651	
Son John b. (d. June 1652)	16 March 1651	
M. licenser of newspaper *Mercurius Politicus*	23 Jan. 1651–22 Jan. 1652	
M. becomes completely blind	Nov. 1651–Feb. 1652	
M. living in Petty France, Westminster	Dec. 1651–1660	

I	II	III
Sonn 19 ('When I consider')		1652–5
Daughter Deborah b.	2 May 1652	
Mary Powell Milton d.	5 (?) May 1652	
Sonn 16 (Cromwell)	May 1652	
Sonn 17 (Vane)	3 July 1652	
Ps 1–8	August 1653	*Ps* 1 earlier?
Period of Cromwell's Protectorate	1654–8	
Def 2 pub.	*c.* 30 May 1654	
Sonn 18 (Piedmont)	May–June 1655	
Sonn 20–2		1654–6
Defpro Se pub.	*c.* 8 Aug. 1655	
M. marries Katherine Woodcock (b. 1628)	12 Nov. 1656	
Daughter b. (d. 17 March)	19 Oct. 1657	
Katherine M. d.	3 Feb. 1658	
Sonn 23	1658	Before 12 Nov. 1656 (Parker)
Cromwell d.	3 Sept. 1658	
Cromwell's funeral: M. presumably in procession with Marvell and other secretaries	23 Nov. 1658	
M. working on *HistBr*, *DocCh*.	1655–60	
PL begun		1658?
CivP pub.	Feb. 1659	
Hirelings pub.	August 1659	

I	II	III
REW pub.	3 March, or slightly earlier, 1660	
LetMonk	March 1660	
BrNotes; *REW* (enlarged)	April 1660	
Charles II enters London	29 May 1660	
M. secluded by friends in Bartholomew Close	Summer 1660	
Parliamentary order for M.'s arrest and burning of *Eikon* and *Def* I	16 June 1660 (public proclamation, concerning books only, 13 Aug.)	
M. not named among those exempted from Act of Pardon	29 Aug. 1660	
M. in custody	Some period between 13 Sept. and release (15–17 Dec. 1660)	
M. living in Holborn		Sept. (?), 1660– early 1661 (Parker)
M. living in Jewin St.		1661–3 (French, *L.R.* 4, 388); till *c.* 1669–70 (Parker, 608, 1125)
M. marries Elizabeth Minshull (b. 1638)	24 Feb. 1663	
PL finished	1663 ?–5	
M. and family at Chalfont St Giles (because of plague)	July 1665–Feb. (?), 1666	
Great Fire in London	2–5 Sept. 1666	

	I	II	III
PL (in 10 bks.) pub.	August 1667	
Acced pub. (see under 1645 above)	June 1669	
M. living in Artillery Walk, Bunhill Fields		From *c.* 1669–70 (Parker, 608) or 1663 (French, *L.R.* 4, 388) till 1674
HistBr (6 bks.) pub.	1670	
PR and *SA* pub.	1671	
Log (written *c.* 1648?) pub.	1672	
TR pub.	1673	
Poems (2nd ed., enlarged)	1673	
Epistol and *Prol* pub.	July (?), 1674	
PL (2nd ed., in 12 bks.)	July 1674	
Milton died	8 (?) Nov. 1674	
M. buried in St Giles Cripplegate	12 Nov. 1674	
CharLP (omitted from *HistBr* of 1670)	1681	
HistMosc (written *c.* 1648?) pub.	1682	
Letters of State, ed. E. Phillips (incl. *Sonn* 15, 16, 17, 22)	1694	

ABBREVIATIONS FOR THE TITLES
OF MILTON'S WRITINGS

Variorum *Commentary*		*Columbia* *Works*
Acced	Accedence Commenc't Grammar	G
AddCM	Additional Correspondence and Marginalia	ACM
AddCorr	Additional Correspondence	AC
Animad	Animadversions upon the Remonstrants Defence	A
Apol	An Apology against a Pamphlet	AP
Arc	Arcades	ARC
Areop	Areopagitica	AR
Asclep	'Asclepiads' (called 'Choriambics,' *Works* 1, 327)	
BrNotes	Brief Notes upon a late Sermon	BN or N
Bucer	The Judgement of Martin Bucer concerning Divorce	M
CarEl	Carmina Elegiaca	CE
Carrier 1, 2	On the University Carrier; Another on the same	UC
CharLP	Milton's Character of the Long Parliament	TC
Circum	Upon the Circumcision	CI
CivP	A Treatise of Civil power	CP
Colas	Colasterion	C
ComBk	Commonplace Book	CB
Comus	Comus	CO
DDD	The Doctrine and Discipline of Divorce	*D. and D.*
DecDut	Declaration against the Dutch	DEC

Abbreviations: Titles of Milton's Writings

Variorum Commentary		Columbia Works
Def 1	First Defence of the English People	1D
Def 2	Second Defence	2D
Defpro Se	Pro Se Defensio	SD
DocCh	De Doctrina Christiana	CD
EC	English Correspondence	EC
Educ	Of Education	E
EffSc	In Effigiei Ejus Sculptorem	IEE
Eikon	Eikonoklastes	K
El 1, &c.	Elegia 1, &c.	EL
Eli	In obitum Praesulis Eliensis	PE
EpDam	Epitaphium Damonis	ED
Epistol	Familiar Letters of Milton	FE
EProl	Early Prolusion by Milton	EP
EpWin	Epitaph on the Marchioness of Winchester	EM
FInf	On the Death of a fair Infant	I
Hirelings	Considerations touching The likeliest means to remove Hirelings out of the church	H
HistBr	History of Britain	B
HistMosc	Brief History of Moscovia	HM
Hor	Fifth Ode of Horace	HOR
Idea	De Idea Platonica	IPA
IlPen	Il Penseroso	IP
InvBom	In inventorem Bombardae	IB
L'All	L'Allegro	L'A

Abbreviations: Titles of Milton's Writings

Variorum Commentary		Columbia Works
Leon 1, &c.	Ad Leonoram Romae canentem	LR
LetFr	Letter to a Friend	LF
LetMonk	Letter to General Monk	LM
LetPat	A Declaration or Letters Patent of the Election of this Present King of Poland	LP
Log	Art of Logic	LO
Lyc	Lycidas	L
Mansus	Mansus	MA
Mar	Marginalia	MAR
May	Song. On May Morning	MM
MC	Miscellaneous Correspondence	MC
Nat	On the Morning of Christ's Nativity	N
Naturam	Naturam non pati senium	NS
NewF	On the new forcers of Conscience	FC
OAP	Observations on the Articles of Peace	O
Passion	The Passion	PA
Patrem	Ad Patrem	ADP
PE	Of Prelatical Episcopacy	P
PhilReg	Philosophus ad Regem	PAR
PL	Paradise Lost	PL
PR	Paradise Regained	PR
Procan	In obitum Procancellarii medici	PM
ProdBom 1, &c.	In Proditionem Bombardicam 1, &c.	PB

Variorum Commentary		Columbia Works
Prol 1, &c.	Prolusions 1, &c.	PO
Propos	Proposalls of Certaine Expedients for the Preventing of a Civil War Now Feard	PRO
Ps 1, &c.	Psalms 1, &c.	PS
QNov	In quintum Novembris	QN
RCG	The Reason of Church-government urg'd against Prelaty	CG
Ref	Of Reformation Touching Church-Discipline in England	R
REW	The Readie & Easie Way to Establish a Free Commonwealth	W
Rous	Ad Joannem Rousium	JR
RH	Apologus de Rustico et Hero	RH
SA	Samson Agonistes	SA
Salmas 1, &c.	On Salmasius 1, &c.	
Sals	Ad Salsillum poetam Romanum	AS
Shak	On Shakespear. 1630	SH
SolMus	At a solemn Musick	SM
Sonn 1, &c.	Sonnet 1, &c.	S
Tetr	Tetrachordon	T
Time	On Time	TI
TKM	The Tenure of Kings and Magistrates	TE
TR	Of True Religion, Haeresie, Schism, Toleration	TR
Vac	At a Vacation Exercise in the Colledge	V

ABBREVIATIONS FOR THE TITLES OF
PERIODICALS AND SERIALS

AJP   *American Journal of Philology*
CL   *Comparative Literature*
ELH   *Journal of English Literary History*
ELN   *English Language Notes* (University of Colorado)
Explic   *The Explicator*
HLQ   *Huntington Library Quarterly*
JEGP   *Journal of English and Germanic Philology*
JHI   *Journal of the History of Ideas*
MLN   *Modern Language Notes*
MLQ   *Modern Language Quarterly*
MLR   *Modern Language Review*
MP   *Modern Philology*
N & Q   *Notes and Queries*
PBSA   *Papers of the Bibliographical Society of America*
PMLA   *Publications of the Modern Language Association of America*
PQ   *Philological Quarterly*
RES   *Review of English Studies*
SB   *Studies in Bibliography* (University of Virginia)
SCN   *Seventeenth-Century News*
SEL   *Studies in English Literature* (Rice University)
SP   *Studies in Philology*
TLS   [London] *Times Literary Supplement*
UTQ   *University of Toronto Quarterly*

ELEGIARUM LIBER PRIMUS

Elegia prima ad Carolum Diodatum

✥

Charles Diodati (1609–38), the closest friend of Milton's youth and early manhood, was the grandson of a notable citizen of Lucca, one of a group of Protestants who had left Italy for the freedom of exile.[1] Charles's uncle, John Diodati, early attained a professorship of Hebrew and theology at Geneva. His father, Theodore, studied medicine at Leyden, went to England about 1598, and became a tutor and later physician in the household of Sir John Harington of Exton, who was created Baron Harington at King James's coronation. The Haringtons, whose son was a friend of Prince Henry (and whose more famous child was Lucy, Countess of Bedford), were put in charge of Princess Elizabeth. In 1608–9 Diodati married an Englishwoman and set up housekeeping in Brentford, where Charles was probably born. His chief patrons having died or lost the power to help him, Theodore Diodati went back to Leyden to take the medical degree he had not taken before and, apparently in 1617, moved from Brentford to London to begin practice. His house, like that of John Milton senior, was near St Paul's School. Charles presumably entered the school in 1617 or 1618; the somewhat older Milton may have entered in 1620 or earlier.[2] Charles matriculated at Trinity College, Oxford, in February 1623, two years before Milton was admitted to Cambridge. He took his B.A. degree in December 1625, when he was sixteen, but continued in residence working for the M.A. When he was only about fifteen, he had had a Latin

[1] Masson's information has been much enlarged by Donald C. Dorian, *The English Diodatis* (New Brunswick, 1950: cited hereafter as *E.D.*). Some further details are given below in the introductions to *El* 6 and *EpDam*. See Parker, *Milton* (1968), 714, n. 53.

[2] Davis P. Harding (*Ovid*, 1946, 34–40) argued for April 1617. Donald L. Clark (*Milton at St. Paul's School*, 1948, 26–32) suggested 1615. Harris F. Fletcher (*Intellectual Development of John Milton*, 1, 1956, 91, 105, 149) leaves the question open. Cf. Dorian, *E.D.* 250, n. 26; J. M. French, *Life Records of John Milton*, 1, New Brunswick, 1949, 7–8, 27–8. Parker (*Milton*, 709, n. 44) prefers the traditional 1620.

poem included in a volume of tributes to William Camden, *Camdeni Insignia* (1624).

In the Lent term of 1626, at the end of his first year in Cambridge, Milton seems to have been rusticated by his college on account of friction between him and his tutor, William Chappell (who had much larger flocks of students than any colleague). We may guess that there was some clash of temperaments, aggravated by Milton's feeling the contrast between his humanistic school and the predominantly scholastic curriculum and atmosphere of the university.[3] At home in London, he has received an eagerly awaited letter from Diodati, who has been visiting in the neighbourhood of Chester, and *El* 1 is his reply.[4]

In the editions of both 1645 and 1673 all of Milton's elegies were dated by him except the two (1 and 6) addressed to Diodati.[5] Within the two groups, *Elegiarum Liber primus* and *Sylvarum Liber*, Milton evidently placed his poems in chronological order (see, however, the headnote to *El* 7), and in both editions *El* 1 heads the Latin poems. *El* 2 (q.v.) must have been written in the autumn of 1626. *El* 1 was written in springtime (line 48), and Milton was at home. This could not have been the spring of 1625, since he was admitted to Christ's College on

---

[3] The accounts of John Aubrey (*Early Lives of Milton*, ed. H. Darbishire, London, 1932, 10) and Samuel Johnson (*Lives of the English Poets*, ed. Hill, 1, 88–9) are discussed by Masson (*Life*, 1, London, 1881, 159–61), MacKellar (22–3, 191), et al. In the fullest inquiry, 'John Milton and William Chappell' (*HLQ* 18, 1954–5, 329–50), D. L. Clark suggests as one factor that Milton's non-Ramist training collided with Chappell's pronounced Ramism. See n. 6 below.

[4] Two letters in Greek that Diodati wrote to Milton, perhaps in 1625–6, are extant, and some scholars have taken Milton's poem as a possible or probable reply to the second. The Greek texts, with translations, are in *Works* 12, 292–5, and, with notes, in French, *L.R.* 1, 98–9, 104–5; and translations and comments are in Masson, *Life*, 1, 1881, 161–3 and his edition of the *Poetical Works* (London, 1890), 1, 255–7; Dorian, *E.D.* 110–14; Milton's *Complete Prose Works*, ed. D. M. Wolfe et al., 1 (New Haven, 1953), 336–7. In his second letter Diodati expressed his delight in the country and his affectionate longing for his friend's society, and lectured him, half-seriously, on letting immoderate study crowd out the pleasures of youth. But this letter might have been written at any time, and a connection between it and *El* 1 is only a possibility. Parker (30) takes the poem as a reply to a letter now lost; on the two Greek letters see Parker, 748, n. 8.

[5] This paragraph summarizes W. R. Parker, 'Notes on the Chronology of Milton's Latin Poems' (cited hereafter as 'Notes'), in *A Tribute to George Coffin Taylor*, ed. Arnold Williams (Chapel Hill, 1952), 116–17. Cf. his *Milton*, 730, n. 21.

12 February 1625, a month after the Lent term had begun, and was in Cambridge to matriculate on 9 April, a day after the beginning of the spring vacation. The poem must therefore belong to the spring of 1626, and, since Milton was expecting to return shortly to Cambridge, it was evidently written near the close of the spring vacation, that is, a little before 19 April, when the Easter term opened—unless, as D. L. Clark observes (*HLQ* 18, 331), the rustication ended early in that term.

When he went back to the university, Milton was assigned to another tutor, a friend of Chappell's named Nathaniel Tovey, son of the John Tovey who, as tutor and chaplain, had been in the Harington household along with Theodore Diodati.[6] The college authorities do not seem to have considered Milton seriously at fault, since his exile was brief and since he graduated in the usual time.

In the poem Milton does not say much about his academic misadventure (he may have told of that already), and dwells rather on the pleasures of exile, on the literature he is now free to read, the books that 'are my life,' and on the incomparable beauty of the London girls he sees when strolling; but he adds that he is proof against sensual temptation. He ends with an allusion to his return to Cambridge.

Hanford, quoting Milton's lines (9–24) on his rustication, speaks of the real resentment and hurt pride beneath 'the assumed lightness and well-bred indifference which the cultured but naïve youth wears like a borrowed garment.'[7] 'Any touch of disgrace he may have felt is promptly

---

[6] Masson, *Life*, 1 (1881), 130; Dorian, *E.D.* 43, 114; Clark, *HLQ* 18, 332.

    H. F. Fletcher (*Intell. Dev.* 2, 1961, 392–403) is sceptical about Aubrey's story of Milton's being whipped and about the unusual transfer of a student from one tutor to another (which Aubrey reported as an exception to the rules). Also, Fletcher—who does not refer to Parker's 'Notes'—would put *El* 1 in the spring of 1625 (and after *El* 4; see the headnote to the latter, below), instead of the orthodox 1626. He leaves the crucial lines unexplained. Parker (29–30, 729, n. 20) notes the fact of Milton's trouble with his tutor, and the strong probability (inferred from *El* 1) that he was sent down. John Carey (*Poems of John Milton*, London, 1968) thinks Milton's '"exile"' is probably merely the university vacation'; the Chronological Table in this Carey–Fowler edition has 'Perhaps rusticated temporarily.'

[7] 'The Youth of Milton,' 109. This elaborate and classic essay has been reprinted in Hanford's *John Milton poet and humanist* (Cleveland, 1966), but throughout the present work it is cited—as 'Youth'—from *Studies in Shakespeare, Milton and Donne* (New York, 1925), by O. J. Campbell et al. Quotations in this paragraph are from 109–14.

converted to a judgment of the University as no fit place for poets and to a consciousness of satisfaction in his superior surroundings and pursuits at home.' Then the young poet 'has been meditating on the analogy between his own little exile and the fate of Ovid until he has made a kind of imaginative identification of himself with his Roman predecessor... For Milton the fellowship of the great is at once a refuge and a vindication.' In other ways the poem gives evidence of 'Milton's awakening emotional and imaginative life.'

In his defensive retreat from the hostility of the real world he takes refuge not alone in his reverence for the past but in a conscious devotion to beauty in all its forms. The disfavour into which he has momentarily fallen, while not taken too seriously, has had the effect of throwing him back upon himself and has prompted him to reveal sensations which have hitherto found no place in his poetry

—imaginative literature, nature and the spring, beautiful girls. On this last theme 'he expatiates with an ardour which belies the artificial medium in which he writes.' But 'Sensuous desire is never with him a simple lyric force. It is from the beginning complicated by ethical and ideal influences and moulded in its expression by literary traditions.' Milton's concluding reference to the symbolic herb moly carries us up to the all-important account, in the *Apology for Smectymnuus* (1642), of his youthful reading and writing and the growth of his ideal of chastity. Hanford sums up *El* 1 as 'an expression, on the one hand, of Milton's sensitive self-love, on the other of a new and intense delight in beauty, nourished by contact with the most sensuous and romantic of ancient poets and given artistic direction by the typical Renaissance ambition to "overgo" some reputed classic name in his own tongue and upon a kindred theme. These related motives are the basis of an enduring inspiration.' (If we may query one note in a study of seminal insight, Hanford, perhaps a little affected in 1925 by 'the Milton legend,' seems at moments to find egotism in what may be thought quite innocent utterances, in this poem and others.)

Going on from Hanford, Ralph W. Condee ('Ovid's Exile and Milton's Rustication,' *PQ* 37, 1958, 498–502) stresses, as an organizing principle in the poem, the cross-comparison between Ovid's exile and

Milton's: the uncivilized place Ovid was banished to is as hostile to poetry and beauty as the place (a university!) Milton was banished from, while London, the scene of Milton's exile, is like the cultured Rome that Ovid had to leave and supplies what Cambridge lacks, plays and lovely girls (though Condee sees the sections on these last two topics as undigested lumps that have resisted organization). Condee thus emphasizes the parallels and contrasts between *El* 1 and Ovid's *Tristia* and *Epistulae ex Ponto*: e.g. when Milton recalls (see below, 23–24 n.) Ovid's saying, in *Tristia* 1. 1, that Homer, in such exile as his, would have lost his genius, it is implied that a modern poet might lose his at Cambridge.

To speak in more general terms, Ovid's two books were the great models for the epistolary use of elegiac verse and they afford countless parallels in phrasing with Milton's Latin poems. (The *Heroides*, which are constantly echoed too, represent of course a special kind of epistle.) While Ovid can be personal and intimate, even in his most despairing complaints from the shore of the Black Sea he is an instinctive and incurable rhetorician, and his epistles tend to be formal literary developments of a theme or argument. His rhetoric as well as his versification attracted the young Milton; Horace's epistles may yield incidental echoes, but Milton's manner is remote from Horace's colloquial and ambling hexameters. Renaissance poets carried on the Ovidian epistle, sometimes extensively, though one would not ordinarily find so high a proportion of their elegiac poems taking that form as Milton's three out of seven. Two of these, being letters to his one real friend, have, with all their Ovidian rhetoric, an open-hearted ease and warmth that belong to exchanges with such a confidant. Of *El* 1 Tillyard (*Milton*, 1930, 21) remarks: 'Its very redundance too betrays the exuberance of Milton's nature, which can only be seen fully in his prose and which he strove so hard to hide beneath the severity of his versification.'

Parker (*Milton*, 30–1) sees the poem as 'a funny, pathetic, normal effort of an adolescent boy to impress another boy with his indifference to something that has hurt him deeply. It is rich in unintended humour,' especially at the end, where, 'after all the flimsy nonchalance,' Milton reports that he is to return to Cambridge. The poem is a first—and 'pale'—attempt, five or six years before *L'Allegro* and *Il Penseroso*, to catalogue his youthful pleasures. The desire to impress Diodati, along with love of Ovid, accounts for the emphasis on pretty girls. It may be added, as Koehler observed (29), that the innocent young Milton's aesthetic and patriotic delight in the beauty of troops of English girls is very different from the Roman elegists' personal and purposeful concern with one.

NOTES

1–2 *tabellae, /...nuncia charta.* Keightley (2, 388: cited by MacKellar) objected to an un-Roman confusion of terms, since *tabellae* and *charta* refer to the same letter; but cf. Ovid's *tabellae* and *littera* (*Am.* 1. 12. 1–2) and *scripta* and *libellus* (*H.* 11. 1–2). Ovid uses *nuntia* with *epistula* (*P.* 4. 11. 9: Fletcher) and with *verba* (*H.* 16. 10).

3 *occidua Devae Cestrensis ab ora.* Chester (from the Latin *castra*) is on the east bank of the Dee, which flows northward into the Irish Sea. Cf. *Vac* 98; *Lyc* 55; Spenser, *F.Q.* 4. 11. 39.

4 *Vergivium prono qua petit amne salum.* In the first sentence of the section on Ireland in his *Britannia* (1586 and later edd.; tr. P. Holland, 1610, 61), Camden explained the name *Vergivium mare* for the Irish Sea as derived from the ancient British *Mor-weridh* or the Irish *Farigi*; Drayton uses the epithet in *Poly-Olbion* 1. 24, 6. 90, etc. *Prono...amni* is in Virgil, *G.* 1. 203, *pronus amnis* in Grotius, *Adamus Exul* (The Hague, 1601: cited in this work from the text with numbered lines in *The Celestial Cycle*, ed. W. Kirkconnell, Toronto, 1952), line 896. Cf. Horace, *Ep.* 1. 10. 21, *pronum...rivum* (and *C.* 1. 29. 11).

5 *terras...remotas.* In Lucan 5. 774–5. Cf. *terra remota* in *Gratulatio Academiae Cantabrigiensis* (Cambridge, 1623), p. 37.

6 *fidele caput.* In Propertius 2. 1. 36 (Fletcher).

7–8 Milton's saying that a distant land 'owes' his friend to him recalls, as editors note, Horace's farewell to Virgil (*C.* 1. 3. 5–8).

9 *Me tenet urbs reflua quam Thamesis alluit unda.* Todd cited Ovid, *M.* 7. 267, *et quas Oceani refluum mare lavit harenas*, and *refluis...undis* in Buchanan, *S.* 1. 41 and *Ps.* 97. 1. Cf. Tibullus 1. 3. 3, *me tenet...Phaeacia.*

11 *arundiferum...Camum.* Editors cite the Tiber's *harundiferum...caput* in Ovid, *F.* 5. 637. Cf. 89 below and *Lyc* 103–4.

12 *vetiti...laris.* The (god of the) hearth denied him, i.e. Milton's room or college at Cambridge. The exiled Ovid (see 21–4 below) refers to Italy as *vetitas...terras* (*Tr.* 1. 4. 21).

13 *Nuda nec arva placent, umbrasque negantia molles.* Cf. Catullus 62. 49 and Sil. Ital. 7. 168, *in nudo...arvo*; Propertius 3. 3. 1, *molli...in umbra*; Seneca, *Herc. Fur.* 884–5: *sol... | umbras corporibus negat.*

14 *Phoebicolis.* Votaries of Phoebus, i.e. poets and students of letters. Mac-Kellar did not observe the word elsewhere and suggested a Miltonic coinage on the model of *caelicola* (cf. *Mansus* 95) and *Christicola* (cf. *El* 4. 18); cf. Sil. Ital. 14. 443, *Neptunicolae.* I have seen one example of *Phoebicolae*, in Joseph Scaliger, *Carmina Illustrium Poetarum Italorum* (11 v. Florence, 1719–26), 9, 476. (This large anthology is henceforth cited as *C.P.I.*)

15–16 *Nec duri libet usque minas perferre magistri/Caeteraque ingenio non subeunda meo.* The introductory note summarizes the meagre facts and guesses about Milton's trouble with his tutor. Masson (*P.W.* 3, 300) cited Buchanan, *El.* 1. 63–4: *Quid memorem interea fastidia mille laborum, | Quae non ingenua mente ferenda putes?* Cf. Ovid, *Am.* 3. 1. 48, *multa supercilio non patienda tuo*; Virgil, *A.* 10. 695, *minas perfert.*

17 *Si sit hoc exilium patrios adiisse penates. Patrios penates* is a stock phrase, e.g. Virgil, *A.* 2. 717, 4. 598; Horace, *S.* 2. 5. 4, *C.* 3. 27. 49; Tibullus 1. 3. 33; Ovid, *M.* 1. 773, 9. 446, *F.* 6. 603; Lucan 1. 353, 9. 230; Buchanan, *Iamb.* 5. 2, *Med.* 35; Milton, *El* 4. 85. On *adiisse* and other examples Godolphin (*MP* 37, 1939–40, 354) remarks: 'Another stylistic device of the Romans which Milton has utilized is the placing of a perfect infinitive next to the last word in the line even when the present infinitive would be more natural. This is most common in the pentameter but is also found in the hexameter...' Godolphin adds that Milton's practice is in accord with the moderation of Ovid and Propertius rather than with the excess of Tibullus.

18 *Et vacuum curis otia grata sequi.* For *vacuum curis* see, e.g., Cicero, *Fin.* 2. 14. 46; Sil. Ital. 15. 272; Claudian 22. 142–3 (2, 12). Cf. Pontano, *A.C.* 1. 8. 4, *ocia grata sequi*; *Lyra* 6. 14, *otia grata*; Sannazaro, *Epig.* 3. 4. 2, *studiis otia grata meis*; Ariosto, *Carmina* 54. 51, *grata otia.*

19 *Non ego vel profugi nomen, sortemve recuso.* Cf. Ovid, *Tr.* 5. 7. 30, *profugi nomen.*

21–2 *O utinam vates nunquam graviora tulisset | Ille Tomitano flebilis exul agro.* In 8 A.D. Ovid was banished by Augustus to the barbarous Tomis on the Black

49

Sea; the reasons are not fully or certainly known, though the *Ars Amatoria* was evidently one of them (L. P. Wilkinson, *Ovid Recalled*, Cambridge, 1955, 297 f.). Ovid often begins a line with *O utinam*, e.g. *Am.* 2. 5. 7, 2. 11. 5, 2. 15. 9, *H.* 1. 5, 4. 125, etc. Cf. Ovid, *Tr.* 5. 11. 7, *multo graviora tulisti*; *P.* 3. 7. 13, *peiora tulisti*; Senecan *Oct.* 652, *graviora tuli.* Ovid uses *Tomitanus...ager* in *P.* 3. 8. 2 (cf. ibid. 1. 1. 1, 1. 2. 75, 3. 1. 6, *Tr.* 5. 7. 9). Cf. Sannazaro, *El.* 1. 5. 30, *Ille, Tomitana qui jacet exsul humo* (J. Goode, *TLS*, 13 August 1931, p. 621); Beza (*Poëmata*, Geneva, 1599, 27ᵛ): *Namque Tomitanis exul lugetur in oris.*

23-4 *Non tunc...Maro.* While Milton's own 'exile' invites a reference to Ovid's, and while such allusions are not made upon oath, his ranking of Ovid as potentially equal to Homer and above Virgil indicates the degree of his youthful admiration. Ancient tradition made Homer a native of Ionia (cf. the note on *Mansus* 22-3). Milton may have remembered Ovid's saying that Homer, in such exile as his, would have lost his genius (*Tr.* 1. 1. 47-8; *P.* 4. 2. 21-2; cf. *Tr.* 1. 6. 21-2). Apropos of 22-4, Godolphin remarks (*MP* 37, 1939-40, 355): 'Milton uses the same rhyme throughout a couplet four times; Propertius has nine examples in the first book, but Ovid provides only six examples in the whole of the *Amores*.'

25 *placidis...Musis.* The gentle Muses, the poetic studies pursued in solitary peace by the young devotee, are contrasted with the *raucae murmur Scholae* (90 below), the hoarse hum of a class immersed in logic and the other studies Milton did not relish.

26 *Et totum rapiunt me mea vita libri.* In the Latin writers, e.g. Propertius, the metaphorical use of *vita* seems commonly to refer to persons rather than to things, but the extension was easily made. The phrase reveals the intensity of Milton's literary ardor.

27-46 Since Milton's allusions mostly fit the stock characters and plots of Roman comedy (cf. Horace, *A.P.* 153 f.; Ovid, *Am.* 1. 15. 17-18), and since he could not have attended tragedies on Greek themes (45-6), it seems likely that he is describing plays he has read rather than plays seen in London theatres, though he writes as if he had been an actual witness. If he is glancing at comic types in English plays, as G.B. suggests (cf. MacKellar on *El* 1. 29-36), his brief and classical labels do not allow of their being pinned down.

27 *sinuosi pompa theatri.* Editors cite Ovid, *A.A.* 1. 89, *curvis...theatris* (cf. ibid. 1. 497, *Am.* 2. 2. 26, *P.* 2. 4. 20), and Propertius' allusion to theatre awnings, *sinuosa cavo pendebant vela theatro* (4. 1. 15). For Milton's use of *pompa* in this context, which Keightley questioned, cf. Ausonius, *Ephem.* 8. 4, *nunc fora, nunc lites, lati modo pompa theatri.*

29 *Seu catus auditur senior, seu prodigus haeres.* Cf. *prodigus haeres* in Mantuan, *De Calamitatibus Temporum Libri Tres*, ed. G. Wessels (*Analecta Ordinis Carmelitarum*, Annus IX, vol. IV, Rome, 1917: cited hereafter as *Cal. Temp.*), p. 39; and in *Carminum Proverbialium* (London, 1603), p. 21.

30 *posita casside.* In Ovid, *M.* 14. 806, *F.* 3. 171; *C.P.I.* 2, 17.

31-2 *Sive decennali foecundus lite patronus | Detonat inculto barbara verba foro.* The picture of the lawyer has been accepted, since Warton, as a probable reference to George Ruggle's Latin play *Ignoramus*, which delighted King James when acted before him at Cambridge in 1615, and which, after its publication in 1630, was popular in print. There is no record of a performance in London. Even if Milton had a manuscript copy, his description does not fit Ruggle's burlesque lawyer, who spouts shreds of legal Latin but does so in his private role of pedantic lover and butt. There seems to be no character in Roman or English comedy that fits; possibly there is in Italian comedy. Whether or not Milton had heard of *Ignoramus* or some other play, if he wished to give a varied survey of comic themes he might have built his lawyer out of hints in Roman satire, e.g. Juvenal 2. 51-2, 7. 106-49, 8. 49-50, 16. 36-50; Martial 3. 46. 9-10, 4. 5. 4, 5. 20. 6; and Seneca, *Herc. Fur.* 172-4. And cf. Secundus, *Epig.* 1. 61. 27-30: *Dumque reus, dum actor erit, dum causidicorum | Perstrepet insano vendita lingua foro*, etc.; and Buchanan, *Epig.* 1. 1, *In Aulum*, which includes the lines *Quam mihi dum peragit decimumque extendit in annum, | Pene decem decies jam periere minae. | Ne lis quod superest exhauriat aeris & aevi, | Vito reum pariter caussidicumque meum.* For Milton's phrasing, cf. also Propertius 4. 1 A. 134, *insano verba tonare Foro* (Fletcher); Ovid, *A.A.* 3. 542, *Contempto ...foro*; Ovid, *P.* 4. 13. 20, Martial 1. 65. 1, Petrarch, *Ep. ad B. Ruthenensem* (*P.M.* 2, 304), and W. Lily, *Carmen de Moribus* (*A Shorte Introduction of Grammar*, ed. V. J. Flynn, New York, 1945, sig. Dv^v), *barbara verba*; and such general parallels as Statius, *S.* 2. 7. 66, *Pharsalica bella detonabis*; Manilius, *Astron.*, ed. Housman (1932), 3. 112: *fortunamque fori; fundentem verba patronum*; *C.P.I.* 6, 290, *Hunc juvat in rauco verba tonare foro.* Garrod would emend Milton's *foecundus* to *facundus*, thereby turning a witty phrase into a trite one. This and other suggestions were first made by Garrod in *Milton's Poems 1645: Type-Facsimile* (Oxford, 1924: cited hereafter as *Ox. Fac.*).

34 *rigidi...Patris.* Cf. Ovid, *M.* 2. 813, *rigido...parenti*; *F.* 4. 310, *rigidos... senes.*

35-6 *Saepe novos illic virgo mirata calores | Quid sit amor nescit, dum quoque nescit, amat.* If Milton is thinking of the heroines of Roman comedy, the description is somewhat idealized. Editors cite Claudian 10. 3-4 (1, 242): *nec novus unde calor nec quid suspiria vellent, | noverat incipiens et adhuc ignarus amandi*; and Ovid, *M.* 4. 329-30: *pueri rubor ora notavit; | nescit enim, quid amor.* Cf. Ovid, *M.* 10. 637, *quid facit ignorans, amat et non sentit amorem*; ibid. 13. 762, *quid sit amor, sensit*; Virgil, *Cir.* 492, *novo...calore*; *E.* 8.43, *nunc scio, quid sit Amor*; Grotius, *Epith. Guil.* (*S.*, bk. 3, p. 116), *Nec, quid amet, novit, sed amat.*

37-8 For the picture of Tragedy editors cite Ovid, *Am.* 3. 1. 11-13:

> *venit et ingenti violenta Tragoedia passu :*
> *fronte comae torva, palla iacebat humi ;*
> *laeva manus sceptrum late regale movebat.*

Cf. the Virgilian *Cul.* 218-19. With Milton's turgid image, that of a Fury, and perhaps more Senecan than Ovidian, compare the sober personification of *IlPen* 97-8.

38 *effusis crinibus.* In various cases, a stock phrase, e.g. Catullus 64. 391, Lucan 1. 443, 7. 370, Seneca, *Herc. Fur.* 472-3, *Oed.* 417, Juvenal 6. 164.

39-40 For the mingled pain and delight evoked by tragedy Milton needed no source, but he might have remembered St Augustine, *Conf.* 3. 2. With *lacrymis dulcis amaror inest* editors compare Catullus 68. 18, *dulcem...amaritiem.* Cf. *C.P.I.* 2, 49 and Gruter, *Del. I.P.* 2, 220, *dulcis amaror.* On the 'bitter-sweet' mood and the association of love and death, see Edgar Wind, *Pagan Mysteries in the Renaissance* (New Haven, 1958), 135 f.

41-4 Many commentators (see Warton, Todd, Keightley, Masson, MacKellar, Visiak) have seen here a reference to Romeo (*puer infelix*) and, in the Stygian *ferus ultor*, the ghosts of *Richard III, Hamlet*, and *Macbeth*; but, as they admit, Romeo's joys were not untasted and, even if we allow for classical dress, the avenger of Milton's description seems rather remote from the Shakespearian ghosts. In a Latin poem, moreover, a young scholar might have thought it doubtfully decorous to allude to English plays. Finally, lines 45-6, a summary glance at the whole body of ancient tragedy, imply that the particular examples belong to it (and see the note above on 27-46). Here, as in *IlPen* 99-100, Milton refers to the tragedies concerned with 'Pelops line,' with 'the tale of Troy divine,' the city founded by Ilus, and with the fate of the Theban Oedipus, Creon's brother-in-law, and his children. The *puer infelix* might be the Haemon of *Antigone.* The *ferus ultor*—if Milton had specific examples in mind—might be the ghost of Tantalus in the prologue of Seneca's *Thyestes* (cf. *Thy.* 22, *Pelopea...domo*, and Propertius 3. 19. 20, *Pelopea domus*), or the ghost of Thyestes in the prologue of Seneca's *Agamemnon* (cf. *Agam.* 7, 165, *Pelopia... domus*), or the shade of Laius, the *pater inultus*, of Seneca's *Oedipus*, 623 f.; or, if a female ghost can be included, the Clytaemnestra of Aeschylus' *Eumenides* or the Agrippina of the Senecan *Octavia* (593 f.), who carries a Stygian torch.

41–2 *Seu puer infelix indelibata reliquit | Gaudia, & abrupto flendus amore cadit.* Puer infelix (or *infelix puer*) appears, e.g. in Virgil, *A.* 1. 475, Ovid, *F.* 6. 146, the Senecan *Oct.* 167, Mantuan, *E.* 1. 129, 2. 81, Pontano, *Uran.* 5. 711. With other phrases, cf. Virgil, *A.* 4. 292, *rumpi...amores* (Fletcher); Sil. Ital. 15. 271, *indelibata...virgine*; F. M. Molsa (*C.P.I.* 6, 349; Gruter, *Del. I.P.* 2, 51) and Secundus, *S.* 9. 39, *Illibata tibi linquens sua gaudia.*

43–4 *Seu ferus e tenebris iterat Styga criminis ultor | Conscia funereo pectora torre movens.* See the notes on 41–4 and *El* 2. 9. Cf. Ovid, *Ibis* 153–4: *Quidquid ero, Stygiis erumpere nitar ab oris, | Et tendam gelidas ultor in ora manus*; and ibid. 160, *Conscia fumabunt semper ad ora faces.* Fletcher cites Ovid, *M.* 8. 512, *funereum torrem.*

45 *Pelopeia domus.* See the note on 41–4.

48 *Irrita nec nobis tempora veris eunt.* Editors cite *El* 5. 138 and Ovid, *F.* 2. 150, *et primi tempora veris erunt.* Cf. *F.* 1. 496, 4. 902, *tempora veris erunt*, and a similar pattern, *tempora noctis eunt*, in Ovid, *Am.* 1. 6. 24, 32, 40, 48, 56.

49–50 Apropos of Milton's contrasts between the charms of London and the drabness of Cambridge (13–14, 89), Condee (see headnote above) cites Ovid's parallel contrasts between Rome and Tomis, e.g. *Tr.* 3. 10. 71–8, 3. 12. 13–16, *P.* 1. 3. 49–52, 3. 1. 13, 3. 8. 13–16.

50 *suburbani nobilis umbra loci.* Some favourite walks of London citizens are mentioned in the note on *El* 7. 51–2.

51 *blandas spirantia sydera flammas.* Cf. Val. Flacc. 6. 465, *blanda adspiramina formae*; Statius, *Th.* 4. 96, *blanda ad spiramina solis* (Fletcher); Buchanan, *El.* 6. 11, *lethiferas spirantia lumina flammas*; Virgil, *G.* 3. 34, *spirantia signa* (and *A.* 6. 847).

52 *Virgineos...choros.* In various forms a stock phrase, e.g. Seneca, *Herc. Oet.* 593, Ovid, *A.A.* 3. 168, Lucan 9. 362, Vida, *A.P.* 2. 527–8, *C.P.I.* 3, 211, 238, 240, etc. Fletcher cites Seneca and Lucan.

54 *Quae possit senium vel reparare Jovis.* Cf. Ovid, *Am.* 3. 7. 41–2: *illius ad tactum Pylius iuvenescere possit | Tithonosque annis fortior esse suis*; Pontano,

Hen. 1. 4. 19–20; Shakespeare, *Cymb.* 2. 5. 11–12: 'A pudency so rosy, the sweet view on't / Might well have warm'd old Saturn.'

55–6 *Ah quoties vidi superantia lumina gemmas,* | *Atque faces quotquot volvit uterque polus.* MacKellar (p. 196, on lines 51–2) cites Ovid, *A.A.* 1. 59: *Quot caelum stellas, tot habet tua Roma puellas.* Cf. *Tr.* 1. 5. 47, *quot in aethere sidera lucent*; *uterque polus* in Ovid, *M.* 2. 295, *F.* 2. 489–90; Milton, *Prol* 3 (*Works* 12, 170, line 13), *stellulae, quotquot inter polos utrosque sparsae sunt*; Grotius, *In Nuptias J. Milandri* (*Farr.* bk. 3, p. 220): *Luminaque Eois aequale nitentia gemmis,* | *...Gemmantes oculi.* On the two poles MacKellar cites Pliny, *N.H.* 2. 13. 63: *terra a verticibus duobus quos appellaverunt polos centrum caeli est, nec non et signiferi oblique inter eos siti.* Cf. Ovid–Micyllus, 3, 37ᴋ, 74ᴀ, and Buchanan, *Sph., passim.* On *polus* in the sense of heaven MacKellar cites Virgil, *A.* 3. 586, 5. 721, and Horace, *C.* 1. 28. 6.

57 *Collaque bis vivi Pelopis quae brachia vincant.* Pelops was boiled by his father Tantalus as a feast for the gods, who refused it, though Demeter ate part of one shoulder; when Pelops was restored to life by a second boiling, the missing part was replaced by ivory. See Apollodorus, *Epit.* 2. 3 (ed. Frazer, 2, 157); Pindar, *Ol.* 1. 35–51; Hyginus, *Fab.* 83; Virgil, *G.* 3. 7 (where Pelops' ivory shoulder is listed among threadbare commonplaces); Ovid, *M.* 6. 404–11 (MacKellar); Milton, *Prol* 6 (*Works* 12, 244, line 20).

58 *puro nectare tincta via.* The Milky Way. MacKellar cites Pliny, *N.H.* 18. 69. 280–1; Aratus, *Phaen.* 469–76; Milton, *Eli* 60, *lacteas...plagas.*

59 *decus eximium frontis.* A fusion of two stock phrases. Cf. *decus eximium* in Catullus 64. 323; Statius, *S.* 3. 3. 113, *Ach.* 1. 290; Seneca, *Phoen.* 238; Pontano, *Erid.* 1. 41. 31; Buchanan, *Ps.* 91. 15; *C.P.I. passim*; *Lacrymae Cantab.* (1619), p. 8; and *frontis decus* in Seneca, *Herc. Oet.* 1641, Val. Flacc. 4. 241, Prudentius, *Cath.* 10. 102, Pontano, *Parth.* 1. 4. 17.

60 *Aurea quae fallax retia tendit Amor.* In Milton's Latin poems Cupid is mainly the 'sportive, winged boy, armed with the bow, arrows, and firebrands' (C. G. Osgood, *Classical Mythology of Milton's English Poems*, New York, 1900, 25: hereafter cited as *C.M.*), derived from Ovid, *M.* 1. 456–73 and *Amores, passim* (especially 3. 9. 7–12), and such other *loci classici* as the *Anacreontea*, Moschus 1, Propertius 2. 12, the Senecan *Oct.* 557–60, 807–19, and Apuleius, *Met.* 5. 22, 10. 32; cf. also Secundus, *passim*; Pontano, *Erid.* 1. 33, etc.; Palingenius, *Z.V.* 4. 316 f. Cupid's blindness was a medieval addition; see E. Panofsky, *Studies in Iconology* (New York, 1939), ch. 4, 'Blind Cupid.' *Tendere retia* is a stock idiom (Horace, *Epod.* 2. 33; Ovid, *Am.* 1. 8. 69, *H.* 21. 206, etc.;

Propertius 2. 32. 20; etc.). Cf. *retia tendit Amor* in J. A. Taygetus (*C.P.I.* 9, 229; Gruter, *Del. I.P.* 2, 1137) and Campion, *El.* 11. 10; and *retia... | ...teten-dit Amor* in Ovid, *H.* 20. 45–6. *Fallax Amor* is in Seneca, *Hipp.* 634 (Fletcher), Pontano, *Hen.* 2. 29. 4, Gruter, *Del. I.P.* 1, 178, and, in the ablative, in Tibullus 1. 9. 83 (Fletcher). E. S. Le Comte (*Yet Once More*, New York, 1953, 6–7) traces the idea of amorous nets through Milton's verse and prose.

61–2 *Pellacesque genas, ad quas hyacinthina sordet | Purpura.* C. W. Brodribb ('Milton and Persius,' *N&Q* 159, 1930, 39) suggests an echo of both Persius 1. 32, *hyacinthina laena*, and I. Casaubon's note, which explains the adjective as *purpura* or *subrubra* (the latter word I do not find in Casaubon's edition of Persius, Paris, 1615).

62 *ipse tui floris, Adoni, rubor.* Venus made the anemone grow from the blood of Adonis after he had been killed by the boar (Ovid, *M.* 10. 735–9).

63 *laudatae toties Heroides olim.* The heroines of ancient myth in general and of Ovid's *Heroides* in particular. Cf. Ovid, *A.A.* 1. 713–14 (Warton).

64 *vagum...Jovem.* For Jove's amours see the note on *El* 7. 42.

65 *Achaemeniae turrita fronte puellae.* 'Achaemenian' means Persian, from Achaemenes, founder of the Persian dynasty. The word is common, e.g. Ovid, *A.A.* 1. 226, *M.* 4. 212; Horace, *C.* 3. 1. 44, *Epod.* 13. 8; Lucan 2. 49; Statius, *S.* 5. 3. 187, *Th.* 1. 718, 8. 286; Sil. Ital. 15. 23. The description of feminine headdress suggests accounts of Cybele; see under 74 below.

66 *Susa...Memnoniamque Ninon.* Susa, the chief city of Susiana, a part of Persia, was said to have been founded by Tithonus, father of Memnon; hence the appellation 'Memnonian' (Strabo 15. 3. 2; Herodotus 5. 53–4, 7. 151; Diod. Sic. 2. 22; George Sandys, *Relation of a Journey begun An: Dom: 1610*, 1615, 204). Milton either confused Susa with Ninos (Nineveh), the Assyrian city on the Tigris, or was following some unidentified authority; he is orthodox in *PL* 10. 308 (Allan H. Gilbert, *Geographical Dictionary of Milton*, New Haven, 1919, 280–1: cited hereafter as *G.D.*; MacKellar). D. T. Starnes and E. W. Talbert (*Classical Myth and Legend in Renaissance Dictionaries*, Chapel Hill, 1955, 338: cited hereafter as 'Starnes-Talbert') quote C. Stephanus, *Dictionarium*, on Susa, but that does not help here. Carey, citing Strabo (loc. cit.), remarks that 'Memnon was buried in Syria, by the river Badas,' and that Milton may therefore have used 'Memnonian' of Nineveh 'since it was the capital city of Syria.'

67 *Vos etiam Danaae fasces submittite Nymphae.* The epithet, derived from Danaus, the mythical founder of Argos, was equivalent to 'Greek' (Homer, *passim*; Virgil, *A.* 1. 30, 96, etc.). With Milton's figurative use of *fasces*, to which Keightley objected, MacKellar compares Virgil, *G.* 2. 495 (which is hardly figurative) and Cicero, *Brut.* 6. 22. Grotius, addressing Prince Maurice in *Mathematica* (*S.*, bk. 2, p. 54), has *fascesque tibi submittit*. Cf. *C.P.I.* 11, 192 (a poem on Pope Gregory XV): *cui tartara leti | Submittunt fasces*.

68   *Et vos Iliacae, Romuleaeque nurus*. Women of Troy (Ilium) and Rome (the city of Romulus). Cf. Sil. Ital. 3. 151, *Iliacaeque nurus*; Ovid, *Am.* 3. 4. 40, *Romulus Iliades Iliadesque Remus*, and *F.* 2. 431–4, 3. 206.

69   *Tarpëia Musa*. Ovid's house was near the Capitoline hill, on the side of which was the Tarpeian rock (Ovid, *Tr.* 1. 3. 29–30). Pompey's porch or colonnade (*Pompeianas...columnas*), in the Campus Martius, was a fashionable rendezvous; see Catullus 55. 6; Ovid, *A.A.* 1. 67, 3. 387; Propertius 2. 32. 11–12, *umbrosis...Pompeia columnis | Porticus*, and 4. 8. 75; Martial 11. 47. 3; MacKellar.

70   *Ausoniis plena theatra stolis*. Ausonia was a common poetical name for Italy derived from the Ausones, the primitive inhabitants of the middle and lower part of the country (Virgil, *G.* 2. 385, *Ausonii, Troia gens missa*; etc.). *Plena theatra*, in various forms, is a stock phrase, e.g. Ovid, *Tr.* 5. 7. 25, Lucan 7. 44, Juvenal 10. 128. The *stola* was the robe worn by Roman matrons (Ovid, *P.* 3. 3. 52; *Tr.* 2. 252). Coleridge expressed surprise 'that a man of so fine an ear as Milton, should have endured a short syllable before *st—theatra* s*tolis*' (Brinkley, 572). But Buchanan 'regularly allows a short vowel at the end of a word to remain short before another word beginning with *s* followed by another consonant' (James R. Naiden, *The Sphera of George Buchanan*, 1952, 32). Naiden points out that this practice, followed by some other Neo-Latinists, was exceptional among the ancients (eleven instances in Lucretius, nine in Horace, four in Propertius, one in Virgil).

73   *Tuque urbs Dardaniis Londinum structa colonis*. Dardanus was one of the mythical founders of Troy (Virgil, *A.* 6. 650, *Troiae Dardanus auctor*; 7. 422, *Dardaniis...colonis*; Lucan 2. 393, *Dardanii...coloni*). According to the story popularized by Geoffrey of Monmouth and later chroniclers, Britain, like other nations of western Europe, was founded by a Trojan, in this case Brutus, great-grandson of Aeneas. Thanks to such sceptics as the early Polydore Vergil and the later Camden (*Britain*, tr. 1610, 5–9) and Selden (*Works of Michael Drayton*, ed. J. W. Hebel et al., 5 v. Oxford, 1931–41, 4, 21 f., 214: cited hereafter as 'Drayton'), the great body of pre-Roman British history was in the early seventeenth century fading into legend. See MacKellar; D. Bush, *Mythology*

and the Renaissance Tradition in English Poetry (rev. ed. New York, 1963, 37–40, with references: cited hereafter as *Mythol.*); C. A. Patrides, *Milton and the Christian Tradition* (Oxford, 1966), 252–5. The fullest account is Sir T. D. Kendrick's *British Antiquity* (London, 1950). See Milton, *Comus* 921–2, *EpDam* 162 f., and *HistBr* (*Works* 10, 6 f.).

74 *Turrigerum late conspicienda caput.* Editors cite Virgil, *A.* 10. 253, *turrigeraeque urbes*; early maps of London and the frontispiece of James Howell's *Londinopolis* (1657); and Milton's 'Towred Cities' (*L'All* 117) and 'towred Cybele' (*Arc* 21). Lucan 1. 188 and Sil. Ital. 4. 408–9 use *turrigero vertice* of Rome; cf. Virgil, *A.* 7. 631, *turrigerae Antemnae.* The epithet belongs especially to Cybele and her diadem, e.g. Ovid, *F.* 6. 321, *turrigera frontem Cybele redimita corona*; ibid. 4. 219–24 (and *Tr.* 2. 24); Propertius 3. 17. 35; Claudian 33. 181 (2, 306); cf. Lucretius 2. 606–9; Virgil, *A.* 6. 784–5; Spenser, *F.Q.* 4. 11. 28; notes on *El* 5. 61–2, *Arc.* 21–2. Cf. Horace, *C.* 3. 16. 19, *late conspicuum.*

76 *pendulus orbis.* Editors cite Ovid, *M.* 1. 12–13: *nec circumfuso pendebat in aere tellus | ponderibus librata suis* (cf. *Tr.* 2. 217, *pendentem...orbem*); Shakespeare, *Meas.* 3. 1. 126, 'The pendant world'; Milton, *Procan* 3; *PL* 2. 1052, 'This pendant world'; *PL* 4. 1000, 'The pendulous round Earth.'

77–80 On the comparison of London girls to the stars, see the notes on 51 and 55–6 above. *Caelo...sereno* is a stock phrase, e.g. Lucretius 6. 247, Virgil, *G.* 1. 260, 487, *A.* 3. 518, 5. 870; Horace, *S.* 2. 4. 51, *Epod.* 15. 1, Ovid, *M.* 1. 168, 2. 321. With *scintillant* cf. Plautus, *Men.* 829, *ut oculi scintillant.*

78 *Endymioneae turba ministra deae.* Fletcher cites Sil. Ital. 11. 274–5, *non una ministri | turba gregis.* Milton's unusual epithet, *Endymioneus*, appears, e.g., in Ausonius, *Cupido Cruciatur* 41; Grotius, *Epith. Kinschot.* (*S.*, bk. 3, p. 108), and Campion, *El.* 9. 16.

81–4 The picture of Venus, her twin doves and quiver-bearing warrior or warriors (Cupid or Cupids) and favorite resorts, combines such standard items as appear, e.g., in Virgil, *A.* 1. 415–17, 617–18, 680–1, 691–4, and Ovid, *M.* 10. 529 f., and are illustrated in the following notes. Cf. Shakespeare, *Temp.* 4. 1. 92–4.

82 *Alma pharetrigero milite cuncta Venus. Alma Venus* is a commonplace, e.g. Lucretius 1. 2, Virgil, *A.* 1. 618, Ovid, *M.* 10. 230, 13. 759, etc. For Cupid, and the idea of love as military service, see the notes on 60 above and *El* 7. 8. The usual adjective is *pharetratus*, e.g. Ovid, *Am.* 2. 5. 1, *M.* 10. 525, *R. Am.* 379, *Tr.* 5. 1. 22; Statius, *S.* 1. 2. 64; cf. Sil. Ital. 14. 286, *pharetrigeri...regis*, and Grotius (loc. cit. p. 107 under 78 above), *pharetrigeri...Amores.* Cf. also Ovid, *P.* 1. 8. 18, *milite cinctus*; Castiglione, *Carm.* 3. 5, *Mirandula milite cincta est.*

83 Cnidos in Caria had a famous temple of Venus (Ovid, *M.* 10. 531; Horace, *C.* 1. 30. 1, 3. 28. 13–15). The river Simois rose on Mount Ida, the scene of the judgment of Paris and of Venus' giving birth to Aeneas (Virgil, *A.* 1. 617–18; Sandys, *Relation*, 1615, 21). With *riguas...flumine valles,* cf. Virgil, *G.* 2. 485, *rigui...in vallibus amnes.*

84 *Huic Paphon, & roseam posthabitura Cypron.* Paphos, in Cyprus, was another place famous for its temple of Venus (Virgil, *A.* 1. 415–17, 10. 51; Horace, *C.* 1. 30. 1, 3. 28. 14; Ovid, *Am.* 2. 17. 4, *M.* 10. 297, 530; Lucan 8. 456–8). See the note on Cypris, *El* 3. 20. *Posthabitura* echoes the *posthabita* of Virgil, *A.* 1. 16 (cf. *Rous* 65).

85 *Ast ego, dum pueri sinit indulgentia caeci.* Cf. Buchanan, *S.* 4. 39, *Venus, & teneri fuit indulgentia nati.* If *Ast ego* needs examples, cf. Virgil, *A.* 1. 46, 7. 308; Castiglione, *Alcon* 101; Milton, *El* 4. 57, 7. 77.

87–8 *malefidae infamia Circes | Atria.* The *loci classici* for Circe are Homer, *Od.* 10. 133–574 and Ovid, *M.* 14. 242–440. For Milton's phrasing, cf. Ovid, *M.* 13. 968, *prodigiosa...atria Circes*; 14. 9–10, *atria...Circes*; 14. 446–7, *infamataeque...deae.*

88 *divini Molyos usus ope.* The magical herb moly, which protected Odysseus from Circe's spells, had long been an allegorical symbol of moral and religious temperance (see the list in R. M. Adams, *Ikon*, Ithaca, 1955, 14–15): e.g. N. Comes, *Mythol.* 6. 6; Golding's *Ovid*, Epistle, 276–9; Ascham, *English Works*, ed. W. A. Wright (Cambridge, 1904), 225–6; Grotius, *In Symbolum Sculteti (Farr.,* bk. 1, p. 179): *Et fruimur, contra pellacis pocla veneni, | Non intellecto superorum munere moly*; Sandys, *Relation* (1615), 307–8. Sandys' later full interpretation (*Ovid*, 1632, 475, 480–1; 1640, 261, 265) is partly quoted in Bush, *Mythol.* 280. A much fuller account of moly will be in the Variorum note on *Comus* 635–6. The phrase *usus ope* also ends Ovid, *F.* 3. 318 and Milton, *ProdBom* 2. 6.

89 *juncosas Cami remeare paludes.* Cf. line 11, and Virgil, *E.* 1. 48, *limosoque palus...iunco*; Ovid, *M.* 6. 345, *iuncis...paludibus.*

90 *raucae murmur...Scholae.* See the note on 25 above and Milton's references to academic studies in *Prol* 1 (*Works* 12, 119–21), *Prol* 3 (ibid. 159–73), *Prol* 4 (ibid. 173–7), *Prol* 7 (ibid. 247–85), and *Educ. Rauca...schola* is in *Cam. Insig.* (1624), sig. D 3. *Raucum murmur,* in varying cases, is a stock phrase, e.g. Virgil, *G.* 1. 109, Ovid, *M.* 13. 567, 14. 280–1, Sil. Ital. 2. 221, 4. 172, Claudian 33. 258 (2, 312), Buchanan, *S.* 3. 37, *Bapt.* 1139, Grotius, *Mathematica* (*S.,* bk. 1, p. 53), *Epith. Kinschot.* (*S.,* bk. 3, p. 102).

91 *fidi parvum...munus amici*. Cf. *parva munera* in Horace, *C.* 1. 28(1). 3–4, Ovid, *F.* 2. 534, and Claudian, *S.P.* 48. 1–2 (2, 274).

92 *Paucaque in alternos verba coacta modos*. The alternating hexameter and pentameter that make up the elegiac distich. Cf. Ovid, *Tr.* 3. 7. 10, *aptaque in alternos cogere verba pedes* (Fletcher); Seneca, *Oed.* 528, *Coacta verba. Modos*, for 'measures,' appears, e.g., in Ovid, *Am.* 1. 1. 2, 28. *Pauca verba* was a stock tag even for English speakers, e.g. Shakespeare, *L.L.L.* 4. 2. 171, *Wives* 1. 1. 123, 134; Jonson, *E.M. in his H.* 4. 2. 40; cf. Ovid, *Tr.* 1. 8. 20.

Elegia secunda, *Anno aetatis* *17*

IN OBITUM PRAECONIS ACADEMICI CANTABRIGIENSIS

🙟

Richard Ridding, M.A., of St John's College, the Senior Esquire Bedell (Beadle) of the university, resigned on 16 September 1626 the ceremonial office he had held for thirty years, and evidently died soon afterwards; his will, dated 19 September, was probated on 28 November. The elegy would no doubt have been written shortly after Ridding's death, probably in November (Parker, 731, n. 26, 733, n. 30), not long before Milton's eighteenth birthday. (There is some further discussion of chronological problems in the introduction to *Elegia tertia*.) This short elegy on a dignified veteran of the Cambridge scene must have been composed about the same time as the one on the Vice-Chancellor, *In obitum Procancellarii medici*, which is just twice as long. Both are formal exercises in the young poet's earliest elegiac manner. While a plethora of mythological allusions is, in some writers, one of the Neo-Latin conventions, and may appear in passages that are deeply felt, in such poems as these allusions constitute the whole texture and structure. But Leigh Hunt singled out *Magna sepulchrorum regina* (*El* 2. 17) as a Dantesque 'personification of Death, worthy of' Milton's 'maturest imagery' (*Lit. Exam.* 30 August 1823, 131–2; Houtchens, 181). Michael West discusses both Latin and English poems in 'The *Consolatio* in Milton's Funeral Elegies' (forthcoming).

Since Milton did not date *Elegy* 1, *Elegy* 2 introduces the method he followed in dating a number of poems. As the dates of events he commemorated show, he used *Anno aetatis* *17*, to cite the present example, to mean, not 'in his seventeenth year,' but 'at the age of seventeen.' This interpretation of *Anno aetatis*, suggested by Masson (*P.W.* 1, 116), was established by W. R. Parker ('Some Problems in the Chronology of Milton's Early Poems,' *RES* 11, 1935, 276–83); it was unconvincingly disputed by E. Sirluck ('Milton's Idle Right Hand,' *JEGP* 60, 1961, 781–4), and is cogently restated by Parker (784–6), who notes that Milton 'was simply conforming to common usage, even that of official records.' The dates Milton assigned seem to be mainly accurate, though his memory was at fault in two cases, certainly in regard to *Procan* (Parker, 731, 785, and below, the headnote to the poem) and apparently in regard to the *Fair Infant* (Parker, 738, 785; and headnote).

NOTES

1 *baculo fulgente.* The mace carried by the Beadle in academic processions. The Duke of Buckingham, who in 1626 was elected Chancellor (and to whom Ridding bore the official news of his election), 'gave the Beadles their old silver Staves, and bestowed better and bigger on the University, with the Kings, and his own Arms insculped thereon' (Thomas Fuller, *History of the University of Cambridge*, London, 1655, 164). See J. B. Mullinger, *The University of Cambridge*, 3 (Cambridge, 1911), 75; A. P. Humphry, 'On the Maces of the Esquire Bedells,' *Cambridge Antiquarian Communications*, Cambridge Antiquarian Society, 21 (1881), 207–18; H. P. Stokes, 'The Esquire Bedells of the University of Cambridge,' *Cambridge Antiquarian Society Publications* 45 (1911), 39, 93–5; MacKellar.

2 *Palladium...gregem.* The devotees of Pallas Athene, goddess of wisdom and learning. Cf. Horace, *Ep.* 1. 4. 16, *Epicuri de grege porcum*; Petronius, *Sat.* 5, *Socratico...grege*; Martial 12. 11. 4, *Pierio de grege*; *Cantab. Dolor* (1625), p. 49, *Phoebi de grege nemo*; Milton, *Procan* 33, *Patrem* 101.

3–4 *Ultima praeconum praeconem te quoque saeva* | *Mors rapit.* As Milton's title indicates, *praeco* ('crier,' 'herald') is the equivalent of 'beadle.' Such plays on words are common in Latin poetry, especially in Ovid and Propertius (Koehler, 165 f.), e.g. Ovid, *H.* 19. 206, *nisi te sospite sospes ero. Saeva mors* is a stock phrase, e.g. Lucan 2. 100, 3. 605, Buchanan, *Ps.* 6. 6, 78. 50.

5–6 *Candidiora...tempora plumis* | *...delituisse Jovem.* An allusion to Jupiter's assuming the form of a swan when he visited Leda. The whiteness of this celestial swan was proverbial, e.g. Spenser, *Prothal.* 42–3, *F.Q.* 3. 11. 32. Editors cite Ovid, *H.* 8. 68, *in plumis delituisse Iovem*, and *Tr.* 4. 8. 1, *Iam mea cycneas imitantur tempora plumas.* Harding (*Ovid*, 48–9) comments on the fusing of the two phrases.

7–8 *Haemonio juvenescere succo,* | *...in Aesonios...dies.* Medea rejuvenated Aeson by boiling his body in a brew compounded of roots cut in a Haemonian valley, seeds, flowers, and strong juices, *sucos acres* (Ovid, *M.* 7. 265). Haemonia was an old and poetical name for Thessaly, the land of witchcraft (Ovid, *M.* 1. 568, 2.543, 8. 813, *R. Am.* 249–50, etc.; cf. Harding, *Ovid*, 63). Cf. A. Gill, *In Parentis mei Natalem...Feb. 27. 1624* (i.e. 1625 N.S.): *O utinam sparsis per membra trementia succis* | *(Fertur ut Aesonias olim reparasse medullas)* | *Docta tibi posset Colchis renovare juventam* (p. 15).

9 *Stygiis...ab undis.* One of the many Latin commonplaces for the underworld, e.g. Virgil, *A.* 3. 215, 6. 385, Ovid, *Tr.* 1. 2. 65, Propertius 3. 18. 9, Seneca, *Herc. Fur.* 185, *Med.* 804–5.

9–10 *medica revocaret...* | *Arte Coronides, saepe rogante dea.* Coronides is Aesculapius, the god of medicine, son of Apollo and Coronis (Ovid, *M.* 2. 542–6, 596–611; for the name, *M.* 15. 624, *F.* 6. 746). Hippolytus was restored to life by the drugs of Aesculapius and the solicitude of Diana; cf. Virgil, *A.* 7. 769, *Paeoniis revocatum herbis et amore Dianae*; Ovid, *M.* 15. 531 f.; Spenser, *F.Q.* 1. 5. 37–44. Starnes-Talbert (233) quote C. Stephanus, *Dictionarium*, especially for the phrases *Dianae precibus* ('Aesculapius') and *a Diana exoratus* ('Hippolytus'), which Milton may have seen but hardly needed. The pattern of Milton's last phrase might have echoed a phrase from one of Ovid's accounts of the death of Hippolytus, *multum indignante Diana* (*F.* 6. 745). *Medica arte* appears, in various forms, in Ovid, *M.* 2. 618, *Tr.* 5. 6. 12; Manilius, *Astron.* 1. 887; Mantuan, *E.* 3. 138; Vida, *A.P.* 1. 376.

11 *acies...togatas.* The gown-clad lines, a combination of military and civilian (here academic) terms. Cf. the note on *Procan* 30; Milton, *Prol* 7 (*Works* 12, 246, lines 7–8), *togatorum hominum frequentia*; Gill, *Ad...Petrum Trionem...Kal. Ian. 1626* (i.e. 1627), *togatos...Academicos* (p. 20).

12 *Phoebo...tuo.* The Vice-Chancellor of the University.

13–14 *Cyllenius...* | *Alipes.* Cyllenius was a common name for Mercury (Virgil, *A.* 4. 252; Ovid, *M.* 1. 713, 2. 720, 818), who was born on the Arcadian mountain Cyllene (*Homeric Hymn to Hermes* 1–2; Ovid, *F.* 5. 85–8). When he was sent down to Priam (Homer, *Il.* 24. 334–57), the meeting, as editors note, took place on the plain, not in the palace; Milton may have thought of the slightly earlier message from Zeus brought by Iris (*Il.* 24. 159 f.), or he may have had a hazy recollection of Horace, *C.* 1. 10. 13–16. The epithet *Alipes* is in Ovid, *M.* 4. 756, 11. 312, *F.* 5. 100. The phrase *aetherea...ab arce* echoes a commonplace, e.g. Ovid, *M.* 15. 858–9, *Tr.* 4. 3. 5, 5. 3. 19; Statius, *Th.* 3. 222;

Elegia secunda: In obitum Praeconis

Val. Flacc. 2. 444; Sannazaro, *P.V.* 1. 33; Grotius, *In Pascha* (*El.*, bk. 1, p. 157).

15–16 *Talis & Eurybates ante ora furentis Achillei | Rettulit Atridae jussa severa ducis.* Eurybates was one of the squires whom Agamemnon (Atrides, son of Atreus) sent to Achilles to take from him his prize, Briseis (Homer, *Il.* 1. 320–33). In Ovid, *H.* 3. 9 (Briseis to Achilles), the name Eurybates occupies the same place in the line as it does here. Achilles is *furens* in Seneca, *Troad.* 185. *Jussa severa* is in Joseph Scaliger, *C.P.I.* 9, 475; cf. Virgil, *G.* 3. 41 and *A.* 9. 804, *haud mollia iussa*, and Ovid, *M.* 7.14, *iussa...dura.*

17 *satelles Averni.* The servant of Avernus is Death. Lake Avernus, near Naples, was supposed to be an entrance to Hades and hence stood for Hades itself (Virgil, *A.* 6. 126, 201 f.; Lucretius 6. 738 f.). Horace (*C.* 2. 18. 34) calls Charon *satelles Orci.*

19–24 Godolphin (*MP* 37, 1939–40, 355) notes the cumulative and schematic rhyming of *is* and *a*: *tel*i*s* ist*a* petend*a* tu*is*, etc. Koehler (149) remarks that in 15–24 'all except one of the pentameters have the same pairing of the vowels *a a* in the second hemistich. In the three final pentameters, the vowels are bracketed with rime—the same rime in all three instances.'

19 *pondus inutile terrae.* Editors note that the phrase translates a phrase in Homer, *Il.* 18. 104; cf. *Od.* 20. 379. But Milton's phrase is in *Cantab. Dolor* (1625), p. 36; and cf. *inutile pondus* in Ovid, *Am.* 3. 7. 15, *C.P.I.* 1, 76 and 9, 488, and Ariosto, *Carm.* 42. 1. *Telluris inutile pondus* is quoted as a proverbial phrase by Erasmus in his *Adagia*, under chil. IV, cent. X, prov. XCVIII (*Opera*, 2, Leyden, 1703, 1182); this appears in *C.P.I.* 4, 235 and Buchanan, *Jeph.* 1358–9.

21 *Vestibus hunc igitur pullis Academia luge.* Cf. *Vestibus ...pullis* in *Lacrymae Cantab.* (1619), p. 39 and *Gratul. Cantab.* (1623), p. 26; the singular in *Lacrymae*, p. 3 and *Cantab. Dolor* (1625), pp. 1, 16, 57. Editors remark that here, and in the epilogue to *El* 7, the penult of *Academia*, contrary to the usual practice, is made short. But the short *i* is not unusual. E.g., cf. Claudian 17. 94 (1, 344): *in Latium spretis Academia migrat Athenis*; and *C.P.I.* 8, 183 and 9, 331. It is the rule in such Oxford and Cambridge anthologies as *Lacrymae Cantab.* (pp. 12, 78, 85) and *Cantab. Dolor*, pp. 1 (*Deflet & amissum pullata Academia Phoebum*) and 11. the *Dictionarium* of A. Calepine (ed. Basel, 1616), the word appears thus: Ăcădēmiă.

22 *Et madeant lachrymis nigra feretra tuis.* Editors see a reference to the custom of attaching funeral verses to the pall. Cf. Milton, *EpWin* 55–8 and

63

Lyc 14; and Gill's elegy on Bishop Lake (d. 4 May 1626): *Quid feretro lacrymas tristia signa damus?* (p. 10).

23–4 For the personification of Elegy see Ovid, *Am.* 3. 1. 7–10, 3. 9. 3, *R. Am.* 379–80, Martial 5. 30. 4, Statius, *S.* 1. 2. 7–10, Pontano, *A.C.* 1. 1, Campion, *El.* 13. 9. In *Am.* 3. 9. 3, as Koehler observes (45), Ovid, lamenting Tibullus, 'is like Milton appealing to Elegy herself to mourn for the deceased'.

24 *Personet & totis naenia moesta scholis.* Garrod suggests *totas scholas*; but cf., e.g., Livy 41. 2, *totis...personabat castris. Naenia moesta* is in *C.P.I.* 4, 420.

Elegia tertia, Anno aetatis 17

IN OBITUM PRAESULIS WINTONIENSIS

❦

Lancelot Andrewes (b. 1555) died on 25 September 1626; his funeral was solemnized on 11 November. He was an alumnus of Pembroke Hall and was its Master from 1589 to 1605. Along with his early connections and his general eminence, his death had a further concern for Cambridge in that his brother Roger was at the time Master of Jesus. Lancelot Andrewes became Dean of Westminster in 1601 and Bishop of Chichester in 1605, of Ely in 1609, and of Winchester in 1618. He was one of the company of scholars who produced the King James version of the Bible. Andrewes was a notable figure at court and in the world as well as in the church, and was revered for the sanctity of his life, the quality of his sermons, and his learning and patronage of learning (though he was not wholly free from some common weaknesses of Jacobean bishops). But there is no need of a long note on a 'metaphysical' preacher and 'church father' who has, through the modern revival of interest in the early seventeenth century, become much better known to the literary than he used to be.

Milton's *Anno aetatis 17*, in its Miltonic meaning, 'At the age of 17,' is presumably correct, since an obituary poem could not be far removed in time from its occasion, so that the elegy must have been written between September 25/26 and his eighteenth birthday, 9 December 1626. But there are some complications that must be touched upon (a fuller discussion was given in the *Harvard Library Bulletin*, 9, 1955, 392–6). In lines 9–10, in his survey of the recent ravages of death, Milton says:

> *Tunc memini clarique ducis, fratrisque verendi*
> *Intempestivis ossa cremata rogis.*

Editors have agreed in accepting the suggestion made by Lord Hailes to Warton, that the *clarus dux* and *frater verendus* were Christian of Brunswick (1599–6 June 1626) and Count Ernest of Mansfeld (*c.* 1580–*c.* 29 November 1626), who fought on the Protestant side in the Thirty Years War (Mansfeld thus being only a 'brother in arms'). This idea seems very questionable.

In the first place, Milton assumes that the two persons are so clearly recognizable that they need only a brief and vague reference; but it is doubtful if the deaths of Christian and Mansfeld attracted such attention in England that they would be obvious to the reader. Secondly, in the opening lines of his elegy on Bishop Felton (*In obitum Praesulis Eliensis*), who died on 5 October, Milton says that he had barely paid in full the rites due to Andrewes when the news came of Felton's death, and that news must have become generally known within a week or two of the event. Such words can only mean that he had written *El* 3 between 25/26 September and, say, 5–12 October. But the report of Mansfeld's death could not have reached England until early in December, and Parker ('Notes,' 117–18), accepting the traditional identification for want of better, has to push the composition of the elegy on Andrewes (and hence of the one on Felton also) up to December or even January (followed by Shawcross, *Complete English Poetry*, New York, 1963, 547). By that time the funeral baked meats for both bishops would surely be cold; and we cannot override Milton's apparent statement that he wrote *El* 3 before 5–12 October. Carey, questioning my argument, says that 'there is no need to equate the weeping' of *Praesulis Eliensis* 1–6 with the composition of *El* 3; but Milton was surely not referring to a private and inarticulate grief. Parker now (733, n. 30) dates *El* 3 in November, the elegy on Felton in late November or early December.

Mansfeld might be one of another Continental pair—though the dates remain troublesome in regard to Milton's words about the time of composition. Duke John Ernest of Weimar died on 4 December 1626, upon hearing of Mansfeld's death; his heart was found to be as dry and withered as a nut. These circumstances apparently attracted some attention. See *Cambridge Modern History* 4 (1906), 98; Richard Knolles,

Generall Historie of the Turkes (4th edition, 1631, with a continuation, 1621–9), 1482–3; Sir Thomas Browne, who cites the *Generall Historie* (*Works*, ed. Keynes, 1964, 3, 328); *The Prose of Sir Thomas Browne*, ed. N. J. Endicott (New York, 1967), 353, 592, n. 30.

Concerning the two leaders of lines 9–10 of *El* 3, we may assume that, as the word *ducis* suggests, they are public and national figures; that, as no pair of actual brothers has been suggested, and as the acceptance of Mansfeld assumes, *frater* means only an associate of some kind; that untimely death may, in the case of eminent persons, indicate almost any age short of the canonical seventy; and, finally, that the two men had died recently. After a survey of some ninety Britons (including Bacon) who died in 1625–6 (when the plague heightened the normal toll), one cannot find a completely satisfactory pair to replace the quite unsatisfactory Christian and Mansfeld.[1]

By far the most conspicuous personage was King James (1566–27 March 1625), and it is almost unthinkable that Milton, writing of

---

[1] Since Milton's letters to Gill indicate that they at least sometimes exchanged verses, it is likely enough that he saw a manuscript of Gill's elegy on King James, or the printed text in *Oxoniensis Academiae Parentalia* (1625), sig. B 3ᵛ (reprinted in Gill's *Parerga*, 1632, pp. 6–7). Whether he did or not, Gill's piece is of interest here. The first six lines, like the opening lines of Milton's *El* 3, speak of the ravages of death in Britain, especially among the great; this was of course a fairly obvious gambit for anyone writing in 1625–6. Gill's next paragraph is more specific than Milton's lines 9–12. He lists seven recent deaths: Ludovic Stuart, second Duke of Lennox and Duke of Richmond (1574–February 1624); Richard Sackville, Earl of Dorset (1589–March 1624), husband of Anne Clifford; Esmé Stuart (1579–July 1624), brother of Ludovic and his successor, for a few months, as third Duke of Lennox; Henry Wriothesley, Earl of Southampton (1573–November 1624); Charles Howard, Earl of Nottingham (1536–December 1624); Arthur, Baron Chichester (1563–February 1625); and James, Marquis of Hamilton (1589–2 March 1625). Such names are a kind of checklist of deaths in 1624–5 that seemed notable to a young man writing in the spring of 1625, presumably a year and a half before Milton wrote *El* 3. None of them, for various reasons, seem to be strong candidates for Milton's allusion. Other lists, contemporary with Gill's, are more or less similar. In *Cantab. Dolor* (1625), the volume of Cambridge tributes to James and his successor which is cited *passim* in these notes, one poem (p. 16) names, as victims of Libitina, Hamilton, the two dukes of Lennox, Nottingham, Chichester, Sackville, and Southampton and his son. In the Oxford counterpart of 1625, which, as we noted above, contained Gill's poem, a piece signed 'Io. Donne *Aed. Christi alumnus*' (sig. D 4ʳ) catalogues the deaths of Dorset, the dukes of Lennox, Hamilton, and Chichester. Another poem in the same volume, by 'Rich. Corbett S.T.D. *Aedis Christi Decanus*' (sig. I 4ʳ), lists the same men as Donne and also Southampton and Nottingham.

notable deaths in 1625–6, could overlook or ignore that of his sovereign—of whom, at this period, he had a sufficiently favorable opinion (witness the opening of *In quintum Novembris*).[2] Of possible candidates for the role of *frater verendus*, the most likely would seem to be an almost exact contemporary of James, namely Maurice Prince of Orange (1567–23 April 1625), a royal 'brother' and the leader of Protestant Holland. Though further inquiry may bring forth a better running-mate for the king, or a better pair, James and Maurice appear to be, logically and chronologically, much more suitable than Christian and Mansfeld.

Milton's elegies on Andrewes and Felton, which were written so close together, are parallel in length, structure, and manner. They are more ambitious and more successful than the elegies on Gostlin and Ridding of about the same time. The young author is not, to be sure, moved by any strong personal feeling.[3] He is still an undergraduate versifier going through conventional motions, yet he achieves something like a pattern of drama and apocalyptic vision appropriate to the commemoration of two men raised above the common run by their office and their personal character. In each poem the power of Death is challenged and overcome by the appeal to Christian immortality, and each ends with a first glimpse of the radiant order of heaven that is to constitute the triumphant affirmation of *Lycidas* and the *Epitaphium Damonis* (cf. Hanford, 'Youth,' 99; Fletcher, *Intell. Dev.* 2, 403–7).[4] M. Mahood (*Poetry and Humanism*, London, 1950, 203) remarks: 'Milton's vision of Lancelot Andrewes's triumphal entry into the roseate light and rose-scented air of a vinous Heaven might, translated into tempera, adorn the cupola of any Baroque church.'

---

[2] Cf. the phrase from Grotius about James as *magnum Ducem* quoted in the note on *QNov* 3–4.

[3] 'There is no evidence that Milton ever saw either Lancelot Andrewes or Nicholas Felton, the Bishop of Ely, although he could easily have heard the latter when Felton was rector of St. Mary-le-Bow church (1596–1617), just back of the poet's home on Bread Street' (Parker, 'Notes', 118).

[4] Fletcher finds the stress I lay on the death dates of Andrewes and Felton 'out of all proportion to Milton's known habits of composition.' But do we know his habits of composition? In this case we have his explicit statement cited above from the poem on Felton. Also, in apparently accepting the conventional pair of leaders and at the same time dating *El* 3 'probably...almost immediately after Milton's return for Michaelmas term,' Fletcher forgets that Mansfeld did not die till the end of November.

Elegia tertia: In obitum Praesulis Wintoniensis

H. Maclean ('Milton's *Fair Infant*,' *ELH* 24, 1957, 296–305), going on from D. C. Allen (*The Harmonious Vision*, Baltimore, 1954, 47–52), measures the complexity of the *Fair Infant* and the *Nativity* against the relative simplicity of the elegies on Andrewes and Felton. In each of these pieces 'Christian images supersede the classical vision, but do not banish the images of classical story...The Christian victory, so to speak, contains, and even (for its fullest effect) depends upon the continued presence of classical elements, which imaginatively take their place in the eternal scheme.' Also, 'in neither poem is the central figure (once received into heaven) considered to be *acting* further in man's behalf,' whereas the fair infant and of course the Christ of the *Nativity* are active agents (298). Detailed analysis shows that the *Fair Infant* marks an aesthetic advance 'over the relatively simple classical-Christian antithesis of thought and image informing *Elegy III*, as well as over the mild (but not final) rejection of a classical viewpoint made, in Christian terms, by the *Bishop of Ely*' (304).

NOTES

1 *Moestus eram.* The first words of Marrasius Siculus' *Ad Maffeum Vegium* (*C.P.I.* 6, 254).

1 *nullo comitante.* In Seneca, *Hipp.* 425, Martial 11. 51. 3, and *C.P.I.* 9, 408.

3–8 During 1625, in London, its liberties, and outparishes, the record of deaths from the plague ran to over 35,000, at least a sixth of the population (F. P. Wilson, *The Plague in Shakespeare's London*, Oxford, 1927, 174–5). Milton is not thinking merely of the plague, as his reference to heroes in Belgium, and of course his main theme, indicate.

3 *subiit funestae cladis Imago.* Cf. Ovid, *Tr.* 1. 3. 1, *subit illius tristissima noctis imago* (Fletcher); Seneca, *Thy.* 189 and *Phoen.* 635, *clade funesta*; Secundus, *Epist.* 2. 4. 16, *funestae nuncia cladis*; Milton, *Prol* 5 (*Works* 12, 192, lines 11–12), *funestis cladibus*.

4 *Libitina.* The ancient Italian goddess of corpses whose name was used by poets as a synonym of Death, e.g. Horace, *C.* 3. 30. 7, *S.* 2. 6. 19, *Ep.* 2. 1. 49; Juvenal 12. 122; Sannazaro, *El.* 1. 10. 7; Buchanan, *Epig.* 1. 25. 12; Gill, *In...obitum...Henrici, Principis Walliae* (p. 2); *Cantab. Dolor* (1625), p. 16.

5–8 Editors cite the most familiar expression of this commonplace, Horace, *C*. 1. 4. 13–14; *pallida Mors aequo pulsat pede pauperum tabernas | regumque turres.*

6 *Dira sepulchrali mors metuenda face.* Editors cite Ovid, *H*. 2. 120, *suntque sepulcrali lumina mota face*; cf. *Cantab. Dolor* (1625), p. 43, *sepulcrali...face. Dira mors* is a stock phrase, e.g. Tibullus 1. 10. 4; Seneca, *Herc. Fur.* 56, *Herc. Oet.* 928, *Oct.* 322; Castiglione, *Carm.* 3. 2. See the note on *El* 2. 3–4.

7 *Pulsavitque auro gravidos & jaspide muros.* Cf. the Horatian phrase quoted under 5–8; Virgil, *A*. 12. 706, *pulsabant ariete muros*, and 3. 464, *auro gravia*; Rev. 4. 3 (Beza): *Is...qui sedebat, aspectu similis lapidi erat jaspidi & sardio: & in circuitu throni erat iris aspectu similis smaragdo;* and 21. 11 (quoted under *Eli* 62–3).

9–10 On the identity of the *clarus dux* and *frater verendus*, see the introductory note and the fuller discussion there cited. Cf. Statius, *Th*. 8. 27, *Minos cum fratre verendo.*

11–12 *Et memini Heroum quos vidit ad aethera raptos, | Flevit & amissos Belgia tota duces.* Masson (*P.W.* 3, 303) suggested that the heroes whom the Low Countries mourned included Henry de Vere, 18th Earl of Oxford (1593–1625), who died there during military service, and his more famous kinsman, Sir Horace Vere, the chief English commander in the Palatinate in 1620–4, who had returned to England in 1624 and might therefore be called *amissus*. Henry Wriothesley, Earl of Southampton (1573–1624), also died while on service in Flanders. The introductory note above mentions Duke Christian and the Prince of Orange.

15 *Delicui fletu, & tristi sic ore querebar.* Cf. Ovid, *M*. 7. 380–1, *flendo | dilicuit* (Fletcher); *M*. 11. 459–60, Catullus 65. 24, and Mantuan, *E*. 6. 93, *tristi...ore.*

16 *Mors fera Tartareo diva secunda Jovi.* Cf. Sedulius, *Elegia* 1. 69 and 70 (Migne, *Pat. Lat.* 19, 758), *Mors fera*; Castiglione, *Alcon* 32, *fera...mors.* Tartarean Jove is Pluto: cf. Val. Flacc. 1. 730, *Tartareo...Iovi*, and the same phrase, in different cases, in *C.P.I.* 7, 22 and the quotation from Diodati in *Procan* 37 n.; cf. also *Comus* 20, 'neather Jove'. In Homer, *Il*. 8. 13 and Hesiod, *Theog.* 721–819, Tartarus is an underworld of mist and darkness; the word became a general term for hell (Virgil, *A*. 6. 543, 577–9; Ovid, *M*. 1. 113, 2. 260, 5. 371; Seneca, *Herc. Fur.* 709 f.; etc.), and in Milton may include fire (*QNov* 35; *ProdBom* 3. 11; *PL* 2. 69, 6. 53–5: MacKellar, Osgood, *C.M.* 80–1).

18 *Et quod in herbosos jus tibi detur agros.* On the power of Death Todd cited Rev. 6. 8, which Beza renders: *...dataque est eis in quadrantem terrae potestas* *trucidandi gladio, & fame, & morte, & per terrestres feras.* Cf. Mantuan, *E.* 2. 38, *herbosos...agros.*

20 *pulchrae Cypridi sacra rosa.* Cypris was a common Greek name for Aphrodite (Venus) because she had risen from the sea near Cyprus and had her chief temples there (e.g. Homer, *Il.* 5. 330, 883; Euripides, *Hipp. passim*; Horace, *C.* 1. 3. 1, 1. 19. 9–10; Ovid, *M.* 10. 270). For the late use of the name in Latin poetry MacKellar (234) cites Ausonius, *Epig.* 67. 1. It is common in Neo-Latin verse, e.g. in Alciati, Pontano, Secundus, Buchanan, Grotius, in *C.P.I.* and Gruter, and appears again in Milton, *El* 7. 48, *Naturam* 63; the name is also used in Chaucer, *H.F.* 518, *Tr.* 3. 725, and Jonson, *Hymenaei* 528. The association of Venus with roses is familiar, e.g. Ovid, *Am.* 1. 2. 39–40; Ausonius, *De Rosis Nascentibus* 18–22; Secundus, *El.* 1. 9. 42, *Bas.* 1.

21 *fluvio contermina quercus.* Warton noted that *contermina* was a favorite word of Ovid (*M.* 8. 620, *tiliae contermina quercus*; and 1. 774, 4. 90, 8. 553; *P.* 4. 6. 45; *F.* 2. 55).

22 *Miretur lapsus praetereuntis aquae.* Cf. Tibullus 1. 1. 27–8: *sub umbra | arboris ad rivos praetereuntis aquae* (Fletcher); Buchanan, *El.* 2. 60 (*Majae Cal.*): *Nunc strepitum captat praetereuntis aquae* (Todd). The phrase is also in *C.P.I.* 9, 490, 497.

23 *liquido...coelo.* Keightley said that the Roman poets 'never termed *caelum* "*liquidum*,"' but commentators cite Ovid, *M.* 1. 23 and Statius, *Th.* 4. 7. One may add Buchanan, *Sph.* 3. 180, *C.P.I.* 11, 50 (Vida) and 434.

24 *augur avis.* This phrase, censured by Salmasius (*Responsio*, London, 1660, 5; quoted in French, *L.R.* 4, 345–7), might have been suggested by the conjunction *augur avem* in Ovid, *F.* 1. 180.

25. *quae mille nigris errant animalia sylvis.* Cf. Horace, *C.* 1. 21. 7–8, *nigris... silvis*; Seneca, *Herc. Fur.* 836, *nigra...silva* (Fletcher); Virgil, *E.* 6. 40, *errent animalia*; Pontano, *Uran.* 1. 49, *errantque suis animalia silvis.*

26 *quod alunt mutum Proteos antra pecus.* Proteus' herding of the seals or sea-calves of Poseidon was an ancient and modern commonplace, e.g. Homer, *Od.* 4. 410–13; Virgil, *G.* 4. 387–95, 429–36; Horace, *C.* 1. 2. 7; Spenser, *F.Q.* 3. 8. 30; Milton, *EpDam* 99–100. For the phrasing cf. Virgil, *G.* 4. 429, *Proteus...antra*; Horace, *S.* 1. 3. 100, *mutum et turpe pecus.*

28 *Quid juvat humana tingere caede manus?* Cf. Ovid, *P.* 2. 9. 56, *hostili tingere caede manum.*

29 *certas acuisse sagittas.* Cf. Horace, *C.* 2. 8. 15, *acuens sagittas* (Fletcher);

1. 12. 23–4, *certa* / ...*sagitta*; Ovid, *Am.* 1. 1. 25, *certas*...*sagittas*; Secundus, *El.* 1. 1. 9, *acuebat*...*sagittas*; 2. 10. 15, *acuitque sagittas*. On the perfect infinitives *acuisse* and *fugasse* (30), see the comment of Godolphin cited under *El* 1. 17.

30 *Semideamque animam sede fugasse sua?* Editors cite Milton, *FInf* 21: 'Unhous'd thy Virgin Soul from her fair biding place.'

31 *alto sub pectore volvo.* With variations, a stock phrase, e.g. Virgil, *A.* 7. 254, *volvit sub pectore*; 6. 599–600, *sub alto* / *pectore*; Ovid, *M.* 1. 656–7; Milton, *Eli* 19, *Naturam* 3.

32 *Roscidus occiduis Hesperus exit aquis.* Hesperus was the evening star (cf. *PL* 9. 49–50). Editors cite Ovid, *F.* 2. 314, *Hesperos*...*roscidus.* Cf. *occiduas*... *aquas* in Ovid, *F.* 1. 314, *Tr.* 4. 3. 4 (Fletcher), and in *C.P.I.* 8, 16; and Buchanan, *S.* 2. 106: *Tristior occiduas Phoebus descendit in undas.*

33 *Tartessiaco*...*aequore currum.* Tartessus was an ancient city of Spain, so that *Tartessiacus* or *Tartessius* meant Spanish or western or, as here, the Atlantic. MacKellar cites Ovid, *M.* 14. 416, Buchanan, *Sph.* 1. 445, 629, and Milton, *El* 5. 83; and notes that in *Comus* 97 Milton at first wrote 'Tartessian' but substituted 'Atlantick.' Cf. Sil. Ital. 6. 1, *Tartessiaco*...*aequore* (and 10. 537, 17. 590); Martial 9. 61. 1; Virgil, *G.* 3. 359 (end), *aequore currum.*

34 *Phoebus, ab eöo littore mensus iter.* '*Phoebus* Apollo, who was often imagined as a sun-god by the Greeks, was identified by the Roman poets with the other Greek sun-god, Helios, the charioteer' (Hughes; cf. Osgood, *C.M.* 11–13). *Ab Eöo littore* is in *Gratul. Cantab.* (1623), p. 11 and *C.P.I.* 6, 355, 9, 489 (and, with *de*, in 8, 89); cf. Lucan 3. 295, *eoa ad litora*, and similar phrases in Claudian, *S.P.* 29. 14–15 (2, 234–6), *S.P.* 30. 114 (2, 246). With *mensus iter* cf. Catullus 34. 18, *metiens iter*, and *emensus iter* in Ovid, *F.* 1. 544, Statius, *Th.* 2. 375; *permensus iter* in Statius, *S.* 1. 2. 202, Claudian 3. 176 (1, 38), 7. 166 (1, 282).

35 *Nec mora, membra cavo posui refovenda cubili. Nec mora* is an especially Ovidian phrase (*Am.* 1. 6. 13, 1. 11. 19, *A.A.* 1. 146, *H.* 15. 169, 18. 57, *M. passim*) and is frequent in such Neo-Latinists as Vida, Pontano, and Secundus; cf. Milton, *El* 7. 69, *QNov* 208. With the rest of the line cf. Virgilian *Cul.* 213, *refoves*...*membra*; Lucan 9. 25, *populi trepidantia membra refovit*; Sil. Ital. 3. 637, *nec refovere datur torpentia membra quiete.* Koehler (52) sees a possible reminiscence of Ovid's encounter with Corinna (*Am.* 1. 5. 2): *adposui medio membra levanda toro*; cf. below, notes on 53 and 68.

36 *Condiderant oculos noxque soporque meos.* MacKellar cites Virgil, *G.* 4. 496,

Elegia tertia: In obitum Praesulis Wintoniensis

conditque natantia lumina somnus. Cf. Ovid, *Tr.* 3. 3. 44, *labentes oculos condet amica manus*; Propertius 4. 11. 64, *condita sunt vestro lumina nostra sinu.*

37 *lato spatiarier agro.* Cf. Ovid, *M.* 4. 87, *lato spatiantibus arvo.*

39 *Illic punicea radiabant omnia luce.* Cf. Ovid, *F.* 6. 252, *laetaque purpurea luce refulsit humus* (MacKellar); Virgil, *A.* 12. 77, *puniceis...rotis Aurora rubebit*; Claudian 33. 222 (2, 308), *crastina puniceos cum lux detexerit ortus.*

40 *Ut matutino cum juga sole rubent.* Cf. Lucretius 5. 462, *matutina rubent radiati lumina solis*; Ovid, *M.* 1. 62, *radiis iuga subdita matutinis*; Propertius 3. 10. 2, *sole rubente.*

41-2 *cum pandit opes Thaumantia proles, | Vestitu nituit multicolore solum.* Iris, goddess of the rainbow, daughter of Thaumas and Electra (Hesiod, *Theog.* 265-6; Virgil, *A.* 4. 700-1, 9. 5; Ovid, *M.* 4. 480, 11. 589-90, 14. 845; Val. Flacc. 7. 398, 8. 116; Shakespeare, *Temp.* 4. 1. 76; *Comus* 991-7). Cf. Milton, *EProl* (*Works* 12, 290, lines 3-4), *agros...herbis multicoloribus vestitos*; Prudentius, *Cath.* 3. 104, *prataque multicolora*; Buchanan, *El.* 2. 88 (*Majae Cal.*), *Pandit odoriferas fertilis annus opes*; Gruter, *Del. I.P.* 2, 930, *Thaumantia proles | Multicolor pennis.*

43 *Non dea tam variis ornavit floribus hortos. Varios flores*, in various cases, is a stock phrase, e.g. Virgil, *E.* 9. 40-1, Ovid, *Am.* 3. 5. 9, *M.* 10. 123, Tibullus 1. 7. 45, Apuleius, *Met.* 11. 3. Cf. Virgil, *G.* 4. 118-19, *hortos... | ornaret.*

44 *Alcinoi, Zephyro Chloris amata levi.* The most famous references to the garden of Alcinous, after Homer (*Od.* 7. 112-32), are *PL* 5. 341, 9. 441. Cf. Virgil, *G.* 2. 87, Ovid, *Am.* 1. 10. 56. The wooing of Chloris (Flora) by Zephyr, the west wind, is described in Ovid, *F.* 5. 195-378. Cf. Ariosto, *O.F.* 15. 57; Jonson, *Chloridia*; Milton, *CarEl* 11 n., *El* 4. 35, 5. 69, *PL* 5. 16. Seneca has *zephyro levi* in *Oed.* 884; the plural is in the Senecan *Oct.* 973.

45 *Flumina vernantes lambunt argentea campos.* Cf. Gruter, *Del. I.P.* 2, 1456, *vernantes...campi*; Martial 9. 54. 8, *vernat ager*; Seneca, *Herc. Oet.* 380, *silvas...vernantes.* The participle, with various words, seems to be especially used by Neo-Latinists, e.g. Pontano, *Uran.* 2. 978, *Erid.* 2. 21. 5; Secundus, *El.* 1. 2. 21, 1. 5. 91; Grotius, *Myrtilus* (*S.*, bk. 2, p. 58), *Epith. C. v. Mylen* (*S.*, bk. 3, p. 94). For silver streams, cf. Ovid, *M.* 3. 407, *fons...argenteus*; *C.P.I.* 2, 376 and 4, 241, *argenteus amnis*; Spenser and Shakespeare, *passim* (examples from both cited in note on *F.Q.* 6. 10. 7. 2, Var. ed., 6-7, p. 246); Milton, *PL* 7. 437. Koehler (152) notes in 45-8 'the predominance of spirants, nasals, liquids, and semi-vowels over the stops.'

46 *Ditior Hesperio flavet arena Tago.* The river Tagus in Spain and Portugal had been famous since antiquity for its golden sand, e.g. Ovid, *Am.* 1. 15. 34, *M.* 2. 251, Seneca, *Thy.* 354–5. From Hesperus ('evening,' and hence the evening star), Hesperia meant the west—to the Greeks Italy (e.g. Virgil, *A.* 2. 781, 3. 163), to the Italians lands and seas west of Italy (Ovid, *M.* 4. 214, 628, *F.* 1. 140; cf. Milton, *El* 3. 32, *QNov* 102, *Comus* 392, *PL passim*).

47 *Serpit odoriferas per opes levis aura Favoni.* The Greek Zephyr, the west wind (Homer, *Od.* 4. 567), was for the Roman poets the gentle Favonius, associated with spring (Lucretius 1. 11; Catullus 64. 282; Virgil, *G.* 1. 43–4; Horace, *C.* 4. 7. 9; Milton, *Sonn* 20. 6–7, *PL* 4. 329). *Aura Favoni* is a stock phrase, e.g. Lucretius and Catullus, loc. cit.; Claudian 1. 272 (1, 20); *C.P.I.* 2, 361; 5, 80, 278, etc. For *odoriferas opes* see the line from Buchanan quoted under 41–2 (cf. *PL* 4. 156–9). *Levis aura* is a stock phrase, e.g. Lucretius 3. 196; Ovid, *Tr.* 3. 4. 15, *M.* 1. 502–3, 529, 4. 673, etc.; Buchanan, *Ps.* 1. 5, *S.* 2. 16.

49 *Talis in extremis terrae Gangetidis oris.* The region of the Ganges represents the extreme east. Cf. Ovid, *Am.* 1. 2. 47 and Pontano, *Uran.* 4. 127 (cf. 5. 527), *Gangetide terra*; *PL* 9. 82. Virgil (*G.* 2. 171) and Ovid (*M.* 8. 788) have *extremis ...in oris.*

50 *Luciferi regis fingitur esse domus. Lucifer rex* is here literally the 'light-bearer,' the sun; cf. Homer, *Il.* 23. 226; Ovid, *Am.* 1. 6. 65, 2. 11. 56, *H.* 18. 112, *Tr.* 3. 5. 55–6; Claudian 5. 336–7 (1, 82). Ovid has the palace of Phoebus east of India (*M.* 1. 778–9).

51–2. Ovid (*M.* 2. 1–18) does not associate gardens and trees with the palace of the sun; Keightley suggested that Milton was recalling the gardens of the sun in Claudian 22. 467–76 (2, 36). *Ipse racemiferis*, the first words of Milton's line 51, begin Ovid, *M.* 3. 666. *Densas umbras* is a stock phrase, e.g. Catullus 65. 13, Virgil, *G.* 1. 342, *Cul.* 108, 157, Horace, *C.* 1. 7. 20–1, Seneca, *Med.* 609, *Agam.* 94, Milton, *Prol* 1 (*Works* 12, 136, line 2).

53–5 *Ecce mihi... | ...talos.* Koehler (52) quotes Ovid, *Am.* 1. 5. 9: *ecce, Corinna venit, tunica velata recincta.*

54 *Sydereum nitido fulsit in ore jubar.* Editors cite Exod. 34. 29–35: after Moses had talked with God, 'the skin of his face shone.' Cf. Ovid, *A.A.* 3. 74, *Et perit in nitido qui fuit ore color*; Seneca, *Hipp.* 376, *non ora tinguens nitida purpureus rubor*; Martial 8. 65. 4 (end), *ab ore iubar.*

55 *Vestis ad auratos defluxit candida talos.* Cf. Virgil, *A.* 1. 404, *pedes vestis* *defluxit ad imos*; Horace, *Ep.* 2. 2. 4, *candidus et talos...ad imos* (and *S.* 1. 9. 10–11); Ovid, *Am.* 3. 13. 26, *tegit auratos palla superba pedes*; Buchanan, *F.F.* 35. 27, *Et nisi fluxa sinus talos penderet ad imos. Candida vestis* is a stock phrase, e.g. Catullus 64. 307–8, Livy 9. 40. 9, Ovid, *H.* 4. 71, Statius, *S.* 2. 7. 10, Buchanan, *F.F.* 19. 1, *Bapt.* 727.

56 *Infula divinum cinxerat alba caput.* Cf. Virgil, *A.* 10. 639, *divini...capitis*; Lucretius 2. 606, *caput summum cinxere*; Ovid, *A.A.* 3. 392, *cinctus honore caput*; Statius, *Th.* 4. 218, *albaque...infula*; Rev. 1. 14 (tr. Beza): *Caput autem ejus & capilli* erant *candidi ut lana alba tamquam nix*; ibid. 4. 4 (quoted under *Patrem* 30–7).

57 *senex...venerandus amictu.* The last words end Buchanan, *Franc.* 859. *Venerande senex* (the common form) is a stock phrase, e.g. Dante, *E.* 2. 46; *C.P.I.* 2, 406, 4, 295, etc.; Palingenius, *Z.V.* 3. 22; Gill, *In Parentis mei Natalem* (p. 14). In regard to this poem of Gill's (written in Feb. 1625), see the notes on *El* 2. 7–8 and *Patrem* 5.

58 *Intremuit laeto florea terra sono.* Cf. Horace, *C.* 2. 17. 26, *laetum...sonum*; Gruter, *Del. I.P.* 2, 116, *laetos...sonos.*

59 *Agmina gemmatis plaudunt caelestia pennis.* Editors refer to the spirits in Virgil's Elysium (*A.* 6. 644): *pars pedibus plaudunt choreas et carmina dicunt*; and cite two of Ovid's phrases about Cupid: *movit Amor gemmatas aureus alas* (*R. Am.* 39), and *tu pinnas gemma, gemma variante capillos* (*Am.* 1. 2. 41). Cf. Sannazaro, *P.V.* 2. 320–1: *caelestia curvas* | *Agmina pulsantum citharas*; Buchanan, *Ps.* 59. 6, *agminum coelestium.* For *plaudunt...pennis*, see the note on *El* 5. 69.

60 *Pura triumphali personat aethra tuba.* Cf. Milton's letter to Gill, dated 20 May 1628 (*Works* 12, 8, line 15), about Gill's poem on Henry of Nassau: *tam sonora triumphalique tuba canere.* This letter was probably misdated and should be assigned to 20 May 1630 (E. Chifos, *MLN* 62, 1947, 37–9; Milton, *C.P.W.* 1, 317, n. 8); Fletcher (*Intell. Dev.* 2, 438–9) questions this redating.

61 *Quisque novum amplexu comitem cantuque salutat.* Cf. Milton, *Patrem* 30 f., *Lyc* 178–81, and *EpDam* 215–19, and notes on these passages.

62 *placido misit ab ore sonos. Placido ore* is a stock phrase, e.g. Virgil, *A.* 7. 194, Ovid, *M.* 8. 703, 11. 282, Sil. Ital. 6. 536, 8. 199, Sannazaro, *P.V.* 1. 156, 408, Pontano, *Uran.* 2. 1188, 3. 915, 4. 747.

63–4 *Nate veni, & patrii felix cape gaudia regni,* | *Semper ab hinc duro, nate, labore vaca.* Editors cite Rev. 14. 13, which Beza renders: *Tunc audivi vocem e caelo, dicentem mihi, scribe, Beati ab hoc tempore mortui ii, qui Domini causa moriuntur. Etiam, dicit Spiritus: ut requiescant a laboribus suis: & opera eorum sequuntur eos.* Cf. Matt. 25. 21 (Beza): *ingredere in gaudium domini tui. Duro labore*, in various forms, is a stock phrase, e.g. Lucretius 5. 1272; Virgil, *G.* 4. 114, *A.* 8. 380; Seneca, *Herc. Fur.* 137, *Thy.* 303; etc.

65 *aligerae tetigerunt nablia turmae.* Editors cite Rev. 14. 2, which Beza renders: *Et audivi vocem e caelo tamquam vocem aquarum multarum, & tamquam sonum tonitrui magni: & vocem audivi citharoedorum pullantium citharas suas. Nablia* ('harps') seems to be commoner in Judeo-Christian than in pagan writing, e.g. Ovid, *A.A.* 3. 327; 1 Chron. 15. 16, 1 Macc. 13. 51; Buchanan, *Ps.* 33. 2, 57. 8, 81. 4, 108. 3, 137. 2, 150. 3; *Jeph.* 409. Cf. Virgil, *A.* 12. 249 and Grotius, *Epith. Kinschot. (S.,* bk. 3, p. 104), *agminis aligeri;* Sil. Ital. 3. 292, *alipedes turmae. Aliger* is recurrent in Vida, *Christ.* 2. 316, 3. 186, 394, 4. 64, 223, etc.

66 *cum tenebris aurea pulsa quies.* Cf. Ovid, *M.* 8. 828, *expulsa quies;* Sedulius, *Carmen Paschale* 3. 59 (Migne, *Pat. Lat.* 19, 639), *pulsa quies.*

67 *Cephaleia pellice.* The mistress of Cephalus, i.e. Aurora, goddess of the dawn. See Milton, *El* 5. 51–2 (and note), *El* 7. 38, and *IlPen* 122–4 (and note). M. West (see *El* 2, headnote) cites Ovid. *Am.* 1. 13, especially lines 39–40, as close in spirit to Milton's reference.

68 *Talia contingant somnia saepe mihi.* For remarks on this apparent—and, in its context, surprising—echo of Ovid and Tibullus, see above, general Introduction, p. 14. Cf., above, the notes on 35 and 53–5.

Elegia quarta. Anno aetatis 18

AD THOMAM JUNIUM PRAECEPTOREM SUUM, APUD
MERCATORES ANGLICOS HAMBURGAE AGENTES,
PASTORIS MUNERE FUNGENTEM

The Scottish Thomas Young (*c.* 1587–1655), M.A. (1606) of St
Andrews, moved to London to engage in teaching and pastoral work,
and was one of the masters John Milton senior employed to give extra-
curricular instruction to his small son.[1] Milton entered St Paul's School
in 1620 or perhaps earlier, and by 1618, when Young's services seem to
have begun, he would have been ready to start on the Latin poetry which
he happily associates with Young's teaching. In 1620, when the boy was
eleven, Young migrated to Hamburg to be chaplain to the English
merchants there. He gave up this post in 1628, returned to England, and
received the vicarage of Stowmarket in Suffolk, which he held until his
death. He became one of the prominent Presbyterian controversialists
and was the 'ty' of Smectymnuus, the group of divines who attacked
episcopacy (and with whom Milton sided in his ecclesiastical tracts of
1641–2). Young was appointed in 1643 to the Westminster Assembly
and in 1644 to the Mastership of Jesus College, Cambridge; in 1650, on
refusing to accept the Engagement, he was ousted from this post and
retired to Stowmarket. Young would not have approved of Milton's
views as they developed after the Smectymnuan phase; indeed, on
28 February 1644, preaching before parliament, Young made what

---

[1] The account of Young in the *DNB* and Masson, *P.W.* 1, 260–5, has been supplemented by
A. E. Barker, 'Milton's Schoolmasters,' *MLR* 32 (1937), 517–36; W. R. Parker, 'Milton
and Thomas Young, 1620–1628,' *MLN* 53 (1938), 399–407; and H. Fletcher, *Intell. Dev.* 1,
137 f. See also the introduction to *El* 1, note 2, and the note on lines 29–30 below. Parker's
latest opinion (*Milton*, 12, 707, n. 40) favours 1618–20 (three years) as the period of Young's
teaching, but he thinks 1615–17 possible.

appears to be a hostile reference to Milton's first tract on divorce (William Haller, *Liberty and Reformation in the Puritan Revolution*, New York, 1955, 123–4). And Arthur Barker (*Milton and the Puritan Dilemma*, Toronto, 1942, 346–7) remarks that 'Milton can hardly have avoided the thought of his former tutor when he commented in the *History of Britain* (x, 322) on the apostacy of those members of the Assembly who, though in receipt of a public salary, were not unwilling to accept "(besides one, sometimes two or more, of the best livings) collegiate masterships in the universities, rich lectureships in the city, setting sail to all winds that might blow gain into their covetous bosoms."'

The chief facts concerning *El* 4 have been made clear, though a few queries remain. Milton's *Anno aetatis 18* means that the poem was written when he was eighteen, that is, in 1627; rumors that the operations of the Thirty Years War are approaching Hamburg have turned his thoughts to the gratefully remembered tutor of his childhood. In lines 33–8 he says that three vernal equinoxes and two seasons of new herbage and two autumns have gone by since he last saw Young. During his Hamburg pastorate, 1620–8, Young visited England in 1621, perhaps in 1623, and 'almost certainly' (Parker) in February or March 1625, when Milton was just entering Cambridge; in the poem of 1627 the young man is recalling their having met some two years before. (For Parker's later and altered opinion see below, 33 n.) Further, if the classical allusions in lines 33–8 are to be taken literally (which, as Parker says, is likely), they put the composition of the poem between the vernal equinox, 21 March, and the beginning of the ancient festival of Chloris, 28 April.

A complicating item—taken into account in Masson's long discussion (*P.W.* 3, 307–10)—is the prose letter written by Milton to Young, the first of the *Epistolae Familiares* published in 1674 and dated 26 March 1625 (no MS. of the letter survives). Parker has argued cogently that the printed date is an error and should be 26 March 1627. To summarize his conclusions, the letter, written in London during a vacation, promises a companion poem, which must surely be *El* 4; feeling unsatisfied with the poem, and not having acknowledged Young's gift of a Hebrew

Bible, Milton wrote a less formal letter expressing more directly his affectionate esteem, his apologies for not having written oftener, and his thanks for the present (cf. Parker, *Milton*, 37–8).

H. F. Fletcher (*Intell. Dev.* 2, 126–33) holds the unusual opinion that '*Elegy IV* is probably the earliest of Milton's extant Latin elegies.' He assigns it (or the first draft of a poem later polished) to the winter or spring of 1625, before Milton took up residence in Cambridge. This dating is rather assumption than argument (see MacKellar, 212). It enables Fletcher to accept 26 March 1625 as the correct date for the prose letter and it provides a reason (not a necessary one) for Milton's not referring to Cambridge in the *Elegy*. On the other hand, this view ignores Milton's '*Anno aetatis 18*'; his allusions (lines 51, 72–4) to war threatening Hamburg, which could hardly be made before 1626; and Parker's discussion of chronological problems. The chief evidence offered is that the classical authors Milton echoed—that is, the authors cited in illustration by Warton and MacKellar—belong to the grammar-school range. But, to go no further, this is invalidated by Fletcher's own candid statement (131): 'Of course he continued using them for years, dropping none as he progressed.' Besides, other authors could be cited, as in the following notes.

Elegy 4, the longest of Milton's epistolary poems, embodies a good deal of personal feeling, in the way of both self-revelation and devotion to Young. Hanford has seen in it a new phase of the 'sensitive self-love' that he found in *El* 1. In *El* 4

warm personal affection, more strongly felt no doubt in the partly hostile environment of the University, is combined with indignation at the harshness of the English church which has compelled so excellent a man to seek his sustenance abroad. Milton's sympathy for Young is a kind of extension of the mood of defensive self-pity which we have seen implied in *Elegy I*. He reminds him that other preachers of the word—Elijah, Paul, Jesus—have been victims of persecution, as he had earlier reminded himself that Ovid, a poet, was driven into exile. Finally he gives a personal application to the motive of Psalm CXXXVI, assuring his friend that the Lord of Hosts who defended Zion will stand at his side amid the clash of battle which surrounds him. Milton writes with an accent of sincerity which leaves no doubt of the hold which the subject has taken on his emotions, but he indulges in no such aesthetic dreaming as in the first elegy and the suppressed excitement which underlies the erotic imagery of the earlier poem is entirely lacking. ('Youth,' 114.)

Much of this, like so much else in Hanford's essay, is acutely seized, but it may also be thought that 'sensitive self-love' and 'defensive self-pity' are imposed upon a poem which contains no real hint of such qualities. Granted that Milton was not the most selfless of men, or boys, he speaks here as if he were. He might have been expected, even in writing from London, to tell his old tutor of his own life and work at Cambridge, yet he says nothing of that—a negative fact that goes along with other positive evidence of his feeling alienated, temporarily, from his fellow collegians (Woodhouse, 'Notes', 69, n. 8). It is possible too that his ignoring of Cambridge was due partly to a desire to make amends for not having written oftener by giving this verse-letter entirely to his elder's concerns; and it is no reflection on his sincerity that he quite naturally adapts his themes and tone to the character of the person he is addressing. A much more central fact is that, being a serious and religious young man, he is deeply moved by the thought of Young's apostolic piety and poverty and domesticity and of the hard lot of a teacher of the way of salvation forced into exile by an ungrateful country. Whatever self-identification with Young there may be in such sympathy, it is what is felt by any generous spirit who is stirred on behalf of a person or a cause. And this particular situation evokes feelings that can be called embryo Puritanism (L. Hunt, *Lit. Exam.* 30 August 1823, 132–3; Houtchens, 183; Woodhouse, 'Notes,' 73). Those feelings might have been heightened by Milton's changing attitude toward a clerical career, though we do not know when he reached a negative decision.

NOTES

1 *Curre per immensum subito mea littera pontum.* For the poet's addressing his letter editors cite Ovid, *Tr.* 3. 7. 1 f.: *Vade salutatum, subito perarata, Perillam, | littera, sermonis fida ministra mei.* Brodribb (*N&Q* 159, 1930, 129) cites Statius, *S.* 4. 4. 1: *Curre...epistola.* Cf. Ovid, *P.* 4. 5. 1 f., which resembles the pattern

of Milton's much longer epistle. For one phrase cf. Ovid, *M.* 4. 689 and *Tr.* 1. 2. 39, *inmenso...ponto.*

2 *I, pete Teutonicos laeve per aequor agros.* Cf. Virgil, *A.* 4. 381: *i, sequere Italiam ventis, pete regna per undas*; Seneca, *Herc. Fur.* 89, *I nunc...pete.*

3 *Segnes rumpe moras.* In Virgil, *G.* 3. 42–3, Seneca, *Med.* 54, and Sil. Ital. 8. 214–15. *Rumpe moras* (sometimes with *omnes*) is very common, e.g. Virgil, *A.* 4. 569, 9. 13; Ovid, *M.* 15. 583; Martial 2. 64. 9; Val. Flacc. 1. 306; etc.

3 *nil, precor, obstet eunti.* Cf. Ovid, *M.* 3. 568, *nil obstabat eunti*; Statius, *Th.* 11. 349, *non obstat eunti.*

5–6 *Ipse ego Sicanio fraenantem carcere ventos | Aeolon.* Editors cite Ovid, *M.* 14. 224: *Aeolon Hippotaden, cohibentem carcere ventos*; Virgil, *A.* 1. 53–4, *ventos...carcere frenat*; and *Lyc* 96–7. Cf. Ovid, *M.* 4. 663, *carcere ventos.* Sicania (from early inhabitants, the Sicani) was a common name for Sicily, e.g. Virgil, *E.* 10. 4, *A.* 3. 692, 5. 24, etc.; Ovid, *M.* 5. 464, 495; Pliny, *N.H.* 3. 8. 86. Aeolus was associated with the Liparian islands north of Sicily (Pliny, *N.H.* 3. 9. 94; Virgil, *A.* 8. 416–17; Diod. Sic. 5. 7. 1–6).

6 *virides sollicitabo Deos.* Cf. Ovid, *Tr.* 1. 2. 59, *viridesque dei* (MacKellar); Statius, *S.* 1. 5. 15, *deae virides*; Ovid, *M.* 5. 575; Horace, *C.* 3. 28. 10, *virides Nereidum comas*; *Comus* 29. *Sollicitare* is a standard verb with *deos*, etc. (Ovid, *M.* 4. 473, Lucan 1. 65, 5. 69).

7–8 *Caeruleamque suis comitatam Dorida Nymphis*, etc. Doris was the wife of Nereus and mother of the Nereids; MacKellar cites Hesiod, *Theog.* 240–64, Ovid, *M.* 2. 11–14, 269, Apollodorus 1. 2. 7. Cf. Spenser, *F.Q.* 4. 11. 48; and *caerula Doris* in Ovid, *M.* 13. 742, Gruter, *Del. I.P.* 2, 20, and *Epith. Caroli et H. Mariae* (1625), p. 57. For the Nereids' friendliness to sailors, see Apollon. Rhod. 4. 833–61 (MacKellar), Statius, *S.* 3. 2. 13–34.

9–12 *At tu, si poteris*, etc. 'Ovid likewise wishes for the chariots of Triptolemus and Medea to enable him to revisit his friends; see *Tr.* 3. 8. 1–4...cf. *Met.* 5. 648–9' (MacKellar, after Warton).

9 *celeres...jugales.* In *C.P.I.* 9, 234.

10 *Colchis.* The Colchian Medea, who, after killing her and Jason's children and Jason's new bride, fled in a dragon-chariot (Euripides, *Med.* 1321–2; Seneca, *Med.* 1022–5). The use of the single word is common, e.g. Horace, *Epod.* 16. 58, Ovid, *M.* 7. 301, 348, Propertius 2. 1. 54, 2. 34. 8, 3. 11. 9; the quotation from Gill under *El* 2. 7–8.

11–12 *Aut queis Triptolemus Scythicas devenit in oras | Gratus Eleusina missus ab urbe puer.* Ceres sent Triptolemus from Eleusis in a dragon-chariot to sow grain in the uninhabited earth as far as Scythia (Ovid, *M.* 5. 642–50; Apollodorus 1. 5. 2, with Frazer's references; N. Comes, *Mythol.* 5. 14). *Queis* is an archaic ablative plural of *qui.* With Milton's phrasing, cf. Ovid, *M.* 5. 649, *Scythicas advertitur oras; Ibis* 496, *Iliaca missus ab arce puer.*

14 *flecte gradum.* In Val. Flacc. 3. 416. Cf. Seneca, *Herc. Fur.* 678, *gradumque...flectere.*

15–16 *Hama, | Cimbrica...clava.* Warton cited the *Saxonia* (1. 11) of the historian Krantzius (Albert Krantz or Crantz) for the story that Hamburg 'took its name from Hama a puissant Saxon champion, who was killed on the spot where that city stands by Starchater a Danish giant...The *Cimbrica clava* is the club of the Dane.' Starnes-Talbert (319) found all the information needed by Milton under Hama and Hamburg in C. Stephanus, *Dictionarium.*

16 *dedisse neci.* For various forms of this idiom see Virgil, *G.* 4. 90, *A.* 12. 341, Vida, *Christ.* 2. 973.

17 *antiquae...pietatis honore.* Cf. Virgil, *A.* 1. 253, *hic pietatis honos?*; and *pietas antiqua,* ibid. 5. 688, and Beza, *Illustrissimi...Friderici III* (*Poëmata,* 38ᵛ).

18 *Praesul Christicolas pascere doctus oves.* The metaphor of Christ or the pastor feeding sheep is of course very common, e.g. John 21. 15 (tr. Beza): *Pasce agnos meos*; 21. 16, 17, *Pasce oves meas.* Cf. *C.P.I.* 9, 251, *Pascere doctus oves. Christicolas* is frequent in Prudentius (*Cath.* 3. 56, 8. 80, 10. 57, etc., *Perist.* 11. 39, 80, 13. 82); it occurs also in Lily's *Grammar* (*Symbolum Apostolorum,* sig. [Dviᵛ]), in *C.P.I.* 1, 458, 475, 476, etc., Palingenius, *Z.V.* 10. 5 and 35, *Cantab. Dolor* (1625), p. 3, and *Oxon. Par.* (1625), sig. A2ᵛ.

19–20 *Ille quidem est animae plusquam pars altera nostrae, | Dimidio vitae vivere cogor ego.* Editors cite Horace's farewell to Virgil, *animae dimidium meae* (*C.* 1. 3. 8). Cf. ibid. 2. 17. 5, *te meae...partem animae*; Ovid, *M.* 8. 406 and *P.* 1. 8. 2, *pars animae...meae*; *C.P.I.* 1, 485 and 2, 17, *animae pars altera nostrae*; Castiglione, *Alcon* 25: *Pars animae; cordis pars Alcon maxima nostri*; Buchanan, *El.* 4. 1–2: *O animae...meae pars altera, tuque | Altera pars animae...meae.*

21 *Hei mihi quot pelagi, quot montes interjecti.* Editors cite Ovid, *Tr.* 4. 7. 21–2: *innumeri montes inter me teque viaeque | fluminaque et campi nec freta pauca iacent*; Homer, *Il.* 1. 156–7: 'for full many things lie between us—shadowy mountains and sounding sea.'

22 *Me faciunt alia parte carere mei!* Cf. Ovid, *Am.* 1. 7. 24 and *Tr.* 4. 10. 32, *parte carere mei.*

23-4 *Charior ille mihi quam tu doctissime Graium | Cliniadi, pronepos qui Telamonis erat.* 'Alcibiades, as the son of Clinias, was called Cliniades (Ovid, *Ibis* 635 [read 633]). He traced his ancestry to Eurysaces, son of Ajax, who was the son of Telamon (Plato, *Alcib.* I. 121; Plutarch, *Alcib.* 1). In the *Symposium* and *Alcibiades* 1, Plato represents Socrates and Alcibiades as intimate friends.' (MacKellar). Keightley objected that Socrates 'was the *wisest*, not the *most learned* of the Greeks,' but Harding (*Ovid*, 44) cites Ovid, *Ibis* 559–60, where Socrates is *doctissimus*, and notes that *doctus*, in antiquity as well as in the Renaissance, had the secondary meaning of 'wise.' In *Prol* 6 (*Works* 12, 218) Milton calls Socrates *sapientissimus...mortalium*; cf. *PR* 3. 96–9, 4. 274–6, 293–4. Cf. Ovid, *M.* 8. 405, *o me mihi carior.*

25-6 *Stagirites generoso magnus alumno | Quem peperit Libyco Chaonis alma Jovi.* 'The Stagirite' is a traditional appellation for Aristotle, who was born at Stagira in Chalcidice, and became the tutor of Alexander the Great. *Chaonis alma*, the gracious maid of Chaonia (Epirus), is Olympias, wife of Philip of Macedon and mother of Alexander. Milton uses the tale that Alexander's real father was Jupiter Ammon (the 'Libyc *Hammon*' of *Nat* 203); see Plutarch, *Alexander* 2–3, and *PL* 9. 508–9, *PR* 3. 84.

27 *Amyntorides.* Phoenix, son of Amyntor (Homer, *Il.* 9, 448; Ovid, *A.A.* 1. 337, *M.* 8. 307, *Ibis* 259), and one of Achilles' tutors (Homer, loc. cit. 438 f.; Apollodorus 3. 13. 8).

27 *Philyrëius Heros.* The phrase is in Ovid, *M.* 2. 676 and *F.* 5. 391; cf. *Phillyrides Chiron* in Virgil, *G.* 3. 550, Propertius 2. 1. 60, and *Lacrymae Cantab.* (1619), p. 7. Chiron the centaur, son of the nymph Philyra, was a skilful physician and the tutor of Achilles and Aesculapius (Homer, *Il.* 11. 830–1; Pindar, *Nem.* 3. 43 f., *Pyth.* 6. 19 f.; Apollodorus 3. 10. 3; Ovid, *A.A.* 1. 11, 17, *F.* 5. 379–414; N. Comes, *Mythol.* 4. 12, 9. 12).

29-30 *Primus ego Aonios illo praeeunte recessus | Lustrabam, & bifidi sacra vireta jugi.* Parker (*MLN* 53, 1938, 403) listed translators from Cowper on who have taken these lines to mean that 'Milton was introduced to classical studies by Thomas Young,' and cited E. K. Rand's judgment: '*Primus* ought to be translated "I was the first under his guidance to visit Castalia," or, possibly, "I was his *foremost* pupil." Surely the phrase does not mean that Young was Milton's first tutor.' D. L. Clark (*J.M. at St. Paul's*, 28–9) says that by 1618, when Young became his tutor, Milton would already have had two years of Latin and would have been 'ready to begin reading Latin poetry either at St. Paul's School in the Third Class or at home with Thomas Young, or with supplementary instruction from Young while he continued as a regular pupil at St. Paul's. Therefore the usual interpretation of the *Fourth Elegy* may still be accepted, that Young first introduced him to Latin poetry. Young could not have been his first tutor or teacher.' While Clark has Milton entering St Paul's in 1615 (*El* 1, headnote, n. 2), Parker, who holds the more orthodox 1620, gives as his latest opinion (707, n. 40) that these lines 'mean (if judged by classical Latin) that Milton was Young's first pupil in classical studies—*not* that Young was his first teacher.'

It is possible that Milton was echoing Virgil, *G.* 3, 10–11: *primus ego in patriam mecum, modo vita supersit,* | *Aonio rediens deducam vertice Musas*, where *primus* means 'first (I will bring back...)'; cf. *EpDam* 168 n. Milton might have thought also of Virgil's use of *primus* in the sense of 'early, long ago,' as in *A.* 1. 24, 5. 596, 8. 319, 602, and perhaps 1. 1, *E.* 6. 1, and elsewhere. Cf. Horace, *Ep.* 1. 1. 1.

Aonia, a part of Boeotia, was a poetic equivalent for the whole country, especially with reference to Mount Helicon, a haunt of the Muses, and its fountain Aganippe (Hesiod, *Theog.* 1–34; Strabo 9. 2. 31; Virgil, *E.* 6. 65, 10. 12, *G.* 3. 10–11, quoted above; Ovid, *M.* 5. 333, 6. 2; Milton, *El* 6. 17, *Patrem* 75, *Rous* 21, *PL* 1. 15). With Milton's phrasing cf. Sannazaro, *El.* 1. 9. 11, *Sed Phoebi sacros cogor lustrare recessus*; Grotius, *Inaug. Reg. Brit.* (*S.*, bk. 2, p. 64), *Pierios...lustrasse recessus*.

30 *bifidi...jugi.* Parnassus, the two-peaked mountain sacred to Apollo and the Muses, had Delphi and the Castalian spring at its foot (Ovid, *M.* 1. 316–17, 2. 221; Seneca, *Oed.* 227, 281; Lucan 5. 72; Milton, *El* 5. 9, *Patrem* 3, *Rous* 66).

31 *Pieriosque hausi latices.* The Muses, daughters of Zeus and Mnemosyne, were born in Pieria, near Mount Olympus (Hesiod, *Theog.* 52–71). The association of the region with poetic inspiration was one of the commonest of ancient and modern commonplaces, from Hesiod (*W.D.* 1, *Theog.* 53–5) onward. With Milton's phrasing cf. the Virgilian *Culex* 18, *Pierii laticis decus*; Palingenius, *Z.V.* 6. 378–9: *Plato...hausit* | *Divinos latices.*

31–2 *Clioque...* | *Castalio sparsi laeta ter ora mero.* Clio, the Muse of History, comes first in Hesiod's list of the Muses (*Theog.* 77), in G. Linocre's *Musarum Libellum* (see *Idea* 2–3 n.), and in some texts of the mnemonic verses on the Muses once attributed to Virgil (quoted in N. Comes, *Mythol.* 7. 15, *Minor Latin Poets* (L.C.L.), 634, and H. G. Lotspeich, *Classical Mythology in the Poetry of Edmund Spenser*, Princeton, 1932, 83); see Starnes-Talbert, 96 f.

Lines from these were quoted by Spenser's E.K. (on *April* 100, *November* 53). Hence Clio was often named in a broad representative way as the prime Muse or Muse of poetry and literature in general: in *Teares of the Muses* Spenser salutes her first as 'thou eldest Sister of the crew.' Milton here (and in *Patrem* 14) is presumably using the name only in that broad sense. One may be unable to accept the abstruse function assigned to Clio here (and in *Patrem* 14: see note) by Shawcross, as 'guardian of man's individual history, that is, the guardian of what a man was given and what he was to become because of those talents' (*N&Q* 8, 1961, 178–9).

For the Castalian spring, see above, 30 n., and Virgil, *G.* 3. 293, Ovid, *Am.* 1. 15. 35–6, *M.* 3. 14, Horace, *C.* 3. 4. 61, Milton, *El* 5. 9. G. S. Gordon (*Lives of Authors*, London, 1950, 50) takes line 32 to mean that Young 'first introduced him to the poets, and what is more, sealed him of the order of poets,' adding that 'This "thrice" is the ritual of enchantment, of the charm,' as in *Comus* 913–14. Shawcross (*C.E.P.* 26, n. 10) explains thus: 'What Milton says is that Young introduced him to the glories of the arts, and that, while under Young's guidance and as a result of the talents given him by Clio, he had thrice been poetically inspired. These early poems are apparently not extant.' To Parker (707, n. 40; cf. 29–30 n. above) 'line 32 means that the tutor–pupil relationship lasted three years.' This seems the simplest and most likely explanation.

33 *Flammeus at signum ter viderat arietis Aethon.* Aethon ('burning'), one of the four horses of the sun's chariot (Ovid, *M.* 2. 153–4), has three times seen the zodiacal sign of the Ram: i.e. three vernal equinoxes have passed. Parker's early view of the significance of these and following allusions is summarized in the headnote above. He now (707, n. 40) reads 'lines 33–38 as meaning that it has been seven years (three plus two plus two) since Milton has seen Young. Taken together, these lines suggest, but do not prove, that Young was Milton's tutor in the years 1618–20.' The arithmetic of the first of these sentences seems unclear. Cf. Masson, *P.W.* 3, 307 f.; MacKellar, 211–12; Shawcross, *C.E.P.* 27, n. 11: all three are more or less convinced that Milton is recalling a meeting two years before, early in 1625.

35 Chloris ('greenness') is the goddess of flowers, otherwise Flora. The Roman festival associated with her began on 28 April (Ovid, *F.* 4. 947, 5. 185, 195). Cf. *El* 3. 44 above.

36 'The south wind (Auster) steals the wealth of Flora, i.e. betokens the gathering of summer's crops in the month of September when the sirocco blows' (Rand, in a letter to Parker, *MLN* 53, 404, n. 7).

37 *Necdum ejus licuit mihi lumina pascere vultu.* The last phrase, in various forms, is a common metaphor. Cf. Ovid, *Am.* 3. 2. 6, *oculos pascat uterque suos*; *M.* 14. 728, *corpore...crudelia lumina pascas*; Lucretius 1. 36; Virgil, *G.* 2. 285, *A.* 1. 464; *Epith. Caroli et H. Mariae* (1625), 58: *Et sua virgineo pascebat lumina vultu.*

38 *linguae dulces aure bibisse sonos.* Cf. Horace, *C.* 2. 13. 31–2: *pugnas... | ...bibit aure volgus*; loc. cit. 38, *dulci...sono*; Cicero, *Rep.* 6. 18. 18, *dulcis sonus.*

39 *cursuque Eurum praeverte sonorum.* Eurus is the east or southeast wind (Pliny, *N.H.* 2. 46. 119; Ovid, *M.* 1. 61). Editors cite Virgil, *A.* 1. 317, *Harpalyce volucremque fuga praevertitur Hebrum*, and 7. 807, *cursuque pedum praevertere ventos.* Cf. Castiglione, *Carm.* 7. 29: *Saepe fugacis equi cursu praevertitur Euros.*

40 *Quam sit opus monitis res docet, ipsa vides.* Cf. Lucretius 2. 565, etc., *manifesta docet res*; Cicero, *Div.* 2. 15. 36, *cum res ipsa doceat*; Ovid, *R. Am.* 296, *monitis non eget iste meis.*

41 *Invenies dulci cum conjuge forte sedentem.* Editors cite Ovid, *Tr.* 3. 7. 3–4: *aut illam invenies dulci cum matre sedentem, | aut inter libros Pieridasque suas.* Cf. Virgil, *G.* 4. 465 and *A.* 2. 777, *dulcis coniunx.*

42 *Mulcentem gremio pignora chara suo.* Cf. Claudian 1. 143–4 (1, 12), *pignora cara... | ...meo...gremio*; Buchanan, *Ps.* 137. 9, *gremio pignora cara tuo.* *Pignora cara* is a stock phrase, e.g. Virgil, *E.* 8. 92, Ovid, *M.* 3. 134, *F.* 3. 218, *Tr.* 1. 3. 60, Statius, *Ach.* 1. 782–3.

43–4 *veterum praelarga volumina patrum | Versantem, aut veri biblia sacra Dei.* The Greek and Latin fathers of the church, whom Puritan divines studied as well as the Bible. Cf. Virgil, *A.* 5. 408, *immensa volumina...versat*; F. M. Molsa (*C.P.I.* 6, 349; Gruter, *Del. I.P.* 2, 52) and Secundus, *S.* 9. 49: *Priscorum et volvens veneranda volumina patrum*; Milton, *Prol* 3 (*Works* 12, 158, line 18), *doctorum volumina*; *Prol* 4 (ibid. 174, lines 20–1), *ingentia Philosophorum volumina.* *Verus Deus* is a universal phrase, e.g. Vida, *Christ.*, *passim.*

45 *Caelestive...rore.* In Ovid, *F.* 1. 312 (Fletcher) and, in the accusative, in Pontano, *Uran.* 1. 1112.

46 *Grande salutiferae religionis opus.* *Grande opus* is in Ovid, *A.A.* 3. 206, *P.* 3. 3. 36, Statius, *Th.* 11. 100, and Mantuan, *E.* 5. 20. Cf. Sannazaro, *El.* 3. 2. 48, *Primaevum sanctae relligionis opus*; *C.P.I.* 6, 450, *Relligionis opus*; ibid. 9, 376, *sincerae relligionis opus.* In the Roman poets (e.g. Ovid, *H.* 21. 174, *M.*

2. 642, 15. 632, 744) *salutifer* commonly means 'health-bringing,' 'beneficial' (cf. Milton, *El* 5. 73). Some examples of the Christian sense are: Titus 2. 11 (tr. Tremellius): *Illuxit enim gratia illa Dei salutifera quibusvis hominibus*; Prudentius, *Cath.* 3. 7, *Psych.* 14; Ausonius, *Ephem.* 3. 27, *Vers. Pasch.* 1 (1, 34); Buchanan, Psalms *passim*.

49 *oculos in humum defixa modestos.* Editors cite Ovid, *Am.* 3. 6. 67, *illa oculos in humum deiecta modestos.* Cf. Virgil, *A.* 6. 156, *maesto defixus lumina voltu*; Sil. Ital. 8. 73, *terrae defixam oculos.*

50 *Verba verecundo sis memor ore loqui.* Cf. Martial 8. 1. 2, *disce verecundo sanctius ore loqui* (Fletcher). *Sis memor* is a stock phrase, e.g. Virgil, *A.* 12. 439; Ovid, *Tr.* 3. 6. 21; Val. Flacc. 4. 37, 7. 477, etc.; Claudian 35. 234 (2, 334).

51 *si teneris vacat inter praelia Musis.* 'In 1626 the Protestant allies in the Thirty Years' War, under Christian IV of Denmark, were defeated by the Imperialists, under Tilly, at Lutter. The seat of war shifted to lower Saxony and for some time Hamburg was in danger of a siege.' (Hughes; see the *Cambridge Modern History*, 4, 1906, 96 f.) Cf. Lucan 10. 185–6: *media inter proelia semper | Stellarum caelique plagis superisque vacavi.*

56 *Icaris a lento Penelopeia viro.* Penelope (Milton uses the Greek form of the name) was the daughter of Icarius (Homer, *Od.* 1. 329, etc.; Ovid, *H.* 1. 81, *Tr.* 5. 5. 44, *P.* 3. 1. 113, *Ibis* 391). In Ovid, *H.* 1, 1. 66, as editors note, she refers to her husband as *lentus.* Cf. Gill, *Ad D. Ioh. Stonhousium…Kal. Ianuar. 1630* (p. 69): *Et tua Penelope lentum te dicit Ulyssem.*

57 *manifestum tollere crimen.* Cf. Ovid, *M.* 3. 268, *manifestaque crimina.*

59 *noxamque fatetur.* Cf. Ovid, *P.* 2. 9. 72, *noxa fatenda* (Fletcher).

61 *da veniam fasso.* As editors note, a recurrent phrase, with *fasso* or *fassae*, in Ovid (*H.* 4. 156, 17. 225, 19. 4, *P.* 4. 2. 23). *Da veniam* is also common, e.g. *H.* 19. 149, *A.A.* 2. 38, *F.* 4. 755, *P.* 1. 7. 22; Lucan 8. 749, 9. 227, etc. The Columbia *fesso* is a misprint.

61 *veniamque roganti.* Cf. Ovid, *M.* 6. 33, *veniam dabit illa roganti*; Castiglione, *Carm.* 5. 97, *Praestabit veniam mitia deus ille roganti*; Virgil, *A.* 11. 101, *veniamque rogantes.*

64 *Vulnifico pronos nec rapit ungue leo.* Hughes cites Shakespeare, *A.Y.L.* 4. 3. 118–19. H. E. Rollins called my attention to the distich in George Cavendish's *Life…of Thomas Wolsey* (Temple Classics ed., 157): *Parcere prostratis scit nobilis ira leonis : | Tu quoque fac simile, quisquis regnabis in orbem.* I have not found the source of this (cf. Lucan 6. 487, *nobilis ira leonum*), but the idea of the first line, and of Milton's line, is common. Cf. Ovid, *Tr.* 3. 5. 33–4; Statius, *Th.* 8. 124–6; Seneca, *De Clementia* 1. 5. 5; Pliny, *N.H.* 8. 19. 48: *Leoni tantum ex feris clementia in supplices; prostratis parcit*...; Claudian 22. 20–2 (2, 4) and *S.P.* 22. 28–9 (2, 198); *Carminum Proverbialium* (London, 1603), 74: *Parcere subiectis scit nobilis ira leonis*; Josuah Sylvester, *Du Bartas His Divine Weekes And Workes* (London, 1621: cited hereafter as *D.W.W.*, with line numbers from Grosart's ed., 2 v. 1880), 1. 6. 340–1. Milton had probably met most of these. Since this note was written, R. S. Sylvester has edited Cavendish (E.E.T.S. 1959), but is also unable to trace the lines; he cites (238–9) chiefly the Ovid, Seneca, and Pliny given above. Cf. also Petrarch, *Ep. ad A. Senensem* (*P.M.* 2, 50), *vulnificos*...*leones.*

65 *sarissiferi*...*Thracis.* Milton's adjective, which does not seem to have been observed elsewhere, is a compound, analogous to *aurifer, caelifer*, etc., of *ferre* and *saris(s)a*, a Macedonian spear (Ovid, *M.* 12. 466, 479, *P.* 1. 3. 59; Lucan 8. 298; Statius, *Th.* 7. 269; Buchanan, *Sph.* 1. 238). The regular Latin word is *sarisophoros*, a transliteration from the Greek (Livy 36. 18. 2; Q. Curtius 4. 15. 13). (MacKellar, with additions.)

67 *Extensaeque manus avertunt fulminis ictus.* Cf. Ovid, *F.* 3. 872, *extentas*... *manus.* Milton's last two words, in various cases, are a stock phrase, especially at the end of a line, e.g. Lucretius 3. 488, 5. 400, 6. 386, Ovid, *P.* 3. 1. 51, *Consol.* 11, Seneca, *Hipp.* 1132, Juvenal 12. 17, Statius, *S.* 3. 3. 158, *Th.* 10. 618.

68 *Placat & iratos hostia parva Deos.* Cf. Cicero, *Leg.* 2. 9. 22, *placare donis iram deorum*; Tibullus 1. 1. 22, *hostia parva*; Ovid, *A.A.* 3. 376 and *Tr.* 4. 1. 46, *iratos*...*deos*; *C.P.I.* 2, 440: *Mens pia coelestes non grandis victima placat, | Hostia parva Deum sit modo sancta juvat.*

69 *Jamque diu scripsisse tibi fuit impetus illi.* The idiom *impetus fuit* is common in Ovid, e.g. *Am.* 2. 5. 46, *H.* 4. 38, 5. 64, *M.* 2. 663, 5. 287, 6. 461, etc.

70 *Neve moras ultra ducere passus Amor.* Cf. Virgil, *A.* 1. 643–4: *neque enim patrius consistere mentem | passus amor.*

71 *Nam vaga Fama refert, heu nuntia vera malorum!* For the characterization of Fame (Rumor) see *QNov* 181–95 and notes. Cf. Statius, *Th.* 9. 32–4, *Fama*... *vaga*... | ...*refert*; Ovid, *H.* 21. 233 and *M.* 8. 267, *vaga fama*; *P.* 4. 3. 28, *fama refert*; *nuntia fama* in Virgil, *A.* 9. 474, Ovid, *H.* 9. 143–4, 16. 38, *P.* 4. 4. 15–16; Virgil, *A.* 4. 188 (on *Fama*), *nuntia veri*; *A.* 3. 310 and Ovid, *P.* 2. 3. 85, *verus nuntius*; Ariosto, *Carm.* 15. 1, *veri nuncia fama.*

72 *In tibi finitimis bella tumere locis.* On the war's approaching Hamburg, see under 51 above. Cf. Ovid, *H.* 7. 120–1: *moenia finitimis*...*locis. | bella tument.*

75 Enyo was a goddess of war: see Homer, *Il.* 5. 333, 592; Ovid, *H.* 15. 139; Lucan 1. 687; Statius, *Th.* 8. 656; Val. Flacc. 4. 604; Grotius, *Induciae Batav.* (*S.*, bk. 2, p. 84), *Epith. Guil.* (ibid. bk. 3, p. 117).

76 *Et sata carne virum jam cruor arva rigat.* Cf. Homer, *Il.* 4. 451, 8. 65, 20. 494; Virgil, *A.* 12. 308, *rigat arma cruore*; Horace, *C.* 3. 3. 48, *rigat arva Nilus*; Ovid, *Am.* 3. 6. 46, *arva rigas*; Pontano, *Met.* 925, *dulci rigat arva fluore.*

77–8 *Thracia Martem, | Illuc Odrysios Mars pater egit equos.* Thrace (Odrysia in Ovid, *M.* 6. 490, Statius, *Th.* 5. 173, Sil. Ital. 4. 430–1, 13. 441) was the traditional home of Ares or Mars (Homer, *Od.* 8. 361, Statius, *Th.* 4. 794, 5. 173, 7. 40–63, N. Comes, *Mythol.* 2. 7). Cf. *Mars pater* in Ovid, *A.A.* 1. 203, 2. 563, *F.* 5. 465, and Propertius 3. 4. 11; and Claudian, *S.P.* 52. 75–6 (2, 286): *Mavors... | Odrysios impellit equos.*

79 *Perpetuoque comans jam deflorescit oliva.* See the note on *QNov* 15. Cf. Val. Flacc. 1. 429, *silvasque comantes*; Sannazaro, *P.V.* 3. 166, *cedrosque comantes.*

80–1 *Fugit & aerisonam Diva perosa tubam, | Fugit io terris.* The goddess who hates the brazen clangor of the trumpet is 'Eirene,...Latin *Pax*, the goddess of peace, one of the *Horae*, Hours, the other two being *Eunomia* (Order), and *Dike* (Justice). They were daughters of Zeus and Themis, and "minded the works of mortal men" (Hesiod, *Theog.* 901–3).' (MacKellar.) See Ovid, *F.* 1. 709 f.

81–2 *jam non ultima virgo | Creditur ad superas justa volasse domos.* Astraea or Virgo, goddess of justice, lived among men during the golden age and beyond, but finally left the wicked earth to become the constellation Virgo (Aratus, *Phaen.* 100–36; Virgil, *E.* 4. 6, *G.* 2. 473–4; Ovid, *M.* 1. 141–50, *F.* 1. 249–50; Senecan *Oct.* 425; Juvenal 6. 19; Spenser, *F.Q.* 5. 1. 11; Milton, *FInf* 50–1, *Nat* 141–3). In *Prol* 4 (*Works* 12, 174), as here, Milton questions the Ovidian myth and says that Peace and Truth would not have abandoned even hostile mortals many ages after Justice. Lucan 2. 691 uses *ultima Virgo* in the astronomical sense, 'the last part of the Virgin.' *Superas domos* is a common phrase, e.g. Ovid, *F.* 1. 298, 2. 188, *M.* 4. 735–6 (Fletcher); Sannazaro, *P.V.* 1. 178, *Caelestumque domos superas*; Cam. *Insig.* (1624), sig. B2ʳ, *superas ascende domos.*

84 *ignoto solus inopsque solo.* Editors cite Ovid, *M.* 14. 217, *solus inops.* The phrase is also in Buchanan, *Ps.* 102. 8, and Gruter, *Del. I.P.* 1, 240.

85 *patrii...penates.* See the note on *El* 1. 17.

87–8 *Patria dura parens, & saxis saevior albis | Spumea quae pulsat littoris unda tui.* It is a question if Young was driven abroad by anti-Puritan hostility or, as Masson says (*P.W.* 3, 313), 'simply from stress of livelihood.' At any rate, on his return to England in 1628, he received a living and continued to hold it through the Laudian regime. Comparison of the hard-hearted to rocks (though not to the white cliffs of Dover) is common in Latin poetry, e.g. Virgil, *A.* 4. 365-7, Ovid, *H.* 7. 37, 15. 189. For *Spumea unda* see Virgil, *A.* 10. 212, Sil. Ital. 4. 524.

89-90 *Siccine te decet innocuos exponere faetus; | Siccine in externam ferrea cogis humum.* MacKellar notes that *Siccine*, more correctly *sicine*, is a comparatively rare word, used at the beginning of exclamations and questions and implying a reproach (Cicero, *Fin.* 1. 10. 34; Plautus, Terence, *passim*). Cf. Catullus 64. 132, 134, 77. 3. Line 89 refers to the ancient practice of 'exposing' undesired infants (e.g. Plautus, *Cist.* 167, Terence, *Heaut.* 4. 629-30, Cicero, *Rep.* 2. 2. 4, Livy 1. 4. 4-5). The word *ferrea* or *ferreus* is common on the lips of angry lovers (Ovid, *Am.* 1. 6. 27, 1. 14. 28, 2. 5. 11, 2. 19. 4, *H.* 1. 58, 3. 138, etc.). Cf. Ovid, *M.* 15. 443, *externum...arvum.*

91 *terris...remotis.* Cf. *El* 1. 5 and note.

92 *Quos tibi prospiciens miserat ipse Deus.* Cf. *Cantab. Dolor* (1625), 8: *Vidit, & a summa miseratus Iuppiter arce.*

93 *laeta ferunt de caelo nuntia.* Cf. Varro, *L.L.* 6. 86, *de caelo nuntium erit*; Ovid, *P.* 4. 4. 15, *laetarum...nuntia rerum.*

94 *Quae via post cineres ducat ad astra, docent?* Milton gives a Christian meaning to the classical *post cineres* (Ovid, *P.* 4. 16. 3; Propertius 3. 1. 36; Statius, *S.* 2. 1. 97; Martial 1. 1. 6). Cf. Sannazaro, *El.* 1. 5. 36, *Majus post cineres emeruere decus* (the last line of this poem is *Virtus sublimi ducet in astra via*). Cf. Virgil, *A.* 1. 401, *qua te ducit via*; 9. 641, *sic itur ad astra*; Horace, *C.* 4. 2. 23, *educit in astra*; P. Arnolphinus, *C.P.I.* 1, 366: *Ut doceas, quae nos ducat ad astra, viam.*

95-6 *Digna quidem Stygiis quae vivas clausa tenebris*, etc. 'Worthy, that is, to be reduced to the darkness and ignorance of a land under the control of the Roman Catholic Church' (MacKellar). G.B. and B.A.W. prefer a more general meaning; cf. *QNov* 60. *Stygiis tenebris* is a stock phrase, e.g. Virgil, *G.* 3. 551, Lucan 3. 13, Statius, *Th.* 8. 376, Sannazaro, *P.V.* 1. 80. Cf. Virgil, *A.* 6. 734, *clausae tenebris.*

97-100 *vates terrae Thesbitidis olim*, etc. Elijah, when threatened by Jezebel, wife of King Ahab, fled to the desert (1 Kings 19. 1-4). Jezebel, daughter of the king of Sidon (1 Kings 16. 31), is here apostrophized as *Sidoni dira*; *Sidonis* is a recurrent epithet in Ovid (*A.A.* 3. 252, *M.* 14. 80, *F.* 5. 610, 617). In the

Tremellius-Beza Bible the epithet for Elijah is *Thischbites*; in the Vulgate it is *Thesbites*; cf. the notes on *PR* 2. 16 and 313. Leigh Hunt remarked that, a year after recording the pastoral virtues of Bishop Andrewes, Milton was now 'zealous for the Puritans; and calling Charles the First and his troublesome wife, Ahab and Jezebel' (*Lit. Exam.* 30 August 1823, 133; Houtchens, 183).

98   *Pressit inassueto devia tesqua pede.* Cf. Grotius, *In praetoria quaedam Regia Angliae: Nonswich* (*Epig.* bk. 1, 269): *Lustranti silvas & devia tesqua Iacobo.* The word *tesqua*, though classical (e.g. Horace, *Ep.* 1. 14. 19, Lucan 6. 41), seems to be much commoner in Neo-Latin, e.g. *C.P.I. passim*; Pontano, *Uran.* 5. 565; Sannazaro, *P.V.* 2. 209; Grotius, *Apologus* (*Farr.* bk. 3, 224); and especially Buchanan, *F.F.* 28. 1, *Misc.* 3. 11, *S.* 2. 2, 4. 114, *Bapt.* 1070; and Milton, *Prol* 3 (*Works* 12, 162, line 8).

100   *Sidoni dira.* See the note on 97–100.

101   *horrisono laceratus membra flagello.* Cf. Val. Flacc. 7. 149, *horrisoni... flagelli* (Fletcher); Virgil, *A.* 6. 570–3, *flagello | ...horrisono...cardine*; Juvenal 15. 102, *membra lacerabant*; Prudentius, *Perist.* 4. 122, *lacerata membra*.

102   *Paulus ab Aemathia pellitur urbe Cilix.* Paul, a native of Tarsus in Cilicia, was scourged and imprisoned at Philippi in Macedonia (Acts 16. 22–40, 21. 39). Aemathia or Emathia, a part of Macedonia, often stood for the whole country, e.g. Virgil, *G.* 1. 492, Ovid, *Tr.* 3. 5. 39, Lucan 1. 1 and *passim*; Milton, *Sonn* 8. 10, *PR* 3. 290.

103–4   *Piscosaeque ipsum Gergessae civis Jesum*, etc. When Jesus caused the evil spirits possessing two men to enter and destroy a herd of swine, the people of Gergessa besought him to leave their coasts (Matt. 8. 34). *Piscosus* is a stock epithet, e.g. Virgil, *A.* 4. 255, Ovid, *M.* 10. 531 (Fletcher), *F.* 3. 581, Vida, *Christ.* 2. 451; it doubtless came from the *ichthuoeis* common in Homer (*Od.* 4. 381, 390, etc.).

105   *At tu sume animos, nec spes cadat anxia curis.* A tissue of stock phrases. For *sume animos*, see Ovid, *R. Am.* 518, Seneca, *Thy.* 242, Sannazaro, *P.V.* 1. 260, *Epig.* 1. 5. 9, Grotius, *Inaug. Reg. Brit.* (*S.*, bk. 2, p. 60); and cf. Ovid, *M.* 3. 544–5, *F.* 1. 147. For *spes cadat*, cf. Ovid, *H.* 9. 42, *speque timor dubia spesque timore cadit*; and *spes...cadit* in ibid. 13. 124, *Tr.* 2. 148 (MacKellar), *P.* 1. 2. 62, 1. 6. 36. For *anxia curis*, see Ovid, *M.* 9. 275 (MacKellar), Statius, *S.* 3. 4. 71, Val. Flacc, 2. 113, 4. 7, Buchanan, *Ps.* 49. 6, *Epig.* 1. 37. 2; cf. Statius, *Th.* 1. 322, *spes anxia*; Claudian 1. 65–6 (1, 6), *non anxia mentem | spes agit.*

106 *Nec tua concutiat decolor ossa metus.* Cf. Ovid, *H.* 3. 82, *miserae concutit ossa metus*; Grotius, *Epist. Palladii* (*El.*, bk. 1, p. 156): *Exanimi gelidus concutit ossa tremor.*

107 *fulgentibus...armis.* A stock phrase, in varying cases, e.g. Virgil, *A.* 6. 217, 490, 861, 10. 550, 11. 6, 188, 12. 275; Ovid, *Tr.* 3. 1. 33, *P.* 4. 7. 31; Sil. Ital. 11. 514, 15. 551; Buchanan, *Epig.* 1. 48. 1; Pontano, *Uran.* 4. 841.

108 *Intententque tibi millia tela necem.* Editors cite Virgil, *A.* 1. 91: *praesentemque viris intentant omnia mortem.*

109 *At nullis vel inerme latus violabitur armis.* Editors cite *Comus* 420 and the rather remote Horace, *C.* 1. 3. 9; see 111 n. below. Cf. *inerme latus* in Petrarch, *Ep. ad Socratem Suum* (*P.M.* 2, 156), Sannazaro, *Epig.* 1. 12. 4, and Pontano, *Uran.* 3. 991.

110 *Deque tuo cuspis nulla cruore bibet.* Cf. Virgil, *A.* 11. 803–4, *hasta... | bibit...cruorem*; Claudian 3. 77–8 (1, 30), *cruorem | ... bibit.*

111 *Namque eris ipse Dei radiante sub aegide tutus.* Behind 109–11, as Hughes remarks, are passages like Ps. 91. 4–5 (tr. Buchanan: *Certusque promissae salutis | Sub clypei latitabis umbra*); cf. Ps. 3. 3. With the figurative shield of God's protection Milton combines the shields of Zeus and Athene (Homer, *Il.* 2. 447–9, 5. 738–42, 17. 593). MacKellar cites Tasso, *Gerusalemme Liberata*, tr. E. Fairfax (London, 1600), 7. 80[–82]. Cf. Spenser, *F.Q.* 1. 7. 33–6.

113–14 When Sennacherib attacked Jerusalem, the angel of the Lord destroyed the Assyrian army (2 Kings 19. 35–6). *Nocte silente* is a stock phrase, e.g. Virgil, *A.* 4. 527, 7. 87, 102–3; Ovid, *Am.* 2. 19. 40, *H.* 6. 96, 16. 284, *M.* 4. 84, *F.* 2. 692; Seneca, *Oed.* 178; Milton, *Idea* 27 (and *PL* 4. 647, 654).

115–22 The Syrian king of Damascus, besieging Samaria, took to flight when the Lord made the army hear the noise of the chariots and horses of a great host (2 Kings 7. 6–7). The piling up of hard consonants has a strident effect comparable to passages in Milton's English verse where he uses similar means.

118 *Aere...vacuo.* Cf. Horace, *C.* 1. 3. 34, *vacuum...aëra*; Statius, *Th.* 10. 861, *vacuoque sub aere* (Fletcher); Buchanan, *Sph.* 1. 372, *Aëre...vacuo.*

119 *Cornea pulvereum dum verberat ungula campum.* For a comment on this line see the general Introduction, p. 13 above. In addition to Virgil, *A.* 8. 596, editors cite *A.* 11. 875 and *G.* 3. 88.

120 *Currus arenosam dum quatit actus humum.* For *quatit* see Virgil, *A.* 8. 596 (see the preceding note) and Horace, *C.* 4. 1. 28, *quatient humum.* Cf. Ovid, *R. Am.* 596, *in harenosa...humo*; *M.* 2. 62, *aget hos currus*; 2. 388, *agat...currus.*

122 *Et strepitus ferri, murmuraque alta virum.* Cf. Milton, *Prol* 5 (*Works* 12, 192, line 7), *strepitus armorum*; Seneca, *Oed.* 922, *altum murmur.*

123 *Et tu (quod superest miseris) sperare memento.* Cf. Virgil, *A.* 7. 126, *sperare ...memento*; Ovid, *Tr.* 2. 145: *ipse licet sperare vetes, sperabimus usque*; ibid. 3. 5. 53, *spes igitur superest*; Lucan 2. 15, *liceat sperare timenti;* ibid. 7. 615, *Cum moriar, sperare licet*; ibid. 9. 243-4; Seneca, *Med.* 162: *Spes nulla rebus monstrat adflictis viam. Quod superest* is recurrent in Virgil and Ovid, e.g. *A.* 5. 691, 796, 9. 157, *M.* 4. 166, 9. 629.

124 *tua magnanimo pectore vince mala.* Cf. Claudian 24. 9 (2, 42), *excipe magnanimum pectus*; Lucan 2. 234, *magnanimi...pectora Bruti*; 9. 133, *magnanimi...pectora patris.*

125 *Nec dubites quandoque frui melioribus annis.* On the fulfilment of Milton's wish, see the introductory note. Cf. Pontano, *Parth.* 2. 13. 51, *frui melioribus annis.* The last two words are a stock phrase, e.g. Virgil, *A.* 6. 649, Ovid, *Tr.* 4. 10. 93, Prudentius, *Cath.* 10. 94, Secundus, *Epist.* 2. 4. 12, Mantuan, *E.* 10. 108; Buchanan, *Franc.* 798, *El.* 3. 173, *Valentiniana* 7. 5 (*Epig.* bk. 3).

126 *patrios...lares.* In various cases, a stock phrase, e.g. Horace, *Epod.* 16. 19, *S.* 1. 2. 56, Ovid, *R. Am.* 237, 239, Lucan 1. 278, Seneca, *Agam.* 392, 782, *Herc. Oet.* 359.

Elegia quinta, Anno aetatis 20

IN ADVENTUM VERIS

Since *Elegy* 5 was clearly written in the season it describes, and since *Anno aetatis 20* presumably means 'at the age of 20,' the poem may be assigned to April or May 1629. (The statement in lines 31–2 that the vernal equinox has now come cannot—as the late F. R. Johnson remarked in a letter—be taken literally: the poem pictures the whole course of spring.) This date accords with the apparent chronological order of the elegies: the fourth was evidently written in the spring of 1627 and the sixth certainly in December–January of 1629–30.

While in a number of his early Latin poems the young craftsman is obviously seeking a subject, the subject of this one has taken hold of him; and, while the texture of course remains highly rhetorical, an individual intensity of feeling burns through the rhetoric. In comparison, Secundus' poem on spring (*El.* 3. 6), for instance, is, though pleasant, quite conventional and pallid; some kindred pieces will be noticed later. Moreover, although the return of spring has for ages been almost a prescribed theme for young poets, Milton here reveals for the first time that intoxication with the idea of nature's fecundity that is a distinct strain in his temperament, a strain that reappears notably in *Comus* (where it is subjected to a religious and moral discipline) and in the descriptions of Eden in *Paradise Lost*. Mario Praz speaks of lines 119–30 as 'the best commentary on Poussin's "Bacchanalian Dance"' (*Seventeenth Century Studies Presented to Sir Herbert Grierson*, Oxford, 1938, 200). Koehler remarks (161): 'Throughout the elegy, the renewal of poetic impulse in Milton has generated a fundamentally dactylic movement...which keeps the lines moving with a nervous energy not found in any of the other elegies.'

Elegia quinta: In adventum veris

But the fifth *Elegy* is more than a conventional spring poem of unusual intensity, and its full character is brought out in the comment of A. S. P. Woodhouse ('Notes,' 71–2):

Elegy 5...(May 1629), the peak of Milton's earlier Latin poetry, adopts the language and the pagan spirit of the tradition in which it consciously takes its place. Not that one can point to any single model in Ovid and his fellows, or (save in the most general terms) in the Renaissance. Even in Tibullus nature plays a small part; and, despite the invitation in much of classic myth and popular custom, the theme of love and spring-time rarely come together in Roman poetry save in one or two of Horace's odes and the late *Pervigilium Veneris*. The development belongs rather to the Renaissance; and Milton's source has been sought in the *Maiae Calendae* of Buchanan, but there are important differences between the poems. [Woodhouse cites Hanford, 'Youth,' 116–17, and MacKellar.] Buchanan's chief strength lies in the vivid portrayal of individual scenes, while his relatively loose structural pattern is controlled by the commonplace *carpe diem* motif of Horace. Milton's firmer and more closely knit pattern turns on ideas, more interesting in themselves, whose origin is obviously his own experience. *Elegy* 5 is a sort of distillation of the whole body of classic myth relatable to love and the coming of spring. How else is one to account for the fact (already noticed by Mr Tillyard) that in some ways the closest analogue comes two centuries and a half later in Swinburne's 'When the hounds of Spring are on Winter's traces'? The question sufficiently attests the note of frank acceptance, which is the true source of the pagan effect of *Elegy* 5. At the same time, because it is a record and a realization of Milton's experience, and expressive of his personality, the paganism is once more tempered by the beauty of innocence that is his own.

To mix summary of Woodhouse with quotation, the poem is not, as a casual first impression of exuberance might suggest, a formless overflow of powerful feelings; its theme receives comprehensive and coherent development. First the renewed greenness of the earth is linked with the renewal of the poetic impulse: the poet and the nightingale become 'respectively civic and sylvan heralds of the spring; and the rest of the elegy is presented as the poet's song.' The potent energies of spring are shown at work successively in the heavens, in terrestrial nature, and in the senses and sexual impulses of youth. 'Finally, through the shepherds of Arcady and the deities of forest and field, the poet proceeds to the gods of high Olympus, who desert the sky for earth'; and the concluding prayer to these deities to remain in the groves 'merges in the vain wish that the days of spring may pass slowly, postponing the return of winter and night.'

'The essence of the experience which the poem records is Milton's recognition that the emotions whose dawning power over him is recorded in *Elegies* 1 and 7, are universal in their sway. Common to all humanity, and having their counterpart in the life of nature, they not only inform classic myth, but are intimately connected with the poetic impulse itself: from these emotions springs the very power by which the poet gives them utterance. So much Milton clearly states. But in thus objectifying the emotions in terms of an aesthetic pattern, he in a way establishes his ascendancy over them. This Milton does not say, but he verifies it in the poem.'

Milton's joyful welcome to the pagan divinities and his desire for their continued sojourn on earth may appear to be a complete contradiction of the mainly joyful triumph in their overthrow that he expressed in the *Nativity* at the end of the same year. But, while both poems are manifestly 'sincere,' the element of contradiction is really not large or central. For one thing, 'decorum' prescribes or permits adherence to a single point of view, a wide difference in emphasis. For another, while in *Elegy* 5 much of the imagery of nature is sexual, and some pagan divinities have their traditional lustfulness, even they personify the excesses of an essentially innocent nature, while in the *Nativity* the oriental and classical gods represent the unnatural corruptions of pagan religions. There remains, to be sure, enough in *Elegy* 5 to testify to the strength of Milton's 'natural' sensibility.

Elegy 5 is the principal subject of D. C. Allen's 'Milton as a Latin Poet' (see above, general Introduction, notes 2 and 7), but one can hardly summarize his wide-ranging survey of the ancient motifs and traditions of springtime poetry and their perpetuation by Neo-Latinists and Milton in particular. Allen indicates his underlying and unifying theme when he says (47) that *In Adventum Veris* 'is more a poem on the ecstasy of poetic insight in its apollonian manifestation than on the ancient topic of the annual renewal of earthly life. But the "advent of spring" is not to be read under, for the poem intends to remind us that the force of poetry is also renewed with each generation. Standing on the margin of promised poetic achievement, Milton recognized the eternal revival in himself.' Comments by David Daiches are cited above on pp. 19–20.

NOTES

1–4   With Milton's response to the returning warmth of spring compare, e.g., Virgil, *G*. 1. 43–4, 2. 330–1; Horace, *C*. 1. 4. 1–4.

1   *In se perpetuo Tempus revolubile gyro*. Editors cite Buchanan, *Sph*. 2. 308: *In se praecipiti semper revolubilis orbe*, and *El*. 2. 9 (*Majae Cal.*): *Dum renovat Majus senium revolubilis aevi*. Cf. Palingenius, *Z.V.* 10. 717, *revolubile tempus*; Buchanan, *Sph*. 2. 169, 3. 13, *Perpetuo…gyro. Gyro(s)* occurs in Manilius, *passim*.

2   *Jam revocat Zephyros vere tepente novos*. See the note on *El* 3. 44 and cf. Virgil, *A*. 4. 223, *voca Zephyros. Vere tepente* is a stock phrase, e.g. Ovid, *A.A.* 3. 185; Seneca, *Herc. Oet.* 1576; Buchanan, *Sph*. 3. 50; Vida, *Christ.* 2. 30; Pontano, *Met*. 554, *H.H.* 1. 461. MacKellar cites Virgil, *G*. 2. 330 and Ovid, *M*. 1. 107–8.

3   *brevem Tellus reparata juventam*. Unlike the more mythical Greek Ge, the Roman Tellus was more simply the earth as the source and scene of growth (Hughes). See, e.g., Cicero, *N.D.* 3. 20. 52; Ovid, *F*. 1. 671–4, *M*. 2. 272; and the note on *Patrem* 87. Cf. *reparasse* and *juventam* in the extract from Gill in the note on *El* 2. 7–8.

5–8   In later years Milton apparently would not have associated the return of spring with returning inspiration. Editors quote Edward Phillips (*Early Lives*, ed. Darbishire, 73): '…his Vein never happily flow'd, but from the Autumnal Equinoctial to the Vernal, and…whatever he attempted [at other seasons] was never to his satisfaction, though he courted his fancy never so much.'

5   *Fallor? an…?* An especially Ovidian mannerism (e.g. *Am*. 3. 1. 34, *F*. 1. 515, 5. 549, *Tr*. 1. 2. 107; cf. *H*. 7. 35), especially carried on by Secundus (*El*. 1. 1. 9, 1. 7. 62, 2. 2. 30, etc.); cf. Sannazaro, *E*. 3. 61, *El*. 1. 11. 69. Milton may have recalled Ovid, *F*. 2. 853–4, where *Fallimur* introduces the question whether spring has come. Cf. Milton, *ProdBom* 1. 3, *El* 7. 56, *Comus* 220–2.

6–7   *Ingeniumque mihi munere veris adest? | Munere veris adest*. The echo of a phrase or half-line (cf. lines 13–14, 132–3) is, as Godolphin notes (*MP* 37,

1939–40, 355), a device of Propertius (e.g. 2. 6. 41–2, 2. 7. 5, 2. 8A. 27–8, 2. 15. 36) and Ovid (e.g. *Am.* 1. 1. 7–8, 1. 6. 24–5 f., 1. 13. 27–9, 2. 5. 43–4).

8 *aliquod jam sibi poscit opus.* Rand (*SP* 19, 1922, 133 n.) cites Ovid, *Am.* 3. 7. 68, *nunc opus exposcunt.* Cf. Gill, *Ad eundem, Kal. Ian. 1632* (72), *Nomen poscit opus*; *C.P.I.* 2, 185, *Egregium sibi poscit opus.*

9 *Castalis ante oculos, bifidumque cacumen oberrat.* For the Castalian spring and the two-peaked Parnassus, see the note on *El* 4. 30. Cf. Buchanan, *El.* 1. 2: *Grataque Phoebaeo Castalis unda choro* (Warton); Ovid, *Tr.* 3. 4. 57, *ante oculos errant domus....*

10 *Pyrenen.* The fountain of Pirene in the citadel of Corinth was associated with the Muses through Pegasus: according to one story (told more commonly of Hippocrene), it started from a blow of Pegasus' hoof; according to another, Pegasus, when drinking there, was caught by Bellerophon. See Pindar, *Ol.* 13. 60–9; Ovid, *M.* 2. 240, 5. 254–64; Persius, *Prol.* 4; Statius, *S.* 2. 7. 1–4, *Th.* 4. 60–1; Milton, *Rous* 36.

11 *Concitaque arcano fervent mihi pectora motu.* Cf. Seneca, *Herc. Fur.* 1095, *mens vesano concita motu* (Fletcher); *Med.* 506, *ira concitum pectus doma*; Ovid, *M.* 6. 158, *divino concita motu*; Horace, *Ep.* 1. 1. 33, *Fervet...pectus.*

12 *Et furor, & sonitus me sacer intus agit.* Cf. Ovid, *H.* 13. 34, *huc illuc, qua furor egit, eo.*

13–14 *Delius ipse venit, video Penëide lauro | Implicitos crines, Delius ipse venit.* The epithet for Apollo comes from his birthplace, Delos (Apollodorus, 1. 4. 1; Ovid, *M.* 6. 189–91, 1. 454, 5. 329, etc.). Daphne, daughter of the river-god Peneus, fleeing from Apollo, was changed into a laurel; he entwined laurel with his hair, his lyre, and his quiver, and it became a symbol of poetry (Ovid, *M.* 1. 452–567). Allusions are very common, e.g. Callimachus, *Hymn to Apollo* 1; Virgil, *E.* 7. 62; Ovid, *A.A.* 2. 495–6, 3. 389, *Consol.* 459; Tibullus 2. 5. 5. Cf. Val. Flacc. 1. 386 and *C.P.I.* 1, 182 and 4, 275, *laurus Peneia.* Cf. Milton, *El* 7. 31–4, *Comus* 660–1. Cf. Virgil, *A.* 4. 148, *crinem...implicat*; Horace, *Epod.* 5. 15–16, *implicata... | crines*; Ovid, *H.* 9. 94, *inplicitis...comis.*

15 *Jam mihi mens liquidi raptatur in ardua coeli.* Editors cite Apollon. Rhod. 3. 1151: 'For her soul had soared aloft amid the clouds'; and Virgil, *G.* 3. 291–92:...*sed me Parnasi deserta per ardua dulcis | raptat amor; iuvat ire iugis.* *Ardua coeli* is a common phrase, e.g. Petrarch, *Afr.* 2. 415, Buchanan, *Ps.* 113. 6, Secundus, *Epig.* 1. 50. 1, *C.P.I.* 2, 383, and 10, 27 and 65, and phrases from Gruter cited under *QNov* 180. For *liquidi coeli*, see the note on *El* 3. 23.

17 *perque antra feror penetralia vatum.* Poetic and prophetic inspiration is commonly associated with caves and grottoes, e.g. Virgil, *A.* 6. 9 f.; Horace, *C.* 2. 1. 39; ibid. 3. 4. 40 and Juvenal 7. 59–60, *Pierio…antro*; Horace, *C.* 3. 25. 3–5, *quibus | antris…audiar | …meditans*; Propertius 3. 1. 5, 3. 3. 14, 27; Statius, *S.* 5. 3. 284–93; Claudian 6. 15 (1, 268), *Pieriis…antris*; Milton, *Prol* 6 (*Works* 12, 216, line 16), *in Trophonii antro vaticinari*; *Patrem* 15; *IlPen* 131–54 (for secluded dreams, though not a cave). With Milton's phrasing, cf. Virgilian *Cul.* 23, *feror inter et antra*; Claudian 33. 25 (2, 294), *sacrarum penetralia…rerum*; Vida, *A.P.* 1. 109, *penetralia vatum*; *C.P.I.* 7, 101, *Aonii montis ad antra feror.*

19 The classical Olympus was: (1) the mountain in Thessaly on whose peak was the home of the gods (Hesiod, *Theog.*, Homer, *Iliad*, *passim*); (2) the conception of the heavens where the gods dwelt (Homer, *Od.* 6. 41–6; Lucretius 3. 18–24; Virgil, *Aeneid*); (3) simply the heavens or sky (Virgil). For a Christian of Milton's time the name was much less concrete and more figurative than it had been even for the Roman poets, and his uses of it are not always distinguishable. Allowing for that, we might under (1) put *El* 5. 117, *El* 7. 21, *PL* 1. 515–16, 7. 7, 10. 583; under (2), *El* 5. 19, *EpDam* 190; under (3), *El* 5. 79, *Naturam* 46, *FInf* 44; and in *QNov* 8, *Eli* 63, *Patrem* 30, *Mansus* 100, and perhaps *EpDam* 190, Olympus is the Christian heaven. In *El* 5. 19–20 the poet's disembodied spirit has a range of vision like that of the Heavenly Muse in *PL* 1. 27–8; cf. *Patrem* 35–7.

20 *Tartara caeca.* See the note on *El* 3. 16.

21 *grande sonat.* In Juvenal 6. 517. For variant forms, see Ovid, *H.* 15. 30, *R. Am.* 375, Statius, *S.* 3. 1. 50 (MacKellar and Fletcher, augmented).

22 *Quid parit haec rabies, quid sacer iste furor?* Cf. Lucan 7. 551, *Hic furor, hic rabies*; Vida, *A.P.* 2. 395, *sacer…furor*; Pontano, *'Iran.* 3. 1189, *sacrumque… furorem.*

25–6 *Jam Philomela tuos foliis adoperta novellis | Instituis modulos, dum silet omne nemus.* Milton uses only the name of the nightingale; for the myth, see Ovid, *M.* 6. 424–674, Virgil, *E.* 6. 78–81, *G.* 4. 511, etc. Cf. the first lines of *Sonn* 1 and *IlPen* 56. While *adoperta* is not a rare word, cf. Ovid, *M.* 15. 688–9, *iniectis adopertam floribus… | …humum*; and Tibullus 1. 1. 70, *tenebris Mors adoperta caput.* Leigh Hunt (*Lit. Exam.* 30 Aug. 1823, 134; Houtchens, 185) thought the idea of the nightingale and her new leaves came from 'our poet's favourite story of Cambuscan,' i.e. Chaucer, *Squire's Tale* 52–7; cf. Homer,

Od. 19. 518–23. *Omne nemus* is a stock phrase, e.g. Virgil, *E.* 7. 59, *G.* 2. 429, *A.* 5. 149, 8. 305, 12. 722, Ovid, *M.* 3. 44, 179–80.

29–30 *Veris io rediere vices, celebremus honores | Veris.* Cf. Claudian 10. 303 (1, 264), *rediere vices*; Virgil, *A.* 5. 58 and Buchanan, *Ps.* 95. 1 (cf. 68. 20), *celebremus honore(m)(s)*; *veris honorem* or *honos* in Claudian, *S.P.* 30. 7 (2, 238), Vida, *Christ.* 1. 316, Buchanan, *Sph.* 2. 356, *El.* 2. 90 (*Majae Cal.*), and Pontano, *A.C.* 2. 3. 13, 3. 4. 56, etc.

30 *hoc subeat Musa perennis opus.* 'Salmasius (*Responsio*, 1660, p. 5) pointed out certain false quantities in Milton's Latin poems; among them was *quotannis*, which in the edition of 1673 was changed to *perennis*. Heinsius (Burman, *Sylloges Epistolarum* 3. 669) also complained of Milton's false quantities.' (MacKellar.) The last syllable of *quotannis* is long, the last one of *perennis* short. Salmasius is quoted in French, *L.R.* 4, 345–7.

31–2 *Jam sol Aethiopas fugiens Tithoniaque arva, | Flectit ad Arctöas aurea lora plagas.* The time is, or is just after, the vernal equinox (see the first paragraph of the introduction). The sun has left the equator (cf. 'the Ethiop line,' *PL* 4. 282) and the East (the region of Aurora, the Dawn, the wife of Tithonus) for the northern sky of the Great and Lesser Bears (cf. Virgil, *G.* 1. 245–6, Ovid, *F.* 2. 153–92). Cf. Ovid, *A.A.* 1. 550, *aurea lora* (Warton).

33 *Est breve noctis iter, brevis est mora noctis opacae.* Cf. Lucan 10. 333, *Noctis iter mediae*; Ovid, *P.* 1. 4. 32, *brevius...iter*; *A.A.* 2. 357, *mora...brevis*; 3. 473, *brevem...moram. Noctis opacae*, in varying cases, is a stock phrase, e.g. Virgil, *A.* 4. 123, 8. 658, 10. 161–2 (Fletcher), Ovid, *H.* 16. 47, Seneca, *Thy.* 790, Statius, *Th.* 1. 520, Sil. Ital. 6. 70–1, 15. 591, Claudian 5. 525 (1, 96), Buchanan, *Sph.* 5. 428.

34 *Horrida cum tenebris.* Cf. Prudentius, *Cath.* 1. 17, *tenebris horridis.*

35 *Lycaonius plaustrum caeleste Boötes.* The *plaustrum* ('wagon,' 'wain') is the constellation Charles's Wain, the Great Bear (Ovid, *M.* 10. 447; Martial 4. 3. 5–6), driven by the 'ploughman,' Boötes (Ovid, *M.* 2. 171–7; Seneca, *Med.* 314–15). Lycaon's daughter Callisto was changed into the constellation of the Great Bear (Ovid, *M.* 2. 505–7; Apollodorus 3. 8. 2), so that *Lycaonius* means 'northern' (Virgil, *G.* 1. 138; Ovid, *Tr.* 3. 2. 2, *F.* 3. 793; Pontano, *Uran.* 1. 524; MacKellar; Harding, *Ovid*, 45–7). Camden, *Britain* (tr. Holland, 1610, 2) cites the phrase *Sicca Lycaonius resupinat plaustra Bootes.* Cf. Milton, *Eli* 51–2, *Mansus* 37, and notes. Starnes-Talbert (261–2) show that *Lycaonius* as 'northern' was established in the dictionaries of Calepine and R. and C. Stephanus.

Elegia quinta: In adventum veris

37 *Jovis atria.* In Ovid, *F.* 3. 703. Cf. Statius, *Th.* 2. 49, *nigrique Iovis vacua atria.*

38 *Excubias agitant sydera rara polo.* Editors cite Virgil, *A.* 4. 200–1, *vigilemque sacraverat ignem,* | *excubias divum aeternas,* and Milton, *Nat* 21. Cf. Ovid, *F.* 3. 245, *excubias ubi rex Romanus agebat;* Apuleius, *Met.* 9. 3, *excubias agitaverant* (Fletcher); Seneca, *Herc. Fur.* 125, *Iam rara micant sidera.*

39–40 *Nam dolus, & caedes, & vis cum nocte recessit,* | *Neve Giganteum Dii timuere scelus.* Editors cite Ovid, *M.* 1. 130–1: *in quorum subiere locum fraudesque dolusque* | *insidiaeque et vis et amor sceleratus habendi,* and ibid. 151–3, on the Giants. Cf. Ovid, *M.* 11. 270, *sine vi, sine caede regebat;* Statius, *Th.* 3. 341, *vim,...scelus,...dolos.* Cf. the notes on Milton, *El* 4. 81–2, *QNov* 174, and *PL* 1. 197–8.

41 *Forte aliquis scopuli recubans in vertice pastor.* MacKellar cites Virgil, *A.* 2. 307–8, *stupet inscius alto* | *accipiens sonitum saxi de vertice pastor;* and Godolphin (*MP* 37, 356) notes the skilful introduction of *recubans,* with its pastoral associations, from the line familiar to every schoolboy, Virgil, *E.* 1. 1, *Tityre, tu patulae recubans sub tegmine fagi.* Echoes of the line or the word were not uncommon, e.g. *C.P.I.* 5, 294, 315, and 8, 139. Cf. Sannazaro, *E.* 2. 2, *Piscator, qua se scopuli de vertice.*

42 *Roscida cum primo sole rubescit humus.* Cf. Ovid, *M.* 2. 116, *terras mundumque rubescere;* 9. 93, *primo...sole;* Virgil, *A.* 6. 255, *primi...solis.*

43 *Hac, ait, hac certe caruisti nocte puella.* Cf. Ovid, *A.A.* 2. 249: *Saepe tua poteras, Leandre, carere puella* (Warton). Hughes cites the talk of the shepherds in Thomas Randolph's *Amyntas* 4. 4 (*Works,* ed. W. C. Hazlitt, London, 1875, 1, 336).

44 *Phoebe tua, celeres quae retineret equos.* See the note on *El* 3. 34. Cf. Ovid's *lente currite, noctis equi* (*Am.* 1. 13. 40), embalmed by Marlowe in Faustus' last speech, and also Ovid's line 10, *roscida purpurea supprime lora manu.*

46 *Cynthia.* Artemis or Diana the huntress (the moon), born with her twin brother Apollo (the sun) on the island of Delos, near Mount Cynthus (Apollodorus 1. 4. 1). Cf. Milton, *Nat* 103, *IlPen* 59.

46 *Luciferas ut videt alta rotas.* See the note on *El* 3. 50. Warton cited Ovid, *H.* 11. 46 and *A.A.* 3. 180, *luciferos...equos.* Cf. Pontano, *A.C.* 1. 4. 70, *luciferasque rotas;* Tibullus, 1. 9. 62, *rota Luciferi;* Ovid, *Tr.* 3. 5. 55–6, *P.* 2. 5.50; Virgil, *E.* 8. 17.

47–8 When the sun brings day, the work of the moon is cut short. With *ponens radios* cf. Ovid, *M.* 2. 41. *deposuit radios*; with *fratris ope* cf. Ovid, *H.* 21. 174, *fratris opem*; Virgil, *G.* 1. 396, *nec fratris radiis obnoxia surgere Luna*; and Ovid, *M.* 15. 196–8.

49–50 Allusion to Aurora, the Dawn, leaving the bed of her aged and immortal husband, Tithonus, is found everywhere, e.g. *Homeric Hymn to Aphrodite* 218–38, Ovid, *Am.* 1. 13. 37–48, 2. 5. 35–6, *H.* 4. 93–6, Virgil, *G.* 1. 446–7, Spenser, *F.Q.* 3. 3. 20; Milton, *El* 5. 31–2, *QNov* 133–4, *EpDam* 189, *PL* 6. 12–15. With *Desere…thalamos…seniles*, cf. Virgil, *A.* 10. 649, *thalamos ne desere pactos*. With *effoeto procubuisse toro*, cf. Ovid, *H.* 8. 108, *in maesto procubuique toro*; Milton, *Asclep* 4 n.

51–2 *Te manet Aeolides viridi venator in herba, | Surge, tuos ignes altus Hymettus habet.* Cephalus, son of Aeolus (called Aeolides in Ovid, *M.* 7. 672) and husband of Procris, was a hunter loved by Aurora (see the notes on *El* 3. 67, 7. 38; Hesiod, *Theog.* 986–7; Ovid, *M.* 7. 700–13, *H.* 4. 93–6). Cephalus and Aurora are placed on Hymettus in Ovid, *A.A.* 3. 687, *M.* 7. 702 (cf. Ovid–Micyllus, 3, 144K–L, 145A–F), and Pontano, *Parth.* 1. 12. 11–12. For the common *viridi in herba* see Virgil, *E.* 6. 59, *Cul.* 115 (plural in *G.* 3. 162, *A.* 5. 330), Ovid, *M.* 2. 864, 3. 502, Buchanan, *Sph.* 5. 158. For *tuos ignes* (the once poetical and later vulgar or facetious 'flame'), see Virgil, *E.* 3. 66, 5. 10, Horace, *Epod.* 14. 13, Ovid, *Am.* 2. 16. 11, 3. 9. 56, Seneca, *Herc. Oet.* 378.

53 *Flava verecundo dea crimen in ore fatetur. Dea flava* is in Ovid, *Am.* 3. 10. 43, *F.* 4. 424. Cf. Martial 8. 1. 2, *verecundo…ore loqui*; and *El* 4. 50 and note.

54 *matutinos ocyus urget equos.* See the note on 44 above and Ovid, *F.* 5. 160, *in matutinis lampada tollet equis.*

55–6 The vernal earth's courting the embraces of the sun is a traditional idea. Among references given by MacKellar are: Lucretius 1. 250–1, 2. 992–3, 5. 318; Virgil, *G.* 2. 325–7; the first sentence of Sidney's *Arcadia*; Giles Fletcher, *C.V.* 1. 41. 1–4; Milton, *El* 5. 95, *Nat* 36. Hughes adds Pontano, *Uran.* 1. 500–6. Cf. Ovid's *Alma Tellus*, *M.* 2. 272 f. With Milton's *Exuit invisam Tellus rediviva senectam*, cf. Pliny, *N.H.* 8. 49. 111, *senectutem exuere*; 20. 95. 254, *serpentes…senectam exuendo.*

57 *Et cupit, & digna est.* Cf. Ovid, *H.* 5. 85, *dignaque sum et cupio fieri matrona potentis.*

58 *Pandit ut omniferos luxuriosa sinus.* Editors cite Buchanan, *El.* 2.96 (*Majae Cal.*): *Omniferos pandens copia larga sinus.* In Ovid, *M.* 2. 275, where

Elegia quinta: In adventum veris

Tellus *sustulit oppressos collo tenus arida vultus*, the word *omniferos* commonly appeared in place of *oppressos* in Renaissance editions, e.g. R. Regius (Parma, 1505), f. 22; J. Micyllus (Frankfurt, 1571), 55; Aldus (Venice, 1600), 18; Ovid–Micyllus (1601), 3, 37; T. Farnaby (Paris, 1637), p. 8, line 273. Cf. Virgil, *A.* 8. 712, *pandentemque sinus*; the Senecan *Oct.* 404–5, *Tellus...sinus | pandebat*; Pontano, *Uran.* 5. 896, *Pande sinus*; Milton, *PL* 5. 338, 7. 313–19.

59 *Arabum spirat messes.* Cf. Statius, *S.* 3. 3. 34, *messes Cilicumque Arabumque superbas*; Ariosto, *Carm.* 12. 21 and *C.P.I.* 9, 521, *messes Arabum*; and the note on *PL* 4. 162–3.

60 *Mitia cum Paphiis fundit amoma rosis.* For Paphos see the note on *El* 1. 84. Cf. Statius, *S.* 3. 4. 82, *multo Paphie...amomo*; Claudian 10. 93 (1, 248), *mitis amomi*; Sil. Ital. 11. 402; Secundus, *Fun.* 24. 22–3: *tenerisque rosis miscebit amomum, | ...lilia fundet.*

61–2 *Ecce coronatur sacro frons ardua luco, | Cingit ut Idaeam pinea turris Opim.* Earth is described in terms of Ops (Terra), wife of Saturn and goddess of fertility, who was identified with Cybele (Rhea), mother of the gods. She wore a turreted headdress. Cf. the note on *El* 1. 74; Tibullus 1. 4. 68, *Idaeae... Opis* (Warton); Virgil, *A.* 6. 784–7, 10. 252–3; Ovid, *F.* 4. 219–24, 6. 321; *Tr.* 2. 24, *turrigerae...Opi*; Spenser, *Ruines of Rome*, 71–6, *F.Q.* 4. 11. 28; Milton, *Arc* 21–5 (MacKellar, with additions). Garrod (cf. *Ox. Fac.*) proposes *Opem*, but *Opim* appears in Renaissance texts, e.g. Ovid, *M.* 9. 498 in the editions of Micyllus (Frankfurt, 1571), p. 337; Aldus (Venice, 1600), p. 109^v; Ovid–Micyllus (1601), 3, 183; Farnaby (Paris, 1637), p. 52, line 499. For *sacro luco* see Virgil, *A.* 5. 761.

63 *Et vario madidos intexit flore capillos.* Cf. Ovid, *H.* 4. 71, *praecincti flore capilli* (MacKellar); *M.* 5. 53, *madidos...capillos*; and, for *vario flore*, the note on *El* 3. 43.

65 *Floribus effusos ut erat redimita capillos.* Cf. Ovid, *Am.* 3. 10. 3, *F.* 1. 711, and 5. 79, *redimita capillos* (cf. *F.* 6. 483); Catullus 64. 193, *redimita capillo.*

66 *Tenario placuit diva Sicana Deo.* Taenarus was a promontory and later a town in Laconia in Greece; a cavern there was supposed to lead to the underworld. Cf. Propertius 1. 13. 22, *Taenarius...deus*; Virgil, *G.* 4. 467, *Taenarias...fauces, alta ostia Ditis*; Horace, *C.* 1. 34. 10–11, *invisi horrida Taenari | sedes*; Statius, *Th.* 1. 96, 2. 32 f.; Ovid, *F.* 4. 612; Seneca, *Herc. Fur.* 587, 662 f. (MacKellar, augmented). The *diva Sicana* is of course Proserpine (*El* 4. 5–6 and note). Koehler (147) notes in 63–6 'the four main rimes in *os*'

and 'the effect of balancing *floribus...suis* and *Taenario...Deo* at the beginning and end of their respective pentameters; an effect accentuated by the correspondence of *madidos* and *effusos* in the two hexameters, and the repetition of *capillos* in the final position.'

67 *faciles hortantur amores.* Cf. Propertius 1. 13. 22, *facili...amore* (Fletcher); Campion, *El.* 4. 1, *faciles...amores.*

68 *Mellitasque movent flamina verna preces.* Cf. Statius, *Th.* 3. 671–2, *verna... / flamina* (Fletcher). *Mellitus* recurs in Catullus, 3. 6, 48. 1, 99. 1.

69 *Cinnamea Zephyrus leve plaudit odorifer ala.* See the notes on *El* 3. 44 and 47. Cf. Virgil, *A.* 5. 515–16, *alis | plaudentem*; Ovid, *M.* 14. 507 and 577, *plausis...alis*; and the common *plaudentibus alis* in Vida, *Christ.* 1. 573 (cf. ibid. 6. 58) and *C.P.I.* 11, 110; ibid. 11, 426 (Gruter, *Del. I.P.* 2, 1472); Gruter, 2, 1475. Cf. the note on *El* 3. 59.

71–2 *Nec sine dote tuos temeraria quaerit amores | Terra, nec optatos poscit egena toros.* Cf. Horace, *C.* 3. 29. 56, *Pauperiem sine dote quaero*; *Epig. Gr.* (Paris, 1570), p. 30, *non sine dote*; Virgil, *G.* 1. 31, *teque sibi generum Tethys emat omnibus undis*; *optatosque toros* in *C.P.I.* 1, 129 and Gruter, *Del. I.P.* 1, 1183. *Optato(s)* recurs in Catullus, 64. 141, 372, 66. 79.

73–4 *Alma salutiferum medicos tibi gramen in usus | Praebet.* Apollo the healer, the father of Aesculapius, is assisted by the medicinal herbs the earth yields (cf. Ovid, *M.* 1. 521–2). For *Alma Terra*, see Lucretius 2. 992, 5. 230; Ovid, *M.* 2. 272, *Alma Tellus.* For *salutifer* see the note on *El* 4. 46; the word is applied to *herba(m)(s)* in Buchanan, *Misc.* 22. 3, and Statius, *Ach.* 1. 117, and to *medicamen* in Buchanan, *Sph.* 5. 142.

76 *muneribus saepe coemptus Amor.* Cf. Ovid, *A.A.* 2. 275: *Carmina laudantur, sed munera magna petuntur*; ibid. 278, *auro conciliatur amor*; Propertius 2. 16. 15, *muneribus quivis mercatur amorem*, and 2. 20. 25; Tibullus 1. 5. 60.

77–8 For treasures hidden under the sea and mountains, see the note on *Naturam* 63–5. *Aequor vastum*, in various forms, is a stock phrase, e.g. Virgil, *A.* 2. 780, 3. 191, Ovid, *F.* 4. 419, *P.* 1. 4. 35. With *superinjectis montibus*, cf. Ovid, *F.* 5. 533 and 6. 570, where the participle is used with *terra* and *togis*.

79 *clivoso...Olympo.* Olympus is here the sky, across which Apollo drives the sun-chariot; see the note on 19 above. Cf. Ovid, *F.* 3. 415, *clivosum...Olympum* (Fletcher).

80 *In vespertinas praecipitaris aquas.* Cf. Ovid, *M.* 4. 92, *praecipitatur aquis* (Fletcher); Buchanan, *El.* 4. 72, *cum sol vitreis praecipitatur aquis*; *Sph.* 1. 468,

Elegia quinta: In adventum veris

Hesperias cito praecipitaret in undas; Grotius, *Canaria insula expugnata* (*Epig.*, bk. 2, p. 292), *In Vespertinis...aquis.*

81–95 D. P. Harding comments minutely on this passage in *The Club of Hercules* (1962), 11–17.

82 *Hesperiis recipit Caerula mater aquis.* On 'Hesperian' as 'western', see the notes on 80 above and on *El* 3. 46. The *Caerula mater* is Tethys, wife of Oceanus and mother of sea-nymphs and river-gods (Hesiod, *Theog.* 136, 337–70; Ovid, *F.* 5. 81). The phrase is used of Thetis in Horace, *Epod.* 13. 16, Ovid, *M.* 13. 288, Propertius 2. 9. 15, and Statius, *Ach.* 1. 650. Cf. Seneca, *Hipp.* 571, *Hesperia Tethys*; Val. Flacc. 2. 36–7: *palmas Tethys grandaeva sinusque | sustulit et rupto sonuit sacer aequore Titan*; Milton, *Comus* 869. See the following note.

83–4 *Quid tibi cum Tethy? quid cum Tartesside lympha, | Dia quid immundo perluis ora salo?* In 81–4 Koehler (158) sees 'perhaps the best, and certainly the most sustained example of the use of spondaic movement to support the meaning.' For the Ovidian pattern, editors cite *H.* 6. 47–8, *Am.* 3. 6. 87–8, *F.* 2. 101, 4. 3. For *Tartesside* see the note on *El* 3. 33. With Milton's lines 80–3 cf. Ovid, *M.* 2. 68–9: *tunc etiam quae me subiectis excipit undis, | ne ferar in praeceps, Tethys solet ipsa vereri.* With line 84 cf. Petronius, *Sat.* 128, *sudor... perluit ora.*

85 *Frigora Phoebe mea melius captabis in umbra.* Editors cite Virgil, *E.* 1. 52, *et fontis sacros frigus captabis opacum.* Cf. ibid. 2. 8, *umbras et frigora captant*; Sannazaro, *P.V.* 3. 304: *Aestivum viridi captabant frigus in umbra.*

86, 88, 94 *Huc ades.* A stock phrase, e.g. Virgil, *E.* 2. 45, 7. 9, 9. 39, 43; Ovid, *Am.* 1. 6. 54, 2. 12. 16, 3. 2. 46, *H.* 15. 95.

86 *ardentes imbue rore comas.* Cf. Virgil, *A.* 11. 77, *arsurasque comas*; Ovid, *M.* 12. 275, *arserunt crines.*

87 *Mollior egelida veniet tibi somnus in herba.* Cf. Horace, *Ep.* 1. 14. 35 (end), *somnus in herba*; *mollis somnus* (or plural) in Virgil, *G.* 2. 470, 3. 435; Tibullus 1. 2. 74; Ovid, *M.* 1. 685. Cf. Virgil, *E.* 3. 55, *in molli...herba*; 7. 45, *somno mollior herba.*

88, 94 *gremio lumina pone meo.* Cf. Ovid, *H.* 21. 113, *luminaque in gremio veluti defixa tenebam*; Pontano, *Met.* 168–9: *in gremio telluris amatae | Exercet sua iura deus, latonia proles.*

89–90 *mulcebit lene susurrans | Aura per humentes corpora fusa rosas.* Cf. Ovid, *M.* 11. 624–5, *corpora...mulces*; Propertius 4. 7. 60, *mulcet...aura...rosas* (Fletcher); Virgilian *Cul.* 155–6: *leniter adflans | aura susurrantis...venti*;

Horace, *C.* 1. 9. 19, *lenesque...susurri*; Ovid, *Am.* 2. 16. 36: *frigidaque arboreas mulceat aura comas*; Buchanan, *Ps.* 98. 8, *Leni susurrans murmure*.

91 *Nec me (crede mihi) terrent Semelëia fata.* Semele, loved by Zeus, was persuaded by the jealous Hera to ask her lover to appear to her in his divine splendor; as a result, she was consumed by fire, though her unborn child Dionysus was saved (Hesiod, *Theog.* 940–2; Ovid, *Am.* 3. 3. 37, *M.* 3. 253–315, *F.* 3. 715–18, 6. 485; and *proles Semeleia* in *M.* 5. 329, 9. 641). Cf. Milton, *PR* 2. 187. See D. P. Harding's comment on the last phrase of line 91 (above, Introduction, p. 14). Cf. Virgil, *A.* 12. 894–5: *non me tua fervida terrent | dicta, ferox*; and *Eli* 51 and note. *Crede mihi* is an especially Ovidian phrase, e.g. *Am.* 2. 2. 51, 3. 4. 11, *H.* 11. 63, 16. 344, 17. 137, 20. 109; cf. Milton, *El* 6. 6, 43, 7. 91, *ProdBom* 2. 10 (all these Miltonic examples, and some Ovidian ones, begin a line).

92 *Phäetonteo fumidus axis equo.* Phaethon, son of Apollo and Clymene, attempting for a day to drive his father's sun-chariot, lost control of the horses and was destroyed by Jove (Ovid, *M.* 2. 19–328); cf. Milton, *Patrem* 97–100. Cf. *Phaethonteos...ignes* (Ovid, *M.* 4. 246). Harding (*Club of Hercules*, 15) observes that the epithet 'is almost unique in classical literature and that no poet except Ovid had associated it directly with the idea of burning.' [Claudian at least does so: *quis Phaëthonteis erroribus arserit annus* (*S.P.* 27. 107: 2, 230).] Harding goes on to say that Milton's echo of *M.* 4. 245–6 works in an allusion to Ovid's tale of Clytie and Leucothea, both goddesses of the sea and rivals for the love of Phoebus: Clytie's jealousy led to the death of Leucothea at the hands of her father—a tale relevant to the substance of Milton's lines.

93 *Cum tu Phoebe tuo sapientius uteris igni.* An allusion, as MacKellar says, to Tellus' protest in Ovid's tale of Phaethon (*M.* 2. 272–300). Harding (*Club of Hercules*, 15) remarks that *igni* suggests sexual desire as well as literal fire, an ambiguity 'which helps to color the interpretation we are to put on the word *lumina* in the next line; the rays of the sun are a source of life as well as of light.' For Milton's phrasing cf. Ovid, *P.* 1. 7. 46: *usus et est modice fulminis igne sui.*

95 *Sic Tellus lasciva suos suspirat amores.* Cf. *suspirat amores* in Tibullus 1. 6. 35 and 3. 11. 11 (Fletcher), and in Pontano, *A.C.* 2. 7. 19 (and *Uran.* 2. 282, *suspiret amores*); Grotius, *Myrtilus* (*S.*, bk. 2, p. 58), *Zephyrus suspirat amores*.

96 *turba ruunt.* In Ovid, *H.* 1. 88, 12. 143 (quoted under 105 below), and Statius, *Th.* 6. 651. Cf. *turba ruit* in Ovid, *M.* 15. 730 and Buchanan, *El.* 1. 67.

97–114 In this passage on Cupid's power Milton may be thinking, among other things, of Lucretius' exordium, Virgil's picture of the frenzy of love in the animal world (*G.* 3. 209–83), and Seneca, *Hipp.* 184–203, 274–357. Cf. Pontano, *Uran.* 5. 409 f. See the note on *El* 7. 27 f.

97 *toto currit vagus orbe Cupido.* See the notes on Cupid under *El* 1. 60 and 7. 3–12. Cf. Ovid, *M.* 14. 680, *toto vagus errat in orbe*; Sil. Ital. 2. 701–2, *vagus exul in orbe* / *errabit toto.* *Toto* (*in*) *orbe* is a common phrase, e.g. Ovid, *M.* 1. 6, Lucan 3. 230, 4. 232, etc.

98 *Languentesque fovet solis ab igne faces.* Cf. Buchanan, *El.* 2. 26 (*Majae Cal.*), *renovat flamma lucidiore faces*; *El.* 9. 5, *Dumque facem rotat, ut languentes colligat ignes*; Ovid, *M.* 1. 417–18, *ab igne* . . . / *solis.* In Ovid's elegy on Tibullus (*Am.* 3. 9. 8) the sorrowing Cupid has *sine luce facem.*

99 *Insonuere novis lethalia cornua nervis.* Cf. Ovid, *M.* 1. 455, *cornua nervo.*

100 *Triste micant ferro tela corusca novo.* Cf. Statius, *Th.* 4. 153–4, *enses* / *triste micant*; Lucan 1. 320, *gladii* . . . *triste micantes*; *corusca* . . . *tela* in Seneca, *Oed.* 1029 and Pontano, *Erid.* 1. 2. 14. Koehler (142) notes in 100–4 the interlacing effect of both end rhyme and internal rhyme (in *o*, *am*, and *at*).

101 *invictam* . . . *Dianam.* Artemis (Diana) was granted eternal chastity by Zeus (Callimachus, *Hymn to Artemis* 6; N. Comes, *Mythol.* 3. 18). Cf. *Comus* 440–5.

102 *sacro Vesta pudica foco.* Vesta, daughter of Saturn and Ops, and younger sister of Juno and Ceres, was goddess of the hearth and of purity (Cicero, *N.D.* 2. 27. 67, *Leg.* 2. 12. 29; Ovid, *F.* 6. 249 f.; Virgil, *G.* 1. 498–9; N. Comes, *Mythol.* 8. 19); cf. *IlPen* 23–30, and Starnes-Talbert, 278–80. Cf. Horace, *Epod.* 2. 43, *sacrum* . . . *focum*; Ovid, *F.* 3. 30, *sacros* . . . *focos.*

103–4 *Ipsa senescentem reparat Venus annua formam,* / *Atque iterum tepido creditur orta mari.* See the note on *El* 1. 84 and cf. Ovid, *Am.* 1. 8. 53: *forma, nisi admittas, nullo exercente senescit*; Statius, *S.* 1. 2. 277, *forma senescat*; Ovid, *H.* 15. 213 and 16. 24, *orta mari.* Milton may have thought of the allegorical interpretation of Venus as matter, perpetually united with Adonis, 'the Father of all formes' (Spenser, *F.Q.* 3. 6. 47. 8). Cf. Pico della Mirandola, *A Platonick Discourse upon Love*, tr. T. Stanley (ed. E. G. Gardner, Boston, 1914, bk. 2, sec. 13; *Poems and Translations of Thomas Stanley*, ed. G. M. Crump, Oxford, 1962, 211): 'Venus is said to be born of the Sea; Matter the Inform Nature whereof every Creature is compounded, is represented by Water, continually flowing, easily receptible of any form'; N. Comes, *Mythol.* 4. 13; Leone Ebreo (Leo Hebraeus), *Dialoghi d'Amore*, ed. S. Caramella (Bari, 1929), 131–2; Eng. tr., *The Philosophy of Love* (London, 1937), 151; *Comus* 997–1001 and notes.

105   *Marmoreas juvenes clamant Hymenaee per urbes.* Cf. the refrain in Catullus 61 and 62; Ovid, *H.* 12. 143: *turba ruunt et 'Hymen,' clamant, 'Hymenaee!' frequenter*; *H.* 14. 27, *vulgus 'Hymen, Hymenaee!' vocant*; *M.* 9. 765, 10. 1–5.

106   *cava saxa sonant.* In Gruter, *Del. I.P.* 2, 118 and 199. Cf. Seneca, *Hipp.* 38, *cava saxa sonent. Cava saxa* is a stock phrase, e.g. Ovid, *Am.* 3. 6. 45, Virgil, *A.* 3. 450, 566, Horace, *C.* 3. 13. 14, Lucan 4. 455, etc. B.A.W. cites *PL* 2. 285, 'hollow Rocks.'

108   *Puniceum redolet vestis odora crocum.* Editors cite Ovid, *M.* 10. 1–2: *croceo velatus amictu | . . .Hymenaeus*; Catullus 68A. 93–4: *Cupido | fulgebat crocina candidus in tunica*; William Browne, *Brit. Past.* 2. 5. 785–6 (*Poems,* ed. G. Goodwin, 2 v. London, 1894): 'a robe unfit / Till Hymen's saffron'd weed had usher'd it'; Milton, *L'All* 125–6. Cf. Ovid, *F.* 5. 318, *punicei...croci* (Fletcher); *M.* 4. 393, *redolent...crocique*; Virgil, *A.* 9. 614, *picta croco et... murice vestis.*

112   *Cytherea.* A common name for Venus, from the island of Cythera, near which, in some myths, she arose from the sea (Virgil, *A. passim*; Horace, *C.* 1. 4. 5; Ovid, *Am.* 2. 17. 4, etc.).   . .

113   *septena modulatur arundine pastor.* Cf. Sil. Ital. 14. 471, *septena modulatus harundine carmen. Modulatur arundine carmen* occurs in the Virgilian *Cul.* 100, Ovid, *R.Am.* 181 and *M.* 11. 154.

114   *Phyllis.* Any shepherdess of the pastoral world, e.g. Virgil, *E.* 3. 76–9, 5. 10, 7. 63, 10.37, 41; Sannazaro, *E.* 1 (*Phyllis*); Milton, *L'All* 86.

115   *Navita nocturno placat sua sydera cantu.* Keightley explained *sua sydera* as 'the stars, or constellations, that are favourable to him,' citing *vere suo,* 'the spring they love,' in Virgil, *G.* 4. 22 (a better example would be Val. Flacc. 2. 71, *regunt sua sidera puppem*). But Milton's verb suggests placating stars that might be unfavorable (cf. Virgil, *G.* 1. 204–7).

116   *Delphinasque leves ad vada summa vocat.* The musical taste of dolphins was signalized in the tale of Arion's being saved from drowning by dolphins which he charmed with his lyre and song (Herodotus 1. 23–4; Ovid, *F.* 2. 83 f.; Pliny, *N.H.* 9. 8. 28; Plutarch, *Dinner of the Seven Wise Men*, 161–2 (L.C.L. 2, 430–9). Full references are given in Eunice B. Stebbins, *The Dolphin in the Literature and Art of Greece and Rome* (Menasha, 1929). K. Svendsen notes that the dolphin's sociability and love of music 'recur in the encyclopedias from Bartholomew to Goldsmith' (*Milton and Science*, Cambridge, Mass., 1956, 155: cited hereafter as *Science*).

117–18 *Jupiter...* | *Convocat & famulos ad sua festa Deos.* Cf. Ovid, *F.* 6. 321–2: *Cybele...* | *convocat aeternos ad sua festa deos.*

119 *cum sera crepuscula surgunt.* See the note on *QNov* 54.

120 *Pervolitant celeri florea rura choro.* Cf. *florea rura* in Virgil, *A.* 1. 430 (Fletcher), Pontano, *Uran.* 2. 976, and Sannazaro, *P.V.* 2. 27; Ovid, *H.* 5. 135–6: *Satyri celeres...* | *rapido, turba proterva, pede.*

121–2 *Sylvanusque sua Cyparissi fronde revinctus,* | *Semicaperque Deus, semideusque caper.* Silvanus, the Italian wood-god, loved the boy Cyparissus, who died of grief for the deer that Silvanus killed and was changed into a cypress tree; Silvanus carried cypress as a token. This, the version of Servius on Virgil, *G.* 1. 20 (*et teneram ab radice ferens, Silvane, cupressum*; see MacKellar and C. Stephanus, *Dict.*), is the one Milton has in mind, not that of Ovid, *M.* 10. 106 f., in which Silvanus does not appear. The former version is the more familiar in later allusions, e.g. Spenser, *F.Q.* 1. 6. 16–17; Marlowe, *H. and L.* 1. 154–6. Cf. Virgil, *A.* 4. 459, *fronde revinctum* (Fletcher); Horace, *Ep.* 2. 1. 110, *fronde comas vincti.*

On line 122 editors cite Ovid, *F.* 4. 752, *semicaperque deus*; 5. 101, *semicaper...Faune*; *M.* 14. 515, *semicaper Pan*; Statius, *Th.* 6. 111–12, *Silvanusque arbiter umbrae* | *semideumque pecus.* Cf. Ovid, *Ibis* 81–2, *Fauni Satyrique...* | *semideumque genus.* The lesser rural divinities might be goat-footed as well as Pan; Ovid identified Pan with Faunus in *F.* 2. 424, and cf. Horace, *C.* 2. 19. 4, *capripedum Satyrorum*; Secundus, *El.* 2. 1. 7, *capripedes Sylvani*; 3. 13. 1, *Capripedes Satyri.* As James Goode observed (*TLS,* 13 August, 1931, 621), Sannazaro has a line, *Semideusque caper, semicaperque deus* (*El.* 2. 4. 28), which, with the order of phrases reversed, is the same as that of Milton, who may have echoed it. Todd, unaware of Sannazaro, cited what may have been his (or Milton's) model, Ovid's notorious *Semibovemque virum semivirumque bovem* (*A.A.* 2. 24). Cf. Alciati, *Natura* (*Emblemata,* Paris, 1618, no. 97, p. 445; *C.P.I.* 1, 67; Gruter, *Del. I.P.* 1, 25): *Semicaprumque hominem, semivirumque Deum*; cf. also *Emblemata,* no. 145, p. 682: *Semiferum doctorem, & semivirum Centaurum.*

124 *Per juga, per solos expatiantur agros.* *Per juga* is a stock phrase, e.g. Virgil, *A.* 1. 498, Ovid, *H.* 4. 42, 5. 20. Cf. Martial 9. 61. 13, *solos nocturnum Pana per agros*; *solis...in agris* in Virgil, *G.* 3. 249 and Ovid, *A.A.* 2. 473; and Ovid, *M.* 1. 285, *exspatiata ruunt per apertos flumina campos.* Cf. PL 1. 774.

125 *Per sata luxuriat fruticetaque Maenalius Pan.* Pan's haunt was the Arcadian mountain range, Maenalus, e.g. Ovid, *F.* 4. 650, *Maenalio...deo* (Masson);

ibid. 2. 271–8; Virgil, *G.* 1. 17; Milton, *Arc* 102. Cf. Ovid, *Tr.* 4. 1. 80, *per sata*; *F.* 1. 156, *in pratis luxuriatque pecus.*

126 *Vix Cybele mater, vix sibi tuta Ceres.* On Cybele, see the note on 61–2, and Catullus 63. 9, *Cybelles…Mater*; Ovid, *A.A.* 1. 507 and *Ibis* 453, *Cybeleïa mater.* The pattern of the line may owe something to Ovid, *Am.* 1. 1. 16, *Vix etiam Phoebo iam lyra tuta sua est.* MacKellar records without comment Keightley's suggestion that the *sibi* of both 1645 and 1673 should be *ibi*, which to Hughes 'seems inevitable'; Garrod takes no account of the matter. The presumption is in favor of the text. Milton might be making an emphatic and strained extension of the usual idiom, e.g. Catullus 30. 8, *quasi tuta omnia mi forent*; Virgil, *E.* 2. 40, *nec tuta mihi valle reperti*; Juvenal 9. 139, *quo sit mihi tuta senectus*; Secundus, *Epig.* 2. 4. 2, *dum sint omnia tuta mihi.* Or he might be echoing Ovid, *M.* 6. 528 (without the essential *videtur*), *nondum sibi tuta videtur.*

127 Faunus, father of Latinus, king of Latium, was a minor divinity of woods and fields, sometimes identified with Pan (Virgil, *E.* 6. 27–8, *G.* 1. 10–11, *A.* 7. 47–9, 81–6; Ovid, *F.* 2. 268 f., 3. 285–322, 5. 99–102, etc.). Cf. Milton, *SalS* 27, *EpDam* 32, *PL* 4. 708, and the note on 121–2 above.

128 *Consulit in trepidos dum sibi Nympha pedes.* Keightley doubted 'the correctness of *in trepidos pedes*, for *trepidis pedibus*.' Cf. Ovid, *M.* 4. 100, *trepido pede* (Fletcher), a variant reading for *timido.*

129 *Jamque latet, latitansque cupit male tecta videri.* Editors cite Virgil, *E.* 3. 65, *et fugit ad salices, et se cupit ante videri*, and Horace, *C.* 1. 9. 21–2, *latentis proditor intumo | gratus puellae risus ab angulo.* Cf. Ovid, *H.* 5. 135, *silvis ego tecta latebam*; Martial 9. 61. 14, *saepe sub hac latuit rustica fronde Dryas*; Buchanan, *Sph.* 5. 126–8: *Dryades sub fronde latentes | …cuperent fugiendo videri.*

131 *Dii quoque non dubitant caelo praeponere sylvas.* Cf. Virgil, *E.* 2. 60, *habitarunt di quoque silvas*; Ovid, *F.* 1. 247–8: *patiens cum terra deorum | esset, et humanis numina mixta locis*; Seneca, *Hipp.* 294–5: [Cupid] *iubet caelo superos relicto | vultibus falsis habitare terras.* With Milton's last phrase, cf. Virgil, *Cat.* 9. 43, *castra foro, te castra urbi praeponere*, and Horace, *S.* 2. 6. 92.

132 *Et sua quisque sibi numina lucus habet.* Cf. Ovid, *M.* 7. 95, *lucoque foret quod numen in illo*; Virgil, *A.* 8. 351–2: *hoc nemus, hunc…collem, | quis deus incertum est, habitat deus.*

135–6 *Te referant miseris te Jupiter aurea terris | Saecla, quid ad nimbos aspera tela redis?* As the gods had one by one abandoned the earth when mankind grew wicked (Ovid, *M.* 1. 150), Milton thinks of their returning in a new Golden Age (Virgil, *E.* 4). Apparently, as Keightley observed, *aspera tela* is in apposition to *nimbos*, although it is *from* the clouds that Jove sends his lightning and thunder (Virgil, *G.* 1. 328–9, etc.). Along with this Virgilian passage Milton may be recalling again (cf. 91 above) the story of Semele; cf. *nimbos* and *tela* in Ovid, *M.* 3. 300–7. Garrod (cf. *Ox. Fac.*) suggests *ad nimbis aspera cela*. Cf. Pontano, *Uran.* 4. 396, *tela aspera*; and *aurea saecula* in Virgil, *A.* 6. 792–3, 8. 324–5, Calpurnius Siculus, *E.* 4. 6–7, and Buchanan, *S.* 7. 3. Cf. also Milton, *Vac* (1628), 42: 'lofts of piled Thunder.'

137 *lente rapidos age Phoebe jugales.* Cf. 43–4 above and the note on *El* 4. 9.

138 *Qua potes, & sensim tempora veris eant.* See the note on *El* 1. 48, and Secundus, *Epist.* 1. 11. 6, *tempora veris eant.*

139 *Brumaque productas tarde ferat hispida noctes.* Cf. Tibullus 1. 4. 5, *hibernae producis frigora brumae*; Secundus, *El.* 1. 10. 34, *Tardaque productae tempora noctis eant*; Grotius, *Hyemis Commoda* (*El.*, bk. 1, p. 147), *Dulcia productae gaudia noctis amat.*

140 *Ingruat & nostro serior umbra polo.* Editors cite Virgil, *G.* 2. 410, *ingruit umbra*, and *A.* 12. 284, *ferreus ingruit imber.* The pattern may echo Ovid, *M.* 15. 868: *tarda sit illa dies et nostro serior aevo.*

Elegia sexta

The circumstances and the date of this poem are made clear by Milton's prefatory note and by his concluding reference, in the text, to his having just written *On the Morning of Christ's Nativity*, which itself is dated 1629. On 13 December 1629 Diodati, who was visiting in the country, had sent Milton a poetical letter in Latin or Greek (see the note below on lines 3–4) in which he had craved an assurance of Milton's affection and had playfully apologized for his mediocre verses on the ground that, in the midst of his friends' Christmas merriment, he could not cultivate the muse with zeal and felicity. As we observed in the introduction to *El* 1, in the second of the two extant letters in Greek that Diodati had written to Milton (1625–6?), he had urged his friend not to let immoderate study of the ancients cut him off from the natural pleasures of youth which he, Diodati, knew how to enjoy; and in this letter of December 1629, to judge from Milton's reply, he may have followed up his account of seasonal festivities with a similar exhortation—or possibly with the promise of his own return to temperate ways. In any case it seems clear that the writing of verse was for Diodati only a casual recreation; and his kind of seriousness was to lead him, a few months after this exchange of letters, to begin the study of theology in preparation for holy orders—an intention we may assume to have been already conceived and shared with Milton (Dorian, *E.D.* 129).

Milton's poetical answer, cast somewhat in the form of an academic prolusion presenting two sides of a case, combines the ease and warmth of intimate friendship with a statement of his earnest and exalted ideal of poetry, a statement none the less deeply felt for being put—like the theme of *Lycidas*—in oblique and impersonal terms. The lover of 'the smooth Elegiack poets' begins with a half-playful, half-serious defence of the kinds of classical verse associated with wine and love.[1] But then, as Diodati had perhaps turned from conviviality to temperance, Milton turns from convivial to heroic poetry, and, 'by way of the antithesis between elegy and epic, which was a commonplace from the days of the Roman elegists' [see the note on 55 f. below], he 'passes to the poet of heroic themes. At first the terms adopted do not differ from those employed in *At a Vacation Exercise*. Only when Milton speaks of the nature of the heroic poet, and the character of his preparation for his task, is something new added, with a deepening of the note. Unlike the elegist, he must adopt the ascetic discipline of the Pythagoreans.' The sudden transition at the end, from the pagan poet-priest to the *Nativity*, 'can have but one meaning. It is in no sense an heroic poem (the time for which is not yet); but it is the first earnest of Milton's resolve to become such a poet as he describes. The Ode teaches us to read the contrast of the elegiac and the heroic vein as a repudiation of the former, to transliterate the description of the heroic poet into Christian terms as the account of a dedicated spirit divinely inspired, and to see in the ascetic discipline referred to, a turning towards that moral and religious preparation for his life-work on which Milton finally entered at Horton. Thus *Elegy* 6 throws light upon the *Nativity Ode* and receives light back from it.'[2]

Although we do not know precisely when Milton gave up the idea of taking orders, for which he had been destined from childhood (and toward which at the time of *El* 6 Diodati was moving), his fervent eulogy of the priestlike character and calling of the heroic poet suggests that he could now at least contemplate the poetical vocation as a not inferior alternative. And his reference at the end to the first great English poem

[1] Z. S. Fink ('Wine, Poetry, and Milton's *Elegia Sexta*,' *English Studies* 21, 1939, 164–5) noted that Milton's remarks on verse of vinous inspiration were solidly grounded in literary theory (Scaliger; Minturno; Comes, *Mythol.* 5. 13; Spenser, *S.C.*, *October* 103–18; et al.), and that his antithesis between this and other kinds appears in some of them, notably Scaliger and Owen Felltham's 'Of Poets and Poetry' (*Resolves*). J. M. Steadman (*Italica* 40, 1963: see Index below) also discusses Milton's ideas of different kinds of inspiration, citing Scaliger, Minturno, et al.

[2] Woodhouse, 'Notes,' 75.

he had written might, as we have seen, stand in his own mind as a sort of vindication of the poet-priest. He had, moreover, come of age on 9 December, and the significance of that event might well communicate itself to the poem and prompt special consideration of the future.

The serious and personal interpretation of *El* 6, given above from Woodhouse, had been touched by Masson (*P.W.* 1, 267–8) and emphasized by Hanford ('Youth,' 122–3), who saw the poem as marking a definite stage in Milton's inner history: 'The formula here given for the discipline of the epic poet is, allowing for the more exalted language of poetry, so precisely identical with that of the statement in the *Apology* [*Works* 3, 302–6] as to make it clear that Milton is in the latter statement looking back to and thinking in terms of his meditation of 1629. We may infer that the Latin utterance represents a definite resolution regarding his life work.' Tillyard went along with Hanford ('The Growth of Milton's Epic Plans,' *The Miltonic Setting*, Cambridge, 1938, especially 177–9).

Two dissenters from this view are W. R. Parker and L. L. Martz. In reviewing Tillyard's book (*MLN* 55, 1940, 216–17) Parker objected to the serious reading of *El* 6, which he took as written rather by L'Allegro than by Il Penseroso. In his *Milton* (1968, 67–70) Parker reaffirms his opposition to the idea that Milton is making a positive commitment to exalted and religious poetry. Martz ('The Rising Poet,' *The Lyric and Dramatic Milton*, ed. J. H. Summers, New York, 1965, 3–33) thinks that *El* 6, placed 'between the pagan celebration of Spring in Elegy Five and the mildly Ovidian eroticism of Elegy Seven,' 'does not lend itself easily to the widely held interpretation expressed, for example, by Woodhouse' (22). Milton's opening jocularity and praise of convivial poetry lead into 'a hyperbolical account of the ascetic life required' for the heroic poet, 'but he does not wholly lay aside the tone of "Ovidian banter" that Rand has found in the earlier part. Milton no doubt hopes to reach that higher vein himself; but he does not appear to be saying so here.' Even when he turns to describe the *Nativity* (*At tu si quid agam, scitabere*: 79), 'he maintains the familiar tone with which the poem has opened.' In line 88 'Milton seems to be saying only that the thought of writing such a poem came to him at dawn; there seems to be no indication of some special experience of religious conversion.' [It might be observed that Milton mingles jocularity with intense seriousness, and uses similar modest epistolary formulas, in the prose letter written to Diodati at the time of *Lycidas* (*Works* 12, 22–8, especially 24–6). And, as a devout Christian from childhood, he could hardly undergo 'religious conversion.'

NOTES

1 *Mitto...salutem.* An epistolary formula, subject to variations. Cf. Ovid, *H.* 18. 1, *Tr.* 5. 13. 1, *P.* 1. 3. 1, 1. 10. 1, 2. 2. 1–3.

1–2 *non pleno ventre... | ...distento.* Cf. *pleno ventre* in Mantuan, *E.* 1. 61 and Beza, *In Philopatrum* 2 (*Poëmata*, 79ᵛ); Plautus, *Cas.* 4. 1. 777, *ventres distendant. Ventre pleno melior consultatio* is one of Erasmus' Adagies (*Opera*, 2, 1703, 893).

3–4 *At tua quid nostram prolectat Musa camoenam, | ...optatas...tenebras?* The Camenae, water-deities associated with a spring in a sacred grove near Rome, came to be identified with the Muses but apparently retained something of a national connotation (see Horace, *C.* 1. 12. 39, 2. 16. 38). In juxtaposing Diodati's Greek *Musa* (whether or not Diodati had written in Greek) with *nostram camoenam*, Milton may be not merely using a variant term but modestly deprecating his own verses. Cf. Ausonius, *Ep.* 24. 12, *adsurgit Musae nostra Camena tuae.* Cf. Sil. Ital. 1. 556, *optatis...tenebris.*

6–8 MacKellar quotes Milton's letter to Thomas Young (*Works* 12, 4), where Milton says that his boundless and singular gratitude cannot be cramped within metrical restraints; cf. his note appended to *Rous.* Koehler (73–5) suggests that Milton, while imitating Ovid's comments on metre (*Am.* 1. 1. 3–4, etc., 3. 1. 10) and expressing affection for Diodati, is also feeling artistically cramped by the elegiac distich—which he apparently did not use again for a long time and then only in epigrams. For the Ovidian *Crede mihi,* see the note on *El* 5. 91.

7 *modulis includitur arctis.* More correctly *artis* (MacKellar). Cf. Buchanan, *Ps.* 4. 2, 5. 3, etc., *rebus in arctis.*

8 *Nec venit ad claudos integer ipse pedes.* The elegiac metre was said to hav 'lame feet' because of its alternating hexameter and pentameter lines. Cf. Ovid, *Tr.* 3. 1. 11, *clauda...carmina*; *A.A.* 1. 264, etc., and Milton, *Sals* 1. Horace's *pede...claudo* (*C.* 3. 2. 32) has of course a different meaning.

9 *solennes epulas, hilaremque Decembrim.* Editors suggest that Milton had in mind the Roman Saturnalia as well as the month of Christmas. The thought of ancient and modern festivities is combined with that of such emblematic personifications as Spenser's (*F.Q.* 7. 7. 41: Hughes). Cf. *sollemnes epulas* in Statius, *Th.* 1. 667 and Vida, *Christ.* 2. 538; Ovid, *F.* 3. 58, *acceptus geniis... December*; *Tr.* 2. 485–92; Grotius, *Hyemis Commoda* (*El.*, bk. 1, p. 146): *Conveniunt soli genialia festa Decembri.*

10 *Festaque coelifugam quae coluere Deum.* Coelifugam has not been observed elsewhere and may be a Miltonic coinage.

11 *Deliciasque refers, hyberni gaudia ruris.* Milton would remember such things as Virgil's *multo...hilarans convivia Baccho,* | *ante focum* (*E.* 5. 69–70) and *genialis hiems* and *mutuaque convivia* (*G.* 1. 301–2; cf. 2. 527–9). Cf. Pontano, *E.* 1. 234 (*Pompa Quinta*), *Delicias ruris*; Ariosto, *Carm.* 6. 41 and *C.P.I.* 1, 363 and 401, *gaudia ruris.*

12 *per lepidos Gallica musta focos.* Garrod (cf. *Ox. Fac.*) would emend *focos* to *iocos* ('jests'), which would perhaps make the figure more logical at the cost of its boldness.

13–16 MacKellar cites Spenser, *S.C., October* 103–8.

14 *Carmen amat Bacchum, Carmina Bacchus amat.* Hughes cites N. Comes, *Mythol.* 5. 13—and cf. Stephanus, *Dict.*—on the association of Bacchus with the Muses and the potent effects of wine. Cf. Virgil, *G.* 2. 388: *et te, Bacche, vocant per carmina laeta*; Horace, *Ep.* 1. 5. 19: *fecundi calices quem non fecere disertum*; *Ep.* 2. 1. 138: *carmine di superi placantur, carmine Manes*; Ovid, *F.* 5. 345, *Bacchus amat flores*; Virgil, *G.* 2. 113, *Bacchus amat colles.*

15 *Nec puduit Phoebum virides gestasse corymbos.* For the association of Bacchus with ivy, see, e.g. *Homeric Hymn to Dionysus* 7; Euripides, *Bacch., Phoen.* 650–6; Ovid, *M.* 3. 664–7; *F.* 1. 393, *festa corymbiferi...Bacchi*; 3. 767, *hedera est gratissima Baccho*; *Tr.* 1. 7. 2; Propertius 2. 30. 39, 3. 17. 29; Sannazaro, *El.* 2. 4. 1, *virides...corymbos*; Milton, *L'All* 16, *Comus* 54–5 (MacKellar, augmented). For Apollo see e.g. *El* 5. 13–14 n.

17–18 *Aoniis...collibus Euoe* | *Mista Thyoneo turba novena choro.* For Aonian hills, see the note on *El* 4. 29–30. *Euoe* was the festal cry of Bacchic devotees (Euripides, *Bacch.* 142; Catullus 64. 255; Ovid, *A.A.* 1. 563). Semele, the mother of Bacchus (see the note on *El* 5. 91), was known as Thyone after Zeus took her to heaven (*Homeric Hymns to Dionysus*, 1. 21, 7. 56–8; Cicero, *N.D.* 3. 23. 58; Horace, *C.* 1. 17. 22–3; Ovid, *M.* 4. 13); hence *Thyoneus* means Bacchic. The phrase *turba novena*, often with *chori*, for the nine Muses (see under 14 above) appears in Secundus, *El*. 3. 8. 18; *C.P.I.* 7, 101 and 9, 363; *Oxon. Par.* (1625), sig. H4ᵛ; Gill, *Epithalamium...1631* (p. 54); cf. Milton, *Idea* 2, *noveni...numinis*, and note.

19–20 For Ovid's banishment to Tomis see the note on *El* 1. 21–2. The Coralli were one of the barbarous peoples near the Danube, in the region of his exile (*P*. 4. 2. 37, 4. 8. 83). On the lack of wines and feasts at Tomis, see *Tr*. 3. 10. 71, 3. 12. 14, *P*. 1. 3. 49–52, 1. 7. 13, 1. 10. 30–2, 3. 1. 13, 3. 8. 13–14. For Ovid's acknowledgement of *mala carmina*, see e.g. *Tr*. 1. 11. 35–40, 3. 1. 18, 3. 14. 25–52, 5. 7. 55–68, 5. 12, *P*. 1. 5, 4. 2. 15–22, 4. 13. The phrase is in Horace, *Ep*. 2. 2. 106, *S*. 2. 1. 82, 2. 5. 74.

21–2 *Quid nisi vina, rosasque racemiferumque Lyaeum | Cantavit brevibus Tëia Musa modis?* The distich evidently echoes, and refines, Ovid, *Tr*. 2. 363–4: *quid, nisi cum multo Venerem confundere vino | praecepit lyrici Tëia Musa senis?* (MacKellar; Harding, *Ovid*, 48). Lyaeus ('the looser') is a common name for Bacchus, e.g. *Anacreontea* 8. 13, 37. 3, 8; Virgil, *G*. 2. 229, *A*. 4. 58; Ovid, *M*. 4. 11, 8. 274; Horace, *C*. 1. 7. 22, *Epod*. 9. 38. *Tëia Musa* is an Ovidian label (*Tr*. 2. 364, quoted just above, and *A.A*. 3. 330, *R. Am*. 762) for Anacreon, the Greek lyrist born at Teos in Asia Minor; the Anacreontic line is short. Cf. Ovid, *M*. 15. 413, *racemifero...Baccho* (Fletcher); *F*. 6. 483, *Bacche, racemiferos hedera redimite capillos*; *Am*. 2. 17. 22, *breviore modo*.

23 *Pindaricosque inflat numeros Teumesius Evan.* Milton refers to Pindar's celebration of chariot races in the Olympic games held in Elis. *Evan* is a name of Bacchus derived from the cry of his followers; see the note on 17–18 above and Lucretius 5. 743, Ovid, *M*. 4. 15. *Teumesius* means Boeotian, from the mountain range and town called Teumessus. Pindar was a Boeotian, born at Thebes, and Bacchus was associated with Thebes through his Theban mother, Semele, and his Theban devotees (Euripides, *Bacch*.; etc.). Cf. Statius, *Th*. 5. 92–4, *Teumesia thyias | ...Euhan.* In regard to Pindar's vinous inspiration Milton may have remembered Juvenal 7. 62: *satur est cum dicit Horatius 'euhoe!'*

25 *gravis everso currus crepat axe supinus.* Cf. Horace, *C*. 1. 12. 58, *gravi curru*; Virgilian *Cir*. 26, *gravidum currum*; Gill, *Ad Honoratiss. Episcop. Lond. Kalend. Ianuar. 1631* (p. 59): *Effractus aut axis crepat?*

26 *Et volat Eleo pulvere fuscus eques.* *Eleo* (see under 23 above) echoes a common allusion, e.g. Virgil, *G*. 3. 202, Ovid, *H*. 18. 166, Statius, *S*. 4. 4. 31, Sil. Ital. 1. 224. For Milton's phrasing, cf. Horace, *C*. 1. 6. 14–15, *pulvere Troico |*

nigrum; Ovid, *F.* 2. 314, *fusco...equo*; and *Eleo pulvere* (with or without *in*) in Secundus, *Epist.* 2. 6. 51, and *C.P.I.* 2, 220, 7, 197, 9, 180.

27–8 *Quadrimoque madens Lyricen Romanus Iaccho | Dulce canit Glyceran, flavicomamque Chloen.* Horace calls himself *Latinus fidicen* (*Ep.* 1. 19. 32); *Lyricen* is a rare word but not, as Keightley said, a Miltonic coinage. Iacchus was a cult name for Bacchus (Virgil, *E.* 7. 61, *G.* 1. 166; Ovid, *M.* 4. 15), here meaning only wine, as in Virgil, *E.* 6. 15, Val. Flacc. 1. 140, etc. Horace speaks of *quadrimum merum* in *C.* 1. 9. 7–8; of Glycera in 1. 19, 1. 30. 3, 1. 33; of Chloe in 1. 23, 3. 7. 10, 3. 9, 3. 26. 12; in 3. 9. 19 she is *flava* (MacKellar). Cf. Ovid, *Am.* 2. 4. 25, *dulce canit*; and Juvenal 7. 62 (quoted under 23 above).

29 *lauta tibi generoso mensa paratu.* Cf. Lucan 4. 376, *lautae...mensae*; Juvenal 14. 13, *lauto cenare paratu*; Val. Flacc. 2. 651–2, *mensaeque paratu | regifico*.

31 *Massica foecundam despumant pocula venam.* Allusions to Massic wine (produced on the slopes of the Campanian mount Massicus) are common, e.g. Virgil, *G.* 2. 143, 3. 526–7; Horace, *C.* 1. 1. 19, *veteris pocula Massici*; 2. 7. 21, 3. 21. 5. Brodribb (*N&Q* 159, 39) cites Persius 3. 3: *indomitum quod despumare Falernum | sufficiat.* Cf. Virgil, *G.* 1. 296, *et foliis undam trepidi despumat aëni*; Manilius 3. 663: *pinguiaque inpressis despumant musta racemis.* As in *El* 1. 31, Garrod would needlessly and unhappily emend to *facundam;* cf. Ovid, *Tr.* 3. 7. 16, *fecundae vena...aquae*; 3. 14. 34, *fons infecundus parvaque vena.*

32 *condita metra.* Cf. Virgil, *E.* 3. 43, *condita servo*; 10. 50–1, *condita versu | carmina*; Horace, *S.* 2. 1. 82, *si...condiderit...quis carmina*; *A.P.* 436, *si carmina condes*; *C.P.I.* 3, 222, *Carmina condo.*

33–4 *Addimus his artes, fusumque per intima Phoebum | Corda, favent uni Bacchus, Apollo, Ceres.* Editors cite Horace, *Ep.* 1. 5. 16–18, *ebrietas... | ...addocet artes.* Cf. Sil. Ital. 13. 319–20, *subit intima corda...mitis deus* (Fletcher); ibid. 10. 545, *intima corda*; Milton's quotation from Claudian cited below under 77–8 and the note on *EpDam* 80. Propertius 3. 2. 9 links two of the deities with his poetry: *nobis et Baccho et Apolline dextro.*

35 *dulcia carmina.* A stock phrase, e.g. Virgil, *Cat.* 9. 19, *Cul.* 146–7; Manilius 3. 38; Castiglione, *Carm.* 4. 5, 9. 1; Milton, *Patrem* 33. Cf. Quintilian 12. 10. 33, *dulce carmen.*

37 *Thressa tibi caelato barbitos auro.* The lyre is Thracian because of Orpheus, 'the Thracian Bard' (*PL* 7. 34); cf. Ovid, *Am.* 2. 11. 32, *H.* 3. 118, *Threiciam lyram*; *M.* 11. 2, *Threicius vates.* With the phrasing, cf. Horace, *C.* 1. 1. 34,

Lesboum...barbiton; ibid. 1. 32. 4; Gill, *Dispensatio petita...Iun.* 3. 1629 (p. 31), *pulsans lyrica Sappho barbiton*; Ovid, *M.* 9. 189, *caelatus...auro*; Virgil, *A.* 1. 640, *caelataque in auro*; Sil. Ital. 11. 278, *caelati...auri*; Sannazaro, *El.* 2. 5. 19, *crater caelato maximus auro.*

38 *Insonat arguta molliter icta manu.* Against Keightley's objection to *arguta manu* as an unclassical combination, MacKellar cites Cicero, *De Orat.* 3. 59. 220, *manus...minus arguta.* Cf. Martial 7. 84. 2, *arguta picta tabella manu*; A. Gellius 1. 5. 2, *manusque eius inter agendum...argutae.*

39 *Auditurque chelys suspensa tapetia circum. Chelys* (lyre) is especially frequent in Statius. That word and *tapetis* (tapestries) occur close together in Val. Flacc. 1. 139, 147. Cf. Gill (loc. cit. under 37 above), *canoram verberans plectro chelym.*

40 *Virgineos...pedes.* In Sannazaro, *P.V.* 2. 78.

43 *Crede mihi dum psallit ebur. Ebur* (ivory) is 'Probably a reference to the keys of the virginal or harpsichord,' according to MacKellar, who cites Shakespeare *Sonn.* 128. S. G. Spaeth (*Milton's Knowledge of Music*, Princeton, 1913, 100, n. 1) explained otherwise: 'Not the dancing of ivory keys, as interpreted by Cowper and Masson, but rather the strokes of the plectrum, with which the lyre was often played.' [Cf. Virgil, *A.* 6. 647: *iamque eadem digitis, iam pectine pulsat eburno.*] Spaeth thinks that 'Milton would hardly introduce a contemporary keyed instrument, such as the virginal, into such classical surroundings'; but the scene is contemporary, in spite of the allusions to the Thracian lyre and the plectrum (37, 43), and Milton may have wanted to suggest both ancient and modern instruments. He is using the verb *psallit* intransitively, in the general sense of 'plays' or 'sounds.' Spaeth's explanation of the original Greek verb *psallo* (to play with the plectrum, not with the fingers) is the reverse of that in Liddell and Scott. The Latin verb (used, e.g., in Horace, *C.* 4. 13. 7, *Ep.* 2. 1. 33; Apuleius, *Met.* 5. 15) is especially frequent in Biblical translations, e.g. Tremellius, *Ps.* 47. 7, 98. 4; Beza, 1 Cor. 14. 15; Buchanan, Ps. 47. 7, 98. 4. 113. 1.

44 *Implet odoratos festa chorea tholos.* Cf. the very different context of *QNov* 62–3: *fremitusque canentum | Saepe tholos implet vacuos.* Cf. *festas choreas* in Ovid, *M.* 8. 582, 746 (Fletcher), and in Vida, *A.P.* 3. 81, Sannazaro, *P.V.* 3. 120, Grotius, *Ad H. Borbonium* (*El.*, bk. 1, p. 127), and the *Epith. Caroli et H Mariae* (1625), p. 20.

45 *tacitum per pectora serpere Phoebum.* Cf. Claudian 1. 56 (1, 6), *ruat centum per pectora Phoebus.*

46 *Quale repentinus permeat ossa calor. Quale* is 'Used in the sense of the adverb *qualiter*; cf. Virgil, *Georg.* 4. 511; *Aen.* 3. 679; Ovid, *Met.* 3. 682' (MacKellar). Cf. Virgil, *A.* 8. 388–90: *repente | ...notusque medullas | intravit calor et labefacta per ossa cucurrit*; *A.* 3. 308, *calor ossa reliquit*; *G.* 3. 272, *vere calor redit ossibus*; Gill, *Ad Eundem In agro...1627* (25), *pascitur ossa calor.*

47 *digitumque sonantem.* Cf. Virgil, *A.* 6. 647 (quoted under 43 above); Statius, *Ach.* 1. 574, *digitosque sonanti | ...citharae*; Propertius 2. 1. 9, *digitis percussit eburnis*; Pontano, *Uran.* 2. 1221, *citharamque sonantem.*

48 Thalia, the Muse of Comedy, was associated also with social and bucolic verse. See Virgil, *E.* 6. 1–2; Horace, *C.* 4. 6. 25, *argutae...Thaliae*; Ovid, *H.* 15. 83–4, *A.A.* 1. 264, *Tr.* 4. 10. 56, 5. 9. 31, *F.* 5. 54; Statius, *S.* 5. 3. 98; Buchanan, *Iamb.* 1. 39 f.

49 *Elegia levis multorum cura deorum est.* Elegy is called *levis* in Ovid, *Am.* 2. 1. 21, 3. 1. 41, *R. Am.* 379–80, *P.* 4. 5. 1, Martial 12. 94. 8. *Cura deorum* or *deum* is a common phrase, e.g. Virgil, *A.* 3. 476, Tibullus 3. 4. 43, Lucan 5. 340, Statius, *S.* 4. 2. 15. Cf. Ovid, *Am.* 3. 9. 17, *at sacri vates et divum cura vocamur*; *A.A.* 3. 405, *Cura deum fuerant olim regumque poetae.*

51 *Liber adest elegis, Eratoque, Ceresque, Venusque.* Liber was a primitive Italian divinity of wines and agriculture who became identified with Bacchus. See the note on 21–2 above, and Cicero, *N.D.* 2. 24. 62; Virgil, *E.* 7. 58, *G.* 1. 7; Horace, *C. passim, Ep.* 1. 19. 4, 2. 1. 5; Ovid, *Am.* 1. 6. 60, 3. 8. 52, *H.* 18. 153, *A.A.* 1. 525–6, 3. 101, *F.* 3. 777; etc. *Liber adest* is in Ovid, *M.* 3. 528, and Pontano, *Parth.* 1. 18. 39. Erato was the Muse of lyrical and amatory poetry; Ovid derives her name from Eros (*A.A.* 2. 16, *F.* 4. 195–6; see Osgood, *C.M.* 56–8).

52 *cum purpurea matre tenellus Amor.* For *Amor*, Cupid, see the notes on *El* 1. 60, 7. 3–12.

55 f. In turning from erotic and convivial to heroic poetry Milton reverses the elegiac poets' common repudiation of the latter in favour of the former. Some examples—in addition to the non-elegiac Virgil, *E.* 6. 1 f., and Horace, *C.* 1. 6 and 2. 12—are: Ovid, *Am.* 1. 1, 2. 1, 18, 3. 1, *Tr.* 2. 313–578; Tibullus 2. 4. 15–20, 3. 7. 18 f.; Propertius 1. 7, 2. 1, 10, 2. 34. 29–94, 3. 1, 5, 9, 4. 1; Secundus, *El.* 1. 1, 1. 2. 87–104, 2. 1, *Epist.* 2. 6. And cf. Pontano, *Elegiam Alloquitur* (*A.C.* 1. 1). Koehler (66) says that 'it was almost equally conventional' for the Roman elegists 'to picture themselves occasionally as dissatisfied with themes of such modest pretensions, and eager to venture into more serious material,' and he cites some of the ancient poems just mentioned; but these pseudo-declarations are only oblique and dramatic heightening of the poets' real and predominant concern.

Milton's glance, in 55–8, at earth, heaven, and hell embraces ancient pagan epics (Aeneas is obviously one of the *Heroas pios*), and also presumably, in spite of the classical language, modern Christian poems, such as Tasso's. For other early surveys of heroic themes and statements of Milton's belief in the consecrated life of the true poet, see *Vac* 29–52, *Prol* 7, *IlPen* 45–8, 116–20, *Patrem* 17–66, *RCG* (*Works* 3, 235–42), *Apol* (ibid. 302–5); and Ida Langdon, *Milton's Theory of Poetry and Fine Art* (New Haven, 1924), 154–75, 259–69, and J. S. Diekhoff, *Milton on Himself* (New York, 1939), 107 f.

55 *adulto sub Jove coelum.* Milton seems to recall the contrast in Ovid, *F.* 3. 437 f., between the unarmed *Iuppiter...iuvenis* and the older god who used thunderbolts against the warring Giants.

56 *semideosque duces.* Heroes of partly divine parentage, like Achilles and Aeneas. Cf. Statius, *Th.* 3. 518 and *Ach.* 2. 77, *semideos reges*; *Th.* 5. 373, *semideum heroum.*

58 *latrata fero regna profunda cane.* The infernal world guarded by the three-headed Cerberus. Cf. Virgil, *A.* 6. 417–23: *Cerberus haec ingens latratu regna*, etc.; Ovid, *M.* 4. 450–1, 7. 413–15; 13. 732, *feris...canibus*; Claudian 33. 85–6 (2, 298): *latratum triplicem compescuit ingens | ianitor*; Mantuan, *Sylv.* 7. 5 (*Opera*, Bologna, 1502, fol. 103ʳ), Sannazaro, *P.V.* 1. 404, and *Gratul. Cantab.* (1623), 23, *regna profunda.*

59–60 *Ille quidem parce Samii pro more magistri | Vivat.* Pythagoras, born at Samos *c.* 580 B.C., established in Croton a religious society that followed ascetic rules (see under 67–70 below). Cf. Buchanan, *Sph.* 1. 327, *Samii...magistri*; Ovid, *M.* 15. 60, *Vir...Samius*; *F.* 3. 153, *Samio*; *Tr.* 3. 3. 62 and Sannazaro, *Epig.* 3. 3. 2, *Samii...senis*; Cicero, *De Officiis* 1. 30. 106, *vivere...parce*; the praise of Pythagoras in Milton, *Prol* 2 (*Works* 12, 151–6); and the note on *EpDam* 7.

61–2 *Stet prope fagineo pellucida lympha catillo, | Sobriaque e puro pocula fonte bibat.* Cf. Tibullus 1. 6. 27–8, *bibebam | sobria...pocula*; Statius, *S.* 5. 1. 121, *sobria pocula tradit* (Fletcher); Tibullus 1. 10. 8, *faginus astabat cum scyphus ante dapes*; 2. 1. 46, *sobria lympha*; Virgil, *E.* 3. 36–7, *pocula ponam | fagina*; Ovid, *F.* 5. 522, *pocula fagus erant*; Seneca, *Herc. Oet.* 653, *tenet e patula pocula fago*; Sil. Ital. 7. 188, *fagina...pocula*; Grotius, *Epith. J Borelii* (*S.*, bk. 3, p. 111), *Sobria...pocula*; Propertius 3. 1. 3, *primus ego ingredior puro de fonte sacerdos*;

Virgil, *A.* 7. 489, *puroque in fonte*; Statius, *Th.* 9. 435–6, *puro / fonte*; Prudentius, *Cath.* 6. 35, *purusque fons* (heaven as a fountain for the human mind).

64 *rigidi mores, & sine labe manus.* Cf. *rigidos mores* in Ovid, *R. Am.* 762 (Fletcher) and Pontano, *Parth.* 1. 25. 4. *Sine labe* is a stock phrase, especially in Ovid, e.g. *H.* 17. 14, 69, *A.A.* 1. 514, *M.* 2. 537, *F.* 4. 335, *Tr.* 2. 110, 4. 8. 33, etc.; Juvenal 14. 69; Sannazaro, *P.V.* 1. 189, 2. 328; Gill, *Ad Dom. G.R.* (p. 17); Heb. 7. 26 (tr. Beza): *Talis enim nos decebat Pontifex, sanctus, ab omni malo alienus, sine labe, separatus a peccatoribus, & sublimior caelis factus.* Cf. Milton, *Apol* (*Works* 3, 303–6).

65 *lustralibus undis.* The water used in rites of purification. The phrase is in Vida, *Christ.* 6. 981, Buchanan, *Franc.* 644 (the singular in 69), Grotius, *Inaug. Reg. Brit.* (*S.*, bk. 2, p. 73), and *Britanniae Natalis* (Oxford, 1630), p. 13. MacKellar cites Virgil, *A.* 6. 229–31; Ovid, *P.* 3. 2. 73, *aqua…lustrali.*

67–70 'So far as I can discover, Keightley is correct in saying that the traditions Milton here assumes concerning Tiresias, Linus, and the others are his own inventions' (MacKellar).

I have not found a source. Possibly a suggestion came from Diog. Laert. 1. 3–7, who tells of Musaeus, Linus, and Orpheus and then of the ascetic habits of primitive 'barbarian' philosophers. For the water-drinking Pythagoras, see ibid. 8. 9, 38, Diod. Sic. 10. 7, and Athenaeus 4. 161. The last, in his account of water-drinking (2. 40 f.), does not mention Milton's bards, except to say (2. 41 *e*) that Tiresias died from drinking the cold water of the Tilphossa (cf. Apollodorus 3. 7. 3); Carey cites the story in C. Stephanus, *Dict.*

67 *Hoc ritu vixisse ferunt.* Cf. Seneca, *Hipp.* 525–6: *Hoc… / vixisse ritu* (and the whole speech).

67–8 *post rapta sagacem / Lumina Tiresian.* The Theban prophet, who appeared in some Greek tragedies, was deprived of his sight for various reasons according to various myths: see Apollodorus 3. 6. 7; Callimachus, *Bath of Pallas* 57–130; Ovid, *M.* 3. 322–38; N. Comes, *Mythol.* 4. 5; Milton, *Prol* 6 (*Works* 12, 240, lines 3–4); *Idea* 25–6 and note. Ovid uses *sagax* of the soothsayer Mopsus (*M.* 8. 316).

68 *Ogygiumque Linon.* The mythical musician of Thebes who was the teacher of Orpheus and Heracles (Virgil, *E.* 4. 56–7, 6. 67–73; Ovid, *Am.* 3. 9. 23–4; Pausanias 9. 29. 7, etc.; Diog. Laert. 1. 4; Apollodorus 1. 3. 2, 2. 4. 9). Ogygia was a poetic name for Thebes, from its first ruler, Ogyges or Ogygus (Seneca, *Oed.* 589; Lucan 1. 675; Val. Flacc. 2. 623, 8. 446; Statius, *Th. passim*; Ralegh, *History of the World* (1614), 1. 1. 7. 2). Cf. Propertius 2. 13. 8, *Inachio…Lino.*

69 Calchas, the prophet in the Greek army at Troy (Homer, *Il*. 1. 69 f., etc.; Virgil, *A*. 2. 100–85; Ovid, *M*. 12. 19 f., etc.), helped later to colonize Pamphylia (Herodotus 7. 91; Strabo 14. 4. 3). He is grouped with Tiresias and others in Cicero, *N.D*. 2. 3. 7. See *La Alessandra di Licofrone*, ed. E. Ciaceri (Catania, 1901), pp. 192–3, 280–1, 292–4.

69–70 *senemque | Orpheon edomitis sola per antra feris*. For Orpheus' taming of wild beasts, see Virgil, *G*. 4. 509–10: *gelidis...sub antris, | mulcentem tigris*; Horace, *A.P*. 392–3: *Orpheus, | dictus ob hoc lenire tigris rabidosque leones*; Ovid, *M*. 10. 143–4, 11. 1, 21, 42, 44; Claudian 34. 25–8 (2, 316). Cf. Secundus, *S*. 5. 1–2, *Orphea... | sola per antra*; Ovid, *M*. 3. 394, *solis...in antris*.

71 Although Horace (*Ep*. 1. 19. 1–6) argued that Homer could not have been a water-drinker, Boccaccio (*Genealogie Deorum Gentilium Libri*, ed. V. Romano, 2 v. Bari, 1951, 14. 19; C. G. Osgood, *Boccaccio on Poetry*, Princeton, 1930, 88) developed the tradition of Homer's blindness and wandering 'into an account of an almost Christian hermit living a life of deprivation among rough crags and mountains, where he composed his poems' (Hughes). The pseudo-Herodotean Life of Homer (A. Westermann, ΒΙΟΓΡΑΦΟΙ: *Vitarum Scriptores Graeci Minores*, Brunswick, 1845; Herodotus, ed. F. E. Palm, Leipzig, 1853: MacKellar), which pictures a poor wanderer, is quoted in Burton's *Anatomy of Melancholy*, 1. 2. 4. 7 (Everyman's Lib., 3 v. London, 1932, 1, 356), on the same page with a Latin tag about the failure of water-drinkers' verse to please or survive. With *dapis exiguus, sic rivi potor*, cf. Ovid, *F*. 2. 362, *exiguas...dapes*; Horace, *Ep*. 1. 19. 3, *aquae potoribus*; *C*. 2. 20. 20, *Rhodanique potor*.

72 *Dulichium vexit per freta longa virum*. Odysseus, ruler of Ithaca and of Dulichium, a small island near it (Homer, *Od*. 1. 246, etc.). For the periphrasis, cf. Virgil, *E*. 6. 76, *Dulichias...rates*; Propertius 2. 21. 13; Sil. Ital. 12. 115; and especially Ovid, *M*. 14. 226, *R. Am*. 272, *Tr*. 1. 5. 60, 4. 1. 31. *Freta*, which MacKellar takes as 'straits,' commonly means seas in the Latin poets, e.g. Virgil, *E*. 1. 60, *G*. 2. 503, Horace, *C*. 1. 3. 16, Ovid, *passim*. With Milton's phrase cf. Ovid, *F*. 3. 868, *vehit per freta longa* and *per freta longa* in *H*. 7. 46, 16. 22, *M*. 7. 67, 8. 142, *F*. 5. 660 (Fletcher).

73 *per Monstrificam Perseiae Phoebados aulam*. A periphrastic allusion to Circe, daughter of the Sun and Perse (Homer, *Od*. 10. 274 f.; Cicero, *N.D*. 3. 19. 48; Ovid, *M*. 14. 10 f., 247 f.; *R. Am*. 263, *Perseïdes herbae*; Buchanan, *El*. 7. 17, *Circe Perseia*; Milton, *El* 1. 87, *Comus* 50–3, 252 f.). 'Phoebas, *-adis*, or *-ados*, means a priestess of Apollo; it would seem here to be used as a patronymic' (MacKellar). Some examples of the uncommon adjective *monstrificus* are:

Pliny, *N.H.* 2. 3. 7, Val. Flacc. 6. 152–3, Secundus, *S.* 5. 144, Mantuan, *E.* 4. 239–40, *C.P.I.* 9, 244, Grotius, *Anapaesti in Morbum…F. Grotii* (*Farr.*, bk. 2, p. 191).

74 *vada foemineis insidiosa sonis.* The shoals of the Sirens. Homer (*Od.* 12. 45) places them in a meadow, Virgil (*A.* 5. 864) on rocks (MacKellar). Virgil (*A.* 7. 24) uses *vada* for the Circean shore. Circe's *pocula* are *insidiosa* in Ovid, *M.* 14. 294. Cf. Milton's allusion to the Sirens in *Leon* 3. 1–3.

75–6 Odysseus' visit to the underworld, in particular the scene described in Homer, *Od.* 11. 34 f. Warton remarked on Milton's illustrating Homer's poetical character by the *Odyssey*, not the *Iliad*, which, Keightley added, 'was quite natural in one who was so fond of Ovid.' But though the young Milton had a strong taste for romance, we may suppose (with Hughes) that here his account of heroic poetry is affected by the Renaissance view, notably exemplified in Chapman, of Odysseus as the wise and magnanimous hero. Cf. Tillyard, *M. Set.* 177. For *sanguine nigro*, cf. Ovid, *M.* 12. 326, *niger…sanguis.*

77–8 *Diis…sacer est vates, divumque sacerdos, | Spirat & occultum pectus, & ora Jovem.* The phrase *sacer vates*, in various forms, is in Horace, *C.* 4. 9. 28, Tibullus 2. 5. 114, Ovid, *Am.* 3. 9. 17, 41, *A.A.* 3. 539, Val. Flacc. 6. 114, Vida, *A.P.* 3. 112. Cf. Ovid, *Am.* 3. 8. 23, *ille ego Musarum purus Phoebique sacerdos*; Propertius 3. 1. 3 (quoted under 61–2); Vida, *A.P.* 1. 562, *Ingredior vates idem, Superumque sacerdos*; 2. 3–5; 2. 580, *Divumque sacerdos*; Sannazaro, *El.* 1. 7. 22, *Quaeque sacer vatum spiritus ore refert*; and the note on 49 above. In his letter to Gill dated 20 May 1628, which probably should be 20 May 1630 (see the note on *El* 3. 60), Milton wrote (*Works* 12, 8): '…*furores illos caelius instinctos, sacrumque & aethereum ignem intimo pectore eluere, cum tua* (*quod de seipso Claudianus*)—Totum spirent Praecordia Phoebum.' See Claudian 33. 6 (2, 294: *De Raptu Proserpinae*): *totum spirant praecordia Phoebum*; and ibid. 22. 340–1 (2, 26), *Minervam | spirat opus.* Cf. Ovid, *A.A.* 3. 548–50, *P.* 3. 4. 93–4.

79–80 *At tu si quid agam, scitabere.* This common locution, in various forms but always with *quid agam*, appears, e.g., in Horace, *Ep.* 1. 8. 3, Ovid, *Tr.* 1. 1. 18, 3. 5. 23–4, 5. 7. 5, *P.* 1. 5. 53 (and cf. *R. Am.* 8), Buchanan, *El.* 4. 3. Cf. Milton's letter to Diodati of 2 September (November?) 1637 (*Works* 12, 20, lines 13–14; *C.P.W.* 1, 325).

81–90 These lines fix the composition of the *Elegy* within the days following Christmas 1629.

81 *Paciferum canimus caelesti semine regem. Pacifer*, used of the olive in Virgil, *A.* 8. 116, is a frequent epithet for the gods, e.g. Mercury, *pacifer…Cyllenius*

Elegia sexta: *Ad Carolum Diodatum*

(Ovid, *M.* 14. 291). Cf. *caelestia semina* in Ovid, *F.* 2. 383, Sil. Ital. 15. 71, Buchanan, *Sph.* 1. 426, P. Fletcher, *Loc.* (p. 109, lines 15–16); and Virgil, *A.* 6. 730–1, *caelestis origo | seminibus.*

83 *Vagitumque Dei.* The *Nativity* does not record 'the infant cry of God' (Parker, 69). Martz (24: see headnote above) suggests that 'Milton is emphasizing the poem's allegiance to the naïve tradition of the Christmas carol, as his next words further indicate.'

83 *stabulantem paupere tecto.* Cf. Horace, *Ep.* 1. 10. 32 and *Oxon. Par.* (1625), sig. A2ʳ, *paupere tecto*; Sannazaro, *P.V.* 1. 70, *Exiguis degit thalamis, & paupere tecto.* Milton's lines 83–4 embody one of the baroque (and medieval) contrasts of *Nat* 8–14.

85 *Stelliparumque polum.* The postclassical epithet was censured by Salmasius (*Responsio*, 1660, p. 5; quoted in French, *L.R.* 4, 345–7). Lines 85–6 are almost a summary of the three main themes or movements of *Nat.*

89 *Te quoque pressa manent patriis meditata cicutis.* Cf. Horace, *Ep.* 1. 20. 17, *hoc quoque te manet.* Editors since Warton have naturally taken 89–90 as a concluding reference to the *Nativity*, the subject of 79–88, but 89 is something of a crux. Three representative translations are: 'These strains composed on my native pipes await you in close keeping' (MacKellar); 'For you other strains too are waiting, strains oft practised, strains struck out from my native country's reeds' (Columbia); 'For you these simple strains that have been meditated on my native pipes are waiting' (Hughes, 1957). MacKellar and Hughes make good sense by ignoring *quoque*; Columbia, taking account of it, makes the line refer to some verse other than the *Nativity*. It is surely a very strong presumption that the reference is to the ode, since a final glance elsewhere would be rather weak and awkward. Since one must take account of *quoque*, and since it should follow the emphatic word, here *Te*, and should not be taken with *meditata* (as by Columbia), the best explanation may be this: Milton has just spoken (87–8) of the *Nativity* as a gift in two senses, a birthday gift for Christ and a gift to the poet, as it were, brought by the dawn; it now awaits Diodati, as a gift for him also. This idea was behind my own translation: 'For you also are waiting these verses, simply fashioned on my native pipes' (*Complete Poetical Works*, Boston, 1965).

Two other views of the problem may be recorded. F. W. Bateson (*English Poetry: A Critical Introduction*, London, 1950, 155–6), following Columbia, took line 89 to refer to other verses and *cicutis* to pastorals, so that the allusion must be to *L'Allegro* and *Il Penseroso*. This idea was refuted by J. B. Leishman

('*L'Allegro* and *Il Penseroso* in Their Relation to Seventeenth-Century Poetry,' *Essays and Studies 1951*, 2 n.), but it was later endorsed, without reference to Leishman and with no stronger evidence (except glosses on *cicutis*), by H. F. Fletcher (*Intell. Dev.* 2, 480–3, 495–6).

John Carey ('The Date of Milton's Italian Poems,' *RES* 14, 1963, 383–6) suggested that, addressing Diodati, Milton used *patriis cicutis* to mean his friend's ancestral language, Italian; the reference would be to Milton's sheaf of Italian poems, which thus would have been written recently, in or before December 1629. Carey notes that this was the month in which Milton bought his volume of Della Casa (French, *L.R.* 1, 205). There are objections to this ingenious idea. It goes against the strong general presumption in favour of the *Nativity*, the theme of 81–8; and it involves not only the awkward, anticlimactic effect of a brief, vague, concluding reference to other verse but here a very jarring shift from religious to erotic poetry (of the kind just repudiated in the second half of the elegy). Further, the idea strains the natural meaning of *patriis*, which in this context surely suggests the poet's native language, the English of the *Nativity*, in contrast with the Latin of the elegy. And, in regard to the pastoral connotation of *cicutis*, the *Nativity*—an obvious descendant of Virgil's Messianic eclogue—is far more of a pastoral than a set of love sonnets.

One particular in line 89, the word *pressa*, has likewise been variously interpreted. Keightley, citing Horace, *A.P.* 388, *nonumque prematur in annum*, paraphrased Milton thus: 'These verses, which are written in English, have not been given to the world, they wait your approval'; cf. MacKellar (101: quoted above), 'in close keeping.' It seems doubtful if the meaning of Horace's verb carries over into orthodox uses of the past participle. Milton appears rather to be using the word in the standard sense of Quintilian (10. 2. 16, 12. 10. 18) and others, as 'concise,' 'plain,' 'Attic'—a modest term which accords with 'native reeds' if not with our view of the *Nativity*. Leishman revived the idea of 'withheld as yet from publication'; but, besides the objection already noted, this implies an impulse that could hardly occur to a poet of the period unless he had a book ready, as Milton had not.

90 *Tu mihi, cui recitem, judicis instar eris.* For phrases similar to the first four words editors cite Ovid, *P.* 3. 5. 39, 4. 2. 37 (quoted under *EpDam* 175), *Tr.* 3. 14. 39–40, 4. 1. 89–90; Horace, *A.P.* 386–8. Cf. also Ovid, *Am.* 3. 11. 47, *magni mihi numinis instar*; *M.* 14. 124, *numinis instar eris semper mihi.*

Elegia septima,
Anno aetatis undevigesimo

The season of *El* 7 is certain, since Milton (line 14) associates it with the first of May. The year is less certain, though the range of possibilities is small. In both 1645 and 1673 the poem came last in the group of numbered elegies, and the preceding six, on Milton's incomplete dating and ours, appear to be in chronological order, extending from the spring of 1626 to late December of 1629. Of the five dated by Milton, *El* 7 is the only one dated with an ordinal numeral, and *Anno aetatis undevigesimo* would normally mean 'in the nineteenth year of his age,' that is, when he was 18, in 1627. However, in view of his use of *Anno aetatis* for 'at the age of,' this elegy has been commonly assigned to the year when he was 19, that is, 1628. But we may then ask why Milton did not, in accordance with his usual practice, say *Anno aetatis 19*. Also, can his use of *Anno aetatis* be carried over to a combination with the ordinal adjective? And it is always possible that he was mistaken in his dating, although the unique ordinal may count somewhat against that. We may conclude that the poem was written either in 1627 or in 1628, and that there is no clear argument for one year against the other.

In either case, as Masson observed (*P.W.* 1, 268), the position of the poem constitutes a violation of the chronological order of the series. Grierson suggested that, after hesitating to include a poem on such a subject, Milton 'Finally, unwilling to lose anything composed by John Milton...printed it at the end, dating it and adding ten lines of apology.'[1] Parker, controverting this 'implausible and ungenerous' idea

---

[1] *Poems of John Milton* (London, 1925), 1, ix. Grierson—apart from the flick at Milton's supposed egoism—was apparently following Masson (*P.W.* 1, 270), though Grierson, making an error in arithmetic, puts the poem back in '1626 when he was eighteen years old,' and Masson says 1627 or 1628—as Grierson does on p. 49.

along with the conventional date, asks why Milton could not have called the poem *Elegia Quinta* and put it in its proper and less conspicuous place, thereby rounding out the elegies with the more serious and mature *El* 6 ('Notes,' 118–21). Since Parker's major premise is that all the numbered elegies are in chronological order, he pushes *El* 7 up to 1630—a plague year, when Milton could have spent May Day in London, where the poem implies he is (lines 14, 51). Parker feels no incongruity in such a poem's following close upon *El* 6, since he declines to see the latter as a self-dedication. In this one instance, being—in 1630—at the significant age of 21, Milton used an ordinal to make the record conspicuous but, Parker thinks, what he actually wrote was *Anno aetatis uno et vigesimo* or *uno & vigesimo*, a phrase which a careless compositor, 'who made plenty of other mistakes not caught in proofreading,' may have misread, especially as Milton's hastily written *et* resembles a *d* with a flourish. Parker summarizes his argument in *Milton* (754, n. 35).

These conjectures (followed by Shawcross, *C.E.P.*, 548) seem both strained and unnecessary. Whether or not Milton was actually in London on May Day in 1627 or 1628, it required no feat of imagination, for the purposes of the poem, to place the scene there or to associate a springtime experience with such a festive day. If he wished to make the dating of the elegy conspicuous, he would presumably have been on the alert for it in reading proof. And a careless and not over-learned compositor would be lucky, even with aid from Milton's script, in happening upon a correct Latin word. We cannot assume that Milton regarded chronological order as absolutely unbreakable but, since he had been following chronology, one possible reason for the unusual way of dating *El* 7 might be just the fact that he was placing it out of order.

Several inferences support the idea that Milton deliberately disregarded chronology in order to put *El* 7 at the end of the series. The experience described in it is a concrete illustration of the beauty of English girls and of the poet's susceptibility, which had been the subject of the second half of *El* 1, so that these two poems make a sort of frame for the group, a frame in keeping with the traditionally erotic character of elegiac verse; cf. E. A. J. Honigmann, *Milton's Sonnets* (London and New York, 1966), 74. *El* 7 is also a concrete example of the springtime activity of Cupid which had been a main theme of *El* 5. Then the apologetic epilogue, which is separated from *El* 7 by a printer's line, and which is commonly taken to refer to that poem, links itself with the apologetic reassurance at the end of *El* 1. However, while the final lines of the epilogue point to *El* 7, the first lines, with their plurals *Haec* and *trophaea*, suggest that Milton was thinking of more than that one poem, probably of *Elegies* 1 and 5; the latter, for all the innocence of its paganism, was erotic enough to awaken qualms in a serious Christian poet who was not indifferent to his moral reputation. Thus another reason for placing *El* 7 at the end would be to have the epilogue there, so that it would cover the several 'wanton' poems of the group; the epilogue would serve that purpose less well if the impersonal *El* 5 had been in the place of 7, and it would have no point if it had followed the mainly serious *El* 6. L. L. Martz ('The Rising Poet,' 13) thinks that 'the placing of this elegy seems to be dictated by the presence of the retractation, evidently written for the seventh elegy alone, and not for this whole set of elegies,' although he allows for wider reference[2] Carey gives the same reason for the placing of the poem.

[2] That the epilogue refers only to *El* 7 has been the view of such scholars as Masson (*P.W.* 1, 269–70), MacKellar, Tillyard (*Milton*, 25 n.), Hughes (1937). The latest upholder is Parker (897, n. 119). Although some scholars, e.g. Harding (*Ovid*, 57), Hughes (1957), and Martz (above), speak loosely of the Elegies in general, the epilogue is directed only against eroticism; it can refer, therefore, only to 5, 7, and part of 1. The question is whether Milton is repudiating 7 alone, or the other two as well, and with them his youthful concern with romantic love, 'amatory trifling' (Hanford, 'Youth,' 126). The second opinion is held, e.g., by Hanford, Harding and Hughes (as qualified above), and Bush; cf. J. W. Saunders in 112 n. below. Further, as was said above, the plurals *Haec* and *trophaea* (1–2) seem to say that Milton has more than one poem in mind. Of course there was no occasion for regrets strong enough to stand in the way of publication.

Opinions about the date of the epilogue have also differed. Masson (*loc. cit.*) thought—as the less informed Warton had—that it was written in 1645, just before the publication of the *Poems*. Hanford is non-committal, but implies some lapse of time after the writing of the Elegies. Tillyard says '1645 or earlier.' Grierson (1, ix and 49) and Fletcher (*Intell. Dev.* 2, 416) follow Masson. Shawcross (*C.E.P.* 62) gives 'late 1630–1631?'; Bush, '1630 or later.' Parker (loc. cit.) prefers 1645, though he admits that Milton might have felt such a revulsion at earlier times.

Internal evidence is not helpful. The *olim* and *Indocilisque aetas* and the past tenses of

Critics' intuitions have differed as to whether the incident was actual or imagined, but not about the actuality of the young poet's sensations. Milton's lifelong capacity for being kindled by feminine beauty, which is manifested in his writing from *El* 1 to *Samson Agonistes*, is to be measured by the intensity of the response, not by the force of the stimulus. The theme and texture and in part the atmosphere of *El* 7 are in the tradition of Roman and Renaissance love poetry, and in the detailed analysis of his reactions (73 f.) Milton perhaps 'approaches most closely the manner and the substance' of the Roman elegists (Koehler, 22). Of course the nemesis that overtakes Milton stops well short of the climax that might be expected from the conventional amorist; as E. K. Rand said (*SP* 19, 112), 'Ovid is often tantalizing, but never to this extent.' The poet's interview with Cupid and the recital of the god's triumphs— a section which, with the later description of amorous pangs, Hanford finds 'academic enough' ('Youth,' 115)—have some general and particular resemblances to Ovid's *Amores* 1 and 2 and *Ex Ponto* 3. 3, and to the encounter of the scornful Apollo and the conquering Cupid in the *Metamorphoses* 1. 452 f. The poem is further allied with such Neo-Latin pieces as the first elegy of Joannes Secundus and George Buchanan's *Elegy* 9 (*De Neaera*); other references are given in the notes on 27 f. and on *El* 5. 97–114. None the less, as Woodhouse observes in noting such models, 'the tone of the elegy is neither Ovid's nor that of his other Renaissance imitators, but Milton's own, marked by a new ardour, but also, like his other early writings, by the beauty of innocence, whose origin Milton correctly divined: in part it sprang from his Christian education, in part from his personal temper, an innate modesty, "a certain niceness of nature" and "an honest haughtiness and self-esteem"' ('Notes,' 71).

most of the verbs suggest a man looking back some distance upon his youth, while the present tenses of *rigent* and *timet* could reflect either closeness to a change of heart or a settled state. But, in apologizing for a phase now ended, whether recently or not, Milton would naturally think of it as remote. Keightley raised a point worth repeating: would Milton in 1645, three years (as we now know) after his marriage, have written the last four lines as they stand? Fletcher (loc. cit.) apparently thinks so; most scholars do not touch the question. Carey raises it again; his dating is '1635?'.

NOTES

1 *Nondum blanda tuas leges Amathusia noram.* Venus was called Amathusia because one of her temples was at Amathus in Cyprus (Virgil, *Cir.* 242, *A.* 10. 51; Ovid, *Am.* 3. 15. 15; Catullus 36. 14, 68A. 11; Pontano, *H.H.* 1. 605). Cf. Ovid, *Am.* 3. 2. 55, *blanda Venus*; *A.A.* 1. 362, *blanda...arte Venus*; Secundus, *El. Solemn.* 3. 77, *cum blando, blandissima Mater, Amore*; *Epig.* 2. 17. 15, *blandem...Venerem.*

2 *Et Paphio vacuum pectus ab igne fuit.* For Paphos see the note on *El* 1. 84. Cf. Lucretius 2. 46, *vacuum pectus*; Ovid, *Am.* 1. 1. 26, *in vacuo pectore regnat Amor*; *M.* 1. 520, *in vacuo...pectore*; Buchanan, *El.* 2. 42 (*Majae Cal.*), *rudis in vacuo pectore flamma calet.*

3 *Saepe cupidineas, puerilia tela, sagittas.* For Cupid as the wanton and powerful bow-boy of amatory convention, see the note on *El* 1. 60 and references at the end of the introduction to *El* 7 and under 27 f. below. MacKellar cites Ovid, *R. Am.* 157: *Vince Cupidineas pariter Parthasque sagittas*; *Tr.* 4. 10. 65–6: *molle Cupidineis nec inexpugnabile telis | cor mihi.* Cf. Claudian 10. 71 (1, 248), *Cupidineas...sagittas*; Buchanan, *El.* 3. 204, *Perque Cupidineas, tela timenda, faces*; and *tela...puerilia* in Virgil, *A.* 11. 578 and Val. Flacc. 1. 269.

4 *tuum sprevi maxime, numen, Amor.* Cf. Ovid, *M.* 6. 4, *numina nec sperni sine poena nostra sinamus.*

5 *Tu puer imbelles dixi transfige columbas.* MacKellar cites Horace, *C.* 4. 4. 31–2: *neque imbellem feroces | progenerant aquilae columbam*; and Ovid, *Am.* 1. 10. 20, on Venus and Cupid as *inbelles deos.* Cf. Secundus, *Bas.* 9. 23, *imbellem columbam*; *imbelles columbas* in Petrarch, *Ep. ad Brunum Florentinum* (*P.M.* 2, 338) and *Afr.* 4. 288, Buchanan, *Misc.* 23. 19, and Grotius, *Ad H. Borbonium* (*El.*, bk. 1, p. 126); and Ovid, *M.* 1. 456 f.

6 *Conveniunt tenero mollia bella duci.* The general idea is in the vein of Ovid, *Am.* 1. 1 and 2 and *P.* 3. 3; and see the note on 8 below. *Tener Amor*, in various cases, is a stock phrase, e.g. Ovid, *Am.* 2. 18. 4 and 19, *A.A.* 1. 7 (cf. *F.* 4. 196), Tibullus 1. 3. 57, 2. 6.1, *C.P.I.* 7, 383 and 10, 210.

7 *tumidos age, parve, triumphos.* Cf. Cupid's 'triumph' in Ovid, *Am.* 1. 2. 25–8, and Milton's letter of 21 July 1628, to Thomas Young: *triumphum agis* (*Works* 12, 14, line 11).

8 *Haec sunt militiae digna trophaea tuae.* The military metaphor for amatory service is especially Ovidian, e.g. *Am.* 1. 9. 1 f., 1. 11. 12, 2. 12. 1 f., *H.* 4. 86,

A.A. 2. 233, 674; cf. Horace, *C.* 4. 1. 16, Propertius 1. 6. 30, 2. 7. 14–18. *Dignus* with the genitive case is relatively uncommon: one example is *dignus salutis* in Plautus, *Trin.* 5. 2. 29, e.g. in editions of 1619 (Amsterdam), p. 708, and 1621 (Wittenberg), p. 1378 (in L.C.L. 5, line 1153, it appears as *salute dignus*).

9 *In genus humanum quid inania dirigis arma?* Perhaps an echo of Virgil, *A.* 1. 542, *si genus humanum et mortalia temnitis arma.*

10 *in fortes...viros.* Cf. *viri fortis* in Ovid, *M.* 13. 121, 383.

11 *Cyprius.* See the note on *El* 3. 20. 'This epithet, so far as I am aware, is not applied to Cupid by the ancient poets' (MacKellar). It is used by P. Fletcher, *In Effigiem Ducissae Matris* (*Sylva*, 1633: *P.W.* ed. Boas, 2, 291).

11–12 *neque enim Deus ullus ad iras | Promptior.* The quick passions and cruelty of Cupid are a commonplace, e.g. Ovid, *M.* 1. 453, *saeva Cupidinis ira*; Seneca, *Oct.* 812–19: *non est patiens | fervidus irae*, etc.; Buchanan, *Hen.* 2. 14, *O saevissime numinum Cupido*; Secundus, *El.* 1. 7. 1, *Insidiose Puer, maternis saevior undis*; Spenser, *F.Q.* 3. 12. 22; Marlowe, *H. and L.* 2. 287–8. Cf. Ovid, *M.* 1. 126, *ad horrida promptior arma.*

12 *duplici jam ferus igne calet.* Cf. Seneca, *Hipp.* 191, *igne tam parvo calet*; Martial 5. 55. 3, *quo calet igne deus*; and Ovid's literal phrase, *Omnia pone feros...in ignes* (*R. Am.* 719).

13 *Ver erat, & summae radians per culmina villae.* Cf. Virgil, *G.* 2. 338, *ver illud erat*; *E.* 1. 82 (and Sil. Ital. 15. 534), *villarum culmina*; *A.* 2. 695, *summa super...culmina tecti*; Ovid, *M.* 1. 295 (end), *mersae culmina villae*; Martial 4. 64. 10, *celsae culmina delicata villae.*

14 *primam...diem.* Cf. *prima dies* in Ovid, *H.* 11. 114 and Virgil, *A.* 10. 508.

15 *lumina noctem.* These words end Virgil, *A.* 10. 746.

16 *Nec matutinum sustinuere jubar.* 'The line is sometimes taken as evidence that Milton was already suffering from weak eyes' (Hughes). This notion (repeated after Warton by Todd, Keightley, and MacKellar) B.A.W. and G.B. reject as far-fetched.

17 *Astat Amor lecto, pictis Amor impiger alis.* Editors cite *Anacreontea* 33 and Herrick, *The Cheat of Cupid*; for more or less parallel situations see the references near the end of the introduction. For Milton's phrasing cf. Vida, *Christ.* 2. 761 (of an angel descending to Christ): *pictis juxta puer astitit alis* (and 3. 617, *pictis...alis*); *impiger alis* in Statius, *Th.* 1. 292, Sil. Ital. 4. 510, and *C.P.I.* 9, 124; Ovid, *M.* 1. 466–7, *percussis...pennis | impiger*; Pontano, *Uran.* 5. 423, *puer impiger*; *C.P.I.* 9, 104, *impiger...Amor.*

19 *dulce minantis ocelli.* Cf. Buchanan, *Hen.* 2. 2, *minacibus. . .ocellis*; *Lacrymae Cantab.* (1619), p. 4, *minax ocellus.*

21–2 *Talis in aeterno juvenis Sigeius Olympo | Miscet amatori pocula plena Jovi.* *Sigeus* means Trojan, from Sigeum, a town and promontory near Troy; Ovid uses the form *Sigeius* in *H.* 1. 33, *M.* 13. 3. Ganymede, the handsome youth taken to heaven to be Zeus's cupbearer, was a Trojan (Homer, *Il.* 20. 231–5; Ovid, *M.* 10. 155; Spenser, *F.Q.* 3. 11. 34; G. Fletcher, *C.T.* 2. 14). Editors cite Tibullus 4. 2. 13, *talis in aeterno felix Vertumnus Olympo ;* and Ovid, *M.* 10. 160 (of Ganymede), *qui nunc quoque pocula miscet.* The Ovidian *pocula miscet*—which Keightley thought unclassical—is, in various forms, a stock phrase, e.g. Horace, *C.* 3. 19. 12, and *C.P.I.* 5, 243, 386, and 7, 56, 330; see comments on the idiom in Harding, *Ovid*, 42–3. *Plena pocula* is also a stock phrase, e.g. Ovid, *F.* 3. 301, *M.* 9. 238; *C.P.I.* 8, 97, etc.; Gruter, *Del. I.P.* 2, 168, 295; Sannazaro, *El.* 2. 10. 26; *Lacrymae Cantab.* (1619), 22.

The evident misprint of 1645, *ærerno*, became *æterno* in 1673, and editors have accepted that. Garrod comments: 'In the copy of 1645 given by Milton to the Bodleian. . .the first *r* of *ærerno* has been corrected in ink to a *t*. But an asterisk (such as is found elsewhere in Milton's manuscripts) directs the reader to a marginal correction; of which there survive only the last two letters, *io.* These point, I think, to *ætherio*, as Milton's own correction. He has *ætherio. . . Olympo* in *Mansus* 100; and it is found in Martial 9. 3. 3.' But Milton's spelling, in *Mansus* and elsewhere, is *aethereo*, not *aetherio*; and, even though 1673 had its uncorrected errors, we may ask why, since this word was corrected in 1673, it was not made *aethereo*. Also, it seems likely that Milton was echoing the phrase from Tibullus quoted above. Shawcross (*C.E.P.* 548) says that Garrod misread the marginal letters.

23–4 *Aut qui formosas pellexit ad oscula nymphas | Thiodamantaeus Naiade raptus Hylas.* Hylas, son of Theiodamas, going to fetch water from a pool, was drawn down into it by an enamored nymph. The story is told in Theocritus 13; Apollon. Rhod. 1. 1207–60; Propertius 1. 20. 5–52; Val. Flacc. 3. 535 f.; Pontano, *Uran.* 5. 649–780. Cf. Ovid, *A.A.* 2. 110, *Naïadumque tener crimine raptus Hylas* (MacKellar); Propertius 1. 20. 6, *Theiodamanteo. . .Hylae* (Fletcher); Val. Flacc. 3. 561 (end), *ad oscula Nymphae*; and Milton's allusions in *EpDam* 1–2, *Apol* (*Works* 3, 300), and *PR* 2. 353.

25 *Addideratque iras,* etc. Cf. Ovid, *M.* 3. 306, *minus addidit irae.* For examples of anger heightening beauty editors cite *Anacreontea* 17. 12; Theocritus 23. 14–15; Statius, *Th.* 9. 704–6; Shakespeare, *Twel.* 3. 1. 157–8, *Antony* 1. 1. 49–

51, *Venus* 70. Godolphin (*MP* 37, 1939–40, 355) notes in 25–6 the *abba* rhyme-scheme (*iras...putares* / *...truces...min*as), reinforced by anaphora; cf. his comment cited under *El.* 2. 19–24.

26 *nec sine felle minas.* Cf. Buchanan, *El.* 2. 16 (*Majae Cal.*), *sine felle sales*; ibid. 25, *linit illas felle sagittas*; Ovid, *A.A.* 2. 520, *multo spicula felle madent.* Garrod (cf. *Ox. Fac.*) suggests *melle* for *felle.*

27 f. For some accounts of Cupid's power over gods and men see the references near the end of the introduction to *El* 7, the note on *El* 5. 97–114, and Ovid, *M.* 5. 365–70, and Petrarch, *Triumphus Cupidinis*, Spenser, *F.Q.* 3. 11–12. Koehler (21) observes that 'Milton's Cupid reveals a loquacity not found in Latin [i.e. Roman] elegy.'

28 *testis eris.* In Ovid, *Am.* 1. 6. 70 and *P.* 4. 7. 4.

31–4 *strato Pythone superbum* / *Edomui Phoebum*, etc. Apollo, proud of having slain the Python, scorned Cupid, who in revenge wounded him with a golden dart (love) and Daphne, daughter of Peneus, with a leaden one (antipathy); see the *Homeric Hymn to Pythian Apollo* 300–74, Ovid, *M.* 1. 438–567, and the note on *El* 5. 13–14. 'The frontispiece of Cowley's *The Mistress* showed Apollo victorious over Python but vanquished by Cupid' (Hughes). Milton refers to the myth in *Prol* 1 (*Works* 12, 146); and in *RCG* (ibid. 3, 275) the Python is prelacy and the Sun's darts are 'beams of Gods word.' With the phrasing of *El* 7. 31–2 cf. Claudian (?), *Laudes Herculis* (*Opera*, Paris, 1602, 218), *strato Pythone*; Ovid, *M.* 1. 447, *perdomitae serpentis*; 1. 454, *victa serpente superbus*; 1. 460, *stravimus...Pythona*; Sannazaro, *El.* 3. 3. 23, *nitidis stratum Pythona sagittis*; *C.P.I.* 9, 124, *Perdomui Phoebum*; Gruter, *Del. I.P.* 2, 73, *stravisse manu Pythona superbum.*

34 *gravius tela nocere mea.* Cf. Ovid, *H.* 16. 354, *et mea tela nocent*; *A.A.* 3. 30, *Parcius haec video tela nocere viris*; *M.* 10. 311.

35–42 Milton's list seems to show a slight confusion in logic. The two generalized examples, the Parthian soldier and the Cydonian hunter, yield to Cupid in the sense of being inferior bowmen, while the particularized Cephalus, Orion, Hercules, and Jove yield in the sense of being victims of Cupid's amorous darts, though the first three were likewise famous bowmen.

35 *adductum curvare...arcum.* Cf. Virgil, *A.* 5. 507, *adducto...arcu*; Ovid, *M.* 1. 455, *adducto...nervo*; Statius, *Ach.* 1. 487, *curvaret Delius arcum.*

36 *Qui post terga solet vincere Parthus eques.* After Crassus' defeat in 53 B.C., the tactics of the Parthian cavalry became proverbial in Roman poetry, e.g.

Elegia septima, Anno aetatis undevigesimo

Virgil, *G.* 3. 31; Horace, *C.* 1. 19. 11–12, 2. 13. 17–18; Ovid, *A.A.* 1. 209–11; *F.* 5. 591, *solitae mitti post terga sagittae*; *Tr.* 2. 228, *Parthus eques*; Lucan 1. 230; Seneca, *Thy.* 382–4; Milton, *PR* 3. 322–5. Garrod suggests the punctuation *nequit, adductum…arcum, Qui…solet, vincere*, which does not seem to improve the sense.

37 *Cydoniusque mihi cedit venator.* Since Cydonia was a port of Crete, the adjective is equivalent to 'Cretan.' Crete was famous for its archers, e.g. Horace, *C.* 4. 9. 17, Ovid, *M.* 8. 22, Sil. Ital. 2. 109. Parthian and Cretan are linked in Virgil, *E.* 10. 59, *A.* 12. 856–9, Seneca, *Hipp.* 815–16.

38 *Inscius uxori qui necis author erat.* The story of Cephalus' unintentional shooting of his wife Procris is told by Ovid, *A.A.* 3. 687–746, *M.* 7. 835–62. Cf. Milton's allusions in *El* 3. 67, 5. 51–4, *IlPen* 121–4, and notes; and *Apol* (*Works* 3, 300). The phrase *necis auctor* (*author* is less correct) appears in Ovid, *M.* 8. 449 (Fletcher), 9. 214, Claudian 8. 94 (1, 292), and the Senecan *Oct.* 617.

39 *ingens…Orion.* The myths of Orion's erotic career vary. In Apollodorus 1. 4. 3–5 he married Side, wooed Oenopion's daughter Merope, was loved and carried off by Eos (Dawn), and was killed by Artemis for attempting her chastity or that of a maiden Opis or Upis. Cf. N. Comes, *Mythol.* 8. 13; Homer, *Od.* 5. 121 f.; Aratus 637–44; Horace, *C.* 3. 4. 70–2; Ovid, *A.A.* 1. 731; Val. Flacc. 4. 122–3. Orion is *magnus* in Virgil, *A.* 10. 763.

40 *Herculeaeque manus, Herculeusque comes.* Hercules' most notorious yielding to Cupid was his affair with Omphale (Sophocles, *Trach.* 351 f.; Ovid, *H.* 9. 53 f., *F.* 2. 305–58; Seneca, *Herc. Oet.* 371–6, *Hipp.* 317–24). Milton's first phrase, a common classical idiom for 'mighty Hercules,' appears in the plural in Ovid, *F.* 2. 312 and Martial, *De Spect. Liber* 15. 6; in the singular in Horace, *C.* 2. 12. 6 (Fletcher), Seneca, *Herc. Fur.* 882 (cf. 1260), *Med.* 701, and in *C.P.I.* 2, 443.

The Roman poets name many men as a *comes* of Hercules: e.g. Antores (Virgil, *A.* 10. 779), Hylas (Propertius 1. 20. 23, Val. Flacc. 3. 579, 734, 4. 37), Lichas (Seneca, *Herc. Oet.* 99), Melampus (Virgil, *A.* 10. 319–21), Philoctetes (Seneca, *Herc. Oet.* 1717), Sthenelus (Val. Flacc. 5. 90), Telamon (Val. Flacc. 2. 451; cf. 2. 384), Theseus (Seneca, *Herc. Fur.* 646–7; Val. Flacc. 4. 701). Editors have suggested Telamon (Keightley), Hylas (MacKellar), Jason (Hughes). Hylas, the closest and most famous companion, was not himself in love, though he could be intended here as a victim. Perhaps the most likely candidate is Theseus, a notable lover and Hercules' companion in the journey up from the underworld (Seneca, *Herc. Fur.* 592 f.; Val. Flacc. 4. 701–2).

41 *Jupiter ipse licet sua fulmina torqueat in me.* Cf. Ovid, *P.* 3. 6. 27, *Iuppiter in multos temeraria fulmina torquet. Fulmina torquet*, with variations in the verb form, is a stock phrase, e.g. Virgil, *A.* 4. 208, Seneca, *Agam.* 802, Statius, *Th.* 1. 258, Val. Flacc. 2. 22–3. See the following note.

42 *Haerebunt lateri spicula nostra Jovis.* Jove's amatory escapades, which hardly need references, are more or less listed, e.g. in Homer, *Il.* 14. 315 f.; Ovid, *M.* 6. 108–14; Apollodorus, *passim*; N. Comes, *Mythol.* 2. 1; Spenser, *F.Q.* 3. 11. 29 f.; Ralegh, *History* 1. 1. 6. 5; Milton, *PL* 9. 396, *PR* 2. 186–91. 'Cupid, with a quiver of arrows hanging to his back, catching and breaking the thunderbolts of Jove, was a familiar "emblem"' (Hughes); Hughes cites Alciati's *Emblemata*. Cf. Senecan *Oct.* 809–10, where Cupid *extinxit fulmina saepe | captumque Iovem caelo traxit*; and *Herc. Oet.* 558. With Milton's phrasing, cf. Virgil, *A.* 4. 73, *haeret lateri letalis harundo*, and 12. 415, *tergo... haesere sagittae*; Ovid, *Am.* 1. 2. 7, *haeserunt tenues in corde sagittae*; Sannazaro, *P.V.* 3. 253, *Haesuramque hastam lateri*; Buchanan, *El.* 9. 10, *Pectoribusque haerent spicula mille meis*.

44 *non leviter.* In Ovid, *H.* 16. 277.

45 *Nec te stulte tuae poterunt defendere Musae.* See the note on *El* 1. 25. Cf. Ovid, *Am.* 3. 9. 21, *quid pater Ismario, quid mater profuit Orpheo*; and, despite the immense difference in tone, *Lyc* 58–9 and *PL* 7. 37–8, and the notes on these lines.

46 *Nec tibi Phoebaeus porriget anguis opem.* Aesculapius, the son of Phoebus (cf. Ovid, *M.* 15. 742, *Phoebeius anguis*), in the form of a serpent went from Epidaurus to Rome and put an end to a pestilence (Ovid, *M.* 15. 622–744). Milton means that love is a plague beyond medical aid. Direct statements of the idea are common, e.g. Ovid, *H.* 5. 149, *amor non est medicabilis herbis*; *M.* 1. 523, *nullis amor est sanabilis herbis*; Propertius 1. 5. 28, 2. 1. 58; Tibullus 2. 3. 13–14; Burton, *Anat.* 3. 2. 4 (3, 185). Hughes cites Spenser, *F.Q.* 6. 10. 31. 5–6.

47 *aurato quatiens mucrone sagittam.* For the gold-tipped arrow, see under 31–4 above; Ovid, *M.* 1. 468–71; Milton, *PL* 4. 763–4.

48 *Evolat in tepidos Cypridos ille sinus.* For the name Cypris see the note on *El* 3. 20. *In tepidos sinus* is a favorite Ovidian phrase: *A.A.* 3. 212, *R. Am.* 354, *F.* 4. 522, Grotius, *Hyemis Commoda* (*El.*, bk. 1, p. 147); in the singular, Ovid, *A.A.* 2. 360, 3. 622, *H.* 3. 114, Martial 8. 59. 8, Pontano, *Parth.* 1. 3. 20.

51–2 'In the first half of the seventeenth century the favorite walks of the citizens of London were in Gray's Inn Fields, Lincoln's Inn Fields, Moorfields, and the Temple Garden' (MacKellar); and, as MacKellar observes, Milton might have walked as far as Hampstead, Highgate, etc. There is no good evidence that the Miltons had a summer home outside the city (Parker, 779). With *rura placent*, cf. Virgil, *G.* 2. 485, *rura mihi...placeant.*

53 *Turba frequens.* The phrase is in Seneca, *Oed.* 777, Buchanan, *Epig.* 3. 1. 1, and Gill, *In ruinam* (p. 11); cf. *PL* 1. 797. With *turba dearum*, cf. Ovid, *Tr.* 4. 1. 53–4, *deorum | cetera...turba*; *Cantab. Dolor* (1625), p. 22, *turba Deorum.*

54 *Splendida per medias itque reditque vias.* Cf. Ovid, *Tr.* 5. 7. 14: *per medias in equis itque reditque vias.* The jingle of verbs, with or without *vias*, is a commonplace, e.g. Virgil, *A.* 6. 122, Ovid, *H.* 15. 118, Statius, *Th.* 1. 102, 8. 49, Claudian *S.P.* 36. 4 (2, 264), Val. Flacc. 1. 725, 8. 331, Buchanan, *El.* 2. 12 (*Majae Cal.*), *Sph.* 2. 336.

55 *Auctaque luce dies gemino fulgore coruscat.* Editors cite Spenser, *F.Q.* 3. 1 43. 8–9, and *Ideas Mirrour* 48. 1–3 (Drayton, 1, 122). Cf. Virgil, *G.* 4. 98, *fulgore coruscant*; Luke 17. 24 (tr. Beza), *fulgur coruscans.*

56 *Fallor? an*, etc. See the note on *El.* 5. 5.

58 *Impetus & quo me fert juvenilis, agor.* Cf. Ovid, *M.* 2. 203, *quaque inpetus egit.*

59 *Lumina luminibus.* Cf. Secundus, *El.* 1. 6. 14, *Aemula Phoebeis lumina luminibus*; *C.P.I.* 2, 363, *Et modo luminibus lumina grata suis*; ibid. 3, 236, *vestris Phoebi lumina luminibus*, and 4, 93 and 5, 395. Lucretius 3. 364 has the same conjunction, though not in the same sense. Such verbal plays are common in Latin and especially Ovidian verse, e.g. Virgil, *A.* 4. 628, Ovid, *Am.* 1. 8. 80, *H.* 2. 95, 14. 100, etc. Cf. Milton, *El* 2. 3, *Eli* 24. Ovid has *obvia lumina* (meaning 'torches') in *M.* 14. 419.

60 *Neve oculos potui continuisse meos.* For the use of the perfect infinitive see the note on *El* 1. 17. *Contineo* seems to be used with *lacrimas* rather than *oculos*; cf. Ovid, *Am.* 3. 9. 46, *H.* 15. 174, *A.A.* 2. 582.

61 *Unam forte aliis supereminuisse notabam.* Cf. Virgil, *A.* 1. 501, *gradiensque deas supereminet omnes*; Ovid, *M.* 3. 182, *ipsa dea...supereminet omnis*; and, with the whole passage, Mantuan, *E.* 2. 94 f.

62 *Principium nostri lux erat illa mali.* MacKellar cites Virgil, *A.* 4. 169–70, *ille dies primus leti primusque malorum | causa fuit*, which would of course be in Milton's mind, but his line is closer to Ovid, *P.* 4. 2. 32, *principium nostri res sit ut ista mali.* Cf. Buchanan, *Hen.* 1. 4 (*In Neaeram*), *Illa principium fuit malorum.*

63 *Sic Venus optaret mortalibus ipsa videri.* MacKellar cites the meeting of Venus and Aeneas in Virgil, *A.* 1. 314–417, and the judgment of Paris (cf. *PL* 5. 381–2).

64 *Sic regina Deum conspicienda fuit.* Juno, sister and wife of Jupiter, is often referred to as *regina deum* or *regina deorum*, e.g. Virgil, *A.* 1. 9, 46, Ovid, *M.* 2. 512, Sil. Ital. 7. 78, Claudian, *S.P.* 31. 23 (2, 258). Cf. Ovid, *Am.* 2. 4. 42, *Leda fuit nigra conspicienda coma.*

67 *ipse vafer latuit.* For the erotic use of *vafer* ('sly rogue') cf. Horace, *C.* 3. 7. 12, *temptat mille vafer modis*; Ovid, *H.* 20. 30; J. C. Scaliger (Gruter, *Del. I.P.* 2, 888), *vafer...Amor.*

68 *Et facis a tergo grande pependit onus.* Cf. Ovid, *F.* 2. 760 (and *C.P.I.* 3, 345), *dulce pependit onus*; *R. Am.* 18 (and *C.P.I.* 4, 241), *triste pependit onus*; *H.* 9. 98 (and Secundus, *El.* 1. 5. 14), *pependit onus*; *M.* 7. 625, *grande onus.*

69 *Nec mora, nunc ciliis haesit, nunc virginis ori.* Koehler (153) notes the quick movement of 69–70, achieved partly by the multiplication of *i* sounds and by the balancing and echoing of sounds (*Nec...nunc...nunc*; *Insilit...insidet*; *hinc...inde*). For *Nec mora*, see the note on *El* 3. 35. For *haesit*, cf. the citations under 42 above, and Propertius 1. 19. 5 (on Cupid), *puer haesit ocellis. Virginis os* (*ora*, etc.) is a stock phrase, e.g. Virgil, *A.* 1. 315, Ovid, *M.* 5. 553, 11. 308, 13. 733.

72 *mille locis pectus inerme ferit.* Cf. the Horatian phrase quoted under 67 above, and *pectus inerme* in Pontano, *Erid.* 1. 31. 12, Secundus, *El.* 1. 11. 18 and *Od.* 10. 7, and *C.P.I.* 9, 13, and *pectus inermum* in Virgil, *A.* 10. 425. Cf. also Buchanan, *El.* 9. 10 (quoted above in 42 n.).

73 *Protinus insoliti subierunt corda furores.* Cf. Statius, *Th.* 1. 125–6, *protinus... | animos subiit furor* (Fletcher); Claudian 10. 1 (1, 242), *insolitos... ignes*; Sil. Ital. 13. 319, *subit...corda.*

74 *Uror amans intus.* Cf. Pontano, *Erid.* 1. 15. 13 and H. Angerianus (Gruter, *Del. I.P.* 1, 218), *uror amans*; Ovid, *H.* 4. 19, *urimur intus*; and *uror* in *H.* 7. 23, 15. 9, 16. 10, 18.167, *Am.* 1. 1. 26, 2. 4. 12, *M.* 3. 464, 13. 867; Horace, *C.* 1. 13. 9; Buchanan, *Hen.* 3. 10.

75 *Interea misero quae jam mihi sola placebat.* Cf. Virgil, *A.* 2. 70, *quid iam misero mihi denique restat.*

76 *Ablata est oculis non reditura meis.* Cf. Lucan 3. 5–6, *litora numquam | Ad visus reditura*; Gill, *Ad Eundem In agro...1627* (25), *Phyllis | Non oculis iterum conspicienda meis.*

77 *Ast ego progredior tacite querebundus, & excors.* See the note on *El* 1. 85; Propertius 3. 1. 3 (quoted under *El* 6. 61–2); and Buchanan, *Hen.* 1. 27–8, *me relicto | Excorde, exanimo.*

79 *Findor.* Brodribb (*N&Q* 159, 39) notes this verb similarly used in Persius 3. 9. With *haec remanet, sequitur pars altera votum,* cf. Ovid, *M.* 8. 711, *vota fides sequitur*; Dante, *Purg.* 2. 12, *che va col cuore e col corpo dimora.*

80 *Raptaque tam subito gaudia flere juvat.* Cf. *El.* 1. 41–2, and Ovid, *Tr.* 3. 2. 19, *nil nisi flere libet*; 4. 3. 37, *est quaedam flere voluptas.*

81–2 *Sic dolet amissum proles Junonia coelum,* etc. This Homeric reference is commented upon in the Introduction, 13–14. The story is told also in Val. Flacc. 2. 87 f. Vulcan (Hephaestus) is called the son of Juno because, according to some stories (Hesiod, *Theog.* 927–8; Apollodorus 1. 3. 5), he was conceived without a father. Cf. Milton, *Naturam* 23–4, and the phrase *amissi coeli solatium* in *Prol* 5 (*Works* 12, 190, line 19).

83–4 *Talis & abreptum solem respexit, ad Orcum,* etc. Amphiaraus, the Greek prince and seer, forced to join what he knew to be the impious war of the seven against Thebes, fled after the attack failed, and Zeus, to save him from disgrace, opened the earth and swept him and his chariot down to Hades (Pindar, *Ol.* 6. 12–14, *Nem.* 9. 13–27; Apollodorus 3. 6. 8; Ovid, *M.* 9. 406–7; Dante, *Inf.* 20. 31–9). Milton's distich is commented upon in the Introduction (13–14), where the apparent sources in Statius and Ovid, as noted by editors, are quoted, and with these an added phrase from Ovid, *Ibis* 578.

   Orcum. 'The lower world (Virgil, *Aen.* 2. 398; 4. 699; Lucretius 1. 115; Propertius 3. 19. 27). In the Latin poems Milton uses Orcus as the name of the place (*Ad Pat.* 118; *Mansus* 18; *Damon.* 201), but in *P.L.* 2. 964 he applies it to Pluto, a usage common in classical writers (Virgil, *Georg.* 1. 277; Ovid, *Met.* 14. 116; Horace, *Carm.* 1. 28. 10)' (MacKellar). Starnes-Talbert (229) cite C. Stephanus, *Dict.*, for both meanings.

85 *Quid faciam infelix.* In Ovid, *H.* 11. 51.

85–6. *amores | Nec licet inceptos ponere.* Cf. Virgilian *Cir.* 328–9: *non ego te incepto...conor | flectere, Amor.*

87 *O utinam,* etc. On this Ovidian mannerism see the note on *El* 1. 21–2.

88 *coram tristia verba loqui.* Cf. Ovid, *H.* 16. 283, *coram ut plura loquamur*; Virgil, *A.* 8. 122–3, *coramque parentem | adloquere. Tristia verba* is a stock phrase, e.g. Ovid, *Tr.* 1. 3. 80, 2. 133; Tibullus 3. 4. 42, 3. 6. 38; *C.P.I.* 1, 362, 463, 6, 347, and 11, 416; *Cantab. Dolor* (1625), 43.

89 *Forsitan & duro non est adamante creata.* A reference to adamant and kindred substances was common among impassioned or angry lovers in classical poetry (see the note on *El* 4. 87–8). Editors cite Theocritus 3. 39. Cf. Ovid, *H.* 2. 137; Statius, *S.* 1. 2. 69, *duro nec enim ex adamante creati* (Fletcher); Shakespeare, *Dream* 2. 1. 195 (Hughes). Beginning a line with *Forsitan et* is an especially Ovidian habit, e.g. *Am.* 1. 6. 45, 2. 6. 28, 3. 8. 21, *H.* 1. 77, 2. 104, 7. 133, 9. 131, 10. 86, etc.

90 Carey says there is no verb *surdeo.* It is not in DuCange and is presumably a Renaissance coinage.

91 *Crede mihi nullus sic infeliciter arsit.* For the Ovidian *Crede mihi,* see the note on *El* 5. 91. Cf. Ovid, *R. Am.* 13, *feliciter ardet* (Fletcher); Secundus, *El.* 1. 5. 97, *non infeliciter arsit.*

93 *Parce precor teneri cum sis Deus ales amoris. Parce precor* is a common Ovidian beginning for a line, e.g. *H.* 7. 163, 16. 11, 18. 45, 20. 117, *F.* 2. 451, 4. 921, etc.; it is also in Horace, *C.* 4. 1. 2, Juvenal 6. 172, and Statius, *S.* 5. 1. 179, 5. 2. 84. For *teneri...amoris,* see under 6 above; for *Deus ales,* Ovid, *M.* 2. 714.

96 *Nate dea.* In Virgil, *A.* 1. 582, 615, 2. 289, Ovid, *M.* 7. 690, 12. 86, 13. 168, etc.

97 *Et tua fumabunt nostris altaria donis.* Cf. Lucretius 6. 752, *fumant altaria donis* (Fletcher); *altaria donis* in ibid. 4. 1237, Virgil, *A.* 5. 54, 11. 50, and Buchanan, *Ps.* 107. 22; *altaria fumant* in Virgil, *E.* 1. 43, Ovid, *H.* 1. 25, *F.* 2. 193.

100 *Nescio cur, miser est suaviter omnis amans.* The idea of love as a welcome pain is, as Koehler says (25), 'a commonplace in many love traditions'; he quotes Tibullus 3. 12. 17–18. Cf. Plautus, *Cist.* 69–70: *Amor et melle et felle est fecundissimus; | gustui dat dulce, amarum ad satietatem usque oggerit.* This is partly quoted in Burton, *Anat.* 3. 2. 3 (3, 141).

101–2 *Tu modo da facilis, posthaec mea siqua futura est, | Cuspis amaturos figat ut una duos.* Editors cite the epigram of Rufinus in the Greek Anthology 5. 97 (L.C.L. 1, 175): 'Love, if thou aimest thy bow at both of us impartially thou art a god, but if thou favourest one, no god art thou.' There is a closer parallel in Guarini, *Pastor Fido* 4. 5 (ed. Venice, 1605, 285; *Opere,* ed. L. Fosso, Turin, 1950, 184): *Ferirà pur duo petti un ferro solo.*

Elegia septima, Anno aetatis undevigesimo

Epilogue

Some comment on the epilogue, lines 103–12, was made in the introduction to *El* 7. E. H. Riley ('Milton's Tribute to Virgil,' *SP* 26, 1929, 157) remarks that Milton 'actually deprecates his most Ovidian elegies in a postscript that imitates the epilogue at the end of Virgil's *Georgics*.'

103 *mente...laeva*. A stock phrase, e.g. Virgil, *E.* 1. 16, *A.* 2. 54 (Fletcher), Vida, *Christ.* 3. 400, 6. 586, *C.P.I.* 2, 263, 379, 3, 408, 5, 388, etc.

104 *Nequitiae posui vana trophaea meae*. Cf. Ovid, *Am.* 2. 1. 2, *ille ego nequitiae Naso poeta meae*; Secundus, *El. Solemn.* 2. 22, *Annua nequitiae ponere sacra meae* (and *tropaea*, ibid. 18).

105 *sic me malus impulit error*. Editors cite Virgil, *E.* 8. 41, *me malus abstulit error*. The same phrase is in Ovid, *Tr.* 2. 109. Cf. Mantuan, *E.* 10. 127, *malus error*.

106 *Indocilisque aetas prava magistra fuit*. The first phrase, though not the idea, recalls Milton's later reference to the academic sow-thistles and brambles offered to students in 'their tenderest and most docible age' (*Educ, Works* 4, 280). The line links itself remotely with the allusion to the quarrel with his tutor in *El* 1. 15, *Nec duri libet usque minas perferre magistri*. With the phrasing cf. Ovid, *H.* 5. 96, *quis aetas longa magistra fuit*; *F.* 3. 119, *animi indociles*.

107–12 *Socraticos umbrosa Academia rivos*, etc. As the best comment on these lines editors cite *Apol* (*Works* 3, 305), where, tracing the growth of his ideal of chastity and love, Milton says that 'from the Laureat fraternity of Poets, riper yeares, and the ceaselesse round of study and reading led me to the shady spaces of philosophy, but chiefly to the divine volumes of Plato,' etc. For the metaphor cf. Horace, *C.* 3. 21. 9–10, *Socraticis madet | sermonibus*; F. M. Molsa (*C.P.I.* 6, 338; Gruter, *Del. I.P.* 2, 40), *Socraticis...de fontibus haustus*; Milton, *PR* 4. 276–7.

109 *extinctis...flammis*. Cf. Ovid, *A.A.* 2. 441, *extinctas...flammas*; *M.* 7. 77, *exstinctaque flamma*.

110 *Cincta rigent multo pectora nostra gelu*. A common idiom, in the literal sense, e.g. Livy 21. 32. 7, *animalia inanimaque omnia rigentia gelu*; and *gelu riget* in Pontano, *Met.* 192, 309, 793; *C.P.I.* 8, 54; and Secundus, *El.* 3. 4. 14.

111 *puer ipse Sagittis*. See the notes on *El* 7. 3 and 31–4.

112 *Et Diomedeam vim timet ipsa Venus*. Aphrodite, appearing in the battle before Troy to protect her son Aeneas, was wounded by Diomedes (Homer, *Il.* 5. 334–417; Ovid, *M.* 14. 477–8, 15. 769; cf. Ovid, *P.* 2. 2. 13). *Diomedeam*

141

vim translates a phrase in Homer, *Il.* 5. 781. J. W. Saunders, 'Milton, Diomede and Amaryllis' (*ELH* 22, 1955, 254–86), takes these last lines as a text for an acute but overstated account of the young Milton divided between Amaryllis and Diomede, that is, between the Renaissance ideal of sensuous and courtly verse for a private audience on the one hand and, on the other, moral, ascetic, and religious poetry for an ideal middle-class audience not as yet in being.

[EPIGRAMMATA]

The epigram was a classical genre immensely cultivated by Renaissance writers in all the literary countries of Europe, in both Latin and the vernaculars.[1] Many of Milton's English predecessors and early contemporaries, from Sir Thomas More up to Campion, Donne, Jonson, Herrick, Herbert, and Crashaw, were more or less notable practitioners, in Latin or English or both. The schoolmaster John Owen, whom Jonson disparaged, devoted himself wholly to Latin epigrams and achieved Continental fame. The work of Martial, the great ancient model (the Greek Anthology, though widely translated, was less familiar), and the names of the English poets remind us that the epigram was a short, terse poem on almost any kind of subject, not merely satirical but amatory, obituary, complimentary, reflective, religious, and what not. But though subject and tone varied widely, the normal epigram was built so as to lead up to a climax in an ingenious turn of thought or a *sententia*. The satirical and witty type was the most popular, and Milton's anti-Catholic epigrams on the Gunpowder Plot belong to it; the first four are all variations on one idea, going to heaven in the course of nature or being blown thither. The much later epigrams on Leonora Baroni's singing belong to the encomiastic line, but have the desired ingredient of ingenuity. The epigrams, being in the elegiac metre, were included in the *Elegiarum Liber*.

[1] For England authorities are: T. K. Whipple, *Martial and the English Epigram From Sir Thomas Wyatt to Ben Jonson* (University of California Publications in Modern Philology, 10, 1925, 279–414); L. Bradner, *Musae Anglicanae* (1940), 77–98; Hoyt H. Hudson, *The Epigram in the English Renaissance* (Princeton, 1947).

Epigrammata

Milton's four epigrams on the Gunpowder Plot and another on the inventor of gunpowder may be called grace-notes to the small epic of 1626, *In quintum Novembris*, and like it they were presumably contributions to the elaborate academic observance of Guy Fawkes Day (Masson, *P.W.* 1, 271; MacKellar, 36, 45–8; French, *L.R.* 1, 122; Fletcher, *Intell. Dev.* 2, 411). While we do not know when four of the epigrams were written, the second evidently came after the death of King James on 27 March 1625 (see line 5), and since the second, third, and fourth were entitled *In eandem*, we may assume that they were put in the order of composition; Fletcher suggests that the epigrams and *In quintum Novembris* were written in successive years, 1625–30 (the epic belonging probably to 1626). On the other hand, the fact that the first four are all variations on the same idea suggests the possibility that these were all done, in one small burst of ingenuity, about the same time. Parker (732, n. 28) sums up our ignorance in saying that the epigrams (apart from the second) 'may have been written either at St. Paul's School or at Cambridge, either at one time or in different years.' Since, as our later commentary indicates, the question has been raised whether *In quintum Novembris* was indebted to Phineas Fletcher's *Locustae*, it may be added that these epigrams do not seem to be.

In Proditionem Bombardicam [ProdBom 1]

2 *Ausus es infandum perfide Fauxe nefas.* Cf. Virgil, *A.* 6. 624, *ausi...immane nefas.*

3 *Fallor? an.* For this Ovidian mannerism see the note on *El* 5. 5.

4 *pensare mala cum pietate scelus.* Cf. Seneca, *Thy.* 1103, *Scelere qui pensat scelus?*; *Herc. Oet.* 986, *hoc erit pietas scelus*; Ovid, *M.* 6. 635, *scelus est pietas in coniuge Tereo.*

5–8 The decorum of the epigram permits the ironical use of Elijah's ascent to heaven in a fiery chariot; cf. the serious allusions in *Eli* 49–50, *Passion* 36–7, and *PR* 2. 16–17.

143

5 *atria caeli.* In Statius, *Th.* 1. 197 (Fletcher). Cf. P. Fletcher, *Loc.* (*P.W.* 1, 105, lines 4–3 from foot), *ingentia coeli | Atria.*

6 *Sulphureo curru flammivolisque rotis.* Cf. 2 Kings 2. 11 (tr. Tremellius), quoted under *Eli* 49–50.

7 *feris caput inviolabile Parcis.* The Parcae, the three Fates (Clotho, Lachesis, and Atropos), appear everywhere in literature from Hesiod (*Theog.* 218, 905) onward; here they are equivalent to Death. Cf. *Procan* 2, 21, *Patrem* 29, *Mansus* 19, *EpWin* 28, *Arc* 65, *Lyc* 75. Cf. *caput inviolabile* in Sil. Ital. 3. 127, 16. 16–17.

8 *Liquit Jördanios turbine raptus agros.* Cf. 2 Kings 2. 11 (the Tremellius translation is quoted below in *Eli* 49–50 n.); Buchanan, *Ps.* 1. 5: *subito sed turbine rapti | Pulveris instar erunt.*

In eandem [*ProdBom* 2]

1 *Siccine.* See the note on *El* 4. 89–90.

2 *Quae septemgemino Belua monte lates?* 'The Papacy, resting on the seven hills of Rome, and regarded by zealous Protestants as the Beast of the Apocalypse (Rev. xiii.)' (Masson, *P.W.* 3, 324). MacKellar quotes Bishop Jewel, *Works*, ed. J. Ayre (4 v. Parker Society, 1845–50), 2, 915. Hughes quotes Bishop Bale, *Select Works*, ed. H. Christmas (Parker Society, 1849), 496. Cf. Spenser, *F.Q.* 1. 7. 16–18, 1. 8. 12–15; P. Heylyn, *Microcosmus* (Oxford, 1621), 101 (on Rome): 'The description of the whore of Babylon sitting on the beast with 7 heads, can be understood of no place but this, being built on 7 hills...' For Milton's phrasing, cf. Statius, *S.* 1. 2. 191, *septemgeminae...Romae*; 4. 1. 6–7, *septemgemino... | Roma iugo*; Claudian 12. 19–20 (1, 234), *septemgeminas... | arces*; Sannazaro, *P.V.* 2. 262, *septemgeminos...montes*; *C.P.I.* 11, 193 and 410, *septemgemini...colles.*

3 *Ni meliora tuum poterit dare munera numen.* The line, and *numen* in particular, suggest the pagan, anti-Christian character many Protestants ascribed to Rome.

4 *Parce precor donis insidiosa tuis.* For *Parce precor*, see the note on *El* 7. 93. The last phrase may be a veiled allusion to Sinon and the wooden horse (cf. Virgil, *A.* 2. 49, *timeo Danaos et dona ferentis*, and 195, *Talibus insidiis... Sinonis*) or to Circe and the Sirens (cf. *El* 6. 73–4 and notes).

5–6 *Ille...serus adivit | Astra, nec inferni pulveris usus ope.* This line obviously dates the epigram as written after the death of James (27 March 1625). Editors cite one of Horace's tributes to Augustus, *serus in caelum redeas*, etc. (*C.* 1. 2. 45–9). Cf. *Cantab. Dolor* (1625), 34: *Ad coelum serus redijsset & astra Iacobus.* Cf. *usus ope* in *El* 1. 88 and Ovid, *F.* 3. 318.

8 *brutos Roma profana Deos.* Cf. *Nat* 211, 'The brutish gods of Nile.'

10 *Crede mihi caeli vix bene scandet iter.* For the Ovidian *Crede mihi*, see the note on *El* 5. 91. Cf. Sannazaro, *El.* 1. 7. 35: *his superas meritis sit scandere in arces*; Lily, *Grammar* (*Symbolum Apostolorum*, sig. [Dvi^v]), *Stelligeras scanditque domos*; sig. [Dvii], *Christus ad aethereas cum vellet scandere sedes.*

In eandem [*ProdBom* 3]

1 *Purgatorem animae derisit Iācobus ignem.* Cf. Augustine, *Civ. D.* 10. 10, *purgator animae.* MacKellar quotes King James's condemnation of 'Purgatorie and all the trash depending thereupon' (*Political Works of James I*, ed. C. H. McIlwain, Cambridge, Mass., 1918, 125). See also MacKellar, 'Milton, James I, and Purgatory,' *MLR* 18 (1923), 472–3; Milton, *DocCh* 1. 16 (*Works* 15, 339–40).

2 *Et sine quo superum non adeunda domus. Non* (sometimes *vix*) *adeunda* is a stock phrase in this position, e.g. Ovid, *H.* 18. 8, *F.* 4. 496, 5. 374, 6. 412, 450, Tibullus 1. 6. 22, 3. 5. 2, etc.

3 *trina monstrum Latiale corona.* For the triple crown, see the note on *QNov* 55; for *monstrum*, the note on *ProdBom* 2. 2. *Latiale:* Roman, from Latium, the region of Italy in which Rome was.

4 *cornua dena.* Cf. Rev. 13. 1, 'a beast...having seven heads and ten horns' (tr. Beza: *bestiam...quae habebat capita septem & cornua decem*).

5 *nec inultus.* Cf. *QNov* 44 and note.

6 *Supplicium spreta relligione dabis.* Cf. Catullus 64. 386, *spreta pietate.*

7 *si stelligeras unquam penetraveris arces.* Cf. the Virgilian *Cul.* 42, *aetherias iam Sol penetrarat in arces* (Fletcher). *Stelliger* is not one of the commonest epithets, though it appears in Lily's *Grammar* (see note on *ProdBom* 2. 10). Examples are: Seneca, *Herc. Fur.* 1204, *Herc. Oet.* 1344, 1907; Statius, *S.* 3. 3. 77, *Th.* 12. 565; Sil. Ital. 13. 863; Claudian 28. 175 (2, 86); Buchanan, *Sph.* 1. 654, 657, 658; Vida, *Christ.* 1. 596, 2. 761; *C.P.I.* 2, 9 and 3, 488; Grotius, *Ad. Ex.* 1626.

8 *triste...iter.* In Ovid, *Tr.* 3. 9. 32.

9 *O quam funesto cecinisti proxima vero.* Cf. Horace, *A.P.* 338, *proxima veris*; Grotius, *Ad Dousam (El.,* bk. 1, p. 128), *proxima vero*; *Epist. Palladii (El.,* bk. 1, p. 153), *proxima veris.*

10 *Verbaque ponderibus vix caritura suis!* For partly similar contrasts between *verba* and *pondus,* cf. Ovid, *H.* 6. 110, *pondere verba carent*; ibid. 3. 4, 98; *Am.* 3. 12. 20; Propertius 3. 7. 44.

11 *Tartareo...igni.* See the notes on *El* 3. 16 and *QNov* 35, 161.

12 *Ibat ad aethereas umbra perusta plagas.* Cf. *aetheria plaga* in Virgil, *A.* 1. 394, 9. 638, Vida, *Christ.* 4. 13; *C.P.I.* 4, 122, *plagas...in aethereas.*

In eandem [*ProdBom* 4]

1 James, baptized a Roman Catholic but reared a Protestant, would be regarded by the Roman Church as excommunicate (MacKellar, quoting the *Cath. Encyc.* 5, New York, 1909, 681; cf. new 1967 ed., 5. 704 f.). On the whole problem of Catholic and royal claims see, e.g., McIlwain (*ProdBom* 3. 1) and D. H. Willson, *King James VI and I* (New York and London, 1956).

2 *Taenarioque sinu.* See the note on *El* 5. 66.

3 *Hunc vice mutata jam tollere gestit ad astra. Vice mutata* is in Ovid, *Tr.* 4. 1. 99. *Tollere ad astra* is a stock phrase, e.g. Virgil, *E.* 5. 51, Horace, *S.* 2. 7. 29, Sil. Ital. 3. 164, Val. Flacc. 4. 555; Sannazaro, *El.* 1. 8. 18, 2. 2. 4.

In inventorem Bombardae [*InvBom*]

Parker (732, n. 28) remarks: 'The verses in praise of the inventor of gunpowder may be intended literally instead of ironically; and, if so, they are not necessarily Fifth of November verses.' Hughes, citing *PL* 6. 503–4, observed that the traditional ascribing of artillery to diabolic inspiration (cf. Ariosto, *O.F.* 9. 91, 11. 21–8; Daniel, *Civil Wars* 6. 26–7) was shifting toward Cowley's view that 'for above a thousand years together nothing almost of Ornament or Advantage was added to the Uses of Humane Society, except only Guns and Printing' (preface to

Epigrammata

A Proposition For the Advancement of Experimental Philosophy, 1661);
Bacon named these two and added the magnet (*Novum Organum* 1. 129).
Milton may here be chiefly concerned with constructing a neat epigram.
Editors cite William Drummond's *The Cannon* (*Poetical Works*, ed. L. E.
Kastner, 2 v. Edinburgh and London, 1913, 1, 107).

1–2 *Japetionidem laudavit caeca vetustas,* | *Qui tulit aetheream solis ab axe
facem.* Prometheus' bringing the heavenly torch from the car of the sun points
to the version of the myth given by Servius on Virgil, *E.* 6. 42, and repeated,
e.g., in N. Comes, *Mythol.* 4. 6, C. Stephanus, *Dict.*, and Bacon, *De Sapientia
Veterum* 26. Hesiod (*Theog.* 521 f.) had apparently less praise for Prometheus
than Aeschylus, though Aeschylus' total view included blame as well (cf.
Osgood, *C.M.* 80, and MacKellar). Prometheus, the son of Iapetus, is called
Iapetionides in Hesiod, *Theog.* 528 f. The name is used of Atlas in Ovid,
M. 4. 632. Cf. Claudian 20. 490–1 (1, 220), *fratres* | *Iapetionidas*; Horace,
C. 1. 3. 27, *audax Iapeti genus*; Ovid, *M.* 1. 82, *satus Iapeto*; and the note on
Procan 4.

4 *Et trifidum fulmen surripuisse Jovi.* As Warton noted, this idea was put in
Satan's mouth (*PL* 6. 490–1). Cf. Milton, *Prol* 1 (*Works* 12, 124, line 3), *Jovis
fulmen*; Manilius 1. 104, *eripuitque Iovi fulmen*; Ovid, *M.* 2. 325, *trifida...
flamma*; Poliziano, *Sylvae* 4. 499 (*P.V.* 401), *trifidum...fulmen*; Grotius,
Ad. Ex. 1792, *fulminis trifidi.*

Ad Leonoram Romae canentem

Leonora Baroni, the Neapolitan singer, was famous enough to evoke in
1639 a volume of tributes, *Applausi Poetici Alle Glorie Della Signora
Leonora Baroni*, which ran to five languages (though chiefly in Italian)
and 267 pages. We do not know when Milton heard her and wrote his
epigrams. He was present at the grand operatic performance given at the
Palazzo Barberini on 27 February 1639, which he described in a letter
to Lukas Holste (30 March), and which Masson and others took to be
the occasion; but women were not allowed to sing at the Palazzo.[1] We

---

[1] See Masson, *Life*, 1 (1881), 792, 802–4, and *P.W.* 1, 271–2; MacKellar, 37–9; French, *L.R.*
1, 391–2, 406–7. The traditional view was questioned by Gretchen L. Finney (*PMLA* 58,
1943, 658; *Musical Backgrounds for English Literature: 1580–1650*, New Brunswick, 1962,

might expect Milton's epigrams to have been among those he showed to his Italian literary friends (*RCG, Works* 3, 235–6). If he saw any of the poems that went into the *Applausi,* they do not seem to have left clear marks on his own; the volume has many allusions to the Sirens and some to Parthenope (pp. 74, 157, etc.; cf. *Leon* 3. 1–4 below), but these were almost inevitable (the phrase cited under *Leon* 2. 12 is insignificant). Of Milton's many testimonies of his lifelong devotion to music these epigrams are perhaps the least familiar. While his praise of the Italian singer may have been touched by Italian extravagance, the first poem at any rate is characteristic in its association of music with divine beauty and order.

1–2 Belief in a guardian angel is too familiar an element of Christianity to need illustration. Editors cite the Attendant Spirit in *Comus* and *SA* 1431–2. Hughes quotes Burton, *Anat.* 1. 2. 1. 2 (1, 181): 'Socrates had his *daemonium*...; Plotinus his; and we Christians our assisting Angel.' Cf. Sylvester, *D.W.W.* 1. 1. 830–1: 'O sacred Tutors of the Saints! you Guard / Of Gods Elect.' MacKellar cites Thomas Heywood, *Hierarchie of the blessed Angells* (London, 1635), pp. 194–5, on the angelic orders, and p. 228, on the Platonic doctrine of a guardian spirit. Robert H. West (*Milton and the Angels*, Athens, Ga., 1955) discusses Protestants' mixed views (e.g. 49–50), and (132) cites Milton's use here of 'the Catholic idea,' adding that 'no more can be made of it than a fanciful compliment to Leonora's voice.'

4 *Nam tua praesentem vox sonat ipsa Deum.* Cf. Virgil, *A.* 1. 328, *nec vox hominem sonat* (Fletcher); ibid. 6. 50–1; *E.* 1. 41, *praesentis...divos*; Ovid, *Tr.* 2. 54, *praesentem...deum.*

5–6 *Aut Deus, aut vacui certe mens tertia coeli / Per tua secreto guttura serpit agens.* Leigh Hunt took *mens tertia* as 'the intelligence of the third heaven (the heaven of love)' (*Lit. Exam.* 6 Sept. 1823, 146; Houtchens, 191). Keightley could hardly suppose that Milton meant the third person of the Trinity, and

228–30), who cited Alessandro Ademollo, *I teatri di Roma nel secolo decimosettimo* (Rome, 1888). See J. Arthos, *Milton and the Italian Cities* (London, 1968), 60, 81–86.

In the Chronological Table in Carey it is said (xviii) that Milton attended the 'Barberini concert' in October 1638 and heard L. Baroni on his second visit to Rome in January–February 1639. In his headnote to the epigrams on her (254) he says, more accurately, that it is not certain on which visit Milton heard her, and also that 'the Barberini entertainment was not a concert but an opera.' Cf. Parker, 177, 828, n. 42.

suggested 'the presiding power of the third sphere, i.e. that of Venus,' and cited Plato's Sirens (cf. *Arc* 63 f. and notes). Masson (*P.W.* 3, 324) said 'some third mind, intermediate between God and Angel,' which is theologically vague. Hughes asks if Milton alludes to 1 John 5. 7: 'For there are three that bear record in heaven, the Father, the Word, and the Holy Ghost'—which Milton was to quote in *DocCh* 1. 6 (*Works* 14, 399); in the same place (398) he uses *tertio loco* for the Holy Ghost. In the Tremellius–Beza Bible of 1603, note *q* on 1 John 5. 6 has *Spiritus noster tertius testis*. Since Milton seems clearly to be using *Deus*, especially in 9–10, for the Christian God, there would seem to be small doubt that *mens tertia* means the Holy Ghost. And whatever else he had in mind, he was surely thinking of 'the third heaven' of 2 Cor. 12. 2, 4 (tr. Beza): *Novi hominem in Christo ante annos quatuordecim, (an in corpore, nescio : an extra corpus, nescio : Deus novit) raptum in tertium usque caelum. . .Raptum fuisse in paradisum, & audisse ineffabilia verba, quae non liceat homini loqui.* A marginal note explains *In sublimissimum usque caelum. . .* Cf. Virgil, *A.* 5. 515, *vacuo. . . caelo.*

7 *facilisque docet mortalia corda.* Cf. Virgil, *G.* 1. 122–3: *haud facilem esse viam voluit,. . . | curis acuens mortalia corda.* The last two words are a stock phrase, e.g. Virgil, *G.* 1. 330; Claudian, *S.P.* 32. 10 (2, 262); Manilius 1. 79, 2. 452; Val. Flacc. 3. 93–4; Pontano, *Uran.* 2. 458.

9–10 *Quod si cuncta quidem Deus est, per cunctaque fusus, | In te una loquitur, caetera mutus habet.* Editors cite Virgil, *A.* 6. 724–7, on Universal Nature moved by Universal Mind; and Hughes adds that these Virgilian lines were 'constantly cited by Italian Neo-Platonists in proof of pantheistic theories like those of Giordano Bruno. . .' (Cf. also Virgil, *E.* 3. 60 and Pontano, *Uran.* 1. 633, *Iovis omnia plena*; and Virgil, *G.* 4. 221–2: *deum namque ire per omnia, | terrasque tractusque maris caelumque profundum.*) MacKellar likewise sees Milton as momentarily dipping into fashionable Italian pantheism for an extravagant compliment. But, while Milton did later arrive at a metaphysical monism (cf. *PL* 5. 468 f. and notes), the idea here does not necessarily go beyond the orthodox conception of God's omnipresence—though the phrasing is rather unguarded. Cf. Vida, *Christ.* 4. 25–6: *Quicquid erat, Deus illud erat, quodcunque, ubicunque | Complexus circum, penitus sese omnis in ipso*; ibid. 50–3: *Nempe locis nullis, spatiis non clauditur ullis, | Omnibus inque locis idem omni tempore praesens | Suffugiens nostras acies, sensuque remotus | Cuncta replet Deus, ac molem se fundit in omnem*; Sylvester, *D.W.W.* 1. 3. 808: 'I find God every-where'; ibid. 828–9: 'Th' Almighty Voice, which built this mighty Ball, / Still, still rebounds and ecchoes over all'; Grotius, *Ad. Ex.* 389–90: *Deus ipse Mens est, universum quae replet | Superatque mundum.* To come back to Milton, Rand remarked (*SP* 19, 134): 'Truly it is only a training in the Classics that could induce a Puritan to fling this theological bouquet at the feet of a prima donna.'

Ad eandem [Leon 2]

1–2 'The insanity of Torquato Tasso (1544–95), from which he suffered intermittently during the last twenty years of his career, was due to many causes—among them his difficulties with the critics of the *Jerusalem Delivered*. His attachment to Leonora d'Este, the sister of his patron, Alfonso, the Duke of Ferrara, has played a larger part in the literature about him than it did in his life.' (Hughes). MacKellar gives references for two other Leonoras of whom Tasso was enamored.

2 *insano...amore.* In various cases, a stock phrase, e.g. Virgil, *E.* 10. 44, *A.* 2. 343; Horace, *C.* 3. 21. 3; Ovid, *H.* 15. 176, *A.A.* 2. 563, *M.* 9. 519; Propertius 2. 14. 18; Castiglione, *Carm.* 7. 21.

5 *Et te Pieria sensisset voce canentem.* For *Pieria voce* see the note on *El* 4. 31. Cf. Castiglione, *Alcon* 3, *Quem toties Fauni, & Dryades sensere canentem.*

6 *Aurea maternae fila movere lyrae.* Leonora's mother, Adriana Baroni, was also a musician. Editors cite Buchanan, *El.* 7. 32, *Aureaque Orpheae fila fuisse lyrae. Fila lyrae* is a stock phrase, e.g. Ovid, *A.A.* 2. 494, *M.* 5. 118, *F.* 5. 106; etc. It occurs several times in Sannazaro, e.g. *El.* 2. 4. 2, *auratae fila canora lyrae*; cf. *C.P.I.* 4, 450, *auratae fila movere lyrae.*

7 *Dircaeo...Pentheo.* The adjective means Theban (from Dirce, a fountain near Thebes), e.g. Virgil, *E.* 2. 24, *Amphion Dircaeus*; Propertius 3. 17. 33, *Dircaeae...Thebae.* Pentheus, king of Thebes, opposed the Dionysian orgies and was torn to pieces by the enraged Bacchantes, his mother among them. As editors note, Milton's allusion glances especially at Ovid, *M.* 3. 577–8: *Adspicit hunc Pentheus oculis, quos ira tremendos | fecerat.* Cf. Euripides, *Bacch.* 918–19.

11 *aegro spirans sub corde quietem.* Cf. Propertius 1. 3. 7, *mollem spirare quietem. Aegro corde* is a stock phrase, e.g. Juvenal 7. 52, Ovid, *Tr.* 3. 2. 16, Val. Flacc. 5. 131–2, 264, Sil. Ital. 8. 288.

12 *Flexanimo cantu.* Examples of the rather uncommon adjective are: Catullus 64. 330 and Gill, *Epithalamium...1631* (p. 48), *flexanimo...amore*; Cicero, *De*

Epigrammata

Orat. 2. 44. 187; *C.P.I.* 9, 477 and 10, 194; J. C. Scaliger (Gruter, *Del. I.P.* 2, 861), *flexanimae...carmina linguae*; *Applausi...Leonora Baroni* (Bracciano, 1639), p. 202, *Carmen flexanimum.*

Ad eandem [Leon 3]

1–4 Since Leonora Baroni was a Neapolitan, Milton, like some poets of the *Applausi*, associates her with the local myth of Parthenope, daughter of Achelous, one of the Sirens who was said to have been washed ashore near Naples and been given a tomb there (Lycophron 717–21; Strabo 1. 2. 13; Pliny, *N.H.* 3. 5. 62; Comes, *Mythol.* 7. 13; Sandys, *Relation*, 1615, 253; *Comus* 878). The city's early name, Parthenope, was used by the Roman poets, e.g. Virgil, *G.* 4. 564, Ovid, *M.* 14. 101, 15. 712. Starnes-Talbert (271) quote a full account from C. Stephanus, *Dict.*

1 *liquidam Sirena.* Cf. Ovid, *M.* 1. 704 (of water nymphs), *liquidas...sorores* (MacKellar); *Applausi*, p. 19, *ò bella Sirena*; p. 63, *numerisque blandas* | *Sola Sirenas.*

2 *Parthenopes fana Achelöiados.* See under 1–4 above. The Sirens are called Acheloides in Apollon. Rhod. 4. 893 and Ovid, *M.* 5. 552, 14. 87. Cf. Sil. Ital. 12. 34, *Parthenope...Acheloïas.*

3 *defunctam Naiada.* Editors have not found classical authority for calling Parthenope a naiad, but Milton is using the term loosely; cf. *Comus* 252–3. Rand (*SP* 19, 117, n. 14) remarks in this connection on Ovid's general use of *nymphae* (*H.* 1. 27, 9. 103, 16. 128).

4 *Chalcidico...rogo.* 'The region of Cumae was called Chalcidian because Greek colonists from Chalcis in Euboea settled there (Statius, *Sil.* 1. 2. 260–5; 2. 2. 94; 3. 5. 12–13; Livy 8. 22; Virgil, *Aen.* 6. 17)' (MacKellar). Starnes-Talbert (300) quote R. Stephanus, *Thesaurus.* Cf. *EpDam* 182.

5 *amoena Tibridis unda.* Editors cite Virgil, *A.* 7.30, *hunc inter fluvio Tiberinus amoeno*, and 8. 31, *huic deus ipse loci fluvio Tiberinus amoeno.* Cf. ibid. 7. 436, *Thybridis undam.*

6 *rauci murmura Pausilipi*, i.e. Naples, which Leonora has left for Rome. Warton, Todd, MacKellar and Hughes take this as a reference to the famous grotto or tunnel under Mount Posilipo, the latter two mentioning the noise of city traffic that went through it. Keightley and Masson take it as referring only to the sound of waves at the foot of the mountain. For the stock phrase *raucum* *murmur*, which can apply to various things, see the note on *El* 1. 90. Sannazaro's half-dozen allusions do not refer to noise of any kind (though he mentions water in *E*. 2. 31–2 and *Epig*. 2. 36. 7, 2. 51. 43–6); nor does Sandys, *Relation* (1615), 262–3, 299–300.

7 *Romulidum*. See the notes on *El* 1. 68 and *Patrem* 79. For *Romulidae*, 'the sons of Romulus,' i.e. Romans, see, e.g., Lucretius 4. 683, Virgil, *A*. 8. 638, Persius 1. 31.

8 *homines cantu detinet atque Deos*. Since *cantus* means both song and spell, Milton is doubtless thinking of Orpheus, Medea et al., as well as of the Sirens. Cf. Tibullus 1. 8. 20: *cantus et iratae detinet anguis iter*; Ovid, *A.A*. 3. 311–12: *Sirenes...quae voce canora | Quamlibet admissas detinuere rates*.

Apologus de Rustico & Hero

Since this piece did not appear in Milton's volume of 1645 but was included in that of 1673, it could be inferred that it was written between those dates. If it had some topical and political significance, as Leigh Hunt suggested (*Lit. Exam*. 6 Sept. 1823, 148; Houtchens, 194) and Masson thought (*P.W*. 1, 272), it might have been written before 1645 and withheld. No one seems to have offered a topical interpretation, and none is needed. The two early English poems, the *Vacation Exercise* and the *Fair Infant*, were likewise first printed in 1673. D. L. Clark (*J.M. at St. Paul's*, 177, 206, 233) and H. F. Fletcher (below) are presumably right, as Parker says (720, n. 64), in taking the piece to be a school exercise (perhaps revised), a bit of imitative verse-making in accordance with the common practice of double translation, into and out of English. The fable, taken from Mantuan, had appeared in various versions more or less close to Milton's. MacKellar (39) cites two, in English prose and verse, in William Bullokar's *Aesop's Fables in True Orthography* (1585: repr. by Max Plessow, *Palaestra* 52, 1906: see especially pp. 48–9), where it is called 'a fable taken out of Mantuan,' and the Latin version of Gilbert Cousin. (In the edition available to me, *Narrationum Sylva...* *Autore D. Gilberto Cognato*, Basel, 1567, the fable, *De annosa Arbore transplantata*, is on p. 76.) I found Mantuan's 10-line fable as quoted by Fr. Gabriel Wessels in his edition of Mantuan, *Cal. Temp.* (1917), p. 17; in *JEGP* 55 (1956), 230–3 and *Intell. Dev.* 1, 238–40, H. F. Fletcher quotes it from *Sylvarum, Lib.* 4, in Mantuan's *Opera*, Tome 3 (Paris, 1513), fol. cxciiii^v, under the title *Apologus alter ad eundem.* A few verbal parallels between Milton and Mantuan, especially in the first lines, are closer than those between Milton and Cousin (and these latter seem to be due to a common model).

1–2 *Rusticus ex Malo sapidissima poma quotannis | Legit, & urbano lecta dedit Domino.* Cf. Mantuan: *Rusticus ex malo dulcissima poma legebat: | Unum dare urbano sola solebat hero.* In Wessels' text the second line is *Unde dare urbano dona solebat hero.*

3 *dulcedine Captus.* With variations in case, a stock phrase, e.g. Virgilian *Cul.* 126; Ovid, *M.* 1. 709, 11. 170; Juvenal 7. 84; Statius, *Th.* 10. 79; Castiglione, *Carm.* 4. 9; Vida, *Christ.* 4. 869, *A.P.* 1. 184, 288; Campion, *Umbra* 319; etc.

5 *longo debilis aevo.* Cf. Lucretius 5. 832, *aevo debile*; Seneca, *Med.* 258, *senio trementem debili atque aevo gravem*; and the note on *Mansus* 25.

7 *spe lusus inani.* Cf. Ariosto, *Carm.* 62. 9–10, *lusus inani | spe*; *spe captus inani* in Virgil, *A.* 11. 49 and Claudian 21. 345 (1, 388) (Fletcher); Castiglione, *Alcon* 130, *spe ductus inani*; Palingenius, *Z.V.* 9. 484, *spe delusus inani. Spes inanis*, in various forms, is a stock phrase, e.g. Virgil, *A.* 10. 627, 648, Val. Flacc. 4. 578, 5. 526, Buchanan, *Ps.* 21. 12, 25. 2, *Franc.* 131.

[*In Salmasii Hundredam*] [*Salmas* 1]

Claude de Saumaise (1588–1653), whose Latinized name was Claudius Salmasius, was a French Protestant who in 1631 became a professor at Leyden and was recognized as the leading classical scholar of Europe. In a book of 1645 (revised from an earlier one) he challenged papal authority, and he was consulted as a sympathizer by English Presbyterians; he came, however, to advocate a limited episcopacy. In 1649, at the solicitation of the exiled Charles II's adherents, he published *Defensio Regia, pro Carolo I. Ad...Regem Carolum II.* This attack on the

Commonwealth was ponderous and pedantic, but its author's name—which was well known, though the work was anonymous—carried weight, and the resentment of the Puritans in power was heightened by what seemed to be his defection from a common cause. As Secretary for Foreign Languages to Cromwell's Council of State, Milton was commissioned to make the official reply, *Pro Populo Anglicano Defensio*, which was published in February 1651. This work, which cost Milton what was left of his eyesight, achieved its purpose partly through political argument, partly through personal abuse, and it gave its author considerable fame on the Continent (Parker, 386 f., 975, n. 96). Salmasius, who had lately been enjoying the hospitality of Christina of Sweden, continued to receive marks of favour (*C.P.W.* 4, 964 f.); contrary evidence is summarized by Parker (1028, n. 62). Two years after his return home he died—from chagrin, some said, but apparently from natural causes.[1]

Milton's epigram, embedded in his *Defensio* (*Works* 7, 428; cf. *C.P.W.* 4, 487), starts from the fact that in his *Defensio Regia* 'Salmasius had paraded a knowledge of English law and government and had expatiated on the term "hundred," which was applied to the subdivisions of the English counties' (Hughes). Warton noted that Milton's lines were modeled on Persius' *Prologus* 8–14. Milton evidently indicated his borrowings and echoes by italics; in the following notes these are in roman type.

1–2 Quis expedivit *Salmasio suam Hundredam*, / Picamque docuit nostra verba conari? Cf. Persius, *Prol.* 8–9: *quis expedivit psittaco suum chaere, / picamque docuit verba nostra conari?* Salmasius becomes the bird that echoes what it is taught. *Picamque*, being from Persius, should have been italicized. 'In *Defensio Regia* 204, Saumaise...gives the plural of "Hundred" as "Hundreda", a mistake not corrected in the *Errata*' (Carey).

3–4 Magister artis venter, *et Jacobaei* / Centum, *exulantis viscera marsupii regis*. Cf. Persius 10–11: *magister artis ingeniique largitor / venter, negatas artifex sequi*

---

[1] For Salmasius' career MacKellar (42) cites several authorities, including Masson, *Life*, 4 (1877), 162–75, 251–71. For later accounts see Parker, *Milton's Contemporary Reputation* (Columbus, 1940), 32 f.; French, *L.R.* v. 2, 3, and 4; K. A. McEuen, 'Salmasius: Opponent of Milton,' *C.P.W.* 4 (1966), 962–82, and other materials in the same volume.

voces. 'The persistent rumor was that Charles, to reward Salmasius for writing the *Defensio Regia*, gave him a hundred Jacobuses, a gold coin of James I valued at about twenty-two shillings. I have not found incontestible evidence to support the story' (MacKellar). See French, *L.R.* 2, 246–50. Milton alludes to the money repeatedly (*Works* 7, 15, 285, 337, 399, 481). The latest comment is in *C.P.W.* 4, 308–9, notes 14–16, and 979–82; it is necessarily inconclusive.

5–8   Quod si dolosi spes refulserit nummi, | *Ipse Antichristi qui modo primatum Papae* | . . .Cantabit *ultro Cardinalitium* melos. Cf. Persius 12–14: *quod si dolosi spes refulserit nummi,* | *. . .cantare credas Pegaseium melos.* In modern editions of Persius the *melos* of early editions is *nectar*. On Salmasius' antipapal book, *De Primatu Papae* (1645), see the headnote above.

[*In Salmasium*] [*Salmas 2*]

The anonymous attack on the Commonwealth regicides, *Regii Sanguinis Clamor ad Coelum*, written by the Anglo-French cleric Peter Du Moulin, evoked Milton's *Pro Populo Anglicano Defensio Secunda* (1654), a more Miltonic work than his first *Defensio*. This book contained the second epigram against Salmasius (*Works* 8, 56; cf. *C.P.W.* 4, 580), written, Milton said, in expectation of Salmasius' reply to his first attack. Neither epigram was included in Milton's *Poems*. See the note on *De Moro* below, under 'Latin Poems Attributed to Milton'; Masson, *Life*, 4 and 5 (1877), French, *L.R.* 3, 306 and *passim*, and especially *C.P.W.* 4.

1–4   'The condemnation of bad verses to wrap fish was proverbial' (Hughes). Editors cite Catullus 95. 7–8, Martial 3. 2. 1–5, 3. 50. 9–10 (cf. 4. 86. 8), Persius 1. 43, and Milton, *Apol* (*Works* 3, 333). Cf. Gill, *Xenium...Farnabio* (19), *Charta timet scombros*; Milton, *Def* 1 (*Works* 7, 24, line 9). W. A. Oldfather (*PQ* 19, 1940, 88–9) observed that, while eight of Milton's ten lines are good senarii, lines 1 and 8 are not (and for the same reason, 'an impossible cretic in the fifth foot'). Assuming errors in printing and proof-reading, he proposed emendations: deleting *est* in line 1 and, in line 8, reading *omne forum cetarium*. G. L. Hendrickson (*PQ* 20, 1941, 597–600) defended the text, citing Catullus 31. 13–14: *gaudete vosque...* | *ridete, quicquid est domi cachinnorum*, which Milton parodies in his first line.

3   *Salmasius eques.* 'The salmon knight.' 'Milton punned on the resemblance

of Salmasius' name to the Latin *salmo*, a salmon. Salmasius had the doubtful honour of the Order of St. Michael, with which Louis XIII had invested him.' (Hughes.)

7   *Insignia nomenque & decus Salmasii.* 'Milton sneers at a circumstance which was true: Salmasius was really of an ancient and noble family' (Warton: see MacKellar). Cf. Virgil, *A.* 2. 89, *nomenque decusque* (Fletcher), and the same phrase in Sil. Ital. 10. 474 and Pontano, *Met.* 1569, and Martial 10. 103. 4, *decus et nomen famaque*; cf. Milton, *Mansus* 50.

8   See Oldfather in 1–4 n. above. Hendrickson (599) remarks that 'the absence of a connecting or resumptive pronoun after *gestetis* in vs. 8, to indicate that *cucullos* is its object, has been apparently a source of confusion, heightened by the traditional punctuation, a colon after *Salmasii* in vs. 7.'

9–10   The point of the whole epigram is 'that Salmasius from the outset did not compose his volumes for scholars to read, but only to furnish fish with handsome jackets bearing his name and dignities. However, as books, their destination was presumptively to grace the shelves of a library,' as in fact they do—the 'shelves' (*scrinia* and *capsulae*) of fishmongers (Hendrickson, 599). *mungentium | Cubito.* 'According to Warton this was "a cant appellation among the Romans for fishmongers. It was said to Horace, of his father, by way of laughing at his low birth." Warton cites Suetonius, *Vit. Horat.*: Quoties ego vidi patrem tuum cubito emungentem?' (MacKellar.) (Early and modern texts of Suetonius vary: some read *cubito*, some *brachio*.) The same story is told of Bion the sage (Diogenes Laertius, 4. 46). *Cubito emungere* is one of Erasmus' Adagies (*Opera*, 2, 1703, 525); he cites Diog. Laert. and the Ciceronian *Ad Herennium* (4. 54. 67). Milton had alluded to the Horatian anecdote in *Prol* 6 (*Works* 12, 244, lines 6–7).

SYLVARUM LIBER

Anno aetatis 16

❦

'John Gostlin, M.D., Master of Caius (1619–1626) and Professor of Physic (1623–1625), was Vice-Chancellor during the academic year 1625–1626, and died on October 21, 1626, when Milton was aged seventeen.'[1] While the date Milton attached to his memorial poem, *Anno aetatis 16*—i.e. 1625—was obviously a mistake (a typographical error is possible but unlikely), there is the fact that it was the earliest of his assigned dates. Also, the *Sylvarum Liber* was apparently arranged, like the *Elegiarum Liber*, in what Milton, in 1645, remembered as chronological order, and in both editions of 1645 and 1673 the poem on Gostlin headed the group. Parker therefore infers 'that it was written *first* of the four poems commemorating persons who died in the autumn of 1626, antedating elegies II and III (on Ridding and Andrewes) and the verses on the Bishop of Ely.'

But all that we can really infer is that in 1645 Milton thought this poem had been written first. Some facts—discussed more fully in the introduction to *El* 3—suggest that his memory was at fault in regard to the order of composition as well as the year of the poem on Gostlin. Bishop Andrewes had died on 25 September, and in the opening of the elegy on Bishop Felton of Ely, who died on 5 October, Milton says—as we observed before—that he had scarcely paid his full tribute to Andrewes when he heard of the other bishop's death; in other words, he had written the poem on Andrewes by about 5–6 October, two weeks before the death of Gostlin. Since he was apparently dating these poems

---

[1] Parker, 'Notes,' 121. Parker adds that Gostlin's funeral took place on 16 November (Joseph Mead, in a letter of 18 November 1626: *The Court and Times of Charles the First*, ed. T. Birch and R. F. Williams, 2 v. London, 1848, 1, 171). Cf. Parker, *Milton*, 731, n. 26.

nearly twenty years after their composition, and since there were four obituary pieces in the busy autumn of 1626, Milton may well have been hazy about their order.[2]

It seems likely then that the poem on Gostlin (and the shorter but similar *El* 2, on Ridding) followed rather than preceded the two longer pieces on Andrewes and Felton, which also resemble each other. The comparative quality of the two pairs might suggest the reverse, but, if we can distinguish degrees of rhetorical thinness, the shorter and poorer poems on Gostlin and Ridding might be explained by the relative remoteness of the subjects from Milton's range of interests and also perhaps by his increasing realization that his pen could not keep pace with the shears of Atropos.

The poem on the Vice-Chancellor is a mythological and periphrastic elaboration of what Masson called 'the truism that even the most skilful medical man must die, like others, when his time comes' (*P.W.* 1, 283). Whereas in his poems on bishops Milton uses Christian ideas, even in pagan dress, in celebrating secular figures like Gostlin and Ridding (for whom he doubtless desired a heavenly reward) he keeps within an antique pagan decorum. Apart from the excess of allusion, the poem on Gostlin has a somewhat Horatian tone as well as a Horatian metre. Tillyard remarks (*Milton*, 20) that the young Milton, while imitating Ovid's elegiacs and mythological circumlocutions with skill and zest, had too ardent a temperament to 'find proper expression in so narrow a form, or, to vary the metaphor, he cannot really accommodate his huge stride to the twinkling little steps of the Ovidian metre. Horace was really a more effective model; and the Alcaics *In Obitum Procancellarii Medici* contain lines as good as any we have before the *Nativity Ode*... The last verse has a dignity very remarkable in a writer only seventeen

[2] We do not know why Milton chose to celebrate Gostlin and ignored three other heads of Cambridge colleges who died during 1626. Parker ('Notes,' 117) lists Barnaby Googe, Master of Magdalene, who died in February; Samuel Walsall, Master of Corpus Christi (31 July); and John Hills, Master of St Catharine's (26 September). Parker suggests (122) that 'Possibly the young poet had a comforting interview with Gostlin as Vice-Chancellor in the spring of 1626, when he returned to the University after his humiliating rustication. If so, the affection expressed in the closing lines may be more than conventional.'

years of age.' D. C. Dorian quotes the text of Charles Diodati's one known printed poem, the elegy on William Camden that appeared in *Camdeni Insignia* (1624), and comments on similarities between it and Milton's elegy on Gostlin. Diodati's poem is in Alcaics and this is Milton's only piece in that metre. 'One will notice the similarity of the occasion; the similar opening theme, that the Parcae and Death call away whom they will to the realm of darkness, without regard to the dignity or arts of their victims; and the reference to Proserpine and the thread of life near the close. Such parallels, of course, are too commonplace to suggest imitation, even if Milton's poem were not in other respects so different and so well adapted to his special purpose; but they are enough to suggest familiarity with his friend's composition.' (*The English Diodatis*, 108–9, 255.)

NOTES

1 *Parere fati discite legibus.* Cf. Milton, *Prol* 2 (*Works* 12, 150, line 10), *fixam fati legem.*

2 *Manusque Parcae jam date supplices.* For the three Fates—Milton's one Fate is less common—see the note on *ProdBom* 1. 7 and cf. 21 below. *Supplices manus*, usually in the plural, is a stock phrase, e.g. Ovid, *M.* 11. 279; Seneca, *Oed.* 71, *Herc. Oet.* 1316; Sallust, *Cat.* 31. 3; Buchanan, *Ps.* 44. 21, 142. 1.

3 *pendulum telluris orbem.* See the note on *El* 1. 76.

4 *Iäpeti...nepotes.* 'Iapetus,...the Titan, son of Uranus and Gaia, that is of Heaven and Earth, and father of Atlas, Menoetius, Prometheus, and Epimetheus (Hesiod, *Theog.* 132–6, 507–12), was regarded as the common ancestor of all mankind (Pindar, *Ol.* 9. 53–9)' (MacKellar). Cf. *InvBom* 1–2 and note; Ralegh, *History* 1. 1. 8. 7, 1. 2. 6. 4; Sandys, *Ovid* (1632), 25, (1640), 13. Iapetus was sometimes identified with Japhet the son of Noah (Gen. 10. 1–2); see Osgood, *C.M.* 46; Starnes-Talbert, 259–60; and the notes on *PL* 1. 508, 4. 717.

5 *relicto mors vaga Taenaro.* For Taenarus, see the note on *El* 5. 66; for *mors*, the note on *Eli* 32.

9–10 *destinatam... | Mortem.* Cf. Cicero, *Tusc.* 5. 22. 63, *ad horam mortis destinatam.*

10-12 Milton follows the story of Hercules' end as it is told in Ovid, *M.* 9. 134-272, though his phrase *Nessi venenatus cruore* is less close to Ovid's *inbutam Nesseo sanguine vestem* (153) than to the Horatian phrase cited by Warton, *atro delibutus Hercules / Nessi cruore* (*Epod.* 17. 31-2). Cf. *PL* 2. 542-6, where Milton recalls Ovid's *victor ab Oechalia* (*M.* 9. 136).

12 *Aemathia...Oeta.* For Aemathia, Macedonia, see the note on *El* 4. 102. Oeta was the mountain in southern Thessaly where the tortured Hercules cast himself on a funeral pyre (Sophocles, *Trach.* 200, etc.; Seneca, *Herc. Oet.*; Ovid, *M.* 9. 165, etc.).

13-14 *Nec fraude turpi Palladis invidae*, etc. Pallas Athene brought on the death of Hector by appearing to him in the form of his brother Deiphobus and urging him to fight with Achilles (Homer, *Il.* 22. 226-404).

15-16 *Quem larva Pelidis peremit / Ense Locro, Jove lacrymante.* The Locrian Patroclus, wearing the armor of Achilles, killed Sarpedon, whose death was mourned by his father Zeus (*Il.* 16. 458-505). If *larva Pelidis*, 'the phantom of Peleus's son,' is not 'a strange expression' (Keightley), it is a bold one. In *Prol* 1 (*Works* 12, 144, line 1) and *Prol* 4 (ibid. 184, line 7) Milton uses *Larvas* and *Larvis* in the common sense of 'ghosts.' In the title of Alciati's Emblem 153, *Cum larvis non luctandum* (*Omnia...Emblemata*, 1618, p. 709), the word refers to the dead Hector maltreated by Achilles. It means an actor's mask in Horace, *S.* 1. 5. 64 and Palingenius, *Z.V.* 9. 714. Cooper's *Thesaurus* (1584) gives: 'Larva. Horat. A visard: one disguised.'

17-19 Non-Homeric tradition made Circe and Odysseus the parents of Telegonus (Hesiod, *Theog.* 1011-14 [1014 is accounted spurious]; Apollodorus, *Epit.* 7. 16-17; Hyginus, *Fab.* 125, 127: MacKellar). *Telegoni parens* is a not very apt periphrasis for Circe in her role as witch, but it was no more so in its Ovidian context, *P.* 3. 1. 123 (cf. Ovid, *Tr.* 1. 1. 114; Horace, *C.* 3. 29. 8); the phrase is cited under Circe in Ravisius Textor, *Epitome*, p. 86. Milton's *triste fatum* is in Horace, *S.* 1. 9. 29. For *verba Hecatëia* editors cite Ovid, *M.* 14. 44, *Hecateia carmina*. See the following note.

19-20 *potentique / Aegiali soror usa virga.* Medea, when fleeing with Jason, killed her brother Absyrtus (more rarely called Aegialeus, Cicero, *N.D.* 3. 19. 48) and scattered fragments of his body on the sea so that her father would pause in his pursuit to gather them up (Cicero, *N.D.* 3. 26. 67; Ovid, *H.* 12. 113-16; Apollodorus 1. 9. 24; Stephanus, *Dict.*, 'Aegialeus'); a different version is in Apollon. Rhod. 4. 452-81. In Ovid, *M.* 7. 74, 194, 14. 405, Medea and Circe call upon Hecate for aid. *Virga potenti* is in Ovid, *F.* 5. 447 and

Statius, *Th.* 4. 482; cf. *virga dea dira* (Ovid, *M.* 14. 278) and *virga* (ibid. 295, 300).

21 *Numenque trinum fallere.* For the triune divinity, the Fates, see the note on *ProdBom* 1. 7. Cf. Virgil, *A.* 6. 324, *fallere numen.*

22 *Artes medentum, ignotaque gramina.* The arts of physicians and medicinal herbs unknown to the laity. Cf. Ovid, *M.* 15. 629, *nihil artes posse medentum*; Statius, *S.* 5. 1. 158, *ars operosa medentum*; Claudian 15. 173–4 (1, 110), *ignota novercis | gramina*; Virgil, *A.* 12. 414–15, *illa...incognita... | gramina*; Pontano, *Uran.* 4. 380, *Haerbarum medicaeque artis*; Milton, *EpDam* 152–4.

23–4 *Non gnarus herbarum Machaon | Eurypyli cecidisset hasta.* Machaon, son of Asclepius (Aesculapius), was a healer in the Greek army at Troy (Homer, *Il.* 2. 732, etc.). He often appears in Latin poetry as the type of the physician, e.g. Ovid, *A.A.* 2. 491, *R. Am.* 546, *P.* 1. 3. 5–6, *Ibis* 256; Propertius 2. 1. 59; Statius, *S.* 1. 4. 113–14; Vida, *A.P.* 1. 376; Grotius, *Epistola Jocosa* (*Farr.*, bk. 2, p. 199). Machaon's being killed by Eurypylus is reported in Quintus Smyrnaeus 6. 391–428, the Scholia on Lycophron 1048, Pausanias 3. 26. 9, and Hyginus, *Fab.* 113. Starnes-Talbert (234) cite Stephanus, *Dict.* Cf. Gill, *Ad Eundem In agro...1627* (25): *Nam neque Patroclus notis felicior herbis, | Eurypylo cujus munere parta salus; | Nec medica fuerat praeclarior arte Machaon, | Quum minor Atrides cuspide laesus erat.*

25–6 *Laesisset & nec te Philyreie | Sagitta echidnae perlita sanguine.* Chiron the centaur (see the note on *El* 4. 27) died through being accidentally wounded by an arrow poisoned with the blood of the Lernaean hydra (Ovid, *M.* 2. 649–54, *F.* 5. 379–414). In Propertius 2. 1. 59–60, Machaon and Chiron are mentioned together. Cf. Ovid, *F.* 5. 405, *sanguine centauri Lernaeae sanguis echidnae.* Starnes-Talbert (235) cite Stephanus, *Dict.* ('Chiron') for the words *sagitta* (also in Ovid, *F.* 5. 398) and *perlita.*

27–8 Apollo, in killing the unfaithful Coronis, took their child Aesculapius from her womb and gave him into the care of Chiron, who taught him the arts of healing; since Aesculapius could even restore the dead to life, Zeus, to prevent men's gaining immortality, slew him with lightning (Pindar, *Pyth.* 3. 8–67, Virgil, *A.* 7. 770–3, Ovid, *M.* 2. 569–648, 15. 531–4, *F.* 6. 759–60, Apollodorus 3. 10. 3–4). With Milton's *Caese puer genitricis alvo* (for which Starnes-Talbert, 235, cite Stephanus, *Dict.*, *secto...utero*), cf. *infans genetricis ab alvo* in Ovid, *M.* 3. 310 and Vida, *Christ.* 4. 455. With *fulmenque avitum* cf. Ovid, *M.* 2. 646, *flamma...avita*, and *H.* 12. 191.

29 *Tuque O alumno major Apolline.* This phrase, 'Greater than your pupil Apollo,' has been queried because of its extreme and illogical hyperbole. Masson (*P.W.* 3, 328) took *alumno* in the classical though not common sense of 'tutor,' 'foster-father,' a solution accepted by MacKellar. But Milton elsewhere (*El* 4. 25, *Sals* 9, *Mansus* 10, *Prol* 7 [*Works* 12, 268, line 11]) uses *alumnus* in its common meaning. Medical knowledge in 1626 had got somewhat beyond that of prehistoric Greece, and Milton's extravagance was wholly in the tradition of addresses to physicians. Cf. Poliziano, *Ad Antonium Benivenium, medicum* 14–16: *Cui sua concessit munera cuncta Deus! | Namque Coronidem tibi cedere jussit Apollo, | Jussit et aemonium cedere Phylliriden* (*P.V.* p. 237); Pontano, *Tumulus Iacobi Solimaei Medici Salernitani* (*Tum.* 2. 59. 13): *Par Phoebo, par Phoebigenae atque Machaone maior | Et melior*; Vida, *Ad Scipionem Vegium, medicum* 5: *Ipse suas artes ultro, sua munera Apollo | Concessit tibi*; Grotius, *Christus Patiens*, Act 4 (*Poemata*, 369), where a chorus of Roman soldiers speak of Christ as *Intonso medicus major Apolline.*

30 *Gentis togatae.* An adaptation of Virgil's *gentemque togatam* (*A.* 1. 282) to the gowned students (cf. *El* 2. 11 and note). The phrase is also in Martial 14. 124. 1 (quoted from Virgil) and Buchanan, *Sph.* 5. 194–5, and *C.P.I.* 3, 159, 186. Cf. *Cam. Insig.* (1624), sig. A[v], *Heu gentis decus, & dolor togatae.*

31 *Frondosa...Cirrha.* Cirrha, the port of Delphi, was a common equivalent for the oracle and Apollo, e.g. Seneca, *Oed.* 269, *Herc. Oet.* 92, 1475; Juvenal 13. 79; Statius, *Th. passim*; Claudian 34. 23 (2, 316); Palingenius, *Z.V. passim.* Here the name stands for Cambridge and the world of learning. *Frondosa* might have been suggested by Statius, *S.* 3. 1. 141, *Cirrhae...opacae*, or *Th.* 3. 474–5, *Cirrha* and *frondes.*

32 *mediis Helicon in undis.* The haunt of Apollo and the Muses (cf. the note on *El* 4. 29–30) here represents learned and literary Cambridge. Cf. Catullus 64. 167 and Ovid, *M.* 2. 242, *mediis...in undis*; Mantuan, *Sylv.* 1. 1 (*Opera,* 1502, fol. 28[v]), *heliconidis undae*; Secundus, *Epist.* 2. 1. 25, *vitreis Heliconis undis*; *Cantab. Dolor* (1625), 24, *sacris Helicon scatet fluentis.*

33 *Palladio gregi.* The students of Cambridge. See the note on *El* 2. 2.

34 *Laetus, superstes, nec sine gloria.* Cf. Ovid, *Tr.* 3. 7. 50, *fama superstes erit*; ibid. 1. 2. 44, *dimidia...parte superstes ero*; Horace, *C.* 3. 26. 2, *militavi non sine gloria.*

35–6 *Nec puppe lustrasses Charontis | Horribiles barathri recessus.* For Charon as the ferryman of the Styx see Virgil, *A.* 6. 299, 326; Ovid, *M.* 10. 73; etc.

In obitum Procancellarii medici

Cf. phrases from Sannazaro and Grotius cited at the end of the note on *El* 4. 29–30; Claudian 3. 379 (1, 52), *imo barathri...recessu*; 33. 37 (2, 296), *ferali monstra barathro*; Milton, *Prol* 1 (*Works* 12, 136, line 1), *deserta Barathri sede*.

37–40 See, at the end of the introductory note above, Dorian's comment on this bit and Diodati's poem; and cf. Castiglione, *Carm.* 8. 9–10 (*De Morte Raphaelis Pictoris*): *Movisti superum invidiam; indignataque Mors est, | Te dudum exstinctis reddere posse animam.*

37 *At fila rupit Persephone tua.* Persephone (Milton uses the Latin Proserpina in 46 below) has acted toward Gostlin as Jove had toward Aesculapius (see the note on 27–8 above). Editors have found no classical authority for Persephone's breaking the thread of life, a function of the third Fate, Atropos. Dorian (*E.D.* 108–9, 255, n. 57) suggests that by a trick of memory Milton combined the alternative references to Proserpine and Atropos in the opening lines of Diodati's elegy on Camden: *Sic furua conjux Tartarei Iovis, | Sic quae tremenda fila secat manu.* Milton may well have remembered these lines, but he is unlikely to have made a slip on such an elementary point (cf. 'the blind *Fury*' of *Lyc* 75–6 and the note thereon). He may have chosen here to follow unorthodox precedent: e.g. Persephone is named as one of the Furies by E.K. (on Spenser's *November* eclogue, 164) and is so taken by Spenser in *Virgils Gnat*, 422–4 (translating *comites Heroidas* as 'her fellow Furies') and perhaps in *Teares of the Muses*, 164 ('Fit for Megera or Persephone'). We may remember also Milton's frequent instinct for giving a fresh turn to commonplaces and Persephone's role as 'Queen of Death.' Cf. Virgil on the death of Dido (*A.* 4. 698–9): *nondum illi flavum Proserpina vertice crinem | abstulerat Stygioque caput damnaverat Orco*; the Virgilian *Cul.* 286–7; Ovid, *H.* 21. 46; Horace, *C.* 1. 28 (1). 20, *Epod.* 17. 2; Tibullus 3. 5. 5; Propertius 2. 28A. 1–2; Claudian 35. 300–6 (2, 340); Buchanan, *El.* 6. 35 f.; Secundus, *El.* 1. 5. 4, 2. 6. 20, *Epist.* 1. 3. 24. To hazard a more specific guess, reading Ovid on the death of Chiron, with which he was concerned earlier in the poem, and particularly *M.* 2. 654, *triplicesque deae tua fila resolvent*, Milton might have been reminded of Persephone-Proserpina as the 'triple goddess' (see the note on *Eli* 57) and given her the function of the third Fate.

39 *Succoque pollenti.* Cf. Ovid, *F.* 2. 425, *pollentibus herbis.*

40 *Faucibus eripuisse mortis.* In various forms, a stock phrase, e.g. Vida, *A.P.* 3. 88–9: *atris e mortis amicos | Faucibus eripere*; Buchanan, *Ps.* 9. 14: *atrae | Mortis faucibus eripe*, and *Ps.* 79. 11, 86. 13, 116. 8; etc.

41-2 *membra precor tua | Molli quiescant cespite.* Todd cited Virgil, *E.* 10. 33, *o mihi tum quam molliter ossa quiescant*, and the more remote Juvenal 7. 207-8: *di, maiorum umbris tenuem et sine pondere terram | spirantisque crocos et in urna perpetuum ver.* Cf. Ovid, *Am.* 1. 8. 108, *ut mea defunctae molliter ossa cubent*; ibid. 3. 9. 67-8; *A.A.* 3. 688, *viridi caespite mollis humus*; Sannazaro, *El.* 1. 2. 30, *molli cespite.*

43 *rosae, calthaeque.* Cf. Ovid, *P.* 2. 4. 28, *calthaque...rosas*, and the quotation from Milton, *Prol* 1, given under *CarEl* 9.

44 *Purpureoque hyacinthus ore.* For the story of Apollo and Hyacinthus and the sanguine flower inscribed with woe, see Ovid, *M.* 10. 162-219, 13. 395, and the note on *Lyc* 106. *Purpureo ore* is a common phrase, e.g. Catullus 45. 12; Horace, *C.* 3. 3. 12; Statius, *Th.* 3. 441.

45 *judicium Aeaci.* Having been a just ruler of the island of Aegina, Aeacus, a son of Zeus and Aegina, was associated with Minos and Rhadamanthus as a judge of the dead in Hades (Plato, *Gorg.* 523-4, *Apol.* 41A; Cicero, *Tusc.* 1. 41. 98; Horace, *C.* 2. 13. 22; Ovid, *M.* 13. 25; Apollodorus 3. 12. 6).

46 *Aetnaea Proserpina.* The story of Pluto's carrying off Proserpine to be queen of the underworld is told in the *Homeric Hymn to Demeter* 1-89; Ovid, *M.* 5. 385 f., *F.* 4. 417 f.; Claudian 32-6 (2, 292-376); for Milton's explicit quotation of Claudian see the note on *El* 6. 77-8. *Aetnaea* means either 'of Mount Etna' or, more loosely, 'Sicilian' (as in Ovid, *M.* 8. 260, Martial 7. 64. 3); see the notes on *PL* 4. 268 f. Garrod actually alters the text, with ill-informed confidence: '*I have written* Ennæa *for* Aetnæa *The legend of Proseropine* [sic] *connects her with Enna, not with Aetna.*' Proserpine is placed on Etna by Hyginus, *Fab.* 146 and Claudian 36. 85, 220, 438-40 (2, 350, 360, 376). Cf. Petrarch, *Afr.* 3. 245: *Rapta olim, ut fama est, Sicule sub vallibus Ethne* [*Etnae*]; 5. 657, *Ethneo raptam sub vertice*; A. Naugerius (*C.P.I.* 6, 481 and Gruter, *Del. I.P.* 2, 119), *Sicula Proserpina ab Aetna*; Titus Strozza, *C.P.I.* 9, 100; and *Gratul. Cantab.* (1623), 26: *Persephonen... | ...imis in vallibus Aetnae.*

48 *Elysio spatiere campo.* The classical abode of the good is here the Christian heaven. *Elysio campo*, in various forms, is a stock phrase, e.g.: Virgil, *G.* 1. 38 (cf. *A.* 5. 735, 6. 542, 744), Ovid, *Ibis* 173, Tibullus 1. 3. 58, 3. 5. 23, Lucan 3. 12, Martial 12. 52. 5, Sil. Ital. 13. 552, Apuleius, *Met.* 11. 6. Cf. Castiglione, *Alcon* 95: *Et nunc Elysia laetus spatiaris in umbra.*

In quintum Novembris,
Anno aetatis 17

The impact of the Gunpowder Plot of 1605 on the English imagination is attested by the survival down to our own time of celebrations of 'Guy Fawkes Day.' Protestant and Puritan hostility to Roman Catholicism, sufficiently and increasingly strong on religious grounds, had been greatly exacerbated by the Catholic plots against Elizabeth, the missionary or subversive work of Jesuits in England, and the fear of the combined powers of the Pope and France and Spain, a fear which had been crystallized by the Spanish Armada and had not been dissolved with its defeat. The feelings expressed in Milton's miniature epic, written twenty-one years after the event, were those shared alike by the populace and by the universities, which regularly commemorated the nation's deliverance. *In quintum Novembris*, like the epigrams, was presumably Milton's contribution to such an occasion. Although the poem has a weak and abrupt ending (the author may have grown tired of it or been pressed for time), and is in the main strident and unattractive, it has undeniable energy; the young poet's emotions were engaged. And, as critics have long recognized, the picture of Satan, however crude, anticipates *Paradise Lost*. Such a skilled and captious craftsman in Latin verse as Landor pronounced the piece, despite its poor conclusion, 'a wonderful work for a boy of seventeen' ('Southey and Landor,' *Works* 5, 328). Tillyard, on the contrary, sees 'a vigorous failure' which has been 'a little over-admired' by Masson and Rand (*Milton*, 22).

The latest and fullest study, by Macon Cheek (*SP* 54, 1957, 172–84), stresses what the poem reveals of Milton's earliest conceptions of epic technique and style and of Satan, his imitation of Virgil, and foreshadowings of *Paradise Lost*. Virgilian affinities appear in structure, in details, and in refinements of style and rhythm. Cheek sees more or less of the *Aeneid* behind the four large movements of the poem: (1) Satan's aerial flight, his survey of western Europe and Britain in particular, and his arrival in Rome; (2) Satan's view of Rome, his appearance to the pope in a vision, and his urging the recapture of Britain; (3) the pope's report to his consistory of Satan's idea and the hatching of the plot: (4) the account of Fame (i.e. Rumor) and the exposure of the plot. These motifs recall, in Virgil, the aerial surveys of Jupiter, Juno, and Venus and Aeneas' view of Carthage and burning Troy; celestial messages, dream-visitations, and councils; and, most obviously, the figure of Fama (whose activities, for Milton's purpose, are beneficent). As in Virgil, such things contribute to the cosmic setting and the epic scope of the fable. Many details suggest imitation of Virgil: in the first two lines, for example, the *pius* King James rules over the broad realms of a nation descended from the Trojans. (The notes below include numerous other items, and also a multitude of miscellaneous phrases, since Milton is by no means exclusively Virgilian.) Cheek likewise illustrates, more amply than previous commentators, the elements in Satan—the exile from heaven, the envious destroyer and plotter—that reappear in his later and far greater self.

Facts and speculations concerning the date of composition have been thus summarized by Parker ('Notes,' 122–3; largely repeated in *Milton*, 732–3, n. 29):

In both 1645 and 1673 Milton gave the date 'Anno ætatis 17' to his long poem on the anniversary of the Gunpowder Plot. In both volumes it appears between two poems presumably composed during or shortly after October of 1626. It is natural to infer, therefore, that it was written late in 1626 and before (if Milton's memory is accurate) December 9, the poet's eighteenth birthday. It is also natural to infer that a poem celebrating the Fifth of November was written near that date. And so I believe.

There are, however, two reasons for questioning Milton's memory in this instance. Critics have traced in the poem the influence of Phineas Fletcher's *Locustæ*, which was first printed, at Cambridge, in 1627. If such an influence is real, we must infer either that Milton saw Fletcher's poem in manuscript or that *In quintum Novembris* belongs one year later than Milton dated it. It was possible, of course, for Milton to have seen a manuscript of the poem, which was complete (in an early version) as long before as 1611, when its author was a fellow of King's College. Still, it remains doubtful that a second year student at Christ's, however poetically inclined, would have had access to such a manuscript, even assuming (without evidence) that one was available in Cambridge in November of 1626. There is another fact to be considered. When Milton assigned dates to his Latin poems (probably in 1645), he perhaps remembered *In quintum Novembris* as composed about a year later than the poem on Gostlin, which, as we have seen, must have been written after October 21, 1626. It so happens that he gives an incorrect date to the poem on Gostlin, but if we believe that Milton's *intention* with regard to the Gunpowder Plot poem is what really matters, we may be tempted to assign the latter to early November of 1627, despite the fact that we know the following poem to have been written in 1626 or early 1627 ['early 1627,' however, is hardly admissible for the elegy on the bishop of Ely; see the introductory note]. But this would raise unanswerable questions regarding all the *other* poems dated 'Anno ætatis 17.' My respect for the evidently chronological arrangement of the *Poemata* persuades me that *In quintum Novembris* is no exception.

Parker, then, accepts the early autumn of 1626. We may suppose, however, since Guy Fawkes Day was as sure to come around as Christmas, that Milton did not wait until autumn to write a poem that could not be despatched in a few days (especially at a time when he was paying tribute to deceased Cantabrigians), and much or most of *In quintum Novembris* may have been written in the long vacation.

The question of Milton's possible debt to Fletcher's *Locustae, vel Pietas Jesuitica* cannot, in the nature of the case, be settled decisively, but, as we have seen, all the external probabilities are negative, and the internal evidence may be thought inadequate. Before we come to that, a brief outline of Fletcher's poem, a small epic of over 800 lines, may be convenient. It opens with an infernal council called by Dis or Lucifer, who complains that the world is peaceful and growing in scriptural knowledge and piety, while he and his fellows endure their punishments; they must shake off inertia and stir up trouble on earth. Æquivocus, the prince of Jesuits, rises, boasts of the Jesuit capacity for spreading disorder, and volunteers to start something at Rome. Arriving at the seat of Romanist power and corruption, he joins an assembly that is addressed by Pope Paul. The Pope laments Protestant defections from the faith; above all, the unconquerable British scattered the Armada and are now led by a new and wise sovereign. A Jesuit leader, inspired by Æquivocus, proposes to destroy the British king and parliament with one blow, and he gives an exultant picture of the havoc to be wrought by gunpowder. The plan is applauded, the Jesuit gathers some choice spirits in England, and they go about the work. The customary splendors of the opening of parliament are described. But the Olympian Father sends down a warning message and the conspiracy is exposed. The poem ends with thanksgiving, more praise of James, and an apology for the writer's youthful effort. Both the narrative and the speeches have of course revealed the virtues of the British people and the royal family and the wickedness of Rome and the Jesuits.

Comparison of Fletcher and Milton would seem to indicate that general resemblances are only such as would be natural, almost inevitable, in two poems written in the same period on the same public and conventional subject by two young academic Protestant poets.[1] The same obvious consideration would seem to account sufficiently for particular parallels in idea and phrase. Obviously, too, both writers were committed to more or less stereotyped imitation of ancient and Neo-Latin diction and idiom, and, in cases where Fletcher is cited in the notes, Milton may be less close to him than to other authors; indeed a number of such items would not have appeared worth recording if this were not a special case.[2] While, then, it remains possible that Milton had

---

[1] Hanford, 'Youth,' 101. Tillyard (*Milton*, 22–3) takes the *Locustae* as probably 'Milton's general model' and thinks his Cave of Phonos (139 f.) is extremely like numerous passages in Fletcher's *Purple Island*, which was not published until 1633. Tillyard disregards the matter of dates, except to say, somewhat loosely, that 'Phineas published his poems during Milton's residence' at Cambridge. In *HLQ* 3 (1939–40), 47–67, Tucker Brooke edited *Pareus* (1585), a Latin poem on Dr William Parry, executed in 1585, and noted that its machinery was 'very similar' to that of Fletcher and Milton: Pluto, unable to subvert peaceful England, sends Fraud to Rome to suggest a plot to the pope, who, through a cardinal, persuades Parry, etc.

[2] The parallels I have observed are cited in the notes on lines 3–4, 5, 5–6, 7, 35, 55, 57, 92–130, 94, 96, 98, 102, 106, 111, 112, 113–15, 117–18, 120, 141–56, 149–50, 158, 161, 168, 177, 178–9, 188, 192–3, 202, 204–10, 212, 215–16, 218, 221. None of these should give one even momentary pause. (Since the standard edition (*Poetical Works of Giles and Phineas Fletcher*, ed. F. S. Boas, 1908–9, 1, 102–23) does not number lines, references here give the number of the line on the page.)

seen a manuscript copy of Fletcher's poem, there is no plausible evidence that he had. If, as we may suppose, he read it later in print, one or two items may have lodged in his mind and given hints for *Paradise Lost*, but that also is only a possibility.

In this ambitious poem, so different in length, character, and tone from the main body of Milton's early Latin verse, he is, as usual, eclectic in style; and one thing of interest, for those who can plough through the notes, is the way in which remote phrases from Ovid and others are embedded in or adapted to a very alien texture. That, of course, we have seen him doing from the start. To mention some verse that is not alien but akin to *In quintum Novembris*, it has long been recognized that the anti-Catholic satires of George Buchanan—whose work in general Milton seems to have known—contributed some specific items to this poem (see the note on 80–5 below), and they may also have contributed to the acrid tone, which, to be sure, was traditional in such writings. A word may be added about one minor piece. Since Milton's letters to his friend Alexander Gill indicate that the two sometimes sent each other their poems, it is likely that he knew Gill's violent anti-Catholic *In ruinam Camerae Papisticae, Londini Octob. 26. 1623*, first published in Gill's *Parerga* (1632). 'This poem rejoices in the collapse of a Popish place of worship which killed almost one hundred Roman Catholics in London. As this happened on the Fifth of November (new style), Gil naturally assumed that it was God's judgment for the Gunpowder Plot.'[3]

E. S. Le Comte, in a succinct commentary (*A Milton Dictionary*, New York, 1961, 157–8), says that 'Milton had probably read the *Locustae*,' and goes on: 'As regards Marini's *La Strage degli Innocenti* (the British Museum Catalogue gives bracketed dates of 1610 and 1620 for two Venetian editions), there is a basic resemblance with Book I (to be translated by Crashaw in 1646), resting on the two Satans and their

---

[3] D. L. Clark, *J.M. at St. Paul's*, 87 f. Clark leaves open the question of influence. For possible echoes of Gill in *QNov*, see the notes below on lines 17, 66, 127, 139–54, 140, 158, 222. Millar MacLure quotes comments on the accident from two preachers, the well-known Thomas Adams and a converted Catholic, John Gee (*The Paul's Cross Sermons, 1534–1642* Toronto, 1958, 106–7).

stirring up of trouble, in disguise, in a dream. Stanzas 6–8 give similar details about the fiery-eyed, teeth-grinding fiend.' On these last details see below, 33–39 n. Le Comte also catalogues details that anticipate the pictures of Satan in *PL* (cf. his *Yet Once More*, 1953, 8–9).

NOTES

1 *pius...Iäcobus ab arcto*. The epithet, and James's coming from outside to rule 'the Teucrian-born peoples' (line 2), suggest the Trojan Aeneas' coming to Italy. The young poet's outlook was still conventional enough to allow him to acknowledge James's moral virtues and theological learning, and of course his theme was Providence's protection of the Protestant king from the Catholic plot. Cf. Grotius' panegyric on James's inauguration, cited below under 3–4, etc. Later Milton saw James as a timid equivocator with the papacy (*Eikon*, *Works* 5, 196, and 181, 226–7, and the Index: MacKellar). *Arctos*, with or without a preposition, is a stock line-ending, as in Ovid and Lucan *passim*.

2–3 *Teucrigenas populos, lateque patentia regna | Albionum tenuit*: Peoples descended from Teucer, the founder of Troy (Virgil, *A.* 1. 38, 89, 235, etc.). For the tradition of the Trojan settlement of Britain see *El.* 1. 73 n. For Albion as a name of Britain see the notes on 25 and 27–9 below, and Geoffrey of Monmouth, *History of the Kings of Britain* (tr. S. Evans, rev. C. W. Dunn, London, 1963), 1. 16; *Holinshed's Chronicles*, ed. Sir Henry Ellis (London, 1807–8), 1, 8; Camden, *Britain* (tr. 1610), 5–8; and further references in MacKellar. With one of Milton's phrases cf. Virgil, *A.* 1. 21, *populum late regem*; Vida (*C.P.I.* 11, 74), *patentia regna*; Secundus, *El.* 1. 1. 13, *regna patentia late*; Ovid, *H.* 7. 119, *lateque patentia... | moenia*.

3–4 *inviolabile foedus*, etc. James's succession to the English throne brought England and Scotland under one ruler, although the two nations remained politically separate until the Act of Union, 1707. Cf. Grotius, *Inaug. Reg. Brit.* (*S.*, bk. 2, p. 59): *Bina Caledoniae sociantur regna coronae, | ...Tria sceptra profundi | In magnum coïere Ducem*; P. Fletcher, *Loc.* (p. 113, lines 6–7): *junctum uno foedere triplex | Imperium*; and similar phrases in *Cantab. Dolor* (1625), *passim*. The sonorous *inviolabile* occurs in the same position in *ProdBom* 1. 7.

5 *Pacificusque...felix divesque*. James's efforts to keep peace with Spain were commonly approved, though some Englishmen thought his failure to assist the Protestant cause in the Palatinate was of the nature of appeasement. His relatively peaceful reign, at any rate the high hopes he inspired, might justify

felix; dives proved more applicable to James's spending than to the state of the Treasury. The full title of the Cambridge memorial volume, *Cantab. Dolor* (1625), includes *Jacobi Pacifici*, and the theme recurs in the verses (and in the Oxford counterpart, *Oxon. Par.* 1625); so too does *felix*. Cf. the note on 26 below, and P. Fletcher, *Loc.* (p. 122, lines 10–9 from foot): *placidam tu pacis olivam | Angligenis infers felix.*

5–6 *sedebat | In solio.* The phrase occurs, divided in the same way, in Ovid, *M.* 2. 23–4, where the subject is Phoebus in his palace. Was Milton merely borrowing a phrase or paying indirect homage to the royal Apollo? Fletcher openly salutes *gelida consurgens Phoebus ab Arcto* (*Loc.*, p. 113, line 1). And cf. the line from *Cantab. Dolor* (1625) quoted under *El* 2. 21.

6 *occultique doli securus & hostis.* Milton forgets, or for the sake of dramatic contrast ignores, the Watson and Cobham plots, which were exposed before the Gunpowder plot (MacKellar).

7 *ferus ignifluo regnans Acheronte tyrannus.* Acheron, one of the rivers of Hades, conventionally stood, like the other rivers (cf. *Phlegetontius* in 74 below), for the underworld in general (cf. *Comus* 603). The fiery stream, as Milton would be well aware, was not 'Sad Acheron' (*PL* 2. 578; cf. Virgil, *A.* 6. 295–316; Dante, *Inf.* 3. 70–129) but Phlegethon (e.g. Virgil, *A.* 6. 550; *PL* 2. 580–1); but cf. Sil. Ital. 11. 473, *flammisque Acheronta sonantem*, and Shakespeare, *Tit.* 4. 3. 43–4. Milton's phrases make the common identification of Satan with Pluto: cf. Ovid, *M.* 4. 444, *imi tecta tyranni*; 5. 508, *inferni...tyranni*; 6. 549, *feri...tyranni* (of Tereus); Claudian 35. 264 (2, 336), *Stygio...tyranno.* Cf. Fletcher, *Loc.*, p. 102, lines 1 f.; Vida's picture of Satan and his infernal council, *Christ.* 1. 121 f.; Sannazaro, *P.V.* 1. 387, *tartarei...tyranni.*

8 *Eumenidum pater.* Another link between Satan and Pluto, who, in Virgil, *A.* 7. 327, is father of the Furies. Keightley also cited *Orphic Hymns*, 70 (*Orphei Hymni*, ed. G. [W.] Quandt, Berlin, 1962).

8 *aethereo vagus exul Olympo.* Olympus represents the Christian heaven (see the note on *El* 5. 19). Editors cite Virgil, *A.* 8. 319–20: *primus ab aetherio venit Saturnus Olympo, | arma Iovis fugiens et regnis exsul ademptis. Aetherius Olympus* is a stock phrase, e.g. Virgil, *A.* 6. 579, 8. 319 (just quoted), 10. 621, 11. 867; Martial 9. 3. 3; Buchanan, *Ps.* 18. 32, 78. 23, *Sph.* 2. 360; Pontano, *Met.* 1083; Vida, *Christ.* 4. 114, 1001; Castiglione, *Carm.* 2. 39. Cf. also Cicero, *Pro Cluentio* 62. 175, *vagus et exsul erraret*; Sil. Ital. 2. 701–2, *vagus exul in orbe | errabit toto*; Buchanan, *Franc.* 263, *vagus, exul...erro*; and *vagus exul* in Ovid, *M.* 11. 408, Seneca, *Thy.* 297, Statius, *Th.* 1. 312, 12.394; etc.

9 *per immensum terrarum erraverat orbem.* The adjective may carry its literal sense of 'immeasurable', as in *PL* 2. 829, 7. 620, etc. *Immensum orbem* appears, e.g. in Manilius 1. 330 (cf. 1. 23); Sannazaro, *P.V.* 1. 253; Secundus, *El.* 2. 1. 13; Grotius, *Inaug. Reg. Brit.* (*S.*, bk. 2, pp. 60, 74). *Orbis terrarum* is a stock phrase, e.g. Cicero, *Verr.* 2. 4. 38. 82; Virgil, *A.* 1. 233; Ovid, *M.* 2. 7; Milton, *Prol* 3 (*Works* 12, 166, line 14), *Prol* 7 (ibid. 268, line 8).

10 *sceleris socios, vernasque fideles.* The first phrase is in Cicero, *Cat.* 1. 4. 8, 3. 1. 3. Cf. Lucretius 3. 61, *socios scelerum;* Milton, *PL* 1. 606, 'The fellows of his crime' (Todd).

11 *Participes regni post funera moesta futuros.* There is an ironical contrast with Christ's followers who are to share in his kingdom. Cf. Heb. 3. 14 (tr. Tremellius): *Participes enim facti sumus cum Christo* (cited in *DocCh*, *Works* 16, 4); ibid. 6. 4 (tr. Beza), 12. 10 (Tremellius and Beza). Cf. Ovid, *F.* 6. 660, *maestis...funeribus* (Fletcher).

12 *Hic tempestates medio ciet aëre diras.* For the 'middle air,' the special haunt of demons who caused storms, see the notes on *Vac* 41 and *PR* 2. 117. MacKellar cites Virgil, *A.* 4. 122, *tonitru caelum omne ciebo.*

13 *Illic unanimes odium struit inter amicos.* Editors cite Juno's words about Allecto, Virgil, *A.* 7. 335–6: *tu potes unanimos armare in proelia fratres | atque odiis versare domos.* Cf. Cicero, *De Orat.* 2. 51. 208, *in alios odium struere discemus.*

14 *Armat & invictas in mutua viscera gentes.* Editors cite Virgil, *A.* 6. 833, *neu patriae validas in viscera vertite viris.* Cf. ibid. 12. 191, *invictae gentes;* Ovid, *R. Am.* 59, *Nec dolor armasset contra sua viscera matrem;* Lucan 1. 3, *In sua victrici conversum viscera dextra,* and 7. 490–1; Grotius, *Grat. Ad Dousam* (*Farr.*, bk. 1, 177), *versam mox in sua viscera dextram.*

15 *Regnaque olivifera vertit florentia pace.* For the association of olives with peace, see, e.g., Virgil, *G.* 2. 425, *A.* 8. 116, Ovid, *P.* 1. 1. 31, Shakespeare, *Sonn.* 107, Milton, *Nat* 46–52, and n. Editors cite the word *olivifera* in Virgil *A.* 7. 711, Ovid, *F.* 3. 151, *Ibis* 317, and Martial 12. 98. 1. Cf. *florentia regna* in the Virgilian *Cir.* 464 and Vida, *Christ.* 1. 56, and *regna pia florentia pace* in *Pareus* (cf. headnote, note 1 above), p. 60.

17 *fraudumque magister.* Editors cite *PL* 4. 121, 'Artificer of fraud,' and 1. 645–6, 3. 152, 6. 794, 7. 143; and *fraudis artifex* in line 3 of the Latin version of *Christus Patiens,* the play formerly attributed (as in Milton's preface to *SA*) to Gregory Nazianzen (Migne, *Pat. Gr.* 38, 138). Cf. Sil. Ital. 13. 738, *fraudum genitor;* Gill, *In ruinam* (p. 13), *callidi artifices doli; De Gestis...Gustavi*

Adolphi...1631 (ibid., p. 86), *Anti-christe, pater scelerum, fraudisque repertor*; and note on 215–16 below. Milton's phrase is an ironical echo of ancient Roman and papal titles, such as *magister morum* or *magister domus sacri palatii apostolici*.

19–20 *Insidiasque locat tacitas, cassesque latentes | Tendit.* Cf. Plautus, *Rud.* 2. 5. 474, *ne illa mulier mi insidias locet* (cf. Plautus, *Curc.* 1. 1. 25); Tibullus 1. 6. 5, *mihi tendentur casses.*

20 *Caspia Tigris.* Cheek (178) compares Virgil's simile of the wolf (*A.* 9. 59–66). Milton's phrase is in Statius, *Th.* 10. 288–9. as editors note. Caspian is a less common epithet for tigers than Hyrcanian or Armenian (Virgil, *A.* 4. 367, Ovid, *M.* 8. 121, 15. 86), but all three words refer to the same savage region (MacKellar).

For the preceding *seu* of 1645 and 1673, editors (except Columbia) read *ceu*.

21 *deserta per avia.* In the Lactantian *De Ave Phoenice* (*Minor Latin Poets*, L.C.L.), 67, Vida, *Christ.* 3. 749, Buchanan, *Ps.* 78. 18, 136. 16, and Palingenius, *Z.V.* 2. 61.

22 *Nocte sub illuni, & somno nictantibus astris.* Cf. Pliny, *Ep.* 6. 20 (1, 494), *nox, non quasi illunis*; Sil. Ital. 15. 616, *illunem...noctem*; Grotius, *Ad. Ex.* 559, *Nox ut illunis silet*; Lucretius 6. 182, *nictantia fulgura flammae*; the Virgilian *Cir.* 218, *nictantia sidera.*

23 Summanus was a somewhat shadowy being, sometimes identified with Pluto but most commonly taken as a nocturnal deity who caused lightning (Cicero, *Div.* 1. 10. 16; Ovid, *F.* 6. 731; Pliny, *N.H.* 2. 53. 138; Augustine, *Civ. D.* 4. 23). Milton evidently had the orthodox idea in mind. Starnes-Talbert (280) quote C. Stephanus, *Dict.*

24 *Cinctus caeruleae fumanti turbine flammae.* Cf. Virgil, *A.* 3. 573, *turbine fumantem piceo.*

25 *fluentisonis albentia rupibus arva.* The white cliffs of Dover. See the note on Spenser, *F.Q.* 2. 10. 6, in the Variorum ed.; Camden, *Britain* (tr. 1610, 23–4), who cites the legends and the name Albion as due to England's being 'environed...with white rocks'; P. Heylyn, *Microcosmus* (1621), 242: 'The whole Iland was once called Albion, not from the Giant Albion; but *ab albis rupibus*, the white rockes toward Brittaine'; Selden, in Drayton, 4, 24. Milton's first adjective is used with *litore* in Catullus 64. 52 (Fletcher), with *undis* in Vida, *Christ*, 2. 346, with *ripis* by J. C. Scaliger (Gruter, *Del. I.P.* 2. 841). Cf. Val. Flacc. 2. 73, *albet ager.*

26 *terra Deo dilecta marino.* A traditional patriotic sentiment, e.g. Shakespeare,

R. II, 2. 1. 40–64, *Comus* 27–8. See J. W. Bennett, 'Britain Among the Fortunate Isles.' *SP* 53 (1956), 114–40. The idiom is common, e.g. Horace, *C.* 1. 21. 3–4, *Latonamque | ...dilectam...Iovi*; Lucan 3. 184–5, *dilecta Iovi... | Creta;* Claudian 7. 96 (1, 276), *o nimium dilecte deo; Gratul. Cantab.* (1623), p. 26, *O multum dilecte Deo; Epith. Caroli et H. Mariae* (1625), 13, *Pacifici soboles multum dilecta Iacobi.*

27–9 *Cui nomen dederat quondam Neptunia proles | Amphitryoniaden... | furiali poscere bello.* Editors quote Milton, *HistBr* (*Works* 10, 4): 'Albion a Giant, Son of Neptune: who call'd the Iland after his own name, and rul'd it 44 years. Till at length passing over into Gaul, in aid of his Brother Lestrygon, against whom Hercules was hasting out of Spain into Italy, he was there slain in fight, and Bergion also his Brother.' MacKellar cites also *Holinshed's Chronicles*, ed. Ellis, 1, 7; Pomponius Mela, *De Chorographia* (ed. C. Frick, Leipzig, 1880), 2. 5. 78.

Cf. Camden, *Britain* (tr. 1610), 24, and Drayton, 4, 24, 43, 70, 'Albion, Neptunes sonne.' *Neptunia proles* is a stock phrase, especially at the end of a line, e.g. Virgil, *A.* 7. 691, 9. 523, 10. 353, 12. 128, Ovid, *M.* 10. 639, 665, Val. Flacc. 1. 415, 4. 209, 256. Heracles (Hercules), the son of Zeus and Alcmena, wife of Amphitryon, is often called Amphitryoniades, e.g. Pindar, *Ol.* 3. 14, Catullus 68A. 112, Virgil, *A.* 8. 103, 214, Ovid, *M.* 9. 140, 15. 49, Propertius 4. 9. 1, Statius, *Th.* 8. 499, *Ach.* 1. 190, Val. Flacc, and Sil. Ital. *passim.* Fletcher cites Sil. Ital. 8. 409, *furialia bella.*

30 *Ante expugnatae crudelia saecula Troiae.* 'From the somewhat confused dates given in Holinshed (*Chronicles*, 1807, pp. 8–9) the reign of Albion would seem to have been about 1700 years before the Christian era' (MacKellar). Cf. Statius, *S.* 1. 4. 125–6, *Troica... | saecula.*

31 *opibusque & festa pace beatam.* Editors cite Ovid, *M.* 2. 790–6, especially 795, *ingeniis opibusque et festa pace virentem.* Cf. Ovid, *H.* 17. 221, *opibus... beato*; Pliny, *N.H.* 14. 1. 2, *societate festae pacis.*

32 *pingues donis Cerealibus agros. Cerealia dona* is a stock phrase, e.g. Ovid, *M.* 11. 122, *F.* 6. 391, Statius, *S.* 5. 3. 226, Sil. Ital. 7. 183. Cf. Lucretius 5. 1248, *agros pinguis*; Columella, *R.R.* 1. 4. 1, *agri pinguis.*

33–4 *venerantem numina veri | Sancta Dei populum, tandem suspiria rupit.* Cf. Ovid, *M.* 6. 44, *venerantur numina* [*Palladis*] (Fletcher); ibid. 15. 680, *venerantur numen*; Lucretius 5. 309, *sanctum numen*; 6. 70, *numina sancta* (also in Virgil, *A.* 3. 543); Virgil, *A.* 2. 141 (end), *conscia numina veri. Suspiria rupit* is in Claudian 15. 235 (1, 114), Pontano, *Met.* 140, Vida, *Christ.* 2. 951, and *C.P.I.* 10,

281. With *Quodque magis doluit* (33), cf. Ovid, *M.* 1. 757, *quo...magis doleas*; 3. 448, *quoque magis doleam*.

33–9 Todd quoted from Crashaw's amplification of Marino's description of the Devil (*Poems*, ed. L. C. Martin, Oxford, 1927, 1957, 111, st. 7). A somewhat similar crude concreteness appears in Tasso, *G.L.* 4. 6–8. The Satan of *QNov*, said Leigh Hunt (*Lit. Exam.* 13 Sept. 1823, 163; Houtchens, 200), 'is the devil of Tasso and others, not of the Paradise Lost'; though even here Satan has less suggestion of the Italian grotesque and more of power and terror (A.S.P.W.).

35 *Tartareos ignes & luridum olentia sulphur.* For Tartarus see the note on *El* 3. 16. Cf. Ovid, *M.* 14. 791, *lurida...sulphura* (Fletcher); ibid. 5. 405, *olentia sulphure*; Sil. Ital. 12. 133: *Tartareae...urbis. tum sulphure et igni*; Fletcher, *Loc.* (p. 104, line 4), *flammis & vivo sulphure tecti.*

36–7 *Trinacria...Aetna | ...Tiphoeus.* The monstrous rebel, Typhoeus, was imprisoned by Jove under Sicily (Trinacria); he belched fire through the volcano of Etna. See Pindar, *Pyth.* 1. 15–28; Aeschylus, *Prom.* 353–74; Ovid, *M.* 5. 346–58; Val. Flacc. 2. 24–33; Milton, *Prol* 1 (*Works* 12, 122); *PL* 1. 199, 2. 661, and notes. Cf. Virgil, *A.* 3. 554, *Trinacria...Aetna.*

38–9 *Ignescunt oculi, stridetque adamantinus ordo | Dentis, ut armorum fragor, ictaque cuspide cuspis.* The *adamantius* of 1673 was corrected in the Errata. Editors cite *PL* 1. 193–4, 6. 848–9. Cf. Tasso, *G.L.* 4. 7. 3, *rosseggian gli occhi*; Crashaw's version of Marino (ed. Martin, p. 111, st. 8); Ovid, *M.* 3. 34, *triplici stant ordine dentes*; Statius, *Th.* 6. 790, *dentibus...stridens*; Mark 9. 18 (tr. Tremellius and Beza), *stridet dentibus suis*; Acts 7. 54 (Beza), *stridebant dentibus*; Statius, *Th.* 8. 399, *et cuspide cuspis*; and *cuspidis ictus* or *ictu* in Val. Flacc. 3. 284, Ovid, *M.* 12. 74, and Sil. Ital. 13. 197. *Armorum fragor* is in Lucan 1. 569, Val. Flacc. 3. 218, Buchanan, *Jeph.* 293, *Misc.* 23. 63, and Vida, *A.P.* 2. 382.

40–2 Editors compare Satan's soliloquy in *PL* 4. 358–92.

40 *pererrato...mundo.* In Vida, *Christ.* 6. 864. Cf. *pererrato* with *orbe* in Ovid, *M.* 3. 6, *F.* 1. 234, 4. 589, and with *ponto* in Virgil, *A.* 2. 295.

42 *Contemtrixque jugi, nostraque potentior arte.* Cf. Ovid, *M.* 1. 161, *contemptrix superum*; Buchanan, *Ps.* 1. 5, *Contemtrixque poli*; Ovid, *M.* 11. 494, *potentior arte est.*

44 *Non feret hoc impune diu, non ibit inulta.* Cf. Ovid, *M.* 8. 279–80: *at non impune feremus, | ...non et dicemur inultae*; *F.* 4. 595: *verum impune ferat, nos haec patiemur inultae.* For other phrases akin to Milton's first one, cf. Ovid, *M.* 2. 474, 8. 494, 11. 207, 12. 265, 14. 383; Propertius 1. 4. 17; Catullus 78. 9.

45 *piceis liquido natat aëre pennis.* The *notat* of 1673 was corrected in the Errata. Fletcher cites Lucan 5. 554, *Ardea sublimis pinnae confisa natanti. Liquido aere*, in various cases, is a stock phrase, e.g. Virgil, *G.* 1. 404, *A.* 6. 202; Ovid, *Am.* 2. 6. 11, *M.* 4. 667, 11. 194; Statius, *Th.* 1. 294, 5. 524; etc.

46–7 *Qua volat, adversi praecursant agmine venti, | Densantur nubes, & crebra tonitrua fulgent.* Editors compare *PL* 1. 225–7, 11. 739–43. Cf. Lucan 4. 76–8 (of clouds): *densantur in imbres | ...nec servant fulmina flammas | Quamvis crebra micent*; Virgil, *A.* 1. 82, *venti, velut agmine facto*; 1. 90: *intonuere poli, et crebris micat ignibus aether*; 2. 416, *adversi...venti*; Ovid, *H.* 21. 71, *adverso...vento*; Pontano, *Uran.* 1. 330, *nullae densentur...nubes.*

48 *Jamque pruinosas velox superaverat alpes.* Editors cite Lucan 1. 183: *Iam gelidas Caesar cursu superaverat Alpes.* Cf. Sannazaro, *El.* 3. 2. 77, *Bisque pruinosas cursu superavimus Alpes*; Claudian 1. 255 (1, 20), *Alpinasque... pruinas*; Gill, *Ad Dom. G.R.* (1625: 17), *Alpes superare juvat.*

49 *tenet Ausoniae fines.* See the note on *El* 1. 70. Cf. Ovid, *F.* 4. 290, *Ausoniamque tenet.* With the stock phrase *Ausoniae fines* cf. Ovid, *Tr.* 1. 2. 92, 1. 3. 6; Virgil, *A.* 6. 345–6; Sil. Ital. 17. 222–3.

50 *Nimbifer Appenninus erat, priscique Sabini.* MacKellar cites Ovid, *M.* 2. 226, *nubifer Appenninus*; cf. the same phrase in Gill, *Ad Dom. G.R.* (1625: p. 17); Ovid, *P.* 4. 8. 60, *nimbifero...igne.* The Sabines, an ancient people of central Italy, with whom early Rome had conflicts, came to represent old-fashioned *mores.* Cf. Ovid, *F.* 2. 477 and Martial 10. 33. 1, *priscis...Sabinis* (they are *veteres* in Virgil, *G.* 2. 532, Juvenal 10. 299); Pliny, *N.H.* 3. 12. 108–9; Milton on Cato's 'old Sabin austerity' (*Areop, Works* 4, 301).

51 *veneficiis infamis Hetruria.* Editors query Milton's phrase, since, according to Livy 5. 1 and common reference, the people of ancient Etruria (Tuscany) were noted for religious devotion, not witchcraft. Possibly, by a kind of metonymy frequent in Latin poetry, he used Etruria for Marsia; the Marsians of central Italy were associated with witchcraft, e.g. Virgil, *A.* 7. 750–8; Horace, *Epod.* 17. 29; Ovid, *Med. Fac.* 39, *A.A.* 2. 102, *F.* 6. 142; Sil. Ital. 8. 495–507; A. Gellius 16. 11; Pliny, *N.H.* 25. 5. 11.

52 *Te furtiva Tibris Thetidi videt oscula dantem.* That is, the Tiber passes gently through its delta to join the sea (Thetis, the sea-nymph, for the sea, as in Virgil, *E.* 4. 32, etc.).Cf. Claudian 11. 24 (1, 230), *furtiva carpent oscula Naides*; Poliziano (*C.P.I.* 7, 391; Gruter, *Del. I.P.* 2, 354), *Ut furtiva* [*lasciva* in Poliziano, *P.V.*, 162] *suo furtim daret oscula lauro*; Gruter, ibid. 1, 1207, *furtiva dat oscula Phyllis.*

53 *Mavortigenae...Quirini.* The epithet ('offspring of Mars') has not been observed elsewhere; Milton may have met it, or he may have coined it on the model of similar compounds. The usual word is *Martigena*, e.g. Ovid, *Am.* 3. 4. 39, Sil. Ital. 12. 582, 16. 532; it is joined with Quirinus in Ovid, *F.* 1. 199 (Fletcher) and Sil. Ital. 13. 811. Quirinus was the name given to Romulus after his deification (Cicero, *Leg.* 1. 1. 3; Ovid, *F.* 2. 475–6; Virgil, *A.* 1. 292; Florus 1. 1. 18). (MacKellar, augmented.)

54–67 Satan reaches Rome on the eve of the festival of St Peter's Day (i.e. 28 June), the occasion of an elaborate procession and service at St Peter's. See MacKellar.

54 *Reddiderant dubiam jam sera crepuscula lucem.* Cf. Ovid, *M.* 11. 596, *dubiaeque crepuscula lucis* (Fletcher); 15. 651, *seram...crepuscula lucem*; 4. 400–1; *sera crepuscula* in Ovid, *M.* 1. 219, Sil. Ital. 2. 215, and Buchanan, *Ps.* 109. 23, *Sph.* 3. 411; and Seneca, *Hipp.* 41, *lux dubia*. The note on Ovid, *M.* 1. 219, in Ovid–Micyllus (13H) is: *crepusculum dicitur dubia lux.*

55 *Tricoronifer.* 'The bearer of the Triple Crown', the Pope. Cf. 94 below and note; *ProdBom* 3. 3; and *Sonn* 18. 12, 'The triple Tyrant.' The papal tiara came into being by degrees, as a non-liturgical symbol, in the later Middle Ages. 'The tiara is placed on the Pope's head at his coronation...with the words "Receive the tiara adorned with three crowns, and know that thou art Father of princes and kings, Ruler of the world, Vicar of our Saviour Jesus Christ"' (*Catholic Dictionary*, ed. W. E. Addis, T. Arnold, rev. P. E. Hallett, 15th ed. St Louis, 1951, p. 779). The views of Reformation Protestantism, and the common use of the symbol, may be illustrated by some quotations: Beza, *Paulo Quarto, Pontifici Romano* (*Poëmata*, 96: misprinted 87), *Cuius nunc onerat terna tiara caput*; Jewel, *Works* (1845–50), 3, 104: 'he [the pope], sitting in his chair, with his triple crown full of labels'; 4,846: 'Felinus, your [i.e. Roman Catholic] doctor, saith thus: '...The pope hath Christ's lieutenantship, not only over things in heaven, over things in earth, and over things in hell, but also over the angels, both good and bad"'; P. Fletcher, *Apoll.* 3. 16: 'Three mitred crownes the proud Impostor weares, / For he in earth, in hell, in heav'n will raigne'; *Purple Island*, 7. 62: 'A Miter trebly crown'd th'Impostour wore; / For heav'n, earth, hell he claims with loftie pride. / Not in his lips, but hands, two keyes he bore, / Heav'ns doores and hells to shut, and open wide'; *Loc.* (quoted under 94 below); Burton, *Anat.* 1, 54, 'their three-crowned Sovereign Lord the Pope'; Gill, *De Gestis...Gustavi Adolphi...1631* (p. 86): *calviciem triplici redimite corona, / Anti-christe*; and, from a poem of 1655 addressed by a

Catholic, one William Metham, to Pope Alexander VII (quoted by J. McG. Bottkol, *PMLA* 68, 1953, 619): 'Three powers, three scepters and a triple crowne... / Whose threefold scutchian from the Trinitie / Displayes three mightie powers Heav'n Earth and Hell.'

56 *Panificosque Deos*: 'gods wrought of bread'—a Protestant view of the Host. Cf. Buchanan, *Franc.* 740, *De pane ut numen faciant.*

57 *submisso* [1645: *summisso*] *poplite.* In Catullus 64. 370; Ovid, *M.* 7. 191; Val. Flacc. 6. 245, Cf. P. Fletcher, *Loc.* (p. 110, last line), *flexo...poplite.*

58 *mendicantum series longissima fratrum.* The four orders of mendicant friars were the Franciscans, Dominicans, Carmelites, and Augustinian Hermits. Cf. *PL* 3. 474–80. Cf. Virgil, *A.* 1. 641, *series longissima rerum* (Fletcher); Vida, *Christ.* 3. 121, *series longissima patrum;* Buchanan, *S.* 4. 262, *Fortunatorum series longissima Regum;* Milton, *Prol* 7 (*Works* 12, 278, line 13), *longa annorum series.*

59–60 *caeci,* / *Cimmeriis nati in tenebris, vitamque trahentes.* The mythical Cimmerii, located by various writers in various regions, lived in darkness and provided a stock epithet, e.g. Homer, *Od.* 11. 13–19, Ovid, *M.* 11. 592, Val. Flacc. 3. 398–405, Sil. Ital. 12. 130 f., Sandys, *Relation* (1615), 263. Cf. Virgil, *A.* 2. 92, *vitam in tenebris...trahebam* (Fletcher); Lily's *Grammar* (*Carmen de Moribus*, sig. Dvᵛ), *in tenebris vivere Cimmeriis;* Buchanan, *Franc.* 28, *immersam caeca caligine mentem;* Milton, *Prol* 1 (*Works* 12, 146, line 17), *Cimmeriis occlusus tenebris; L'All* 10. Starnes-Talbert (303) quote C. Stephanus, *Dict.*, on the Cimmerians' wicked ways as well as their dark abode.

62 (*Vesper erat sacer iste Petro*) *fremitusque canentum.* Cf. Mantuan, *E.* 2. 63, *lux ea sacra fuit Petro.* Fletcher cites Ovid, *Tr.* 4. 2. 53, *fremituque canentum* [other readings are *canentes, -is, -e*].

63 *tholos implet vacuos, & inane locorum.* With the first phrase cf. *El* 6. 44. *Inane* is an especially Lucretian word (1. 223, 330, 342, etc.), but is used by Manilius, Virgil, Ovid et al. Cf. the note on *Naturam* 53.

64 *Bromius.* 'The noisy one,' one of the surnames of Dionysus (Euripides, *Bacch.* 66, etc.; Diod. Sic. 4. 5. 1; Ovid, *M.* 4. 11). With 64–7 Cheek (178) compares Virgil's Bacchic allusions, *A.* 4. 300–3, 7. 385–91.

65 *Orgia cantantes in Echionio Aracyntho.* Echion was one of the warriors who sprang from the dragon's teeth sowed by Cadmus and was father of Pentheus (Euripides, *Bacch.* 229, 265, 537–41, etc.); hence the adjective means 'Theban' (Virgil, *A.* 12. 515; Horace, *C.* 4. 4. 64; Ovid, *Tr.* 5. 5. 53; Statius, *Th.* 6. 14;

Val. Flacc. 7. 301, 554, 8. 343). The mountain Aracynthus, on the coast of Aetolia, was by some writers placed on the border of Boeotia and Attica (Servius on Virgil, *E.* 2. 24; Propertius 3. 15. 42: MacKellar). Rand (*SP* 19, 115) remarks that Milton's line shows his awareness 'that Virgil allowed Greek words at the end of a verse a certain metrical liberty—a spondee in the fifth foot, or a hiatus there, or a short syllable under the ictus, or all of these licenses in a general riot.' Cf. Virgil, *E.* 2. 24, *in Actaeo Aracyntho*. Rand also observes (120–1) how the pagan imagery reinforces the satire.

66 *tremit attonitus vitreis Asopus in undis.* Asopus was a Boeotian river (and river god): Euripides, *Bacch.* 749, 1044; Apollodorus 3. 12. 6; Propertius 3. 15. 27; Statius, *Th.* 3. 337, etc. Cf. Gill, *In ruinam* (p. 12), *serus attonitus tremor. Vitreis undis*, in various forms, is a stock phrase, e.g. Virgil, *A.* 7. 759 (Fletcher), Ovid, *M.* 5. 48, Martial 6. 68. 7, Claudian 10. 128 (1, 250), Mantuan, *E.* 10. 30, Vida, *A.P.* 1. 349, Buchanan, *S.* 3. 24, Sannazaro and Pontano, *passim.*

67 *cava responsat rupe Cithaeron.* A range of hills separating Boeotia and Megaris from Attica on which Dionysian rites were celebrated (Euripides, *Bacch.* 62, 661, etc.; Ovid, *M.* 2. 223, 3. 701–3; Virgil, *A.* 4. 303, *orgia nocturn-usque vocat clamore Cithaeron; G.* 3. 43; Statius, *Th.* 2. 72–80. *Cava rupe*, with variations, is common.

68 *solenni more.* In Lucretius 1. 96, Claudian, *S.P.* 31. 37 (2, 258).

69 *Nox senis amplexus Erebi taciturna reliquit.* Night and Erebus were children of Chaos and, as a wedded pair, the progenitors of Aether and Day (Hesiod, *Theog.* 123–5; Cicero, *N.D.* 3. 17. 44). Cf. Milton, *Prol* 1 (*Works* 12, 126, line 19), where Night *ad incestos Erebi fratris amplexus...se corripit.* The line of verse is on the model of many allusions to Aurora and Tithonus; cf. *El* 5. 49–50 and note. *Tacita* is the common epithet for night, e.g. Ovid, *H.* 18. 78, *F.* 2. 552. Erebus might be Hades, the home of the dead (Homer, *Od.* 11. 37; Ovid, *M.* 14. 404) or the god of darkness; Virgil uses both meanings (*G.* 4. 471, *A.* 4. 26, 510, 6. 247, 404, 671, 7. 140). Erebus is the place in *Comus* 803 and *PL* 2. 883, the god in *QNov* 69 and *Eli* 33. See Osgood, *C.M.* 33, 62–4; Stephanus, *Dict.* (Starnes-Talbert, 250–1).

70 *Praecipitesque impellit equos stimulante flagello.* Night drove a chariot corresponding to that of Aurora or the sun, e.g. Virgil, *A.* 5. 721, *Cul.* 202; Tibullus 2. 1. 87, 3. 4. 17–18; Ovid, *P.* 1. 2. 54; Sil. Ital. 15. 284–5; Claudian 33. 276–7 (2, 312). *Praecipites* begins Ovid, *M.* 2. 207 (on Phaethon). Cf. Statius, *Th.* 7. 83, *Mars impellit equos*; Pontano, *Uran.* 3. 17, *celeres impellit equos*; Sil. Ital. 4. 439, *quadriiugos atro stimulat Bellona flagello.*

71–3 Milton adds Greek names (and explanatory epithets for three of them) to the horses of Night. He doubtless had in mind the names of Apollo's horses (Ovid, *M.* 2. 153–4) and Pluto's in Claudian 33. 284–6 (2, 314). Editors cite Spenser, *F.Q.* 1. 5. 20, 28. For Milton's *Captum oculis* (71), see Virgil, *G.* 1. 183, Cicero, *Div.* 2. 3. 9; etc. For *Acherontaeo* see the note on 7 above. With *hirsutis...capillis* (73), Fletcher compares Ovid, *H.* 9. 63, *hirsutos...capillos*; cf. Palingenius, *Z.V.* 3. 428, *hirsutisque capillis.*

74 *regum domitor, Phlegetontius haeres.* The first phrase—applied to Paul V (1552–1621) and other modern popes—is an ironical reminder of the temporal power wielded by some of the great medieval popes. For the second phrase, see the notes on 7 and 55 above.

75–6 The character or reputation of such popes as Alexander VI had reinforced traditional charges of immorality; see, e.g. Burton, *Anat.* 3. 4. 1. 3 (3, 366–8). Milton's *secretus adulter* is in Juvenal 6. 237. With *Producit steriles molli sine pellice noctes*, cf. Buchanan, *Franc.* 549, *cum pellice noctes / Ducere*; *Epith. Caroli et H. Mariae* (1625), p. 5, *steriles noctes*; Lucan 10. 173 (quoted under *EpDam* 46–7); Claudian 7. 48 (1, 274), *vigiles producere noctes*; *C.P.I.* 9, 483, *longas producere noctes.*

77 *compositos somnus claudebat ocellos.* Cf. Propertius 1. 3. 33, *compositos... ocellos*; 2. 13. 17, *nostros mors claudet ocellos.*

78 *niger umbrarum dominus, rectorque silentum.* Cf. Ovid, *M.* 10. 16, *umbrarum dominum*, and, with *dominos*, Seneca, *Herc. Fur.* 570 and Boethius, *C.P.* 3, met. 12. 28; Ovid, *M.* 5. 356 and Claudian, *S.P.* 52. 45 (2, 284), *rex...silentum* (*reges* in Lucan 3. 29); Seneca, *Oed.* 869, *rector umbrarum*; Claudian 35. 156 (2, 328), *animarum rector*; Virgil, *A.* 6. 432–3, *silentum / conciliumque* (cf. 6. 264, *umbraeque silentes*).

79 *falsa sub imagine tectus.* Cf. Ovid, *H.* 17. 45–6, *falsa sub imagine... / ...pluma tectus adulter erat. Falsa imagine* is a stock phrase, e.g. Ovid, *M.* 2. 37, *F.* 6. 489, *Consol.* 325; Virgil, *A.* 1. 408 (plural); Vida, *Christ.* 2. 414, 6. 369, 434, *A.P.* 1. 226; Buchanan, *S.* 3. 11; etc. B.A.W. cites *Comus* 156, 'false presentments.'

80–5 Editors compare this picture of Satan in Franciscan garb with *PR* 1. 314–20 and 497–8, and observe Milton's debt here to two passages in Buchanan, *Franciscanus* 45–8 and, in *Fratres Fraterrimi* 34 (*Somnium*), lines 5–9 (MacKellar; cf. Brodribb, *N&Q* 158, 1930, 185). These and other possible echoes of these two works are recorded in the notes on lines 8, 56, 59–60, 75–6, 80, 81–2, 82–3, 84, 85, 215–16 (see also 144). We might observe also the picture of the followers of *Sathanas cucullatus* in Beza's *Abrahamus Sacrificans* (*Poëmata*, 1599, 154ʳ). The disguised Satan links himself with such figures as Spenser's Archimago, *F.Q.* 1. 1. 29, 34–5, etc.

80 *tempora canis.* A stock phrase, e.g. Ovid, *M.* 3. 516, 8. 568, 12. 465, 14. 655, 15. 211; Statius, *Th.* 10. 706; Buchanan, *Franc.* 277.

81 *Barba...promissa.* In Virgil, *E.* 8. 34 and Pontano, *Uran.* 2. 537.

81–2 *cineracea longo | Syrmate verrit humum vestis.* Cf. Buchanan, *F.F.* 9. 4, *Qui semper longo syrmate verrit humum*; *Franc.* 87–88, *longo syrmate talos | Usque tegi*; *El.* 1. 90, *Turgidus aut tragico syrmate verris humum. Verrit humum* is a stock phrase, e.g. Ovid, *H.* 12. 102, *M.* 6. 706, 11. 166, *R. Am.* 192, *F.* 4. 736.

82–3 *pendetque cucullus | Vertice de raso.* Cf. Buchanan, *Franc.* 20, *Obrasumque caput duro velante cucullo*; 45, *longo sub syrmate rasum | Cerno caput*; 86–7, *raso vertice calvum | ...caput*; 721–2, *rasi...verticis*; *F.F.* 35. 21, *Rasus erat vertex. Vertice raso* is in Juvenal 5. 171, 12. 81.

84 *Cannabeo lumbos constrinxit fune salaces.* Cf. Buchanan, *Franc.* 19, *cum cannabe cinctus*; 46, *tortum funem*; 125, *fuscam cum cannabe vestem*; 178–9, *fune | Cingimur*; *F.F.* 24. 9, *tunicam fluxam nodosa cannabe cingas*; 34. 5, *Franciscus nodosa cannabe cinctus.* To the friars' unsavory reputation there are many familiar witnesses, from Boccaccio and Chaucer onward.

85 *Tarda fenestratis figens vestigia calceis.* Sandals are 'latticed' because of the spaces between the straps. Cf. Buchanan, *Franc.* 47, *fenestratum...cothurnum*; *F.F.* 34. 8, *fenestratus calceus.* Fletcher cites Virgil, *A.* 6. 159, *vestigia figit*, and the same phrase, with different verb forms, in Claudian 17. 324 (1, 362), 26. 170 (2, 138).

86–9 Both context (see references to Buchanan above, 80–5 and notes) and particulars make it likely that Milton was thinking of St Francis of Assisi, founder of the Franciscan Order, rather than of St Francis Xavier, the Jesuit missionary to the Indies. The former, who preached to the birds and converted the wolf of Agobio, and who was said to have set out for Africa, has a better claim to the added lions (MacKellar; Hughes).

86 *uti fama est.* A stock phrase (usually with *ut*), e.g. Lucretius 5. 17, 412, Virgil, *A.* 6. 14, Horace, *S.* 2. 1. 36.

87 *Tetra vagabatur solus per lustra ferarum. Lustra ferarum* is a stock phrase, e.g. Virgil, *G.* 2. 471, Sil. Ital. 3. 438, Mantuan *E.* 10. 203, Pontano, *Uran.* 3. 989, Campion, *Ad Daphnin* 8. Cf. Mantuan, *E.* 3. 144, *solivagum...per lustra ignota ferarum.*

88 *pia verba salutis. Pia verba* is a stock phrase, e.g. Ovid, *M.* 14. 813, Ausonius, *Ephem.* 2. 9, Pontano, *L.D.* 7. 11, Castiglione, *Carm.* 4. 4 and 40. Cf. Acts 13. 26 (tr. Tremellius and Beza), *sermo salutis*; Beza (*Poëmata*, 21ᵛ), *verbumque Salutis.*

89 *Lybicosque leones.* Libyan lions are a classical commonplace, e.g. Ovid, *F.* 2. 209, 5. 177–8, 371, Seneca, *Oed.* 919, Lucan 1. 206.

90–1 'Here as well as in the picture of Satan "collecting all his Serpent wiles" in *P.R.* III, 5, Milton followed the biblical conception of him as "that old serpent." (Rev. xii, 9 and xx, 2.)' (Hughes). Cf. Gen. 3. 1, *PL* 4. 347, 7. 495.

90 *velatus amictu.* With variations in the verb form, a stock phrase at the end of a line, e.g. Catullus 64. 266, Virgil, *A.* 3. 545, Ovid, *A.A.* 3. 179, *F.* 3. 363, *M.* 10. 1, Val. Flacc. 1. 659, Pontano, *Uran.* 1. 348.

92–130 This speech of reproach and exhortation has some general resemblances to speeches in P. Fletcher, *Loc.* pp. 102 f., but some such dramatic utterance was almost inevitable in both poems.

92 *Dormis nate? Etiamne tuos sopor opprimit artus?* Editors cite Homer, *Il.* 2. 23; Virgil, *A.* 4. 560: *nate dea, potes hoc sub casu ducere somnos?*; Tasso, *G.L.* 10. 8; and *PL* 5. 673, 'Sleepst thou Companion dear?' Cf. Virgil, *G.* 4. 190, *fessosque sopor suus occupat artus*; *A.* 2. 253, *sopor fessos complectitur artus.*

93 *pecorumque oblite tuorum.* Cf. Ovid, *M.* 13. 763, *oblitus pecorum...suorum. Oblite tuorum* is a stock phrase at the end of a line, e.g. Virgil, *A.* 4. 267 (*tuarum*), Ovid, *H.* 1. 41, Lucan 4. 212, Sil. Ital. 12. 69, Grotius, *Responsum J. Bavari* (*El.*, bk. 1, p. 143).

94 Bacchus is addressed as *venerande* in Ovid, *M.* 4. 22; cf. Sil. Ital. 16. 248 and the note on *El* 3. 57. The Columbia translator mistranslates—as if the word were *venerandam.* For the meaning of *diademaque triplex*, see the note on 55 above (and *ProdBom* 3. 3, *trina...corona*). For the phrase, cf. e.g. *C.P.I.* 7, 173 and P. Fletcher, *Loc.* (p. 111, line 11 from foot): *diademate Paulus | Tempora praefulgens triplici.* King James is given a *diadema triplex* in *Cantab. Dolor* (1625), pp. 26, 34, 54.

95 *Hyperboreo gens barbara nata sub axe.* MacKellar cites Virgil, *G.* 3. 381 and Ovid, *Tr.* 4. 8. 41, but Milton's phrase is closer to the *Hyperboreum... ad axem* of Juvenal 6. 470 and Buchanan, *El.* 1. 97; cf. Grotius, *Epiced. J. Heemskerckii* (*S.*, bk. 2, p. 78), *Hyperboreum...sub axem.* Milton may have intended only the common meaning, 'northern,' or he may have recalled that Diod. Sic. 2. 47 (quoted in C. Stephanus, *Dict.*) placed the Hyperboreans in the ocean beyond

Gaul; Pliny (*N.H.* 4. 12. 89) placed them behind the Rhipaean mountains. (MacKellar, augmented.)

96 *pharetrati spernunt tua jura Britanni.* A patriotic reminder both of England's prolonged friction with the papacy and final revolt and of battles won with the English longbow. Such a tribute, from the mouth of an enemy, was a natural device in such a poem; cf. Fletcher, *Loc.* pp. 112–13. The Roman poets use *pharetratus* of various peoples, e.g. Virgil, *G.* 4. 290, Horace, *C.* 3. 4. 35, Claudian 15. 32–3 (1, 100). *Iura Britannis* ends a line in Claudian 15. 19 (1, 100), Pontano, *Parth.* 2. 13. 15, and Gruter, *Del. I.P.* 1, 792.

97 *Surge, age, surge piger, Latius quem Caesar adorat.* Medieval, if not later, history offered impressive examples of the submission of emperors of the Holy Roman Empire to the popes; Burton gave a list in *Anat.* 3. 4. 1. 2 (3, 335; cf. 1, 54). Lines 97–8 ironically link the popes' earthly and heavenly power. *Surge, age* is a stock ejaculation, e.g. Virgil, *A.* 3. 169, 8. 59, 10. 241; Ovid, *A.A.* 1. 548, *H.* 14. 73, *M.* 11. 669; etc., and Milton, *CarEl* 1 and 19.

98 *Cui reserata patet convexi janua caeli.* Based of course on Jesus' saying to Peter (Matt. 16. 19, tr. Beza): *Et tibi dabo claves regni caelorum*; see the notes on 55 above and 101 below and *Lyc* 110–11. The line may be called a tissue of stock phrases. Cf. Ovid, *F.* 2. 455–6, *reserata...* | *...ianua...patet* (Fletcher); *patet...ianua* in ibid. 1. 280, Virgil, *A.* 2. 661, 6. 127; Vida, *Ad J. M. Gibertum* 165 and *C.P.I.* (Vida), 11, 19 and 112, *patet alti janua coeli;* Fletcher, *Loc.* (p. 102, lines 1–2), *patet intima Ditis | Janua ;* and *convexi caeli*, with variations, in Virgil, *A.* 4. 451, Ovid, *M.* 1. 26, Seneca, *Thy.* 993, Sannazaro, *P.V.* 1. 209, 3. 280; etc.

99 *Turgentes animos, & fastus frange procaces.* Cf. Pliny, *N.H.* 9. 58. 119, *procaci fastu* (Fletcher).

101 *Et quid Apostolicae possit custodia clavis.* 'The Roman Catholic doctrine of "the power of the keys," to which Milton here refers, is that Christ, in giving to Peter (Matt. 16. 19) the keys of the kingdom of heaven, bestowed on him ecclesiastical authority in the widest sense' (MacKellar). See his full note and references, and the notes on 55 and 98 above; also *Lyc* 110 and n.

102 *Et memor Hesperiae disjectam ulciscere classem.* Hesperia, which usually meant the west in general, here means Spain, as in Horace, *C.* 1. 36. 4 and Milton, *El* 3. 46 (see note). The reference is of course to the defeat of the Armada; cf. Fletcher, *Loc.* p. 112, and the reference to Beza in the next note. Cf. Virgil, *A.* 1. 128, *disiectam Aeneae...classem.*

103 *Mersaque Iberorum lato vexilla profundo.* Cf. Horace, *C.* 4. 4. 65, *merses profundo*; Sil. Ital. 4. 800 and Buchanan, *Sph.* 2. 194 (in the latter not the sea), *mersa profundo*; and Beza's poem on the Armada (*Poëmata*, 32ʳ), *Hispanum vasto nunc gurgite mergitur agmen.* Examples of the Latin use of *profundus* for the sea are: Ovid, *M.* 7. 65, 11. 202, 14. 223, Lucan 3. 536, 636, 651, Statius, *S.* 1. 5. 54; cf. *PL* 2. 980.

104–5 Satan naturally omits the burning of many Protestants under Mary and recalls only the Roman Catholics, conspirators and Jesuit missionaries, put to death under Elizabeth.

105 *Thermodoontea nuper regnante puella.* The Amazonian maiden is Elizabeth. The Amazons were said to live on the river Thermodon in Pontus (Diod. Sic. 2. 45–6; Herodotus 4. 110 f.; C. Stephanus, *Dict.*) and allusions were common, e.g. Virgil, *A.* 11. 659, Ovid, *P.* 4. 10. 51, Seneca, *Herc. Fur.* 246, Val. Flacc. 4. 601–5. MacKellar emends to *Thermodontea* and says: 'The common form of the Latin adjective is *Thermodontiacus* (Ovid, *Met.* 9. 189; 12. 611; Statius, *Sil.* 1. 6. 56), but Propertius 3. 14. 14, cited by Todd, may be Milton's authority for *Thermodonteus*, although the word has since been emended to *Thermodontiacis*. But Milton uses the apparently unauthorized form *Thermodoontea*, with which it is impossible properly to scan the line.' This statement is not quite clear, since Todd's Propertian word was *Thermodoontëus* (in Scaliger's ed., Antwerp, 1582, Heidelberg, 1600, it was *Thermodoonteis*). *Thermodoontaea* appears in Gruter, *Del. I.P.* 1, 750.

106 *At tu si tenero mavis torpescere lecto.* Cf. Fletcher, *Loc.* (p. 105, line 26), *Quin soliti lento Reges torpescere luxu.*

108 *Tyrrhenum...Pontum.* The part of the Mediterranean along the west side of Italy, e.g. Virgil, *A.* 1. 67, *Comus* 49. With *numeroso milite*, cf. Ovid, *H.* 16. 368, *innumeri militis*; *P.* 1. 8. 18, *innumero milite.*

109 *Signaque Aventino ponet fulgentia colle.* The Aventine is the southernmost of the seven hills of Rome. Cf. Virgil, *A.* 7. 659, *collis Aventini. Signa fulgentia* is a stock phrase, e.g. Lucan 2. 576, Sil. Ital. 3. 282, 408, Manilius 1. 667, Pontano, *Uran.* 1. 546 (cf. Horace, *C.* 1. 7. 19). Milton may have recalled Juvenal 10. 156, *media vexillum pono Subura.*

110 *Relliquias veterum franget, flammisque cremabit.* Many Catholic shrines, images, and relics had been destroyed in the reign of Henry VIII and later. Cf. Virgil, *A.* 8. 356, *reliquias veterumque* (and 1. 30, 3. 87, *reliquias Danaum*), *A.* 7. 74, *flamma...cremari.*

111   *Sacraque calcabit pedibus tua colla profanis.* Cf. Fletcher, *Loc.* (p. 106, lines 23–4): *ipsum coeli calcare tyrannum | Sub pedibus videor.* Both phrases probably go back to Joshua 10. 24 (tr. Tremellius): *imponite pedes vestros cervicibus istorum regum.* Cf. Beza (*Poëmata*, 20ᵛ), *pedibusque polos & sydera calcant*; Jewel, *Works* 4, 700 f.

112   *Cujus gaudebant soleïs dare basia reges.* MacKellar cites two Catholic documents on the kissing of the pope's feet as a symbolic form of salutation (Luke 7. 37–8; Isa. 49. 23). Cf. Mantuan, *Opera* (1502), fol. 243ᵛ; *Opera* (1513), 1, 239ʳ: *Sancta procul positi subeunt tua limina reges: | Et pedibus figunt oscula prona tuis*; P. Jovius, *C.P.I.* 5, 439: *Pontificis sanctis oscula dat pedibus*; Jewel, *Works* 3, 76 and 4, 687 f.; Fletcher, *Loc.* (p. 111, last two lines): *sacris | Blanda etiam pedibus libantes oscula Reges*; Burton, *Anat.* 1, 54.

113–15   *Nec...aperto Marte lacesses, | Irritus ille labor, tu callidus utere fraude, | ...fas est.* Protestants associated fraud with Catholics in general and Jesuits in particular. See MacKellar; Spenser's Duessa, Archimago, et al.; editors' notes on the 'equivocator,' *Macbeth* 2. 3. 9. f.; *PL* 1. 645–7, 4. 121–2; and Fletcher's *Æquivocus* (see the outline of *Locustae* in the introduction above). *Aperto Marte*, with variations in case, is a common phrase, e.g., Ovid, *M.* 13. 208–209; Seneca, *Oed.* 275; *C.P.I.* 3, 258; Grotius, *Ad. Ex.* 1922; Fletcher, *Loc.* (p. 111, line 12 from foot). *Irritus labor* is also common, e.g., Ovid, *M.* 1. 273, Seneca, *Med.* 748, Quintilian 12. 1. 13, Palingenius, *Z.V.* 9. 489, Pontano, *H.H.* 2. 97, *E.* 2. 38. Cf. Seneca, *Hipp.* 502–503, *Callidas... | ...fraudes.*

117–18   *Patricios* refers to the House of Commons, *procerum de stirpe creatos* to the peers of the House of Lords, and *Grandaevosque patres trabea, canisque verendos* to the bishops of the upper House and Privy Councillors (Masson, *P.W.* 3, 332). Fletcher, *Loc.* (pp. 116 f.) uses *Proceres, Patresque Equitesque.* In *Inaug. Reg. Brit.* (*S.*, bk. 2, pp. 59 f.), *passim*, Grotius uses *proceres.* With Milton's *procerum...creatos* cf. Ovid, *M.* 1. 760, 3. 543, 14. 699, Lucretius 1. 733. *Grandaevosque patres*, with variations in case, is in Ovid, *M.* 7. 160, Petronius, *Sat.* 123, line 230, and Buchanan, *Sph.* 1. 215. Seneca, *Herc. Fur.* 1248–9, has *venerandos... | canos.*

120   *nitrati pulveris igne.* MacKellar cites *pulvis nitratus* from Du Cange and compares *PL* 2. 936–8, 4. 814–15, 6. 512–13. Cf. *C.P.I.* 1, 31, *nitrati & pulveris ignem*; ibid. 9, 447, *Pulvere nitrato*; Fletcher, *Loc.* (p. 121, lines 8–9), *nitroso | Pulvere*; (line 2 from foot), *Pulvere sulphureo.* With *dare in cineres*, cf. Ovid, *H.* 7. 192, *dabis in cineres.*

124 *jussa facessere Papae.* Cf. *iussa facessunt* in Virgil, *A.* 4. 295 (Fletcher) and Vida, *Christ.* 1. 224; *iussa facessere divum* in M. Vegius, *Aeneid* 13. 28 (*Maphaeus Vegius and his Thirteenth Book of the Aeneid*, ed. A. C. Brinton, Stanford, 1930). **125** *Perculsosque metu subito.* Cheek (*SP* 54, 178) compares the idea of sudden fear in Virgil, *A.* 1. 92, 3. 30, 6. 559.

125 *casumque stupentes.* Warton, Todd, Keightley, Masson, MacKellar, and Hughes (1937) keep the *casuque* of 1645. Columbia editors regularly follow the 1673 text; Garrod, who gives the text of 1645, prefers here the *casumque* of 1673 (xviii, 261). The ablative seems commoner than the accusative with *stupeo* (as in 216 below), though that does not settle the question.

126 After the king and parliament had been blown up, some of the conspirators were to get aid from the Continent. See MacKellar, 276; S. R. Gardiner, *History of England . . . 1603–1642* (10 v. London, 1883–4), 1, 242–3, and *What Gunpowder Plot Was* (London, 1897), 58–9, 64–6.

127 *Saecula sic illic tandem Mariana redibunt.* Cf. Virgil, *E.* 4. 6, *redeunt Saturnia regna.* A grim pun is involved. The speaker means the age of Mary, the golden age of later English Catholicism; in Roman language (e.g. Florus 1. 47. 12; cf. 2. 13. 2) the phrase means *Mariana . . . Sullana tempestas*, the evil time of Marius and Sulla (MacKellar; Hughes). Cf. Gill, *In ruinam* (p. 11), *Marianaque precantes redire saecula*; *Cantab. Dolor* (1625), p. 65, *Mariana . . . | Asperitas.* We may remember that the Marian persecution had ended less than fifty years before the Gunpowder Plot and was still vivid in memory and hearsay (A.S.P.W.)

129–30 *divos divasque secundas | . . . numina fastis.* Pagan phrases for Catholic saints and feast days suggest an affinity with ancient polytheism. Cf. *Prod Bom* 2. 8.

132 *ad infandam, regnum illaetabile, Lethen.* Cheek (178) compares Virgil, *A.* 2. 4, *lamentabile regnum*; cf. Vida, *Christ.* 1. 179, *illaetabile regnum.* Keightley objected to Milton's using Lethe 'to express the underworld,' for which he recalled no previous instance except Statius, *Th.* 8. 97 (see MacKellar). But Lethe, though not listed with the four underworld rivers (see the note on 7 above), and though often not precisely located (e.g. Sil. Ital. 13. 554, beyond the ocean stream), is commonly placed in the underworld proper or a related region, e.g. Virgil, *A.* 6. 705, 714, 749, *Cul.* 215; Ovid, *M.* 11. 603; Seneca, *Herc. Fur.* 680 f., *Herc. Oet.* 1162; Claudian 33. 282 (2, 314), *S.P.* 52. 46 (2, 284); etc. See Osgood, *C.M.* pp. 72–3; cf. *PL* 2. 582–614.

133–4 *Jam rosea Eoas pandens Tithonia portas*, etc. A Homeric and common transition, e.g. *Od.* 5. 1–2, Virgil, *A.* 4. 584–5, 6. 535–6, Ovid, *Am.* 1. 13. 1 f.,

M. 2. 112–14, *F.* 3. 403, Milton, *El* 5. 49–50, *PL* 5. 1–2, 6. 2–4, 12–15. See the notes on *El* 5. 31, 49. With Milton's *Vestit...lumine terras,* cf. Virgil, *A.* 6. 640, *lumine vestit*; 9. 459 (end), *lumine terras.*

135–6 *Maestaque adhuc nigri deplorans funera nati | ...montana cacumina guttis.* Memnon, son of Eos (Aurora) and Tithonus and king of the Ethiopians, fought in the Trojan war and was killed by Achilles (Hesiod, *Theog.* 984–5; Homer, *Od.* 4. 188, 11. 522; Virgil, *A.* 1. 489, *nigri Memnonis arma ;* Ovid, *Am.* 1. 13. 3–4, *M.* 13. 576–622, *F.* 4. 713–14; Milton, *IlPen* 18). For Aurora's continuing to shed tears (i.e. dew) over the earth, see Ovid, *M.* 13. 621–2, and note on Milton, *EpWin* 35–46. Cf. Catullus 64. 401, *funera nati*; for *Maestaque funera,* the note on 11 above; and *montana cacumina* in Ovid, *M.* 1. 310 (Fletcher) and Claudian, *S.P.* 2. 1 (2, 174).

137 *stellatae janitor aulae.* The pope as holder of the keys of heaven (see MacKellar, Hughes, and the note on 101 above); Shawcross glosses as 'Jove.' *Stellatae...aulae* is in *Gratul. Cantab.* (1623), 7. Janus is *caelestis ianitor aulae* in Ovid, *F.* 1. 139 (this phrase is also in *Oxon. Par.* 1625, sig. D 1ᵛ); Cerberus is *immanis... | ianitor aulae* in Horace, *C.* 3. 11. 15–17, and *lacrimosae Ianitor aulae* in Sil. Ital. 2. 552; and the pope is *aethereae...janitor aulae* in *C.P.I.* 3, 488 and Gruter, *Del.I.P.* 2, 1217.

139–54 Todd found some resemblance to Claudian 3. 123–31 (1, 34); the passage is quoted in MacKellar. Cf. Claudian 5. 466 f. (1, 92). *Est locus,* with which Milton and Claudian begin, is a stock phrase, e.g. Virgil, *A.* 1. 530, 3. 163, 7. 563, Ovid, *H.* 16. 53, *F.* 4. 337, Gill, loc. cit. under 127 above.

139 *septus caligine noctis.* Cf. Sil. Ital. 11. 513, *nigrae caligine noctis*; Vida, *Ad J. M. Gibertum* 106, 171, *noctis caligine pressus* and *pressi*; Gruter, *Del. I.P.* 1, 664, *caligine septus ; Cantab. Dolor* (1625), p. 32, *caeca caligine noctis.*

140 *Vasta ruinosi...fundamina tecti.* Cf. Gill, *In ruinam* (p. 12), *Tecti ruentis machina.*

141–56 Such lists of personifications begin with Hesiod's catalogue of the children of Night; the most famous is in Virgil, *A.* 6. 274–81. Milton's list is eclectic. To quote most of MacKellar's partial summary of possible sources or analogues: 'Strife, Toil, Murders (Φόνους), and Disputes, appear in Hesiod, *Theog.* 225–30; Terror, Rout, and Strife in Homer, *Il.* 4. 440–3; Discord in Virgil, *Aen.* 6. 280; 8. 702;...*Timor* in Virgil, *Aen.* 9. 719;...*Mors* in *Aen.* 11. 197; *Fama* in *Aen.* 4. 173.' Cf. Sil. Ital. 13. 581 f.; Spenser, *F.Q.* 2. 7. 21–3, 3. 12. 7–19; the abstractions in Fletcher's *Apoll.* (1627), 1. 15–16, and *Purple*

Island (1633), 7. 14–85; Milton, *Prol* 1 (*Works* 12, 132); and the notes below on individual items.

141–2 *Phoni, Prodotaeque bilinguis | Effera quos uno peperit Discordia partu.* In Hesiod, *Theog.* 226–8, Eris gives birth to *Phonous* (Murders) along with Lying Words, Lawlessness, etc. Warton noted *Phonos* in Fletcher's *P.I.* (1633), 7. 69, and said *Prodotes* (Treason) was there too; he may have meant *Dichostasis* ('Sedition or Schisme') in 7. 61. Cf. Virgil, *A.* 1. 661, *Tyriosque bilinguis*; Claudian 15. 284–5 (1, 118), *bilingues | insidias. Discordia* is one of the commonest abstractions, e.g. Virgil, *A.* 6. 280, 8. 702; Petronius, *Sat.* 124, lines 271–95; Sil. Ital. 13. 586; Val. Flacc. 2. 204, 7. 468; Claudian 3. 30 (1, 28); Prudentius, *Psych.* 442, 477, etc.; Manilius 1. 923, *adamanteis discordia vincta catenis.* Cf. Lucretius 5. 1305, *peperit discordia tristis*; Virgil, *A.* 12. 846–7: *quas...Nox... | uno eodemque tulit partu.*

143 *praeruptaque saxa.* A stock phrase, e.g. Ovid, *R. Am.* 179, Sil. Ital. 2. 33, Sannazaro, *E.* 4. 67, *El.* 2. 4. 49 (cf. Virgil, *G.* 2. 156). In 1673 *praeruptaque* replaced the *semifractaque* of 1645, which involved a false quantity noted by Salmasius, *Responsio* (1660), 5 (quoted in French, *L.R.* 4, 345).

144 *Ossa inhumata virum, & trajecta cadavera ferro.* Cf. Buchanan, *Sat. Car. Lothar. Cardinalem* 77–8, *inhumataque passim | Ossa virum*; Ovid, *H.*1.55–6, *semisepulta virum... | ...ossa*; Virgil, *G.* 1. 497; *A.* .1 355, *traiectaque pectora ferro* (and 353, *inhumati*); Statius, *Th.* 9. 309, *traiectus pectora ferro.*

145 *Dolus*: Guile. In Cicero, *N.D.* 3. 17. 44, Val. Flacc. 2. 206, Prudentius, *Psych.* 465, Milton, *Prol* 1 (*Works* 12, 132, line 16). With *intortis...ocellis,* cf. Virgil, *G.* 4. 451, *oculos...intorsit.*

146 *stimulis armata Calumnia fauces.* I have not observed any close original for Milton's one descriptive item. Cf. *Patrem* 107 and n.; Spenser's Blatant Beast (*F.Q.* 6. 1. 8–9, 6. 12. 22 f.; Lucian's account of Apelles' picture of Slander (L.C.L. 1, 364–7); and S. C. Chew, *The Virtues Reconciled* (Toronto, 1947), 77, 86–8, 138–40. Lucian is cited by L. Giraldus, *Historiae Deorum* (*Opera*, Basel, 1580, 1, 35–6), and Sandys' description, which includes Deceit and Treachery, is loosely similar (*Ovid*, 1632, 77): 'The figure of Calumnie seemed full of hast; and although neatly trickt, yet with such a looke and gesture as expressed the wrath and rancor of her bosome. In her left hand she held a flaming fire-brand; and haled a youth with the right by the haire...' E. Panofsky gives further references (*Renaissance and Renascences*, Stockholm, 1960, 26, n. 2; and *Studies in Iconology*, 158–9).

147 *Furor* is in Seneca, *Herc. Fur.* 98, Statius, *Th.* 10. 558, Petronius, *Sat.* 124

(lines 258–63), Sil. Ital. 4. 325. With *viae moriendi mille*, cf. Tibullus 1. 3. 50, *leti mille repente viae*.

148 *Timor* is in Virgil, *A.* 9. 719 (cf. *Metus*, ibid. 6. 276); Claudian 3. 34 (1, 28): Milton, *Prol* 1 (*Works* 12, 132, line 16); Fletcher, *Apoll.* (1627), 1. 16, 'feare, fright.'

148 *exanguisque...Horror.* In Claudian 5. 130 (1, 66) (Fletcher). Cf. Seneca, *Oed.* 591, *Horror*; Spenser, *F.Q.* 2. 7. 23, 'sad Horrour', etc.; Fletcher, *Apoll.* 1. 16, 'horrour'.

149–50 *Perpetuoque leves per muta silentia Manes,* | *Exululat tellus & sanguine conscia stagnat.* This, the reading of the 1695 edition, is followed by the Columbia editors. Their textual note (*Works* 1, 587) is this: '*Exululat*] so 1673, but with a comma after the word and no comma after *Manes* (l. 149). The Errata of 1673 directs that *Exululat* stand, but that the comma after it be deleted, and a comma inserted after *Manes*. These directions were followed by 1695. This seems to be a deliberate change from the reading of 1645, *Manes* | *Exululant tellus*, in which *Manes* is the subject of *Exululant*. The change chiefly accomplished by means of the Errata of 1673 seems to have been designed to make *Manes* the subject of *circumvolant* understood [cf. *circumvolat* in 148], and *tellus* the subject of both *Exululat* and *stagnat*. Such a change, especially as the Errata had to be used to effect it completely, cannot well be regarded as accidental, or as one which a printer or publisher's proofreader would, or indeed could, have taken upon himself. It seems to come too near to a correction, made at Milton's direction, possibly only on account of the belated discovery of *Exululat* of 1673, to warrant editors like Warton and Masson in following as they do, the text of 1645...The fact that Milton, or whoever acted for him, could have restored in the Errata of 1673 the reading of 1645, but did not do it seems to determine the balance in favor of the text of 1695, which is here followed.' There seems to be no appeal against an apparently deliberate change by the author. Garrod, in *Ox. Fac.*, remarked that 'it does not follow that the change from *Exululant* to *Exululat* was deliberate'; in his 1955 edition he makes no comment. The change makes Milton's phrases less conventional but somewhat strained, as the textual comment has indicated. Examples akin to the conventionality of 1645 are: Seneca, *Thy.* 670, *ululantque manes*; Fletcher, *Loc.* (p. 110, last two lines), *ululantes* | *...manes*; Ovid, *F.* 2. 553–4: *ululasse per agros* | *deformes animas*. The idea of *Manes* [*circumvolant*], on the other hand, might be supported by, e.g. Ovid, *M.* 15. 797–8: *ululasse canes umbrasque silentum* | *erravisse ferunt*. The single activity of *tellus* in 1645 is more in keeping with such items as Sil. Ital.

12. 43–4, *stagnantia regna | sanguine* (Fletcher), ibid. 6. 36, *stagnantem caede...* *terram*, and Homeric phrases cited in *El* 4. 76 n. Milton may have some general recollection of Ovid, *M*. 14. 403–11. See Carey's extended comment on the textual problem (4).

For some details not affected by the change, Ovid (*M*. 10. 14), Seneca (*Herc. Fur.* 708, *Oct.* 522), and Horace (*C*. 1. 10. 18–19) use *levis* of the shades. *Per muta silentia* is a stock phrase, e.g. Ovid, *M*. 4. 433, 7. 184, 10. 53, Pontano, *Uran.* 3. 378, Buchanan, *S*. 2. 39; cf. *IlPen* 55. For Milton's use of *conscia* cf. Virgil, *A*. 4. 167, Ovid, *H*. 18. 105, 20. 180, *M*. 2. 438, etc., and Milton, *Naturam* 64–65, *PL* 6. 521.

153 *atrum feralibus umbris*. Cf. Lucan 6. 623, *feralis...umbra*.

155–6 The pope summons the champions of Rome, Murder and Treachery; Milton is thinking of such things as the Inquisition and the Massacre of St Bartholomew. The Babylon of Rev. 14. 8, 17. 5, was identified with Rome by such Catholics as Petrarch in Sonnet 108, part of which—as Hughes (p. 393) observes—Milton translated in *Ref* (*Works* 3, 27). Jewel lists such Catholics, *Works* 3, 81 and 4, 628, 740 f. English Protestants gladly carried on the idea: MacKellar cites John Philpot, *Examinations and Writings* (Parker Soc. 1842), 428–9, and John Bradford, *Writings* (Parker Soc. 1848–53), 1, 443–4. Cf. Jewel, *Works* 1, 401 and 4, 681; Spenser, *F.Q.* 1. 2. 13, 1. 7. 16, 1. 8. 6, 12–13, 29; Milton, *Sonn* 18.14. *Per saecula longa* is a stock phrase, e.g. Ovid, *M*. 4. 67, 15. 446 (cf. Martial 8. 8. 2).

157 *circumfusum...aequor*. Cf. Virgil, *Cir.* 493, *circumfusum aequore corpus*.

158 *Gens exosa mihi*. Cf. Juno's phrase about the Trojans, *gens inimica mihi* (Virgil, *A*. 1. 67); Gill, *In ruinam* (p. 13), *Papistae invisa gens*; Fletcher, *Loc.* (p. 102, line 11), *Coelo infensa cohors, exosa*; (p. 112, line 12), *Exosum genus*.

160 *celeri...gressu*. In Mantuan, *Cal. Temp.*, p. 21. Cf. Sil. Ital. 6. 499, *celerem gressum*, and the plural in Seneca, *Med.* 847–8.

161 *Tartareoque leves difflentur pulvere in auras*. See the notes on 120 above and *El* 3. 16. Hughes quotes an anticipatory picture of the explosion from the Jesuit speaker in Fletcher, *Loc.* (p. 116, line 10 from foot). *Leves...in auras*, in various forms, is a stock phrase, especially in Ovid, e.g. *A.A.* 3. 100, *H*. 5. 53, *M*. 1. 502–3, 529, 8. 524, 14. 432, 538, 597; Virgil, *G*. 3. 274, *A*. 11. 595.

162 *satrapae*: nobles. The word is used also in *ProdBom* 1. 1, *El* 3. 8. *Scelerata propago* appears in Petrarch, *Afr.* 6. 264; in *C.P.I.* 2, 420 and, in the same author, I. F. Bonhomus, in Gruter, *Del. I.P.* 1, 485.

164 *Consilii socios adhibete, operisque ministros.* Cf. Virgil, *A.* 5. 712, *hunc cape consiliis socium*; Lucretius 3. 61, *socios scelerum atque ministros*; and the note on 10 above.

166 *longo flectens curvamine coelos.* Editors cite Ovid, *M.* 6. 64, *inficere ingenti longum curvamine caelum* (cf. 2. 130, 3. 672, 8. 194); Ps. 18. 9 and 144. 5; and *Comus* 1014.

167 *Despicit aetherea dominus qui fulgurat arce.* A variation on a common kind of phrase, e.g. Virgil, *A.* 1. 223–4, *Iuppiter aethere summo | despiciens*; Ovid, *M.* 1. 163. *Aetherea arce*, in either number, is a stock expression, e.g. Virgilian *Cul.* 42; Ovid, *M.* 15. 858–9, *Tr.* 5. 3. 19.

168 *Vanaque perversae ridet conamina turbae.* Editors quote Ps. 2. 4: 'He that sitteth in the heavens shall laugh: the Lord shall have them in derision' (tr. Tremellius: *Sedens in caelis ridet; Dominus subsannat eos*), which is echoed in *PL* 2. 731, 5. 736–7, 8. 78. Cf. Sil. Ital. 12. 405, *risit nube sedens vani conamina coepti* (Fletcher); and P. Fletcher, *Loc.* (p. 108, line 12 from foot), *vana manu conamina ludas* (and *conamina* on p. 106, line 6, p. 120, line 8).

170 *ab Aside terra.* In Buchanan, *Sph.* 3. 170 (end). Cf. Ovid, *M.* 9. 448 (end), *in Aside terra*; 5. 648, *Asida terram*.

171 *spectat Mareotidas undas.* Lake Mareotis is west of the Nile, near Alexandria (Ovid, *M.* 9. 773, *Mareoticaque arva*). Gilbert (*MLN* 28, 1913, 30; *G.D.* 183), MacKellar, Hughes, and apparently Harding (*Ovid*, 51) take Milton to be referring, by metonymy, to Egypt and Africa in general: the tower of Fame is equidistant from Asia and Europe and faces Africa, as the House of Fame in Ovid (*M.* 12. 39–42) and Chaucer (*H.F.* 713–15) is equidistant from heaven, earth, and sea. Although the texts of both 1645 and 1673 have *Mareotidas*, Keightley, Masson (*P.W.* 3, 334), and apparently the Columbia translator have thought the word was a printer's error, that Milton wrote *Maeotidas* for Lake Maeotis, now the Sea of Azof. D. T. Starnes, in *N&Q* 196 (1951), 515–18, and Starnes-Talbert (253–7) argue further for the recognized central position of Maeotis between Europe and Asia, citing, e.g. Lucan 3. 271–8, Stephanus, *Dict.* (who quotes Lucan), Pomponius Mela 1. 1. 7–15 and Isidore of Seville, *Etymol.* (ed. W. M. Lindsay, Oxford, 1911), 14. 3; the last two in some editions had maps showing Maeotis in the center of the known world. One might add, e.g., P. Heylyn (*Microcosmus*, 1621, 283), who names *Palus Maeotis* as one of half a dozen regions of land and water by which 'Asia is separate from Europe' (cf. Strabo 7. 1. 1). But while allusions to the much more significant Maeotis are so common, and while it is possible that there was an uncorrected misprint, there seems to be no sufficient ground for altering Milton's *Mareotidas*, which makes sense.

172f. The account of Fame's tower and activities combines details from Ovid, *M.* 12. 43–63 and Virgil, *A.* 4. 173–97; the description of the tower is mainly Ovidian, the details that vivify the personified Fama are mainly from Virgil (Harding, *Ovid*, 51–3). Milton analyzed most of the Virgilian passage in his *Log*, *Works* 11, 274–8 (E. H. Riley, *SP* 26, 1929, 158, n. 11). The picture of Fama in Val. Flacc. 2. 116 f. seems to contribute nothing specific (see the note on *El* 4. 71). Editors cite some details in Chaucer, *H.F.* 714–20, 1184–1200, 1526–32. Rand (*SP* 19, 116) remarks that Milton's description 'inevitably suggests Ovid, and it lacks the incomparable grace and fluency with which in Ovid's picture each image glides, before you know it, into the current of the verse. Milton is less at his ease, but his picture is striking, and for all its borrowed details, his own.'

172 *Titanidos...Famae.* Fama was the youngest of the Titans (Virgil, *A.* 4. 178–80); cf. Ovid, *M.* 13. 968, *Titanidos...Circes.* With *turris...ardua*, cf. Ovid, *M.* 12. 43 and Virgil, *A.* 4. 186–7; the phrase is in Ovid, *M.* 11. 392.

173 *Aerea, lata, sonans.* Cf. Ovid, *M.* 12. 46, *tota est ex aere sonanti.*

174 *superimpositum vel Athos vel Pelion Ossae.* The giants, warring against the gods, according to various versions piled Pelion on Ossa (Ovid, *P.* 2. 2. 9, Statius, *Th.* 8. 79, Claudian 8. 108 and 21. 12 [1, 294, 364]), or Ossa on Pelion (Seneca, *Thy.* 811–12), or tried to heap one or both on Olympus or vice versa (Homer, *Od.* 11. 313–16, Apollodorus 1. 7. 4, Virgil, *G.* 1. 281–2, Horace, *C.* 3. 4. 52, Propertius 2. 1. 19–20, Ovid, *Am.* 2. 1. 13–14, *F.* 1. 307–8, *M.* 1. 155, Seneca, *Agam.* 346–7, *Herc. Fur.* 971–2, *Troad.* 829–30, Statius, *Th.* 6. 721–2). Athos, the peak in Macedonian Chalcidice, is usually mentioned merely as a famous mountain (Virgil, *G.* 1. 332, Ovid, *M.* 2. 217, 11. 554, Val. Flacc. 1. 664, 4. 322), but Seneca (*Herc. Oet.* 1152–3) names Athos and Pindus along with Pelion and Ossa. Cf. Claudian, *S.P.* 52. 68 (2, 284).

175 *Mille fores aditusque patent, totidemque fenestrae.* Cf. Ovid, *M.* 12. 44–6: *innumerosque aditus ac mille foramina tectis | ...nocte dieque patet*; ibid. 4. 439, *mille capax aditus et apertas undique portas*; Seneca, *Phoen.* 153, *mille ad hanc aditus patent.*

176 *Amplaque per tenues translucent atria muros.* Cf. Virgil, *A.* 1. 725–6, *per ampla... | atria.*

177 *Excitat hic varios plebs agglomerata susurros.* Cf. Ovid, *M.* 12. 47–9: *tota* *fremit vocesque refert...* | *...nec tamen est clamor, sed parvae murmura vocis*; 53: *atria turba tenet: veniunt, leve vulgus, euntque*; 61, *dubioque auctore Susurri*; Chaucer, *H.F.* 1521–5; Fletcher, *Loc.* (p. 117, line 6 from foot), *visi sub nocte susurros* | *Percipere.*

178–9 The simile of the flies, as Warton noted, is Homeric (*Il.* 2. 469–71, 16. 641–3); cf. *PR* 4. 15–17. With Milton's *circum mulctralia bombis* | *Agmina muscarum*, cf. Fletcher, *Loc.* (p. 104, lines 6 and 2 from foot), *glomerantque per auras agmina muscae*, | *...bombis.*

180 *Canis aestivum coeli petit ardua culmen.* The Dog Star is a common symbol of summer heat, e.g. Tibullus 1. 1. 27, *Canis aestivos ortus*; 1. 4. 6, *aestivi tempora sicca Canis*; 3. 5. 2, *aestivum...Canem*; Ovid, *F.* 4. 939–40; Pliny, *N.H.* 2. 40. 107. With Milton's last phrase, cf. the note on *El* 5. 15 and *petit arduus* in Ovid, *M.* 1. 316 and 2. 306 and Pontano, *Uran.*1.124; Prudentius, *C. Or. Symm.* 2. 251 and 458 (end), *ardua culmen*; Gruter, *Del.I.P.* 1, 1257, *petit ardua coeli*; 2, 546, *petere ardua coeli.*

181 *summa sedet ultrix matris in arce.* Starnes (*N&Q* 196, 1951, 515) and Starnes-Talbert (252–3) suggest that Milton knew N. Perottus' *Cornucopiae* (Venice, 1518, col. 909, 30 f.) because Perottus, under Fama, brought together the Ovidian and Virgilian passages and referred to Fama as the sister of giants and avenger of her mother Terra and because this last point is not accounted for by Ovid or Virgil. But Milton did not need to go so far afield. Virgil's story of Fama (*A.* 4. 178–80) makes Terra, *ira inritata deorum*, the mother of Fama and the two giants; see Milton's comment on the quoted phrase in *Log* (*Works* 11, 274). The point was quite clear to Bacon, who, in his discussion of poetry, just before quoting Virgil says 'the giants being overthrown in their war against the gods, the Earth their mother in revenge thereof brought forth Fame' (*Advancement of Learning, Works* 3, 345); cf. *Sap. Vet.* 9 (ibid. 6, 645, 718). The point is clear also in Ravisius Textor, *Epitome*, 125–6; Sandys, *Ovid* (1632), 27, (1640), 15. Cf. Claudian, *S.P.* 52. 1–35 (2, 280–2). *Summa...in arce* is in Ovid's account of Fama (*M.* 12. 43; Harding, *Ovid*, 52) and is, with variations, a stock phrase, e.g. Catullus 64. 241, Ovid, *M.* 1. 27, 163, *F.* 2. 70, 6. 429, *R.Am.* 57, 450, Virgil, *A.* 6. 519, 9. 86. Cf. Virgil, *A.* 4. 473, *ultricesque sedent.*

182 *Auribus innumeris cinctum caput.* Cf. Virgil, *A.* 4. 183, *tot subrigit auris*; Ovid, *M.* 12. 41–2; and *cinctum caput* in Virgil, *A.* 4. 248–9, Ovid, *M.* 1. 625, and *Cantab. Dolor* (1625), p. 26.

183–4 *sonitum exiguum...levissima...* | *Murmura.* Cf. *exiguo...sono* in Ovid, *H.* 14. 52 and *F.* 1. 344; Ovid, *F.* 3. 18, *leve murmur*; *M.* 12. 49.

184 *ab extremis patuli confinibus orbis.* Cf. Horace, *A.P.* 132, *patulumque... orbem* (metaphorical); Ovid, *M.* 12. 40, *triplicis confinia mundi.*

185–8 *Aristoride servator inique juvencae,* etc. Argus, in some accounts the son of Arestor (Ovid, *M.* 1. 624, *Arestoridae...Argo*), was set by the jealous Juno as a spy upon Io, whom she had changed into a heifer after Jupiter's affair with her (Ovid, *M.* 1. 588–667). MacKellar finds no ancient authority for Milton's use of *inique* and *immiti...vultu,* but Val. Flacc. in his full version (4. 346–421) calls Argus *durus* (383) and has him whipping Io onward. Carey finds *inique* justified by the fact of Argus's forcing Io away from her father, Inachus (Ovid, *M.* 1. 664–5). Cf. Aeschylus, *Prom.* 568–74, 677–9.

185–6 *juvencae | Isidos, immiti volvebas lumina vultu.* Io was identified with the Egyptian goddess Isis, who was represented as a woman with cow's horns (Herodotus 1. 1, 2. 41; Ovid, *A.A.* 1. 77, 3. 393, *M.* 1. 747, 9. 687–94; Val. Flacc. 4. 416–18; Comes, *Mythol.* 8. 18). See the preceding note. For *lumina vultu* at the end of a line, cf. Virgil, *A.* 6. 862, Claudian 24. 197 (2, 56).

187 *Lumina...tacito nutantia somno.* Cf. Virgil, *A.* 4. 185, *nec dulci declinat lumina somno*; Seneca, *Agam.* 714, *nutant lumina*; Mantuan, *Parthenices, lib.* 3 (*Opera,* 1502, fol. 181; Paris, 1513, tom. 1, 70ʳ), *blando nutabant lumina somno*; Secundus, *Basia* 10. 5, *oculis nutantibus.*

188 *Lumina subjectas late spectantia terras.* Cf. Ovid, *M.* 6. 66 and Buchanan, *Sph.* 2. 165, 275, *spectantia lumina*; Fletcher, *Loc.* (p. 109, line 11), *Subjectasque...terras*; *Lacrymae Cantab.* (1619), p. 65, *subiectam...terram*; *C.P.I.* 11, 456, *subjectis...terris*; Milton, *PL* 12. 640, 'the subjected Plaine.'

189 *loca luce carentia.* Cf. Ovid, *M.* 15. 531, *luce carentia regna*; Virgil, *G.* 4. 255, 472; Seneca, *Oed.* 256.

190 *radianti impervia soli.* Cf. Virgil, *A.* 8. 23, *sole repercussum aut radiantis imagine lunae.*

191 *Millenisque loquax...linguis.* Fama is *loquax* in Ovid, *M.* 9. 137 (cited in the following note) and *P.* 2. 9. 3, the Senecan *Oct.* 762, and Poliziano, *Sylvae* 1. 304 (*P.V.,* p. 301). Cf. Claudian 22. 408–9 (2, 32), *Fama loquacibus alis... | linguis et mille.* With *auditaque visaque,* cf. Virgil, *A.* 4. 83, *auditque videtque.*

192–3 *effundit temeraria, veraque mendax,* etc. As editors note, Ovid mentions *temerarius Error* (*M.* 12. 59) among the frequenters of the house of Fama. For Fama's mixture of truth and falsehood editors cite Virgil, *A.* 4. 188–90 and Ovid, *M.* 12. 54–5. Cf. also Ovid, *M.* 9. 137–9: *Fama loquax... | ...quae veris addere falsa | gaudet*; Sil. Ital. 6. 554, *vera ac ficta simul spargebat Fama*; Fletcher, *Loc.* (p. 108, lines 4–5), *mentitaque veris | Texunt.*

194–219 On 26 October Lord Monteagle—who probably knew of the plot already—received an anonymous letter (apparently from his brother-in-law Tresham, one of the conspirators) warning him to stay away from the opening of parliament. On his reporting the letter to the government, the cellar under the House of Lords was searched, the gunpowder was found, and its custodian, Guy Fawkes, arrested. The other conspirators tried to escape but were captured and executed. (MacKellar, 37; Gardiner, *Hist. Eng.* 1, 1883, 246 f.).

194 *carmine laudes.* These words also end Virgil, *A.* 8. 287.

195 *Fama, bonum quo non aliud veracius ullum.* Editors cite Virgil, *A.* 4. 174: *Fama, malum qua non aliud velocius ullum.*

196 *Nobis digna cani.* Cf. Virgil, *E.* 5. 54, *cantari dignus*; Val. Flacc. 2. 117, *digna atque indigna canentem*; Buchanan, *Iamb.* 1. 41–2: *cani | Est digna Phoebi barbito.*

198 *vaga diva.* Cf. *El* 4. 71 and note.

199 *Te Deus aeternos motu qui temperat ignes.* Cf. Virgil, *A.* 2. 154, *aeterni… ignes*; Sannazaro, *De Morte Christi* 5, *Aeternosque astrorum ignes*; Lucan 4. 109 and Secundus, *El.* 3. 11. 17, *temperat ignes*; Milton, *Prol* 7 (*Works* 12, 256, line 6): *spatia aeternis accensa atque distincta ignibus.*

199–200 The classical image of the Zeus or Jupiter who hurled thunderbolts was often applied to God—mainly by the wicked—in Milton's English poetry (*Comus* 802–4; *PL* 1. 93, 174, 258, etc.).

202 *Conjurata cohors in meque meosque Britannos.* An early hint of one of the animating ideas in Milton's prose tracts, that of the English as a chosen people who, through Wycliffe, had inaugurated the Reformation in Europe. See the anti-episcopal tracts, *passim*, and the famous phrase in *Areop* (*Works* 4, 340). Cf. Virgil, *G.* 1. 280, *coniuratos…fratres*; Fletcher, *Loc.* (p. 102, line 11), *Coelo infensa cohors*; (p. 103, line 18), *conjurato…milite*; (p. 107, line 20), *Foeda, horrenda cohors*; Beza (*Poëmata*, 30ᵛ), *coniuratos in Christi regna tyrannos*; (52ᵛ), *coniuratosque gigantas.*

203 *sceptrigero… Iäcobo.* The adjective, rare or nonexistent in ancient Latin, is common in Neo-Latin, e.g. Palingenius, *Z.V.* 5. 4; Buchanan, *Icones* 23, *Valentiniana* 3. 2 (*Epig.*, bk. 3); Grotius, *Epith. Guil.* (*S.*, bk. 3, p. 117), *In Mortem Scaligeri Epicedia* 4 (*Epig.*, bk. 1, p. 261); J. Barclay, *Poematum Libri Duo* (1615), p. 9; Campion, *Epig.* 1. 1. 12, Cf. *Cantab. Dolor* (1625), p. 54, *sceptrigeri…Iacobi* (and pp. 2 and 38, with *Carolus* and *Regis*). With *nova caedes*, cf. Virgil, *A.* 10. 515, *caede nova.*

204–10   There is some general resemblance to the despatch and flight of celestial messengers in Homer, *passim*, and Virgil, *A.* 1. 297–304, 4. 219–58. Fletcher, *Loc.* (119–21), has the *Pater rerum* send down his eagle with a message which only the royal intellect can interpret. But divine protection of Britain was inevitable in such poems.

204   *mandata Tonantis.* See the note on 199–200. The epithet for Jupiter was a . Latin commonplace, e.g. Horace, *Epod.* 2. 29; Ovid, *H.* 9. 7, *M.* 1. 170, 2. 466, 11. 198, etc.; Lucan, Seneca, Martial, and Claudian *passim.* It was taken over by Christian poets, e.g. Prudentius, *Cath.* 6. 81, 12. 83, *Apoth.* 171, *Perist.* 6. 98; Mantuan, *E.* 7. 37 (and Mustard's note); Sannazaro, *P.V.* 1. 217, 447, etc. Cf. *PL* 2. 28, 6. 491.

205   *stridentes...alas.* In various cases, a stock phrase, e.g. Virgil, *A.* 1. 397, Ovid, *M.* 4. 616, Sil. Ital. 1. 589, 9. 515, 14. 124, Vida, *A.P.* 2. 143, etc. B.A.W cites *PL* 1. 768.

207   *tubam gestat Temesaeo ex aere sonoram.* Temesa, a city of Bruttium, was famous for its copper mines, from Homer (*Od.* 1. 184) onward (Strabo 6. 1. 5). *Temesaea aera* is an especially Ovidian commonplace, e.g. *M.* 7. 207–8, *Med. Fac.* 41, *F.* 5. 441, Statius, *S.* 1. 5. 47–8.

208   *Nec mora jam pennis cedentes remigat auras.* For *Nec mora* see the note on *El* 3. 35. Editors cite Virgil, *A.* 1. 301, *remigio alarum*, 6. 19, *remigium alarum*; Milton, *Rous* 46, *PL* 2. 927–8. *Cedentes auras* is in Ovid, *M.* 10. 59; cf. Horace, *S.* 2. 2. 13, *cedentem aëra.* Editors compare *PL* 2. 841–2, 5. 269–70, 6. 72–3.

209   *cursu celeres praevertere nubes.* Editors cite Virgil, *A.* 7. 807, *cursuque pedum praevertere ventos*; 12. 345, *praevertere ventos*; *Cir.* 203, *praevertite...nubes.* Cf. Sannazaro, *El.* 2. 4. 39, *celeres praevertitur auras*; *Gratul. Cantab.* (1623), p. 38, *celeri...cursu praevertere Famam.*

210   *solis equos post terga reliquit. Solis equos*, in various cases, is a stock phrase, e.g. Ovid, *M.* 2. 154, 4. 214, Lucan 9. 853, Sil. Ital. 16. 231. *Post terga reliquit* (*relicta*, etc.) is a stock ending for a line, e.g. Juvenal 13. 16, Ovid, *M.* 2. 187, 10. 670, *F.* 4. 281, Statius, *Th.* 5. 507, Claudian 5. 245 (1, 74), 26. 297 (2, 148).

211–16   Dorian (*E.D.* 115–16) suggests that Milton may have heard details of the Gunpowder Plot in talk, since Charles Diodati's father had been a member of the household of Lord and Lady Harington, with whom the Princess Elizabeth lived: '...the conspiracy is exposed throughout the land by Rumor in a way interestingly reminiscent of the reports that led Lord Harington first to write to London for advice about protecting the Princess Elizabeth and then

to carry her off hastily from Combe Abbey to the greater safety of Coventry.'
This may have been so, although Milton's lines do not seem to contain anything
beyond common knowledge.

211 *solito de more per urbes.* The first phrase, with or without *de*, is common,
e.g. Ovid, *H.* 21. 55, 127, *P.* 3. 1. 165, Seneca, *Oed.* 374, Statius, *S.* 4. 4. 10.
Virgil (*A.* 4. 173), Ovid (*M.* 8. 267), and Seneca (*Herc. Fur.* 193) end lines
about Fama's activity with *per urbes*; cf. the note on *Eli* 9.

212 *Ambiguas voces, incertaque murmura spargit.* Fletcher, *Loc.* (p. 117, line 5
from foot), has *tenui incertas cum murmure voces,* and (p. 120, line 4), *ambiguo...
sermone,* but Milton is closer to Virgil, *A.* 2. 98–9, *spargere voces | ...ambiguas*
(Fletcher), and Ovid, *M.* 7. 821, *vocibus ambiguis*; cf. Seneca, *Hipp.* 639,
Ambigua voce. Cf. *incerto...murmure* in Ovid, *F.* 3. 273 and Lucan 9. 1008, and
murmure incerto, in different cases, in Seneca, *Thy.* 729 and Grotius, *Christus
Patiens,* Act 3 (*Poemata,* 357). B.A.W. cites *PL* 5. 703, 6. 568, 'Ambiguous words.'

215–16 *Authoresque...sceleris, nec garrula caecis | Insidiis.* See the note on
194–219 above. Milton's first phrase, in either number, is common, e.g. Cicero,
Cat. 1. 11. 27, Petrarch, *E.* 12 (*P.M.* 1, 240), Vida, *Christ.* 1. 225, 2. 974, 4. 674,
Buchanan, *Franc.* 530, *F.F.* 13. 4, Grotius, *Ps.* 82 (*S.,* bk. 1, p. 16), *Ad. Ex.* 1682.
Fletcher, *Loc.* (p. 121, line 8) has *Artificem sceleris* (in the plural in Grotius,
Inaug. Reg. Brit., *S.,* bk. 2, p. 72, and *Induciae Batav.,* ibid. p. 85); Fletcher's
criminis author (p. 121, line 18) is in Ovid, *M.* 15. 40. Cf. *fama...garrula* in
Seneca, *Herc. Fur.* 193–4 and *Oxon. Par.* (1625), sig. E 1ᵛ; and Buchanan,
Ps. 35. 4, *Caecas insidias.*

216–19 On the almost hysterical state of the king and the public mind,
MacKellar quotes a report from the Venetian ambassador (*Cal. State Papers,
Venice,* 10, 293 f.).

218 *Effaetique senes.* Fletcher, *Loc.* (p. 122, line 20) has *Nos anni premit effoeti
properata senectus*; but cf. *effeta senectus* in Virgil, *A.* 7. 440, 452, 8. 508, and
one of Erasmus' Adagies is *Effoeta senecta* (*Opera,* 2, 1703, 938). With *tantaeque
ruinae* cf. Ovid, *P.* 1. 4. 6, *tanta ruina*; Claudian, 15. 74 (1, 104), *tantae...
ruinae.*

219 *ad aetatem...omnem.* For this use of *aetas,* cf. the Ovidian *Consol.* 203,
Seneca, *Oed.* 53.

221 *Aethereus pater.* A pagan phrase given a Christian sense, e.g. Martial
9. 35. 10, 9. 36. 7, Statius, *S.* 3. 1. 108, *Th.* 11. 207, Claudian 22. 26 (2, 4),
Buchanan, *Ps.* 1. 7, 2. 4.

221 *crudelibus obstitit ausis.* In Ovid, *H.* 14. 49 (Fletcher), Secundus, *S.* 9. 141–2, and *C.P.I.* 6, 352 (or Gruter, *Del. I.P.* 2, 54). Fletcher, *Loc.* (p. 109, line 12 from foot), has *ausisque ingentibus obstant.*

222 *Papicolum; capti poenas raptantur ad acres. Papicolas* appears in Gill, *In ruinam* (p. 12), *Epith. Oxon.* (1625), sig. A4ʳ, and *Oxon. Par.* (1625), sig. D4ᵛ. Cf. Lucretius 6. 72, *poenas...acris* (Fletcher).

223 *pia thura.* A stock phrase, e.g. Ovid, *Am.* 3. 3. 33, *M.* 6. 161, 11. 577, *Tr.* 2. 59, Tibullus 2. 2. 3, Lucan 9. 996, Juvenal 13. 116, Martial 8. 8. 3, 8. 66. 1, Castiglione, *Alcon* 141.

224 *Compita laeta focis genialibus omnia fumant.* See Gardiner, *Hist. Eng.* 1 (1883), 265; *Letters of John Chamberlain,* ed. N. E. McClure (Philadelphia, 1939), 1, 213. Cf. *Genethliacum...Caroli & Mariae* (1631), p. 71: *Et caleant crebris compita laeta focis.*

226 *Nulla Dies toto occurrit celebratior anno.* Cf. Ovid, *M.* 7. 430–1: *nullus... celebratior illo | ...dies* (Fletcher).

Anno aetatis 17

Nicholas Felton (1556–5 October 1626) held the Mastership of
Pembroke Hall, Cambridge, during 1617–19 and followed Andrewes
as Bishop of Ely, 1619–26. He was a learned and amiable man and a
noted preacher, whose virtues of head and heart received the praise of
Fuller (*Church History of Britain*, ed. J. S. Brewer, 6 v. London, 1845,
6, 63; MacKellar, 48–9). The 'great...conformity' that Fuller saw
between Felton and the far more prominent Andrewes seems, along
with their being 'both great scholars, painful preachers in London for
many years,' to have been in their partly parallel careers: both were
'scholars, fellows, and masters of Pembroke Hall...both successively
bishops of Ely.' Andrewes had died on 25 September. Some discussion
of the date and character of the poem on Felton will be found in the
introduction to *Elegy* 3 (Andrewes), which is so closely parallel in
length, structure, and manner (though the piece on Felton is in iambic
verse of alternate trimeters and dimeters). Hanford ('Youth,' 99–100),
after remarking on the heavenly vision in the elegy on Andrewes, says
of that on Felton: 'In the second piece he forbears to repeat the description of the Heaven of Heavens, but elaborates instead the journey on
which he is borne by the Muse into the broad spaces of the sky, ... to the
threshold of Olympus. The theme is an equally congenial one and fore-
shadows some of the best known and most characteristic passages in his
mature poetry.' Comments by H. Maclean are quoted in the introduction to *El* 3.

NOTES

1–6 See the introduction to *El* 3.

1 *madentes rore squalebant genae*. Partly similar phrases are common, e.g. Catullus 68A. 16, *tristique imbre madere genae*; Ovid, *A.A.* 3. 378, *lacrimis... madere genas*, and *M.* 10. 46, *Tr.* 1. 9. 34, *Ibis* 100; Prudentius, *Perist.* 6. 82, *genas madentes*; Sannazaro, *E.* 1. 116, *Exhaustae maduere genae*; Sil. Ital. 4. 455 and Grotius, *Epist. Palladii* (*El.*, bk. 1, p. 156), *maduere genae*. Cf. *rore* with *madentes* in Lucan 4. 316, with *madentem* in Virgil, *A.* 5. 854, with *madens* in Statius, *Th.* 5. 198.

2–4 *sicca nondum lumina; | Adhuc liquentis imbre turgebant salis, | Quem nuper effudi pius*. Cf. Tibullus 1. 1. 66, *lumina...sicca*; Lucan 9. 1044, *sicco lumine*; Propertius 1. 21. 3, *nostro gemitu turgentia lumina*; Statius, *S.* 5. 2. 4, *turgentes impellunt lumina guttas*; Lucretius 1. 125, *lacrimas effundere salsas*. For *imber* as 'tears' cf. Catullus, cited under 1 above, and Ovid, *Tr.* 1. 3. 18. The semicolon after *lumina*, introduced in 1673, we may, with Garrod (xix), call a misprint.

5 *maesta charo justa persolvi rogo*. Cf. Seneca, *Oed.* 998, *iusta persolvi patri*; Q.Curtius 6. 6. 19, *ut iusta fratri persolveret*; Castiglione, *Alcon* 102, *Debita nec misero persolvi justa sodali*; *Cantab. Dolor* (1625), p. 2, *persolvit iusta Iacobo*.

6 The Columbia translator makes a slip in rendering *Wintoniensis praesulis* as 'the Bishop of Ely' instead of 'the Bishop of Winchester.'

7–8 *centilinguis Fama (proh semper mali | Cladisque vera nuntia)*. Cf. *QNov* 172–93 and notes. *Centilinguis* may be Milton's coinage, on the model of *centimanus* and *centoculus* (MacKellar); cf. Claudian 22. 408–9 (1, 32), *Fama... | ...linguis et mille*. For Milton's last phrase see the note on *El* 4. 71 and Livy 5. 50. 5, *vocis...quae nuntia cladis*; Ovid, *M.* 6. 654, *nuntia cladis* (and 11. 349–50); Grotius, *Ad. Ex.* 496, *nuntia cladis face*.

9 *Spargit per urbes*. Cf. Ovid, *M.* 8. 267, *sparserat Argolicas nomen vaga fama per urbes*; and *QNov* 211–12 and notes.

10 *Populosque Neptuno satos*. For Albion, son of Neptune and a legendary king of Britain, see *QNov* 3, 27–9, and *El* 1. 73, and notes. Cf. Mantuan, *Apoloniae Agon* (*Opera*, 1502, fol. 238ᵛ; Paris, 1513, Tom. 1, fol. 171ʳ), *neptunicolasque britannos*.

11 *ferreis sororibus*. The Fates. Cf. Ovid, *M.* 15. 781, *ferrea...decreta sororum* (Fletcher). See *ProdBom* 1. 7 n.

12 *Te generis humani decus.* Cf. Lucretius 3. 3, *te...O Graiae gentis decus*; Senecan *Oct.* 534, *Claudiae gentis decus.*

13–14 *Qui rex sacrorum... | ...nomen Anguillae tenet.* Most translators give 'king of holy men' or a similar phrase. *Rex sacrorum* (e.g. Ovid, *F.* 1. 333) was a Roman priestly title surviving from the early times when kings had sacerdotal duties. According to Bede, *Hist. Eccles.* 4. 19 (Migne, *Pat. Lat.* 95, 204: see MacKellar), 'Elge' (Ely) received its name, 'eel-island,' because it was virtually an island and because the fens harbored many snakes (*anguilla*, eel). The etymology is supported by Bosworth-Toller, *Anglo-Saxon Dictionary.* Bede is cited by Camden, *Britain* (tr. 1610), 492.

15–16 *ira... | fervida.* Cf. *fervidus ira* in Virgil, *A.* 8. 230, 9. 736.

17 *Tumulis potentem saepe devovens deam.* The goddess may be Libitina (cf. *El* 3. 4), *Mors* (cf. *El* 3. 6, *Eli* 31 f.), or Proserpine (*Procan* 37 and n.). For *devovens*, see Ovid, *Ibis* (the poem Milton refers to in 18 f.), 55, 56, 95.

18 *Naso in Ibida.* During his exile Ovid wrote *Ibis* (*The Crane*), an invective against an enemy who has not been identified and was probably fictitious (L. P. Wilkinson, *Ovid Recalled*, 355).

19 *alto...pectore.* For this stock phrase see the citations under *El* 3. 31.

21–2 *Turpem Lycambis... | Sponsamque Neobolen suam.* The early Greek poet Archilochus, when his promised bride, Neobule, was refused him by her father Lycambes, was said to have attacked him with such savage invective that he hanged himself. In *Areop* (*Works* 4, 300) Milton says the Spartans drove the poet out of the city. Starnes-Talbert (238–9) quote entries from C. Stephanus, *Dict.*, which give this last item as well as the rest of the story. There are brief allusions in Ovid, *Ibis* 53–4, 521–2; Horace, *Epod.* 6. 11–13, *Ep.* 1. 19. 25 and 30–1 (where Neobule is *sponsae*); Martial 7. 12. 6; *Epig. Gr.*, pp. 191–3; *Cam. Insig.* (1624), sig. A2ᵛ: *impendent tibi tristia fata Lycambae, | Cum gravis Archilochus, cum forte reciprocus Index | Prodeat*; *Oxon. Par.* (1625), sig. H4ᵛ; Gill, *Dispensatio* (1629: p. 32).

24 *imprecor neci necem.* For a few examples of this especially Ovidian kind of verbal play see the note on *El* 7. 59. Editors cite Hosea 13. 14 and W. Browne, *On the Countess Dowager of Pembroke.* Cf. Rev. 6. 8; Donne, 'Death be not proud.'

27 *Caecos furores.* In either number, in Horace, *Epod.* 7. 13, Seneca, *Herc. Fur.* 991, *Thy.* 27, Vida, *Christ.* 2. 35, Buchanan, *Bapt.* 297, Grotius, *Ad. Ex.* 1711, etc. The dead bishop's imagined speech begins here.

27-8 *pone vitream | Bilemque & irritas minas.* 'Greek medical writers attributed madness to a peculiar condition of the black bile. . .which they described as having a specially glittering appearance (Galen. . .*Opera Omnia*, ed. by Kuhn, 7. 245)' (MacKellar). MacKellar cites Horace, *S*. 2. 3. 141, *splendida bilis*; Persius 3. 8, *vitrea bilis*; Burton, *Anat*. 1. 1. 3. 1 f.; see L. Babb, *Elizabethan Malady* (East Lansing, 1951), 21 f. *Irritas minas* is in Buchanan, *Ps*. 2. 4, 37. 13 (cf. *Ps*. 37. 8, *Compesce bilem*).

30 *Subitoque ad iras percita.* Cf. *ira. . .percitus* in Lucretius 5. 399; *percitus ira* in *C.P.I.* 4, 142, 263, etc., and Grotius, *Historia Ionae* (*S*., bk. 1, p. 8).

31-4 The lines summarize and reject pagan notions of death, as a prelude to the dead bishop's Christian view. Cf. *El* 2 and 3, *Procan* 5, and *Eli* 17.

32 *Mors atra Noctis filia.* In Hesiod, *Theog.* 758-9, Sleep and Death are the children of dark Night; cf. Homer, *Il.* 14. 231, Cicero, *N.D.* 3. 17. 44. Milton refers to the Homeric passage in *Prol* 1 (*Works* 12, 146). *Mors atra* is a stock phrase, e.g. Horace, *C*. 1. 28(1). 13, Ovidian *Consol.* 360, Tibullus 1. 3. 5, 1. 10. 33, Seneca, *Oed.* 164, etc.

33 *Erebove patre creta.* See the note on *QNov* 69.

33 *Erinnye.* The Furies were commonly three earth-born monsters who avenged crime (Hesiod, *Theog.* 185; Homer, *Il.* 19. 259; Aeschylus, *Eumen.*; Euripides, *Orest.* 255-61; Ovid, *M*. 4. 452, 490 f., 8. 481; Apollodorus 1. 1. 4). Homer sometimes (*Il.* 19. 87, *Od.* 15. 234) has only one Fury. Cf. *Comus* 640, *Lyc* 75, *PL* 2. 596, 671, 6. 859, 10. 560, *PR* 4. 422 (MacKellar). Carey notes the single Erinys in Virgil, *A*. 7. 447, and Ovid, *M*. 1. 241, 4. 490.

34 *Vastove nata sub Chao.* In Hesiod, *Theog.* 116 (cf. Virgil, *G*. 4. 347, *A*. 4. 510), Chaos first came into being, then Earth. Milton quotes Hesiod, line 123, in *Prol* 1 (*Works* 12, 126). In Ovid, *M*. 1. 5-20, Chaos is rather cosmic than mythological (MacKellar). From Milton's phrase here, as Hughes says, 'it is hard to tell whether Chaos is regarded as a place or a deity.' Cf. Ovid, *M*. 10. 30, *F*. 1. 103 f., 4. 600; *PL* 2. 890 f. and notes; Osgood, *C.M.* 21-2; and Harding (*Ovid*, 70), who cites Renaissance readings of Ovid, M. 14. 404, and comments on the notion of Chaos as a deity.

35-6 *Ast illa caelo missa stellato, Dei | Messes ubique colligit.* Editors cite Rev. 14. 14-16, which, in part, Beza renders: *Misit igitur is qui insidebat nubi falcem suam in terram, & demessa est terra.* For the biblical metaphor of harvesting, and the word *messis*, cf., in Tremellius and Beza, Jer. 8. 20, 51. 33, Joel 3. 13, Matt. 9. 37-8, 13. 39. Cf. Buchanan, *Sph.* 1. 586, *stellati tegmine coeli.*

37–8 *Animasque mole carnea reconditas | In lucem & auras evocat.* Starting from such passages as Plato, *Phaedo* 64 and 82, and Cicero, *De Senectute* 21–2, *Somnium Scip.* (*Rep.* 6), and *Tusc.* 1. 19. 44 f., and from Christian writings, the idea of the rebirth through death of the flesh-bound, earth-bound soul became a central tenet of Christian Platonism. Cf. Davies, *Nosce Teipsum*; Donne, *Second Anniversary* 165–84 and *passim*; Drummond, *A Cypress Grove*; Browne, *Religio Medici* 1. 37–9, etc.; *Comus* 458–68; and the note on 46 below. Milton uses images associated with Mercury, the conductor of the shades, e.g. Virgil, *A.* 4. 242, *animas ille evocat Orco*, and 6. 749–51; cf. Prudentius, *C. Or. Symm.* 1. 91, *in lucem revocasse animas.*

39–40 *fugaces excitant Horae diem | Themidos Jovisque filiae.* In Hesiod, *Theog.* 901, the Hours are daughters of Zeus and Themis (Justice); in Ovid, *M.* 2. 26, 118 (cf. *F.* 1. 125), and Statius, *Th.* 3. 410, they attend the Sun-god. For Milton's adjective cf. Horace, *C.* 2. 14. 1–2, *fugaces… | …anni*; Ovid, *M.* 2. 118, *velocibus…Horis.* For other classical personifications of the Hours, cf. Milton, *Sonn* 1. 4, *Time* 2, *Comus* 985, *PL* 4. 267, 6. 3. (MacKellar, augmented.)

43 *furvi…Tartari.* See the note on *El* 3. 16.

44 *Sedesque subterraneas.* Cf. Juvenal 2. 149, *subterranea regna*; Ovid, *M.* 15. 772, *sedesque…silentum.*

45–54 Early editors thought that lines 27–44 were a speech delivered by Death and that in 45–68 the poet spoke in his own person. Masson (*P.W.* 3, 336–7) first pointed out that lines 27–68 are uttered by the dead bishop—as Cowper had understood in translating the poem (MacKellar).

46 *Foedum reliqui carcerem.* The loathsome prison of both the flesh and earthly life (both meanings are classical). Cf. the note on 37–8 above; Cicero, *Tusc.* 1. 30. 74 (of death), *illa vincla carceris ruperit* (and 1. 31. 75); Chaucer, *Knight's Tale* 3061, 'this foule prisoun of this lyf'; Calvin, *Inst.* 3. 9. 4 (*Opera*, 9, 1667, 187): *Si liberari a corpore, est afferi in solidam libertatem, quid aliud est corpus quam carcer? Si Dei praesentia frui suprema felicitatis summa est, nonne ea carere miserum?*; Sylvester, *D.W.W.* 1. 6. 842–3; Gill, *In…obitum Henrici, Principis Walliae* (p. 3): *corporisque ergastulo | Nondum solutos*; Milton, *Prol* 7 (*Works* 12, 266, line 1): *non contentus iste spiritus tenebricoso hoc ergastulo.*

47 *Volatilesque faustus inter milites.* For similar references to angels, cf. Milton, *Circum* 1, 'winged Warriours'; Sannazaro, *P.V.* 1. 20–1, *aetheris alti | Militia est*; H. Vaughan, *Peace.*

48 *Ad astra sublimis feror.* Similar phrases, not with the same meaning, are common, e.g. Virgil, *E.* 5. 52, *A.* 1. 259, 9. 641; Horace, *C.* 1. 1. 36; Ovid, *M.* 15. 875-6, *super alta perennis | astra ferar*; Seneca, *Herc. Fur.* 958, *in alta mundi spatia sublimis ferar*; Claudian 7. 158-9 (1, 282), *securus ad astra | . . . ferar.*

49-50 *Vates ut olim raptus ad coelum senex | Auriga currus ignei.* For the translation of Elijah to heaven, see 2 Kings 2. 11 (tr. Tremellius): *ut ecce currus igneus & equi ignei separationem facerent inter utrosque: sic ascendit Elija turbine in caelum.* Cf. Milton, *El* 4. 97, *ProdBom* 1. 7-8, *PL* 3. 522, *PR* 2. 16-17. Cf. 2 Cor. 12. 2 (tr. Beza): *Novi hominem. . .raptum in tertium usque caelum*; Prudentius, *Cath.* 7. 31 f. (on 'Elias'): *sed mox in auras igneis iugalibus | curruque raptus evolavit praepete*; Ausonius, *Ephem.* 3. 40-2; Vida, *Christ.* 1. 949-51, and 2. 398-400: *haec rapido gens turbine quondam | Sublatum vatem coeli per aperta repente | Vidit flammifero ferri super aethera curru.*

51-64 For the flight of the soul through the stars to heaven, editors cite pagan and Christian parallels: Cicero, *Somnium Scip.* (*Rep.* 6. 15 f.); Ovid's account of Phaethon, *M.* 2. 167 f.; Dante, *Parad.* 1 f.; Chaucer, *H.F.* 529 f., *P.F.* 29 f.; Sylvester, *D.W.W.* 1. 4. 12-21; Donne, *Second Anniversary* 185-210.

51-2 *Non me Boötis terruere lucidi | Sarraca tarda frigore.* The pattern of 51 may echo Virgil, *A.* 12. 894-5: *non me tua fervida terrent | dicta*; cf. Milton, *El* 5. 91. The constellation Bootes, 'the Ploughman,' which follows 'the Wain' or the Great Bear, contains the bright Arcturus (hence *lucidi*); cf. Seneca, *Agam.* 70, *lucida versat plaustra Boötes*; Cicero, *N.D.* 2. 42. 110. Ancient poets often referred to its slow setting: Homer, *Od.* 5. 272, Catullus 66. 67, Ovid, *M.* 2. 176-7, *F.* 3. 405, Senecan *Oct.* 233-4, Claudian 21. 123 (1, 372), 35. 190 (2, 332). For Milton's phrase editors cite Juvenal 5. 23, *frigida circumagunt pigri serraca Bootae.* Starnes-Talbert (241-2) take Milton's spelling *sarraca* and his use of *tardus* as pointing to Stephanus' *Dict.* (which quotes Juvenal, with *sarraca*); but, out of a random six editions of Juvenal, 1583-1620, four, including Farnaby's, read *sarraca*, and Bootes is *tardus* in Catullus, Ovid, *M.* 2. 177, Seneca (loc. cit.), Claudian 21. 123, Boethius, *C.P.* 4, met. 5. 3, and in Grotius, *Inaug. Reg. Brit.* (*S.*, bk. 2, p. 65).

54 *Formidolosi Scorpionis brachia.* Editors cite Virgil, *G.* 1. 34-5: *bracchia contrahit ardens | Scorpios*; and Ovid, *M.* 2. 82-3, 195-200. Cf. Horace, *C*, 2. 17. 17-18, *Scorpios. . . | formidolosus* (Fletcher), and the lines translated from Aratus in Cicero, *N.D.* 2. 42. 107-9.

54 Orion is regularly represented with a sword, e.g. Ovid, *A.A.* 2. 55-6. *comesque Bootae | Ensiger Orion*; *M.* 8. 207, 13. 294, *F.* 4. 388; Lucan 1. 665;

Seneca, *Herc. Fur.* 12; Manilius 1. 391; Claudian 28. 176–7 (2, 86); Statius, *S.* 1. 1. 44–5; Sannazaro, *P.V.* 3. 125 (following a reference to Bootes, 121–2); Pontano, *Uran.* 3. 565 f., 738–40, *Met.* 1322–3.

55 *Praetervolavi fulgidi solis globum.* Cf. Lucretius 5. 471–2, *solis lunaeque... | ...globi*; the note on *Idea* 18; and Prudentius, *Cath.* 1. 9, *solis ortum fulgidi.*

56–8 *Longeque sub pedibus deam | Vidi triformem, dum coercebat suos | Fraenis dracones aureis.* The moon as the triune divinity, Luna, Diana, and Proserpine or Hecate (Comes, *Mythol.* 3. 15–18; C. Stephanus, *Dict.*, 'Hecate'; T. W. Baldwin, *William Shakspere's Small Latine & Lesse Greeke*, Urbana, 1944, 2, 436 f.; Harding, *Ovid*, 49–50). Cf. Virgil, *A.* 4. 511, *tergeminamque Hecaten, tria virginis ora Dianae*; the *diva* or *dea triformis* of Horace, *C.* 3. 22. 4, Ovid, *M.* 7. 94, and Sil. Ital. 1. 119–20; Ovid, *H.* 12. 79, *triplicis...Dianae*; *F.* 1. 141–2, 389; Seneca, *Hipp.* 412, *Hecate triformis.* Since no classical authority has been found for Luna's—or Cynthia's (*Il Pen* 59)—driving a yoke of dragons (Osgood, *C.M.*, 28–29), it has been suggested (Keightley, MacKellar) that Milton confused Luna with Ceres, who had a dragon team (Ovid, *M.* 5. 642–3, etc.). But Milton was unlikely to err on such an item without authority. Harding (loc. cit.), following Baldwin and R. K. Root on Shakespeare, pointed out that the Ovidian 'Medea's prayer to Hecate and other divinities was followed soon afterwards by the descent of a dragon-drawn chariot' (Ovid, *M.* 7. 218–19), and that 'apparently some of Ovid's Renaissance commentators thought that he strongly implied Hecate's ownership, for they do not hesitate to attribute the chariot to her.' The dragons of Hecate–Luna–Diana were familiar in English, e.g. Marlowe, *H. and L.* 1. 107–11; Shakespeare, *Dream* 3. 2. 379, 'night's swift dragons,' and 5. 391, 'the triple Hecate's team'; *Man in the Moone* 431 (Drayton, 2, 585): 'Calls downe the Dragons that her Chariot draw.' With Milton's phrasing cf. Virgil, *E.* 5. 57: *sub pedibusque videt nubes et sidera Daphnis*; *G.* 1. 243, *sub pedibus Styx atra videt*; Ovid, *M.* 5. 643, *frenisque coercuit*; Q. Curtius 3. 13. 11, *aurei freni.*

59 *Erraticorum syderum.* The planets or wandering stars, as distinguished, in the old astronomy, from the fixed stars. Cf. Jude 13 (tr. Beza), *stellae erraticae*; A. Gellius 3. 10. 2, *stellas...'erraticas,'* and 14. 1. 11; Hyginus, *Poet. Astron.* 2. 42; Cicero, *Div.* 2. 42. 89, 2. 71. 146; Seneca, *Quaestiones Naturales* 7. 23 f.

60 *lacteas...plagas.* The Milky Way. Commentators cite Ovid, *M.* 1. 168–9, *via... | lactea*; Statius, *S.* 1. 2. 51 and Ausonius, *Versus Pasch.* 7 (1, 36), *plaga lactea* (Fletcher). This last phrase is also in Sannazaro, *El.* 1. 7. 36. Cf. Milton, *El* 1. 58, *PL* 7. 577–81.

62–3 *nitentes ad fores | ...Olympi.* Olympus is of course the Christian heaven (cf. *PL* 3. 501–9). Editors cite Rev. 21. 11, which Beza renders: *Habentem gloriam Dei: & cujus lumen* erat *simile lapidi pretiosissimo, tamquam lapidi jaspidi instar crystalli splendenti*; and 21. 21: *Duodecim autem portae, duodecim margaritae sunt, & singulae portae ex singulis margaritis sunt: & e platea civitatis, aurum purum tamquam vitrum perlucidum*; and Ovid's picture of the Sun's palace, *M.* 2. 1 f. Cf. Seneca, *Herc. Oet.* 1438, *video nitentem regiam clari aetheris.*

63 *regiam Chrystallinam.* Milton is presumably thinking only of the crystalline city of heaven and not of the ninth or crystalline sphere. Cf. Rev. 21. 11 and 21, quoted in the preceding note; Sannazaro, *P.V.* 1. 216, *Crystalli domus*; *Cantab. Dolor* (1625), p. 29, *crystallina tecta.*

64 *Stratum smaragdis Atrium.* Cf. Ovid, *M.* 2. 24, *in solio Phoebus claris lucente smaragdis*; Rev. 21. 11 and 21 (quoted under 62–3 above); Rev. 21. 19, *smaragdus*; 4. 4 (quoted under *Patrem* 30–7).

65–7 *nam quis effari queat | Oriundus humano patre | Amoenitates illius loci.* MacKellar cites 1 Cor. 2. 9, which Beza renders: *Sed praedicamus, sicut scriptum est, quae oculus non vidit, nec auris audivit, nec in mentem hominis venerunt, quae paravit Deus iis a quibus ipse diligitur.* Cf. Lucretius 2. 991–2: *Denique caelesti sumus omnes semine oriundi; | omnibus ille idem pater est.* Milton copied this bit of Lucretius into his text of Aratus (*Works* 18, 325; M. Kelley and S. D. Atkins, *PMLA* 70, 1955, 1092, 1102). Cf. Gill, *In ruinam* (p. 13), *Satanae oriundi, Iesuitae, semine.*

68 *Sat est in aeternum frui.* Cf. the quotation from Calvin under 46 above; Castiglione, *Alcon* 96: *Alcone & frueris dulci, aeternumque frueris.*

Naturam non pati senium

❧

On 2 July 1628 Milton wrote to his friend Gill that he was sending him a printed copy of a poem he had lately produced: '...a certain Fellow of our College who had to act as Respondent in the philosophical disputation in this Commencement chanced to entrust to my puerility the composition of the verses which annual custom requires to be written on the questions in dispute, being himself already long past the age for trifles of that sort, and more intent on serious things' (*Works* 12, 11). It has commonly been assumed that these verses were *Naturam non pati senium*, though they might equally well have been the other philosophical piece, *De Idea Platonica*. There is no proof that either poem is the one mentioned in the letter, but nothing else among the published poems fits the occasion. Masson, after thorough investigation, had little doubt that *Naturam* was the poem sent to Gill.[1]

W. R. Parker ('Notes,' 123–4; *Milton*, 773–4, n. 79) does not accept either poem as the one referred to in Milton's letter. He notes that in the editions of 1645 and 1673 *Naturam* followed the elegy on the Bishop of Ely (late 1626) and preceded the undated *Idea Platonica*, and that the next piece that can be confidently dated is the Greek translation of Psalm 114 (1634). *Naturam* is obviously an academic exercise; 'The problem is to find the occasion which prompted it.' After speaking of the

---

[1] *P.W.* 1, 289. In the manuscript of Thomas Baker, the Cambridge antiquary, Masson found a record of divinity respondents and their subjects for the Commencement of July 1628, but nothing about the philosophical 'act' (ibid. 291–2), Two Latin poems, akin to Milton's in character and date, are quoted and discussed in W. T. Costello's fresh and lively account of Cambridge disputations, *The Scholastic Curriculum at Early Seventeenth-Century Cambridge* (Cambridge, Mass., 1958), 18 f., 172–3.

Carey thinks that Milton's description, *leviculas illiusmodi nugas* (see text above) fits *Idea* far better than the serious *Naturam*, but in *Patrem* 115 he describes as *lusus* (sports, diversions) his *juvenilia carmina*, which include the *Nativity* and other serious poems in English and Latin.

traditional assumption, and quoting Milton's letter, Parker proceeds ('Notes'):

'This, of course, is no identification of *Naturam non pati senium;* the verses *De Idea Platonica* would suit as well; indeed, they are more "frivolous." But beginning with Todd (in 1801), editors and critics have found support for their guess in the fact that George Hakewill's *Apologie* (a "Censure of the Common Errour Touching Nature's Perpetual and Universal Decay") had been published in the preceding year, 1627. That the Cambridge authorities chose a "timely" topic for the philosophical disputation in 1628 is, of course, only another conjecture. It may be true, but it is no more nearly true now as a result of a century and a half of uncritical repetition. Against it is the possibility (to my mind, the probability) that Milton may later have decided against including among his collected poems a piece which he had hastily ghost-written for another person. Against it is the fact that *Naturam no pati senium* owes absolutely nothing to Hakewill's book unless it be the general subject, which was not even of Milton's choosing if the general conjecture be right.

'A printed copy of the poem distributed at the Commencement of 1628 may eventually come to light, and then we shall know something. Meanwhile, there seems to be only one factor worth serious consideration in tentative dating of both *Naturam non pati senium* and *De Idea Platonica.* That is Milton's omission of his age in these two instances, although he had dated twelve other poems as written when he was twenty or younger.[11] In the absence of other evidence I submit that both of these poems belong to the period 1630–1632, and are academic exercises of his last years at Cambridge.'

While Parker's close scrutiny of traditional assumptions is always salutary, and while the particular one he here controverts does not rest on what can be called positive evidence, his own solution (cf. Shawcross, *C.E.P.* 550) is pure and questionable conjecture. Whatever his Commencement verses were, Milton presumably knew they would be printed, and for that as well as other reasons he would not spare pains. So far as we know, he was not given to discarding things he had written, and he would not be likely to throw away a piece that had been printed for academic circulation; and both *Naturam* and *De Idea Platonica* are

---

[11] *Naturam non pati senium* is a longer poem than five for which Milton gave his age; *De Idea Platonica* is longer than one, the *Elegia Secunda.* [Parker's note.]

better than some other poems that he chose to publish. His omitting dates does not prove anything; he did not date poems of such length and personal significance as the early *El* 1 and the later *El* 6, *Ad Patrem*, *Mansus*, and *Epitaphium Damonis*. It is not necessary to assume that the Cambridge authorities' choice of a subject was prompted by the appearance of Hakewill's book, since the question of nature's decay had been active for a long time; and we do not know how close *Naturam* might have been to the chosen topic, or how much latitude was allowed the poet (Dorian, *English Diodatis*, 117). Nor—as the notes below indicate—is it possible to say that *Naturam* owed nothing to Hakewill's book except the general subject. Finally, there is no external or internal support for the suggestion that both philosophical poems belong to the years 1630–2. Both, with their flamboyant rhetoric and profusion of mythology, seem to associate themselves with the earlier Latin poems and the earlier prolusions; it is hard to imagine either as written in the period of *L'Allegro*, *Il Penseroso*, and the seventh Prolusion. For want of evidence, therefore, we may think that 1628 is a reasonable date for either *Naturam* or *De Idea Platonica*, that one of the two was the poem referred to in Milton's letter, and that the other was not far removed from it in time of composition.

In regard to *Naturam*, some other small straws point toward 1628. Parker has argued (*TLS*, 17 December 1938) that *On the Death of a Fair Infant* was written in that year, presumably in the first third of it (in the summer, says Fletcher, *Intell. Dev.* 2, 455–6). While we might not expect affinities between an English and a Latin poem on such different subjects, actually the *Fair Infant* contains many parallels with *Naturam*: allusions to Venus and Adonis (*FInf* 5–7; *Naturam* 62–3); 'grim Aquilo' (*FInf* 8) and *Trux Aquilo* (*Naturam* 55); Apollo and Hyacinth (*FInf* 23–7; *Naturam* 62–3); 'that high first-moving Spheare' (*FInf* 39), *rota prima* (*Naturam* 37); 'the ruin'd roofe / Of shak't Olympus' and 'carefull' Jove's restoring a star (*FInf* 43–46) and the convulsions the supposedly *imprudens Jupiter* could have prevented and God's founding the stars more firmly (*Naturam* 8–36); the war of the giants and gods (*FInf* 47–8; *Naturam* 14–15, 31–2); the gods' visiting the earth to do good (*FInf* 50, 55–6) and the mainly beneficent planetary gods (*Naturam* 39–50); the end of the world (*FInf* 77; *Naturam* 65–9). Granted that most of these are, individually, stock items, their coming together in these very dissimilar poems suggests that they were running in the writer's mind about the same time.

Modern scholarship has shown how conspicuous, in English writing of the late sixteenth and early seventeenth centuries, was the idea of the decay of nature, and how it was opposed by supporters of the rising doctrine of progress.[3] Since the subject is both familiar and complex, only a broad and unqualified summary can be given here. In the Christian world-view inherited from the Middle Ages (see, e.g. C. S. Lewis, *The Discarded Image*, Cambridge, 1964), man's life on earth was only a prelude to eternity and amelioration of that life was not a prime concern; nature was to be contemplated rather than investigated and controlled. Along with acceptance of things as they are went belief in a fixed cosmos, which comprised the pure and unchanging world beyond the moon and the flux of nature on the base earth. A fixed view of history comprised the two thousand years before Moses, the two thousand of the Law, and the two thousand of the Christian era. As Donne could say, more than three-quarters of this last were already spent: and for Sir Thomas Browne, born in 'this setting part of time,' it was too late to think of lasting monuments. In his seventh Prolusion of 1631–2 (?), Milton put this pessimistic view in the mouth of Ignorance, and opposed to it the immortality of the well-deserving (*Works* 12, 279–81).

The revival of the classics, the expansion of the known world, and the growth of secular knowledge in general could foster both pessimism and optimism. On the one hand, modern man seemed immeasurably inferior

---

[3] See, e.g., J. B. Bury, *The Idea of Progress* (London, 1920); George Williamson, 'Mutability, Decay, and Seventeenth-Century Melancholy,' *ELH* 2 (1935), 121–50 (repr., *Seventeenth Century Contexts*, Chicago, 1961); Richard F. Jones, *Ancients and Moderns* (St. Louis, 1936; 2nd ed. 1961); E. M. W. Tillyard, *The Elizabethan World Picture* (London, 1943); Victor Harris, *All Coherence Gone* (Chicago, 1949); E. L. Tuveson, *Millennium and Utopia* (Berkeley, 1949); C. A. Patrides, *Milton and the Christian Tradition* (Oxford, 1966), 264–72. *Naturam* is briefly discussed by J. A. Bryant, 'Milton's Views on Universal and Civil Decay' *SAMLA Studies in Milton*, ed. J. M. Patrick (Gainesville, 1953), 1–19, and by Fletcher, *Intell. Dev.* 2, 439–42. Patrides (110–11) gives full references.

to the ancients; scientific discovery—including the appearance of new stars—demolished the belief in an immutable world beyond the moon; the extension of knowledge widened and deepened man's consciousness of ignorance and confusion and might lead to cynicism and atheism or— as it led Cornelius Agrippa in 1530—to a revulsion against all learning and inquiry and to complete dependence on the Bible and religious faith. On the other hand, modernists of various types—Vives, Loys le Roy, Bacon—could maintain that nature was not running down; that it, and man, were as potent as ever; that it was the modern world that was really ancient, through its accumulated experience and knowledge; that exploration of the globe and of nature was enlarging man's horizons and powers in all directions; and that defeatism must give way to confidence and effort.

The bulkiest statements of these opposed attitudes came from two clerics: *The Fall of Man* (1616; other edd. 1618, 1629), by Godfrey Goodman, later a bishop, and George Hakewill's *An Apologie of the Power and Providence of God in the Government of the World. Or an Examination and Censure of the Common Errour Touching Natures Perpetuall and Universall Decay* (1627; enlarged edd. 1630, 1635). While Milton is, as we might expect, on Hakewill's side in opposing the idea of decay, he says nothing of man and civilization and concerns himself only with cosmic and terrestrial nature[4] (the theme of a large part of the *Apologie*); and whereas Hakewill can use such semi-scientific arguments as the conservation of matter through endless change, Milton merely asserts in mythological terms that the order and powers of nature are unimpaired and will continue to operate until the final conflagration of the world.[5] Such a poetic texture can hardly yield any clear evidence of

[4] Hanford, 'Youth,' 105; Tillyard, *Milton*, 27.
[5] We may observe that, while the final conflagration was a Christian commonplace, it was the culminating argument in Hakewill (see the note on 69 below), without being preluded, as in Goodman, by general decay (A.S.P.W.).

Milton's attitude in the seventh Prolusion, noted above, Fletcher (who, by the way, would date the Prolusion in the autumn of 1629) finds 'the exact opposite' of his attitude in *Naturam,* and sees both as merely representative of his skill in debate (*Intell. Dev.* 2, 493). But the religious belief in the end of the world and belief in nature's decay were distinct ideas, which might or might not go together. Milton's acceptance of the one and denial of

indebtedness to Hakewill. As the following notes partly indicate, Hakewill had ideas, and quotations ranging from Lucretius to Sylvester's translation of Du Bartas, that Milton might have used; yet he already had in his head quite enough for the embroidering of his central affirmation. There seems to be no sufficient evidence for either a negative assertion like Parker's or for a positive one.

NOTES

1 *perpetuis erroribus acta.* Cf. *longis erroribus acto* (or *actum, actus*) in Ovid, *H.* 2. 107, *Tr.* 4. 10. 109, *M.* 15. 771; Molsa, *C.P.I.* 6, 348 (or Gruter, *Del.I.P.* 2, 51); and Secundus, *S.* 9. 23; *non tantis erroribus actus* in Grotius, *Epith. C. v. Mylen* (*S.*, bk. 3, p. 95) and *Epith. J. Borelii* (ibid. p. 110). Cf. Ovid, *M.* 4. 567 and Virgil, *A.* 6. 532.

1–2 *fatiscit | Avia mens hominum.* Cf. Statius, *Th.* 4. 187, *mens...fatiscit*; Lucretius 3. 463–4, *avius errat | saepe animus* (Fletcher); Beza, *Praefatio Poetica in Psalmum Dauidis LI. Sylua IV* (*Poëmata*, V^v): *Mens quoque victa labat, flammisque oppressa fatiscit.*

3 *Oedipodioniam volvit sub pectore noctem.* Cf. Statius, *Th.* 1. 46–8: *Impia iam merita scrutatus lumina dextra | merserat aeterna damnatum nocte pudorem | Oedipodes.* Milton's adjective occurs in ibid. 2. 505, 10. 801 (cf. 1. 313, 4. 491, 7. 216), Ovid, *M.* 15. 429, Lucan 8. 407. For the stock phrase *volvit sub pectore*, see the note on *El* 3. 31.

4–5 *Quae vesana suis metiri facta deorum | Audet.* Editors cite Isa. 55. 8: 'For my thoughts are not your thoughts, neither are your ways my ways, saith the Lord.' Hakewill (*A.P.P.G.* 1. 2. 4, p. 21) expresses, like many other men, the orthodox attitude: 'But how long this age shall last, it is still doubtfull, it being one of those secrets which the Almighty hath lockt up in the cabinet of his owne counsell, a secret which is neither possible neither profitable for us to know, as being not by God revealed unto us in his Word, much lesse then in the booke of

the other (a position like Hakewill's) may be thought to represent his real convictions. Also, Milton's orthodox view of the end of the world indicates that preceding phrases about nature's perpetual order are not to be taken with technical literalness; he would not share the Averroistic heresy about the eternity of the world (cf. O. B. Hardison, *Texas Studies in Literature and Language* 3, 1961–2, 121–2).

D. C. Allen (*Harmonious Vision*, 50) suggests that Milton had in mind the conclusion of Seneca's *Ad Marciam: De Consolatione.*

Nature.' Cf. Milton, *De Curiositate, ComBk* (*Works* 18, 138); *SA* 307–14. Cf. Ovid, *M.* 5. 320 and *C.P.I.* 4, 252, *facta deorum.*

5 *incisas leges adamante perenni.* Cf. Ovid, *M.* 15. 813–14, *incisa adamante perenni* | *fata* (Fletcher); Statius, *Th.* 7. 68, *adamante perenni*; Sil. Ital. 17. 620, *incisae leges*; Poliziano, *Sylvae* 3. 119–20 (*P.V.* p. 342; *C.P.I.* 7, 344): *aeterno incisas adamante...* | *...leges*; Sannazaro, *Sal.* 94, *duro leges adamante.*

7 *Consilium fati perituris alligat horis. Consilium fati* means of course the will of God; cf. *PL* 7. 173. Cf. Grotius, *Grat. Ad Dousam* (*Farr.*, bk. 1, p. 178), *perituris horis*; *Mathematica* (*S.*, bk. 2, p. 54), *Horarum pars nulla perit*; and the note on *Eli* 39.

8–9 *marcescet sulcantibus obsita rugis* | *Naturae facies.* Cf. Ovid, *M.* 3. 276, *sulcavitque cutem rugis* (Fletcher); Mantuan, *Parthen.* (*Opera*, 1502, fol. 171ʳ; 1513, 1, 45ᵛ), *cava sulcantes crispabant tempora rugae.* Hakewill (2. 1. 4, p. 74) speaks of the opinion that the moon's spots were 'contracted by age and continuance of time, as wrinkles are in the most beautifull faces.' In 2. 9 (pp. 128 f.) he discusses the 'pretended decay of the Earth, together with the Plants, and beasts, and minerals.' See the following note.

9 *Naturae facies, & rerum publica mater.* The earth. Todd quoted Shakespeare, *Tim.* 4. 3. 177–8: 'Common mother, thou | whose womb unmeasurable.' Cf. *Romeo* 2. 3. 9–12. See references in MacKellar; Pliny, *N.H.* 24. 1. 1, 27. 1. 2; and the note above on *El* 5. 3. Hakewill (2. 9. 3, p. 133) cites Columella (*R.R., Praef.* 2) on the earth (*tellurem*) as *communis omnium parens. Naturae facies*, in various forms, occurs in Pliny, *N.H.* 24. 1. 1; Manilius 1. 206; Palingenius, *Z.V.* 11. 8; and Grotius, *Ad. Ex.* 285.

10 *contracta...ab aevo.* Cf. the first quotation from Hakewill under 8–9, although the meaning of the participle differs.

11 *male certis passibus.* Cf. Ovid, *M.* 3. 175, *non certis passibus.*

12 *Sidereum tremebunda caput.* Cf. *caput sidereum* in Ovid, *M.* 15. 31 (of *Nox*), in Seneca, *Hipp.* 677 (of the sun), and in *C.P.I.* 11, 457.

13 *Annorumque aeterna fames, squalorque situsque.* Cf. Seneca, *Thy.* 149, *aeterna fames*; Calpurnius Siculus, *E.* 1. 43, *squalore situque* | *...posito*; Vida, *A.P.* 1. 166–7, *veterum squalore situque* | *Deterso*; *Gratul. Cantab.* (1623), p. 32, *picti squalore situque.*

14–15 *an & insatiabile Tempus* | *Esuriet Caelum, rapietque in viscera patrem?* In Hesiod (*Theog.* 453–96, 617 f.) Cronos, the son of Heaven and Earth, devoured the children Rhea bore him (though she contrived to save Zeus, who later fought against his father and the Titans). In keeping with the idea of imagined decay, of a reversal of the natural order, Milton reverses the myth. He touches the semi-allegorical tradition based on the identification of Cronos with *Chronos*, Time, or Saturn, e.g. Cicero, *N.D.* 2. 25. 64; Lactantius, *D.I.* 1. 12 (Migne, *Pat. Lat.* 6, 185–6); Comes, *Mythol.* 2. 1 and 2; cf. Pindar, *Ol.* 2. 17. E. Reiss ('An Instance of Milton's Use of Time,' *MLN* 72, 1957, 410–12) suggests that Milton is using ideas, much later put into *DocCh*, of the world as created out of God, who was also the creator (and hence father) of time, and that he is here rebuking 'the folly of thinking that time could destroy matter in which resided the spirit of God.' This is perhaps possible, but had Milton already arrived at his later metaphysical monism? MacKellar cites Virgil, *A.* 2. 324, *et ineluctabile tempus.* Milton's adjective may echo the derivation (Cicero, loc. cit.) of Saturnus from his being 'saturated' with the years and ages he devoured.

18   *gyrosque...perennes.* See the note on *El* 5. 1.

19–20   *sono dilapsa tremendo | Convexi tabulata ruant.* Editors cite 2 Pet. 3. 10: 'The heavens shall pass away with a great noise' (tr. Beza: *caeli cum stridore praeteribunt, elementa vero aestuantia solventur, terraque & quae in ea sunt opera exurentur*).

21   *Stridat uterque polus.* See the note on *El* 1. 55–6.

22   *horribilisque retecta Gorgone Pallas.* Pallas Athene's shield bore the head of the Gorgon Medusa, which Perseus had severed and which turned the beholder to stone (Homer, *Il.* 5. 741–2; Hesiod, *Theog.* 270–81; Ovid, *M.* 4. 772–803; Virgil, *A.* 2. 615–16, 8. 435–8; Val. Flacc. 4. 605, 6. 173–6).

23   *proles Junonia.* Vulcan, Hephaestus. See the note on *El* 7. 81–2.

25–8   As Phaethon, after his wild drive through the sky, fell into the river Eridanus (Ovid, *M.* 2. 324), so his father Phoebus, the sun, would fall into the ocean.

26   *Praecipiti curru, subitaque ferere ruina.* For *Praecipiti* or *praeceps* cf. Ovid, *M.* 2. 69, 185, 207, 320, 12. 128; and 1. 202, *subitae terrore ruinae.*

27   *extincta fumabit lampade Nereus.* The oldest of the children of Ocean (Hesiod, *Theog.* 233–6) and hence the sea itself (Homer, *Il.* 18. 141; Virgil, *E.* 6. 35, *G.* 4. 392, *A.* 2. 419, etc.; Ovid, *M.* 2. 268–9, etc.). Cf. Sil. Ital. 4. 694, *lampade Vulcanus mersit fumantibus undis.*

28   *dabit attonito feralia sibila ponto.* Cf. Ovid, *M.* 4. 494, *sibila dant*; 15. 684, *dedit...sibila* (Fletcher); Secundus, *El.* 3. 4. 12 and Grotius, *Ad Gernandum* (*Farr.* 1, p. 183), *attonitas...aquas.*

29–32   There was some confusion in antiquity, as there has been ever since, between the war of the gods and Titans and that of the gods and Giants (MacKellar; Osgood, *C.M.* 37–8, 82–3; Apollodorus, Frazer's index and notes). Hesiod (*Theog.* 617–735) describes the former; Homer (*Od.* 11. 313–16), Ovid (*M.* 1. 151 f.), and Claudian, *S.P.* 52 (2, 280–90) describe the latter; Horace (*C.* 3. 4. 42–64) links the two together; Apollodorus gives an account of each (1. 2. 1, 1. 6. 1–3). In Apollodorus 1. 2. 1, Pluto is allied with Zeus and Poseidon against the Titans; in ibid. 1. 6. 3, Typhon fights against Zeus at Mount Haemus and heaves mountains. In *FInf* 47–48 Milton speaks of the war of 'earths Sonnes' against heaven. See the note on 30–2 below.

29   *aërei…Haemi.* See the preceding note. Haemus was a Thracian range, often named simply as a high, cold mountain (Herodotus 4. 49; Ovid, *M.* 2. 219, 6. 87, etc.; Virgil, *G.* 1. 492, 2. 488).

30–2   *imoque allisa barathro | Terrebunt Stygium dejecta Ceraunia Ditem | In superos quibus usus erat, fraternaque bella.* There seem to be more difficulties here than editors have recognized. Since the Columbia rendering is awkward and free to the point of mistranslation, MacKellar's version (p. 139) may represent orthodoxy: 'and the Ceraunian hills, which he used in the war on his brother immortals, broken and cast down to the lowest depths shall terrify Stygian Dis' (much the same in *The Student's Milton*, ed. F. A. Patterson, rev. ed. New York, 1933, 100; Hughes, 1957, 33–4; Shawcross, 64; Bush, 52). This may be what Milton meant, though it may somewhat strain the Latin to take *fraterna bella* as parallel to *In superos* and the object of *in* understood (*in* meaning 'in,' 'for,' not 'against' as in *In superos*). It seems possible that *fraterna bella* is, along with *Ceraunia*, the subject of *Terrebunt*, so that this bit could read: 'the Ceraunian mountains…and fraternal wars shall terrify…Dis.' Also, no authority has been found for Pluto's hurling mountains, though in Claudian, *S.P.* 52. 66–73 (2, 284–6), the giants do (and see 29–32 n. above); nor do the Ceraunians (a range on the coast of Epirus) seem to come into pictures of these wars. Perhaps Milton was not making Pluto a hurler of mountains but was using *quibus usus erat* simply for 'which had been used.' Perhaps also the epithet 'Ceraunian' was, after the Latin way, an oblique equivalent for 'Thessalian' or 'Thracian.' In speaking of the alarm of the underworld and its king Milton probably had some or all of these passages in mind: Hesiod, *Theog.* 681–2, 850, Homer, *Il.* 20. 56–66, Virgil, *A.* 8. 243–6, Ovid, *M.* 2. 260–1, 5. 356 f.; but these do not help to clarify his lines. (The Homer and Virgil are quoted in the note on *Nat* 140.)

Sylvarum Liber

MacKellar remarks: 'Neither the war with the Titans nor that with the giants was a war of brother against brother; both were, however, "fraternal wars" in that brothers united to oppose brothers.' Cf. Milton, *Prol* 1 (*Works* 12, 124, lines 4–8): *Terrigenas fratres...consternatos plerosque a Jove Fratres.* In *fraterna bella* Milton could be thinking of Pluto either as an ally of his brothers Zeus and Poseidon (see Apollodorus under 29–32 above) or as a jealous enemy of his brothers. In *Prol* 1 (*Works* 12, 139, lines 25–6; cf. ibid. p. 125, lines 1–3) Milton speaks of Pluto's having 'sought many times the dominion of heaven'; and cf. the Fate's appeal to Pluto, in Claudian 33. 64 (2, 298): *neu foedera fratrum | civili converte tuba.*

With *imoque allisa barathro*, cf. Virgil, *A.* 3. 421, *imo barathri ter gurgite*; Vida, *Christ.* 2. 24, *imo emissa barathro*; Buchanan, *Ps.* 107. 26, *tartarei...ad ima barathri.* MacKellar cites *fraternaque bella* in Statius, *Th.* 11. 460 (cf. 1. 1, *Fraternas acies*); Milton's phrase appears also in Petrarch, *Ep. ad Io. de Columna* (*P.M.* 3, 60).

33f.   Having pictured, in 8–32, the idea of violent change and final collapse as reflected in pagan myths of the origin and government of the universe, Milton turns to describe—now through myths related to the planetary orbits and the processes of nature—the enduring order established by God, an order which contradicts any notion of change or decay. To quote one of Hakewill's summaries (2. 6. 1, p. 102): 'Hauing thus prooued at large, in the former Chapters touching the Heauens, that there neither is, nor in the course of Nature can be, any decay either in regard of their matter, their motion, their light, their warmth or influence, but that they all continue as they were euen to this day by Gods ordinance, it remains that I now proceed to the consideration of the sublunary bodies, that is, such as God & Nature hath placed under the Moone.' On pp. 82 (2. 2. 2) and 102 (2. 6. 1) Hakewill quotes Boethius, *C.P.* 4, met. 6, on the planetary and terrestrial order.

Hakewill (2. 5. 4, pp. 55 f.) translates a long passage from Arnobius, *Adversus Gentes* 1. 2 (Migne, *Pat. Lat.* 5, 720 f.), the first part of which is akin to Milton: 'Those first Element [*sic*], whereof it is agreed that all things are compounded, are they changed into contrary qualities? Is the frame of this engine and fabricke which covereth and incloseth us all in any part loosed or dissolved? Hath this wheeling about of Heaven swaruing from the rule of its primitive motion either begun to creepe more slowly, or to be carried with headlong volubilitie? Doe the Stars begin to raise themselues up in the West, and the Signes to incline towards the East? The Prince of Stars the Sun whose light clotheth, and heat quickneth all things, doth hee cease to be hot, is he waxen cooler, and hath he corrupted the temper of his wonted moderation into contrary Habits? Hath the Moone left off to repaire herselfe, and by continuall restoring of new to transforme herselfe into her old shapes?...Doth the Earth refuse to receiue the seeds cast into her? Will not trees budde forth?' The Latin text, which Hooker's editors suggest may have inspired a famous passage in him (*Eccles. Pol.* 1. 3. 2), is quoted in his *Works*, ed. Keble, Church, and Paget (1888), 1, 208 (Everyman ed. 1, 157). Hakewill occasionally refers (1. 3. 2, p. 28; 1. 4. 1, p. 39) to Philo Judaeus' *De Mundi Incorruptibilitate* (L.C.L. 9, *De Aeternitate Mundi*, e.g. 11. 61-2). Manilius (1. 518 f.) gives a picture of undecaying regularity: *at manet incolumis mundus suaque omnia servat*, etc. (Brodribb, *N&Q* 159, 129). Cf. Lucretius, 1. 165 f.; Buchanan, *Sph.* 2. 601-15.

33 *At pater omnipotens.* So Lucretius (5. 399) and Ovid (*M.* 2. 304) begin their accounts of Jupiter's acting to end the cosmic disorder caused by Phaethon. But *pater omnipotens* was a stock phrase (Virgil, *G.* 2. 325, *A.* 1. 60, etc.; Ovid, *M.* 1. 154, etc.) which needed no adaptation to Christian use (Vida, *Christ. passim*; Sannazaro, *P.V.* 1. 182; Buchanan, *Ps.* 78. 60; Diodati, poem on Camden, in Dorian, *E. D.* 109; etc.).

fundatis fortius astris. Cf. Gen. 1. 16-17, and the extract from Arnobius under 33 f. above, and Plato, *Tim.* 40 A-B.

34 *Consuluit rerum summae.* Editors cite *PL* 6. 673, 'Consulting on the sum of things.' Cf. Ovid, *M.* 2. 300, *rerum consule summae*; Caesar, *B.C.* 3. 51, *ad summam rerum consulere*; Cicero, *Rep.* 1. 26. 42, *Pro Roscio Amerino* 32. 91, and Prudentius, *C. Or. Symm.* 2. 392, *summa rerum.*

34-5 *certoque peregit | Pondere fatorum lances.* Cf. Virgil, *A.* 12. 725-6: *Iuppiter ipse duas aequato examine lances | sustinet et fata imponit diversa duorum*; and *PL* 4. 996 f. A. S. Ferguson, discussing the imitation in *PL* 4 of the final combat between Aeneas and Turnus, in particular *A.* 12. 725-7 and *PL* 4. 990-1002, remarked that in *Naturam* Milton 'had given the same hyperbole a cosmic setting, but had not as yet transformed the figure itself' (*MLR* 15, 1920, 169-70).

35-8 Hakewill, though more scientifically minded than Milton, also follows the old system (2. 2. 2, p. 80): 'The most signall motions of the heavens...are the diurnall motion of all the fixed starres and Planets, and all the Coelestiall spheres from East to West in the compasse of every foure and twenty houres, and the proper motion of them all from the West to the East againe.' Cf. Cicero, *N.D.* 2. 19. 49, 2. 21. 54-6, *Rep.* 6. 17. 17.

36 *Singula perpetuum jussit servare tenorem.* Cf. Claudian 1. 17 (1, 4), *continuum simili servantia lege tenorem* (Fletcher); Columella, *Arbor.* 2, *eundem tenorem servarint*; Pontano, *Met.* 1411, *Perpetuum quoniam servat natura tenorem*; ibid. 1557, *Singula et inceptum alternat natura tenorem*; P. Beroaldus, *C.P.I.* 2, 156, *Perpetuum discet vitae servare tenorem*; Buchanan, *Sph.* 1. 42, *Perpetuum servat solida & sincera tenorem*; *Ps.* 45. 3, *perpetuum...tenorem.* Hakewill (2. 8. 1, pp. 124–5) quotes Pontano, *Met.* 1555–8; and quotes 1556–8 in 1. 4. 1, p. 40.

37 *Volvitur hinc lapsu mundi rota prima diurno.* The *rota prima*, 'First Wheel,' is the *primum mobile*; see the note on *Idea* 17. Cf. Virgil, *A.* 4. 524, *medio volvuntur sidera lapsu.*

38 *Raptat & ambitos socia vertigine caelos.* Cf. Ovid, *M.* 2. 70, *adsidua rapitur vertigine caelum*; 1. 37, *ambitae...litora terrae*; 15. 287, *Fluctibus ambitae.*

39 *Saturnus.* See the note on *Idea* 17. Saturn was the slowest of the planets in moving through the signs of the zodiac, e.g. Cicero, *N.D.* 2. 20. 52; Claudian 22. 438–9 (2, 34), *semita... | pigraque Saturni*; Pontano, *Uran.* 1. 770, *Ultimus extremo torpet Saturnus in orbe.* Hakewill (2. 2. 2, p. 81), remarking on the orbits of the planets, says: 'Neither do we find that they haue either quickned or any way slackned these their courses, but that in the same space of time they allwayes run the same races which being ended, they begin them againe as freshly as the first instant they set forth...'

40 *Fulmineum rutilat cristata casside Mavors.* Mavors is an old and poetic name for Mars (Virgil, Ovid, *passim*). The planet, noted for its red light, is described in terms of the god of war. Cf. Cicero, *N.D.* 2. 20. 53, *Rep.* 6. 17. 17; Pontano, *Uran.* 1. 778, *rutilus...Mavors*; Buchanan, *Sph.* 2. 101, *Mars sanguineo rubet igne*; and, for Milton's phrasing, Claudian 7. 194 (1, 284), *fulminea...in casside* (Fletcher); Ovid, *M.* 8. 25, *cristata casside*; 14. 806, *posita...casside Mavors*; Sil. Ital. 1. 401, *cristatae cassidis.*

41-4 Phoebus (Apollo), the sun-god or the sun itself, in Latin poetry generally. As in the myth of Phaethon, he was imagined as driving the chariot of the sun across the heavens from the east to the western ocean; cf. 25–8 above and *El* 5. 81–94; and Cicero, *N.D.* 2. 19. 49, 2. 40. 102. Hakewill (1. 4. 4, pp. 45–6) quotes Boethius, *C.P.* 3, met. 2, lines 27–33. Milton takes no account of what disturbed Spenser (*F.Q.* 5, proem, st. 7) and others, that is—to quote Hakewill, who argues against it—'a supposed approach of the Sun neerer the earth then in former ages' (2. 4. 3, pp. 93–4), and 'a supposed removall of the Sun more

Southerly from us then in former ages' (2. 4. 4, pp. 94–7). Cf. Selden, in Drayton, 4, 300–1. *Signa rotarum* (44) is in Claudian 36. 431 (2, 376).

45–8 Venus, the planet that appears as Lucifer, the morning star, and as Hesperus, the evening star (Cicero, *N.D.* 2. 20. 53). Cf. Milton, *El* 3. 32, *Nat* 74, *PL* 4. 605–9, 7. 104, 366. The phrase *odoratis. . .ab Indis* is in Sil. Ital. 17. 647 (Fletcher) and *C.P.I.* 6, 294; cf. Virgil, *G.* 4. 293, *coloratis. . .ab Indis*.

46 *Aethereum pecus albenti qui cogit Olympo.* Olympus here is the sky. Cf. Caesar, *B.C.* 1. 68, *albente caelo*; Sil. Ital. 5. 283, *albenti. . .in aethra*; Vida, *Christ.* 2. 965, *albentes coeli. . .oras*; Virgil, *E.* 3. 20, *coge pecus*; 6. 85, *cogere. . . ovis stabulis*; Ovid, *M.* 2. 114–15, *stellae, quarum agmina cogit | Lucifer.*

49–50 *Delia.* Diana, born, with her brother Apollo, on the island of Delos. Editors compare Virgil, *G.* 1. 427–8; allusions to the phases of the moon in terms of the goddess-huntress are common. Ovid (*M.* 15. 188–98) speaks of both Apollo and Diana in his Pythagorean picture of everlasting change, which Renaissance poets echoed but which Milton here ignores or reinterprets in his argument for unchanging order and undiminished vitality.

51 *Nec variant elementa fidem.* Editors cite Claudian 33. 42–3 (2, 296): *paene reluctatis iterum pugnantia rebus | rupissent elementa fidem.* Cf. Claudian, *S.P.* 17. 35 (2, 190), *senserunt elementa fidem*; *C.P.I.* 2, 165, *Cui jurant elementa fidem*; ibid. 3, 27, *Quam teneant elementa fidem.* Ovid (*M.* 1. 21 f.) describes the primal elements as ordered by God or Nature (in ibid. 15. 237 f., they are in continual flux). Two of Hakewill's headings are: 'That the Elements are still in number foure, and still retaine the ancient places and properties' (2. 6. 1, p. 102); 'That the Elements still hold the same proportions each to other, and by mutuall exchange the same dimensions in themselues' (2. 6. 2, p. 106). Hakewill (2. 6. 1, p. 102) cites Boethius, *C.P.* 4, met. 6. 19–33. Among his many extracts from Sylvester, *D.W.W.*, are 1. 2. 219–34 (*A.P.P.G.* 2. 6. 1, p. 103) and 1. 2. 267–82, 207–10, 164–75 (*A.P.P.G.* 2. 6. 2, p. 108).

52 *Lurida perculsas jaculantur fulmina rupes.* Cf. Ovid, *M.* 2. 61, *qui fera terribili iaculatur fulmina dextra.*

53 *Nec per inane furit leviori murmure Corus.* Corus or Caurus was the north-west wind, e.g. Virgil, *G.* 3. 356; Seneca, *Hipp.* 737, 1013, 1131; Sil. Ital. 1. 469, *vasto Cauri cum murmure*; *Cantab. Dolor* (1625), p. 63, *nec murmura Coris | Ulla.* For *per inane*, see Lucretius *passim*, Virgil, *E.* 6. 31, Ovid, *M.* 4. 718, 6. 230, etc., and the note on *QNov* 63.

54 *armiferos. . .Gelonos.* A Scythian people, in the modern Ukraine; a stock example of a remote and savage nation, e.g. Virgil, *G.* 2. 115, 3. 461, *A.* 8. 725, Horace, *C.* 2. 9. 23, 3. 4. 35.

55 *Trux Aquilo.* The north or northeast wind. A stock allusion in Virgil, Ovid, *passim,* et al. Cf. Virgil, *G.* 1. 370, *Boreae...trucis*; *C.P.I.* 3, 374, *trucibusque Aquilonibus*; Milton, *FInf* 8, 'grim Aquilo.'

56 *Siculi...Pelori.* In the genitive and other cases, in Ovid, *M.* 15. 706, Seneca, *Med.* 350, *Herc. Oet.* 80–81, Lucan 2. 438, and Claudian 36. 255 (2, 362). Pelorus was a northeastern promontory of Sicily. Cf. *PL* 1. 232–3.

57–8 *Rex maris, & rauca circumstrepit aequora concha | Oceani Tubicen.* For Neptune, the king of the sea, cf. Ovid, *M.* 1. 331, *rector pelagi,* 10. 606, *regis aquarum.* Editors remark that Triton was the trumpeter of Neptune (cf. Ovid–Micyllus, 3, 17D and 30E, and C. Stephanus, *Dict., tubicen Neptuni*), not of the Titan Oceanus, but the shift is natural. Cf. Virgil, *A.* 6. 171, *cava dum personat aequora concha*; Statius, *S.* 3. 4. 5, *aequora concha*; Ovid, *M.* 1. 330–8; Grotius, *Myrtilus* (*S.* bk. 2, p. 56), *at concha mihi perstrepit aequora Triton.*

58–9 *nec vasta mole minorem | Aegaeona ferunt dorso Balearica cete.* Aegaeon, more familiarly Briareus, was a hundred-armed giant (Hesiod, *Theog.* 147–52; Homer, *Il.* 1. 403–4; Virgil, *A.* 10. 565–8). Ovid, whom Milton is following, makes him a sea-god: *ballenarumque prementem | Aegaeona suis immania terga lacertis* (*M.* 2. 9–10). Ovid–Micyllus (3, 30H–1) describes Aegaeon as a giant or a sea monster, and cites Homer for his being the same as Briareus; cf. C. Stephanus, *Dict.,* and Starnes-Talbert, 242–3. Balearic whales, by a common Latin figure, stand for whales in general. Cf. Virgil, *A.* 3. 656, *vasta mole* (Fletcher). Garrod (cf. *Ox. Fac.*) suggests *iusta* for *vasta.*

60 *Terra.* See the note on *El* 5. 3. Hakewill argues that trees and plants are as fruitful as ever (1. 3. 3, p. 32, 2. 9. 3–5, pp. 133–41). Cf. Cicero, *N.D.* 2. 47. 120.

61 *Narcissus.* 'The name of the flower is capitalized in allusion to Ovid's story of its origin in the metamorphosis of the youth, Narcissus. (*Met.* III, 509–10)' (Hughes).

62–3 *Et puer... | Phoebe...Cypri.* Apollo, having accidentally killed his favorite, Hyacinthus, changed the boy into the flower and marked its petals with Al, Al, the Greek cry of sorrow. Cf. Ovid, *M.* 10. 162–219, Milton, *FInf* 25–7, *Lyc* 106. For Venus and Adonis, see the note on *El* 1. 62, where the hyacinth and anemone are also linked. For the name Cypris, see the note on *El* 3. 20.

63–5 *nec ditior olim | Terra datum sceleri celavit montibus aurum | Conscia, vel sub aquis gemmas.* MacKellar cites Ovid, *M.* 1. 137–42 [cf. *Am.* 3. 8. 35–8, 53];

Horace, *C.* 3. 3. 49–52; Boethius, *C.P.* 2, met. 5. 27–30; Chaucer, *The Former Age* (which follows Boethius). Cf. Sylvester, *D.W.W.* 1. 3. 914–19. The 'precious bane' of *PL* 1. 692 may echo Boethius' *Pretiosa pericula*. Hakewill (1. 5. 3, pp. 50–1) quotes and translates a passage from Cyprian (*Ad Demetrianum* 3, Migne, *Pat. Lat.* 4, 546) on nature's decay. One bit is this: 'and the emptied Mines yeeld lesse quantity of gold and siluer, their veines daylie diminishing and decreasing.' MacKellar suggests that Chaucer, who has gems under rivers (*F.A.* 30), supplied the original of Milton's *sub aquis gemmas*. That may be, but such allusions—especially to the Red Sea (the Persian Gulf)—are common in Latin and Neo-Latin, e.g. Propertius 1. 14. 12, *Rubris gemma sub aequoribus*, and 2. 16. 17; Tibullus 2. 2. 15–16; Seneca, *Thy.* 372, *gemmis mare lucidis*; Claudian 10. 168 (1, 254), *S.P.* 29. 15 (2, 236), ibid. 31. 14 (2, 256), ibid. 39 (2, 266), ibid. 46. 10 (2, 272); Secundus, *El.* 1. 10. 35; Pontano, *A.C.* 1. 1. 6, *Quae legitur Rubro lucida gemma mari*. For *Conscia*, see the note on *QNov* 150, and Propertius 2. 13A. 42, *conscia terra*.

65–9 God's final destruction of the world by fire (2 Pet. 3. 10) is very different from the imagined collapse of 19–32 above, since the conflagration of Christian belief is a prelude to the perfect renewal of eternity—a vision that was to lift Milton's thoughts as he lost hope of a reformation on earth (*Pl* 3. 333–41, 11. 65–6, 900–1, 12. 458–65, 546–51). Cf. Sylvester, *D.W.W.* 1. 1. 392–409. See the notes below on 67–8 and 69.

66 *cunctarum series justissima rerum.* Cf. the Virgilian and other phrases cited under *QNov* 58. '"The righteous course of all things": it is precisely this sense of control and ultimate rightness that Milton seeks to establish in the final cadences of *Lycidas*' (I. G. MacCaffrey, '*Lycidas*: The Poet in a Landscape,' *The Lyric and Dramatic Milton*, ed. J. H. Summers, New York, 1965, 91).

67–8 *flamma orbem populabitur ultima, late | Circumplexa polos, & vasti culmina caeli.* Cf. Ovid, *F.* 4. 856, *ultima...flamma*, and Manilius 1. 149–50: *ignis... | summaque complexus stellantis culmina caeli* (Fletcher); Boethius, *C.P.* 4, met. 6. 3, *Aspice summi culmina caeli*. Hakewill (2. 2. 2, p. 82) quotes from this metrum, of which the theme is cosmic and terrestrial order.

69 *Ingentique rogo flagrabit machina mundi.* While the final conflagration was familiar doctrine (see the end of the headnote above, and C. A. Patrides, *Milton and the Christian Tradition*, 276–8), it may be noted that the theme of Hakewill's chapter 13 in book 4 (441–53) is 'That the world shall have an end by Fire, and by it be entirely consumed.' *Machina mundi* is a stock phrase (e.g. Pontano, *Uran.* 1. 932, *Parth.* 1. 6. 37, Vida, *Christ.* 1. 584, etc.), but Milton may have

remembered Lucretius 5. 95–6: *una dies dabit exitio, multosque per annos |*
sustentata ruet moles et machina mundi; and Lucan 1. 80: *Machina divolsi*
turbabit foedera mundi. Both Lucretius (5. 92–6) and Lucan (1. 72–80) are
quoted by Hakewill, 443–4. In connection with Milton's *rogo*, cf. Lucan
7. 812–15 (quoted by Hakewill, 4. 13. 3, p. 445):

> *Hos, Caesar, populos si nunc non usserit ignis,*
> *Uret cum terris, uret cum gurgite ponti.*
> *Communis mundo superest rogus ossibus astra*
> *Mixturus.*

Cf. Milton's reference to the final conflagration in *Prol* 7 (*Works* 12, 278,
lines 18–19), *quae vicinus mundi rogus cremarit.*

De Idea Platonica quemadmodum Aristoteles intellexit

※

Whether or not this undated poem was connected with a public occasion, it is in character a sort of brief and satirical prolusion or appendage to a serious prolusion. As we observed in the introduction to *Naturam non pati senium*, the *Idea Platonica* may have been the verses, referred to in Milton's letter to Gill of 2 July 1628, which he had just written for an elder to deliver at the Commencement of that month. Orthodox conjecture would apparently put the poem in or about 1628; if *Naturam* is to be assigned to 1628, the *Idea*, which follows it in Milton's arrangement, might have come later in that year or in 1629. (Parker, as we have seen, would assign both poems to Milton's last years at Cambridge, 1630–2.)

Although handled in half-burlesque fashion, the theme is large: Platonic realism or idealism versus Aristotelian nominalism or conceptualism. Masson (*P.W.* 1, 294–5 and 3, 341–2) seems to have been the first to make quite clear the nature of the piece.[1] Milton, himself

---

[1] Cf., however, Coleridge: 'This is not, as has been supposed, a ridicule of Plato; but of the gross Aristotelian misinterpretation of the Platonic Idea, or Homo *Archetypus*' ('Notes in Anderson's *British Poets*,' *Coleridge's Miscellaneous Criticism*, ed. T. M. Raysor, 190; Brinkley, 552. MacKellar (52) and Carey give references: Plato, *Rep.* 10. 596–7, *Crat.* 389, 439–40, *Phaedo* 75–6, *Parm.* 135, *Soph.* 246–7; Aristotle, *Meta.* 1. 9, 7. 8, 13. 4–5.

A.S.P.W. cites the comment of Atticus from Eusebius, *Preparation for the Gospel*, 15. 13 (tr. E. H. Gifford, Oxford, 1903, 2, 876):

'But the chief point and power of Plato's system, his theory of ideas, has been discredited, and abused, and insulted in every way, as far as it was in Aristotle's power. For as he was unable to conceive that things of a grand, divine, and transcendent nature require a certain kindred power for their recognition, and trusted to his own meagre and petty shrewdness, which was able to make its way through things terrestrial, and discern the truth in them, but was not capable of beholding the plain of absolute truth, he made himself the rule and judge of things above him, and denied the existence of any peculiar natures such as Plato affirmed, but dared to call the highest of all realities triflings and chatterings and nonsense.'

Fletcher (*Intell. Dev.* 2, 427–31) does not feel so sure as other commentators do of Milton's anti-Aristotelian irony.

ardently devoted to 'the divine volumes of Plato,' ironically assumes the role of a flat-footed Aristotelian who challenges the actuality of the Platonic or Neoplatonic Idea or archetype of man; his objections expose the literal-minded myopia of the Aristotelian and, by implication, uphold Platonic doctrine. 'In the background are Platonic passages such as the discussion in the *Republic* (x, 596 b–597 d) of the Eternal ideas or divinely established patterns upon which all things were supposed to be moulded, but the archetypal man is a Neo-Platonic conception and may owe something to the Hermetic Books (*e.g.*, *Poimander* I, 12–4) and to Kabbalistic interpretations of the story in Genesis i, 27, of the creation of man in the image of God. In his college exercises Milton is sometimes ironical with "Aristotle, the envious and perpetual calumniator of Pythagoras and Plato" (Second *Prolusion*), and here he satirizes the unimaginative objections to the doctrine of ideas in Aristotle's *Metaphysics*. Even the study of natural science seemed to him to confirm the Platonic doctrine. "For who can contemplate and examine attentively the ideal forms of things, human and divine," he asked in the seventh *Prolusion*, "unless he has a mind saturated and perfected by Knowledge?"' (Hughes). In its general spirit the *Idea Platonica* is akin to *Prol* 2 on the harmony of the spheres (with its praise of Pythagoras and Plato), and *Prol* 3 (against the scholastic philosophy), and the Platonic portions of *Prol* 7.

In *English* 5 (1944–5), 195, C. S. Lewis gave a verse translation of lines 1–34 which, he modestly feared, might not preserve 'the goblin quality' of 'a neglected and exquisite grotesque.'

The metre is iambic trimeter, which permits a spondee in the odd feet or sometimes other substitutions. Keightley of course complained of Milton's excessive licenses.

De Idea Platonica

NOTES

1 *Dicite sacrorum praesides nemorum deae.* MacKellar, citing Virgil, *A.* 9. 404-5 and Horace, *C.* 3. 22. 1-4, takes the goddesses to be Diana and her nymphs, who attend at births and are associated with groves, 'not necessarily the sacred groves.' E. H. Visiak also names 'Diana and her train.' But these seem to be remote from philosophy and poetry, and Hughes is probably right in taking them as the nine Muses, whose mother is addressed in lines 2-3. Cf. Virgil, *E.* 7. 21. The grove of the Muses, on the slopes of Helicon, and the grove of the Camenae near Rome (see the note on *El* 6. 3-4) occasioned endless allusions, ancient and modern, which were not confined to these particular groves. E.g. cf. Horace, *C.* 1. 1. 29-32, *me gelidum nemus*, etc.; Statius, *S.* 5. 3. 209-11: *Me quoque vocales lucos Boeotaque tempe | pulsantem... | admisere deae*; *Th.* 4. 34-5, *nemoris regina sonori, | Calliope*; *Ach.* 1. 10 and Propertius 3. 3. 42, *Aonium nemus*; Sannazaro, *P.V.* 1. 9 (to the Muses), *vestras nemora ardua rupes*; Buchanan, *Sph.* 1. 19, *Castalidum nemora*; Milton, *Patrem* 16, *nemoris laureta sacri Parnassides umbrae*; and the notes on 2-3 below and *El* 4. 29-31. The phrase *sacrorum nemorum*, and the singular, are common, e.g. Virgil, *G.* 2. 21, Seneca, *Med.* 608, *Herc. Oet.* 957, Statius, *Th.* 5. 186.

2-3 *Tuque O noveni perbeata numinis | Memoria mater.* Memory, the most blessed mother of the goddesses nine, is clearly Mnemosyne, mother of the nine Muses (Hesiod, *Theog.* 36-103; Plutarch, *Education of Children*, 9E (L.C.L. 1, 44); Ovid, *M.* 6. 114; Statius, *S.* 1. 2. 4: *demigrant Helicone deae quatiuntque novena | lampade*; Milton, *El* 6. 18, *turba novena*, and note. Hughes cites the first chapter of Geoffrey Linocre's *Musarum Libellum* (printed at the end of Comes, *Mythol.*), which interprets Hesiod's account of the Muses, daughters of Zeus and Mnemosyne, 'as an allegory of the Platonic doctrine that all knowledge is memory or—in Christian terms—innate ideas implanted by God.'

3-10 *quaeque in immenso procul | ...Aeternitas*, etc. Todd noted the general resemblance between these lines and Claudian 22. 424-40 (2, 32-4), the picture, to quote Hughes, 'of a mysterious old man who controls the events of time from a cave "somewhere beyond the range of human minds and hardly approachable by the gods"; but it was Boccaccio, in the opening chapter of the *Genealogy of the Gods*, who gave to Claudian's old man the name of Eternity.'

5 *ratas leges Jovis. Ratas leges* is in Seneca, *Oed.* 942 and Buchanan, *Jeph.* 1044-5. Claudian 22. 433-6 (see the note on 3-10 above) has *mansura...iura* and *fixis...legibus.*

6 *Caelique fastos atque ephemeridas Deum.* Cf. Claudian 22. 476 (2, 36), *aetheriis...fastis*; Ovid, *Am.* 1. 12. 25, *ephemeridas.*

7–12 To summarize, 'Who was the original from which the Deity modeled the human race? Surely not a mere conception in the Divine Mind, a sort of twin brother of Pallas.' (After Masson, *P.W.* 3, 341; MacKellar.)

8 *Natura solers finxit humanum genus.* Cf. Vida, *Christ.* 4. 115, *genus humanum fingens.*

9 *Aeternus, incorruptus, aequaevus polo.* Cf. Claudian 26. 54 (2, 130), *urbs aequaeva polo* (Fletcher); Grotius, *Epith. Guil.* (*S.*, bk. 3, p. 115), *Aequaevusque polo.*

11–12 *Haud ille Palladis gemellus innubae | Interna proles insidet menti Jovis.* For the birth of Athene from the head of Zeus, see Hesiod, *Theog.* 933ᵃ–946ᵃ and Apollodorus 1. 3. 6 (MacKellar), and Milton, *PL* 2. 757–8 and notes. Hughes cites Comes, *Mythol.* 4. 5, on the myth as an allegory of the mind as the seat of memory and wisdom. With Milton's phrasing cf. Val. Flacc. 1. 87, *innuba Pallas* (Fletcher) and 4. 605, *divaque Gorgonei gestatrix innuba monstri*; 4. 542, *Iovis optima proles*; 5. 653, *proles Iovis*; Sil. Ital. 4. 476, *vera Iovis proles*; Ariosto, *Carm.* 19. 5 and *Epith. Oxon.* (1625), sig. E2ʳ, *Pallas...innuba.*

13–24 While human nature is universal, men are individual persons. Since the archetype must have an actual existence, where is it to be found?

16 *sempiternus...syderum comes.* Cf. Cicero, *Rep.* 6. 15. 15, *sempiternis ignibus, quae sidera et stellas vocatis*; 6. 17. 17, *stellarum cursus sempiterni.*

17 *Caeli...ordines decemplicis.* In the old astronomy the number of spheres varied, but here (cf. *PL* 3. 481–3) there are ten: seven carrying the seven planets, the moon, Mercury, Venus, the sun, Mars, Jupiter, and Saturn; the eighth, with the fixed stars; the ninth or crystalline sphere; and the *primum mobile* (the *rota prima* of *Naturam* 37), which revolved daily and imparted its motion to the inner spheres. See the note on *Naturam* 35–8. Cf. Mantuan, *Sylv.* 7. 5 (*Opera*, 1502, fol. 103ʳ), *coelique decemplicis astra.*

18 *Citimumve terris incolit Lunae globum.* Cf. Cicero, *Rep.* 6. 16. 16, *citima terris*; Lucretius, 5. 69, *lunaique globum*; and *globum* (*globo, globus*) *lunae* in Virgil, *A.* 6. 725, Prudentius, *Cath.* 9. 15, Buchanan, *Sph.* 5. 282.

19–20 'Milton thought of Virgil's Pythagorean passage where Anchises explains the doctrine of metempsychosis to Aeneas— how all spirits drink the oblivion-bringing waters of Lethe after death and suffer various purifications before rebirth is possible. (*Aen.* VI, 713–51.)' (Hughes). MacKellar cites Plato,

De Idea Platonica

Meno 81 b–c, *Phaedo* 70–2, *Phaedrus* 248–9, *Rep.* 10. 617. Cf. Ovid, *M.* 15. 158–72, 456–78. For Milton's *Obliviosas...Lethes aquas*, cf. Virgil, *A.* 6. 714–15: *Lethaei ad fluminis undam | ...longa oblivia potant*; and the notes on *QNov* 132 and *PL* 2. 583.

21–2 *Sive in remota... | ...archetypus gigas.* A being like the Giants, or the Titans, whom—with Atlas—Hesiod (*Theog.* 729–31, 746–7) placed in a gloomy region at the ends of the earth. Cf. Juvenal 2. 7, *archetypos...servare Cleanthas*; Palingenius, *Z.V.* 7. 474, *archetypus mundus* (and 12. 478); 7. 484, *Mentali archetypo*.

23 *Et diis tremendus erigit celsum caput.* The *diis* of 1645 was misprinted as *iis* in 1673. *Celsum caput* is a stock phrase, e.g. Seneca, *Hipp.* 656, Statius, *S.* 1. 1. 32, Sil. Ital. 3. 264, 456, Vida, *Christ.* 1. 928.

24 *Atlante major portitore syderum.* For Atlas see Hesiod, *Theog.* 507–20, and the note on 21–2 above; Homer, *Od.* 1. 52–4; Virgil, *A.* 4. 246–51, 480–2; Ovid, *M.* 4. 631–62, 6. 174–5. The use here of *portitor* is postclassical; the word properly means a boatman (Virgil, *G.* 4. 502, *A.* 6. 298) or a carter.

25–34 Even the most renowned seers have never beheld the archetype. Of his Utopians Sir Thomas More says, ironically, that 'so far are they from ability to speculate on second intentions that not one of them could see even man himself as a so-called universal—though he was, as you know, colossal and greater than any giant, as well as pointed out by us with our finger' (*Utopia*, ed. E. Surtz and J. H. Hexter, New Haven, 1965, 159, and notes, 437–8; ed. J. R. Lumby, Cambridge, 1879 f., 103; Everyman ed., 71).

25–6 *Dircaeus augur*, etc. Dirce was a Theban fountain. Tiresias, the blind prophet of Thebes, could not even see the archetype in a mental vision. Cf. *PL* 3. 36, 51–5. and *Def* 2 (*Works* 8, 63).

27–8 *Non hunc silenti nocte Plëiones nepos | Vatum sagaci praepes ostendit choro.* Hermes (Mercury) was the son of Maia, who was one of the Pleiades, the seven daughters of Atlas and the sea-nymph Pleione (Ovid, *F.* 5. 83–90). The phrase *Plëiones nepos* occurs, e.g. in Ovid, *H.* 16. 62, *M.* 2. 743, Val. Flacc. 1. 737–8. Horace (*C.* 4. 3. 15) uses *vatum...choros* with reference to poets. Milton's line 28 is taken to refer to seers, and the word *sagaci* favors that (cf. the note on *El* 6. 67–8), although Mercury is more familiarly linked with poetry than with prophecy. There seems to be no point in Keightley's notion (embalmed in the Columbia translation, *Works* 1, 269) that Milton confounded Hermes with Hermes Trismegistus; he would not mention the latter here and again, as another example, in 32–4, nor would he be likely to apply to Trismegistus the Ovidian label for Mercury. He may have thought of Mercury's association with wisdom and of his power to give and take away sleep (Virgil, *A.* 4. 244); hence Mercury could not exhibit the archetype to the sages even at night, the time of contemplation—and invisibility. Cf. Comes, *Mythol.* 5. 5 (end), where Mercury is said to have been the messenger of the gods not merely because of his eloquence and wisdom, *sed pro illa divina vi, quae divinitus in mentes hominum infunditur, quaeque res humanas omnes mirifice in suo ordine componit, & conservat. Hanc, ubi somnia in mentes hominum infundere opinabantur, Mercurium somniis praeesse dixerunt.* Cf. also Milton's reference, in the opening of *Prol* 7 (*Works* 12, 249) to 'that retreat of Prometheus under the leadership of Mercury into the deepest solitudes of Mount Caucasus, where he became the wisest of gods and men...'

29–30 *sacerdos...Assyrius, licet | ...commemoret atavos Nini.* Warton suggested that Milton had in mind the legendary Phoenician sage, Sanchuniathon; Visiak names 'Berōsus, priest of Bēl at Babylon, *c.* 250 B.C.' Hughes plausibly thinks that 'Milton vaguely individualized a figure among those learned orientals to whom Herodotus referred (1, 1) as authorities for his account (1, 7) of the half-mythical Assyrian king, Ninus, the husband of Semiramis'. Ninus was the traditional founder of the Assyrian empire and of the city of Nineveh (Diod. Sic. 2. 1–20; C. Stephanus, *Dict.*; Ralegh, *History* 1. 1. 10. 2–3, 1. 1. 12. 1; Milton, *El* 1. 66 and note). Warton's idea might get support from Eusebius (tr. Gifford), 1, 34 f. and 2, 519–20, if Milton at this time knew an author he often quoted later. Cf. Carey's note.

31 *Priscumque Belon, inclytumque Osiridem.* Cf. Ovid, *M.* 4. 213, *prisco... Belo*; Boccaccio, *Gen. Deor.* 2. 21–2; Sandys, *Relation* (1615), 207: 'Belus Priscus, (reputed a God, and honoured with Temples; called Bel by the Assyrians, and Baal by the Hebrewes).' MacKellar cites Ralegh's description (*History* 1. 1. 12. 5) of the temple of Bel, which Diod. Sic. (2. 9. 4) attributed to Semiramis. See the notes on *Nat* 197 and *PL* 1. 720. Osiris and Isis, his sister and wife, were the chief Egyptian deities. See Herodotus 2. 42; Diod. Sic. 1. 11–27; Plutarch, *Isis and Osiris* (L.C.L. 5) and notes on *Nat* 212–20 and *PL* 1. 478.

33 *Ter magnus Hermes.* Hermes Trismegistus ('thrice great Hermes,' *IlPen* 88). The Greek god Hermes was identified with the Egyptian Thoth and his name was attached to religious and philosophic books which were actually written in Egypt in the second and third centuries A.D. The Hermetic writings, through Ficino's Latin version, affected religious and mystical thought in the sixteenth and seventeenth centuries (e.g. Sir Thomas Browne). See Cicero,

N.D. 3. 22. 56; Iamblichus, *De Mysteriis*, etc. (Geneva, 1607), 1. 1, etc.; Ralegh, *History* 1. 2. 6. 6; MacKellar; Hughes; Starnes-Talbert (283–4), who quote R. Stephanus, *Thesaurus*. For the texts and full information see *Hermetica*, ed. W. Scott (4 v. Oxford, 1924–36), and the more reliable *Hermès Trismégiste*, ed. A. D. Nock and A.-J. Festugière (4 v. Paris, 1945–54; 2nd ed. 1960 f.); Festugière, *La Révélation d'Hermès Trismégiste* (2nd ed. 4 v. Paris, 1950–4). In connection with *IlPen*, D. C. Allen (*Harmonious Vision*, 13–15) quotes substantial bits from Scott's *Hermetica*, 5. 4, 1. 26a, 11. (ii). 20b. See the Variorum note on *IlPen* 88.

34 *Isidis cultoribus*: Egyptians. See the notes on 31 above and *QNov* 185–6, and on *Nat* 211–26.

35 *At tu perenne ruris Academi decus*. Plato's Academy was outside the city of Athens (*PR* 4. 244–6). Cf. *perenne decus* in Claudian, *S.P.* 17. 48 (2, 190): *C.P.I.* 2, 496 and 11, 239; Beza, *Abrahamus Sacrificans* (*Poëmata*, 174^r); and *Cantab. Dolor* (1625), 5.

36 *induxti*. The word, misprinted *induxit* in 1673, is a colloquial form, e.g. Terence, *And.* 572. Cf. Propertius 1. 3. 27, *duxti suspiria*.

37–9 Plato's banishment of poets from his ideal state (*Rep.* 3. 398A, 8. 568B, 10. 595–608), because they falsified truth and undermined morality, was continually cited and countered by Renaissance defenders of poetry. Sir Philip Sidney, opposing Platonic rigor with partly Platonic arguments, anticipated Milton's unimaginative Aristotelian by pointing out, with a sympathy akin to Milton's, that Plato himself was a poet (*Eliz. Critical Essays*, ed. G. G. Smith, Oxford, 1904, 1, 152, 190; Hughes; MacKellar). In *PR* 4. 295 Milton's Christ was to repeat the charge of fabling more seriously.

39 *migrabis foras*. Cf. Plautus, *Curc.* 2. 1, *Migrare...e fano foras*.

Ad Patrem

❧

Of the Latin poems that were not dated by Milton, or that have not so far been dated with fair precision, *Ad Patrem* is the most important. Conjectures have ranged from 1631–2 to 1645. In recent decades opinion has in the main favoured *c.* 1637; a minority has preferred 1634. The point of the two dates is the idea that Milton's definite decision to embrace a poetic vocation is most probably to be associated with either the publishing or the writing of *Comus*. E. Sirluck has listed an impressive array of witnesses for *c.* 1637: Grierson, Tillyard, Hanford, Diekhoff, and Barker; and Sirluck himself adds a complex argument for that time; Parker and Hughes are named as supporters of 1634.[1] But the counting of heads, however notable they may be, is of small avail if the feet rest on what may be considered few and unsubstantial reasons; and most of these testimonies were given before the problem had received any real examination, so that they are subject to a discount.

Masson (*Life*, 1, 1881, 334; *P.W.* 1, 299) dated *Ad Patrem* in 1632–3 because he linked it with the 'Letter to a Friend' in which Milton tried to explain and defend his studious retirement and in which he copied the sonnet 'How soon hath time' (*Works* 12, 320–5; *C.P.W.* 1, 318–21). French, as Sirluck also notes, followed Masson (*L.R.* 1, 274). As Sirluck puts it, 'Woodhouse ("Notes on Milton's Early Development," pp. 89–91), although repudiating Masson's reason, argues for his date.' One

---

[1] E. Sirluck, 'Milton's Idle Right Hand,' *JEGP* 60 (1961), 784–5. As Sirluck notes, Hanford and Hughes have changed their minds. In 1925 Hanford ('Youth,' 130–1) went along with Masson's 1632–3; in 1953 (*Poems*, 151) he shifted to 1637. Hughes, who in 1937 dated the poem in 1636–7, changed in 1957 to Parker's date, 1634. B.A.W., commenting on the first draft of this introduction, dismissed 1631–2 and upheld 1634; he gave no reasons. E. Saillens (*Milton*, New York, 1964, 43, n. 2) follows Masson and the earlier Hanford.

The present introduction largely reproduces my article, 'The Date of Milton's *Ad Patrem*,' *MP* 61 (1963–4), 204–8. There is some further discussion below in the notes on 71–2 and 83–4. See also the Chronological Survey in the forthcoming Variorum volume on the minor English poems.

would not guess from this scant reference that Woodhouse's article (*UTQ* 13, 1943–4) offered new and, it may be thought, cogent arguments for 1631–2, arguments not known to a number of witnesses for 1637 or apparently to Parker when he wrote his 'Notes on the Chronology of Milton's Latin Poems' in 1952. One may therefore review the problem, rehearsing and sometimes augmenting Woodhouse's discussion.

The chief point in the conventional view, advanced by Grierson and repeated by others, is that the publication of *Comus* in 1637 (or early 1638) would have crystallized both Milton's sense of his vocation and his father's uneasiness over his not seeking a means of livelihood. If such feelings arose only after Milton had had five years of reading at home, they would seem to prove much more 'belatedness' in both father and son than the son had, five years earlier, recognized in himself. The idea that he might take orders was presumably much weakened by the time Milton left Cambridge and could hardly have continued to deceive both him and his father up to 1637. What were they both thinking about during that long period? Moreover, far from publicly proclaiming himself in 1637 a dedicated poet, Milton only allowed Lawes to publish the masque while withholding his own name; was he still too unresolved to commit himself? The associating of the problem of a profession with the writing of *Comus* in 1634 is less irrational to the degree that it cuts three years off the time during which Milton and his father were not questioning themselves or each other about the son's future; in itself it seems hardly more tenable.

Tillyard (*Milton*, 1930, 384) accepted Grierson's argument—against Masson and Hanford's early view—that 'the sonnet and the letter accompanying it are an apology for waiting and learning; the Latin poem is an apology for poetry.' He accepted also Grierson's opinion that 'it would be after *Comus* had made clear Milton's poetical purpose that so emphatic an apology for poetry would be apt.' Tillyard went on to say: 'Stronger almost to my mind is the argument from style. *Ad Patrem*, *Mansus*, and *Epitaphium Damonis* make an inseparable group. They show a common sureness of touch that belongs to the period round

Lycidas.' If 'sureness of touch' can be so clearly assessed and used as an argument for dates, one might say that nowhere in Milton's Latin poetry is it more evident than in the early *Elegy* 5; and I would say—though doubtless many others would not—that his touch in the *Epitaphium* is quite unsure. One certain case of non-progression is the fact that the *Passion*, an avowed failure, was written after the *Nativity*.

Tillyard proceeds to details. '*Inenarrabile carmen* of *Ad Patrem* is related to the *unexpressive nuptial song* of *Lycidas* (as has been often noted).' But, as Woodhouse urged (loc. cit. notes 38 and 41, pp. 91 and 93–4), the fiery spirit of *Ad Patrem* 'is not more closely linked with *Lycidas* than with *Il Penseroso*'; and see D. C. Allen, *Harmonious Vision*, 15–16, and J. Carey under 35–7 below. Tillyard then cites two lines of *Ad Patrem* (46 and 102), which are repeated—as Warton observed—with slight changes as lines 43 and 6 of *Mansus*. But Milton's echoes of himself are not reliable evidence for chronology, as Le Comte's *Yet Once More* abundantly demonstrated. It would be wholly natural, and in Milton's way, in the writing of such a poem about poetry as *Mansus*, to recall phrases from *Ad Patrem*. Tillyard's final point is that lines 82–4 of *Ad Patrem*, about the Italian language and the barbarian invasions, are parallel to the passage on Milton's reading in medieval Italian history in the letter to Diodati of 23 September 1637 (dated in the *C.P.W.* 1, 325, 329, as probably of 23 November). But Milton knew long before 1637 that Italian was a 'corruption' of Latin.

Parker's argument for 1634 ('Notes,' 1952: see *El* 1, introduction, n. 5) starts from the conviction that the Latin poems in each of Milton's two groups are in chronological order and that *Ad Patrem* was therefore written between the *Idea Platonica* (which he dates 1630–2, later than most scholars put it) and the Greek Psalm of the end of 1634. His other arguments are, in brief, that the performance of *Comus* in 1634 would more naturally crystallize the problem of Milton's vocation than its anonymous publication, that this year would preserve the chronological position of *Ad Patrem*, and that the poem fits Milton's situation in 1634. He has had two years of studious leisure at home, reflected in lines 73–6 (this point is queried below); he has thought it worth while to interrupt his studies to write the most elaborate of his early works, and both composition and performance would seem to confirm a poetical destiny accepted with confidence in *Ad Patrem*; his father, retired from business, might well be uneasy (especially if he had read Prynne's *Histriomastix*); and Milton's continuing interest in Latin verse is attested in his letter to Gill of 4 December 1634. Further, if Milton's arrangement of poems had been based on artistic grounds, he would probably have allowed *Ad Patrem* to introduce the Latin section or would have placed it beside *Mansus*: 'Its present position, if not chronological, is meaningless.' So Parker would have the poem written in 1634, 'probably between September 29, when *Comus* was performed, and November 29, when the Greek translation of Psalm 114 had been composed.'

Before we look at Parker's latest statement we may take account of two intervening commentators. Sirluck supports '1637 or early 1638' for *Ad Patrem*. His appendix, already quoted from, is mainly a summary of scholarly opinions. His discussion in the text (766–67) is part of a large argument and needs to be read in its context; he sees Milton renewing and deepening his religious and poetic self-dedication with pledges of celibacy in 1637 and *Ad Patrem* as related to this phase. One may not be convinced by either the main thesis or its application to this poem. Sirluck imagines Milton, in conversations preceding the poem, defending his position on the ground that a poet is God's priest.

But at this point either the father or the poet's own conscience...must have said something like the following: 'It was on this ground that you refused to take orders; it was with this argument that you met the suspicion that you were surrendering to the allurements of a life of retirement and books; but many years have gone by, and the work 'doctrinal and exemplary to a Nation' is nowhere to be seen. How can you know that you are not deceiving yourself: avoiding a duty which you find distasteful, not performing the duty which you proclaim its surrogate, taking all—a life of ease and scholarly pleasure—and giving nothing?'

But if the father or the poet's conscience put the question in such terms, it is odd that in the poem Milton did not try to answer on the same high ground. In fact the imaginary conversation has no recognizable connection with either the substance or the manner of the poem. There is in *Ad Patrem* no sign of a troubled conscience: Milton is completely serene and confident in the obvious rightness of his case. It was perhaps natural to avoid the fact that he had been brought up with the expectation of becoming a clergyman, but Milton barely touched the exalted conception of the poet-priest. Almost everything that he says and does not say would rather confirm than remove the qualms Sirluck puts into words. The poetic vocation described and implied in *Ad Patrem* is not like that set forth in the personal passages of the early tracts. It is, on the contrary, the perfect picture of the Renaissance humanist-poet, classical and largely secular, the scholar-artist of the elite. Both the substance and the tone of the poem are a world away from the religious vision of *Lycidas* and the religious additions to *Comus* on which Sirluck lays much stress (although we do not know that these were written in 1637).

J. T. Shawcross (*N&Q* 6, 1959, 358–9) gives reasons, based on problems in the physical make-up of some pages in the *Poems* of 1645, for thinking that *Ad Patrem* was placed out of chronological order; his reasoning is concrete but his conclusion seems speculative. Following H. A. Barnett's argument for the time of year (see 38 n. below), the opinions of Grierson and Tillyard, and H. Darbishire's suggestion that *Comus* was published early in 1638, Shawcross puts *Ad Patrem* 'around March 1638.' Like a number of opinions mentioned above, this takes no account of contrary reasons. In 'Milton's Decision to Become a Poet' (*MLQ* 24, 1963, 21–30) Shawcross reaffirms his date for *Ad Patrem*, in the course of an argument that reaches an astonishing conclusion: 'None of the works before 1637 which have usually been adduced to indicate leanings toward a poetic career prove so under scrutiny. The writings before this date are all casual, or occasional, or done on commission.' (These loosely derogatory headings cover the *Vacation Exercise*, the *Nativity*, *Elegy* 6, *Il Penseroso*, 'How soon hath time,' *Arcades*, and *Comus*.) 'It was not until 1637 that he recognized this calling and took steps to become more fit'—having, it appears, loafed and drifted through five years at Hammersmith and Horton.

Ad Patrem

Parker, in his latest argument (*Milton*, 788–9, notes 25, 26,) brings further support to 1634, now specifically March or April, four or five months before the performance of *Comus* (see Barnett, 38 n. below). The poem must have been written after Milton left Cambridge (July 1632), since he is at leisure (lines 73–6), is not forced into business or law (68–72), and has more time to study the history not provided at Cambridge (14); the ministerial career is not mentioned but is 'simply assumed.' As against 1637, Parker thinks *Ad Patrem* reflects the Milton who 'is still composing Latin verse' and is 'not yet dedicated to English'; the poem is 'youthful in attitude and tone,' the work of 'an obscure poet who has not yet tasted the triumph of *Comus*.' And 'although he professes to rise above his hitherto trivial songs...he nevertheless classes *Ad Patrem* among his *juvenilia carmina* (115), which can hardly include *Comus* or *Lycidas*.' And the opening of *Lycidas* breaks 'a long poetic silence.' Some of Parker's reasons are stronger for 1631–2 than for 1634; others will come up shortly.

Some of Woodhouse's arguments have been anticipated, but they must be summarized in coherent fashion. His discussion of *Ad Patrem* is only one item in his tracing of Milton's early artistic and spiritual development. He would assign the poem to the poet's last year at Cambridge, 1631–2. The approaching end of his academic career would inevitably raise in his own mind, and in his father's, the question of his future. Other reasons emerge from the course of his writing. In the time between early 1630 and early 1631 Milton wrote the epitaphs on Shakespeare, Hobson, and the Marchioness of Winchester, all 'exercises' in the sense that they were outside or on the fringe of his inner life. Then in the rest of 1631 and in 1632 came *L'Allegro and Il Penseroso* (and, in Woodhouse's view, *Ad Patrem* and *Arcades*), and in December 1632 the earnestly religious self-dedication, 'How soon hath time.' The last four of these pieces, says Woodhouse (84), both carry on something of the abstraction of the epitaphs and bear a closer relation to Milton's inward evolution. 'Through each of *Il Penseroso*, *Prolusion 7* and *Ad Patrem* there run two or more of these themes: leisure, learning and poetry' (88). The invocation, in *Prolusion 7*, of the glades and streams of

Milton's summer with the Muses recalls the scene and mood of *Il Penseroso,*

just after the position of *Ad Patrem,* on leisure, learning and poetry has been anticipated. For that poem is not adequately described as Milton's Apology for Poetry, which conceals its common ground with *Il Penseroso* and *Prolusion* 7. It must be described as Milton's plea for the leisure necessary to learning, and the learning necessary to poetry: his defence of poetry indeed, but also of the contemplative life which alone renders it possible: his assertion, finally, of the delight as well as the dignity of means and end—a description which immediately reveals the common ground. (89)[2]

Woodhouse showed the fallacies of Grierson's arguments for 1637, arguments that would, along with other things, place *Ad Patrem* after, long after, *Sonnet* 7, although the sonnet 'is the record of a religious experience which adds to Milton's conception of himself as poet elements lacking in *Ad Patrem*' (90).

Some preoccupations (with the absence of others) and the tone of *Ad Patrem* are alike foreign to the later Horton period. They seem to place the poem in the lighter air of Cambridge and with the Companion Pieces, *Prolusion* 7, and *Arcades*...The connections suggested by *Ad Patrem* are nearly all with the writings of the Cambridge period. (90)

Milton has no wealth except that given by Clio, which, if it means historical reading, recalls *Prolusion* 7; heroic poetry means, not a British theme, but something vaguely classical, as in the *Vacation Exercise* and *Elegy* 6.[3] The allusion to the poet as priest is in terms reminiscent of *Elegy* 6, and the poet's joining the angels' song, which is echoed by the music of the spheres, recalls the *Nativity*; his poetry to date is 'my boyish verses and amusements,' which hardly covers *Comus,* especially if that work fixed his wavering choice. And is it credible, Woodhouse asks, that, throughout the Cambridge period and five years at home,

---

[2] Though mindful of the cautious scepticism registered above concerning parallels as evidence for dating, I might refer, as an example of common ground, to the image of philosophy or nature offering herself naked to man's view in *Patrem* 90-2 (see note) and *Prolusion* 6 (*Works* 12, 216, lines 1-3). *Patrem* has in fact a good many parallels, general or particular, with the poems and prolusions of 1626-32.

[3] This seems to me a mistaken interpretation of Milton's allusion to Clio: see 14 n. below.

Milton drifted, until the success of *Comus* showed him where he was going? 'On the contrary, Milton's hopes and plans in poetry date back to his earliest days at Cambridge and appear to manifest a steady growth and clarification'—witness the *Vacation Exercise, Elegy* 6, *Nativity*, and *Prolusion* 7. Then there is the mainly secular tone of *Ad Patrem*, 'the absence...of any stress on the religious calling and ethical function of the poet,' which suggests 'some fading of the religious experience of December 1629,' an experience to be strongly renewed in 'How soon hath time' (91–2). Thus *Ad Patrem* belongs to a period, from the spring of 1631 to the summer of 1632, marked both by rapid maturing and by tranquility, the period of *L'Allegro* and *Il Penseroso* in which, in the words of *Ad Patrem*, Milton was able to banish 'sleepless cares and complaints' and 'walk with heart secure.'

Some other considerations may be added. The argument that the 'maturity' of *Ad Patrem* favors a late date seems very tenuous; like a number of Milton's Latin poems, this one is both mature and immature. Then in lines 71–6, after the one imperfect tense, *jubebas*, Milton says to his father, in brief, that 'you do not drag me to the law,' 'you do not condemn my ears to foolish clamor,' but 'you allow me' to attend Phoebus and the Muses. He is clearly referring to his situation at the moment of writing; if he were writing *c.* 1637, or even *c.* 1634, it would be hard to imagine his using present tenses about an attitude his father must have taken before or soon after he left Cambridge. In these lines, moreover, Milton says that his father, eager to enrich his son's mind, took him away from the noisy city into lettered peace—a phrase which fits removal from London to Cambridge but does not fit removal at a later time from Cambridge to Hammersmith or Horton. Several reasons appear, in or between the lines. While it would be quite proper for Milton to say that his father 'drew' him (75, *Abductum*) away from the city to the university, it would be hardly correct to say that his father 'drew' him back home; so far as we know, he just went. Then we may remember that during his candidacy for the M.A., 1629–32, Milton was free from the more irksome demands of his undergraduate years; and the language of *Ad Patrem* implies that he is not in studious isolation but is a member of a cultivated community. Although the atmosphere of Cambridge had not at first been congenial, it became so increasingly, and it was there that Milton did most of his early writing. At the end of a letter written 'amid city distractions' to Thomas Young (dated 26 March 1625, but probably of 1627: *C.P.W.* 1, 310–12; *Works* 12, 7), Milton promised a fuller one 'as soon as I have returned to the haunts of the Muses.' In his letter to Gill of 2 July 1628 he spoke of himself, in Cambridge, as being 'in Athens itself, nay in the very Academy' (i.e. of Plato);[1] and, though he complained of the scarcity of literary companions, he contrasted London with the immediate prospect of summer retirement 'into a deeply literary leisure... in the bowers of the Muses,' that is, the university.

Finally, if Milton was living under his father's roof, in daily contact with him, it would surely be straining even the artificial inspiration of much Neo-Latin verse to address him in a poem.

To sum up the matter, advocates of 1637 or 1634 have not met the reasons given for 1631–2, and the case for the earliest date may be thought far stronger than that so far made for either of the later dates.

NOTES

1–2 *Nunc mea Pierios cupiam per pectora fontes | Irriguas torquere vias.* For *Pierios* see *El* 4. 31 n. Cf. Manilius: *Ducite Pierides... | ...inriguos in carmina ducere cantus* (3. 3–4: ed. Scaliger, p. 59, lines 17–18; Housman reads *ignotos... census*); Statius, *S.* 1. 2. 6, *Pieriis...fontibus*; Virgil, *G.* 4. 32, *inriguumque... fontem.*

3 *gemino de vertice.* Parnassus. See the note on *El* 4. 30.

[1] This rendering of *Academia* (*C.P.W.* 1, 314) seems to be more accurate than 'the University itself' (*Works* 12, 11, line 24).

In *Patrem* 74 Milton says his father removed him *urbano strepitu*, 'from the din and the uproar of the city' (presumably London) to the haunts of Apollo and the Muses (Cambridge). In his letter to Young (21 July 1628), in which he accepted Young's invitation to visit him at Stowmarket (see Parker, 740–1, n. 60), Milton, writing from Cambridge, used the words *ab urbano strepitu subducam me* (*Works* 12, 14, lines 5–6; *C.P.W.* 1, 315–16); but here he was playfully emphasizing the philosophic peace of Young's rural abode in contrast with crowded Cambridge.

4 *tenues oblita sonos audacibus alis.* Milton's implied apology for former trivia need not have been serious, since it enhances his present theme. Cf. Virgil, *E.* 4. 1: *Sicelides Musae, paulo maiora canamus*; Horace, *C.* 1. 6. 8–9: *nec... | conamur, tenues grandia, dum pudor | ...vetat*; Ovid, *M.* 1. 708, *sonum tenuem.* Fletcher cites *audaces...alas* in Ovid, *H.* 18. 49 and Sil. Ital. 12. 103; cf. *PL* 1. 12–16, and 3. 13, 'with bolder wing.'

5 *venerandi...parentis.* The phrase needs no precedents, but cf. *venerand(a) (e) parens* in Claudian 1. 177 (1, 14) and Grotius, *Anapaesti In mortem Bezae (Farr.,* bk. 3, p. 216). In *JEGP* 49 (1950), 345–51, M. Little finds some rather tenuous resemblances between Milton's poem and his friend Gill's *In Parentis mei Natalem,* published in *Parerga* (1632) but written in 1625 and probably seen by Milton. Gill refers (p. 14) to his father as *venerande senex* (a stock phrase: *El* 3. 57 and note). For other Miltonic parallels with this poem see the notes on 111 below and on *El* 2. 7–8 and *El* 3. 57.

6 *pater optime.* A phrase applied in Virgil (*A.* 1. 555) to Aeneas, in Horace (*S.* 1. 4. 105, 2. 1. 12) to his father and Trebatius, in Ovid (*Tr.* 3. 1. 49) to Augustus, in Val. Flacc. (4. 65) to Jupiter, in Ariosto (*Carm.* 12. 4) to his father, in Buchanan (*Sph.* 1. 70, 5. 419) to God.

7 *Exiguum...opus.* In Ovid, *F.* 2. 4, *P.* 3. 4. 5.

11 *vacuis quae redditur arida verbis.* Cf. Sallust, *Jug.* 90. 1, *ager...aridus et frugum vacuus.*

12 *census.* The financial rating or wealth of a Roman citizen; here Milton's poetic capacity, which is all he possesses. Ovid speaks in the same way: *Am.* 2. 17. 27, *sunt mihi pro magno felicia carmina censu*; *M.* 3. 588, *ars illi sua census erat*; *P.* 4. 8. 34, *Naso suis opibus, carmine gratus erit*; *A.A.* 3. 172, *M.* 7. 739, *F.* 1. 217–18. Cf. Petrarch, *Ep. Zoilo* (2): *Census honestus | Est mihi, Musarum studium (P.M.* 2, 242).

14 *aurea Clio.* Clio is golden partly because she is a substitute for gold coin. MacKellar follows Masson (*P.W.* 3, 342) in explaining Milton's reference to the Muse of history on the ground that 'what he is to say about his Father is strictly true,' and cites Ovid, *A.A.* 1. 27 and Horace, *C.* 1. 12. 2. Hughes suggests, if Milton had any particular meaning, a patriotic ambition to write 'poetry based on the heroic past of England.' These interpretations—and those of Woodhouse and Parker mentioned in the headnote (237–8)—seem over-literal. The context shows that Milton is only naming Clio, in a traditional way, as the prime and general representative of poetry; she had acquired that function because, from Hesiod (*Theog.* 77) onward, she commonly came first in lists of the Muses;

see the note on *El* 4. 31–2 above. Here, as there, Carey takes Clio as 'holy guardian of lustration' (Simonides, quoted in Plutarch, *The Oracles at Delphi* 402, L.C.L. 5, 303), but the aptness of such a reference is not clear.

15 *Quas mihi semoto somni peperere sub antro.* For the association of caves and poetic inspiration see *El* 5. 17 n.

16 On sacred groves, laurel, and Parnassus, see the notes on *Idea* 1, *El* 5. 13–14, and *El* 4. 30.

17–55 The praise of poetry has general affinities with many panegyrics ancient and modern, e.g. Horace, *Ep.* 2. 1. 119 f., *A.P.* 391–407; Ovid (see the note on 21 f. below); Sidney's *Apologie*; Puttenham, *Arte of English Poesie*, ed. G. D. Willcock and A. Walker (Cambridge, 1936), 3 f.

17 *Nec tu vatis opus divinum despice carmen.* Cf. Ovid, *P.* 4. 8. 67, *non potes officium vatis contemnere vates*; Vida, *A.P.* 1. 11, *sacras ne despice Musas*; Lucretius 1. 731, *carmina...divini pectoris*; Horace, *A.P.* 400, *divinis vatibus atque | carminibus*; and *divino carmine* in Catullus 64. 321, Virgil, *E.* 6. 67, and Pontano, *Uran.* 1. 450.

18–20 *aethereos ortus, & semina caeli, | ...Sancta Prometheae retinens vestigia flammae.* Although Milton is perhaps thinking of Prometheus' gift of fire (Hesiod, *Theog.* 510–69, *W.D.* 42–58; Aeschylus, *Prom.* 106–10, etc.; Milton, *InvBom* 1–2 and note) more than of his making men of clay (Apollodorus 1. 7. 1, Lucian, *Prometheus*, and Spenser, *F.Q.* 2. 10. 70 tell of both), he seems to have in mind Ovid's account of the creation of man, *M.* 1. 76–81: *Sanctius his animal mentisque capacius altae | ...divino semine... | aethere cognati retinebat semina caeli.* Cf. also Catullus 64. 294–5: *Prometheus, | extenuata gerens veteris vestigia poenae.* Promethean fire was allegorized as philosophic and poetic inspiration, e.g. Comes, *Mythol.* 4. 6; Chapman, *Poems*, ed. P. B. Bartlett (New York, 1941), 22, 388, 426; Milton, *Prol* 7 (*Works* 12, 248, lines 13–16, quoted in translation under *Idea* 27–8). Cf. *vestigia flammae* in Virgil, *A.* 4. 23, Buchanan, *S.* 3. 36, and Grotius, *Epist. Palladii* (*El.*, bk. 1, p. 155); and Poliziano, *Sylvae* 4. 74 (*P.V.*, p. 374; *C.P.I.* 7, 296), *Prometheae coelestia semina flammae.*

21 f. *Carmen amant superi*, etc. Although the details illustrative of the power of song differ, the repetition of *Carmen* at the beginning of several lines recalls Ovid, *Am.* 2. 1. 23–38, *Tr.* 1. 1. 39–43, Virgil, *E.* 8. 69–71, and Secundus, *El.* 3. 1. Cf. also the celebration of the power of poetry in Ovid, *P.* 4. 8. 43–82; Horace, *Ep.* 2. 1. 138, *Carmine di superi placantur, carmine Manes*; and the notes on 17 above and 56 below. Cf. Milton, *El* 6. 14, *Carmen amat Bacchum*, etc.

21–3 *tremebundaque Tartara carmen | Ima ciere valet*, etc. The generalized allusion to Orpheus includes possible echoes of Virgil's story, *G.* 4. 454–527: *regemque tremendum*, 469; *de sedibus imis*, 471; *Tartara*, 482 (cf. Seneca, *Oed.* 869, *Tartara ima*); *coercet*, 480. There seem to be no echoes of such other accounts of Orpheus as Ovid, *M.* 10. 1–63 and Boethius, *C.P.* 3, met. 12. Cf. *L'All* 145–50, *IlPen* 105–8; the latter is obviously closer in tone. See the note on Orpheus under 52–5 below.

23 *triplici duros Manes adamante coercet. Triplex* is more familiar with the *aes* of Horace, *C.* 1. 3. 9 and Virgil, *A.* 10. 784. Cf. Virgil, *A.* 6. 552, *solidoque adamante*; Ovid, *M.* 4. 453, *carceris ante fores clausas adamante sedebant*; Milton, *Prol* 1 (*Works* 12, 122–4, *catenis adamantinis...Briareus* (where Milton goes on to speak of the *Deos manes* aroused a third time to a hope of heavenly dominion); and the note on *Naturam* 5. Todd cited Val. Flacc. 3. 408, *carmina turbatos volvit placantia manes.*

24 *Carmine sepositi retegunt arcana futuri.* Cf. Lucan 5. 137–8: *farique sat est arcana futuri | Carmina* (Fletcher); Horace, *C.* 3. 21. 15–16: *arcanum iocoso | consilium retegis Lyaeo*; Seneca, *Oed.* 522: *arcana sacri voce ni retegis tua*; Vida, *A.P.* 1. 1–2, *vulgare arcana... | ...recludere.*

25 *Phoebades.* 'Priestesses of Apollo, especially at Delphi, where the answers of the oracle were usually made in verse' (Hughes). Editors cite Ovid, *Am.* 2. 8. 12, *Tr.* 2. 400; Lucan 5. 128–30; Vida, *A.P.* 1. 36–8; and Milton, *El* 6. 73 (see the note).

25 *tremulae pallentes ora Sibyllae.* Without comment Columbia keeps *pallantes*, the misprint of 1673. Milton would think especially of the Cumaean Sibyl who conducted Aeneas to Hades (Virgil, *A.* 6. 46–51, 77–80). For prophetic *carmina* MacKellar cites ibid. 3. 445–6; Lucan 5. 136–8; and Vida, *A.P.* 1. 539–41. Cf. Claudian, *S.P.* 3 (2, 176).

26 *Carmina sacrificus sollennes pangit ad aras. Pangere* means to 'compose' (e.g. Lucretius 1. 25, 933–4, 4. 8–9, Horace, *Ep.* 1. 18. 40) and editors find no authority for a priest's composing verses. Milton may have used the word in the sense of 'sing,' 'recite.' Thomas Cooper's *Thesaurus* (ed. 1584) gives 'to write: to make: to sing: to tell.' The verb occurs some fourteen times, with or without *laudes*, in Buchanan's version of the Psalms (9. 12, 26. 7, 29. 2, 33. 1, 47. 1, 71. 15, 96. 1, 98. 1, 103. 20, 21, 22, 117. 1, 147. 12, 148. 5), where the King James Bible has 'sing,' 'shout,' 'bless,' 'praise.' *Solennes aras* is a common phrase, e.g. Virgil, *A.* 2. 202; Pontano, *Uran.* 1. 373, *L.D.* 6. 5; Sannazaro, *El.* 1. 2. 35, 3. 3. 7, *Epig.* 2. 36. 26, 2. 37. 7.

27 *Aurea seu sternit motantem cornua taurum.* For the gilding of the sacrificial bull's horns MacKellar cites Homer, *Od.* 3. 437–8 (cf. also 384, 426) and Seneca, *Oed.* 137, *aureo taurus...cornu.* Cf. Seneca, *Herc. Oet.* 785, *tauris... auratis;* Ovid, *M.* 10. 271; Virgil, *G.* 1. 217, Val. Flacc. 1. 89, and Pliny, *N.H.* 33. 12. 39, *auratis...cornibus;* Sannazaro, *P.V.* 1. 413, *Taurus: cui cornua fronti | Aurea;* Prudentius, *Perist.* 10. 1024–5.

28–9 Milton would know of ancient rituals of augury from many sources, e.g. Ovid, *M.* 15. 130–7. MacKellar cites Cicero, *Div.* 2. 12–16, on the inspection of entrails. Cf. Virgil, *G.* 1. 484, 2. 194. For the *Parcae* (here singular), see the notes on *ProdBom* 1. 7 and *Procan* 2.

30–7 The picture of the Christian heaven has something of the ecstatic glow of the crowning vision of *Lyc* and *EpDam* (and cf. the conclusion of *Eli*). Editors cite Rev. 4. 4, 5. 8, 14. 2. These verses are, in Beza's version: 4. 4: *Et in circuitu throni, erant throni viginti quatuor: & super eos thronos vidi viginti quatuor Seniores sedentes, amictos vestibus albis, & habentes impositas capitibus suis coronas aureas;* 5. 8: *Quumque accepisset librum, quatuor illa animalia & viginti quatuor illi Seniores prociderunt in conspectu Agni, habentes singuli citharas & phialas aureas plenas suffituum, quae sunt preces sanctorum;* 14. 2: *Et audivi vocem e caelo tamquam vocem aquarum multarum, & tamquam sonum tonitrui magni: & vocem audivi citharoedorum pulsantium citharas suas.*

30 *patrium...Olympum.* In various cases, in Vida, *Christ.* 3. 533, Buchanan, *Sph.* 1. 549, and Grotius, *Annales Dousarum (S.,* bk. 2, p. 46). Cf. Milton, *Prol* 7 (*Works* 12, 254, lines 4–5), *ad nativum coelum.*

31 *Aeternaeque morae stabunt immobilis aevi.* At the end of life and time and the beginning of eternity. See Tillyard's comment on the line, quoted above in the general Introduction, p. 21. Cf. Buchanan, *Sph.* 2. 613, *aeternoque immobilis aevo;* Claudian 22. 435 (2, 34), *stabilesque moras.* The latter passage Milton apparently recalled in his picture of *Aeternitas* in *Idea* 3–6.

32 *Ibimus auratis per caeli templa coronis.* There seems to be a deliberate contrast between these golden crowns and the bull's gilded horns—that is, between Christianity and paganism. Cf. *coronas aureas* in Rev. 4. 4 (quoted under 30–7). *Caeli templa* is in Lucretius 1. 1014, 1064, 1105, 2. 1039, 6. 286, Secundus, *Fun.* 26. 162, and Milton, *Prol* 1 (*Works* 12, 124, line 5) and *Prol* 3 (ibid. 162, line 20).

33 *Dulcia suaviloquo sociantes carmina plectro.* Cf. Ovid, *M.* 11. 5, *percussis sociantem carmina nervis* (Fletcher); Rev. 14. 2 (quoted above under 30–7); Lucretius 1. 945–6, *suaviloquenti | carmine.*

34 *geminique poli convexa.* Fletcher cites Claudian 15. 2 (1, 98), *alterius convexa poli.* Cf. Ovid, *F.* 3. 106 and 6. 718, *geminos...polos*; Petrarch, *Afr.* 2. 263, 329, *convexa poli*; Grotius, *Ad. Ex.* 283, *Geminique Poli*; Vida, *Christ.* 1. 596, *Stelligeri convexa poli*; and the note on *QNov* 98. Svendsen (*Milton and Science*, 62–3) says that 'the "twin poles" of *To My Father* and the "wheeling poles" of the Vacation Exercise refer to the imaginary axle of the universe, which was thought to coincide with the Pole or North star.'

35–7 *Spiritus & rapidos qui circinat igneus orbes, | Nunc quoque sydereis intercinit ipse choreis | Immortale melos, & inenarrabile carmen.* These lines have received diverse explanations. Masson (*P.W.* 3, 342–3), following Keightley, took the fiery spirit to be the Empyrean, enveloping the spheres; but this strains the meaning of *Spiritus, circinat,* and *ipse intercinit.* In what seems to be the only occurrence of *spiritus* in the Prolusions (*Prol* 7, *Works* 12, 266, line 1, quoted in *Eli* 46 n.), the word means the soaring mind of man, and is obviously an individual spirit. Le Comte (*Yet Once More*, 108) quotes *Comus* 111–14 as a parallel. Woodhouse ('Notes,' 93–4, n. 41) cited Thomas Heywood's *Hierarchie of the blessed Angells* (1635), 272, for a parallel between the natural and the celestial worlds, in particular 'what reference the Seraphim / Hath with the Primum Mobile. Then, what kin / The Cherub from the Starry Heav'n doth claime...' Woodhouse commented: 'It is this traditional association of the cherubim with the starry heaven that explains Milton's allusion...to the fiery spirit flying through the swift spheres and singing his *inenarrabile carmen.* The spirit is, I take it, not the Platonic soul of the world (as Tillyard supposes [*Milton*, 377, n. 1; and cf. MacKellar, 310]) or the interfused and sustaining spirit and mind of Virgil's *Aeneid* 6. 724–7 (as Hughes suggests [cf. Keightley]), but the cherub, whose song harmonizes with the music of the spheres, and (because it is angelic) is by man "unutterable." The link is with the Cherub of *Il Penseroso*.' Behind both he sees (87) Ezek. 10 (and 1 ?). On the music of the spheres and Neoplatonic conceptions of music see the long note on *Nativity* 125–32 in the Variorum Commentary. Shawcross (*C.E.P.*) takes the *spiritus* as Apollo.

J. Carey ('Milton's *Ad Patrem*, 35–37,' *RES* 15, 1964, 180–4) sees basic errors in 'all' previous commentators, though he cites only Keightley, Masson, and MacKellar. Masson 'is wrong in every particular.' Carey ignores Woodhouse, but dismisses Keightley's reference to Ezekiel as irrelevant, since Ezekiel lacks 'the two features which distinguish the *spiritus* in *Ad Patrem*: extra-spherical flight and song.' Carey argues persuasively that the *spiritus* is Milton's own disembodied spirit. Illustrating the traditional idea of the soul's upward voyage (see above, the notes on *Eli* 37–8 and 46), Carey quotes Cicero's

Somnium Scipionis (Rep. 6. 15, 17, and 18); Macrobius' *Commentary* on Cicero (*Opera*, ed. L. Janus, Quedlinburg, 1848–52, 1, 76–7); and *Hermetica*, ed. W. Scott (Oxford, 1924–36), 1, 220. 'Milton claims, then, that his fiery spirit soars even now, while he is still alive, to the outermost sphere of the universe and there, whirling around the other spheres, joins in the immortal song of the starry choir.'

With Milton's phrasing, cf. *circinat orbe(m)(s)* in Manilius 1. 638 and Buchanan, *Sph.* 1. 278, 2. 185, 507, 3. 91; Ovid, *M.* 2. 73, *rapido...orbi*; Virgil, *A.* 8. 97 (end), *igneus orbem.* Along with examples of *inenarrabilis* in Harpers' Latin Dictionary cf. Prudentius, *Perist.* 2. 553–4, Vida (*C.P.I.* 11, 64), Grotius, *Epith. Guil.* (*S.*, bk. 3, p. 117); and *non* or *haud enarrabile* in Virgil, *A.* 8. 625, Persius 5. 29, and Vida, *Christ.* 1. 586. In *Prol* 2 (*Works* 12, 152, line 10) Milton describes the music of the spheres as *ineffabile illud Astrorum melos.*

38–40 H. A. Barnett ('A Time of the Year for Milton's "Ad Patrem,"' *MLN* 73, 1958, 82–3) explains that the position of the stars described in 38–40 would fit about March 5 at midnight or April 5 at 10 p.m., roughly, the vernal equinox, the season of renewed life and confidence.

38 *Torrida dum rutilus compescit sibila serpens.* 'Milton thought of Ovid's account of Phaeton riding the chariot of the sun, when he was threatened by the Serpent (the constellation which winds between the two celestial bears) and by all the other formidable constellations in the sky. (*Met.* 11, 173–5).' (Hughes). Cf. Virgil, *G.* 1. 205, 244–5.

39 *Demissoque ferox gladio mansuescit Orion.* See *Eli* 54 n. and the description of Orion with *demissus ensis* in Manilius 1. 391 (Brodribb, *N&Q* 159, 1930, 129). Orion is *ferox* (*saevus* in Virgil, *A.* 7. 719) because the constellation was associated with storms; cf. *PL* 1. 305, 'with fierce Winds Orion arm'd.'

40 *Stellarum nec sentit onus Maurusius Atlas.* See *Idea* 24 n. The mountain was in Mauretania (Maurusia to the Greeks), i.e. Morocco (Diod. Sic. 3. 53. 4–5; Pliny, *N.H.* 5. 1. 6–16). Cf. Claudian 28. 104 (2, 82), *Maurusius Atlas*; Ovid, *M.* 9. 273, *sensit Atlas pondus*; 15. 694, *sensit onus*; Lucan 1. 57, *Sentiet axis onus*; Virgil, *A.* 4. 206, 246–51.

41–9 For bards singing at royal feasts, see Homer, *Il.* 1. 601–4, *Od.* 8. 62 f., 254 f., 499 f.; Virgil, *A.* 1. 740–6. For the exalted themes of poetry, see Virgil, *E.* 4 and 6; Horace, *C.* 1. 6; Ovid, *Am.* 2. 1. 11–32, etc.; a multitude of Renaissance poets and critics; and Milton, *Vac* 29–52, *Mansus* 78–84, *EpDam* 161–8, etc. *Regales epulas* is a stock phrase, e.g. Ovid, *M.* 6. 488, Statius, *Th.* 2. 306, Sil. Ital. 11. 42, Vida, *A.P.* 2. 357, Pontano, *Uran.* 4. 627.

42–3 *vastaeque immensa vorago | Nota gulae.* The Roman poets, even Ovid (*F*. 1. 191–226, etc.), were given to looking back from an age of luxury to the simplicity of primitive Rome or the mythical golden age long before that. For Milton's phrasing cf. Cicero, *Verr*. 2. 3. 9. 23, *immensa aliqua vorago* (Fletcher), and, in Sil. Ital. 5. 617 (end) and Mantuan, *Cal. Temp*., p. 38, *immensa vorago*; Virgil, *A*. 6. 296 and Lucan 4. 99, *vastaque voragine*; Ovid, *M*. 8. 843–6, *altaque voragine ventris | …flamma gulae.*

43 *modico spumabat coena Lyaeo.* For Lyaeus, a common name for Bacchus or wine, see the note on *El* 6. 21–2. Cf. *multo…Lyaeo* in Ovid, *A.A*. 3. 645, 765, Propertius 2. 33. 35, 3. 5. 21, and Gill, *Epith*. (p. 43); Ovid, *P*. 1. 10. 29, *immodico…Lyaeo*; Horace, *C*. 1. 18. 7, *modici…munera Liberi.*

44 *festa…convivia.*In Martial 4. 55. 17.

45 *Aesculea intonsos redimitus ab arbore crines.* Cf. Ovid, *M*. 8. 410, *aesculea… ab arbore*; 9. 3, *redimitus harundine crines. Intonsus* is a stock epithet for Apollo, e.g. Horace, *C*. 1. 21. 2; Ovid, *M*. 1. 564, *Tr*. 3. 1. 60; Tibullus 1. 4. 37–8, 2. 5. 121; cf. Homer, *Il*. 20. 39, Pindar, *Pyth*. 3. 14, Milton, *Vac* 37.

46 *Heroumque actus, imitandaque gesta canebat.* Todd cited Vida, *A.P*. 1. 544, *Post epulas laudes heroum, & facta canentes*; cf. ibid. 1. 4, *Heroum qui facta canat.* See Tillyard's comment quoted under 47. Milton's line reappears, with very slight changes, as line 43 in *Mansus*; see the note on 102 below.

47 *Et chaos, & positi late fundamina mundi.* Editors cite the song of Iopas, Virgil, *A*. 1. 740–6; cf. Virgil, *E*. 6. 31–40. Cf. Ovid, *M*. 10. 17, *positi…mundi*; Milton, *Nat* 123, 'And cast the dark foundations deep.' Apropos of *Patrem* 44–9, Tillyard remarks: 'The acts of heroes and their function as "examples" fit in perfectly with Renaissance theory and Spenserian practice and a possible *Arthuriad*. But chaos and the creation show that Milton continued to be haunted by the theme of Hesiod and Du Bartas' (*M. Set.* 182–3).

48 *Reptantesque Deos, & alentes numina glandes.* The Roman poets often refer to acorns as the food of primitive people before Ceres taught agriculture, e.g. Lucretius 5. 939–40, 965, 1363, 1416, Horace, *S*. 1. 3. 100, Virgil, *G*. 1. 148, Claudian 36. 43–7 (2, 348). With or without authority, Milton may be extending the idea to the infancy of the gods (cf. Tillyard, *M. Set.* 182, n. 1). Hughes suggests that he is thinking of the Titans and cites Apollon. Rhod. 4. 988–9. Or Milton may have thought of the serpentine Aesculapius and other primitive deities such as the Egyptian (Visiak); cf. *PL* 1. 489, 'all her bleating Gods.' Cf. Lucan 9. 727–8: *qui cunctis innoxia numina terris | Serpitis…dracones*; and

Milton, *Prol* 7 (*Works* 12, 270, lines 19–20, and 272, lines 1–3). Milton might, however, be using *reptare* in the sense of 'stroll,' as in Horace, *Ep.* 1. 4. 4, and Pliny, *Ep.* 1. 24 (and perhaps 9. 26), thinking of the gods mingling with mankind on earth. Cf. *PL* 1. 481–2, on Egypt's 'wandring Gods disguis'd in brutish forms / Rather then human.' Cf. also the 'creeping things' of Ezek. 8. 10 and Rom. 1. 23. Carey cites the account of creation in Ovid, *M.* 1. 73 and 106.

49 *Aetneo quaesitum fulmen ab antro.* Jove's thunderbolts were forged by Vulcan and his assistant Cyclopes under Mount Etna (Virgil, *G.* 1. 471–3, 4. 170–5, *A.* 8. 416–28). Cf. Seneca, *Hipp.* 102–3, *Aetnaeo... / antro*; Val. Flacc. 4. 104, *Aetnaeis...Cyclopes in antris.*

50–5 *Denique quid vocis modulamen inane juvabit,* etc. Here, as in *SolMus* 1–3 and *Sonn* 13, Milton is 'expressing his attachment to the traditional conception of the two arts as vitally related to each other' (Hughes). MacKellar cites I. Langdon, *Milton's Theory*, 39–40, 228–30, and Vida, *A.P.* 1. 181–4. Cf. Pontano, *Uran.* 2. 1303, *vocis...modulamine.*

52–5 *Orphea... / Qui tenuit fluvios & quercubus addidit aures / Carmine, non cithara, simulachraque functa canendo / Compulit in lacrymas.* See the note on 21–3 above. Milton seems, as often, to be adapting and fusing phrases from several sources. Cf. Ovid, *M.* 10. 14–15, *perque leves populos simulacraque functa sepulcro* (cf. ibid. 4. 435, *simulacraque functa sepulcris*); 10. 41, *exsangues flebant animae*; 10. 45–6, *lacrimis... / Eumenidum maduisse genas*; 10. 90, *non Chaonis afuit arbor*; Virgilian *Cul.* 117–18: *tantum non Orpheus Hebrum / restantem tenuit ripis silvasque canendo*; ibid. 278–82: *rapidi steterant amnes... / ...imam viridi radicem moverat alte / quercus humo*; Horace, *C.* 1. 12. 10–12 (on Orpheus), *fluminum lapsus... / ducere quercus*; Claudian 34. 22 (2, 316, on Orpheus), *comitem quercum pinus amica trahit.* Todd cited Manilius 5. 327: *et sensus scopulis et silvis addidit aures.*

56 *Nec tu perge precor sacras contemnere Musas.* Cf. Ovid, *P.* 4. 8. 67 (quoted under 17 above); Propertius 2. 13. 3, *graciles vetuit contemnere Musas*; Vida, *A.P.* 1. 501, *contemnere Musas*; Campion, *Epig.* 1. 1. 5 (to Prince Charles): *At tenues ne tu nimis (optime) despice musas.*

57–66 *quarum ipse peritus / Munere,* etc. John Milton senior, if not in the first ranks of composers in the golden age of English music, was still of enough repute to be a contributor to Thomas Morley's *Triumphs of Oriana* (1601) and Thomas Ravenscroft's *Whole Book of Psalms* (1621). See Ernest Brennecke, Jr., *John Milton the Elder and His Music* (New York, 1938).

58 *mille sonos numeros componis ad aptos.* Cf. Ovid, *Tr.* 4. 10. 25, *carmen numeros veniebat ad aptos* (Fletcher); Milton, *Sonn* 13. 1–4.

59 *Millibus & vocem modulis variare canoram.* Cf. *L'All* 137–44, 'Married to immortal verse / ... The melting voice through mazes running.' *Vocem canoram,* in various cases, is a stock phrase, e.g. Cicero, *Brut.* 66. 234; Ovid, *A.A.* 3. 311 (quoted under *Leon* 3. 8); Seneca, *Med.* 356; Manilius 3. 655–6; Secundus, *Od.* 7. 4.

60 *Arionii...nominis haeres.* For Arion see the note on *El* 5. 116, and Virgil, *E.* 8. 56, Propertius 2. 26. 18, Ovid, *A.A.* 3. 325–6. Fletcher cites Ovid, *F.* 2. 93, *nomen Arionium; M.* 6. 239, *aviti nominis heres;* and 15. 819, *nominis heres;* cf. *nominis heres* in Ovid, *F.* 5. 155, Claudian 10. 39 (1, 244).

63 *Cognatas artes, studiumque affine sequamur.* Cf. Manilius 4. 260, *cognatas...artes.*

64 Allusions to Phoebus Apollo as god of music and poetry begin with Homer, *Il.* 1. 603. Cf. Milton, 76 below; *Vac* 37, *Passion* 23, *Shak* 12, *Comus* 477, *Sals* 26, *Mansus* 2, 24, *Lyc* 77.

65 *dona parenti.* Also the end of Virgil, *A.* 3. 469.

66 *Dividuumque Deum genitorque puerque tenemus.* 'The Latin adjective "*dividuus*" for "divisible" or "divisible into two" had fastened on Milton; and he turned it into English. See *Par. Lost,* VII. 382 and XII. 85; also *On Time,* 12' (Masson, *P.W.* 3, 343). The word recurs in Ovid, e.g. *Am.* 2. 10. 10 (Fletcher), 1. 5. 10. *A.A.* 2. 488, *F.* 1. 292.

67 *teneras odisse camoenas.* See the notes on *El* 6. 3 and on 56 above. Cf. Grotius, *Ad I. Reigersbergium (Epig.,* bk. 2, 301), *teneras...Camoenas; In Natalem Patris (Farr.,* bk. 2, 209), *Et quas nunc etiam non possum odisse Camoenas;* Sannazaro, *Sal.* 13, *tenues ne dedignare Camoenas.*

69 *Qua via lata patet, qua pronior area lucri.* Cf. Ovid, *H.* 1. 72, *et patet in curas area lata meas; F.* 2. 456, *ianua lata patet;* Cicero, *Verr.* 2. 4. 53. 119, *una via lata.*

70 *Certaque condendi fulget spes aurea nummi.* Keightley cited Persius, *Prol.* 12, *spes refulserit nummi* (echoed also in *Salmas* 1). Cf. Velleius Paterculus 2. 103. 5, *refulsit certa spes liberorum parentibus* (Fletcher); Campion, *Epig.* 1. 122. 7, *spes aurea.*

71–2 *Nec rapis ad leges, male custoditaque gentis | Jura, nec insulsis damnas clamoribus aures.* Masson took the present tense of *sinis* (76) to confirm his view that the poem was written soon after Milton left Cambridge. H. F. Fletcher

Sylvarum Liber

('Grierson's Suggested Date for Milton's "Ad Patrem,"' *Fred Newton Scott Anniversary Papers*, Chicago, 1929, 203), arguing that the poem was written after Milton's Italian tour of 1638–9, says that the present tenses are not 'actual presents' and that therefore *sinis* (76) is not; they all refer to the past. This seems forced and arbitrary. The past tense of *jubebas* (68) refers to the original decision, a broad rejection of money-making, which could include Milton's having been destined from childhood for the church. The present tenses of the other verbs give his father credit for his present happy state.

Editors cite Ovid, *Am.* 1. 15. 5–6: *nec me verbosas leges ediscere nec me | ingrato vocem prostituisse foro*; Propertius 4. 1 A. 133–4: *tum tibi pauca suo de carmine dictat Apollo | et vetat insano verba tonare Foro*; Milton, *El* 1. 31–2 and note; and the scorn for lawyers expressed in *Prol* 7 (*Works* 12, 276) and in *Educ.* Cf. Campion, *Epig.* 1. 205. 4, *male custodita*.

73–6 These lines, and *procul urbano strepitu* in particular, presumably do not refer to Horton (as Masson and others have thought) or to Hammersmith, but to Cambridge. See the latter part of the introduction above. Cf. Horace, *C.* 3. 29. 12, *fumum et opes strepitumque Romae* (and *Comus* 5).

75 *Aoniae...ripae.* See the note on *El* 4. 29–30.

76 *Phoebaeo lateri comitem.* Cf. Val. Flacc. 4. 468, *Phoebi comes.*

78–85 Cf. Milton's grateful tributes to his father's care for his education in *RCG* (*Works* 3, 235) and *Def* 2 (ibid. 8, 118–20). It is of interest, as Masson and MacKellar observe, that in the poem Milton says his father's persuasions added French, Italian, and Hebrew to the normal Latin and Greek. It is not clear why Masson (*P.W.* 3, 344) assumes that these three languages were added while Milton was at Cambridge. See Clark, *J.M. at St. Paul's*, 18 f.

79 *Romuleae...facundia linguae.* For the ancient Romans and Renaissance poets Romulus was the progenitor of the Roman people (Livy 1. 4–7; Virgil, *A.* 1. 275–7; etc.). Cf. Ovid, *P.* 1. 2. 67, *Romanae facundia...linguae*; 2. 3. 75, *Latiae facundia linguae* (Fletcher); *Tr.* 3. 5. 29, 4. 4. 5.

81 *elata vocabula.* Cf. Cicero, *Orator* 36. 124, *elatis...verbis.*

83–4 *degeneri novus Italus ore loquelam | Fundit, Barbaricos testatus voce tumultus.* Cf. Claudian 19. 53 (1, 182), *barbarico...tumultu* (Fletcher); Ovid, *P.* 3. 5. 7, *patrii non degener oris*; Prudentius, *C. Or. Symm.* 2. 643, *degeneri... ore*; Virgil, *A.* 5. 842, *funditque has ore loquellas*; 6. 619, *testatur voce.* H. F. Fletcher (see above, 71–2 n.) took Milton's lines to refer to the Italian accent and hence found support for dating the poem after his Italian travels (an idea tentatively endorsed by J. Carey, *RES* 15, 184: above, 35–7 n.). But Milton might have observed the speech of Italians, or met such comments, in England. Anyhow, the lines do not seem to refer to the modern Italian's defective enunciation but rather to the Italian language as a decline from classical Latin brought about by the barbarian invasions. Tillyard (*Milton*, 384) linked these lines with Milton's remark, in his letter to Diodati of 23 September (November?) 1637, that he has been 'long engaged in the obscure business of the state of Italians under the Longobards, the Franks, and the Germans' (*Works* 12, 29; *C.P.W.* 1, 325–8), and thought it probable 'that *Ad Patrem* and this letter are not very many months separated in time.' However, as we observed above, Milton did not have to wait for special study of medieval Italian history to know that the language was a 'barbarian' adaptation of Latin. Cf. P. Heylyn, *Microcosmus* (1621), 90: 'The language is very courtly and fluent, the best whereof is about Florence and Siena, it retaineth the greatest portion of Latin, but not without the mixture of Barbarous languages so long in use amongst them.' In *Mansus, EpDam*, and elsewhere Milton amply attested his regard for Italian literature and the Italian language and for the cultivated friends he made in Italy, though he recalled their bemoaning 'the servil condition into which lerning amongst them was brought' (*Areop, Works* 4, 329–30).

85 *Quaeque Palaestinus loquitur mysteria vates.* The language and matter of the Hebrew prophets and (Visiak) the Psalmist—here referred to in terms befitting a classical poet-prophet—and hence of the Old Testament in general.

86–92 References are not needed for the Renaissance conception of the poet, especially the heroic poet, as a universal scholar, versed in science as well as letters and history. Cf. the sketch of poetic themes in *Vac* 40–6, and *Prol* 3 (*Works* 12, 168–70) and *Prol* 7; and the note on 47 above.

87 *Terra parens.* A stock phrase, e.g. Virgil, *A.* 4. 178 (cf. 6. 595); Petronius, *Sat.* 127; Juvenal 8. 257; Claudian, *S.P.* 52. 1 (2, 280); Sannazaro, *P.V.* 2. 393; Secundus, *Epist.* 2. 4. 89; *Lacrymae Cantab.* (1619), p. 58.

88 *Quicquid & unda tegit, pontique agitabile marmor.* Cf. Ovid, *M.* 1. 290, *unda tegit*; 2. 263, *quosque altum texerat aequor.* For the 'marble' sea, cf. Homer, *Il.* 14. 273; Catullus 63. 88, *marmora pelagi*; Virgil, *A.* 6. 727–9: *mens agitat molem... | ...et quae marmoreo fert monstra sub aequore pontus*; 7. 28, *in lento...marmore*; Val. Flacc. 1. 313; *C.P.I.* 10, 466, *sub aequoreo...marmore*, and 11, 196, *marmora ponti.*

90–2 *spectanda scientia... | Nudaque...inclinat ad oscula vultus. Scientia* is presumably much broader than our 'science' and includes all knowledge, but here has special emphasis on 'natural philosophy.' Cf. *Prol* 6 (*Works* 12, 216, lines 1–3): *ille Philosophiam nihili facit, quia scilicet formossima Dearum Natura nunquam illum tali dignata est honore, ut se nudam illi praebuerit intuendam.* See above, headnote, n. 2.

92 *Ni fugisse velim, ni sit libasse molestum.* With *libasse* understand *oscula,* as Keightley said, citing Virgil, *A.* 1. 256, *oscula libavit natae.* Granted again that *scientia* embraces more than natural science, the phrase suggests a response less ardent or constant than Milton's devotion to letters.

93 *I nunc, confer opes.* Editors cite Ovid, *H.* 12. 204: *i nunc, Sisyphias, inprobe, confer opes;* and Horace, *Ep.* 1. 6. 17–18. The scornful *i nunc* is common in Ovid (*H.* 3. 26, 4. 127, 9. 105, etc.) and Martial (1. 42. 6, 2. 6. 1, 17, etc.), and occurs also in Virgil (*A.* 7. 425), Horace (*Ep.* 1. 6. 17, 2. 2. 76), and others. Cf. *El* 4. 2 and note.

93–4 *avitas | Austriaci gazas, Perüanaque regna.* Heylyn's *Microcosmus* (1621 and later edd.) has a section on Peru. Cf. Grotius, *Induciae Batav.* (*S.*, bk. 2, p. 82), *fulvi dives Peruana metalli.* Milton had read Gill's poem, *Sylva-Ducis* (see *Works* 12, 8, and the note on *El* 3. 60 above), which includes the phrase *divesque Peruvia mittit | Auriferas classes* (*Parerga,* p. 40) and *Austriacus* on pp. 36, 38, and 40. Cf. also Gill, *Ad Honorat. Episcop. Lond. Kalend. Ianuar. 1631* (p. 61): *auri dives abditissimis | Perua fodinis.*

98 *Publica qui juveni commisit lumina nato.* An echo of the speech of Phaethon (the *juvenis*) to his father Apollo, *O lux inmensi publica mundi* (Ovid, *M.* 2. 35). See the note on *El* 5. 92.

99 *Hyperionios currus.* Hyperion, son of Heaven and Earth and father of the sun-god, often stands for the sun itself, e.g. Hesiod, *Theog.* 134, 371; Ovid, *M.* 4. 192–203; Virgilian *Cul.* 101; Claudian 35. 44 (2, 320). Cf. Val. Flacc. 2. 34–5, *Hyperionius... | currus* (Fletcher).

101 *Ergo ego jam doctae pars quamlibet ima catervae.* Ergo ego at the beginning of a line is an Ovidian mannerism, e.g. *Am.* 1. 4. 3, 1. 7. 11, 1. 12. 27, 3. 11 *a.* 9, 11, etc.; cf. *Mansus* 24. Cf. *C.P.I.* 2, 439 and *Gratul. Cantab.* (1623), p. 29, *docta caterva.*

102 *Victrices hederas inter, laurosque sedebo.* Editors cite Virgil, *E.* 8. 13, *inter victrices hederam tibi serpere laurus;* Horace, *C.* 1. 1. 29–32: *me doctarum hederae praemia frontium | dis miscent superis... | secernunt populo; Ep.* 1. 3. 25, *hederae victricis praemia.* Cf. Ovid, *Tr.* 2. 119, *turbaque doctorum Nasonem novit;* Claudian 8. 609 (1, 330), *hederis victricibus;* and the notes on *El* 5. 13–14 and 6. 15. As editors have noted, Milton's line is also (with *sedebis* for *sedebo*) line 6

of *Mansus*. Grierson (*Poems*, 1, xxii) used the item as an argument for dating *Patrem* in or after 1637, and Tillyard added the almost complete identity (noted by Warton) of *Patrem* 46 and *Mansus* 43; but Milton's echoes of himself are not reliable evidence for dating (see Le Comte, *Yet Once More*); witness 'barbarous dissonance' in *Comus* 549 and *PL* 7. 32. *Patrem* might have been among the early poems Milton had with him in Italy, in memory or in manuscript (*Works* 3, 235).

103-4 *nec obscurus populo miscebor inerti, | Vitabuntque oculos vestigia nostra profanos*. The passage reflects the classical and Renaissance conception of the scholar-poet set apart from the unlettered crowd. Cf. the citations under 102 and Horace, *S*. 1. 10. 73-4; *C*. 3. 1. 1, *Odi profanum vulgus et arceo*; Vida, *A.P.* 3. 362, *turbam quo longe arceret inertem*; Ovid, *M*. 3. 710 and Claudian 26. 102 (2, 132), *oculis...profanis*; Ovid, *M*. 7. 256, *oculos...profanos*.

105 *Este procul vigiles curae, procul este querelae*. Cf. M. Vestrius (*C.P.I.* 10, 462 and Gruter, *Del.I.P.* 2, 1383): *Ite procul curae tristes, procul ite querelae*; Virgil, *A*. 6. 258, *procul o, procul este, profani*; Ovid, *Am*. 2. 1. 3, *procul hinc, procul este, severae*; and *vigiles curae* in Ovid, *M*. 3. 396 (cf. 2. 779), Lucan 8. 161, Statius, *S*. 1. 4. 55, Val. Flacc. 3. 447, and Buchanan, *S*. 3. 5, *Sph*. 5. 10. Such personifications as those in 105-7 are common in Latin and Neo-Latin poetry; cf. *QNov* 141 f. and notes, and *Prol* 1 (*Works* 12, 132). MacKellar cites Care in Spenser, *F.Q.* 2. 7. 25. 1, 3. 12. 25. 4, and Envy, ibid. 5. 12. 33-8. V. M. Chaney (*Elegies of George Buchanan*, 134) quotes Ovid, *A.A.* 2. 151: *Este procul, lites et amarae proelia linguae*, and Buchanan, *El*. 2. 7: *Este procul lites, et amarae jurgia linguae*.

106 *Invidiaeque acies transverso tortilis hirquo*. A difficult twisting, as editors say, of Virgil's *transversa tuentibus hircis* (*E*. 3. 8). Cf. Horace, *C*. 4. 3. 15-16: *vatum ponere me choros, | et iam dente minus mordeor invido*. B.A.W. cites the epigraph in *Poems* (1645), which Milton took from Virgil, *E*. 7. 27-8.

107 *Saeva nec anguiferos extende Calumnia rictus*. Possibly an adaptation of two neighbouring phrases (about Cerberus) in Seneca, *Herc. Fur*. 797-8, *feros | ...rictus*, and 812, *cauda pulsat anguifera latus*. Cf. *QNov* 146 and note.

108-9 *faedissima turba... | Nec vestri sum juris ego*. Cf. Ovid, *Am*. 1. 1. 5-6: *Quis tibi, saeve puer, dedit hoc in carmina iuris? | Pieridum vates, non tua turba sumus*; *M*. 10. 37, *iuris erit vestri*; and 10. 724-5.

109-10, 115-20 Renaissance celebrations of the immortality of poetry and the poet's power to confer immortal fame start especially from Horace, *C*. 3. 30, and the last lines of Ovid, *M.* 15; cf. Ovid, *Am.* 3. 9. 17–32. Cf. Milton, *Shak*; *Mansus* 1–26; *Comus* 514–15; *Sonn* 8. 5–8.

111   *chare pater.* In Gill, *In Parentis mei Natalem* (p. 14).

113   *Sit memorasse satis.* Cf. Statius, *Th.* 5. 38, *hoc memorasse sat est.*

115–20   There seems no reason to accept Masson's suggestion that these lines were added just before the collected poems were published in 1645–6. The lines sustain the tone of what has preceded and appropriately conclude a piece in which the writer is claiming poetry as his vocation.

115   *O nostri, juvenilia carmina, lusus.* Cf. *juvenalia carmina* in Ovid, *Tr.* 2. 339, 4. 10. 57, and *P.* 3. 3. 29. Ovid refers to his looser poems as *lusibus . . . ineptis* (*Tr.* 2. 223); cf. *F.* 2. 6.

117   *Et domini superesse rogo, lucemque tueri.* Cf. Ovid, *Am.* 3. 9. 28, *defugiunt* [*effugiunt* in some texts] *avidos carmina sola rogos*; *M.* 4. 166, *quodque rogis superest*; Lucretius 4. 337 (312), *e tenebris autem quae sunt in luce tuemur.*

118   *sub Orco.* See the note on *El* 7. 83–4.

119–20   *decantatumque parentis | Nomen.* For one example of the participle, see the full title, in the Index, of *Epith. Caroli et H. Mariae* (1625).

The Greek Poems

❦

Apart from comments on technical errors, which are conveniently on record and need not be repeated here, not much can be said about Milton's three Greek poems, which make a total of 31 lines. These are the translation of Psalm 114, the five-line fable, *Philosophus ad regem*, and the quatrain *In Effigiei Ejus Sculptorem*. This last appeared under the author's portrait in the *Poems* of 1645; the other two pieces came between *Ad Patrem* and *Ad Salsillum*, and in 1673 the quatrain was put with them. Whatever the technical slips in Greek compositions done before a rigorous standard of correctness prevailed in England, there is small question of Milton's general competence. There is of course no question at all of his general mastery of Greek literature: the evidence is in the facts of his education, in the close and scholarly reading of Greek texts that is attested by his marginalia in surviving books,[1] and, most importantly, in the substance and texture of his English verse and prose. The meagre amount of Milton's Greek verse, as of most other men's, is naturally explained by the more familiar use of Latin and the far larger audience for it. In his letter to Gill of 4 December 1634 Milton remarked, in connection with the Psalm he had just translated, that 'whoever spends study and pains in this age on Greek composition runs a risk of singing mostly to the deaf' (*Works* 12, 17).

The fullest commentary on Milton's Greek verses is the appendix by Charles Burney in Warton's edition of the minor poems (ed. 1791, 593–605). To quote Masson's summary of Burney (*P.W.* 1, 307), the poems 'show imperfect Greek scholarship...lax constructions...

---

[1] *Works* 18, 304 f. Marginalia on Pindar (ibid. 276–304) must be discarded, since M. Kelley has shown, on external and internal grounds, that the annotated copy of Pindar in the Harvard library—accepted since 1871 as Milton's—is almost certainly not his (*SB* 17, 1964, 77–82). For an analysis of Milton's notes on Aratus see Kelley and S. D. Atkins, *PMLA* 70 (1955), 1090–1106.

questionable usages of words, and even false quantities.' Landor, of course, was magisterially severe: 'We will pass over the Greek verses. They are such as no boy of the sixth form would venture to show up in any of our public schools.'[2] A page of comments was supplied by S. H. Butcher for Masson's edition (*P.W.* 3, 345–6). Garrod corrects punctuation, accents, breathings, and missing iotas subscript.

[2] 'Southey and Landor,' *Works*, 5, 327.

Psalm CXIV

This translation, according to Milton's account a quite spontaneous effort, can be assigned definitely to the end of November 1634. In the letter to Gill of 4 December with which he enclosed a copy of the verses he said—to quote the Columbia rendering of Milton's Latin: 'I send, therefore, what is not exactly mine, but belongs also to the truly divine poet, this ode of whom, only last week, with no deliberate intention certainly, but from I know not what sudden impulse before daybreak, I adapted, almost in bed, to the rule of Greek heroic verse.'[3] Milton added, by way of apologizing for shortcomings, that, 'since I left your school, this is the first and only thing I have composed in Greek,— employing myself, as you know, more willingly in Latin and English matters.' H. F. Fletcher's argument (*Intell. Dev.* 1, 258–60) that Milton was only polishing up a translation done at school was more convincing to D. L. Clark (*JEGP* 56, 1957, 635) than it is to me.

Burney (Warton, p. 594), notwithstanding his censure of some details, endorsed Joseph Warton's judgment that Milton's translation was more vigorous than the Greek version of the same psalm by James Duport, professor of Greek at Cambridge during 1639–54 and in 1660 (see his ΔΑΒΊΔΗΣ ΈΜΜΕΤΡΟΣ, Cambridge, 1666). Butcher (Masson, *P.W.* 3, 345), while noting a number of wrong forms, false quantities, and misapplied words, remarked: 'This translation is interesting owing to a certain rhythmical swing in the verses rather than to any accuracy of diction. It may be noted as a special point, which indicates the delicacy of Milton's ear, that he observes Epic usage as regards the hiatus between

---

[3] *Works* 12, 17. One may fail to understand Sirluck's query (*JEGP* 60, 1961, 785): 'what reason is there to share Masson's odd assumption that the "ode" Milton sent Gill…is the Greek psalm?' The assumption, by the way, is at least as old as Warton. Milton's 'description fits a Greek paraphrase of a psalm of David, and fits nothing else known to have been composed by Milton' (Parker, 795, n. 65).

vowels, although he could not have known anything of the grounds on which it rested.' The amateur Leigh Hunt thought the Greek translation 'not so good as his English version of the same psalm, written at fifteen' (*Lit. Exam.* 13 Sept. 1823, 161; Houtchens, 197). If the King James version may be taken as a criterion, both of Milton's renderings, and especially the Greek, were freely expanded; and such early additions as 'froth becurled head' and 'Chrystal Fountains' had their equivalents in the later Greek. The only comment made since Butcher seems to be an emendation, or correction of a possible misprint, in line 19—a change from ἐκτυπέοντα to ἐκκτυπέοντα—by G. S. Gordon ('The Youth of Milton,' *Lives of Authors*, 1950, 63); this was accepted by Garrod (*Ox. Fac.* 1924), by Grierson (*Poems*, xxxviii), and by Garrod in 1955. H. Stephanus (*Thesaurus Graecae Linguae*, ed. Geneva, 158—, 3, 1696-7) and J. Scapula (*Lexicon Graecolatinum*, ed. Geneva, 1628, 1680) seem to have recognized such forms as κτυπέω and ἔκτυπ(ε)(ον) but not ἐκτυπέω, which Liddell and Scott list as an error for ἐκκτυπέω.

Since this note was written, Carey has noticed and augmented some of Burney's and Butcher's strictures.

Philosophus ad regem

❧

The possibility that this little fable may have some topical significance depends largely on whether it is assigned a late or an early date, and there is no concrete evidence for either.

Masson's view was this (*P.W.* 1, 308):

As these Hexameters appear in the Edition of 1645, and as their tenor suggests that they were done after the Civil War had begun, we may date them between 1642 and 1645. Milton probably imagined himself coming, by some possibility, into the situation of the 'Philosophus,' and the imaginary 'Rex' in that case might be Charles I. The piece has a touch in it of the peculiar spirit of Sonnet VIII, beginning 'Captain or Colonel.'

This topical conjecture is not very satisfying. A.S.P.W. comments:

The poem differs from *Sonn* 8 in this: the latter pleads for immunity as poet; it does not condemn the Puritan cause as does the heading of *PhilReg*. Would Milton thus belie his convictions to save his own skin (for otherwise the piece is purposeless on this hypothesis)? It is a serious charge—unless indeed one regards the piece as at once topical and a *jeu d'esprit*: 'this is what Milton might say, but won't'; and for the notion of a *jeu d'esprit* there is perhaps some support in the not wholly serious air of *Sonn* 8. There is, I suppose, an alternative—namely, that *PhilReg* is an exercise done some time after December 1634.

It might be added that in attacking the bishops Milton spoke respectfully of the monarchy and that he did not attack Charles until his first political tract in 1649; and that, if these verses were seriously topical, they were out of date by 1645, when the king was in no position to punish a Puritan.

Parker ('Notes,' 128–9) suggested another topical explanation (briefly repeated in his *Milton*, 144): 'If Alexander Gill was any kind of a teacher, he probably encouraged Milton, soon after receiving Psalm 114, to try his hand at *more* Greek verse... The poem could indirectly allude to Gill's unfortunate clash with Laud and the Star Chamber, and his subsequent pardon by King Charles (November 30, 1630), better than to any known incident in Milton's personal experience.' Since *Philosophus* was placed between Psalm 114 of November 1634 and *Ad Salsillum* of 1638, Parker would date it near the first Greek verses (also in hexameters), that is, at the end of 1634 or early in 1635; his latest conjecture is December 1634 or 'perhaps much later' (*Milton*, 144, 796, n. 67). If the poem had the topical reference Parker suggested, Milton's reaction would be oddly belated.

While Milton's statement to Gill in connection with Psalm 114 allows for composition of the *Philosophus* anywhere between 1634 and 1645, it also allows for the poem's having been a school exercise. This view (Clark, *J.M. at St. Paul's*, 206; Fletcher, *Intell. Dev.* 1, 262–3) is plausible in itself and gets rid of all difficulties. It is no doubt possible that Milton, having kept a school exercise, came to see a topical relevance in it, but that would leave us in the dark again.

Masson remarked that 'The Greek is very much found fault with by Dr. Burney, whose criticism of the five lines extends over a greater number of closely-printed pages.' Butcher (in Masson, *P.W.* 3, 345), after commenting on Psalm 114, pronounced this piece 'An inferior production, consisting of a mixture of Epic dialect and that of Attic prose,' and he cited details. Milton had enough interest in the poem to revise line 4 between 1645 and 1673; Garrod misquotes the revised line. In illustration of the concluding line 5, Carey quotes the praise of a wise man in Prov. 24. 3–6, and Comenius, *The Great Didactic*, tr. M. W. Keatinge (London, 1896), 453.

In Effigiei Ejus Sculptorem

William Marshall, the engraver of the portrait of Milton which appeared in the 1645 volume, was the most popular craftsman of his age; his services were called upon by the booksellers far more than any other man's. In this case, Milton later alleged his bookseller's importunity and the fact that no other engraver was available in London in wartime.[4] The handsome poet had good reason to dislike Marshall's picture, and he took sardonic revenge in these iambics, which the Greekless and unsuspecting engraver put below the portrait. The censorious Dr Burney, enjoying a kind of revenge in his turn, remarked that 'the Poet does not appear to have suspected, that while he was censuring the *Effigiei Sculptor*, he was exposing himself to the severity of criticism, by admitting, into his verses, disputable Greek and false metre' (Warton, 602–3). 'The moral,' says Masson (*P.W.* 1, 308), 'is that, when one makes a practical joke, it may be dangerous to do it in Greek.' Burney thought the epigram far inferior to those on bad painters in the Greek Anthology and without point. The complaint was repeated, along with strictures on metre and diction, by Butcher: 'The thought is very confusedly expressed. There seems to be no real antithesis between the first and the second couplet' (Masson, *P.W.* 3, 345). The various translations do leave the second couplet a virtual repetition of the first.

The presumed antithetical point of the epigram is blurred by our uncertainty about two key words, ἐκτυπωτὸν and δυσμίμημα. Mabbott (*Explicator* 8, 1950, no. 58) takes the first word as 'exact copy,' saying, mistakenly, that it is not in Liddell and Scott; it is there, equated

---

[4] An account of Marshall's work in connection with many notable books is given by F. L. Huntley, 'The Publication and Immediate Reception of *Religio Medici*,' *Library Quarterly* 25 (1955), 203–18. See also Masson, P.W. 1, 92–4, 308, and *Life*, 3 (1873), 456–9; and Milton, *Defpro Se* (*Works* 9, 124–5). Comments on the portrait by L. L. Martz are quoted below at the end of the headnote on *Rous*.

with ἔκτυπος, 'worked in relief,' 'distinct,' 'formed in outline'—meanings which do not seem to favor Mabbott's view. Mabbott's other point is that Milton's last phrase is intentionally ambiguous and means a bad picture either *by* or *of* an artist, so that 'the picture represents the man who made it, not the supposed subject'; and the best rendering would be McCrea's 'poor reproduction of a worthless artist' (*Student's Milton*), though this does not point up the ambiguity. But δυσμίμημα, as Butcher says (Masson, *P.W.* 3, 346), should mean 'a thing hard to imitate' [Liddell and Scott give δυσμίμητος in that sense], not 'a bad imitation.' In view of Milton's Greek usages, we cannot be sure of the sense he intended. The Columbia translator (*Works* 1, 283), by the way, takes Γελᾶτε as 'you laugh'; it is surely imperative.

Ad Salsillum poetam Romanum aegrotantem

SCAZONTES

☙

Giovanni Salzilli was one of the men who in 1638–9 welcomed Milton to Italian literary circles. Since Milton at 30—and indeed through most of his life—seems to have had little personal acquaintance with English writers, and since he had as yet published no collection of poems, his cordial reception in Italy gave him confidence in his choice of a vocation and remained a bright spot in his memory, as *Mansus, Epitaphium Damonis,* letters to Italian friends, and the *Second Defence* amply testify. A quatrain by Salzilli, which ranked the young Englishman above Homer, Virgil, and Tasso, was one of the commendatory pieces printed in the volume of 1645, and Milton's epistle to the ailing poet was evidently written as an answer (see lines 7–8). *Ad Salsillum* precedes *Mansus* in the editions of 1645 and 1673 and was therefore, we may assume, composed earlier—that is, during Milton's first visit to Rome, in or about November 1638 (Parker, 'Notes,' 130; *Milton,* 173, 826, n. 30). In such exchanges, especially in Latin, a man was not upon oath, and Milton's verse-letter is graceful enough as an acknowledgement of literary courtesies and companionship. Landor's opinion was characteristic: 'The scazons to Salsilli are a just and equitable return for his quatrain; for they are full of false quantities, without an iota of poetry.' Warton, on the other hand, did not know 'any finer modern Latin lyric poetry' than the latter half of the piece (lines 23–41): 'The close... is perfectly antique.' Dr Johnson, as we should expect, was more moderate than either.[1]

[1] Landor, 'Southey and Landor,' *Works,* 5, 330; Warton, *Poems...by John Milton* (1791), 534; Johnson, *Lives,* 1, 95; MacKellar, 57–8.

Sylvarum Liber

NOTES

1 *O Musa gressum quae volens trahis claudum*. In the scazontic or choliambic metre the final spondee or trochee, in departing from the iambic norm, gives a 'limping' effect. One particular requirement is that the penultimate foot be iambic; in 19 out of 41 lines Milton has a spondee in the fifth foot (Garrod, xviii). As some editors remark, Milton may have followed the greater license of Greek scazons. In *R. Am.* 378, Ovid refers to this metre in the phrase *extremum seu trahat ille pedem*; he uses *claudus* (e.g. *Tr.* 3. 1. 11) for the halting rhythm of the elegiac distich.

2 On Vulcan's fall from heaven, which left him lame, see the note on *El* 7. 81–2.

4–5 Juno promised Aeolus the nymph Deiopea as a reward for sending a storm upon the Trojan fleet (Virgil, *A.* 1. 65–75; cf. *G.* 4. 343). Dëiope is here given the comely ankles of Hebe (Homer, *Od.* 11. 603; Theocritus 17. 32; cf. the *teretes suras* of Ovid, *M.* 11. 80 and Horace, *C.* 2. 4. 21). Milton may have had some authority for her dancing before Juno's couch, or he may have invented a function parallel to Hebe's being cup-bearer to Jupiter.

6–7 *Adesdum & haec s'is verba pauca Salsillo | Refer*. '*Dum* is used colloquially as an enclitic with imperatives and interjections, a usage common in Plautus and Terence. *s'is*. Contracted from *si vis*, . . . a colloquialism' (MacKellar). On the stock phrase *pauca verba*, see the note on *El* 1. 92, and cf. Virgil, *A.* 4. 333, 10. 17, *pauca refert*.

7–8 *camoena nostra cui tantum est cordi*, etc. See Salzilli's quatrain (*Works* 1, 156–7) and the introductory note above. For *camoena nostra*, see the note on *El* 6. 3–4; cf. Tibullus 4. 1. 191, *nostrae . . . camenae*. The common idiom in Milton's line occurs in his prose letter to Diodati of 2 September [November?] 1637 (*Works* 12, 20, line 12; *C.P.W.* 1, 325, n. 6): *res tuae cordi mihi sunt*.

9–16 With this brief survey of the first part of Milton's travels, compare the commendatory verses of another Italian friend, Antonio Francini (*Works* 1, 156–65; Hughes, 6–10; Masson, *Life*, 1, 1881, 783–5), and *Def* 2 (*Works* 8, 120–6).

9 Among the several Latinized forms of Milton's name used by himself and his Italian friends, *Milto* is the one that appears in Salzilli's quatrain.

11–13 *pessimus . . . ventorum*, etc. Aquilo (the Greek Boreas) is *trux* in *Naturam* 55 and 'grim' in *FInf* 8. Cf. Virgil, *G.* 1. 370, 460, 2. 113, 261, etc. With Milton's *impotens* (12), Hughes compares Horace's *Aquilo impotens* (*C.* 3. 30. 3).

13 *sub Jove*. A stock phrase, 'under the sky,' e.g. Horace, *C*. 1. 1. 25, Ovid, *F*. 3. 527, etc.

14 *Venit feraces Itali soli ad glebas*. Cf. Secundus, *El*. 2. 7. 61, *Ad fines veni Latios, glebamque feracem*; *Epig. Gr*., p. 4, *Glebane...Ibera ferax*.

18 *fesso corpori*. Cf. Lucretius 4. 848, *fessum corpus*; etc.

19–20 According to the physiological theory of the four humours, an excess of one—here bile—caused a corresponding disease. See Burton, *Anat*. 1. 1. 2. 2, 1. 1. 3. 3 (1, 147–8, 173–4); L. Babb, *Elizabethan Malady*, 1–72, and, on Milton, 178–80; and the notes on *L'All* 1–10.

20 *damnosum spirat*. For the idiom, cf. Virgil, *A*. 7. 510, *spirans immane*; Horace, *Ep*. 2. 1. 166, *spirat tragicum satis*.

21–2 *tu Romano | ...ore Lesbium condis melos*. Lyric poetry in the tradition of Alcaeus and Sappho, both natives of Lesbos. Editors cite Horace, *C*. 1. 1. 32–4 1. 32. 4–5, and Ovid, *Tr*. 3. 7. 20. Masson (*P.W*. 3, 346) took *Romano ore* to mean Italian, not Latin, because 'it seems to have been by his Italian poetry that Salzilli was best known in Rome.'

23–41 In appealing to Apollo as the god of both healing and poetry Milton gives a medical turn to the pastoral conception of the poet as the singer and priest of nature.

23–4 *O salus Hebes | Germana*. Hebe, daughter of Zeus and Hera (Homer, *Il*. 4. 1–3, *Od*. 11. 603–4; Hesiod, *Theog*. 922, 950–5; cf. note on 4–5 above), became known as the goddess of youth, *hebe* being the Greek word for 'youth.' Salus, 'Health,' was a Roman goddess. In linking her with Hebe, Milton may have thought of Hebe's Roman equivalent, Iuventas (Ovid, *M*. 9. 400–17; Servius on Virgil, *A*. 1. 28, 5. 134) (MacKellar); cf. Cicero, *Tusc*. 1. 26. 65, *N.D*. 1. 40. 112. Cf. Vida, *Ad Scipionem Vegium, medicum* 23: *Ipsa Salus tecum pariter mihi visa subisse*; Grotius, *Anapaesti in Morbum...F. Grotii* (*Farr*., bk. 2, p. 190): *Si respiciat nos alma Salus, | Et placato numine Paean*.

24–5 As the god of healing Apollo acquired the name Paean (Aeschylus, *Agam*. 146; Sophocles, *O.T*. 154; Cicero, *Verr*. 2. 4. 57. 127; Ovid, *M*. 1. 566; Juvenal 6. 172–4 (MacKellar; Hughes); cf. the phrase from Grotius in the note on 23–4. For Apollo's slaying of the Python see *El* 7. 31–4 and note. Sandys (*Ovid*, 1632, 34; 1640, 20), citing Pontano, *Uran*. 1. 381–4, speaks of the Python as 'that great exhalation' which followed the flood: 'The word signifies putrefaction.' In calling Apollo *morborum terror* Milton may have echoed Ovid's

Sylvarum Liber

maxime Python | ...terror eras (*M.* 1. 438–40). With Milton's *Pythone caeso*, cf. *caeso Pythone* in E. Vaughan's commendatory poem in Gill's *Parerga* (1632).

26 *Libenter audis, hic tuus sacerdos est.* For the poet as priest see the note on *El* 6. 77. For the classical idiom of the first phrase cf. Horace, *S.* 2. 6. 20, *seu 'Iane' libentius audis* (Fletcher), and ibid. 2. 7. 101, *Ep.* 1. 7. 38, 1. 16. 17; Claudian 5. 387 (1, 86); Spenser, *F.Q.* 1. 5. 23. 7; *Cam. Insig.* (1624), sig. A2ᵛ, *merito Clarentius audis*; Gill, *Epith.* (50): *Luna... | Quae in terris Hecate frequenter audit*; Milton, *EpDam* 209; *Areop* (*Works* 4, 317), 'for which England hears ill abroad'; *PL* 3. 7.

27 *Querceta Fauni.* See the notes on *El* 5. 121–2 and 127.

27–8 *rore vinoso | Colles benigni, mitis Evandri sedes.* Evander, son of Hermes and an Arcadian nymph, established a kingdom in Italy, including the town Pallanteum on the Tiber. Milton would recall his welcome of Aeneas (Virgil, *A.* 8. 51–584) and also Ovid, *F.* 1. 471–542, as the possible echo of *colles* (*F.* 1. 515) suggests; cf. *F.* 5. 91–100; Statius, *S.* 4. 1. 6–7, *Evandrius... | collis.* MacKellar cites Pausanias 8. 43, etc. Cf. Petrarch, *Ep. ad Nicolaum Florentinum* (*P.M.* 2, 118), *in colle benigno.*

32 *Vicina dulci prata mulcebit cantu.* A variation on a stock theme and stock phrases, e.g. Virgil, *A.* 7. 34, *aethera mulcebant cantu*; Seneca, *Hipp.* 10–11, *prata... | ...mulcens*; *Med.* 229, *saxa cantu mulcet*; Horace, *C.* 2. 12. 13–14, *dulces...cantus* (cf. 3. 11. 24); Petrarch, *E.* 1 (*P.M.* 1, 10), *dulci mulcentem sydera cantu*; Castiglione, *Alcon* 73: *Non tua vicinos mulcebit fistula montes*; Sannazaro, *P.V.* 3. 255, *dulci mulcebant aethera cantu.*

33–5 *Ipse inter atros emirabitur lucos | Numa,... | ...Aegeriam.* Numa, the second of the legendary kings of Rome, learned—according to Livy 1. 19. 5 and Lactantius, *D.I.* 1. 22 (Migne, *Pat. Lat.* 6, 242–3) pretended to learn—religious and civil wisdom in nightly colloquies with the nymph Egeria; she was one of the Camenae or water-nymphs who became identified with the Muses. See Ovid, *M.* 15. 482–92, *F.* 3. 261–84, 4. 641–72; Cicero, *Rep.* 2. 13–15; Plutarch, *Numa* 4; Spenser, *F.Q.* 2. 10. 42. 8. In Milton's picture of eternal contemplation (which, as Keightley suggested, may owe something to Lucretius 1. 31–40, on Mars and Venus), Numa becomes an even more ideal figure than in Roman legend. The grove or valley of Egeria was a famous beauty spot in the time of the Empire (Juvenal 3. 12–20). Milton's *atros...lucos* recalls Ovid's *silva opaca* (*F.* 3. 263), though his phrase may come from *F.* 3. 801. With *degit otium*, cf. Catullus 68A. 64, *otia...degeret.*

36–41 The most familiar allusion to the swelling Tiber is Horace, *C.* 1. 2.

13–20 (quoted by MacKellar), where reference is apparently made to the low left bank as especially subject to floods.

37 *Spei favebit annuae colonorum.* Cf. *anni spem* in Virgil, *G*. 1. 224 and Ovid, *M*. 15. 113; Buchanan, *Sph.* 2. 359, *spem...coloni.*

38 *Nec in sepulchris ibit obsessum reges.* Milton's phrase corresponds to Horace's *monumenta regis* (*C*. 1. 2. 15; see the note above on 36–41), and may refer to Augustus' mausoleum in the Campus Martius, although Horace was probably thinking of other buildings (MacKellar; *Horace*, ed. E. C. Wickham, 1, 8).

40 *fraena melius temperabit undarum.* The metaphor might have been suggested by the juxtaposed phrases in Horace, *C*. 1. 8. 6–8: *Gallica nec lupatis | temperet ora frenis. | cur timet flavum Tiberim tangere?*

41 *curvi salsa regna Portumni.* Portumnus or Portunus was the Roman god of harbors and gates (Cicero, *N.D.* 2. 26. 66; Virgil, *A*. 5. 241; Ovid, *F*. 6. 547); he was identified with the Greek Palaemon (Ovid, loc. cit. and the notes on *Lyc* 164, 183–5). *Curvi* seems to apply to the shore the god protects (MacKellar). Milton may have thought of his general function or, more particularly, of the temple which tradition placed at the mouth of the Tiber (Frazer's appendix, pp. 440–2, in the Loeb *Fasti*, and his large edition, 4, 288). Harding (*Ovid*, 56–7), noting the broad Renaissance conception of Portunus as god of the sea, and hence the sea itself, takes Milton's phrase as a variation on Ovid's *curvum... aequor* (*M*. 11. 505: 'writhing' or 'vaulted' waters), but this, though possible, seems less likely.

Mansus

❦

During his visit to Naples, in the early winter of 1638, Milton was introduced to Giovan Battista Manso, Marquis of Villa (1560?–1645), author of a life of Tasso and other works but noted chiefly as a generous patron of the arts. In the eyes of the young English poet, Manso's beneficent friendship with Tasso—not to mention such later and lesser poets as Marino—must have invested him with a special glamor. As Milton says in his introductory note, and much later in the *Second Defence* (*Works* 8, 122–4), he received abundant courtesies from Manso. As he also says in that note, he sent the poem to Manso before he left Naples, so that it was presumably written in or about December 1638 (Parker, 'Notes,' 130; *Milton*, 175). Dr Johnson remarked that the poem 'must have raised an high opinion of English elegance and literature'; and Landor, who damned *Ad Salsillum*, exclaimed: 'But how gloriously he bursts forth again in all his splendour for Manso; for Manso, who before had enjoyed the immortal honour of being the friend of Tasso!'[1] If a bread-and-butter epistle became a poem of impassioned energy, it was because the name and associations of the recipient kindled Milton's feelings about poetry and poets and about the place he had not yet won—at least in public repute—in the great succession.

The poem praises Manso for his patronage of Tasso and Marini, through whose immortality Manso's name too will be remembered, but not without reminding him that the northern island has had its poets too and that he, Milton, is meditating a great poem about his own native land. The two themes are blended with a perfect tact. Milton's insisting (quite simply and calmly) on his own merit raises the importance of Manso's attention to him and is really but an added compliment. His tact prevents him from direct statement...Indeed we see

[1] Johnson, *Lives* 1, 96; Landor, 'Southey and Landor,' *Works* 5, 330; MacKellar, 60.

Milton here in his most charming mood, responding with sweetness and courtesy and a grave warmth to Manso's kind attentions.

But *Mansus* is more than a mere compliment. Its sustained sweetness and dignity, rising at times to positive grandeur, make it the best of all Milton's Latin poems (the *Epitaphium Damonis* included), and the one which as a whole can seriously compete with say *L'Allegro* or *Arcades*...Certainly the way in which he here writes—with complete grasp of his medium and with hardly a falter from beginning to end—is quite astonishing. (Tillyard, *Milton*, 89–90; cf. *M. Set.* 188–92.)

The unexpected theme and tone of the conclusion—'sixteen lines so charged with personal feeling that Manso may have puzzled over their significance'—have, with other reasons, led Parker to suggest that Milton had learned of Diodati's death (*MLN* 72, 1957, 488):

Milton imagines himself dying. But the spiritual dilemma of *Lycidas* is absent, as already resolved; he imagines, instead, his death at the end of a long and productive life. The problem now is the need, even of a great poet, for an intimate, understanding, and lifelong friend. From this note of brooding and pathetic dependence, this wistful lingering over imagined obsequies, the poem rises in its last four lines to a confident statement of happiness in the hereafter.

In repeating these comments in his *Milton* (175–6), Parker does not repeat the suggestion that the emotional conclusion of *Mansus* might have been inspired by news of Diodati's death, a suggestion which has been disputed but may be thought a plausible possibility (see below, the note on 85 f.).

Ralph W. Condee, in his full and close study, '"Mansus" and the Panegyric Tradition' (*Studies in the Renaissance* 15, 1968, 174–92), gives the body of his paper to elaborating and illustrating this view of the poem:

'Mansus', like so many of Milton's mature poems, refuses to rest passively within its genre as a panegyric—it combines praise with the contemplation of death, it turns poetic conventions upside down, and in the end it creates not merely an encomium of Manso but a celebration of the harmony of things.

In order to do this, Milton uses the panegyric tradition not merely as a framework for a note of praise to his Italian host. The poem gathers together *topoi* that have come down through centuries of stylized adulation, but it also weaves these *topoi* into a fabric which establishes a continuity of poetic tradition and then uses this continuity as a means of expanding 'Mansus' to a significance beyond that of the simple occasion of its composition. The poem stresses not only Manso's assistance of and spiritual kinship with Marino and Tasso; it also points out Manso's resemblance to Herodotus, Gallus, and Maecenas, and then it relates to Manso this honorable line of patrons by both direct and inverse use of devices occurring in countless other panegyric poets for centuries before. The conventions of the panegyric are not merely devices to praise Manso; they are also the means by which the poem achieves its vision of a harmonious universe. (174). Ultimately the poem finds its integrity not merely in the theme of praise for Manso, but more importantly in its embodiment of a universe united by mutual trust, respect, and affection, transcending human mortality. (192.)

For Milton's whole Italian tour see Masson, *Life*, 1 (1881); Hanford, 'Milton in Italy,' *Annuale Medievale* 5 (1964), 49–63; *Mansus*, n. on 85 f.; Arthos (*Leon* 1, n.); and Parker.

NOTES

1–2 *Haec quoque*, etc. As a patron of poets Manso had received many tributes before Milton's (see the note on 70–2 below). Hence the *quoque* and, in line 2, *choro notissime Phoebi*, where Milton recalls Virgil's saying (*E*. 6. 64–6) that *Phoebi chorus...omnis* rose up to honor Gallus (see the note on 4 below). For *Pierides*, see the note on *El* 4. 31.

3 *ille...dignatus honore*. Cf. Castiglione, *Carm*. 2. 10, *dignatus honore est*; Virgil, *A*. 1. 335.

4 *Post Galli cineres, & Mecaenatis Hetrusci*. C. Cornelius Gallus (*c*. 69–26 B.C.), the poet and friend of Virgil (see *E*. 10 and the note on 1–2 above). See also Ovid, *Am*. 1. 15. 29–30, 3. 9. 64, *Tr*. 2. 445–6. Maecenas (d. 8 B.C.), the friend of Augustus and patron of Virgil, Horace, and other poets, has long been the symbol of patronage. For his Etruscan descent, see Propertius 3. 9. 1, *Maecenas, eques Etrusco de sanguine regum*, and Horace, *S*. 1. 6. 1–6 (cf. *C*. 1. 1. 1.).

5 *nostrae...Camoenae*. See the notes on *El* 6. 3–4 and *Sals* 7–8.

6 *Victrices hederas inter, laurosque sedebis*. See the note on *Patrem* 102, with which this line is almost identical, and also the note on ibid. 46. For ivy and laurel see under *El* 5. 13–14 and 6. 14–16, and 92–3 below.

7 *Te pridem magno felix concordia Tasso*. The phrase recalls a famous pair of mythological friends: Ovid, *M*. 8. 303, *et cum Pirithoo, felix concordia, Theseus*. The phrase is also in Grotius,|*Epith. J. Borelii* (*S*., bk. 3, p. 111) and *Epith. Oxon.* (1625), sig. D1ᵛ.

9–16 Giambattista Marino (1569–1625), author of *L'Adone* (1623), an immense poem on Venus and Adonis, and other works. His conceits, which have made Marinism a critical term (see, e.g. Crashaw's *Sospetto d'Herode*, translated, freely,from Marino's *La Strage degli Innocenti*), are doubtless comprehended in Milton's *dulciloquum* (9) and *mollis* (12). See F. J. Warnke, 'Marino and the English Metaphysicals,' *Studies in the Renaissance*, 2 (1955), 160–75; J. V. Mirollo, *The Poet of the Marvelous: Giambattista Marino* (New York, 1963).

10 *ille tuum dici se gaudet alumnum*. Cf. Claudian 8. 128 (1, 296), *te gaudet alumno*.

11 *Assyrios divum...amores*. Adonis, whose Babylonian prototype was Tammuz or Thammuz, was the son, in the most familiar versions of the myth, of Myrrha and her father Cinyras, king of Cyprus. Venus was identified with the Semitic Astarte or Ashtoreth. See Frazer's notes in Apollodorus, 2, 84–8; Cicero, *N.D.* 3. 23. 59; Ovid, *M*. 10. 503 f.; Comes, *Mythol.* 5. 16; G. Sandys, *Ovid*, ed. 1632, 366–7, ed. 1640, 198–202; Milton, *Nat* 204, *Comus* 1001, *PL* 1. 446–52, and notes.

12 *Ausonias stupefecit carmine nymphas*. Italian girls (see the note on *El* 1. 70). Cf. Virgil, *E*. 8. 3, *stupefactae carmine* (Fletcher).

13–23 Masson (*P.W.* 1, 311) says that 'when Marini died, in 1625...the charge of his burial and of erecting his monument was left to Manso. It was understood that Manso was preparing a biography of Marini similar to that he had written of Tasso.' MacKellar comments: 'Masson has translated Milton's language into specific terms; I have not, however, found the authority for his statements. Milton, we may assume, knew whereof he spoke, and he implies something very close to what Masson has said.' MacKellar adds that Marino's epitaph would appear to make the Academy of the Humoristi chiefly responsible for the monument; he cites Mario Menghini, *La Vita e le Opere di Giambattista Marino* (Rome, 1888), 271–4. See Angelo Borzelli, *Storia della Vita e delle Opere di Giovan Battista Marino* (rev. ed. Naples, 1927), 256 f., 267–8; Mirollo (above, 9–16 n.), 93.

13 *debita*. 'Doomed or fated. Servius (*ad Aen*. 8. 375) glosses *debita* as *fataliter ad exitium destinata*' (MacKellar). Here, however, the context suggests that Marino was conscious of a debt to Manso.

16 *Vidimus arridentem operoso ex aere poetam*. Milton refers to Marino's monument at Naples; see under 13–23 above. Cf. Ovid, *H*. 3. 31, *operoso ex aere*.

18 *Orco*. The underworld, death. See the note on *El*. 7. 83–4.

19 *avidas Parcarum...leges*. See the note on *ProdBom* 1. 7.

20 *Amborum genus*. Cf. Virgil, *A*. 8. 142 and Ovid, *M*. 6. 153, *genus amborum*. Manso had written a life of Tasso (published in part in 1621), but his MS. life of Marino has been lost (M. Manfredi, *Gio. Battista Marino*, Naples, 1919, 21, 114, 259).

21 *dona Minervae*. Intellectual gifts (see the note on *El* 2. 2). In Virgil, *A*. 2. 189 (cf. 2. 31) the phrase describes the Trojan horse.

22–3 *illius Mycalen qui natus ad altam*, etc. The eloquent writer, born at high Mycale, who wrote a life of Aeolian Homer, is evidently Herodotus, though he has not in modern times been regarded as the author of that work. His birthplace, Halicarnassus, was not very near the promontory of Mycale (cf. Homer *Il*. 2. 869). Western Asia Minor was settled by Aeolian Greeks. Seven cities which claimed to be Homer's birthplace were named in a famous distich which is quoted, e.g., in Sandys, *Relation* (1615), 13; cf. Sannazaro, *Epig*. 2. 5, *De patria Homeri*.

24 *Ergo ego te Clius & magni nomine Phoebi*. For Clio and Phoebus, see the notes on *Patrem* 14 and 64; for *Ergo ego*, the note on ibid. 101.

25 *jubeo longum salvere per aevum*. *Iubeo salvere* was a Latin formula for good wishes. *Longum per aevum* is, with variations, a stock phrase, e.g. Horace, *Ep*. 1. 3. 8, 2. 1. 159, Ovid, *A.A*. 3. 657, *P*. 4. 8. 7, *M*. 3. 445, 7. 176, etc.

26 *Hyperboreo...ab axe*. See the note on *QNov* 95, and the letter to Diodati of 2 September (November?) 1637 (*Works* 12, 20; *C.P.W*. 1, 323–5) in which Milton used the Greek word for Hyperboreans with playful reference to the people among whom Diodati was then living.

27–8 *musam, | Quae nuper gelida vix enutrita sub Arcto*. For Milton's consciousness of the possible effect of a cold climate on poetic powers, MacKellar cites *El* 5. 5–8 (see the note on these lines, above), *RCG* (*Works* 3, 237), *Areop* (ibid. 4, 296), *HistBr* (ibid. 10, 325), *PL* 9. 44–5. See the discussions of Z. S. Fink ('Milton and the Theory of Climatic Influence,' *MLQ* 2, 1941, 67–80) and

T. B. Stroup ('Implications of the Theory of Climatic Influence in Milton,' ibid. 4, 1943, 185–9). *Gelida sub Arcto* is, in various forms, a stock phrase, e.g. Virgil, *A.* 6. 16, Ovid, *M.* 4. 625, Val. Flacc. 5. 155, 6. 140, Sil. Ital. 15. 227, Buchanan, *Sph.* 1. 303. Cf. Milton, *El* 5. 31–2 and note.

29 *Imprudens Italas ausa est volitare per urbes. Imprudens* seems to be a modest reference to the poems Milton had shown to friends or read in public in Italy; see Masson, *Life*, 1 (1881), 782, 792, *EpDam* 125–38, *RCG* (*Works* 3, 235). MacKellar suggests that the word also glances at the dangers that attended Milton's Protestant outspokenness (*Def 2, Works* 8, 124–5). The last phrase, in various forms, is common, e.g. Virgil, *A.* 7. 104, *volitans...Fama per urbes* (cf. 9. 473); Ariosto, *Carm.* 4. 24, *Interea Eoas volitat vaga fama per urbes*; and *C.P.I.* 8, 189 and 11, 190.

30–4 *Nos etiam in nostro modulantes flumine cygnos*, etc. A reminder that England is not so wanting in culture and in poetry as Italians might suppose. Some commentators have seen a special reference to Spenser because he was born in London and because of the wedding of the Thames and the Medway (*F.Q.* 4. 11) and the *Prothalamion*. Tillyard (*Milton*, 95–6) thinks that Milton means 'Chaucer, Spenser, and no more,' and that 'the passage implies that Milton saw himself...the third great English poet in the tradition of the Renaissance.' This view perhaps makes Milton more selfconsciously assured than at this time he was. He had already paid formal tributes to Shakespeare and Jonson (*Shak*; *L'All* 132–4), and probably had Spenser in mind in *IlPen* 116–20, so that here he is presumably thinking of these and others. Though he admired Spenser (cf. *Areop, Works* 4, 311), the Thames may be only a general symbol for England; editors cite Jonson's 'Sweet Swan of Avon.' See the note on 34 below. The last phrase of Milton's line 30, *flumine cygnos*, is the last in Virgil, *G.* 2. 199.

31 *Credimus obscuras noctis sensisse per umbras.* Milton seems to suggest the slow or recent rise of English poetry in comparison with that of Italy. Cf. Catullus 63. 41, *noctis umbras*; Sannazaro, *E.* 1. 112, *obscuras...umbras.*

32 *Thamesis...puris argenteus urnis.* Cf. Ovid, *M.* 3. 407, *fons...argenteus*; Vida, *Christ.* 2. 464, *Taphua...argenteus*; and the note above on *El* 3. 45. The association of personified rivers with urns is common, e.g. Virgil, *A.* 7. 792.

34 *Quin & in has quondam pervenit Tityrus oras.* Milton's earliest reference to Spenser's *Shepheardes Calender*. Spenser alluded to Chaucer as Tityrus in *February* 92, *June* 81, and *December* 4 (and in *C.C.C.H.A.* 2). Chaucer had visited Italy in 1372–3 and 1378. Milton's reference would presumably have been lost on Manso. Tillyard (*Milton*, 96) takes Milton's use of Spenser's name for Chaucer to indicate 'Spenser as the other poet he has in mind' (see the note above on 30–4). Tillyard (ibid. 90) remarks that line 34, closing a paragraph, has almost precisely the same effect as 'And old Damaetas lov'd to hear our song,' closing a paragraph in *Lyc.*

35–48   Cf. the celebration of early British culture in *Areop* (*Works* 4, 339–40).

35   *genus incultum, nec inutile Phoebo.* Cf. Horace, *C.* 1. 14. 13, *genus et nomen inutile.*

36   *Qua plaga septeno mundi sulcata Trione.* See the note on *El* 5. 35. Cf. Ovid, *M.* 2. 171, *radiis gelidi caluere Triones*; Virgil, *G.* 3. 381–2: *Hyperboreo septem subiecta trioni | gens effrena*; Seneca, *Herc. Oet.* 95, *mundi plaga.*

37   *Boöten.* See the notes on *El* 5. 35 and *Eli* 51–2.

38–48   Editors cite Selden's 'Illustrations' of Songs 8 and 9 of *Poly-Olbion* (Drayton, 4, 156, 194) for the ancient Britons' worshipping Apollo, to whom Selden related Belinus, the Druid god of healing. 'Milton...identifies the Hyperborean nymphs, whom Herodotus (4. 35) mentions as coming to Delos with offerings to Apollo and Artemis, as British Druidesses; but in Herodotus only Upis [Opis] and Arge appear; Loxo comes from Callimachus (*Hymn* [4] *to Delos* 291–2). But Milton further characterizes the three as Loxo the daughter of Corineus, Upis a prophetess, and Hecaerge the yellow-haired. Moreover, they are all three stained with woad—*Caledonio variatas...fuco*—as was the custom among the Britons...' (MacKellar). The name Hecaerge is in Callimachus, loc. cit. Milton may also have remembered the reference to her and Opis in Claudian 24. 253–6 (2, 60). For woad, MacKellar cites Caesar, *B.G.* 5. 14, and Pliny, *N.H.* 22. 2. 2. Corineus was the companion of Brutus (Brute) after whom Cornwall was supposedly named (Geoffrey of Monmouth, *Hist. Brit.* 1. 12 f.; Giraldus Cambrensis, *Hist. Works*, ed. T. Wright, London, 1881, 479).

38   *Nos etiam colimus Phoebum, nos munera Phoebo.* Perhaps a distant echo of Virgil, *E.* 3. 62–3: *Et me Phoebus amat ; Phoebo sua semper apud me | munera sunt.*

39   *Flaventes spicas, & lutea mala canistris.* The last two words end Ovid, *M.* 8. 675. Cf. Seneca, *Oed.* 50, *altis flava cum spicis.*

40   *Halantemque crocum (perhibet nisi vana vetustas).* Cf. Virgil, *G.* 4. 109, *croceis halantes floribus horti*; Buchanan, *Ps.* 135. 18, *halantes...flores. Vana vetustas* is in Lucan 10. 239 and *C.P.I.* 2, 56, 451.

43   *Heroum laudes imitandaque gesta canebant.* For the common notion of the

Druids as priests and philosophers rather than poets, MacKellar cites Caesar, *B.G.* 6. 14 (who speaks of their learning much poetry by heart in their schools); Diod. Sic. 5. 31; Lucan 1. 450–6, 3. 399–428; Camden, *Britain* (ed. 1637), 4, 12–14; Milton, *DDD* (*Works* 3, 376), *HistBr* (ibid. 10, 50). Cf. Selden (Drayton, 4, 122, 192–7, 215–17). Milton here, as in *Lyc* 53, makes the Druids poets. Cf. Camden, *Britain* (tr. 1610, 4): 'the *Druidae*, who being in olde time the Priests of the Britans and Gaules, were supposed to have knowen all that was past; and the *Bardi*, that used to resound in song all valorous and noble acts, thought it not lawfull to write and booke any thing.' See A. L. Owen, *The Famous Druids: A Survey of three centuries of English literature on the Druids* (Oxford, 1962). Milton's line 43 is almost identical with *Patrem* 46 (see the notes on *Patrem* 46 and 102). Cf. Vida, *A.P.* 1. 544 (quoted under *Patrem* 46); Virgil, *E.* 4. 26 and *C.P.I.* 1, 21 and 4, 216, *heroum laudes*; Pontano, *Uran.* 1. 1171, *canere heroum laudes.*

44 *festo cingunt altaria cantu.* Cf. Statius, *S.* 2. 7. 88, *festis cantibus* (Fletcher); Virgil, *E.* 8. 64, *cinge haec altaria*; Val. Flacc. 1. 90, *altaria cingent.*

45 *Delo in herbosa Graiae de more puellae.* See the note on 38–48 above and, for Delos, notes on *El* 5. 13–14 and *Naturam* 49–50. Warton cited Ovid, *M.* 2. 711, *castae de more puellae.*

46–7 *Corinëida Loxo, | Fatidicamque Upin, cum…Hecaërge.* See under 38–48 above. *Fatidicus* is a fairly common adjective, e.g. Virgil, *A.* 7. 82, 8. 340, Ovid, *M.* 1. 321, etc., Seneca, *Oed.* 302, Statius, *Th.* 4. 187, 8. 208, etc.

49 *Fortunate senex.* A happy application, as editors note, of Virgil, *E.* 1. 46, *Fortunate senex, ergo tua rura manebunt.* It had been often made before, e.g. Dante, *E.* 2. 55; *C.P.I.* 2, 146 and 3, 164, 193, etc.; Beza, *Ad Andream Tiraquellum* (*Poëmata*, 84ᵛ); Secundus, *Fun.* 26. 90; Grotius, *Grat. Ad Dousam* (*Farr.*, bk. 1, pp. 176, 177), *In filium G. Martinii* (loc. cit., p. 186); *Cam. Insig.* (1624), sig. A3ʳ.

50 *Torquati decus, & nomen…ingens.* See the note on *Salmas* 2. 7.

51 *Claraque perpetui succrescet fama Marini.* See the note on 9–16. The line is doubtless further from Milton's critical opinion than the *prolixus* of line 11.

52 *Tu quoque in ora frequens venies plausumque virorum.* Editors cite Propertius 3. 9. 32, *et venies tu quoque in ora virum* (cf. 3. 1. 24), and Virgil, *G.* 3. 9, *victorque virum volitare per ora*, both perhaps echoes, as MacKellar notes, of Ennius' epitaph on himself, *volito vivos per ora virum* (Cicero, *Tusc.* 1. 15. 34), though the idiom is common.

55 *Cynthius.* A name for Apollo derived from Mount Cynthus on the island of Delos, where he was born (*Homeric Hymn to Delian Apollo* 26; Virgil, *E.* 6. 3; Horace, *C.* 1. 21. 2). Cf. Cynthia, *El* 5. 46.

56–8 When Zeus killed Apollo's son Aesculapius (see *Procan* 27–8 and note), Apollo in revenge killed the Cyclopes who made Zeus's thunderbolts; Zeus would have sent him to Tartarus but was persuaded by Leto to commute his punishment to a year's service with a mortal, and Apollo went as herdsman to Admetus, son of Pheres and king of Pherae (Euripides, *Alc.* 1. f., 569 f.; Apollodorus 3. 10. 4; and the note on 59 below). Milton is saying that Apollo (i.e. poetry) voluntarily dwelt in Manso's house, whereas his stay with Admetus was enforced exile from heaven, even though Admetus had entertained great Heracles. No authority has been found for Admetus' having received Heracles before the coming of Apollo (MacKellar), and Milton may have altered the item to enhance the dignity of Admetus and, by implication, the higher merit of Manso. For Milton's *Pheretiadae*, cf. Ovid, *A.A.* 3. 19 (Fletcher), *M.* 8. 310; for *magnum Alciden*, Seneca, *Agam.* 815, *Herc. Oet.* 771, etc.

59 *ubi clamosos placuit vitare bubulcos.* Perhaps suggested by the picture of Apollo's servitude in Tibullus 2. 3. 11–30, especially 19–20: *O quotiens ausae, caneret dum valle sub alta, | rumpere mugitu carmina docta boves!* Cf. Ovid *M.* 2. 676–85.

60 *Nobile mansueti cessit Chironis in antrum.* For Chiron see the notes on *El* 4. 27 and *Procan* 25–6. Milton may have had some authority for Apollo's visiting Chiron's cave during his year of servitude, or he may have invented the item on the strength of Chiron's being the tutor of Aesculapius and Achilles. In Pontano, *Uran.* 2. 1215 f., Chiron says: *Inde deos mihi concilians divertit ad antrum | Saepe meum Clarius vates, aviumque volatus | Et voces didici*, etc. The difficulties of distance noticed by Masson (*P.W.* 3, 350) and MacKellar might not have troubled a god. The point of the passage 56–69 is that Manso had befriended Tasso and Marino as Admetus and Chiron had been hospitable to Apollo. *Chironis in antrum* is also the ending of Ovid, *M.* 2. 630 and (with *antro*) of Val. Flacc. 1. 407; the latter is cited by Brodribb, *N&Q* 175 (1938), 399.

61–2 *Irriguos inter saltus frondosaque tecta | Peneium prope rivum: ibi saepe sub ilice nigra.* Editors cite Ovid's description (*M.* 1. 568–76) of the river Peneus flowing through the vale of Tempe in Thessaly; cf. Milton, *El* 5. 13, 7. 33. Cf. *C.P.I.* 7, 232, *irriguos saltus*; Claudian 35. 5 (2, 318), *riguos saltus. Sub ilice nigra* is in Virgil, *E.* 6. 54 (cf. *A.* 9. 381) and Ovid, *M.* 9. 665 (cf. *Am.* 2. 6. 49, *F.* 3. 295); cf. Seneca, *Thy.* 654, *nigra ilice.*

63 *Ad citharae strepitum blanda prece victus amici.* Editors cite Horace, *Ep.* 1. 2. 31, *ad strepitum citharae,* and 2. 1. 135, *docta prece blandus. Blanda prece* (or the plural) is a stock phrase, e.g. Horace, *C.* 4. 1. 8, *A.P.* 395, Ovid, *A.A.* 1. 710, *M.* 10. 642, Tibullus 3. 6. 46, Seneca, *Herc. Fur.* 1014.

64 *Exilii duros lenibat voce labores. Duros labores* is a stock phrase, e.g. Virgil, *A.* 6. 437, 8. 291, Tibullus 1. 4. 47, Sil. Ital. 389, Pontano, *Uran.* 2. 511, 4. 673, Mantuan, *E.* 3. 16. Cf. *C.P.I.* 11, 423, *durum cantu...lenire laborem.*

65-9 Milton gives to Apollo's music the power over nature more familiarly associated with that of Orpheus, e.g. in Ovid, *M.* 10. 86-105 and Claudian 34. 17-28 (2, 316). The idea may be taken over from the praise of Hesiod in Virgil, *E.* 6. 69-73, as the particular reference to mountain ash trees suggests (68 n. below).

65-6 *Tum neque ripa suo, barathro nec fixa sub imo, | Saxa stetere loco.* With *barathro...sub imo* cf. *Naturam* 30 and note. Cf. the Virgilian *Cul.* 278, *iam rapidi steterant amnes*; Virgil, *E.* 8. 4; Ovid, *M.* 11. 1-2, 45.

66 *nutat Trachinia rupes.* Mount Oeta, in southern Thessaly, where the town of Trachis was (Ovid, *M.* 11. 269, 627; Lucan 3. 178; Milton, *Procan* 12, *PL* 2. 545). Milton may be particularizing the *saxa sequentia* of Ovid, *M.* 11. 2 and similar allusions, or varying the particulars of Claudian's account of Orpheus, 34. 19-20 (2, 316): *porrexit Rhodope sitientes carmina rupes, | excussit gelidas pronior Ossa nives.* Seneca has several references to rocky Trachis (*Troad.* 818, *Herc. Oet.* 135, 1432).

67 *Nec sentit solitas, immania pondera, silvas.* Cf. Virgil, *A.* 10. 496, M. Vegius, *Aen.* 13. 288-9, and Gill, *Sylva-Ducis* (39), *immania pondera*; Ovid (on Orpheus), *M.* 10. 90-105, 11. 1, 11. 45-6: *te carmina saepe secutae | ...silvae.* Cf. also Milton, *Patrem* 40.

68 *Emotaeque suis properant de collibus orni.* Editors cite Virgil, *E.* 6. 70-1 (on Hesiod): *ille solebat | cantando rigidas deducere montibus ornos*; and *A.* 4. 490-1: *mugire videbis | sub pedibus terram et descendere montibus ornos.* Cf. Ovid, *M.* 10. 101.

69 *Mulcenturque novo maculosi carmine lynces.* Editors cite Virgil, *E.* 8. 3, *stupefactae carmine lynces.* Cf. Virgil, *A.* 1. 323, *maculosae tegmine lyncis*; Mantuan, *E.* 6. 27, *maculosaque tergora lyncis.* For Orpheus' taming of animals, see the note on *El* 6. 69-70.

70-2 'For thirty years before Milton's visit, says Angelo Borzelli in *Giovan Battista Manso* (Naples, 1916, p. 101), Manso had received countless poetical tributes which compared him to Jove, Apollo and Mars' (Hughes).

See also Manfredi (cited above in 20 n.). For *Diis dilecte senex* see the note on *QNov* 26. *Jupiter aequus* is in Virgil, *A.* 6. 129–30. With *miti lustrarit lumine Phoebus* cf. Virgil, *A.* 8. 153, *lustrabat lumine* and, though the sense is different, Lucretius 5. 693, *lumine lustrans.*

72 *Atlantisque nepos.* The appellation for Mercury is, in various forms, in Horace, *C.* 1. 10. 1; Ovid, *M.* 2. 742–3, *F.* 5. 663; Claudian 33. 89 (2, 300); Pontano, *Uran.* 2. 1103. Cf. *Idea* 27–8 and note.

74–5 *Hinc longaeva tibi lento sub flore senectus | Vernat.* Warton found 'much elegance' in *lento sub flore* but objected to *senectus Vernat.* MacKellar cites Claudian 21. 316 (1, 386) *senioque...vernante.* Cf. Propertius 2. 13. 47, *longaevae...fata senectae* (readings vary between *longae* and *longaevae*; the latter appeared, e.g. in Scaliger's edition of Catullus, Tibullus, and Propertius, 1582 and 1600); Castiglione, *Alcon* 1: *Ereptum fatis primo sub flore juventae*; Virgil, *E.* 10. 40, *lenta sub vite.*

75 *Aesonios lucratur vivida fusos.* For Medea's restoring the aged Aeson to youth, see Ovid, *M.* 7. 251–93 and Milton, *El* 2. 7–8 and note. Milton's condensed and oblique phrase was displeasing to Keightley.

76 *Nondum deciduos servans tibi frontis honores.* In a long note, quoted in MacKellar, Masson (*P.W.* 3, 351) cites contemporary evidence for Manso's good-humored willingness to remove his wig and expose his baldness, if asked to do so by fellow members of the club of the Blessed Virgin. Masson concludes that 'the old nobleman's wig was a good one, and he had worn it carefully when Milton and he were together.' Fletcher cites Statius, *S.* 1. 2. 113, *frontis honores*; *Th.* 9. 705, *frontis servat honorem.* The former phrase, with variations, is common, e.g. Statius, *S.* 2. 1. 26; Val. Flacc. 6. 296; Grotius, *Inaug. Reg. Brit.* (*S.*, bk. 2, p. 65), *Epith. Kinschot.* (*S.*, bk. 3, p. 106).

77 *mentis acumen.* In Claudian 35. 201 (2, 332); Pontano, *Uran.* 4. 1048, 2. 553, *H.H.* 1. 372; Beza, *Nihil* (*Poëmata*, 100ʳ); Buchanan, *Misc.* 15. 23, *Sph.* 2. 640, 5. 12.

78 *O mihi si mea sors talem concedat amicum.* Cf. Ovid, *F.* 3. 477, *o utinam mea sors.*

79 *Phoebaeos decorasse viros.* The epithet—*Phoebe(i)us*—is fairly common in Ovid, Statius, and Lucan (MacKellar). Todd noted that it was frequent in Buchanan (e.g. *El.* 1. 68, *Sph.* 1. 28, 2. 201, 346, 3. 38, etc.).

80–4 These lines are Milton's earliest statement of his desire to write an epic about Arthur; cf. *EpDam* 162–71. For the genesis of his epic plans see the commentary on *PL* in the present work.

80 *Si quando indigenas revocabo in carmina reges.* The ancient epics established for Renaissance theory and practice the principle that a heroic poet should deal with the early history or legends of his country; witness Ariosto, Tasso, Ronsard, Spenser et al. Tillyard (*M. Set.* 190) asks 'to whom does *indigenas reges* refer? Certainly to the British kings of legend other than Arthur. But if only to them, what point in referring to the prophecy of Merlin that Arthur was still alive below ground? I can only think that Milton meant to reiterate the legend that Arthur was re-embodied in the house of Tudor.' See the next note.

81 *Arturumque etiam sub terris bella moventem.* If Milton had no precise authority for Arthur's carrying on wars beneath the earth (MacKellar), he would know 'the tradition that Arthur was alive in the other world and would return to rule over the Britons' (Hughes). And, if he was not acquainted with Wace and Layamon, who end with a reference to Arthur's return, such a devotee of romance would surely have read Malory (*Le Morte Darthur*, Globe ed. London, 1868 f., 21. 7) (Hughes). That the Arthurian line was renewed in the Tudor sovereigns was an idea cultivated by Henry VII, and its potency is exemplified by *The Faerie Queene*. On the continued vitality and later decline of the Arthurian story in the sixteenth and seventeenth centuries, see Edwin Greenlaw, *Studies in Spenser's Historical Allegory* (Baltimore, 1932), C. B. Millican, *Spenser and the Table Round* (Cambridge, Mass., 1932), Josephine W. Bennett, *The Evolution of "The Faerie Queene"* (Chicago, 1942), Roberta F. Brinkley, *Arthurian Legend in the Seventeenth Century* (Baltimore, 1932), and Kendrick (cited under *El* 1. 73). For Milton's later scepticism about Arthur see his *HistBr* (*Works* 10, 127 f.). *Bella movere* is a standard idiom, e.g. Ovid, *Am.* 2. 12. 21, 3. 12. 4, *A.A.* 2. 146; Seneca, *Herc. Fur.* 123, *Oct.* 753, 776, 806; Lucan 1. 119.

82-3 *invictae sociali foedere mensae, | Magnanimos Heroas.* The knights of the Round Table (Malory, 3. 1-2, etc.). Todd cited Statius, *Th.* 8. 240-1: *Tunc primum ad coetus sociaeque ad foedera mensae | semper inaspectum. Sociali foedere,* in various forms, is a common phrase, e.g. Ovid, *H.* 4. 17, *M.* 14. 380, Sil. Ital. 16. 168, 274, Mantuan, *E.* 6. 57. For *Magnanimos Heroas* see Virgil, *G.* 4. 476, *A.* 6. 307, 649; *C.P.I.* 3, 26, 164, 170, etc.

84 *Frangam Saxonicas Britonum sub Marte phalanges.* 'What a glorious verse,' exclaimed Landor (see the introductory note above). 'There is great power in the crash of *frangam* after the hushed parenthesis of *O modo spiritus adsit*' (Tillyard, *Milton,* 91). For Arthur as the leader of British resistance to Germanic invaders see Geoffrey of Monmouth, 9. 1 f., *Holinshed's Chronicles* (1807),

1, 574. Do Milton's first two words embody a sort of pun? Cf. Virgil, *G.* 1. 267, *frangite saxo*; *A.* 1. 179, *frangere saxo*; Seneca, *Phoen.* 571, *haec saxa franges?* In Latin poetry, and sometimes in prose, the name Mars was virtually a common noun, 'war,' 'battle,' e.g. Virgil, *A.* 2. 335, 6. 165, Ovid, *Am.* 2. 18. 36, *M.* 3. 123, Milton, *QNov* 113. For Milton's last word cf. Virgil, *A.* 6. 489, *Agamemnoniaeque phalanges*, and 12. 551, 662; Caesar, *B.G.* 1. 25, *phalangem perfregerunt*.

85f. Rose Clavering and J. T. Shawcross ('Milton's European Itinerary and His Return Home,' *SEL* 5, 1965, 54–8) oppose Parker's suggestion (*MLN* 72, 1957, 486–8) that it was the news of Diodati's death that chiefly led Milton to cancel his visit to Sicily and Greece, but their arguments partly touch the matter that concerns us, Parker's further suggestion that the news of his friend's death might have inspired the unexpected conclusion of *Mansus* (see the end of the headnote above). The objections are: (1) the impossibility of Milton's receiving such news in Naples along with news of political disturbance, since the latter did not begin until late November [but the report of Diodati's death might have come in separate letters, since he had died in August]; (2) the lack of any 'logical connection' between the news of Diodati and Milton's abandoning his projected visit [this has no relevance to *Mansus*]; (3) lines 9–13 of *EpDam* 'deny the possibility that he received news of Diodati's death while in Naples' [I think Shawcross misreads these lines: see the note on them below].

Petrarch offers a rather close parallel to Milton: *Post ubi longaevo finem factura labori | Affuerit suprema dies, solamen et ipsum | Mortis erit, tanti in gremio lachrymantis amici | Lassatum posuisse caput, manibusque sepulchro | Invectum iacuisse piis* (*Ep. ad Amicum Transalpinum, P.M.* 2, 142).

85 *tacitae permensus tempora vitae.* Cf. Castiglione, *Alcon* 117, *securae peragemus tempora vitae*; and *tempora vitae* in Ovid, *M.* 3. 469, Lucan 9. 233, and Statius, *S.* 5. 1. 205.

86 *Annorumque satur cineri sua jura relinquam.* Cf. Lucretius 3. 938, *ut plenus vitae conviva*; 3. 960, *quam satur ac plenus possis discedere rerum*; Horace, *S.* 1. 1. 119, *cedat uti conviva satur*; Gill, *In obitum D. Guil. Stonhousij...1632* (p. 79), *annorum satur*.

87 *madidis...ocellis.* In Sannazaro, *El.* 1. 4. 3 and Pontano, *E.* 1 (*Pompa Secunda*). 36.

89 *artus liventi morte solutos.* Cf. Statius, *Th.* 1. 617, *liventes in morte oculos.*

90 *Curaret parva componi molliter urna.* Cf. Ovid, *Tr.* 3. 3. 65, *parva...in urna*; Tibullus 3. 2. 26, *sic ego componi versus in ossa velim.*

91 *Forsitan & nostros ducat de marmore vultus.* An audible echo, as editors note, of Virgil, *A.* 6. 848, *vivos ducent de marmore voltus.* On *Forsitan et*, see the note on *El* 7. 89.

92–3 *Nectens aut Paphia myrti aut Parnasside lauri | Fronde comas.* For the association of Venus and Paphos, see the note on *El* 1. 84. For the myrtle's association with Venus, see Virgil, *E.* 7. 62, *G.* 1. 28, *A.* 5. 72; Ovid, *Am.* 1. 2. 23, *necte comam myrto*; *F.* 4. 15, 139 f., 869; etc. *Paphia myrti*, in various forms, is a stock phrase, e.g. Virgil, *G.* 2. 64, Ovid, *A.A.* 3. 181, Seneca, *Oed.* 539, Statius, *Th.* 4. 300. For Parnassus and the Muses see the note on *El* 4. 30; for Apollo and the laurel, the note on *El* 5. 13–14, and Ovid, *M.* 11. 165, *lauro Parnaside*; Milton, *Prol* 6 (*Works* 12, 214, line 1), *Parnassi Lauros. Fronde comas* also begins Horace, *Ep.* 2. 1. 110 and, with *comam*, Statius, *Th.* 3. 467 and Buchanan, *S.* 7. 7, and is in Virgil, *A.* 8. 274.

93 *ego secura pace quiescam.* Cf. Virgil, *A.* 1. 249, *placida compostus pace quiescit* (Fletcher); Vida, *Christ.* 1. 57, *Pax...secura.*

94 *si qua fides, si praemia certa bonorum. Si qua fides* is a stock phrase, e.g. Virgil, *A.* 3. 434, 6. 459, Ovid, *Am.* 1. 3. 16, Lucan 2. 550, 9. 78, Grotius, *Inaug. Reg. Brit.* (*S.*, bk. 2, p. 72), *Cantab. Dolor* (1625), p. 14. For the second phrase editors cite Virgil, *A.* 1. 603–5, 2. 142–4; see also the note on *EpDam* 36.

95 *Ipse ego caelicolum semotus in aethera divum.* One of Milton's many visions of heaven. *Caelicolae* was a common word which readily took on a Christian meaning, e.g. Catullus 30. 4, 64. 386; Virgil, *A. passim*; Ovid, *M.* 1. 174, 8. 637, etc.; Statius, Sannazaro, *P.V.*, and Vida, *Christ., passim.*

96 *Quo labor & mens pura vehunt, atque ignea virtus.* Editors cite Virgil, *A.* 6. 130, *ardens evexit ad aethera virtus*; 6. 730, *igneus est ollis vigor.* Fletcher adds Lucan 9. 7–9: *quos ignea virtus | Innocuos vita patientes aetheris imi | Fecit.* Cf. *ignea virtus* in Mantuan, *Margaritae Agon* (*Opera*, 1502, fol. 222ᵛ) and *C.P.I.* 8, 230; Buchanan, *Misc.* 2. 7–8 (*In Castitatem*): *Pura mens puris radiantis aulam | Incolet aethrae*; and the phrase from Beza cited under *EpDam* 206–7.

98 *Quantum fata sinunt.* In Vida, *A.P.* 3. 192. For similar phrases cf. Virgil, *A.* 1. 18, Ovid, *M.* 5. 534, Propertius 2. 15. 23, Tibullus 1. 1. 69, Seneca, *Herc. Fur.* 177, Statius, *Th.* 10. 216, etc.

99 *Ridens purpureo suffundar lumine vultus.* Editors cite Virgil, *A.* 6. 640–1, *lumine vestit | purpureo* (cf. 1. 590–1, *lumenque... | purpureum*) and Statius, *S.* 5. 1. 256, *lumine purpureo.*

100 *Et simul aethereo plaudam mihi laetus Olympo.* For *aethereo...Olympo*, see the note on *QNov* 8. Cf. Horace, *S.* 1. 1. 66–7, *mihi plaudo | ipse domi.*

Epitaphium Damonis

※

Although the first and last poems Milton addressed to Diodati were *Elegies* 1 and 6, of 1626 and 1629–30, the two friends had kept in touch with each other. The second of Milton's two letters of September (November?) 1637 (*Works* 12, 22–8; *C.P.W.* 1, 325–8) shows him pouring out his private ambitions to Diodati more freely than he would have done to any other person. Diodati, though slightly younger than Milton, had had a more rapid academic career and taken his M.A. at Oxford in 1628, at the age of 19 or thereabouts. After a period of indecision he embarked upon theology at Geneva (1630–1). Some time after his return to England he took up the study of medicine, probably under his father (see the introduction to *El* 1), and in 1637 he began to practise himself. During the autumn and winter of 1637 he was apparently often in London or at Horton. He died in August 1638 (he was buried on 27 August), while Milton was in Italy. It has been commonly assumed that Milton received the news during his second visit to Florence or when, on his way home, he visited Charles's uncle, John Diodati, professor of theology at Geneva. But Parker (*MLN* 72, 1957, 486–8; cf. *Milton*, 826–7, n. 33) argues that Milton learned of the event at Naples in December or January 1638–9, and that his second stay at Florence, the side-trip to Lucca, and the visit in Geneva were afterthoughts prompted by the knowledge of his friend's death (this view has been disputed: see note on *Mansus* 85 f.). He arrived in England in or about August 1639 and, after nearly a year in lodgings near Fleet Street (Parker, 186, 192, 838, n. 2, 844, n. 20), he established himself in a house in Aldersgate Street, probably in the autumn of 1640, with the purpose of taking pupils.

The *Epitaphium Damonis* was printed by itself, anonymously and

privately, probably in 1640;[1] Milton sent copies to his Italian friends and
no doubt to relatives and friends of Diodati in England. As for the date
of composition, in lines 9–13 Milton says that twice the grain has risen
high and been harvested between Diodati's death and the writing of the
elegy, a statement that seems to place the poem late in 1639 or early in
1640 (see the note below on 9–13). What may appear a long delay in the
commemoration of his closest friend is at least partly explained by a
number of circumstances: his possibly not knowing of Diodati's death
until some time after it occurred; the obvious difficulties of writing
adequately while he was travelling; the business of getting settled, both
domestically and pedagogically, in London; and the very depth of his
feelings, the realization of his loss that came upon him when he took up
life again in scenes associated with years of intimate friendship (lines
14–17, etc.). Among the evidences of close attachment, Masson noted

---

[1] An apparently unique copy was discovered by Leicester Bradner in the British Museum and
described by him in the *TLS*, 18 August 1932, 581. The text is the same as that printed in
the *Poems* of 1645, apart from some slight variations (recorded in *Works* 18, 641–3, Garrod,
370, and Fletcher, facsimile cited below). This first text was reprinted, with a translation
by W. W. Skeat, in 1933 (see Index below) and by H. F. Fletcher in his facsimile edition
of the complete poetical works (1, 1943, 354 f.). Bradner at first assigned the printed text
to 1639 or 1640; in his later *Musae Anglicanae* (358) he assumed 1640. Fletcher, in his
reprint, gave 'ca. 1640.' Later Fletcher argued ('The Seventeenth-Century Separate
Printing of Milton's *Epitaphium Damonis*,' *JEGP* 61, 1962, 788–96), chiefly on the basis of
type and format and Milton's correspondence with Carlo Dati, that the separate printing
was not the first but came soon after the *Poems*, 'early in 1646 perhaps'—a date pronounced
'incredible' by Parker (840, n. 4). Shawcross ('The Date of the Separate Edition of Milton's
"Epitaphium Damonis,"' *SB* 18, 1965, 262–5) opposed Fletcher and held that 'certain
textual and compositorial matters show that the separate printing was a source for the text
of 1645,' that the text 'is frequently altered in 1645 to improve certain readings.'

Prose translations of the *Epitaphium* appear of course in the various complete editions of
Milton. Cowper's couplets are not very satisfactory for the modern reader; nor is Skeat's
archaic style in his partly different versions of 1933 and 1935 (the latter is cited in the Index,
and in the following notes, under the name of its editor, E. H. Visiak). For the non-Latinist
the most attractive versions are those of Helen Waddell and Edmund Blunden (*UTQ* 16,
1946–7, 341–8 and 25, 1955–6, 16–22: the former is reprinted in *Milton's Lycidas*, ed. C. A.
Patrides, New York, 1961).

Besides editions of the Latin poems that have been normally quoted, the notes cite *The
Lycidas and Epitaphium Damonis of Milton*, ed. C. S. Jerram (2nd ed. rev. London, 1881)
and Harrison and Leon (see note 2 below).

Information about Diodati is taken—as in the introduction to *El* 1—from D. C. Dorian,
The English Diodatis (1950).

Milton's making a visit to Lucca, the town where Diodati's forebears had lived (*Def* 2, *Works* 8, 126; Milton's headnote to the *Epitaphium*), and the letter to Carlo Dati of 21 April 1647 (*Works* 12, 44–52), in which 'the death of Diodati, then nine years past, is mentioned, with peculiar solemnity, as still in his thoughts and ever to be sacredly present there' (Masson, *P.W.* 1, 317, 327). On the other hand, it has been suggested (Tillyard, *Milton*, 99–101) that, because of the Italian tour, Milton's past had somewhat receded from his consciousness and that the writing of the poem, the evocation of that past, required an effort.

II CRITICISM

The history and character of pastoral elegy are outlined (with references to the many scholarly and critical studies) in the commentary on *Lycidas*, and here, as in the voluminous notes that follow, only particulars that bear directly upon the *Epitaphium* can be touched. It is significant that, for the utterance of actual, personal grief, Milton not only turned again to the pastoral convention but chose to write in Latin. For him, to be sure, Latin had been the language of intimate feeling and communication, especially communication with Diodati, and the *Epitaphium* is, as Woodhouse says, the last of the epistles to his old friend. Yet when we think of *Elegies* 1 and 6 we realize that the *Epitaphium* is conceived and executed in the formal and rhetorical manner the genre prescribed, a manner heightened in Latin, and that the old epistolary tone appears only at moments. For, no matter how great the poet, or how poignant his emotions, to write an elegy in Latin was to be swept at once into the stream of stereotyped motifs and phrases. That is not to say that the *Epitaphium* does not have the power to move us, that it does not have strength and originality; it is to say that a good many parts of the poem are much closer to the common run of Renaissance elegies than the unique and incomparable *Lycidas*. It may be that in attempting to express his grief Milton found a kind of solace or escape in dallying with the pastoral and elegiac clichés that flowed so readily from the learned pen.

The conventions developed in Theocritus' first Idyll and in the *Epitaphium Bionis* attributed to Moschus had been so fully assimilated by Virgil and his successors that the pastoral elegist of the Renaissance did not need, and did not generally feel, direct Greek influence. Such scholars as W. V. Moody and E. K. Rand have said that the *Epitaphium* represents a return to the form and mood of Moschus and Bion, but even if we substitute Theocritus for Bion (whose influence seems very slight), this view requires some qualification. Though Milton was a better Grecian than most of his predecessors, and though he invoked the Sicilian Muses, the themes and elements of structure and texture in which his poem resembles the Greek pastoral elegy had, as we just observed, been long acclimatized in Latin and the vernaculars. On the other hand, since Neo-Latin elegists of the Renaissance do not seem to be especially devoted to the pastoral convention, the *Epitaphium* can be called a return to the Greek mode. At the same time, as the next paragraph suggests, it can be said that 'with all its echoes of Greek pastoral it is the most deliberately Vergilian poem in the book' (L. L. Martz, 'The Rising Poet,' 9).

In his imagery and phrasing Milton is, as always, eclectic. Illustrative citations in the notes, which vary widely in significance but may be taken as a rough guide, come from the whole range of ancient and modern Latin poets that have been regularly drawn upon in this commentary. Yet, to speak only, and in round numbers, of Virgil, the *Eclogues* yield some 70 citations, the *Georgics* 35, and the *Aeneid* 40. The eclogues most cited are the fifth, the poem on the death and deification of Daphnis (presumably Julius Caesar) which was *par excellence* the model for pastoral elegy, and the tenth, on the poet Gallus, which was also a standard model. In the larger concerns of themes and structure Milton is likewise eclectic; we can compare his treatment of this or that motif with that of various other elegists, but we cannot point to any one model. Indeed, apart from two or three novel and important features, the *Epitaphium* is an exceptionally long and elaborate mosaic of pastoral conventions, non-elegiac as well as elegiac. In handling these, of course, Milton displayed more or less originality, as Woodhouse shows in an analysis to be quoted presently.

T. P. Harrison has made a case for one special or partial model,

Castiglione's *Alcon*, a poem that Milton might be expected to know (and one already cited occasionally in notes on his earlier pieces) and that he might have recalled because of its similar situation.[2] Castiglione was lamenting the loss of Falcone, his brother's tutor and the friend of his own Mantuan boyhood, who died while the poet was in Rome. The nearest approach to the pattern of both poems Harrison finds in Virgil's tenth eclogue, and he sees in both a triple division that is partly parallel. The body of *Alcon* has three themes: the mourning of nature (24–82), the author's absence at the time of Alcon's death (83–129), and the concluding invocation of the departed spirit and the promise to erect a tomb (130–54). The *Epitaphium Damonis* also falls into three parts: sorrow for the loss of Damon, the visits of comforters, and the contrast between animals and man (18–111); memories of Damon, regret for absence from his death-bed, plans for the author's British epic, and the description of Manso's cups (112–97); and the concluding vision of Damon in heaven. While Milton may well have had *Alcon* in mind (along with many other poems), this triple division of the *Epitaphium* seems rather arbitrary (cf. Woodhouse below) and for the most part not very close to *Alcon*. Further resemblances in detail do not appear to go much beyond the generic; as Harrison says, verbal parallels are few, and some of those noted were common property.

In the Roman elegy and its successors Greek pastoral realism declined and the personal and autobiographical became a conspicuous, even the dominant, feature, but the *Epitaphium* is marked by an individual and all-embracing subjectivity. To quote Dorian (*English Diodatis*, 177–8):

In every one of the leading classical laments which might have served as precedents—the first *Idyl* of Theocritus, the *Lament for Bion* attributed to Moschus, the fifth and tenth *Eclogues* of Virgil—in every one of these the shepherd's death is mourned not only by the singer, but also by other beings, human or divine, and by Nature in some form. Even in Castiglione's *Alcon*, which is most

---

[2] 'The Latin Pastorals of Milton and Castiglione,' *PMLA* 50 (1935), 480–93. Parallels discussed in this article are recorded briefly in the notes on *EpDam* in the useful anthology of Harrison and Leon, *The Pastoral Elegy* (Austin, 1939), 293–7, so that in annotations here only the book is ordinarily cited (as Harrison-Leon). Some general resemblances were noted by Hanford (see under note 3 below).

nearly his model in this respect, the pathetic fallacy is used extensively to show all Nature mourning Alcon's loss. But the *Epitaphium Damonis* is the mourning of Thyrsis (Milton) and Thyrsis alone. The nymphs of Himera are invoked not to utter their own grief but to assist Thyrsis in his lament for Damon; the crops and the sheep suffer not through their own sorrow for Damon but through Thyrsis' neglect; and though numerous shepherds and shepherdesses named in the poem attempt vainly to console Thyrsis, not one of them mourns Damon as a lost comrade. In this, the *Epitaphium Damonis* is the complete antithesis of *Lycidas*, in which Milton exclaims 'Who would not sing for *Lycidas?*' and represents many mourners, natural and supernatural, as sharing his grief. The *Epitaphium Damonis* was a monument which he erected alone, a memorial of his singular love for his friend.

Critical estimates of the *Epitaphium* have not been unanimous. Dr Johnson characteristically described the poem as 'written with the common but childish imitation of pastoral life' (*Lives*, 1, 97). Masson pronounced it 'beyond all question, the finest, the deepest in feeling, of all that Milton has left us in Latin, and one of the most interesting of all his poems, whether Latin or English' (*P.W.* 1, 320). Masson's verdict has had perhaps enough endorsement to be called the orthodox view. Hanford, for example, sees the *Epitaphium* as 'incomparably the best of the Latin poems' (*Milton Handbook*, New York, 1946, 136), and numerous other scholars have expressed the same opinion. There have, however, been dissenters. E. K. Rand objected to Greek artifice and the lack of the 'epic pastoral' spirit of Virgil and *Lycidas* (*SP* 19, 1922, 121, 126). Tillyard (*Milton*, 90, 99–100), who ranks *Mansus* first, thinks that the *Epitaphium*, though 'containing perhaps the most beautiful passages,' and though characterized throughout by 'grave sweetness,' 'is not the best of Milton's Latin poems. And the reason is that it reveals a troubled, disunited mind,' painful experiences which have not been resolved. Along with sincere grief, the poet suffers, Tillyard feels, from a reaction after his stimulating sojourn in Italy; there his thoughts had been forward-looking, but now he must in piety turn back to the past. And while 'the first 123 lines are almost faultless, and unique in Milton from the peculiar tenderness of tone in which they are written,' Tillyard sees the poem beginning to flag at 124. Moreover, 'there is something a little forced about the poem as a whole,' and 'something hyperbolical and morbid' in the final vision of Diodati's reception in heaven. Tillyard's general view is shared by Leicester Bradner (*Musae Anglicanae*, 114–16) and by E. H. Visiak (90–1), who thinks Milton's feelings too 'raw,' their expression 'too poignant,' for a completely successful result.

The present commentator must enroll himself among the dissenters, in spite of some discerning analyses to be summarized shortly. No one, certainly, could fail to be stirred by a number of passages, the glowing recollections of old companionship, the revelation—especially moving from one so self-sufficient as Milton has been assumed to be—of his sense of dependence and of irreparable loss and loneliness, and the concluding visions of celestial love and of his friend's pure soul welcomed into heaven. Yet this conclusion, intensely felt as it is (and inspired not only by affection and grief but by Milton's ecstatic response to the ideas of goodness, divine love, and heaven), may serve to bring home to us the immeasurable inferiority of the poem to *Lycidas*. In *Lycidas* the beatific vision is the triumphant answer to the poet's questioning of God's ways to men, and, while the debate has swayed to one side or the other, every detail has contributed to the onward pressure and unified complexity of the whole. But in the Latin elegy that great argument is only touched upon, among many other themes, and the poem almost seems to ramble, as if the author, half-benumbed by his emotions, did not quite know how either to stop or go on. Then in *Lycidas* the pastoral convention has the value of a dramatic mask for public theme and private feeling, and the pastoral motifs are actively functional and organic in building up the central tensions; there are variations of mood and tone but no—or no unintentional—discords. In the *Epitaphium*, however, a few passages of poignant directness make most of the pastoralism stand out as artificial literary embroidery. And although the tradition of the pastoral elegy sanctioned an account of the author's own activities,[3] and although

---

[3] Hanford, in 'The Pastoral Elegy and Milton's *Lycidas*,' *PMLA* 25 (1910), 414, remarks on 'the fiction that the writer of the elegy is himself the poetical successor of the dead shepherd,' which 'justifies the writer in allowing himself digressions concerning his own poetic achievements and aspirations.' Hanford cites Theocritus 1, the *Lament for Bion* (97), *Lycidas* (64 f.), and 'the still more personal and explicit' passage in the *Epitaphium*.

Diodati had in fact been a cherished confidant, we may for once find a touch of egotism, or at least want of tact, in the elaboration of Milton's epic plans.

However, after playing briefly the part of devil's advocate, one surrenders gladly to the full and sympathetically penetrating analysis of A. S. P. Woodhouse.[4] This must be quoted at length, though condensed summaries are resorted to at some points.

The introductory paragraph (1–17) establishes the tradition, 'tells how the poet was long held in the Tuscan city by the love of song (poetry and Italy are to be two of the poem's themes) and how he was at last drawn homeward by care of the flock (...the flock is nothing less than the English Church and State),' ...and 'how, when he reached home, the full sense of irreparable loss came upon him, and how he has sought by utterance to lighten the heavy weight of woe. Here is the motive of the poem categorically stated, and it claims precedence (as the refrain reiterates) over that care of the flock which brought him home.

With this the poem proper commences. Its basic pattern is that of Christian monody, with pagan grief and despair freely expressed in the earlier movements, which act as a foil to the Christian conclusion, where these emotions are dispelled or transcended. In the *Epitaphium* the idea of immortality appears almost at the beginning, but dimly and afar off, in the pagan form simply of an immortality of remembrance, incapable of giving life to the departed or comfort to the bereaved. Midway through the poem it is repeated, this time in a form which posits remembrance by, and not merely of, the departed, but briefly, tentatively, and still to the accompaniment of regret. Finally, it swells triumphant in its full Christian form. Upon this framework Milton weaves his detailed pattern of reminiscence and reflection, the stuff of pastoral monody, turning to his own purpose its accumulated store of image and convention.

(1) In the first movement (18–34) the poet finds no help in the powers of earth or heaven which have doomed Damon to death and left his friend alone and inconsolable. (Loneliness is a dominant note through

4 'Milton's Pastoral Monodies,' *Studies in Honour of Gilbert Norwood* (Toronto, 1952), 261–78.

the earlier movements of the poem, though there is a point at which it will be dispelled.)' This part offers 'the first suggestion of immortality—an immortality of fame, merely, in the memories of men.

(2) And it is wholly inadequate to bring consolation, as the second movement (35–56), whose theme is the poet's loneliness, insists. For Damon the reward of fame cannot fail. But what, cries the mourner, is to become of me? And he turns naturally to memories of his dead friend and their life together, presented in simple rural images...'This 'second movement, and the first passage of reminiscence' are 'dominated by loneliness and grief.

(3) It has almost broken through the frame of pastoral convention, to which the poem is always being brought back by its refrain. Now in the third movement (57–123) these conventions are put to novel and effective use. Not only is the flock neglected (as the refrain repeats) but all labour in field and vineyard; and from the maids and shepherds who come to enquire what ails him and to call him to their sports, the poet turns sullenly away. This is Milton's adaptation of the procession of mourners found in pastoral laments from Theocritus onward. And it leads to another brilliant adaptation. In the lament of Moschus for Bion, and commonly thereafter in pastoral monodies, man is contrasted with nature: the life of nature (that is, of each natural species) dissolves only to be renewed, but man (thought of as an individual) perishes for ever. Milton gives the contrast a new turn, and one that escapes the evident fallacy inherent in the conventional form. In nature, he says, in the herd, all are companions together, of like feeling and under a common law... But we men are alien mind from mind, and heart from heart. Scarcely in a thousand do we find one congenial spirit; or, if we do, yet in an hour when we least expect it, fate snatches him from us, leaving eternal loss behind.' Thyrsis was not at hand when Damon died, to whisper, "Farewell, do not forget me as thou goest to the stars." 'Again the suggestion that for Damon death is not the end. The idea of immortality comes as it were a step nearer; but still without comfort to the bereaved. The whole context is one of mourning, intensified by regret and self-reproach for absence.

(4) And now there follows as the fourth movement (124–178) a bold digression on Milton's Italian journey and the plans for poetry which it matured: a digression, indeed, only in appearance, for it has its own justification—and it is as skilful as bold.' It is not, as Tillyard has said, the destruction of the poem. 'It is bold because it *seems* to carry us away from Diodati; skilful because there is nothing arbitrary about it. *For in fact the seeming digression is the turning-point of the poem :* the shadows fall back and a subtle but perfectly recognizable train of associations leads us on to the triumphant close.

For Milton, Italy and Diodati are indissolubly linked together. Not only was his friend of Italian race though English by adoption: Milton's Italian journey, and his gracious reception in the academies, mark the end of a chapter, the culmination of his youth, of that phase of his life so much of which is symbolized by the friendship with Diodati.' Woodhouse cites the letter to Carlo Dati, written in 1647 amid the rigors of Puritanism and the Revolution, in which Milton recalled both his happy memories of Italian friends and the sacred and solemn memory of his grief for Diodati.[5] At the time, among those friends, he had imagined what Diodati was doing, not knowing that he was dead. Medical arts could not save the young physician, and the poet's pipes broke in his hand; yet he will tell of his epic ambition.

'(5) "All these things I was treasuring up for thee," the next movement (179–197) commences (and properly; for the dead friend was Milton's confidant, and the *Epitaphium Damonis* is...the last of the epistles to Diodati).' Among other treasures were the carved cups given by Manso, the description of which 'is Milton's most brilliant adaptation of a convention of pastoral verse...The pattern on the bowl described by Theocritus [*Id.* 1] represents the life and loves of earth; that on the cups described by Milton, the life and love of heaven and the promise of a resurrection thereto. Thus the theme is twofold, presented by the two pictures on the cups: first, the signs on earth which, for those smitten with the heavenly love, point to resurrection and the joys of heaven (and in so doing suffuse the themes of earth with a heavenly light); and,

[5] *Works* 12, 48.

secondly, the heaven to which they point, whose motivating principle is love. The fragrant Spring betokens the beauty of earth (as do all the images in the first picture) but, above all, the symbolic promise of renewal, to be reinforced by later images; the waters of the Red Sea suggest divine protection (as of God's people of old);[6] Arabia, with its trees dropping balm, suggests divine healing (the heavenly completion of Damon's fallible earthly art) and serves to bring in the image of the Phoenix, the symbol of renewal and resurrection, while the dawn rising beyond the waters reinforces this idea by yet another image (also utilized in *Lycidas*). In the second picture the sky is a general symbol of heaven, and Olympus lying open to view represents a prevision of the life of the heavenly host. That life is inspired by heavenly love, as is symbolized by the celestial Cupid as he kindles angelic natures, but also the sanctified mind in man, and this, like all the other images, points on to heaven.

(6) Then, *by a sudden return to Damon*, with no intervention this time of the refrain, the monody reaches its concluding movement (198–219). The idea of immortality (seen in the first movement, afar off, in the dim perception that Damon must not be numbered with the nameless dead, and renewed in the third movement with the metaphorical allusion to his passage to the stars)—the idea of immortality has come at last to its full Christian form: mourning is banished by triumph, and triumph includes consolation. Heaven is presented as the realization and enjoyment of the heavenly love. Milton remembers the passage in Revelation (14. 1–4):

And I looked, and lo, a Lamb stood on the mount Sion, and with him an hundred and forty and four thousand, having his Father's name written in their foreheads. And I heard a voice from heaven, as the voice of many waters, and as the voice of a great thunder: and I heard the voice of harpers harping with their harps. And they sung as it were a new song before the throne...; and no man could learn that song but the hundred and forty and four thousand which were redeemed from the earth. These were they which were not defiled with women; for they are virgins. These are they which follow the Lamb whithersoever he

---

[6] This particular item is perhaps questionable; see the note on 185 below.

goeth. These were redeemed from among men, being the first fruits unto God and to the Lamb.

And so...Damon is among them joining his according voice. The note is not that of triumph only but of ecstasy; and abandoning his usual practice of the quiet close (certainly sanctioned by the tradition of the pastoral monody) Milton ends with the full volume of the orchestra. *It is to this conclusion that the pictures on the cups have been leading us unawares*...In the *Epitaphium Damonis* Milton' finds relief 'through a pattern which carries his thoughts from earth to heaven or from nature to grace. The pattern is necessary to this transition, and the pattern has its own assuaging power. It does not (as...the pattern of *Lycidas* does) return the poet to the world of extra-aesthetic experience. There is no further reference to the flock, which must, had it occurred, have given an effect of anticlimax; but it would be rash to infer that for Milton the poetic experience had no further result.'[7]

Ralph W. Condee ('The Structure of Milton's "Epitaphium Damonis,"' *SP* 62, 1965, 577–94) more or less follows Woodhouse but has his own valuable insights and emphases. He deprecates critics' preoccupation with pastoral conventions; these Milton follows closely but shows to be inadequate as the poem surges upward 'from the humble rustic beginning to the ecstatic...vision of divine Love.' The refrain, for example, is not repeated mechanically but 'develops quite different meanings at different points in the poem, and these changes of meaning are among the most important of the structural elements...'

The conventional pastoralism of lines 1–34 has moments of feeling and elevation. The word *pecus* (25) is arresting: it underlines the contrast between the merely gregarious instinct of the herd and the love of human friends—a contrast to be developed in 94–111 and to reach climactic resolution 'in the beatific vision of the "caelicolae" joined in harmonious and eternal ecstasy' (581). Lines 27–34 are a preliminary 'pseudo-conclusion' in merely pastoral terms: Damon's promised fame seems to

---

[7] W. L. Grant (*Neo-Latin Literature and the Pastoral*, 329) says that 'Woodhouse vastly overestimates the originality of Milton's treatment of the themes of pagan lament and Christian consolation,' but his discussion of the pastoral elegy (306–30) gives next to no evidence of a Christian strain.

resolve the conflict between love and death, but the third occurrence of the refrain brings us back to the lonely Thyrsis. Continuing pastoralism is repeatedly disturbed by outbreaks of personal feeling (37–9, 45–9, 55–61), 'and by the time the poem again interjects its "Ite domum impasti" at line 93 we are hearing not only the irritation of Thyrsis with pastoral duties, but also the restlessness of a deeply emotional poem within its pastoral garments' (584). In 94–111 Milton returns to 'the central dilemma' 'of love and loss which seemed half-solved at line 34...' Thyrsis berates himself (113–23) 'for having gone to Italy, with the result that he was absent when Damon died.' But his happy recollections of Italy, and of his thinking there of Damon, 'can lead nowhere.' At 161 he repeats 'for the next-to-last time the refrain which helped establish the pastoralism early in the poem, but which now is used as a farewell in order to move beyond pastoralism' (586).

Opposing Tillyard, Condee shares Woodhouse's defensive view (section 4 above) of Milton's account of his projected epic. This part of the poem 'acts as an instrument for increasing the excitement which has replaced the melancholy of the lines preceding it'; 'it begins to turn the poem toward the realm of art.' With the last repetition of the refrain (179), Milton 'brushes aside the flocks, but not with anger, despair, or anguish...He lifts up his eyes from the pastoral to the epic, and from the Latin language to the English, and the meaning of the refrain has now changed almost totally. Pastoral poetry is something inferior, something to be surmounted.' (587). The poem 'stresses the inadequacies of pastoralism in assuaging sorrow'; if the nymphs and shepherds were to 'join sympathetically in mourning Damon...it would have the effect of softening the essential clash between profound grief and threadbare pastoralism' (588). Condee finds here 'something of a structural advance beyond the pastoralism of "Lycidas"...: Where "Lycidas" rests within the tradition, and the nymphs, Hippotades, the waves, and the felon winds are conventionally grief-stricken but ineffective, the "Epitaphium Damonis" derives part of its impetus from spurning pastoralism because of the vacuity and misguidance of Mopsus, Tityrus..., Aegon, and the others.' [One may not feel the validity of this comparison.]

Condee thinks that the Renaissance view of the place of pastoral in the hierarchy of genres becomes here 'a poetic device for giving structure and direction to the progression toward the vision of the transfigured Damon in Heaven...Thus the poem derives a great part of its vigor, its upward surge, from using the pastoral metaphor as something to burst through' (590). The symbolism of the decorations on Mansus' pastoral 'cups' must be read in the light of 'the Platonic and neo-Platonic' conception of love as the means of ascent 'to absolute Goodness, Beauty, and Truth'—a doctrine approached in Milton's letter to Diodati of 23 September [November?] 1637 (*Works* 12, 27; [*C.P.W.* 1, 325, 328]). 'Amor functions to resolve the central dilemma of the poem—that of reconciling man's lofty spirit to the grief that death inflicts' (594). 'At last this extremely complex poem achieves its goal, the vision of the transfigured Damon in Heaven, where Love is eternal. And now the last vestiges of pastoralism drop away,' as in line 210 the pastoral name Damon gives place to 'Diodatus, the gift of God, even though "silvisque vocabere Damon" (211). Now the earthly dilemma of love and death, of the need for companionship that is not merely gregariousness, finds its solution in the true and eternal Love of the celestial marriage feast, Bacchic in its ecstasy and divine in its dedication.

As for Thyrsis—he has surmounted the pseudo-conclusion which led him to ask, "At mihi quid tandem fiet modo?" (37). As the intricate structure of the poem reaches its culmination, what remains for him now as a solace for the agony of his loneliness is the glimpse of divine and eternal Love—and also (and this is part of the poem too) the creation of this pastoral-elegiac hymn to celebrate the eternal joy of his friend; this work of art which, like the cups of Mansus, both embodies and makes possible the vision of triumphant bliss.'

W. M. Jones ('Immortality in Two of Milton's Elegies,' *Myth and Symbol*, ed. Bernice Slote, Lincoln, Nebraska, 1963, 133–40) deals with the *Fair Infant* (*q.v.*) and the *Epitaphium*. He imposes upon Milton an overriding belief in 'the natural fertility of God's world' which—the poet's Christian fervour being slighted—becomes the essential consolation in the face of death. 'In the "Epitaphium Damonis" Milton has prepared for his conclusion about the fertility of the actual world from the very beginning,' the picture of harvest; and in the very last lines, 'More subtly than in any other of his poems on death, the movement... is again from heavenly to actual.' 'The green stalks of the opening passage echo throughout the poem and reappear in the fertility symbol of the heavenly staff.' 'True fame may have its root in heavenly soil, but it is achieved in this world. The Christian promise, like the classical metamorphosis, remains too unreal and illusory for Milton's own practical needs'; 'productivity is assurance of fame to the world's end.' This is the key to both poems, and, incidentally (136), to *Lycidas* as well.

D. Daiches (*More Literary Essays*, 1968: Introduction above, pp. 19–20) is concerned with Milton's early efforts, chiefly in his English poetry, to accommodate his classical principles and knowledge to his growing originality. The relatively late *Epitaphium Damonis* is 'perhaps the most personal poem' he ever wrote. 'It is about Diodati in a way that *Lycidas* is not about Edward King.' Its inspiration is clearly and naturally more Latin than Greek.

That Milton, genuinely moved by the death of a dear friend, should have written a Virgilian pastoral elegy replete with classical names taken from Virgil's fifth and, to a lesser degree, his tenth eclogue, suggests that classical literature was more to him than a field for exhibitionist imitation.' While 'a case can always be made for Milton's having tried to sublimate his grief in a formal exercise, the case of the *Epitaphium Damonis* is more complicated than that. The personal note rises in a new way with the question *Pectora cui credam?*' 'The loss of his confidant, the loss of the friend to whom he confided his secret poetic ambitions, forces him to put these ambitions into a poem and tell the world. When he begins to do so, the imagery begins to move away from the classical world and to name features of the English landscape, especially English rivers..."and my own Thames above all."'

Yet this is not merely a shift from exercise to confession. Milton's 'imagination was clearly deeply touched by the classical elegiac notion of the poet as shepherd, because he saw shepherds as *companions*, as *artists* (singers of artful songs), and as *guardians* (of flocks). These three facets of the shepherd's role had already fused' in *Lycidas*, in a central and lasting 'concept of the poet-priest.' In the *Epitaphium* 'the guardian-priest element is less stressed' (though the refrain stresses the grieving poet's neglect of his sheep); 'companionship, emulation, what we would today call literary friendship, is the aspect of the shepherd symbolism that he concentrates on. And wouldn't the turning of an accomplished Latin poem on this theme be precisely what Charles Diodati would have admired?'

NOTES

1 *Himerides nymphae.* There were two Sicilian rivers called Himera; one flowed northward and had at its mouth the city of Himera (see Theocritus 5. 124, 7. 75). With this invocation of the Sicilian Muses—i.e. Greek pastoral elegy—cf. Virgil, *E.* 4. 1, 6. 1; Milton, *Lyc* 85, 133 (MacKellar).

1–2 *Daphnin & Hylan, | ...fata Bionis.* Theocritus' lament for Daphnis (*Id.* 1) was the fountain-head of pastoral elegy. In *Id.* 13 Theocritus told of the nymph's carrying off of Hylas (cf. Milton, *El* 7. 24). Bion, whose *Lament for Adonis* (ΑΔΩΝΙΔΟΣ ΕΠΙΤΑΦΙΟΣ) is a link in the development of pastoral elegy, was himself commemorated in the *Lament for Bion* (ΕΠΙΤΑΦΙΟΣ ΒΙΩΝΟΣ) formerly ascribed to Moschus, the first elegy on an actual poet.

3 *Dicite Sicelicum Thamesina per oppida carmen.* In writing a Sicilian or pastoral elegy Milton takes the most famous of English rivers, the one beside which he was born, as an equivalent of the Himera. Cf. Virgil, *G.* 2. 176: *Ascraeumque cano Romana per oppida carmen* (Jerram); Vida, *A.P.* 3. 558: *Argolicum resonans Romana per oppida carmen.*

4 *Quas miser effudit voces, quae murmura Thyrsis.* Milton gives himself the name of the shepherd who mourns for Daphnis in Theocritus 1 (cf. Virgil, *E.* 7). Cf. *effudit voces* in Lucan 9. 565, Sannazaro, *P.V.* 3. 337, and Vida, *Christ.* 1. 275; *effundit* or *effundere voces* in Virgil, *A.* 5. 482, 723, 8. 70.

5 *quibus assiduis exercuit antra querelis.* Here and later, in accordance with pastoral convention, both the dead shepherd and his elegist are linked with nature, the background of their life and song. Harrison-Leon (294) cite Castiglione, *Alcon* 15, *Languidulus moestis complet nemora alta querelis*, and 138, *antra querelas.* Cf. Buchanan, *S.* 3. 16–17: *deserta querelis | Antra meis, silvasque & conscia saxa fatigo*; and *assiduae querelae*, in various cases, in Cicero, *Div.* 1. 8. 14, Propertius 2. 18¹. 1, and *C.P.I.* 7, 123.

6 *Fluminaque, fontesque vagos, nemorumque recessus.* As a model for the first phrase Jerram cited Virgil, *A.* 3. 91, *liminaque laurusque dei*, remarking on the license of Milton's long *que*, which does not come within Virgil's rules; he referred to Nettleship (cited below under 78). Cf. *nemorumque recessus* in Lucan 5. 125 and Mantuan, *Syl.* 8.6 (*Opera*, 1502, fol. 112ᵛ), and *nemorum recessus* in Sannazaro, *Epig.* 1. 2. 9 and Buchanan. *Misc.* 4. 40.

7 *Damona.* Milton's name for Diodati is that of one of the singers in Virgil, *E.* 8 (cf. 3. 17, 23), and is common in pastoral literature. Woodhouse ('Monodies,' 265–6) suggests that Milton may have thought also of the famous friends Damon and Pythias, both votaries of the Pythagorean discipline praised in *El* 6, addressed to Diodati.

7–8 *altam | Luctibus exemit noctem loca sola pererrans.* Cf. *nox alta* in Val. Flacc. 3. 206 (cf. 3. 730–1, 6. 14). *Loca sola* is a stock phrase, especially in Ovid, e.g. Lucretius 4. 573, 6. 396; Ovid, *Am.* 3. 6. 50, *errabat nudo per loca sola pede*; *R. Am.* 579, *M.* 7. 819, *F.* 1. 502, 4. 514; Buchanan, *Ps.* 104. 12; *C.P.I.* 11, 419 and Gruter, *Del. I.P.* 2, 1465, *loca sola pererro.*

9–13 The time when the stalk was rising high with the green ears of grain would be about as close to reaping as to sowing, so that 9–10 do not indicate two distinct seasons, spring and autumn; rather, the two lines go together and describe one season, in two successive years, of ripening crop and harvest. (This interpretation is endorsed by B.A.W. and—in *MLN* 72, 1957, 486–8; *Milton*, 839, n. 3—by Parker.) Thus Milton is saying that two harvests or autumns have passed since Diodati's death (August 1638). He might be writing late in 1639 or early in 1640.

   Dorian (*E.D.* 286–7, n. 86) interpreted Milton as saying, inexactly, that four seasons had passed before his return from Italy; but this does not fit the text, nor is there any reason for such very inexact chronology. In opposing Dorian, J. T. Shawcross (*MLN* 71, 1956, 322–4; cf. *SEL* 5, 1965, 56–7) argues that in 9–13 Milton is writing as of the time when he was still in Italy, unaware of Diodati's death, and that he is counting Italian harvests (September–October 1638, March–April 1639), almost a year, between the date of the event and his learning of it, so that the lines do not properly concern the date of composition (which Shawcross would put in the autumn of 1639). Parker (*Milton* 839, n. 3) thinks that 'lines 9–13 refer, not to the time between Diodati's death and the poem's composition, but to a period of *absence from England*, and there were two Italian harvests (in August and March) in that time—as any Italian recipient of the privately printed *Epitaphium Damonis* (1639?) would have understood.'

Apart from the date of composition assigned, I am quite unable to understand these views. Even if Milton expected English readers, his chief prospective audience, to be acquainted with Italian agricultural seasons and practices, the idea is wholly irrelevant. The full passage seems to me to clearly rule out the notion that in lines 9–13 Milton is writing as if he were in Italy. Lines 1–8 certainly picture the disconsolate poet in England. There is not the slightest hint that the scene suddenly shifts to Italy. Line 9 (with its *jam*) carries on directly from 1–8: Thyrsis, now in England, is writing a lament for Damon, who died over a year ago, when Thyrsis was not at his bedside. Lines 12–15 (*pastorem scilicet...Cura vocat*) are—with *scilicet* as a signal— a parenthetical explanation of his absence and his return, and 15–17 resume the picture of the elegist at home. The phrase *Nec dum aderat Thyrsis*, by the way, makes no sense in the Columbia translation, 'and Thyrsis was not yet by his side!'

9 *Et jam bis viridi surgebat culmus arista.* Cf. Virgil, *G.* 1. 48, *bis quae solem, bis frigore sensit*; ibid. 1. 49 (quoted in 10 n. below); ibid. 1. 111 (end), *culmus aristis*; Sil. Ital. 8. 61, *dum flavas bis tondet messor aristas.*

10 *totidem flavas numerabant horrea messes.* Cf. Virgil, *G.* 1. 49, *immensae ruperunt horrea messes*; Ovid, *M.* 8. 293 (end), Poliziano, *Sylvae* 2. 147 (end; *P.V.*, p. 311), and Mantuan, *E.* 8. 109 (end), *horrea messes;* Seneca, *Troad.* 547–8, *post hiemes decem | totidemque messes.*

11 *Ex quo summa dies tulerat Damona sub umbras.* A pagan description of death, to be repudiated later. Cf. Ovid's elegy on Tibullus, *Am.* 3. 9. 27, *hunc quoque summa dies nigro submersit Averno*; Virgil, *E.* 5. 34, *postquam te Fata tulerunt*; *A.* 2. 324, *venit summa dies et ineluctabile tempus*; 4. 660, 11. 831, 12. 952, *sub umbras*; and *summa dies* in Lucan 8. 29, 9. 208, Statius, *Th.* 3. 624, Fracastoro, *C.P.I.* 5, 82, and Vida, *Christ.* 2. 681.

12–13 *pastorem scilicet illum | Dulcis amor Musae Thusca retinebat in urbe.* See the note on 9–13. At the time of Diodati's death Milton was having his first sojourn in Florence (August–September 1638); his second was in March and April 1639 (Masson, *Life*, 1, 1881, 769–72, 821–3). Milton attested his special regard for the genius and language of the Florentines in *Def* 2 (*Works* 8, 122–3) and in his letter to Buonmattei (ibid. 12, 34–5). Cf. Virgil, *G.* 3. 291–2: *sed me Parnasi deserta per ardua dulcis | raptat amor*; Vida, *A.P.* 1. 380, *Musarum dulcem sanctique Heliconis amorem*; F. M. Molsa (*C.P.I.* 6, 355; Gruter, *Del.I.P.* 2, 58), *dulci...Musarum...captus amore.* *Dulcis amor* is a stock phrase, e.g. Catullus 64. 120, 66. 6, 68. 24, Sil. Ital. 8. 104, 146, Vida, *A.P.* 2. 227, Castiglione, *Carm.* 4. 37, Buchanan, *Ps.* 42. 3.

14–15 *Ast ubi mens expleta domum, pecorisque relicti | Cura vocat*. Care of the flock left behind may include Milton's family and other private interests, but—according to his own later account (*Def* 2, *Works* 8, 124–6)—refers chiefly to the concern he felt in Italy over news of the mounting tensions at home that were to bring on the civil war—although, as he proceeded to make clear, that concern, which led him to forgo a visit to Sicily and Greece, did not prevent a further prolonged stay in Italy. R. Clavering and Shawcross (*SEL* 5, 1965, 49–59; see above, the note on *Mansus* 85 f.) argue 'that Milton did not originally intend to visit Sicily and Greece, that he decided upon the trip en route, and that he then gave it up as a pleasant excursion not essential to his original purpose,' and 'that his subsequent travelling abroad constituted not a delay but a continuation of his original design.' For Milton's phrasing, cf. Virgil, *A*. 1. 713, *expleri mentem nequit*; Vida, *E*. 1. 10, *pecorisque relicti*; J. Barclay, *Poematum Libri Duo* (London, 1615), 32, *pecori...relicto*.

15 *assueta seditque sub ulmo*. Editors naturally relate the accustomed elm to 'th'accustom'd Oke' of *IlPen* 60, whether or not there was a relationship in Milton's memory. Jerram quoted the *dilectas villarum ulmos* of *Prol* 7 (*Works* 12, 248, line 17). Editors also cite Ovid, *M*. 10. 533–4: *hunc tenet, huic comes est adsuetaque semper in umbra | indulgere sibi*; and the elm under which the rustics sit in Theocritus 1. 21.

17 *Coepit & immensum sic exonerare dolorem*. Fletcher cites Seneca, *Phoen*. 352, *immensus dolor*, and Petronius, *Sat*. 132 (p. 296), *dolorem meum...exoneravi*.

18 *Ite domum impasti, domino jam non vacat, agni*. As editors have noted, this refrain is modeled on Virgil, *E*. 7. 44: *ite domum pasti, si quis pudor, ite iuvenci*. Cf. *E*. 10. 77: *ite domum saturae, venit Hesperus, ite capellae*. Visiak adds Ovid, *M*. 13. 576, *Non vacat Aurorae*, etc. Milton's refrain is used seventeen times. The refrain of the song in Theocritus 1 occurs nineteen times, the last four embodying a slight variation. The refrain in Bion's *Adonis* appears in identical, varied, and partial forms. 'Bion, beginning the refrain early and continuing it as a distinctive mark of theme transition, is Milton's model' (W. A. Montgomery [see Index], p. 216). In the *Lament for Bion* the refrain occurs thirteen times. In Virgil's *E*. 8 the two refrains each occur nine times, and there are two variants. In spite of such precedents the modern reader, with all his conditioning to pastoral conventions, may feel that Milton's refrain becomes, in a deeply emotional context, an obtrusive element of artifice. See, however, the comments of Woodhouse and Condee in the introduction above, and R. L. Brett, *Reason and Imagination* (Oxford, 1960, 48–9, cited by Carey, 18 n.), who takes the refrain as 'a farewell to the pastoral tradition and all that it symbolizes.' Cf. Condee in 73 n. below.

19–20 *Hei mihi! quae terris, quae dicam numina coelo, | Postquam te immiti rapuerunt funere Damon.* Here and elsewhere pagan pastoralism veils hints of what had been the central theme of *Lycidas*, the arraignment and the final justification of God's providence and justice. Cf. Ovid's elegy on Tibullus, *Am.* 3. 9. 35–6: *cum rapiunt mala fata bonos—ignoscite fasso!— | sollicitor nullos esse putare deos.*

21 *sine nomine.* In Virgil, *A.* 6. 776, Ovid, *M.* 3. 288, 9. 532, *P.* 3. 6. 45.

23 *ille, animas virga qui dividit aurea.* For the role of Mercury, MacKellar cites Virgil, *A.* 4. 242–4, but Milton's phrase is closer to Horace, *C.* 1. 10. 17–19: *tu...animas reponis | ...virgaque levem coerces | aurea turbam. Virga aurea* is also in Ovid, *H.* 16. 64, *M.* 11. 109. Milton's *aurea* is a dissyllable.

25 *Ignavumque procul pecus arceat omne silentum.* Keightley objected to *pecus* in this context, citing Virgil's line about the bees, *ignavum fucos pecus a praesepibus arcent* (*G.* 4. 168; cf. *A.* 1. 435). MacKellar, after referring to Keightley, cites the same line in defense of Milton, and also (after Jerram) Horace's *nigro...Mercurius gregi* (*C.* 1. 24. 18). Claudian 35. 214 (2, 332) uses *ignavi... vulgi* of the dead. For *silentum* see the note on *QNov* 78.

27 *nisi me lupus ante videbit.* For the superstitition that a man became dumb (not 'blind,' as Shawcross says: *C.E.P.*) if he was seen by a wolf before he saw it, editors cite Plato, *Rep.* 1. 336D, Pliny, *N.H.* 8. 34. 80, Virgil, *E.* 9. 53–4. Cf. Theocritus 14. 22, *C.P.I.* 3, 393.

28 *Indeplorato non comminuere sepulchro.* Editors cite Ovid, *Tr.* 3. 3. 45–6: *sed sine funeribus caput hoc, sine honore sepulcri | indeploratum barbara terra teget*; *M.* 11. 669–70; *Ibis* 164; Milton, *EpWin* 55, *Lyc* 14, *Mansus* 17–18. Cf. Ovid, *H.* 3. 134, *lacrimis conminuere meis.*

30–2 *Illi tibi vota secundo | Solvere post Daphnin, post Daphnin dicere laudes | Gaudebunt.* Editors cite Virgil, *E.* 5. 76–80. In placing Damon after Daphnis, Milton is not disparaging Diodati but modestly ranking himself, as poet, below Theocritus (*Id.* 1) and Virgil (*E.* 5) (Le Comte, *Yet Once More*, 21). Cf. Theocritus 1. 3; Virgil, *E.* 5. 49, *tu nunc eris alter ab illo.* Virgil, *E.* 6. 6 and Tibullus 1. 3. 31 both end with *dicere laudes.*

32 *Pales...Faunus.* Both belong to Italian religion and myth. For Pales, a female tutelary deity of shepherds and cattle, see Virgil, *E.* 5. 35, *G.* 3. 1, 294,

Ovid, *F.* 4. 721 f. For Faunus, see the note on *El* 5. 127. Carey notes that the form of line 32 imitates Virgil, *E.* 5. 76–8.

33 *priscamque fidem coluisse, piumque.* Commentators cite Virgil's eulogy of Marcellus, *heu pietas, heu prisca fides* (*A.* 6. 878), and Ovid, *M.* 1. 90, *fidem rectumque colebat. Prisca fides* became, not always in the same sense, a stock phrase, e.g. Virgil, *A.* 9. 79; Martial, *De Spect. Lib.* 6 b. 3, 1. 39. 2; Statius, *S.* 4. 6. 92, *Th.* 1. 509, 2. 269; *C.P.I.* 8, 22; *Cantab. Dolor* (1625), p. 11.

34 *Palladiasque artes, sociumque habuisse canorum.* Cf. *Palladias artes* in *C.P.I.* 2, 447; Vida, *Ad...Parentum Manes* 11; Grotius, *Mathematica* (*S.*, bk. 2, p. 48) and *Ad Gernandum* (*Farr.*, bk. 1, p. 183); and *Oxon. Par.* (1625), sig. D1ᵛ; *Palladiae...artis* in Propertius 3. 9. 42 and Martial 6. 13. 2; Vida, *A.P.* 3. 481, *Palladis arte*; and the note on *El* 2. 2. The poetic friend is of course Milton.

36 *Haec tibi certa manent, tibi erunt haec praemia.* Cf. Vida, *Christ.* 1. 88–9, *praemia quando | Certa manent*; 6. 896, *Haec tibi certa manent*; Sallust, *Cat.* 41. 2, *certa praemia*; Virgil, *A.* 5. 348–9, *munera vobis | certa manent*; Claudian 33. 197 (2, 306), *praemia digna manent*; and the note on *Mansus* 94.

37–8 *quis mihi fidus | Haerebit lateri comes, ut tu saepe solebas.* Cf. Naugerius (*C.P.I.* 6, 481; Gruter, *Del.I.P.* 2, 119), *Haerebat lateri semper comes ille*; Claudian 23. 11 (2, 38), *haerebat doctus lateri castrisque solebat* (on the poet Ennius' following Scipio); Seneca, *Agam.* 452, *comes lateri*; Pliny, *Ep.* 7. 27 (2, 68), *comes haeserat*; Grotius, *Epist. Palladii* (*El.*, bk. 1, p. 153), *Haerebam lateri comes.*

39 *Frigoribus duris, & per loca foeta pruinis.* Editors cite Virgil, *A.* 1. 51, *loca feta furentibus Austris.* Cf. Ovid, *M.* 14. 103, *loca feta...undis*; Virgil, *E.* 10. 47, *dura...frigora*; Lucan 9. 376, *duro frigore.*

40 *rapido sub sole, siti morientibus herbis.* Both phrases are common. For *rapido...sole*, with variations, see Catullus 66. 3, Virgil, *G.* 1. 92, 424, 2. 321, Horace, *C.* 2. 9. 12, Ovid, *Am.* 3. 7. 106, *M.* 8. 225, Mantuan, *E.* 2. 45, Pontano, *Uran.* 1. 108, *Met.* 110, 805, 855, 1550. *Morientibus herbis* is in Virgil, *G.* 1. 107, Mantuan, *E.* 2. 47, Castiglione, *Alcon* 38, Pontano, *Met.* 1027, etc. And cf. Virgil, *E.* 7. 57.

41–2 Lions and wolves belong more to the pastoral tradition than to Milton's England. For wolves see Virgil, *E.* 2. 63, 3. 80, 7. 52, 8. 52, *G.* 1. 130, etc.; Ovid, *Tr.* 1. 1. 78 and Statius, *Th.* 11. 30 have *avidi...lupi* (singular in Ovid, *F.* 2. 86). With *in magnos...eminus ire leones* cf. Ovid, *F.* 5. 176, *comminus ire leas*; Pontano, *Uran.* 3. 909 and 1033, *comminus ire leoni*; Virgil, *E.* 4. 22, *magnos...leones. Praesepibus altis* is the end of Virgil, *A.* 7. 275 (Fletcher) and Ovid, *M.* 2. 120.

43 *Quis fando sopire diem, cantuque solebit?* Harrison-Leon (p. 294) cite Virgil, *E.* 9. 51–2: *saepe ego longos | cantando puerum memini me condere soles.* Cf. Virgil, *G.* 1. 293, *longum cantu solata laborem*; *A.* 7. 754, *cantuque manuque solebat.*

45–9 With this nostalgic picture of delightful talk cf. Milton's letter to Diodati of 2 September (November?) 1637 (*Works* 12, 20–1; *C.P.W.* 1, 325): 'Are there in those parts any smallish learned folks with whom you can willingly associate and chat, as we were wont together?' For a similar atmosphere Hughes cites Horace, *Epod.* 13; cf. *C.* 1. 9, and details in both poems noted below under 46–7 and 61. Cf. also Mantuan's account (*E.* 5. 81–5) of winter evenings and roasting chestnuts at the fire.

46 *Mordaces curas.* Editors cite Lucan 2. 681, *curis...mordacibus,* Horace's *curas edaces* (*C.* 2. 11. 18), Marino's *cura mordace* (*La Lira*, Venice, 1602, 40), and the 'eating Cares' of *L'All* 135. *Mordaces curas,* in various cases and usually in the plural, is in Boethius, *C.P.* 3, met. 3. 5, Sannazaro, *El.* 2. 5. 35, Buchanan, *Ps.* 109. 16, and *C.P.I.* 3, 232, 373, and 9, 470.

46–7 *longam fallere noctem | Dulcibus alloquiis.* Editors cite Milton's last phrase in Horace, *Epod.* 13. 18, and Fletcher adds Val. Flacc. 1. 251, *dulcibus adloquiis ludoque educite noctem. Dulcibus alloquiis* is also in Statius, *S.* 2. 1. 232, *C.P.I.* 2, 254, and Milton, *Prol* 1 (*Works* 12, 144, lines 15–16). Cf. Ovid, *H.* 1. 9, *spatiosam fallere noctem*; Lucan 10. 173–4, *longis Caesar producere noctem | Inchoat adloquiis*; M. Vegius, *Aen.* 13. 509–10, *longam | ...fallere noctem*; Secundus, *Epist.* 1. 11. 75, *tecum solitis fallit sermonibus horam*; Grotius, *Anapaesti in Morbum...F. Grotii (Farr.,* bk. 2, p. 194), *longas... | ...fallere noctes.*

47 *grato...igni.* Cf. Ovid, *F.* 4. 698, *grato...igne.*

48–9 *malus auster | Miscet cuncta foris.* For *miscet* commentators cite Virgil, *A.* 1. 124, 4. 160, and *G.* 1. 356–9.

51–2 *aestate, dies medio dum vertitur axe, | Cum Pan aesculea somnum capit abditus umbra.* Commentators cite Theocritus 1. 15–17 and imitations, e.g. Fletcher, *Faithful Shepherdess* 1. 1. 97–9 (*Beaumont and Fletcher*, ed. F. E. Schelling, New York, 1912): 'Lest the great Pan do awake, / That sleeping lies in a deep glade, / Under a broad beech's shade.' See W. P. Mustard, 'Later Echoes of the Greek Bucolic Poets' (*AJP* 30, 1909, 247). Cf. Sannazaro, *Epig.* 1. 19. 1, *Corniger aesculea Faunus recubabat in umbra*; *C.P.I.* 4, 211, *esculea captanti frigus in umbra. Medio...axe* in various cases is a stock phrase, e.g. Virgil, *G.* 3. 351, *A.* 6. 536, Lucan 3. 423, 10. 250, Sil. Ital. 8. 650, Claudian 3. 11 (1, 26), Buchanan, *Ps.* 49. 1–2, *Sph.* 1. 508.

53 *repetunt sub aquis sibi nota sedilia nymphae.* Editors cite Homer, *Od.* 12. 318, and Virgil, *A.* 1. 167–8: *intus aquae dulces vivoque sedilia saxo, | Nympharum domus.* Cf. Ovid, *M.* 5. 316–17.

54 *Pastoresque latent, stertit sub sepe colonus.* Cf. Milton, *Prol* 6 (*Works* 12, 240, line 13): *nunquam ad meridianum Solem supinus jacui septennis bubulcus.*

55–6 *risus, | Cecropiosque sales referet, cultosque lepores?* *Cecropius* means Attic, from Cecrops, the first king of Attica, e.g. Virgil, *G.* 4. 177, 270, *A.* 6. 21, Ovid, *H.* 10. 100, 125, *M.* 6. 446, 667, etc. Jerram cited Martial 3. 20. 9, *lepore tinctos Attico sales. Cecropiosque sales* is in *C.P.I.* 2, 452; in the singular, in Virgil, *Cat.* 9. 14, Buchanan, *Epig.* 1. 43. 4, and *C.P.I.* 2, 360, 6, 368, and 10, 43. Cf. Martial 4. 23. 6, *Cecropio...lepore*; Buchanan, *Franc.* 4: *Quo lepor & rusus abiere, salesque venusti?*; Milton, *Prol* 6 (*Works* 12, 216, line 10), *sales, & lepores.*

59 *ramosae densantur vallibus umbrae.* Cf. Virgil, *G.* 1. 248, *obtenta densantur nocte tenebrae*; ibid. 1. 342, *densaeque in montibus umbrae.*

60 *Hic serum expecto.* On the non-poetic use of *serum* as 'evening,' Jerram quotes Livy, 7. 8. 5, *serum erat diei.* Cf. Suetonius, *Aug.* 17. 2, *Ner.* 22. 2, *Otho* 11. 1. Cf. the adverbial use in Virgil, *A.* 12. 864 and Horace, *S.* 2. 7. 33.

60–1 *supra caput imber & Eurus | Triste sonant.* Cf. Virgil, *A.* 3. 194 and 5. 10, *supra caput adstitit imber*; Horace, *Epod.* 13. 2–3, *silvae | ...sonant*; Seneca, *Herc. Fur.* 688, *triste resonat*; Castiglione, *Alcon* 46 and *Lacrymae Cantab.* (1619), p. 18: *Nil nisi triste sonant & silvae, pascua, & amnes*; *C.P.I.* 8, 39, *nisi triste sonant, & pascua, & amnes.*

61 *fractaeque agitata crepuscula silvae.* A striking fusion of concrete and abstract, a twilight variation of 'the Chequer'd shade' of *L'All* 96. Cf. Virgil, *E.* 9. 9, *veteres, iam fracta cacumina, fagos*; Horace, *C.* 1. 9. 11–12, *nec cupressi | nec veteres agitantur orni*; Lucan 2. 409, *Eridanus fractas devolvit in aequora silvas*; Secundus, *S.* 5. 4, *fracta gravi nemora avia questu.* Cf. also Ovid, *F.* 2. 439, 3. 329.

64 *ipsa situ seges alta fatiscit!* Editors remark that the ground cracks or crumbles from drought, not blight (cf. Virgil, *G.* 2. 249, 1. 72), and that *seges* can mean the ground itself (ibid. 1. 47, 4. 129), but that here *alta* (cf. ibid. 3. 198, *segetes altae* and Ovid, *A.A.* 3. 102, *seges alta*) requires the meaning of 'grain,' which makes difficult sense with *fatiscit* and *situ.* MacKellar, who summarizes editorial comments, takes the verb in its other sense as 'droops,' 'withers,' with blight. Milton may have intended that, or he might, through a factual error, have meant 'the grain gapes open with blight.'

65 *Innuba neglecto marcescit & uva racemo.* The idea of the vine wedded to the elm was a classical commonplace; see P. Demetz, *PMLA* 73 (1958), 521–32. Editors cite Virgil, *G.* 1. 2, 2. 221, 360–1; Horace, *C.* 4. 5. 30, *Epod.* 2. 9–10; Catullus 62. 49–55 (cf. also 61. 34–5, 102–3); Ovid, *M.* 14. 661–5, *P.* 3. 8. 13; etc. Cf. Sylvester, *D.W.W.* 1. 3. 586–7; and Milton, *PL* 5. 215–16. Ovid ends *M.* 3. 484 with *uva racemis.*

66–7 *ovium quoque taedet, at illae | Moerent, inque suum convertunt ora magistrum.* Cf. Virgil, *E.* 10. 16–17: *stant et oves circum (nostri nec paenitet illas, | nec te paeniteat pecoris, divine poeta...).*

69–90 The friends who appear to distract or comfort Thyrsis are a variation on the usual procession of mourners for the dead shepherd; the device may have been suggested by Virgil, *E.* 10. 19 f. (Harrison, *PMLA* 50, 483). Most if not all of them are characterized too slightly and vaguely to be more than representative lay figures with pastoral names. Carey (88–9 n.) thinks that Milton's classical names presumably 'stand for real people, mutual acquaintances of himself and Diodati.'

69 *Tityrus ad corylos vocat.* Cf. Virgil, *E.* 1. 13–14, *Tityre... | hic inter densas corylos.* The name Tityrus appears in Theocritus (3 and 7. 72) but is most familiar through Virgil, *Eclogues, passim.*

69 *Alphesiboeus ad ornos.* The Greek name ('bringer of oxen') appears, e.g. in Virgil, *E.* 5. 73, 8. 1, 5, 62 f.; Sannazaro, *E.* 4. 72, *El.* 1. 1. 26.

70 *Ad salices Aegon.* The name is in Theocritus 4. 2, 26; Virgil, *E.* 3. 2, 5. 72; Sannazaro, *P.V.* 3. 186–91. Cf. Virgil, *E.* 10. 37–9, *Phyllis... | mecum inter salices.*

70 Amyntas appears in Theocritus 7. 2, 132, and Virgil, *E.* 2, 3, 5, and 10, and is common in Renaissance pastorals.

71 *Hic gelidi fontes, hic illita gramina musco.* Editors cite Theocritus 5. 33 and Virgil, *E.* 10. 42, *Hic gelidi fontes, hic mollia prata. Gelidi fontes* is a stock phrase, e.g. Virgilian *Cul.* 148, Ovid, *M.* 14. 786, 15. 550, Seneca, *Agam.* 318, etc. MacKellar cites Jerram's objection to *illita*, 'smeared,' 'spread on the surface,' as a dubious word for moss growing among grass. But cf. Horace, *Ep.* 1. 7. 10, *si bruma nives... illinet agris*; ibid. 1. 10. 7, *musco circumlita saxa*; and *C.* 4. 9. 14, *aurum vestibus illitum.* For the pastoral scene cf. Castiglione, *Alcon* 124: *Hic* *umbrae nemorum, hic fontes, hic frigida Tempe* (Harrison-Leon, 294); Ovid, *F.* 3. 298, *gramen, muscoque adoperta virenti*; and similar phrases in Virgil, *E.* 7. 45, *G.* 3. 144, 4. 18–19.

72 *placidas interstrepit arbutus undas.* Cf. Horace, *C.* 1. 1. 21–2: *nunc viridi membra sub arbuto | stratus, nunc ad aquae lene caput sacrae.*

73 *Ista canunt surdo.* A proverbial phrase. Erasmus has *Surdo canis* in his *Adagia* (*Opera*, 2, 1703, 178). Editors cite Virgil, *E.* 10. 8, *non canimus surdis*; Propertius 4. 8. 47; Ovid, *Am.* 3. 7. 61. Cf. Milton's letter to Gill, 4 December 1634, about his Greek translation of Psalm 114 and the writing of Greek in this age: *periculum est, ne plerumque surdo canat* (*Works* 12, 16, line 18). Milton 'is rejecting the charms of the cool waters and of Vergil's pastorals. He is saying, with the words repeated but the meanings new, "Ite domum impasti, domino iam non vacat, agni" (74)...He is saying that it is Diodati who is dead; the old rituals [cf. 30–2] have no power on such an occasion.' (Condee, 584–5).

75 *frutices ego nactus abibam.* Cf. Ovid, *F.* 6. 117, *frutices haec nacta*; *M.* 2. 455, *nacta nemus.*

75f. Mustard (249: see above, 51–52 n.) cites Theocritus 1. 77–8 (the coming of Hermes), but see note on 69–90 above.

76 *callebat avium linguas, & sydera Mopsus.* Mopsus is both a common pastoral figure (e.g. Virgil, *E.* 5, 8. 26, 29) and a soothsayer (Hesiod, *Shield of Heracles* 181; Cicero, *N.D.* 2. 3. 7; Ovid, *M.* 8. 316, 350, 12. 455–6, 524–31; Seneca, *Med.* 654–6; Val. Flacc. 1. 207 f., 3. 372 f.). Hughes cites Tasso's Mopso who understood the speech of birds and the virtue of herbs and fountains (*Aminta* 1. 2. 457 f.), and Mopsus the burlesque seer of Randolph's *Amyntas* 1. 3, etc. With Milton's description editors compare Virgil, *A.* 3. 359–61, 10. 175–7. Cf. Cicero, *Div.* 1. 57. 131, *linguam avium.*

77 *quae te coquit improba bilis?* With the use of *coquit* for mental disturbance Jerram compares Virgil, *A.* 7. 345 and Sil. Ital. 14. 103. Cf. Vida, *Christ.* 1. 539, Buchanan, *Ps.* 26. 10, 64. 5, 69. 10. For bile, see the notes on *Eli* 27–8 and *Sals* 19–20.

78 *Aut te perdit amor, aut te male fascinat astrum.* On the long final syllable of *amor*, MacKellar refers to Nettleship's discussion of Virgilian usage in *Virgili...Opera*, ed. Conington (1883), 3, 486–91. MacKellar also quotes Virgil, *E.* 3. 103, *nescio quis teneros oculus mihi fascinat agnos*, and remarks (after Keightley) that, in Milton's astrological allusion, *astrum* becomes almost an eye. Cf. Catullus 7. 12, *mala fascinare lingua*; Ovid, *Am.* 1. 6. 41, *somnus, qui te male perdat*; *M.* 4. 148–9, *tua te manus...amorque | perdidit.*

79 *Saturni grave saepe fuit pastoribus astrum.* 'The planet Saturn was by the ancients regarded as cold and as a cause of rain (Virgil, *Georg.* 1. 336; Pliny, *N.H.* 2. 39. 106); thus it was unfavorable to farmers and shepherds. According to the astrological belief, those born under the influence of Saturn were of a melancholy temperament' (MacKellar). See the Variorum introduction to *L'Allegro* and *Il Penseroso*, II. 2; C. Agrippa, *De Occulta Philosophia, passim*; E. Panofsky, *Albrecht Dürer* (2 v. Princeton, 1943), 1, 166 f.; Raymond Klibansky, E. Panofsky, and F. Saxl, *Saturn and Melancholy: Studies in the History of Natural Philosophy, Religion, and Art* (London, 1964). Editors cite Propertius 4. 1. 84, *grave Saturni sidus*, and Cicero, *Div.* 1. 39. 85. Cf. Persius 5. 50–1, *Saturnumque gravem... | ...astrum*; Horace, *C.* 2. 17. 21–5; Juvenal 6. 569–70, *sidus triste minetur | Saturni*; Secundus, *Epist.* 1. 6. 11, *Falciferique senis grave rebus in omnibus astrum*; Pontano, *Uran.* 3. 1306; Gill, *Ad Honoratiss. Episcop. Lond....1631* (p. 60): *Saturne tristis, gelide, moeste, luride, | Tetricoque vultu squallide*; Grotius, *Ad. Ex.* 587–8, *gravis | Saturnus astro.*

80 *Intimaque obliquo figit praecordia plumbo.* The planet Saturn was associated with lead, for which Saturn was the technical name in alchemy. Cf. Camden, *Britain* (tr. 1610), 556: 'Saturne, whom they [alchemists] make the Lord and Dominatour of lead'; John Read, *Prelude to Chemistry* (New York, 1937), 88, 143, etc. With *obliquo* editors compare Horace, *Ep.* 1. 14. 37, *obliquo oculo*; Spenser, *F.Q.* 2. 9. 52. 9, 'oblique Saturne'; Milton, *IlPen* 43, 'With a sad Leaden downward cast'; *Arc* 52, 'the cross dire-looking Planet smites.' Cf. Gill, (loc. cit. under 79), *Obliquus in coelo*; Petrarch, *Ep. ad Io. de Columna* (*P.M.* 3, 58): *Despicit obliquo Saturnus lumine terras. Praecordia intima* is a stock phrase, e.g. Virgil, *A.* 7. 347, Ovid, *H.* 16. 135, *M.* 4. 507, 6. 251, Vida, *Christ.* 2. 113, 5. 349. Cf. Ovid, *H.* 10. 107, *figi praecordia ferrea cornu.*

82 *Mirantur nymphae, & quid te Thyrsi futurum est?* Cf. Virgil, *Cir.* 391, *nymphae mirantur*; Ovid, *M.* 1. 301, *mirantur... | Nereides.* Jerram proposed *de te* for *te.* Garrod (*Ox. Fac.* and again in 1955 ed.) made the same suggestion, apparently without knowledge of Jerram, and was followed by Grierson (xxxviii, 179). The Columbia editors accepted the change as probably right (*Works* 18, 643). But Masson (*P.W.* 3, 355) took *Quid te* as 'A Ciceronian idiom for "*Quid tibi*,"' though he gave no evidence. Cf. Cicero, *Academica* 2. 33. 107, *Quid fiet artibus?*; *Letters to Atticus* 6. 1 (1, 430), *Quid illo fiet...? quid me autem...?*; *Sibyllina Oracula* (Paris, 1599), *lib.* 2, 213: *Eheu me miseram, quid me illo tempore fiet?* Jerram and Masson took *nymphae, et* as legitimately unelided;

Jerram cited Virgil, *pecori et* (*E.* 3. 6) and *pecori, apibus* in *G.* 1. 4 (cf. *E.* 7. 53). Milton's text would seem to be defensible.

84 *Nubila frons, oculique truces, vultusque severi.* Cf. Ovid, *M.* 5. 512, *nubila vultu*; Gill, *Epith.* (p. 43): *Exhilarans convivia tristis* | *Explicat omnia nubila frontis*; Campion, *Umbra* 122, *nubila frontem. Oculi truces*, in various forms, is in Seneca, *Oed.* 921, 962–3, Statius, *Th.* 7. 474, Cicero, *N.D.* 2. 42. 107, Castiglione, *Carm.* 7. 35. With Milton's last phrase cf. Juvenal 14. 110, *vultuque et veste severum.*

85 *choros, lususque leves.* Cf. Horace, *C.* 1. 1. 31, *leves...chori.*

86 *bis ille miser qui serus amavit.* For this apparently proverbial idea editors cite Guarini, *Il Pastor Fido*, 1. 1 (*Opere*, ed. L. Fasso, Turin, 1950, 46; *Il Pastor Fido*, Venice, 1605, 5–6), and Shakespeare, *All's W.* 5. 3. 57–59. Cf. Propertius 1. 7. 26, *saepe venit magno faenore tardus Amor.* Milton might have been echoing an unidentified Latin phrase or embroidering the proverbial *Miser est qui amat* (Plautus, *Pers.* 2. 179; *Carminum Proverbialium*, 1603, p. 8).

88 *Hyas, Dryopeque.* Hyas, a hunter and brother of the Hyades, is in Ovid, *F.* 5. 172–82, but Milton apparently uses the name for a nymph. Dryope in Ovid, *M.* 9. 331–93, is the daughter of Eurytus and mother, by Apollo, of Amphissus; in Virgil, *A.* 10. 550–2, Dryope and Faunus are the parents of the warrior Tarquitus. Milton seems to use the name for any pastoral nymph.

88–9 *filia Baucidis Aegle* | *Docta modos, citharaeque sciens, sed perdita fastu.* *Filia Baucidis* is probably only a filler, since there would be small point in relating Aegle to Ovid's apparently childless old couple (*M.* 8. 629–724). MacKellar notes—as Stephanus et al. had noted—that there were several classical Aegles. If Milton had any of these in mind, it would be the naiad in Virgil, *E.* 6. 20, who appears in a pastoral setting. Editors cite Horace, *C.* 3. 9. 10, *dulces docta modos et citharae sciens.* Cf. Virgil, *E.* 2. 14–15: *Amaryllidis iras* | *atque superba pati fastidia*; Sannazaro, *E.* 5. 66, *Docta Aegle*, and *Epig.* 2. 11, *Ad Aeglen*; Buchanan, *Alc.* 590, *citharae sciens*; Ovid, *A.A.* 3. 511, *Odimus immodicos...fastus.*

90 *Idumanii Chloris vicina fluenti.* The river Chelmer in Essex flows into Blackwater Bay; in Ptolemy's *Geographia* it was *Idumanius fluvius.* Cf. Camden, *Britain* (tr. 1610), 444; Drayton, *Poly.* 19. 94 f., 109–10. 'If any one of the four shepherdesses mentioned was a real person of Milton's acquaintance, this Chloris might be she...It is hardly possible to suppose so precise a local designation adopted without some suggestion from fact' (Masson, *P.W.* 3, 355–6). 'Hardly possible' seems a bit strong.

91 *solantia verba.* In Ovid, *M.* 11. 685 (Fletcher).

92 *Nil me…movet, aut spes ulla futuri.* Cf. Virgil, *A.* 2. 137, *nec mihi…spes ulla videndi*; 8. 580, *spes incerta futuri*; *Lacrymae Cantab.* (1619), p. 48, *sola aevi spes illa futuri.*

94–105 Although Milton's point is the contrast between sociable animals and lonely man, he might have had in mind such a catalogue as that of Ovid, *A.A.* 2. 481–8. See the note on 101 below and, in the introduction above, Woodhouse's and Condee's comments on this adaptation of a pastoral motive.

94 *quam similes ludunt per prata juvenci.* Cf. Virgil, *E.* 7. 11, *per prata iuvenci*; Claudian 8. 17 (1, 286), *ludunt per prata*; Ovid, *F.* 1. 156, *ludit et in pratis luxuriatque pecus*; Seneca, *Herc. Fur.* 141–2, *ludit prato liber aperto | …iuvencus.*

95 *Omnes unanimi secum sibi lege sodales. Unanimi sodales*, in varying forms, is a stock phrase, e.g. Catullus 30. 1 (Fletcher), Claudian 3. 105 (1, 32), Sannazaro, *El.* 2. 7. 11, *Epig.* 2. 15. 24, Secundus, *El.* 3. 10. 41, Campion, *Epig.* 2. 144. 3.

99–100 *deserto in littore Proteus | Agmina Phocarum numerat.* Editors cite Virgil, *G.* 4. 429–32: *Proteus… | sternunt se somno diversae in litore phocae*; and 387–95. See the note on *El* 3. 26. Cf. *deserto in litore* in Catullus 64. 133, Virgil, *A.* 2. 24, Vida, *E.* 1. 37, and *Gratul. Cantab.* (1623), p. 26.

101 *Passer habet semper quicum sit.* Cf. Ovid, *A.A.* 2. 481, *Ales habet, quod amet*; Buchanan, *Valent.* 1. 10 (*Epig.*, bk. 3), *Quisque sibi sociam jam legit ales avem.*

102 *sua tecta revisens.* Cf. Virgil, *G.* 1. 414, *dulcisque revisere nidos.*

103 *si fors letho objecit.* Cf. Horace, *S.* 1. 1. 2, *seu fors obiecerit* (Fletcher).

103–4 *seu milvus adunco | Fata tulit rostro, seu stravit arundine fossor.* Cf. Ovid, *M.* 8. 147 and 371, *rostro…adunco* (Fletcher); Castiglione, *Alcon* 10–11: *Quam procul incautam quercu speculatus ab alta | Immitis calamo pastor dejecit acuto* (Harrison, *PMLA* 50, 489; Harrison-Leon, 295).

106–7 *Nos durum genus, & diris exercita fatis | Gens homines aliena animis.* Editors cite Virgil's *durum genus* (*G.* 1. 63) for the human race engendered from the stones thrown by Deucalion and Pyrrha; the phrase is also in *A.* 9. 603 (cf. 5. 730, *gens dura*) and in Ovid, *M.* 1. 414 (Deucalion). Editors note *exercite fatis* in Virgil, *A.* 3. 182 and 5. 725, and *exercita curis* in *A.* 5. 779. Cf. Secundus, *El.* 3. 10. 56 and *Epist.* 1. 10. 30, *Mens quibus a nobis non aliena fuit.*

108 *Vix sibi quisque parem de millibus invenit unum.* Cf. Ovid, *P.* 2. 3. 11: *nec facile invenias multis in milibus unum.*

109 *sors...non aspera votis.* Cf. Statius, *Th.* 1. 196, *aspera sors*; Claudian 28. 282–3 (2, 94), *aspera fati | sors*; Virgil, *A.* 8. 365, *non asper egenis.*

110–11 *Illum inopina dies qua non speraveris hora | Surripit.* Cf. *C.P.I.* 3, 46: *Felices inopina dies quos funere mergit*; and *mors inopina* in Buchanan, *Ps.* 9. 18 and 88. 6, Gruter, *Del.I.P.* 1, 183, *Lacrymae Cantab.* (1619), p. 83, and *Cantab. Dolor* (1625), p. 34.

113 *Heu quis me ignotas traxit vagus error in oras. Vagus error* is in Val. Flacc. 5. 115, Buchanan, *Ps.* 44. 12, *S.* 3. 16, *Sph.* 1. 247; cf. Ovid, *M.* 4. 502, *erroresque vagos. Ignotis oris* is in Virgil, *G.* 3. 225, Ovid, *Tr.* 3. 3. 37, Propertius 1. 20. 15. Cf. Castiglione, *Alcon* 83, *Heu male me ira deum patriis abduxit ab oris* (Harrison-Leon, p. 295).

114 *Ire per aëreas rupes, Alpemque nivosam!* On his journey to Italy, Milton went by ship from Nice to Genoa; in returning he traveled 'by way of Verona, Milan, and the Paenine Alps, and along the lake Lemano, to Geneva' (*Def 2, Works* 8, 127). Cf. *aëria(e)(s) rupes* in Sil. Ital. 1. 371 and Grotius, *Myrtilus* (*S.*, bk. 2, p. 55); *nivosas Alpes* in Sannazaro, *Epig.* 2. 60. 15–16 and Beza, *In Tolenonem* (*Poëmata*, p. 84ᵛ); Virgil, *E.* 10. 47, *Alpinas...nives* (cf. Secundus, *El.* 2. 5. 38); *G.* 4. 508, *rupe sub aëria*; Ovid, *M.* 2. 226, *aeriaeque Alpes.* B.A.W. cites *SA* 628, 'snowy Alp.'

115 *Ecquid erat tanti Romam vidisse sepultam?* Editors cite Virgil, *E.* 1. 26: *Et quae tanta fuit Romam tibi causa videndi?* Milton had two sojourns in Rome, in October and November 1638 and in January and February 1639; see Masson, *Life,* 1 (1881), 792–807, 820–1, *P.W.* 3, 356. Harrison-Leon (295) cite *Alcon* 122–5, in which Castiglione anticipates his friend's coming to Rome.

117 Tityrus here means Virgil's Tityrus, who saw Rome, not 'buried' but in the early days of its ancient splendor (cf. *E.* 1 and the preceding note), not Chaucer, who is called Tityrus in *Mansus* 34 (see the note thereon). In Milton's time many of the remains that the modern tourist sees had not been uncovered. With *rura reliquit,* cf. Ovid, *M.* 10. 478, *rura relinquit.*

119–20 *Possem tot maria alta, tot interponere montes, | Tot sylvas, tot saxa tibi, fluviosque sonantes.* Editors cite Homer, *Il.* 1. 155–7 (quoted under *El* 4. 21); Ovid, *Tr.* 4. 7. 21–2: *innumeri montes inter me teque viaeque | fluminaque et campi nec freta pauca iacent*; and Milton, *El* 4. 21–2. Cf. *alta...maria* in Catullus 63. 1 and Gruter, *Del.I.P.* 1, 664, 1187, 1218; Catullus 34. 12, *amniumque sonantum*; Ovid, *F.* 2. 704, *sonantis aquae*; and *fluvi(i)(os)...sonantes* in Beza, *I. Quelini...Memoriae* (*Poëmata,* 48ᵛ) and Grotius, *Epith. Kinschot.* (*S.*, bk. 3, p. 104).

121 *certe extremum licuisset tangere dextram.* Cf. Virgil, *A.* 1. 408–9: *cur dextrae iungere dextram | non datur...?*; Ovid, *Am.* 3. 8. 16–17: *dextram tange... | ...potes hanc contingere dextram*; Claudian 15. 231 (1, 114), *da tangere dextram.*

122 *Et bene compositos placide morientis ocellos.* Cf. Virgil, *A.* 1. 249 (quoted under *Mansus* 93). Harrison-Leon (295) and Hughes cite Castiglione, *Alcon* 84–6: *Ne manibus premerem morientia lumina amicis*, etc. Harrison-Leon (loc. cit.) also cite Spenser, *Astrophel* 137–8. Cf. *Oxon. Par.* (1625), sig. H2ʳ, *composuit morientis lumina regis.*

123 *Et dixisse vale, nostri memor ibis ad astra. Vale nostri memor* is in Juvenal 3. 318 and Sannazaro, *Epig.* 3. 7. 3. *Memor nostri* is a stock phrase, e.g. Horace, *C.* 3. 27. 14, Ovid, *Am.* 2. 11. 37, *H.* 11. 125, *Tr.* 4. 3. 10; etc. For phrases akin to *ibis ad astra*, see the note on *Eli* 48.

125f. For Milton's recollections of the 'shepherds of Tuscany'—that is, his Florentine literary friends—see *Def* 2 (*Works* 8, 122–3), his letter to Carlo Dati (ibid. 12, 48), and the eulogies of Francini and Dati (ibid. 1, 156–66), and the notes on 12–13 and 14–15 above and 129–30 below.

127–8 *Hic Charis, atque Lepos; & Thuscus tu quoque Damon, | Antiqua genus unde petis Lucumonis ab urbe.* The personified Charis and Lepos are Grace and Charm; cf. P. Crinitus, *C.P.I.* 3, 513, *gratus Lepor, & Charis.* 'Lucumo was an Etruscan title for princes and priests which was misunderstood by Livy (1, 34) as the personal name of Tarquinius Priscus (of whom Milton thought as the founder of Lucca)...' (Hughes). Diodati's forebears had come from Lucca; see Milton's epigraph to this poem and Dorian, *E.D.* Cf. *urbs antiqua* in Virgil, *A.* 1. 12 and 2. 363.

129–30 *O ego quantus eram, gelidi cum stratus ad Arni | Murmura.* 'The beautiful upper valley of the Arno, the *Valdarno* of *P.L.* 1, 290, became familiar to Milton during his visits to Florence in 1638 and 1639. In a letter written September 10, 1638...to...Buonmattai, he speaks of "visiting with delight the stream of the Arno, and the hills of Faesolae"' (Hughes; *Works* 12, 34–5). Cf. the Horatian phrase quoted under 72.

130 *Murmura, populeumque nemus, qua mollior herba. Murmura* is the first word in Virgil, *A.* 10. 99. Cf. Virgil, *E.* 3. 55, *in molli...herba*; 7. 45, *somno mollior herba*; Ovid, *M.* 4. 314, *mollibus...herbis*; Seneca, *Herc. Fur.* 145, *molli...in herba.* Le Comte (*Yet Once More*, 120) quotes *Acced* (*Works* 6, 350): *Dicite quandoquidem in molli consedimus herba.*

131 *Carpere nunc violas, nunc summas carpere myrtos.* Cf. Virgil, *E.* 2. 47, *violas et summa papavera carpens*; Ovid, *M.* 5. 392, *violas...carpit.*

132 *Et potui Lycidae certantem audire Menalcam.* Lycidas is one of the contestants in Theocritus 7, Menalchas in Theocritus 8 and Virgil, *E.* 3. The pastoral convention of a singing contest represents the literary recitals and discussions Milton had heard and taken part in in Florentine academies. See Masson, *Life*, 1 (1881), 763–6, *P.W.* 3, 356–7; Parker, *Milton*, 169–82 and notes; general references in the headnote to *Mansus*, 270 above.

133–4 In *RCG* (*Works* 3, 235–6) and *Def* 2 (ibid. 8, 122) Milton speaks of his participation in such gatherings and of the favor his own poems received.

134–5 *nam sunt & apud me munera vestra* | *Fiscellae calathique, & cerea vincla cicutae.* 'The gifts represent books or copies of verses like the Ode by Antonio Francini which Milton placed at the head of his Latin poems in the edition of 1645' (Hughes). Editors cite Virgil, *E.* 3. 62–3 (quoted under *Mansus* 38). Cf. Virgil, *E.* 2. 32, *calamos cera coniungere*; 2. 36–7, *compacta cicutis* | *fistula;* 2. 44, *munera nostra.*

136–8 For two of Milton's Italian friends, Dati and Francini, see the notes on 125 f. and 134–5, and Masson, *Life*, 1 (1881), 774–6, 779–80, 783–5. They are imagined as shepherds singing Milton's praises among the trees (Virgil, *E.* 1. 5; 6. 83). 'According to Herodotus (1. 94) the Lydians...migrated from Asia Minor to northern Italy, and thus became the progenitors of the Etruscans and Tuscans. The Roman poets frequently allude to the Lydian origin of the Etruscans; see Virgil, *Aen.* 2. 781; 8. 479–80; 9. 11; Horace, *Sat.* 1. 6. 1' (MacKellar). The information is given in Ovid–Micyllus, 3, 65 F–G.

140 *roscida luna.* Also at the end of Virgil, *G.* 3. 337 (Jerram) and Pontano, *Erid.* 2. 27. 5, and in Claudian 24. 288 (2, 62).

141 *solus teneros claudebam cratibus hoedos.* Editors cite Horace, *Epod.* 2. 45, *claudensque textis cratibus...pecus*, and *Comus* 343, 'The folded flocks pen'd in their watled cotes.' Cf. *teneri...haedi* in Lucretius 2. 367 and the singular in Horace, *C.* 3. 18. 5 and Ovid, *A.A.* 1. 410.

142–78 Harrison-Leon (295) compare *Alcon* 103–29, in which Castiglione 'tells of his dreams of the absent friend.'

142 *cinis ater habebat.* Editors note that the phrase is in Virgil, *A.* 4. 633.

143 *tendit retia.* For this common phrase see the note on *El* 1. 60.

144 *Vimina nunc texit, varios sibi quod sit in usus.* Editors cite Virgil, *E.* 2. 71–2: *quin tu aliquid saltem potius, quorum indiget usus,* | *viminibus mollique paras* *detexere iunco ?* Milton's line is a fusion of common phrases. Cf. Virgil, *E.* 10. 71, *gracili fiscellam texit hibisco* (Harrison-Leon, 295); *G.* 4. 34, *vimine texta*; *A.* 11. 65, *arbuteis texunt virgis et vimine querno*; Ovid, *M.* 2. 554, *texta de vimine*; Claudian 35. 138 (2, 328), *nunc vimine texto*; and *varios...usus* in Manilius 1. 61, Pontano, *Uran. passim*, and Sannazaro, *P.V.* 1. 38, *Sal.* 6.

145–6 Harrison-Leon (295) compare Castiglione, *Alcon* 103–4: *Quin etiam sortis durae, ignarusque malorum, | Vana mihi incassum fingebam somnia demens.*

148 *Imus? & arguta paulum recubamus in umbra.* Cf. Virgil, *E.* 1. 1(quoted under *El* 5. 41). Jerram remarked that we should expect *eamus* and *recubemus*, or else the future, and that Milton might have been led to use the present indicative by Virgil's *paras* in *E.* 2. 71–2 (quoted under 144 above).

149 *ad aquas Colni, aut ubi jugera Cassibelauni.* The river Colne flows near Horton. Dorian (*E.D.* 168) thinks that Milton and Diodati 'undoubtedly met often during the autumn and winter [1637–8], if they did not actually live together either in London or at Horton. No known evidence precludes the latter possibility.' Milton's second phrase seems a little vague. In *HistBr* (*Works* 10, 44), echoing Caesar (*B.G.* 5. 11), he says that the territory of 'Cassibelan' 'from the States bordering on the Sea was divided by the River Thames about 80 mile inward,' and speaks also of Verulam (St Albans) as the supposed town of the chieftain (ibid. 47); cf. Camden, *Britain* (tr. 1610), 391–2, 408–9. Since the chieftain's territory included Bucks, and since we know of no connection Milton or Diodati had with St Albans, commentators take the phrase as another reference to the neighbourhood of Horton: Masson, *P.W.* 3, 358; Gilbert, *G.D.* 76; MacKellar; Hughes. 'A walk from Horton up the Colne would bring Milton to the neighbourhood of St Albans' (Visiak). Fletcher (*Intell. Dev.* 2, 515), following MacKellar (and Camden), names the territory within the points Hammersmith, Eton, Staines, and St Albans.

150–3 As some commentators, e.g. Warton, Todd, Keightley (apparently), Masson (*P.W.* 3, 229), Jerram, MacKellar, and Dorian (*E.D.* 151, 271–2, 288) have said (Masson with some hesitation), these lines favor the idea that the 'certain Shepherd Lad' of *Comus* 618–27 is a reference, by way of friendly fiction, to Diodati. Cf. Milton's tribute to his medical capacity and his character in the letter cited under 200 below. *Medicos...succos* (or *medici succi*) appears in *C.P.I.* 2, 49 and 8, 163.

151 *Helleborumque, humilesque crocos, foliumque hyacinthi.* The herbs are traditional in medicine (Pliny, *N.H.*, L.C.L. v. 7, index). Cf. Ovid, *M.* 10. 208 (on Apollo's marks on the hyacinth), *folioque legatur eodem.*

313

153–4 *Ah pereant herbae, pereant artesque medentum | Gramina, postquam ipsi nil profecere magistro.* Editors cite Ovid, *M.* 1. 524: *nec prosunt domino, quae prosunt omnibus, artes.* Cf. Horace, *Ep.* 2. 2. 150–1, *herba | proficiente nihil*; Pontano, *Parth.* 2. 3. 25, *Nil medicae prosunt artes*; Milton, *Procan* 22 and note.

155–60 The pastoral pipe proved unequal to epic strains. The incoherence of these lines seems to reflect the inward conflict between poetical pride and proper modesty, not grief—since, when in Italy Milton anticipated this talk, he assumed that Diodati was alive and would in time receive his confidences. Cf. Masson, *P.W.* 3, 358–9.

155–6 *grande sonabat | Fistula, ab undecima jam lux est altera nocte.* Editors cite Virgil, *E.* 8. 39, *alter ab undecimo tum me iam acceperat annus.* For *grande sonabat* see the note on *El* 5. 21 and cf. Mantuan, *E.* 1. 18–19, *sonabat | fistula*; Gill, *Ad...Paulum Pindarum...1632* (p. 80), *Grande sonans.*

157 *Et tum forte novis admoram labra cicutis.* Cf. Virgil, *E.* 3. 43, *necdum illis labra admovi*; 2. 36–7, *compacta cicutis | fistula*; Buchanan, *S.* 2. 27, *vix primis admoram labra cicutis*; Sannazaro, *E.* 4. 70, *calamos labris admoverit audax*; C.P.I. 4, 211, *Cumque admovissem teretes ad labra cicutas.*

158 *rupta compage.* The usual phrase, in various contexts, is *compage soluta*, e.g. Statius, *Th.* 8. 31, Lucan 1. 72 (cf. 2. 487, *Discussa conpage*), Claudian 33. 115 (2, 300), *Cantab. Dolor* (1625), p. 27. Cf. Claudian 36. 184 (2, 358), *fractane...compage*; Lucan 3. 629, *ruptis...conpagibus.*

160 *vos cedite silvae.* Editors cite Virgil, *E.* 10. 63, where Gallus, with *concedite silvae*, turns away from pastoralism.

162–8 The plan for the British epic is much more concrete here than it was in *Mansus* 80–4, whether because it has become so in Milton's mind or only because the present context invites a fuller statement. See the remarks of Hanford quoted in note 3 of the introduction.

162 *Dardanias Rutupina per aequora puppes.* For the tradition of the Trojan (Dardanian) origin of Britain, see the note on *El* 1. 73. Cf. Propertius 4. 1. 40 and Sil. Ital. 2. 1, *Dardana puppis.* Rutupiae was identified by Camden, *Britain* (tr. 1610), 340–2, with Richborough in Kent; he quoted Ausonius, Juvenal 4. 139–42 and Lucan 6. 67. Milton (*HistBr, Works* 10, 95; cf. p. 80, note) speaks of Rutupiae as 'on the opposite shoar' from 'Boloigne'; cf. Camden, 78, 'Rhutupiae, a place over against Bologne.' Cf. Drayton, *Poly.* 18. 704, 'the Rhutupian shore' (and note, 'Neere Sandwich'); Grotius, *Inaug. Reg. Brit.* (*S.*, bk. 2, p. 62), *Rutupinaque littora*; and *Rutupinum littus* in *Epiced. J. Heemskerckii* (loc. cit. p. 77).

163 *Pandrasidos regnum vetus Inogeniae.* According to Geoffrey of Monmouth (1. 3–11), 'Pandrasus was a king of Greece defeated in war by Brutus to whom he then gave his daughter Ignoge—the name appears in various forms, as Ignoge, Inogen, and Imogen. The realm of Brutus in Britain is called "in poetical gallantry," as Masson has said, not his but Imogen's.' (MacKellar, citing Milton, *HistBr*, *Works* 10, 7–11). Hughes cites Spenser, *F.Q.* 2. 10. 13. 5, on 'Inogene of Italy.' Cf. Drayton, *Poly.* 1. 353 f. Gill, *In ruinam* (12) has *regnum vetus.*

164 *Brennumque Arviragumque duces, priscumque Belinum.* Moving on some seven centuries, supposedly, from the arrival of Brute in Britain, Milton comes to Brennus and Belinus, sons of Dunwallo Molmutius, king of Britain (Geoffrey of Monmouth, 3. 1–10; Spenser, *F.Q.* 2. 10. 37–40, and Variorum notes). In Geoffrey's and later chronicles Brennus and Belinus achieved Continental conquests which culminated with their taking Rome; this event was telescoped with the historical capture of Rome in 390 B.C. by the Gauls under a chief named Brennus (Livy 5. 36 f.; Milton, *Prol* 5, *Works* 12, 192 and *HistBr*. ibid. 10, 23–5; Selden, in Drayton, 4, 124, 154–7). The later Arviragus, son of King Cymbeline, submitted to Claudius Caesar and married his daughter, but afterwards revolted against Rome. See Geoffrey, 4. 12–16; Juvenal 4. 126–7 (quoted by Geoffrey, 4. 16); Spenser, *F.Q.* 2. 10. 51–2 and Variorum notes; Milton, *HistBr* (*Works* 10, 56, 80); Selden, loc. cit. 161; MacKellar.

165 *Et tandem Armoricos Britonum sub lege colonos.* Camden (*Britain*, 110–11) quotes William of Malmesbury, who says (*Chronicle*, ed. J. A. Giles, London, 1847, 6) that Constantine founded a colony of veteran British soldiers on the west coast of Gaul, now Brittany. Cf. Milton, *HistBr* (*Works* 10, 118); Ussher, *Britannicarum Ecclesiarum Antiquitates* (Dublin, 1639), 421: *Britannorum vero coloniam in Armoricam traductam, a Constantio quidem Chloro significat Radulphus Niger in Chronico, a filio ejus Constantino Magno Guilielmus Malmesburiensis...* (C. Nicholas, *Introduction and Notes to Milton's History of Britain*, Illinois Studies in Language and Literature, 44, 1957, 75).

166–8 According to Geoffrey (8. 19), King Uther Pendragon, falling in love with Igerne, wife of Gorlois, Duke of Cornwall, was enabled by Merlin's magic to gain access to her in the form of her husband and begot a son, Arthur. Cf. the versions in Malory, *Morte Darthur* 1. 2, and Selden, in Drayton, 4, 19–20.

168–71 *O mihi tum si vita supersit, | Tu procul annosa pendebis fistula pinu | Multum oblita mihi, aut patriis mutata camoenis | Brittonicum strides.* Although Milton must have had a clear idea in his mind, and although the general sense of the whole passage 155–78 is mostly clear, there are more difficulties than editors have commonly recognized. Jerram (121) touched on some of them, though his solution may not seem quite satisfying: 'The sense should therefore be, "Either I will abandon poetry altogether, or else change it from Latin verse into English." But if Prof. Masson is right in explaining *fistula* of *Latin* poetry in particular, the alternative "aut–aut" is merely formal, the real meaning being this: "I will abandon Latin verse for English." "Patriis Camenis" will then signify "*its* native Muse," i.e. the Latin.'

In 145 f., Milton had begun an imaginary conversation with Diodati of which his share would have been the communication of his epic plans (155 f.): he had essayed composition but his pastoral pipe (*fistula*) had proved as yet unequal to such lofty strains. However, he will report his plans, and he gives (162–8) an outline of the British epic. There follows (168 f.) the exclamation: 'And then, my pastoral pipe, if life still remains to me, you shall hang forgotten on an old pine far away; or else, changed, you shall sound forth a British theme in native strains.' (My translation). But the logic of *or* (*aut*, 170) is not clear, since the two phrases do not express alternatives (unless the first means giving up poetry altogether, which is inconceivable) but are different statements of the same idea, so that *et* would be more logical than *aut* (there is no *aut–aut* as Jerram says). Perhaps *aut* can be justified by the fact that Milton is continuing to address the pipe, which must be transformed to become a fit instrument for heroic verse. The *tum* (*then*) of 168 is perhaps more logical than temporal: if Milton does not, like Diodati, suffer untimely death, he will give up non-heroic or pastoral poetry and go on with the epic. But he will write it in English. No change of theme is involved in *patriis mutata camoenis* because the British theme has already been specified, because *Brittonicum strides* implies the harsh, crude sounds of English as compared with those of Latin, and because lines 171–8 are wholly concerned with writing in English and the limited audience for an English poem. (This note includes some private comments from A.S.P.W.)

168 *O mihi tum si vita supersit.* Fletcher cites Virgil, *G.* 3. 10, *modo vita supersit*, where Virgil is planning to cultivate the native muse. The Virgilian phrase is in *C.P.I.* 4, 68 and 7, 228. Cf. Sil. Ital. 9. 124, *non ut mihi vita supersit.*

169 *Tu procul annosa pendebis fistula pinu.* Editors cite Virgil, *E.* 7. 24, *arguta sacra pendebit fistula pinu.* Cf. *C.P.I.* 1, 2, *Hic suspensa alta pendebis, fistula, quercu.*

170 *patriis mutata camoenis.* See the note on 168–71 above. MacKellar (p. 169) translates 'forsaking your [the pipe's] native songs' and explains in a note (p. 347) 'its paternal Muses, *i.e.*, Latin.' This may be right, but Ovid (*P.* 4. 13. 33) uses *patria Camena* for his native language in contrast with the Getic, and Milton seems to mean his native language (cf. *El* 6. 89 and note, 126 above) in contrast with his earlier use of Latin. Of course the two readings come to the same thing in the end. With *oblita mihi*, cf. Virgil, *E.* 9. 52, *nunc oblita mihi tot carmina*.

171–8 He cannot hope to succeed in both Latin and English. See Milton's account in *RCG* (*Works* 3, 236: quoted in MacKellar) of his debate with himself over which language to use, and of his patriotic resolve to write in English, even though it would mean addressing only England instead of all Europe. With *omnia non licet uni* (171) editors compare Virgil, *E.* 8. 63, *non omnia possumus omnes*. Cf. ibid. 7. 23, *si non possumus omnes*; Propertius 3. 9. 7, *omnia non pariter rerum sunt omnibus apta*; Mantuan, *E.* 5. 59–60 [*Deus*] *omnia non dat | omnibus;* Vida, *A.P.* 1. 354–5: *Verum non eadem tamen omnibus esse memento | Ingenia.* With *Non sperasse*, etc., cf. the citations under *El* 4. 123.

173–4 *mihi grande decus* (*sim ignotus in aevum | Tum licet...*). Cf. Horace, *C.* 2. 17. 4, *C.P.I.* 3, 54, and Gill, *Epith.* (p. 48), *grande decus.* For *in aevum* Jerram cites Horace, *C.* 4. 14. 3.

175 *Si me flava comas legat Usa, & potor Alauni.* Editors compare Horace's similar idea and phrase, *discet Hiber Rhodanique potor* (*C.* 2. 20. 20). Cf. Ovid, *P.* 4. 2. 37: *hic mea cui recitem nisi flavis scripta Corallis.* Fletcher cites Ovid, *M.* 6. 118, 9. 307, *flava comas.* 'Whether the *Usa* is the Ouse of the Eastern Counties or the Ouse of Yorkshire may remain doubtful; but the former may be preferred, as the river nearest Cambridge (see Spenser, *F.Q.* IV. xi. 34)' (Masson, *P.W.* 3, 361). Cf. *Vac* 92; Gilbert, *G.D.* 222; Camden, *Britain* (tr. 1610), 367: 'For, Isis, commonly called Ouse, that it might bee by originall of Glocester-shire, hath his head there...This is that Isis which afterwards enterteineth Tame, and by a compound word is called Tamisis, Soveraigne as it were of all the Britain rivers in Britaine'; ibid. 373, 'Isis, or Ouse'; 376, 'the Owse or Isis'; 383–4; 396: 'Usa or Ouse, in times past Isa, and the second Isis, which...passeth through the North part of this Province [Bucks] arising in Northampton-shire...' 'According to Camden [*Britain*, 259, 813], the Alne in Northumberland and the united Stour and Avon in Hampshire both bore the Latin name of *Alaunus*' (Hughes; cf. MacKellar).

176 *Vorticibusque frequens Abra, & nemus omne Treantae.* The Abra is probably the Humber (Gilbert, *G.D.* 148–50; *Vac* 99 and note), though the Humber is the Abus in Camden, *Britain* (tr. 1610), 710; cf. Spenser, *F.Q.* 2. 10. 16 and Variorum note. Editors cite Ovid, *M.* 9. 106, *verticibusque frequens*, *F.* 6. 502, *verticibus densi.* 'The river Trent rises in Staffordshire, and by its confluence with the Ouse forms the Humber. Cf. *Vacation* 93; Spenser, *F.Q.* 4. 11. 35. 8–9' (MacKellar).

177 *Thamesis meus ante omnes.* Gilbert (*G.D.* 292–3) lists Milton's many references to the Thames and cites Spenser, *F.Q.* 4. 11. 27–8, and Drayton, *Poly.*, Song 17; see also the Index to the *Works*. Cf. the quotation from Camden (367) in the note on 175 above.

177–8 *fusca metallis | Tamara, & extremis me discant Orcades undis.* Cf. the Horatian phrase cited under 175, and Ovid, *M.* 10. 220, *fecundam Amathunta metallis*; 531, *gravidamve...metallis*. The Tamar, between Cornwall and Devon, passes through a region famous for its mines (Camden, *Britain*, tr. 1610, 187, 196; Spenser, *F.Q.* 4. 11. 31. 1–2; MacKellar). For the Orkney Islands, MacKellar cites Juvenal 2. 159–61 and Milton, *HistBr* (*Works* 10, 80).

180 *Haec tibi servabam lenta sub cortice lauri.* The general sense is clear: that Milton had, in his head or on paper, plans or notes for the British epic which he had been expecting to show Diodati. The metaphor is commonly taken to mean that he was treasuring his plans 'like valuables in a box of laurel bark' (Hughes; MacKellar; Masson, *P.W.* 3, 361), though Hughes finds another explanation in the songs of Apollo which the laurels were to learn (Virgil, *E.* 6. 83). But Milton's metaphor probably comes from Virgil, *E.* 5. 13–14: *haec, in viridi nuper quae cortice fagi | carmina descripsi.* The same pastoral idea of verses carved or written on bark appears, e.g. in *C.P.I.* 1, 149 (*viridi signatum in cortice carmen*) 205, 207. Fletcher cites Ovid, *M.* 9. 353, *lentus...cortex.*

181–2 *quae mihi pocula Mansus, | Mansus Chalcidicae non ultima gloria ripae.* For Chalcidian as meaning Neapolitan, see the note on *Leon* 3. 4. Some commentators, such as Warton (who allowed for 'an allegorical description of some of Manso's favours'), Masson, Jerram, and MacKellar, have taken Milton to refer to actual cups. Keightley thought he was only using a popular pastoral convention that started with Theocritus 1. 29–56 and Virgil, *E.* 3. 36–48. Milton's description owes nothing to either of these poems, and the singularity of his subjects and his pictorial minuteness have been the main arguments for actual cups. But M. de Filippis, in *PMLA* 51 (1936), 745–56, argued—with references to imaginary cups in Renaissance verse—that the 'cups' given to Milton were really two of Manso's books, *Erocallia* (1618; 1628), and an anthology drawn from Manso and others, *Poesie Nomiche* (1635)—an idea put forth in John Black's *Life of T. Tasso* (London, 1810), 2, 467. He elaborated Black's guess that Milton's description of the supposed cups was indebted especially to the dialogues on Platonic love in *Erocallia* and the Italian translation of Claudian's *Phoenix* in the *Poesie* (see the note on 187–9 below). (Dorian, *PMLA* 54, 1939, 612–13, pointed out that Pindar, at the beginning of *Ol.* 7, compared his ode itself to a cup presented to a bridegroom by the bride's father.) De Filippis' argument is quite compatible with Woodhouse's interpretation of Milton's symbolism (see the introduction above). We may conclude, first, that Milton was obviously using the ancient and Renaissance pastoral convention of ornamented cups; secondly, that Manso gave him presents which had some suggestive significance in his mind and were not merely dragged in as a complimentary allusion; and, thirdly, that these presents may well have been books rather than cups, and possibly two particular books of Manso's own authorship or compilation that furnished hints toward a theme always active in Milton's mind, the Christian and Platonic contrast and connection between earthly and heavenly life and love. For one phrase, cf. *C.P.I.* 10, 343, *non ultima gloria gentis*; Poliziano, *Sylvae* 2. 561–2 (*P.V.*, p. 332), *haud ultima Phoebi | Gloria*.

183 *artis opus*. With various adjectives (or none), a stock phrase, e.g. Ovid, *A.A.* 2. 14, *M.* 13. 290, *F.* 1. 268, 6. 662; Tibullus 3. 4. 37; Martial 6. 13. 2; *C.P.I.* 1, 175, *Artis opus mirae*, etc.

184 *gemino caelaverat argumento*. Editors cite Ovid, *M.* 13. 684, *longo caelaverat argumento*. The scenes on Ovid's cup (685–701) do not resemble Milton's.

185–97 For the symbolism of the whole passage see Woodhouse; section 5 of his analysis is quoted in the introduction.

185 *In medio rubri maris unda, & odoriferum ver*. Milton apparently takes the Red Sea in the ancient sense as the Arabian and Persian Gulfs together—more largely, the Indian Ocean (Gilbert, *G.D.* 243; Starnes-Talbert, 334, quoting C. Stephanus, *Dict.*). See, e.g. Seneca, *Herc. Fur.* 903, *rubri maris*; Pomponius Mela 1. 10. 61, 3. 7. 71, 3. 8. 72; Pliny, *N.H.* 9.54. 106, 9. 56. 113, 12. 1. 2 (and the Loeb translator's note, 3, 238). For precious stones gathered from the 'Red Sea,' see Seneca, *Thy.* 371–3, *Herc. Oet.* 660–2, Sil. Ital. 12. 231, and the citations from Propertius, Claudian (the first four), and Pontano in the note on *Naturam* 63–5. Although the classical phrase, *rubrum mare*, is used of the biblical Red Sea (as in Beza, Acts 7. 36, Heb. 11. 29), Milton seems less likely to be thinking of that, both because of classical usage and because of his associating the sea with Arabian odors, as in *PL* 4. 159–65.

186 *Littora longa Arabum, & sudantes balsama silvae*. See the preceding note, and Pliny, *N.H.* 12. 54. 111 f. and Diod. Sic. 3. 46 (MacKellar). Cf. Virgil, *G.* 2. 118–19, *sudantia ligno | balsamaque*; Claudian 1. 252 (1, 20), *sudent...*

spirantia balsama; 10. 96 (1, 248), *sudanti...balsama rivo*; Pontano, *Uran.* 1. 1009, *sudanti balsama ligno.*

187–9   As possible sources for this brief account of the phoenix, commentators cite Pliny, *N.H.* 10. 2. 3–5; Ovid, *M.* 15. 391–407, *Am.* 2. 6. 54; Claudian, *Phoenix* (*S.P.* 27; 2, 222–30) and 22. 414–20 (2, 32); the *De Ave Phoenice* (*Minor Latin Poets*, L.C.L., pp. 643 f.) attributed to Lactantius, which is argued for by K. E. Hartwell, *Lactantius and Milton* (Cambridge, Mass., 1929), 123 f.; Tasso, *Il Mondo Creato*, 5. 1278–1591, mostly translated from the Lactantian poem, with items from Claudian and an original introduction and epilogue (R. B. Gottfried, *SP* 30, 1933, 497–503). But De Filippis (see the note on 181–2 above) is properly sceptical of arguments for particular sources, since Milton's data were common property; he notes that Mary C. Fitzpatrick, *Lactanti De Ave Phoenice* (Philadelphia, 1933), lists 128 passages on the phoenix in ancient literature. (See also Svendsen, *Science*, 146–8.) We may feel the same scepticism in regard to De Filippis' own suggestion, the Italian translation of Claudian in Manso's anthology, *Poesie Nomiche*: if Manso gave Milton books and not cups, and if this was one of the books, the translation might have reminded him of the phoenix, if he needed any reminder. Without contravening the negative principle just enunciated, one may quote Grotius' phrase about the phoenix, *in terris unica semper avis* (*In Pascha, El.*, bk. 1, 157).

189   *Auroram vitreis surgentem respicit undis.* K. E. Hartwell (125, 129: see preceding note) cites the same detail—a stock one—from *De Ave Phoenice* 35: *lutea cum primum surgens Aurora rubescit.* And Gottfried (p. 500: see preceding note) points it out in Tasso; he suggests (502) that Milton might have remembered Claudian and Lactantius in Tasso's version as well as in Latin. Cf. Virgil, *A.* 4. 129, *surgens Aurora*, and the notes on *El* 5. 49–50 and *QNov* 133–4. For the stock phrase *vitreis undis*, see the note on *QNov* 66.

190   *polus omnipatens, & magnus Olympus.* The sky and heaven. See the notes on *El* 5. 19 and 79, and the deified Daphnis' view of the Olympian heaven in Virgil, *E.* 5. 56–7 (partly quoted under 203–4 below). *Omnipatens* may be a Miltonic coinage (Jerram).

191   *hic quoque Amor, pictaeque in nube pharetrae.* For the usual quiver-bearing Cupid see the notes on *El* 1. 60 and 82; for his significance here, see Woodhouse, sec. 5, quoted in the introduction. Cf. the accounts of heavenly love in Spenser's *Hymnes* and *C.C.C.H.A.* 783 f. *Pictae pharetrae*, in various cases, is a stock phrase, e.g. Ovid, *M.* 2. 421, 4. 306, 308, Sannazaro, *P.V.* 2. 128, Vida, *A.P.* 1. 282, 2. 467.

192 *Arma corusca faces, & spicula tincta pyropo.* Cupid's torches are almost as common as his arrows; see the notes on *El* 1. 60 and 5. 97 and 98. *Pyropus* was bronze of a fiery color, e.g. Lucretius 2. 803, *claro. . .rubra pyropo*; Ovid, *M.* 2. 2, *flammasque imitante pyropo*; Propertius 4. 10. 21, *picta neque inducto fulgebat parma pyropo.* Harding (*Ovid*, 90), citing Ovid and *PL* 3. 591–8, shows that Renaissance scholars (e.g. Ovid–Micyllus, 3, 30D) commonly took the word as 'carbuncle.' See also Svendsen, *Science*, 29–30.

193 *Nec tenues animas, pectusque ignobile vulgi.* Cf. *tenues animae* in Ovid, *F.* 2. 565 and *M.* 14. 411. *Ignobile vulgus* is a stock phrase, e.g. Virgil, *A.* 1. 149 (Fletcher), Pontano, *Uran.* 1. 1147, *C.P.I.* 1, 105, 250, 402, *Lacrymae Cantab.* (1619), p. 65, *Cantab. Dolor* (1625), p. 32.

194 *flammantia lumina torquens.* Editors note the same phrase in Virgil, *G.* 3. 433 (cf. *A.* 7. 448–9); it is also in Vida, *Christ.* 5. 33 and *C.P.I.* 3, 163, 165. The idiom, with variations and with or without an adjective, is common, e.g. Propertius 1. 21. 3, Val. Flacc. 2. 184–5, Sil. Ital. 4. 234, etc.

195–6 *spargit sua tela per orbes | Impiger.* The use of *spargere* with *tela* is common, e.g. Virgil, *A.* 12. 50–1, Ovid, *M.* 12. 600–1, Lucan, 3. 327, Secundus, *El.* 1. 1. 6 (of Cupid). Cf. Seneca, *Hipp.* 283–4 (of Cupid), *per orbem | spargit effusas agilis sagittas.* For Cupid as *impiger*, see the note on *El* 7. 17. Garrod (cf. *Ox. Fac.*) suggests *orbem* for *orbes*, which would spoil the sense, since Milton is writing of the celestial spheres, not of 'the world.'

196 *collimat* ('looks with glance askant,' in the painful Columbia translation) is from a ghost-verb *collimo*, once generally accepted but later recognized as an error for *collineare*, 'aim in a straight line' (Jerram; *Harpers' Latin Dict.*).

197 *formaeque deorum.* Also at the end of Ovid, *M.* 1. 73. For Cupid shooting his darts MacKellar cites Ovid, *M.* 1. 455–76 and Moschus 1. 14–19. For Milton's figurative meaning see Woodhouse (quoted in the introduction).

198 *nec me fallit spes lubrica.* Cf. Statius, *Ach.* 1. 547, *me spes lubrica tardat*; Boethius, *C.P.* 4, met. 2. 8, *spes lubrica.*

200 *Sanctaque simplicitas,. . .candida virtus.* Editors cite Milton's reference to Diodati's *morum simplicitas* in his letter of 23 September (November?) 1637 (*Works* 12, 24, line 15). *Candida virtus* is in Buchanan, *Franc.* 43 and Grotius, *Epitaph. F. Junii* (*Farr.*, bk. 2, p. 187).

201 *Lethaeo. . .sub orco.* See the notes on *QNov* 132 and *El* 7. 83–4.

202 *Nec tibi conveniunt lacrymae.* Cf. *SA* 1721, 'Nothing is here for tears.'

203–4 *Ite procul lacrymae, purum colit aethera Damon, | Aethera purus habet,* *pluvium pede reppulit arcum.* Editors cite the deification of Daphnis in Virgil, *E.* 5. 56–9, *sub pedibusque videt nubes et sidera Daphnis,* etc., and *G.* 4. 233, *Plias et Oceani spretos pede reppulit amnis.* Harrison-Leon (295) cite Sannazaro's Italian *Ecl.* 5. 9–10, on the disembodied soul: *Et sotto le tue piante | Vedi le stelle errante* (ibid. 96). Fletcher cites Horace, *A.P.* 18, *pluvius arcus.* Cf. Seneca, *Oed.* 220, *haustusque tutos aetheris puri dabit*; Sil. Ital. 17. 52, *purumque per aethera*; Sannazaro, *E.* 1. 91, *altum felix colis aethera*; the quotation from Buchanan under *Mansus* 96; and George Herbert, *Jordan* (2), 11–12: 'Nothing could seem too rich to clothe the sun, | Much lesse those joyes which trample on his head.' Cf. *Epith. Caroli et H. Mariae* (1625), p. 8, *Ite procul lacrymae.*

206–7 *Aethereos haurit latices & gaudia potat | Ore Sacro.* Editors cite Horace, *C.* 3. 3. 11–12: *quos inter Augustus recumbens | purpureo bibet ore nectar*; and Spenser, *S.C., November* 195–6. Cf. *ore sacro* in Ovid, *M.* 14. 21; *os sacrum* in Claudian 24. 11 (2, 42) and Vida, *A.P.* 1. 165; Manilius 2. 7–9: *ore sacro cecinit... | ...cuiusque ex ore profusos | omnis posteritas latices in carmina duxit*; Virgil, *A.* 6. 715, *securos latices et longa oblivia potant*; Beza (*Poëmata,* 21ʳ), *puraeque bibunt nova gaudia mentes.*

207–8 *Quin tu coeli post jura recepta | Dexter ades, placidusque fave quicunque vocaris.* Although Milton would hardly accept the Catholic tradition of invocation of the saints, Damon is presented, in classical terms, as a deified mortal who can assist those on earth; cf. *Lyc* 182–5. Editors cite Virgil, *E.* 5. 65, *sis bonus o felixque tuis,* and *A.* 8. 302, *et nos et tua dexter adi pede sacra secundo.* Cf. *A.* 4. 578–9: *adsis o placidusque iuves et sidera caelo | dextra feras. Dexter ades* is in Ovid, *F.* 1. 6, 67, 69, and Sil. Ital. 1. 514; cf. Secundus, *Fun.* 26. 11, *Dextera ades.*

209 *sive aequior audis.* For the classical idiom see the note on *Sals* 26.

210–11 *Diodotus, quo te divino nomine cuncti | Coelicolae norint, sylvisque vocabere Damon. Diodotus (Diodatus,* MacKellar, 170) means 'God-given.' For *Coelicolae,* see the note on *Mansus* 95. Cf. Virgil, *E.* 5. 43, *Daphnis ego in silvis.*

212 *purpureus pudor, & sine labe juventus.* Ovid has *purpureus pudor* in *Am.* 1. 3. 14, 2. 5. 34, *Tr.* 4. 3. 70 (cf. Statius, *Th.* 2. 231, Secundus, *El.* 1. 11. 6), but here of course the phrase has a much deeper meaning. For the common and especially Ovidian *sine labe,* see the note on *El* 6. 64. Cf. Pontano, *Uran.* 2. 406, *non sine labe iuventa.*

213 *quod nulla tori libata voluptas.* Cf. *El* 1. 41–2 and note; and Ovid, *H.* 2. 115, *cui mea virginitas avibus libata sinistris.*

215 *caput nitidum cinctus rutilante corona.* Editors cite 1 Pet. 5. 4 (tr. Beza: *amarantinam illam gloriae coronam*); Rev. 2. 10 (Beza: *coronam vitae*), 14. 3–4 (partly quoted under *Patrem* 30–7 and, in English, in the introduction to *EpDam* p. 292); and Jeremy Taylor's echo of 14. 4: 'that little coronet or special reward, which God hath prepared...for those "who have not defiled themselves with women, but follow the" virgin "Lamb for ever"' (*Holy Living* 2. 3: *Works* 3, London, 1861, 56–7). Cf. Milton's comment on the same phrase in *Apol* (*Works* 3, 306). *Caput nitidum* is a stock phrase, e.g. Virgil, *G.* 1. 467, Horace, *C.* 1. 4. 9, Ovid, *M.* 13. 838, 15. 30, Tibullus 1. 8. 16. Cf. Ovid, *M.* 2. 27, *cinctum florente corona*, and *corona* with various forms of *cingo* (with or without *caput*) in Lucretius 2. 606, Virgil, *A.* 11. 475, Lucan 1. 321, Apuleius, *Met.* 11. 24, Fracastoro, *C.P.I.* 5, 18, and *Cantab. Dolor* (1625), p. 12.

216 *Letaque frondentis gestans umbracula palmae.* Editors cite Rev. 7. 9–10 (the end of 7. 9 Beza renders: *& palmae in manibus eorum*).

217 *Aeternum perages immortales hymenaeos.* Editors cite Rev. 19. 6–8.

218 *choreisque furit lyra mista beatis.* Editors cite Horace, *Epod.* 9. 5, *sonante mixtum tibiis carmen lyra.* Cf. Claudian, *S.P.* 25. 22–3 (2, 206): *plausus mixtaeque choreis | auditae per rura lyrae*; Pontano, *Uran.* 2. 1332–3: *Charitumque choreis | Immistus canit Aeneam*; 4. 519, *choreis mistus.*

219 *Festa Sionaeo bacchantur & Orgia Thyrso.* The bold fusion of pagan and Christian images is remarked upon in the general Introduction; and see Hanford, 'Youth,' 153–4. Unlike *Lycidas*, as Woodhouse says (see the introduction to *EpDam*), this poems ends, not with a return to earth, but on the note of climactic ecstasy. On the thyrsus, the vine-leaved staff carried by Bacchic celebrants, editors cite Ovid, *M.* 3. 542; Virgil, *A.* 7. 390; Horace, *C.* 2. 19. 8. Cf. Grotius, *Eucharistia* (*S.*, bk. 1, p. 10), *Coetibusque sancta semper Christianis Orgia*; Gill, *De Gestis...Gustavi Adolphi...1631* (p. 86), *trivijs bacchantes Orgia circum.*

Ad Joannem Rousium
Oxoniensis Academiae Bibliothecarium

This poem addressed to John Rouse or Rous, keeper of the Bodleian Library, was dated 23 January 1646 (i.e. 1647) by its author and was of course first printed in the second edition (1673) of his *Poems*. When the first edition of the *Poems* appeared, in the first days of 1646 or the last of 1645, Milton sent a copy of it to Rouse, along with a collection of the eleven prose pamphlets he had so far published, for deposit in the Bodleian. During the parcel's journey from London to Oxford—which had for some years been the royalist headquarters—the volume of poems was either lost or stolen, and Rouse asked for another copy; Milton complied, enclosing the manuscript of the poem (not apparently in his own hand). Both the book and the manuscript are still in the Bodleian. Rouse, a graduate of Oxford, was librarian from 1620 until he died in 1652. Whether or not Milton was personally acquainted with him, he may, thought Masson, have known of his parliamentary sympathies.[1]

The poem has hardly received its due, even as a personal document, although—like the earlier Sonnet 8, 'Captain or Colonel'—it reveals something of the state of mind of the citizen-artist in wartime. Tillyard (*Milton*, 169–72) helps to right the balance:

Can it be that this ode is not an isolated poem written for an occasion but an experiment in the style of what Milton in *Reason of Church Government* calls the 'magnific odes and hymns, wherein Pindarus and Callimachus are in most things worthy'? Not that the style is predominantly Pindaric: the ode is a

---

[1] Masson, *Life* 1 (1881), 624–6, 3 (1873), 646–50; *P.W.* 1, 329–33; and authorities cited by MacKellar, 63–6. Masson thought it 'almost certain' that Rouse was 'our common Friend Mr. R.' mentioned in Sir Henry Wotton's letter to Milton, the letter that is prefixed to *Comus*; but see Parker, 816–17, n. 96. Sir Edmund Craster had an account of Rouse as librarian in the *Bodleian Library Record* 5 (1955), 130–46. Carey questions Rouse's alleged parliamentary sympathies but, as Craster says (141), his subscription to Charles's funds does not prove him a royalist, since he could not avoid it.

mixture of stateliness and of half-humorous and urbane elegance. About this elegance there is something very pleasing, as there is not always about the elegance of men whose lives, unlike Milton's, have been sheltered and easy. Milton had by his entry into action earned the right to indulge in redundant graces. But though the tone of the poem may not be entirely Pindaric, the metrical scheme has no Latin original and seems to be modelled principally on Pindar. I venture no metrical comparison, but I may record a personal impression that Milton is complete master of his new medium, that he accommodates sound to sense with the greatest skill, and that if read with due quantitative emphasis the ode reveals itself as one of the greater Latin poems, less serious than *Mansus* and the *Epitaphium Damonis*, but in completeness of achievement worthy to rank with them.

...Altogether the poem gives a charming picture of the more amiable Milton, of whom we see but too little during the years of the Commonwealth.

The strophic pattern is highly formal for a partly playful epistolary poem, and both the pattern and the metrics were roughly handled by such a Sixth Form critic as Landor.[2] As Milton's note suggests, he was making an experiment in Latin with a Greek and particularly Pindaric structure, and Rand (*SP* 19, 1922, 115) defended his imitation of the mixed formalism and freedom of a Greek chorus. In his strophes and antistrophes, changing metres, and occasional free verse, Milton was concerned, not with pedantic correctness, but with what he himself called ease and propriety in the reading. His note shows his awareness of the licenses he had taken, licenses which were controlled partly by conventional rule and partly by his ear. He might have had in mind, among other things, the choruses in Grotius' *Adamus Exul*, from which illustrative phrases have often been quoted in the course of this commentary. The metrics of the ode to Rouse have been touched on by scholars concerned with the versification of *Samson Agonistes*, e.g. S. E. Sprott, *Milton's Art of Prosody* (Oxford, 1953), 131; F. T. Prince, *The Italian Element in Milton's Verse* (Oxford, 1954), 148 n.; E. Weismiller, 'The "Dry" and "Rugged" Verse,' *The Lyric and Dramatic Milton*, ed. J. H. Summers (New York, 1965), 128.

---

[2] 'Southey and Landor,' *Works* 5, 331. See also Charles Symmons, *Life of Milton* (1810), 276–85. Both are quoted by MacKellar, 65–6. MacKellar (358–60) discusses Milton's note on the metrics.

The whole poem is an 'envoy' to its volume, and as such may trace its line of descent at least as far back as the *Tristia* of Ovid, which begins with a similar address. Ovid again uses the envoy in the *Epistulae ex Ponto* (4. 5), and Martial has several examples of it [e.g. 1. 70; 2. 1; 3. 2, 4, 5; 4. 86, 89; 7. 97]. In the *Silvae* (4. 4) of Statius it occurs once (MacKellar, 66).

Martz ('The Rising Poet,' 4–5) calls the ode 'a mock-heroic poem of remarkably high spirits,' written with a 'learned wit that makes translation almost impossible.' Quoting the first strophe, he says:

Here is the picture of a youthful poet, free from adult cares, sometimes wandering alone, amusing himself, sometimes making music for his friends or acquaintances, sometimes writing in his native vein, sometimes evoking a strain from idealized antiquity—but with a light and dancing posture that we do not usually associate with John Milton: *et humum vix tetigit pede*. It is clear, from many indications, that Milton has designed his book with great care to create this impression.

The entire volume strives to create a tribute to a youthful era now past—not only the poet's own youth, but a state of mind, a point of view, ways of writing, ways of living, an old culture and outlook now shattered by the pressures of maturity and by the actions of political man. Even the frontispiece, by William Marshall, attempts to set this theme. The aim of the engraving is clearly to present the youthful poet surrounded by the Muses, with a curtain in the background lifted to reveal a pastoral landscape of meadow and trees, where a shepherd is piping in the shade, while a shepherd and a shepherdess are dancing on the lawn. The legend around the portrait identifies it as a picture of the poet in his twenty-first year—but in fact the portrait presents the harsh and crabbed image of a man who might be forty or fifty! Marshall could do better than this, as his engraving of the youthful Donne testifies; one almost suspects deliberate sabotage here.

[For Milton's revenge see above, the headnote to the Greek quatrain inscribed under the portrait.]

J. T. Shawcross ('The Prosody of Milton's Translation of Horace's Fifth Ode,' *Tennessee Studies In Literature* 13, 1968, 81–9) scans and comments upon lines 1–6: 'The ode is a dactylic lyric. Similar to Horace, II, 14, 3–4, is line 1: alcaic enneasyllable (iamb+penthemimer) +dactyl; and line 2: hemiepes (3 dactyls ᴧᴧ). Line 3 consists of

1 hemiepes+2 dactyls; line 4, of 2 dactyls. Line 5 may be a third pæon+1 trochee, or 3 trochees (with the first quantity defective). Line 6 is 1 dactyl+a hipponactean. The complexity one finds in the ode is worthy of Milton's study of Horace and Catullus.'

NOTES

1–2 *Gemelle...liber, | Fronde licet gemina.* Milton's volume of 1645 'was a double book, or two volumes bound in one, first the English poems, then the Latin, with separate pagination and title-pages' (MacKellar). As MacKellar observes, Martial (3. 2. 8), Ovid (*Tr.* 1. 1. 8, 11), and Tibullus (3. 1. 13) use *frons* and *geminae frontes* (*frontes* being 'the edges of the papyrus-roll at each end'), and Milton, probably recollecting such allusions, shifted to *fronde* ('leaf') in a sort of punning metaphor suited to the form of a modern book. The word perhaps takes in both the title-pages and two divisions of the book and 'the double crown deserved by the collections of poems in the two languages' (Hughes). Of course there were, besides, the few poems in Italian and Greek.

3 *Munditieque nitens non operosa.* Cf. Horace, *C.* 1. 5. 5, *simplex munditiis* ('Plain in thy neatness,' in Milton's translation of that poem); and ibid. 4. 2. 31–2, *operosa parvus | carmina fingo.*

4–6 Such a perfectionist as Milton must have been at least partly sincere in deprecating his more youthful efforts, and doubtless what faults he now discerned seemed larger than they were, but his phrases hardly fit the greater English poems; cf. the conclusion. Editors in general from Warton to Hughes have accepted line 6 as printed in 1673: *Sedula tamen haud nimii Poetae.* Garrod emends two words to read *Seduli tamen haud nimis Poetae,* saying that thus '*we get a perfectly good Phalaecian for a verse which yields no kind of metre. Moreover,* Sedula *contradicts* non operosa *in line 3.*' But Milton was not observing strict regularity of metre in this poem; the emendations do not improve the sense; and there is no good reason for going against both text and manuscript (Fletcher, Facsimile ed. 1, 1943, 459).

7–8 *Ausonias...per umbras | Britannica per vireta.* For *Ausonias* see *El.* 1. 70 n. Some of the poems were written in Italy, some (the majority) in England (MacKellar).

9 *Insons populi.* Apart from the invective against the clergy in *Lycidas,* Milton's volume could hardly be called 'public poetry.' His active concern with public affairs had shown itself in his prolusions and pamphlets.

9–10 *barbitoque devius | Indulsit patrio, mox itidem pectine Daunio*, etc. A repetition, in reverse order, of the idea of lines 7–8, but now with reference to the language used; Milton is distinguishing his English poems from those in Latin (and Italian and Greek). He may be recalling Horace, *C.* I. 32. 3–4, *dic Latinum, | barbite, carmen.* Daunia, properly a part of Apulia, was used (e.g. Ovid, *R. Am.* 797; Sil. Ital. *passim*) as another name for Italy. Masson (*P.W.* 3, 366) suggested that Milton used the adjective in a deprecatory way, remembering Horace's reference (*C.* 3. 30. 10–12; and cf. ibid. 4. 6. 27, Ovid, *M.* 14. 510–11) to Daunia as a rather barbaric and sterile part of Italy. This is possible but perhaps over-subtle.

11 *Longinquum...melos.* The phrase for 'a song brought from far-off lands' may have been suggested by Horace's *longum...melos* (*C.* 3. 4. 2). The phrase, along with *Vicinis*, may possibly contain a special reference to the Italian poems; cf. the *Canzone*.

12 *humum vix tetigit pede.* MacKellar cites Keightley's remark that this is not quite in harmony with line 6 (quoted under 4–6 above). B.A.W. comments: 'I take Milton's meaning to be that he was rapt in the ecstasy of song—that he hadn't his feet on the ground, as we say; hence Keightley's remark.' Cf. Catullus 63. 2, *nemus...pede tetigit*; E. Puteanus, *Comus* (Louvain, 1608), p. 24: *Vix pedibus udam terram tetigeram.*

15 *missus ab urbe.* In *El* 4. 12.

16 *jugiter.* This postclassical and relatively uncommon word is used, e.g. by Ausonius, *Parentalia* 19. 4, *Commem. Profess. Burdig.* 15. 14; Prudentius, *Cath.* 4. 54; Poliziano, *In Anum* (Gruter, *Del. I.P.* 2, 364); Buchanan, *Ps.* 19. 12, 37. 4; *Cam. Insig.* (1624), sig. B3ʳ.

17–19 *Illustre tendebas iter | Thamesis ad incunabula | Caerulei patris.* 'Milton refers to Oxford as the birthplace of the Thames because it lies on the river Isis, not far above that river's confluence with the Thames, where the Thames proper begins' (Hughes). Cf. Ovid, *M.* 2. 547, *tendebat iter*; 8. 99, *Iovis incunabula, Creten*; 1. 275, *caeruleus frater*; Statius, *Th.* 6. 309, *caeruleum... patrem*; Secundus, *El.* 2. 7. 12, *Caeruleis Nymphis, caeruleoque Patri.*

20–1 *Fontes ubi limpidi | Aonidum, thyasusque sacer.* The Bacchic throngs are here the devotees of learning at Oxford; cf. Val. Flacc. 3. 540, *thiasos et sacra moventem.* For the Aonian Muses and their fountain Aganippe, see the note on *El* 4. 29; cf. Juvenal 7. 59, *fontibus Aonidum.*

22 *Orbi notus per immensos.* Garrod would change *per* to *super*, to get an anapaestic dimeter.

24 *in aevum.* See the note on *EpDam* 173–4.

25–36 Whatever Milton's intense conviction of the righteousness of the Puritan and parliamentary cause, the nature of this occasion turns his reflections into a channel less partisan than that of his prose and more typical of his cultural and moral interests. The idea of war or conquest as a punishment for slackness and sin is recurrent in his writings, e.g. *HistBr* (*Works* 10, 103–4, 319 f., etc.), *PL* 1. 432–7, 11. 791–807, 12. 90–101, *PR* 4. 131–45, *SA* 268–76. On this strophe J. H. Finley comments: 'For Horace's similar appeal to an unnamed god or hero, cf. *Od.* 1, 2, 25–52. For his expressions of national guilt, cf. *Epod.* 7, 17–20; *Od.* 1, 2, 47; 1, 35, 33–40; 2, 1, 25–36. For the blessings of peace, cf. *Od.* 4, 15, 9–20, especially the last four lines.' ('Milton and Horace,' *Harvard Studies in Classical Philology*, 48, 1937, 54 n.)

28 *Mollique luxu degener otium.* Cf. Sil. Ital. 12. 18, *molli luxu*; Claudian 26. 160 (2, 138), *luxu mollior aetas*; Manilius 2. 146, *mollemque per otia luxum*; Pontano, *Uran.* 3. 640–1, *molli sed degener umbra* | *...luxu languens*; Grotius, *Ad Gernandum* (*Farr.*, bk. 2, p. 196), *otiumve degener*; Milton, *HistBr* (*Works* 10, 1); 'fatally decaying, and degenerating into Sloth and Ignorance.'

30–2 From October 1642 until it surrendered to Fairfax in June 1646, Oxford was the royalist headquarters, and the normal activities of the university were largely suspended. (Sir Charles Mallet, *History of the University of Oxford*, 2, London, 1924, 349–69).

33–6 Phineus, a king and prophet, punished by Zeus with loss of sight and visitations of the Harpies, monstrous bird-women who devoured and defiled his food, was delivered from this torment by two of the Argonauts (Apollon. Rhod. 2. 178–310; Virgil, *A.* 3. 211–62; Val. Flacc. 4. 425 f.). With Milton's *Immundasque volucres* cf. Mantuan, *E.* 4. 236, *immundae Phinei volucres*, and Virgil, 227–8, *contactuque...* | *...immundo*; 216, *virginei volucrum voltus*. For Milton's *pestem* cf. Virgil, 215 and Val. Flacc. 481–2. Milton is thinking of the general disorder of war and of the royalist enemy and also, no doubt, of such Presbyterians as he impaled in sonnets of this period. The arrow of Apollo brings in another myth, the god's slaying of the Python; see the note on *El* 7. 31–4, with the reference to Milton's use of the myth in *RCG*, where the Python is prelacy. The stream of Pegasus is here the Thames, i.e. Oxford as a home of culture; see the notes on *El* 5. 10 and on 46 below. Cf. *PL* 7. 18 and note.

38 *oscitantia.* This uncommon postclassical noun ('drowsy negligence') appears, e.g. in Selden, *De Dis Syris* (ed. Leyden, 1629, p. 7), *tantae monimentum oscitantiae*. Cf. 'John Selden on the *Workes*, 1616' (*Ben Jonson*, ed. Herford and

Simpson, 11, 327), line 9, *Qui pigre trahat oscitationem*; Milton, *DDD* (*Works* 3, 440): God's justice cannot be, 'if I may so say, oscitant and supine.'

39   *Semel erraveris agmine fratrum.* '*Both grammar and metre seem to demand* erraveris ex (*another anapaestic dimeter*)' (Garrod); but Milton's metrical demands, as we have seen, are not over-rigorous. As for grammar and the idea of 'wander from' without a preposition, he had at least such partial precedents as Terence, *Eun.* 245, *tota erras via*; Virgil, *A.* 2. 739, *erravitne via*; and Sil. Ital. 13. 561, *portis omnibus errat.*

42   *institoris insulsi.* Any 'tasteless huckster' who might make use of the paper in the book. See the note on *Salmas.* 2. 1–4.

45   *Lethen,* See the note on *QNov* 132.

46   *remige penna.* See the note on *QNov* 208, and Lucretius 6. 743, *remigi... pennarum.* In his letter to Diodati of 23 September (November?) 1637, speaking of his desire for fame, Milton said: *sed tenellis admodum adhuc pennis evehit se noster Pegasus* (*Works* 12, 26, line 22; *C.P.W.* 1, 325, 328).

50–1   *cujus inclyta | Sunt data virum monumenta curae.* Cf. the famous phrases about good books in the opening pages of *Areop.* Garrod suggests *vatum* for *virum*: 'Milton seems to have intended a choriambic trimeter; and it is difficult to believe that he thought the first syllable of *virum* long.' As usual, emendation is injudicious. Milton may have been echoing Virgil, *A.* 8. 312, *virum monumenta priorum.*

54   *Aeternorum operum custos fidelis.* Cf. Virgil, *G.* 4. 215, *operum custos*; and *fidissim(a)(e) custos* in Ovid, *M.* 1. 562, Statius, *Th.* 1. 530, and Claudian 10. 333 (1, 266).

55–60   'Milton thought of the atmosphere of charmed magnificence thrown around Apollo's Delphian temple in the first act of Euripides' *Ion*' (Hughes). The hero, son of Apollo and Creusa, was brought up at his father's shrine and made guardian of its treasures; for these see especially *Ion* 184 f., 1146 f. Creusa was the daughter of Erechtheus, king of Athens. *Actaea* means Attic, from Acte, an early name for Attica (cf. Ovid, *M.* 2. 720, 6. 711). With Milton's *Opulenta...templa,* cf. Virgil, *A.* 1. 446–7, *templum... | ...donis opulentum.* With *Fulvosque tripodas, donaque Delphica* cf. Vida, *Christ.* 1. 391, *tripodas, fulvoque ex aere lebetas.*

61–2   *lucos | Musarum.* See the note on *Idea* 1.

65   *Delo posthabita.* Editors cite Virgil, *A.* 1. 16, *posthabita...Samo.* For Delos see the note on *El* 5. 13–14.

66 *Bifidoque Parnassi jugo.* For common allusions to the twin-peaked Parnassus see the note on *El* 4. 30, and cf. Lucan 3. 173, *Parnasosque iugo...utroque*; Gill, *Epith.* (p. 41), *bicipitis juga Parnassi.*

69 *dextri prece sollicitatus amici.* Cf. Ovid, *M.* 9. 683, *sollicitat precibus* (Fletcher).

70 *alta nomina.* In Juvenal 8. 131–2 (Fletcher).

72 *Antiqua gentis lumina, & verum decus.* Cf. Sil. Ital. 6. 130–1, *lumen | gentis*; Cicero, *Cat.* 3. 10. 24, *lumina civitatis*; Cicero, *Letters to his Friends*, 10. 12. 5, and Sil. Ital. 7. 388, *verum decus.*

73–4 It is a question if Milton is referring to his poems, or the tracts that had gone to the Bodleian also, or both. In any case, as the rest of this section suggests, he is thinking of the sterile mind of the general public rather than his own; his idealistic ardor has already met disillusionments.

76 *Perfunctam invidia requiem, sedesque beatas.* The last is a stock phrase, e.g. Virgil, *A.* 6. 639, Sil. Ital. 4. 46, *C.P.I.* 3, 211, 518, and *passim*; *Lacrymae Cantab.* (1619), p. 1.

77 *bonus Hermes.* Milton is thinking, not of Hermes Trismegistus (see the note on *Idea* 33), but of the ordinary Hermes of classical myth, the god of eloquence and the lyre and wisdom and marshal of the shades (see the note on *Idea* 27–8).

78 *tutela...solers Roüsi.* Cf. Virgil, *G.* 4. 327, *custodia sollers* (Fletcher.)

79 *lingua procax.* In Tacitus, *Ann.* 1. 16, Sil. Ital. 8. 248, and Buchanan, *F.F.* 35. 108. With Milton's assurance, in 79–80, of fame among the fit and few, editors compare *Patrem* 101–4, *PL* 7. 30–1, and Horace, *C.* 3. 1. 1.

82–5 See the note on 73–4 above. The words *cordatior* (82) and *invidia* (76) echo the Latin preface to the Latin poems in the 1645 volume, where Milton deprecated resentment of excessive praises in the commendations from Italian friends.

85–7 *Tum livore sepulto*, etc. Cf. Ovid, *Am.* 1. 15. 39–40: *pascitur in vivis Livor; post fata quiescit, | cum suus ex merito quemque tuetur honos.* It is interesting that Milton's last formal piece of Latin verse should end with an apparent echo of the poet of his youthful idolatry.

[*Carmina Elegiaca* and *Asclepiads*]

✠

When A. J. Horwood discovered Milton's Commonplace Book in 1874, he found along with it a damaged sheet of paper containing a short Latin essay on early rising and two pieces of Latin verse, related to that theme, of 20 and 8 lines respectively. Horwood printed the several small items along with the Commonplace Book (Camden Society, 1876). It is now agreed that they are in Milton's own hand and that they were written during his last year or two at St Paul's School, when he was fifteen or sixteen. Thus they are his earliest surviving compositions in Latin. The verses were not included in either edition of his poems; presumably he had no thought of preserving them. Examples of the stock diction in the longer poem are given above in the general Introduction (see note 8).[1]

NOTES

1 *Surge, age surge, leves, iam convenit, excute somnos.* For *Surge, age* see the note on *QNov* 97. *Leves somnos,* in various cases, is a stock phrase, e.g. Virgil, *A.* 5. 838, Horace, *C.* 2. 16. 15, *Epod.* 2. 28, Seneca, *Hipp.* 511–12. *Excutere somnos,* in various forms, is also common, e.g. Virgil, *A.* 2. 302, Ovid, *H.* 10. 13, 13. 111, *F.* 1. 547, 4. 555, *Ibis* 156, Senecan *Oct.* 123, Buchanan, *El.* 1. 35, etc. Cf. the excerpt from Milton's *Prol* 1 under 3–4 below.

[1] Texts of the two pieces of verse are in MacKellar, texts and some textual notes in Garrod; texts and translations in *Works* 1, 326–8, and, with some annotation, in Hughes et al.

The little prose essay, headed *Mane citus lectum fuge,* suggests the background of the verses. The text and a translation are in *Works* 12, 288–91; a translation, with introduction and notes, in *C.P.W.* 1, 1034–9. Lily's *Grammar* (ed. 1945, sig. Cv) has: 'Diluculo surgere, saluberrimum est, To arise betime in the morning, is the most holsome thing in the worlde'; and the third line of *Carmen de Moribus* (sig. Dv in the same book) is *Mane citus lectum fuge, mollem discute somnum.* Le Comte (*Yet Once More,* 22) notes that Milton's own Latin Grammar contains the saw *Diluculo surgere saluberrimum est* (*Works* 6, 330). Clark (*J.M. at St. Paul's,* 234–7) shows how the early essay follows the formula of Aphthonius' *progymnasmata,* and quotes a textbook exercise on the theme, 'A counsellor should not sleep all night,' on which Milton's prose might have been modeled.

2 *Lux oritur.* With various adjectives, in Horace, *S.* 1. 5. 39, Ovid, *F.* 1. 71, Claudian 5. 313 (1, 80), *Cantab. Dolor* (1625), p. 48.

3 *tepidi...tori.* Cf. Petronius, *Sat.* 132 (p. 296) and Pontano, *A.C.* 3. 4. 36, *in tepido...toro.*

3–4 *Iam canit excubitor gallus praenuncius ales | Solis et invigilans ad sua quemque vocat.* Cf. Virgil, *Mor.* 2: *excubitorque diem cantu praedixerat ales*; Ovid, *F.* 2. 767, *lucis praenuntius ales*; Prudentius, *Cath.* 1. 1, *Ales diei nuntius*; 1. 51, *gallus canat*; 1. 67, *gallus...canit*; Milton, *Prol* 1 (*Works* 12, 136, lines 15–16): *adventantem Solem triumphat insomnis Gallus, & quasi praeco quivis, monere videtur Homines, ut excusso somno prodeant...*

5 *Flammiger Eois Titan caput exerit undis.* Titan is a common name for the sun, e.g. Ovid, *M.* 1. 10, 2. 118, etc.; Seneca, tragedies *passim*; and Shakespeare and Spenser. For Milton's phrasing cf. Lucan, 1. 415, *Flammiger...Titan*; 5. 598, *ab oceano caput exeris Atlanteo*; Ovid, *M.* 13. 838, *caeruleo nitidum caput exere ponto*; *P.* 2. 5. 50, *ab Eois Lucifer ortus aquis*; Seneca, *Agam.* 554, *exerens undis caput*; Buchanan, *Sph.* 1. 101, *Exserit...caput*; 1. 613, *Eois...caput exserit undis.*

6 *spargit nitidum laeta per arva iubar.* *Nitidum iubar* is a stock phrase, e.g. Ovid, *F.* 2. 149, *M.* 15. 187, Seneca, *Med.* 100, *Agam.* 463, Val. Flacc. 3. 429, Pontano, *L.D.* 4. 33. Cf. Ovid, *F.* 1. 78, *tremulum...spargit...iubar*; Buchanan, *El.* 2. 50 (*Majae Cal.*) and Gruter, *Del. I.P.* 2, 932, 1456, *laeta per arva*; and *laeta arva* in Virgil, *A.* 6. 744, Sannazaro, *P.V.* 3. 306.

7 *Daulias argutum modulatur ab ilice carmen.* The Daulian bird is the nightingale, from the story of Philomela (Ovid, *M.* 6. 668–74). For the epithet, cf. Catullus 65. 14; Ovid, *H.* 15. 154, *Consol.* 106; Seneca, *Herc. Oet.* 192; Ralegh, *History* 1. 2. 13. 3: 'whence also *Philomela* is called *Daulias ales*.' Cf. Virgil, *A.* 1. 1*a*–1*b*, *modulatus avena | carmen*; Ovid, *M.* 11. 154, *modulatur harundine carmen*; Pontano, *Uran.* 3. 520, *arguta carmen modulentur avena.*

8 *Edit et excultos mitis alauda modos.* Cf. Ovid, *F.* 1. 444, *facili dulces editis ore modos.*

9 *Iam rosa fragrantes spirat siluestris odores.* Cf. Virgil, *A.* 1. 403–4, *comae divinum vertice odorem | spiravere*; Milton, *Prol* 1 (*Works* 12, 136, lines 22–4): *Caltha quoque & Rosa...aperientes sinum, Odores suos Soli tantum servatos profuse spirant.*

10 *Iam redolent violae luxuriatque seges.* Cf. Ovid, *H.* 1. 53–4: *iam seges est... | luxuriat...humus*; *A.A.* 1. 360, *seges...luxuriabit.*

11 *Ecce novo campos zephyritis gramine vestit | Fertilis. Vescit* (MacKellar, 361) was Horwood's misreading of the MS. *vestit* (*Works* 1, 597). Cf. Ovid, *F*.1.402, *gramine vestitis...toris*. Zephyritis is not one of the familiar figures of myth and has been taken as a daughter of Zephyr invented by Milton (translation in *Works* 1, 327; Hughes; Woodhouse, 12 n. below); Garrod's solution, of course, was emendation—*Zephyri vis*; since this note was written, Zephyritis has been correctly identified by Shawcross (*C.E.P.*) as Chloris, the wife of Zephyr. Scaliger in his edition of Catullus (1582, p. 71; 1600, p. 88) says that Chloris and Zephyritis are synonymous. The same thing is said several times in the *Epitome* (1595) of Ravisius Textor's *Epitheta* (cited in the general Introduction, note 8), e.g. 84: *Chloris, Zephyritis, candida, verna. Chloris dicitur dea florum, uxor Zephyri venti amoenissimi*; ibid. 395, where Pontano is cited (cf. Pontano *H.H.* 2. 140, *Exsultansque novis plaudat Zephyritis alunnis*); and p. 434. In *Epith.* (1606), under Chloris, Ravisius Textor gives the sentence quoted above (*Chloris dicitur...*) and quotes, as from Claudian, *His tum mulcebat dominam Zephyritida dictis.* (I have not found this line in Claudian.) Thus Zephyritis—the adjective becoming a virtual noun—is the wife of Zephyr and identical with Chloris and Flora (see the notes on *El* 3. 44 and 4. 35). Carey identifies her with Venus. See S. K. Heninger, *Handbook of Renaissance Meteorology* (Durham, N.C., 1960), 125.

12 *vitreo rore madescit humus.* Cf. Ovid, *Am.* 1. 6. 55, *vitreoque madentia rore*; *F.* 1. 312, *caelesti rore madebit humus*; and *rore madesc(i)(a)t humus* in Pontano, *L.D.* 1. 44 and Gruter, *Del.I.P.* 2, 74. Woodhouse ('Notes,' 86, n. 30) cites lines 9–12 and *L'All* 19–23 and *Prol* 1 (*Works* 12, 136–8) and comments 'Here are the ideas and images—*roses, violets, dew* as the symbol of *freshness* and perhaps *fertility*, and *Zephyr as parent of a daughter*...which are adapted and recombined in the parentage of Mirth.' Although the 'daughter' is the wife of Zephyr (see the note on 11), the general comment holds good.

13 *Segnes invenias molli vix talia lecto.* Cf. Tibullus 1. 2. 19, *molli...lecto*; Propertius 2. 4. 11, *lectis mollibus*.

14 *Cum premat imbellis lumina fessa sopor.* Mainly a blending of stock phrases. Cf. Virgil, *G.* 4. 190, *A.* 4. 522; Ovid, *H.* 19. 56 and *C.P.I.* 1, 363 and 3, 40, *lumina fessa sopor*; Senecan *Oct.* 117, *fessa...lumina oppressit sopor*; Tibullus 1. 2. 2, *fessi lumina...sopor*; and *fessa lumina* in Val. Flacc. 4. 639–40 and Sannazaro, *El.* 2. 5. 38; Statius, *Th.* 3. 256, *imbelli...somno*.

15 *Illic languentes abrumpunt somnia somnos.* Cf. Ovid, *Am.* 2. 10. 19, *at mihi saevus amor somnos abrumpat inertes*; Lucan 7. 24, *Ne rumpite somnos*. Ravisius

Carmina Elegiaca

Textor, *Epith.* ('*Somnus*') quotes *languenti...somno* from Mantuan; I find *languentia lumina somno* in Mantuan. *Sylv.* 8. 1 (*Opera*, 1502, fol. 105ʳ).

16 *turbant animum tristia multa tuum.* Cf. Virgil, *A.* 1. 515, *res animos incognita turbat.*

17 *tabifici...semina morbi.* The last two words are in Ovid, *R. Am.* 81 (end). Ravisius Textor, *Epith.* ('*Morbus*'), quotes *tabificum...morbum* from Neo-Latin.

18 *Qui pote.* In Persius 1. 56.

Asclepiads

The metre is the lesser Asclepiad, not (as labeled in *Works* 1, 327), choriambic (Garrod).

1–2 *Ignavus... | Somnus qui populo multifido praeest.* Cf. Ovid, *M.* 11. 593, *ignavi...Somni.* Brodribb (*N&Q* 162, 1932, 188) cites Homer, *Il.* 2. 23–4 (quoted by Milton in *EProl. Works* 12, 288).

3 *Dauni veteris filius armiger.* 'Turnus, the leader of the Volscian, Rutilian and other native Italian tribes with which Aeneas had to contend for the possession of Italy' (Hughes). For Turnus as the son of Daunus, see Virgil, *A.* 10. 616,688, etc., and the note on *Rous* 10. Cf. Virgil, *A.* 9. 330, *armigerumque Remi.*

4 *Stratus purpureo p[rocu]buit st[rato].* So given in *Works* 1, 328. Garrod comments: '*The photograph shows no more than* Str. tus purp. .eo. But Horwood was able to read *procubuit.* For the missing last word I have printed, conjecturally, *thoro* (*toro*): the Columbia edition gives *strato*, reluctante metro...[Since this was written the Columbia Milton...withdraws *strato* and proposes, independently, *thoro.*]' See Brodribb, *N&Q* 162 (1932), 188; Mabbott, ibid. 263–4 and 163 (1932), 170; *Works* 18, 643; Hughes. Cf. Ovid, *H.* 8. 108, *procubuique toro*; Virgil, *A.* 9. 189–90, *somno vinoque soluti | procubuere*; Martial 12. 17. 8, *purpureoque toro*; Grotius, *Induciae Batav.* (*S.*, bk. 2, p. 80), *Auro strata torum.*

5–8 *Audax Eurialus, Nisus,* etc. 'The story of the raid upon the Rutilian and Volscian camp by Aeneas' followers, Nisus and Euryalus, is told in the *Aeneid*, IX, 176–449' (Hughes). Milton's *E Prol* (*Works* 12, 290), also on the subject of sleep, ends with an apparent reference to the story.

6 *nocte sub horrida.* Cf. Prudentius, *Cath.* 1. 27, *nox horrida.*

8 *Hinc caedes oritur clamor et absonus.* Cf. Val. Flacc. 1. 681, *oritur clamor*; Virgil, *A.* 2. 313 and 12. 756, *exoritur clamor*; ibid. 2. 411, *oriturque miserrima caedes*; *absonus clamor* in T. Cooper, *Thesaurus* and, in different cases, in Apuleius, *Met.* 1. 17, 3. 29.

Latin Poems Attributed to Milton

Along with an 'inscription in place of a portrait of Charles I' (*Works* 18, 351, and note, p. 586), five Latin poems have been attributed to Milton.

1. *De Moro.* The scurrilous two-line epigram on Alexander More, whom Milton at first insisted on regarding as the author of *Regii Sanguinis Clamor* (see above, under *Salmas* 2), 'first appeared in England in the *Mercurius Politicus* of Sept. 30, 1652, as from a Dutch correspondent' (Masson, *P.W.* 1, 273; *Life*, 4, 1877, 587 n.). It was reproduced, each time as the work of another (in the second case a Dutch author), in Milton's *Def* 2 and *Def pro Se* (*Works* 8, 36 and 9, 240; *C.P.W.* 4, 1966, 570, 802). Although Milton was a sort of censor of the *Mercurius* in 1651–2, no one (unless perhaps S. B. Liljegren or Robert Graves) would suppose that he wrote the distich himself and then passed it off on someone else; and only inert tradition has kept it in editions of his works. It is printed as Milton's by Garrod (287). 'It seems to have been concocted originally in Holland by some Dutch wit' and 'is all but certainly' not Milton's (Masson, *P.W.* 1, 273); cf. MacKellar, 362–3; French, *L.R.* 3, 253, 270, 292–3. The legend of Milton's authorship is dismissed by the latest editors of the two prose works, D. A. Roberts and K. Svendsen (*C.P.W.* 4, 570, n. 102, and 802, n. 259).

2. *Ad Christinam, Suecorum Reginam, Nomine Cromwelli.* This eight-line epigram to Christina of Sweden (*Works* 18, 356), supposedly written in 1654 to accompany the gift of Cromwell's portrait, is said by Mabbott and French (ibid. 18, 588) to have been 'published as Milton's by Toland, 1698, I, 38–9, although it had already appeared in the 1681 collection of Marvell's *Poems*.' What Toland said was much less positive: '...whether it was he [Marvell] or *Milton* (for both are nam'd for

it) that made the Verses sent with *Cromwel*'s Picture to the Queen of *Sweden*, I am uncertain: but whoever was the Author, they deserve a room in this place' (Darbishire, *Early Lives*, 175; French, *L.R.* 3, 305). Toland's text differs in several small particulars from that in Marvell's *Poems*, so that another version—that is, a slightly garbled one—must have been in circulation. Masson's arguments for Marvell's authorship (*P.W.* 1, 273–81; summarized by MacKellar, 363–4) might be thought conclusive. In brief, these are: that in Marvell's *Poems* the epigram is one of a related group of Latin pieces (one is addressed to a friend, Dr Ingelo, a chaplain of the English ambassador to Sweden, and contains a eulogy of Christina; the second is a distich, *In Effigiem Oliveri Cromwell*; and the third, the epigram in question, is called *In eandem Reginae Sueciae transmissam*); that in *Doctor Ingelo* Christina is *Sceptripotens* and that *Nulla suo nituit tam lucida Stella sub Axe*, while in the epigram she is *Bellipotens virgo* and *Arctoi lucida stella poli*; and that, 'as Milton was totally blind in 1654, lines about a portrait would hardly then be expected from him, even though he was Latin Secretary' (Masson, loc. cit, 280–1). Masson notes (277–8) that Milton asked Bradshaw to make Marvell his assistant in February 1653 and that, although the appointment was not made until 1657, the two men were more or less close during several years before that date (cf. Parker, 1022, n. 39). Margoliouth (*Poems and Letters of Andrew Marvell*, 1927 and 1952, 1, 249), who accepts the poem as unquestionably Marvell's, and French (*L.R.* 3, 305–6) have pointed out that the epigram is ascribed to Marvell in two manuscripts of his poems in the British Museum. Thus, apart from Toland's statement, there had been no reason to doubt Marvell's authorship; after that, editors were divided (they are listed pro and con in French, *L.R.*, loc. cit.). Mabbott and French (*Works* 18, 588) listed, without preference, the several possibilities: that the verses were written by Marvell or Milton or both together.

E. H. Visiak reopened the question in *N&Q* 176 (1939), 200–1. His chief argument was 'two striking parallels to the epigram' in the eulogy of Christina in Milton's *Def* 2 of 1654. One is between *septem regina Trionum* (epigram) and *habet nunc & septentrio reginam suam* (*Def* 2,

Works 8, 108); the other is between *Nec sunt hi vultus regibus usque truces* (epigram) and *nullum me verbum fecisse contra reges, sed contra regum labes ac pestes duntaxat tyrannos* (*Works* 8, 104). Visiak would accordingly 'hazard the conjecture that both ascriptions of authorship are valid, and that Milton and Marvell collaborated.' This view is apparently accepted by French (*L.R.*, loc. cit.). The idea is not impossible, though it would seem rather odd for Milton and Marvell to put their heads together over a small epigram. But the first of Visiak's parallels has no weight, because other poems to Christina naturally referred to her northern realm (e.g. *C.P.I.* 2, 199 and 7, 429), and one (ibid. 2, 200) has a similar phrase, *Teque genu posito septem gens tota Trionum*. Visiak's second pair of phrases are not good evidence either. Marvell might have seen Milton's eulogy in manuscript or in proof, but no such supposition is needed. If Milton had never written a word about Christina, it would be wholly natural, indeed almost inevitable, that a poem sent by the regicide Protector to a foreign queen should contain a declaration that he was not hostile to all monarchs.

So far, then, as available evidence goes, there is no serious argument against Marvell's authorship. The naming of Milton by some men, which Toland recorded, would have been a logical result of the well-known facts that Milton had been Latin Secretary and a poet in Latin as well as English, while Marvell's posthumously printed poems were much less known. Parker (1013) expresses entire disbelief in the notion of Milton's authorship or collaboration.

3. A Latin distich (with a translation) glorifying Prince Charles, printed in 1636 (*Works* 18, 357 and note, p. 588). The author was probably John Meredith; in any case the ascription to Milton is most implausible.

4 and 5. A 6-line epigram against Urban VIII, who was pope from 1623 to 1644, and an *Epitaphium* on Cardinal Mazarin (d. 1661), an invective of 69 lines (*Works* 18, 351–5), were first printed in Charles Gildon's *Miscellany Poems* (1692), 29–33. 'This book claims on the title page to contain poetry by Milton and the lines on Mazarin are expressly

attributed to him in the index as well as in the heading, while the make-up of the book indicates that the epigram on the Pope was ascribed to the same writer as well' (*Works* 18, 587). Mabbott and French (loc. cit.) record further testimony to the belief in Milton's authorship, and a text of the *Epitaphium*, with variants, in *Poems on Affairs of State* (1703), 1, ii, 58. They conclude: 'On the whole, students seem to accept the poem as Milton's—his fondness for humorous epitaphs is known: a man who had written so many polite letters to the old fox Mazarin might well have wished to relieve his feelings, by writing what he really thought to himself, and the Latin is the work of a master whoever he may be.' The piece was welcomed by Cowper as an addition to the Miltonic canon (Mabbott, *N&Q* 172, 1937, 188). Writing to Hayley on March 19, 1793, he said: 'Thanks for Mazarin's epitaph! it is full of witty paradox, and is written with a force and severity which sufficiently bespeak the author. I account it an inestimable curiosity, and shall be happy when time shall serve, with your aid, to make a good translation of it. But that will be a stubborn business.' (*Correspondence of William Cowper*, ed. T. Wright, 4 v. London, 1904, 4, 383).

Mabbott and French remark (*Works* 18, 588) 'that as Urban VIII died in 1644 Milton excluded the lesser poem from his 1645 volume; it is so slight a thing that he well might have done so.' However, he included epigrams equally slight. And, if he wrote the considerable piece on Mazarin, we might wonder why he did not include it in his *Poems* of 1673. Both pieces were printed as Milton's and anonymously, and in some editions of Thomas Brown's *Works* (a list of their appearances in print and in manuscript is given by French, *L.R.* 4, 361). While Mabbott and French 'regard both poems with only slight reservation, as Milton's work,' one may, without evidence, have strong doubts. Milton may, like a number of other Englishmen, have shared the sentiments expressed in both poems but, although he has no Latin verse with which they—or the longer piece—can be compared, they may not in manner seem to suggest him. Parker (1081–2) gives no opinion but appears to be sceptical.

Index

The nature of the material forbids anything like a complete bibliography or index and this one represents a very limited fusion of the two purposes. Classical authors are not ordinarily listed, since almost all are cited from the volumes of the Loeb Classical Library. Abbreviations for the titles of their writings are the more or less standard and obvious ones; a few ancient authors (Cicero, Horace, Ovid, Statius, Virgil) are included because they are cited so often and because some abbreviations may be unfamiliar. In the case of later authors, especially those drawn upon for parallels with Milton (e.g. Buchanan, Grotius, Sannazaro, Secundus), many individual pieces are cited in the notes: the index gives abbreviations for such titles, the divisions of books they belong to (elegies, epigrams, etc.), and descriptions of the editions used. Modern scholarly and critical writings that have been cited in the commentary are fully listed here, with a reference to the place where each was first mentioned; subsequent references are not listed. This mode of reference sometimes obviates the need of repeating long titles or bibliographical descriptions. For long titles, or titles often cited, abbreviations are given. The index includes a few items that were not cited in the commentary.

Arthos, John. *Milton and the Italian Cities.* London, 1968. (*Leon* 1, headnote, n. 1)

Ascham, Roger. *English Works*, ed. W. A. Wright. Cambridge, 1904.

Aubrey, John. See H. Darbishire, *Early Lives.*

Augustine. *Civ. D.* = *De Civitate Dei* (Migne, *Pat. Lat.* 41)
Conf. = *Confessions.* 2 v. L.C.L.

Ausonius (2 v. L.C.L.). *Ephem.* = *Ephemeris. Ep.* = *Liber XVIII Epistularum. Epig.* = *Epigrammata.*

Aylward, Kevin J. *Milton's Latin Versification: The Hexameter* (Columbia University, 1966): *Dissertation Abstracts* 27 (November 1966), 1331–1332A. (Introd. n. 13.)

Babb, Lawrence. *The Elizabethan Malady: A Study of Melancholia in English Literature from 1580 to 1642.* East Lansing, 1951. (*Eli* 27–8 n.)

Bacon, Francis. *Works*, ed. J. Spedding, R. L. Ellis, and D. D. Heath, 7 v. London, 1870–5.

Baldwin, Thomas W. *William Shakspere's Small Latine & Lesse Greeke.* 2 v. Urbana, 1944. (*Eli* 56–8 n.)

Bale, John. *Select Works* (*ProdBom* 2. 2 n.)

Barclay, John. *Poematum Libri Duo.* London, 1615.

Barker, Arthur E. 'Milton's Schoolmasters.' *MLR* 32 (1937), 517–36. (*El* 4, headnote, n. 1)
Milton and the Puritan Dilemma 1641–1660. Toronto, 1942. (*El* 4, headnote)

Barnett, H. A. 'A Time of the Year for Milton's "Ad Patrem."' *MLN* 73 (1958), 82–3. (*Patrem* 38–40 n.)

Bateson, Frederick W. *English Poetry: A Critical Introduction.* London, 1950. (*El* 6.89 n.)

Beaumont and Fletcher [four plays], ed. F. E. Schelling. New York, 1912.

Bede, *Historia Ecclesiastica* (*Opera*, Migne, *Pat. Lat.* 95)

Bennett, Josephine W. 'Britain Among the Fortunate Isles.' *SP* 53 (1956), 114–40. (*QNov* 26 n.)
The Evolution of "The Faerie Queene." Chicago, 1942. (*Mansus* 81 n.)

Beza, Theodore. *Poëmata varia.* Geneva, 1599.

Bible. *Testamenti Veteris Biblia Sacra...Latini recens ex Hebraeo facti...ab Immanuele Tremellio, & Francisco Junio...Novi Testamenti libros ex sermone Syro ab eodem Tremellio, & ex Graeco a Theodoro Beza.* Hanau, 1603.

ΒΙΟΓΡΑΦΟΙ: *Vitarum Scriptores Graeci Minores.* 1845. (*El* 6. 71 n.)

Birch, Thomas. See R. F. Williams.

Black, John. *Life of Torquato Tasso.* 2 v. London, 1810. (*EpDam* 181–2)

Index

Browne, William. *Brit. Past.* = *Britannia's Pastorals. Poems*, ed. G. Goodwin. 2 v. London, 1894.

Bryant, J. A. 'Milton's Views on Universal and Civil Decay.' (*Naturam*, headnote, n. 3)

Buchanan, George. *Opera Omnia*, ed. T. Ruddiman. 2 v. Leyden, 1725. V. 2, *Poemata.*

    Bapt. = *Baptistes. E.* = *Elegiarum Liber. Epig.* = *Epigrammatum Libri* 1–3. *Alc.* = *Euripidis Alcestis. Med.* = *Euripidis Medea. Franc.* = *Franciscanus. F.F.* = *Fratres Fraterrimi. Hen.* = *Hendecasyllabon Liber. Iamb.* = *Iambon Liber. Jeph.* = *Jephthes. Misc.* = *Miscellaneorum Liber. Ps.* = *Psalmorum Paraphrasis. Sph.* = *De Sphaera. S.* = *Silvae.*

Bullokar, William. *Aesop's Fables.* (*RH*, headnote)

Burman, Pieter, ed. *Sylloges Epistolarum a Viris Illustribus Scriptarum.* 5 v. Leyden, 1727. (*El* 5. 30 n.)

Burney, Charles. 'Appendix containing Remarks on the Greek Verses of Milton.' *Poems*, ed. Warton (q.v.), 593–605. (The Greek Poems.)

Burton, Robert. *The Anatomy of Melancholy*, ed. H. Jackson. Everyman's Library, 3 v. London, 1932.

Bury, John B. *The Idea of Progress.* London, 1920. (*Naturam*, headnote, n. 3)

Bush, Douglas. *Mythol.* = *Mythology and the Renaissance Tradition in English Poetry.* Rev. ed. New York, 1963. (*El* 1. 73 n.)

    'An Allusion in Milton's *Elegia tertia.*' *Harvard Library Bulletin* 9 (1955), 392–6. (*El* 3, headnote)

    'The Date of Milton's *Ad Patrem.*' *MP* 61 (1963–4), 204–8. (*Patrem*, headnote)

Butcher, Samuel. In Milton's *Poetical Works*, ed. Masson (q.v.), 3, 345–6. (The Greek Poems)

Calepine. *Ambrosii Calepini Dictionarium Undecim Linguarum.* Basel, 1616.

Calpurnius Siculus, *E.* = *Eclogues. Minor Latin Poets* (L.C.L.)

Calvin, John. *Opera Omnia.* 9 v. Amsterdam, 1667 (v. 1 dated 1671).

Cambridge Modern History 4. Cambridge, 1906. (*El* 4. 51 n.)

Camden, William. *Britain, Or A Chorographicall Description of...England, Scotland, and Ireland...Translated newly into English by Philemon Holland.* London, 1610.

Cam. Insig. = *Camdeni Insignia.* Oxford, 1624.

Campion, Thomas. *Works*, ed. P. Vivian. Oxford, 1909. *El.* = *Elegiarum liber unus. Epig.* = *Epigrammatum Libri II. Umbra.*

344

Index

Cantab. *Dolor* = *Cantabrigiensium Dolor & Solamen: Seu Decessio Beatissimi Regis Jacobi Pacifici: et Successio Augustissimi Regis Caroli.* Cambridge, 1625.

Carey, John. 'The Date of Milton's Italian Poems.' *RES* 14 (1963), 383–6. (*El* 6. 89 n.)

'Milton's *Ad Patrem*, 35–37.' *RES* 15 (1964), 180–4. (*Patrem* 35–7 n.)

Carmina Illustrium Poetarum Italorum. 11 v. Florence, 1719–26. (Cited as *C.P.I.*)

Carminum Proverbialium, Totius Humanae vitae statum breviter deliniantium. London, 1603.

Castiglione, B. *Opere Volgari, e Latine del Conte Baldessar Castiglione*, ed. G. Antonio and G. Volpi. Padua, 1733. *Alcon. Carmina.*

Catholic Dictionary, ed. W. E. Addis et al. (*QNov* 55 n.)

Catulli, Tibulli, Properti, Nova Editio, ed. J. Scaliger. Antwerp, 1582; Heidelberg, 1600.

Cavendish, George. *The Life and Death of Thomas Wolsey.* London, 1899, 1930; ed. R. S. Sylvester. E.E.T.S. 1959. (*El* 4. 64 n.)

Chamberlain, Letters of John, ed. N. E. McClure. 2 v. Philadelphia, 1939.

Chaney, Virginia M. *The Elegies of George Buchanan in Relation to those of the Roman Elegists and to the Latin Elegies of John Milton.* Unpublished dissertation, Vanderbilt University, 1961. (Introd. n. 12)

Chapman, George. *Poems*, ed. P. B. Bartlett. New York, 1941.

Chaucer, Geoffrey. *Works*, ed. F. N. Robinson. 2nd ed. Boston, 1957. *H.F.* = *The House of Fame. P.F.* = *The Parliament of Fowls. Tr.* = *Troilus and Criseyde.*

Cheek, Macon. 'Milton's "In quintum Novembris": An Epic Foreshadowing.' *SP* 54 (1957), 172–84. (*QNov*, headnote)

Chew, Samuel C. *The Virtues Reconciled: An Iconographic Study.* Toronto, 1947. (*QNov*, 146 n.)

Chifos, Eugenia. 'Milton's Letter to Gill, May 20, 1628.' *MLN* 62 (1947), 37–9. (*El* 3. 60 n.)

Cicero (L.C.L.). *Brut.* = *Brutus. Cat.* = *In Catilinam. Div.* = *De Divinatione. Fin.* = *De Finibus. Leg.* = *De Legibus. N.D.* = *De Natura Deorum. Rep.* = *De Re Publica. Tusc.* = *Tusculan Disputations. Verr.* = *Verrine Orations.*

Clark, Donald L. *John Milton at St. Paul's School: A Study of Ancient Rhetoric in English Renaissance Education.* New York, 1948. (Cited as *J.M. at St. Paul's*: Introd., p. 10.)

'Milton and William Chappell.' *HLQ* 18 (1954–5), 329–50. (*El* 1, headnote, n. 3)

Review of H. F. Fletcher, *Intell. Dev.* (q.v.). *JEGP* 56 (1957), 633–6. (*Ps 114*, headnote.)

Claudian. *S.P.* = *Shorter Poems* (L.C.L. v. 2).

Index

De Filippis, Michele. 'Milton and Manso: Cups or Books?' *PMLA* 51 (1936), 745–56. (*EpDam* 181–2 n.)

Demetz, Peter. 'The Elm and the Vine: Notes Toward the History of a Marriage Topos.' *PMLA* 73 (1958), 521–32. (*EpDam* 65 n.)

Diekhoff, John S., ed. *Milton on Himself: Milton's utterances upon himself and his works.* New York, 1939. (*El* 6. 55 f., n.)

Donne, John. *Poetical Works*, ed. H. J. C. Grierson. 2 v. Oxford, 1912.

Dorian, Donald C. *The English Diodatis.* New Brunswick, 1950. (Cited as *E.D.: El* 1, headnote, n. 1)

'Milton's *Epitaphium Damonis*, lines 181–97.' *PMLA* 54 (1939), 612–13. (*EpDam* 181–2 n.)

Drayton, Michael. *Works*, ed. J. W. Hebel, K. Tillotson, and B. H. Newdigate. 5 v. Oxford, 1931–41. (Cited as 'Drayton'.) *Poly.=Poly-Olbion.*

Drummond, William. *Poetical Works*, ed. L. E. Kastner. 2 v. Edinburgh, 1913.

DuCange, Charles, et al. *Glossarium Mediae et Infimae Latinitatis.* 10 v. Paris, 1937–8. (*El* 7. 90.)

Epig. Gr.=Epigrammata Graeca, selecta ex Anthologia, ed. H. Stephanus et al. Paris, 1570.

Epith. Oxon.=Epithalamia Oxoniensia. In Auspicatissimum, Potentissimi Monarchae Caroli...cum Henretta Maria...Connubium. Oxford, 1625.

Epith. Caroli et H. Mariae=Epithalamium Illustriss. & Feliciss. Principum Caroli Regis, et H. Mariae Reginae...A Musis Cantabrigiensibus decantatum. Cambridge, 1625.

Erasmus. *Opera Omnia*, ed. J. Clericus. 10 v. Leyden, 1703–6.

Eusebius, *Praeparatio Evangelica* (Migne, *Pat. Gr.* 21); *Preparation for the Gospel*, tr. E. H. Gifford, 2 v. Oxford, 1903.

Fairfax, Edward. See Tasso.

Ferguson, A. S. '"Paradise Lost," IV, 977–1015.' *MLR* 15 (1920), 168–70. (*Naturam* 34–5 n.)

Festugière, A.-J. See Hermes Trismegistus.

Fink, Z. S. 'Wine, Poetry, and Milton's *Elegia Sexta*.' *English Studies* 21 (1939), 164–5. (*El.* 6, headnote, n. 1.)

'Milton and the Theory of Climatic Influence.' *MLQ* 2 (1941), 67–80. (*Mansus* 27–8 n.)

Finley, John H. 'Milton and Horace.' (*Rous* 25–36 n.)

Finney, Gretchen L. 'Chorus in *Samson Agonistes*.' *PMLA* 58 (1943), 649–64. (*Leon* 1, headnote, n. 1.)

Index

Giraldus Cambrensis. *Historical Works.* (*Mansus* 38–48 n.)

Godolphin, F. R. B. 'Notes on the Technique of Milton's Latin Elegies.' *MP* 37 (1939–40), 351–6. (Introd. n. 7.)

Golding, Arthur. See Ovid.

Goode, James. 'Milton and Sannazaro.' *TLS*, 13 August, 1931, 621. (*El* 1. 21–2 n.)

Goodman, Godfrey. *The Fall of Man.* London, 1616.

Gordon, George S. 'The Youth of Milton.' *The Lives of Authors.* (London, 1950), 44–86. (*El* 4. 31–2 n.)

Gottfried, Rudolf B. 'Milton, Lactantius, Claudian, and Tasso.' *SP* 30 (1933), 497–503. (*EpDam* 187–9 n.)

Grant, W. Leonard. *Neo-Latin Literature and the Pastoral.* Chapel Hill, 1965. (Introd. n. 2.)

Gratul. Cantab. = *Gratulatio Academiae Cantabrigiensis De Serenissimi Principis reditu ex Hispanijs exoptatissimo.* Cambridge, 1623.

Greenlaw, Edwin. *Studies in Spenser's Historical Allegory.* Baltimore, 1932. (*Mansus* 81 n.)

Gregory Nazianzen. *Opera* (Migne, *Pat. Gr.* 35–8.)

Grotius, Hugo. *Ad. Ex.* = *Adamus Exul.* The Hague, 1601 (cited from W. Kirkconnell, q.v.).

    Poemata Omnia. 4th ed. Leyden, 1645. *Christus Patiens. El.* = *Elegiarum Lib. Epig.* = *Epigrammatum Lib.* 1–2. *Farr.* = *Farraginis Lib.* 1–3. *S.* = *Silvarum Lib.* 1–3.

    Individual Poems: *Epith. J. Borelii* = *Epithalamium Joannis Borelii. Epith. Kinschot.* = *Epithalamion Casparis Kinschotii. Epith. C. v. Mylen* = *Epithalamium Cornelii vander Mylen. Epith. Guil.* = *Epithalamium Philippi Guilielmi. Inaug. Reg. Brit.* = *Inauguratio Regis Britanniarum. Induciae Batav.* = *Induciae Batavicae.*

Gruter, *Del. I.P.* = Gherus, Ranutius, *Delitiae CC. Italorum Poetarum, huius superiorisque aevi illustrium.* 2 v. Frankfort, 1608.

Guarini, Battista. *Il Pastor Fido* (Venice, 1605); *Opere,* ed. L. Fasso (Turin, 1950).

Hakewill, George. *An Apologie,* etc. Oxford, 1627. (*Naturam,* headnote.)

Haller, William. *Liberty and Reformation in the Puritan Revolution.* New York, 1955. (*El* 4, headnote.)

Hanford, James Holly. *A Milton Handbook.* 4th ed. New York, 1946. (*EpDam,* headnote, 11.)

    'The Pastoral Elegy and Milton's *Lycidas.*' *PMLA* 25 (1910), 403–47. (*EpDam,* headnote, n. 3.)

De Ave Phoenice. Minor Latin Poets (L.C.L.)
  Lactanti De Ave Phoenice, tr. and ed. Mary C. Fitzpatrick. Philadelphia, 1933.
Landor, Walter Savage. *Works*, ed. T. Earle Welby. 12 v. London, 1927–31.
  (Introd. n. 4.)
Langdon, Ida F. *Milton's Theory of Poetry and Fine Art*. New Haven, 1924.
  (*El* 6. 55 f., n.)
Le Comte, Edward S. *A Milton Dictionary*. New York, 1961. (*QNov*, headnote.)
  Yet Once More: Verbal and Psychological Pattern in Milton. New York, 1953.
  (*El* 1. 60 n.)
Leishman, J. B. '*L'Allegro* and *Il Penseroso* in Their Relation to Seventeenth-
  Century Poetry.' *Essays and Studies 1951* (London, 1951), 1–36. (*El*.
  6. 89 n.)
Leone Ebreo (Leo Hebraeus). (*El* 5. 103–4 n.)
Lewis, C. S. *The Discarded Image ; An Introduction to Medieval and Renaissance
  Literature*. Cambridge, 1964. (*Naturam*, headnote.)
  'From the Latin of Milton's *De Idea Platonica...Intellexit*.' *English* 5 (1945),
  195. (*Idea*, headnote.)
Lily, William. *A Shorte Introduction of Grammar*, ed. V. J. Flynn. New York,
  1945.
Linocre, Geoffrey. *Musarum Libellum* (pr. in N. Comes, *Mythol.*, q.v.).
Little, Marguerite. 'Milton's *Ad Patrem* and the Younger Gill's *In Natalem
  Mei Parentis*.' *JEGP* 49 (1950), 345–51. (*Patrem* 5 n.)
Lotspeich, Henry G. *Classical Mythology in the Poetry of Edmund Spenser*.
  Princeton, 1932. (*El* 4. 31–2 n.)
Lycophron. *La Alessandra di Licofrone*, ed. E. Ciaceri. Catania, 1901. (*El* 6.
  69 n.)
Mabbott, Thomas O. 'Milton's "In Effigiem Ejus Sculptorem."' *Explicator* 8
  (1950), item 58. (*EffSc*, headnote.)
  'The Miltonic Epitaph on Mazarin: Cowper's Opinion.' *N&Q* 172 (1937),
  188. ('Latin Poems Attributed to Milton' [5].)
MacCaffrey, Isabel G. '*Lycidas*: The Poet in a Landscape.' See J. H. Summers
  below. (*Naturam* 66 n.)
MacKellar, Walter. 'Milton, James I, and Purgatory.' *MLR* 18 (1923), 472–3.
  (*ProdBom* 3. 1 n.)
Maclean, Hugh. 'Milton's "Fair Infant."' *ELH* 24 (1957), 296–305. (*El* 3,
  headnote.)
MacLure, Millar. *The Paul's Cross Sermons, 1534–1642*. Toronto, 1958.
  (*QNov*, headnote, n. 3.)

Poems, &c. upon Several Occasions. By Mr. John Milton: Both English and Latin, &c. Composed at several times. London, 1673.

Complete Poetical Works, ed. D. Bush. Boston, 1965.

Poems of John Milton, ed. John Carey and Alastair Fowler (minor poems and *SA* edited by Carey). London, 1968.

C.P.W. = *Complete Prose Works* (see Wolfe below).

Complete Poetical Works Reproduced in Photographic Facsimile, ed. Harris F. Fletcher. 4 v. Urbana, 1943–8.

Milton's Poems 1645: Type-Facsimile [ed. H. W. Garrod]. Oxford, 1924. (Cited as *Ox. Fac.*)

Poemata, ed. H. W. Garrod. In v. 2 of *Poetical Works,* ed. H. Darbishire. 2 v. Oxford, 1952–5.

The Poems of John Milton English Latin Greek & Italian Arranged in Chronological Order with a Preface by H. J. C. Grierson. 2 v. London, 1925.

Poems of John Milton, ed. J. H. Hanford. 2nd ed. New York, 1953.

Milton's Sonnets, ed. E. A. J. Honigmann. London and New York, 1966.

Paradise Regained, the Minor Poems, and Samson Agonistes, ed. Merritt Y. Hughes. New York, 1937. (Cited as 'Hughes').

Complete Poems and Major Prose, ed. M. Y. Hughes. New York, 1957.

The Lycidas and Epitaphium Damonis of Milton, ed. C. S. Jerram. 2nd ed. rev. London, 1881.

Poems, ed. Thomas Keightley. 2 v. London, 1859.

The Latin Poems of John Milton, ed. and tr. by Walter MacKellar. New Haven, 1930.

Poetical Works, ed. D. Masson. 3 v. London, 1890. (Cited as *P.W.*)

Complete Poetical Works, ed. W. V. Moody. Boston, 1899; with translations of the Latin poems rev. by E. K. Rand, 1924.

Milton's Lycidas: The Tradition and the Poem, ed. C. A. Patrides. New York, 1961.

The Works of John Milton, ed. F. A. Patterson et al. 20 v. New York, 1931–40 (cited as *Works*). Latin and Greek poems edited by W. P. Trent and T. O. Mabbott and translated by C. Knapp.

The Student's Milton, ed. F. A. Patterson. Rev. ed. New York, 1933. Latin and Greek poems translated by N. G. McCrea.

The Complete English Poetry of John Milton, ed. John T. Shawcross. New York, 1963. (Cited as *C.E.P.*)

John Milton's Epitaphium Damonis. Printed from the First Edition. With a

Phillips, James E., and Don C. Allen. *Neo-Latin Poetry of the Sixteenth and Seventeenth Centuries.* Los Angeles, 1965. (Introd. n. 2.)

Philpot, John. *Examinations and Writings.* (*QNov* 155–6 n.)

Pico della Mirandola. *A Platonick Discourse upon Love.* (*El* 5. 103–4 n.)

Poliziano, Angelo. *P.V. = Prose Volgari Inedite e Poesie Latine e Greche*, ed. I. del Lungo. Florence, 1867.

Pontano, G. G. *Ioannis Ioviani Pontani Carmina*, ed. B. Soldati. 2 v. Florence, 1902. *A.C. = De Amore Coniugali. E. = Eclogae. Erid. = Eridanus. Hen. = Hendecasyllabi. H.H. = De Hortis Hesperidum. Iamb. = Iambici. L. D. = De Laudibus Divinis. Lyra. Met. = Meteora. Parth. = Parthenopeus. Tum. = De Tumulis. Uran. = Urania.*

Praz, Mario. 'Milton and Poussin.' (*El* 5, headnote.)

Prince, F. T. *The Italian Element in Milton's Verse.* Oxford, 1954. (*Rous*, headnote.)

Prudentius (2 v. L.C.L.). *Apoth. = Apotheosis. Cath. = Liber Cathemerinon. C. Or. Symm. = Contra Orationem Symmachi 1–2. Perist. = Peristephanon Liber. Psych. = Psychomachia.*

Ptolemy. *Cl. Ptolemaei Alexandrini Geographiae Libri Octo*, ed. G. Mercator. Cologne, 1584.

Puteanus, Erycius. *Comus, sive Phagesiposia Cimmeria. Somnium.* Louvain, 1608.

Puttenham, George. *The Arte of English Poesie*, ed. G. D. Willcock and A. Walker. Cambridge, 1936. (*Patrem* 17–55 n.)

Raby, F. J. E. (Introd. n. 2.)

Ralegh, Sir Walter. *History of the World.* London, 1614.

Rand, Edward K. 'Milton in Rustication.' *SP* 19 (1922), 109–35. (Introd. n. 7.)

Randolph, Thomas. *Poetical and Dramatic Works*, ed. W. C. Hazlitt. 2 v. London, 1875.

Read, John. *Prelude to Chemistry.* New York, 1937. (*EpDam* 80 n.)

Reiss, Edmund. 'An Instance of Milton's Use of Time.' *MLN* 72 (1957), 410–12. (*Naturam* 14–15 n.)

Riley, Edgar H. 'Milton's Tribute to Virgil.' *SP* 26 (1929), 155–65. (*El* 7, epilogue.)

Root, Robert K. *Classical Mythology in Shakespeare*, New York, 1903. (*Eli* 56–8 n.)

Ruggle, George. *Ignoramus, Comoedia*, ed. J. S. Hawkins. London, 1787.

Saillens, E. *Milton*, New York, 1964. (*Patrem*, headnote, n. 1.)

Salmasius, Claudius.

 De Primatu Papae. Leyden, 1645.

Defensio Regia, pro Carolo I. 1649.
  Claudii Salmasii ad Johannem Miltonum Responsio. Opus Posthumum. London,
    1660.
Sandys, George. *Relation of a Journey begun An: Dom: 1610.* London, 1615.
Sannazaro, Jacopo. *Jacobi, sive Actii Synceri Sannazarii...Poemata,* ed. J. A.
    Vulpius. Padua, 1731. *E. = Eclogae. El. = Elegiarum Lib.* 1–3. *Epig. =*
    Epigrammaton Lib. 1–3. *P.V. = De Partu Virginis. S. = Salices.*
Jacopo Sannazaro: Arcadia & Piscatorial Eclogues, tr. Ralph Nash. Detroit,
    1966.
Saunders, J. W. 'Milton, Diomede and Amaryllis.' *ELH* 22 (1955), 254–86.
    (*El* 7. 112 n.)
Secundus, Joannes. *Opera Omnia,* ed. P. Burmann and P. Bosscha. 2 v. Leyden,
    1821. *Bas. = Basia. El. = Elegiarum Lib.* 1–3. *Epig. = Epigrammatum Lib.*
    1–2. *Epist. = Epistolarum Lib.* 1–2. *Fun. = Funerum Liber. Od. = Odarum*
    Liber. S. = Silvarum Liber.
Sedulius, Coelius. *Opera* (Migne, *Pat. Lat.* 19).
Selden, John. *De Dis Syris Syntagmata II.* Ed. Leyden, 1629.
  'Illustrations' to *Poly-Olbion, Works of Michael Drayton,* v. 4 (see Drayton
    above).
Semple, W. H. 'The Latin Poems of John Milton.' *Bulletin of The John Rylands*
    Library 46 (1963), 217–35. (Introd. n. 7.)
Servius. *In Vergilii Carmina Commentarii,* ed. G. Thilo and H. Hagen. 3 v.
    Leipzig, 1881–1902.
Shakespeare. *Complete Works,* ed. G. L. Kittredge. Boston, 1936.
Shawcross, John T. 'The Date of Milton's *Ad Patrem.*' *N&Q* 6 (1959), 358–9.
    (*Patrem,* headnote.)
  'The Date of the Separate Edition of Milton's "Epitaphium Damonis."'
    SB 18 (1965), 262–5. (*EpDam,* headnote, n. 1.)
  '*Epitaphium Damonis:* lines 9–13 and the Date of Composition.' *MLN* 71
    (1956), 322–4. (*EpDam* 9–13 n.)
  'Milton's Decision to Become a Poet.' *MLQ* 24 (1963), 21–30. (*Patrem,*
    headnote.)
  'Two Milton Notes: "Clio" and Sonnet 11.' *N&Q* 8 (1961), 178–9. (*El* 4.
    31–2 n.)
Sibyllina Oracula. Paris, 1599.
Sidney, Sir Philip. *Complete Works,* ed. A. Feuillerat. 4 v. Cambridge, 1912–26.
Sills, Kenneth C. M. 'Milton's Latin Poems.' *Classical Journal* 32 (1936–7),
    417–23. (Introd. n. 7.)

Index

Taylor, Jeremy. *Works*. (*EpDam* 215 n.)

Textor, Ravisius. *Epitome = Epithetorum Ioann. Ravisii Textoris Epitome*. London, 1595.

    Epithetorum...Opus Innovatum...Secundaque Cura Meliore et Pleniore Auctum. Basel, 1602.

    Epitheta. Toulouse, 1606.

Tillyard, E. M. W. *The Elizabethan World Picture*. London, 1943. (*Naturam*, headnote, n. 3.)

    Milton. New York, 1930. (Introd. n. 7.)

    M. Set.=The Miltonic Setting Past and Present. Cambridge, 1938. (*El* 6, headnote.)

Tuveson, E. L. *Millennium and Utopia: A Study in the Background of the Idea of Progress*. Berkeley, 1949. (*Naturam*, headnote, n. 3.)

Ussher, James. (*EpDam* 165 n.)

Van Tieghem, Paul. *La Littérature Latine de la Renaissance*. Paris, 1944. (Introd. n. 2.)

Maphaeus Vegius and his Thirteenth Book of the Aeneid, ed. A. C. Brinton. Stanford, 1930.

Vida, M. G. *Christ.=Marci Hieronymi Vidae...Christiados Libri Sex*, ed. E. Owen. Oxford, 1725.

    Poematum...Pars Prima...Pars Altera, ed. T. Tristram. 2 v. Oxford, 1722–3. *A.P.=De Arte Poetica. E.=Bucolica. Carmina*: individual titles.

Virgil. *A.=Aeneid. Cat.=Catalepton. Cir.=Ciris. Cul.=Culex. E.=Eclogues. G.=Georgics. M.=Moretum*.

Visiak, E. H. 'A Miltonian Puzzle.' *N&Q* 176 (1939), 200–1. ('Latin Poems Attributed to Milton' [2].)

Waddell, Helen, tr. 'Lament for Damon: The *Epitaphium Damonis* of Milton.' *UTQ* 16 (1946–7), 341–8. (*EpDam*, headnote, n. 1.)

Warnke, F. J. 'Marino and the English Metaphysicals.' (*Mansus* 9–16 n.)

Weismiller, Edward. 'The "Dry" and "Rugged" Verse.' See J. H. Summers above. (*Rous*, headnote.)

West, Michael. 'The *Consolatio* in Milton's Funeral Elegies' (*HLQ*, forthcoming). (*El* 2, headnote.)

West, Robert H. *Milton and the Angels*. Athens, Ga. 1955. (*Leon* 1. 1–2 n.)

Whipple, T. K. *Martial and the English Epigram*. (Epigrammata, headnote, n. 1.)

Wilkinson, L. P. *Ovid Recalled*. Cambridge, 1955. (*El* 1. 21–2 n.)

William of Malmesbury's Chronicle of the Kings of England, ed. J. A. Giles. London, 1847, 1904.

THE ITALIAN POEMS
OF JOHN MILTON

✤

Edited by the late J. E. SHAW
of the University of Toronto and revised by
A. BARTLETT GIAMATTI
of Yale University

Introduction

Milton's six poems in Italian are love poems in honour of a lady who is addressed directly in four of them (Sonn 2, 3, 5, and 6) and described in two (Sonn 2 and 4). She is presumably Italian or of Italian descent, since it is she who has caused the poet to write in Italian (*Canzone*, 14–16) and because the description in sonnet 4 presents her not as the British type with golden hair and rosy cheeks, exalted in El 1, but as a foreign type of beauty with black eyes (Sonn 4, 5–9). A better reason still is that, as Smart was the first to see, her name is Emilia.

The first two lines of the first Italian sonnet (Sonn 2) are:

> Donna Leggiadra il cui bel nome honora
> L'herbosa val di Rheno, e il nobil varco,...

translated by Smart: 'Bright lady, whose fair name honours the flowery vale of Reno and the famous ford...' The Reno is a river of the *Regione* Emilia in northern Italy, and the 'famous ford', Smart thinks, is that of the Rubicon, also in Emilia. Milton is following the practice, common in both Latin and Italian poetry, of indicating the name of a country by mentioning its rivers. He does so more than once in *Paradise Lost*. He is also following the custom of indicating a lady's name in a roundabout way meant to be understood by the reader, a common custom of Italian poets. The translation of *nobil varco*, 'famous ford', is well supported by Florio's dictionary, which Smart quotes as follows: '*nobil*—noble, famous, excellent, greatly known; *varco*—any ford, ferry, passage, or wading place over a river...' (See Smart, pp. 137–44.)

Professor Livingston's translation of the first lines of the sonnet

(*Works*, vol. I, 49) is: 'Beauteous lady, whose fair name honoreth the grassy vale and the noble gorge of the Reno...' By applying both 'grassy vale' and 'noble gorge' to the Reno alone he showed that he disagreed with Smart, and it is not clear whether he thought that the name Emilia is suggested or not, for the Reno is in Tuscany as well as in Emilia, and the word 'gorge'—which is an unusual meaning for *varco*—would apply better to the part of the river that is in Tuscany, where it flows through a narrow valley between high mountains. Only after it has entered Emilia does it widen into the beautiful valley described by Leandro Alberti. (Smart, p. 138.) It is certain that Milton intended to suggest a name to the reader of these lines, and the name Emilia is happily acceptable.

It is not impossible that Milton may have invented the lady Emilia, but it is more probable that she was a real person. The name Emilia is not an uncommon name for an Italian woman, but, on the other hand, it is not one of the commonest. He certainly intended the reader to believe that she was a real woman, with black eyes, a beautiful singing voice, and speaking more than one language: it is she who has persuaded him to write in Italian. (*Canzone*, 13-14.)

Apart from these peculiar characteristics, however, the descriptions of her in sonnets 2 and 4 are of the conventional kind belonging to the sixteenth-century Italian lyric. All her sweet ways are dignified and simple; only the worthless could fail to be enamoured by them and by her eyes, in which are the bow and arrows of Cupid and burning fire; their effect is very dangerous. The other four poems contain no description of her and in none of them is there a convincing expression of love.

This string of poems seems to be a compliment to a lady, but it is still more an essay in Italian verse, an imitation of Italian Petrarchan poets of love, whose artfulness Milton had learned to appreciate. It is introduced by the Nightingale Sonnet in English, a wistful expression of the hope that love will come to him, and will not come too late. It has not yet come. Almost desperate but not quite, for he hopes (in the last two lines) for another affair in which love will be mutual. The love that he really longed for, for himself, was of a kind that he was well able to imagine, the love of Adam for Eve in *Paradise Lost*, noble, deep and enduring, tender and delicate, and naturally sensuous besides. The fear that it might come too late is openly expressed in the Nightingale Sonnet, and the words *bis ille miser qui serus amavit* (*Epdam* 86) express the same haunting fear.

The unity of subject in these Italian poems argues that they were written within a short time of one another, all in the same period. Smart has shown that they could not have been written either after the poet's visit to Italy or during that visit. Sonnet 4 is addressed to Diodati, who died while Milton was in Italy, and the canzone *Ridonsi donne* could not have been written in Italy. They seem to have been written after most of the Elegies, as is implied by Milton's placement of them between the Nightingale Sonnet and *How soon hath time*. But it must be added that in *RES* 14 (1963), 383–6, John Carey argued persuasively that line 89 in El 6—*Te quoque pressa manent patriis meditata cicutis* (addressed as it is to Diodati) must refer to some recent versifying in Italian, presumably to the Italian sonnets, which should consequently be dated about December 1629. For the approximate dating of *How soon hath time*, see Woodhouse in *UTQ* 13, 78–83, and the references given there. The most probable period for the Italian poems is the summer of 1630.

Milton admired Ovid immensely (El 1, 21–4) and as late as the *Apology against a Pamphlet* defended both the matter and the manner of the 'smooth elegiac poets', going on to say, however, that he came to prefer Dante and Petrarch, who 'never write but honor of them to whom they devote their verse, displaying sublime and pure thoughts, without transgression.' (*Apol. Works* 3, 302–3). His experiments in Latin and Italian poetry are, as Professor Hanford says, '...essentially imitation.... The process of literary composition is with him in each case the result of a cultural enthusiasm which enables the poet to identify himself in it freely and spontaneously without having to resort to a particular model.' (Hanford, 'The Youth of Milton', p. 102). It was in this way that he imitated first the Roman elegies and then the Italian sonneteers. He shrank instinctively from open sensuality, a shrinking which was probably more 'a certain reservedness of natural disposition,' 'a certain nicenesse of nature' as he calls it in the *Apology* (*Works* 3, 304–6) than the result of 'moral discipline' and 'the noblest philosophy' as he says in the same place. It was, perhaps, this quality that earned for him the nickname 'the Lady' at Cambridge. But the kind of literature he chose to imitate took hold of him, and he found it easy to be discreetly sensual in his Latin elegies.

That he did not, in the Italian poems, choose to imitate the *Marinisti* of his own century is not surprising, for these latter poets were reacting against the manner inculcated by Bembo and Tasso, which he himself admired. They called it old-fashioned and decrepit, and they particularly disliked the poems of Della Casa, which were like a textbook for Milton. One of them, Pier Francesco Minozzi, called the followers of Della Casa *casisti* and said that they were living in a ruined *casa*. (See Croce, *Saggi sulla letteratura italiana del seicento*, Bari, 1911, p. 381). The outstanding quality of the Marinistic love-poetry is an exquisitely soft sensuality which Milton, who called a lyric in Sidney's *Arcadia* a 'vain amatorious poem' (*Eikon.* in *Works* 5, 86), did not esteem.

The accepted subject of the Italian sixteenth-century love-poetry was a devotion, described as an irresistible passion for an ideally perfect but unresponsive lady, leading upward Platonically to spiritual perfection, but struggling, often ineffectually, against the fleshly desire aroused by the Lady's beauty and charm. This is the subject of Milton's sonnets 2, 4, and 5, which are conventional. Sonnet 3 and the *canzone* are unconventional, except for the last two lines of the sonnet. Their subject is the experiment in the foreign language, the *raison d'être* of the whole series. Sonnet 6 is also unconventional except for the first and the last sentence. It is a heartily felt commendation of the poet's own character. As far as the content goes, then, only the three conventional sonnets are imitative, and only one of these three, the extremely artificial fifth sonnet, speaks of the suffering inflicted on the lover by the coldness of the lady, so common a subject of the Italian models. The paradoxical delight in suffering, another common subject, is quite absent.

The rhyme-scheme of the sonnets follows Italian, not English, models. The fashion of writing sonnets had died in England with

Shakespeare. When Milton revived it he did not adopt the departures from Italian custom made by the English sonneteers of the sixteenth century. (See Smart's admirable discussion.) The quatrains of his sonnets have only two rhymes, and in all of them the scheme is *abba*, *abba*, the favourite of Petrarch. As for the tercets, two of Milton's Italian sonnets (2 and 6) have the scheme *cde, dce*, which is used by Petrarch, but that of the other three sonnets (3, 4, 5) is *cdc, dee*. This latter is an unusual scheme in Italian verse but not unknown. Smart discovered it in the sonnets of the fourteenth-century poet Fazio degli Uberti, and noticed that it was used also by Antonio Minturno in the sixteenth century, and mentioned in his *Arte Poetica*.[1] Walter Bullock (*MLN.*, 39 (1924), 478) noted that in Volpi's *Rime di trecentisti minori* (Florence, 1907) there are two more examples by Antonio Pucci and Simone Serdini, and that in Massera's *Sonetti burleschi e realistici dei primi due secoli* (2 vols. Bari, 1920) there are many more: no less than seventy-three examples by Niccolò del Rosso and twelve by others. Another example is in the *Lirica italiana antica* of Eugenia Levi (Florence, 1908), p. 157. Still more interesting is the fact—also noted by Professor Bullock in *PMLA* 38 (1923), 741—that Benedetto Varchi used the same scheme in three of his sonnets which are found in the Venetian edition of 1555. In another edition of 1557 an example by Michele Barozio is found addressed to Varchi, and it is followed by Varchi's reply in the same rhyme-scheme. Milton knew Varchi's sonnets in the edition of 1555, which was in his possession bound up with Dante's *Convivio* and the poems of Della Casa. In a description of this volume in the *Bulletin of the New York Public Library* 66 (1962), 499–502, Maurice Kelley observes that almost all its marginalia (in the hands of three of Milton's amanuenses) are in the part containing the Varchi sonnets.

In England the scheme was used by Wyatt and Surrey, and it became

---

[1] Smart (p. 19) mentioned four sonnets by Fazio that have the scheme, but in Renier's edition of the poems (Florence, 1888) there are six sonnets by Fazio that have it as well as two more by Antonio da Ferrara and Luchino Visconti, which have it because they are in reply to two of the above-mentioned sonnets by Fazio. Smart mentions the one in reply by Antonio da Ferrara. In the same edition, p. 245, there is also an anonymous sonnet with the same scheme. In the *Rime del Signor Antonio Minturno*, Venice, 1559, pp. 12, 56, 66, 118, there are four sonnets with this scheme.

part of the English sonnet standardized by Sidney and Shakespeare. The Elizabethans liked to think of the last two verses rhyming together as a couplet with a character of its own, separate from the other verses, and they made of it an important feature of the sonnet. The Italians seem not to have had that intention; for them the rhyming together of the last two lines is only one of the possible arrangements of the tercets; the last two verses are not separate from the rest. Milton's view was the Italian. In his only English sonnet ending with two rhymed verses (Sonn 16), there is no marked pause separating them from the rest of the poem. Of his Italian sonnets that have the scheme *cdc, dee*, sonnet 3 has a pause in the sense before the last two verses like that of the Shakespearian sonnet, but 4 and 5 have no such pause.

One of the Italian poems is entitled 'Canzone', although, since it consists of only a single stanza, it would be more accurate to call it a *Stanza di Canzone*. This was a type of poem recognized as a separate kind, although it differed from the *canzone* only in having no more than one stanza. (See Casini, *Le forme metriche italiane*, Florence, 1915, 15, and Mario Pelaez in *Enciclopedia italiana*, article 'Stanza'.) Leandro Biadene, in his *Indice delle canzoni italiane del secolo xiii* (Asolo, 1886, p. 33) lists seven *cobbole* (one-stanza poems) which, as he says on p. 2, n. 1, are constructed like the stanzas of a *canzone*. Two of them are poems of Guido Cavalcante, usually called *ballate* in the printed editions, but recognized as '*stanze di canzone*' by Ercole in his edition (pp. 374 and 376). Biadene (p. 33, n. 3) agrees with Ercole. Wilkins calls this poem of Milton's a madrigal (*A History of Italian Literature*, Harvard University Press, 1954, 293, note) meaning that it belongs to a kind that 'was called at first *canzone* or *canzonetta*' (in the sixteenth century) 'but the name *madrigale* was soon applied to it though it is quite unlike the Petrarchan madrigal' (p. 179). Milton himself did not think of it as a madrigal. He not only entitled it 'Canzone', but addressed it as 'Canzon' in the *commiato* (verse 13), and Carducci in his essay on 'Luisa Grace Bartolini' (*Opere*, Ediz. Nazionale, 6, 433-4) where he reproduces the poem in full, has no fault to find with the title: he calls it 'questa breve canzone italiana'.

It was natural enough that, experimenting in Italian verse, Milton should try his hand at a *canzone*, which Dante had called the noblest form of poetry (*De Vulgari Eloquentia*, 2, 3, 9) and since Dante had also said that the whole art of the *canzone* is in the construction of the stanza (ibid. 2, 9, 2–3), it is not surprising that Milton should have been content to do his best with one.

The reform brought about by Bembo and continued by Tasso in Italian verse aimed to raise the language and style to a dignity equal with that of Latin. The vocabulary was that of Petrarch and Boccaccio; so was the syntax, but Latinized as much as possible, with a constant endeavour to avoid commonplace words and expressions. Milton, who thought of the Italian language as degenerate Latin ('Et quam degeneri novus Italus ore loquelam...Fundit' he says in *Ad Patrem*, 83–4) would sympathize. For lyric verse the supreme model was Petrarch's *Rime*, which were, Bembo says, a perfect blend of seriousness and pleasantness (*gravità e piacevolezza*). All of Petrarch's constructions were analysed and codified so as to make imitation easy, but scope for originality was left in the ordering of the words with regard to both sound and meaning, and in the versification, both of sonnet and *canzone*. Most original of all was Giovanni Della Casa (1503–56) whose devices, praised, recommended and adopted by Tasso, and illustrated in the anonymous dialogue *Il Tasso, dialogo d'incerto sopra lo stile di Monsignor Della Casa, e il modo d'imitarlo* (see Prince, pp. 18–24) were familiar to all the poets of his own time. Milton, who owned a copy of Della Casa's poems as early as 1629, and a copy of Varchi's sonnets, had access to others of the very many *canzonieri* and anthologies published in Italy again and again during the sixteenth century and welcomed in England.

The most striking features of Della Casa's verse, adopted in these Italian poems, is the disregard of the traditional separation of the different parts of the sonnet and *canzone* as regards the sense, so that the same sentence may flow freely from quatrain to quatrain, from quatrain to tercet, and from tercet to tercet. This occurs in all of our six poems except the very artificial fifth sonnet in which pauses in the sense are maintained in the traditional places. The four sentences of which the sixth sonnet is composed pay no attention to the formal divisions; indeed as far as the punctuation goes, both in the 1645 and 1673 editions, the whole sonnet is only one sentence.

Another feature, derived from Petrarch by his followers, including Della Casa, is that 'parallelism, balance, and antithesis' (Prince, p. 93) which appears in the use of couplets of substantives, with or without adjectives, and sometimes of whole sentences. Prince illustrates this feature with part of Milton's sixth sonnet, which he reproduces and translates as follows:

> Quando rugge il gran mondo e scocca il tuono,
> S'arma di sè, e d'intero diamante,
> Tanto del forse e d'invidia sicuro,
> Di timori e speranze al popol use
> Quanto d'ingegno e d'alto valor vago
> E di cetra sonora, e delle muse;

> When the great heavens roar and flies the thunder,
> (His heart) stands armed in itself and in pure diamond,
> As much secure from envy and from chance,
> From fears and hopes such as the many use,
> As it is fain of virtue and high thought
> And of the sounding lyre and of the Muse.

Each of these six lines contains two substantives balanced against each other—*mondo* and *tuono*, *sè* and *diamante*, *forse* and *invidia*, *timori* and *speranze*, *ingegno* and *valor*, *cetra* and *muse*—and the predicate adjective *sicuro* of the third line corresponds to the predicate *vago* of the fifth; but monotony is avoided by applying a qualifying adjective to only one of the two balanced substantives in each line—*gran mondo*, *intero diamante*, *speranze use*, *alto valor*, *cetra sonora*—and in the third line using no qualifying adjective at all. In his *Lezione...sopra il sonetto Questa vita mortal...di Monsignor Della Casa* (Tasso, *Opere*, Pisa, 1823, 44) Tasso blames Bembo and other Venetians for making too frequent use of balanced correspondences and antitheses, and praises Della Casa for his care to avoid the monotony they may produce.

The vocabulary is old Italian and poetical, that of the poet's models.

It contains a sprinkling of nouns with poetical meanings, such as *spera* for *climate*, *peso* for *misfortune*, *diamante* for *adamant*; adjectives such as *scarco* for *deprived of*, *vago* for *desirous*; old forms such as *volse* instead of *volle*, *dinne* for *dicci*, *dirotti* for *ti dirò*; it never descends to the level of ordinary prose.

Milton's mastery of the language is amazing! These poems were written by a college man of twenty-two who had never yet been away from his own country. All the apparent errors can be justified by examples from Italian poets or as Latinisms, except one in verse 2 of the *Canzone*, on which see the note. Wilkins (*A History of Italian Literature*, p. 293, note) says: 'these poems are quite unidiomatic, and are imperfect metrically at certain points', but he could have said this with equal truth of the sonnets by Italian followers of Bembo, Della Casa and Tasso, who write in a language that no one ever spoke, break up their verses with unconventional pauses, and disregard the divisions of the sonnet. Carducci (*Opere*, Ediz. Nazionale, 6, 433–4), after endorsing Camerini's praise of Milton's *Canzone*, adds that most of his Italian sonnets are 'hard and laboured, and sometimes defy the strictest laws of syntax.' That is an accurate judgment, but the faults mentioned are like the qualities recommended by Tasso, the qualities he admired in Della Casa. 'The style he delineates,' says Prince (p. 38), 'aims at difficulty. Sense and metre have to be preserved; but all the devices of language and versification are intended to produce a certain difficulty, even an obscurity, in the sense, and an equivalent difficulty, even a roughness, in the sound.' Referring to Della Casa's influence in a lecture in Florence ('Milton e Tasso, *Rivista di Letterature Moderne e Comparate*, XIII, 1960, 53–60), Prince regarded the use to which Milton put the sonnet as related to Della Casa's example, for there is no doubt that he knew Della Casa's work well. Tasso's adoption of Della Casa's manner in the *Sonetti Heroici* helped to determine Milton's general ideas of the heroic sonnet.

The disparaging remarks of Allodoli (*Giovanni Milton e l'Italia*, Prato, 1907, p. 57) and Guidi (*Milton*, Brescia, 1940, p. 7) cannot be valued because they give no examples of Milton's errors, but Federico Olivero, who does give examples in his *Saggi di letteratura inglese*, (Bari, 1913, pp. 7–19) and whose objection to the synaloepha in Sonnet 4, 13, between *suoi* and *avventa* is undeniably sound, misunderstands some of Milton's constructions, and has no inkling of the influence of Della Casa and his school. On the other hand Mario Praz—as excellent a judge as could possibly be desired—after mentioning the influence of Della Casa, says of these poems: 'they show a profound understanding of the Bembist manner, and only here and there betray the foreign hand.' (*Storia della letteratura inglese*, Florence, 1942, p. 160.)

These youthful essays in Italian verse are not great poetry, but whereas the second and fourth sonnets are artificially imitative, and the fifth is painfully artificial, the third and the *Canzone* are elegantly original in content, and the sixth is an expression of genuine feeling: these last-mentioned three well deserve to be called poetry.

Though it arrived too late for inclusion in all the proper places, the reader must consult the excellent work of Sergio Baldi, 'Poesie italiane di Milton,' *Studi Secenteschi* 7 (1966), 103–30. Baldi has edited the six Italian poems and has provided valuable glosses which include meanings and usages of Italian words as set out by John Florio in his *Second Frutes* (1591) and *Queen Anna's New World of Words...*(1611). The comments on dating, text, language, meter and Petrarchism which preface the poems are generally consistent with what has been said above. E. A. J. Honigmann's *Milton's Sonnets : The Texts with an Introduction and Commentary* (London and New York, 1966) may also be consulted. Though Honigmann generally follows Smart and others in his texts and brief annotations, he has an interesting discussion of the Italian sonnets in his introduction (76–81). One should also see John T. Shawcross, "Milton's Italian Poems: An Interpretation," *The University of Windsor Review*, 3 (1967), 27–33 and W. R. Parker, *Milton A Biography*, 2 Vols. (Oxford, 1968), 1, 78–81; 11, 747; 755.

Sonnet 2

The lady addressed in this sonnet has all the qualities of the convention-ally adored object of the sixteenth-century love lyric. Her noble spirit, shown generously in her gracious ways, enamors all men of worth and so does the beauty of her eyes and voice. In her eyes are the bow and arrows of Cupid, and when she sings hard trees are moved as by the lyre of Orpheus. Men who are unworthy of her are in grave danger, for the passion of their desire may become incurable. They had better not look or listen.

NOTES

1   *Donna leggiadra.* Charming lady. 'Leggiadra' is a general expression including graciousness and beauty: all the attractive qualities mentioned in the sonnet.

honora. For other Latin *h*'s see *L'herbosa* of line 2 and *l'herbetta* of Sonn 3, 3; *talhor, honesti,* and *hemispero* of Sonn 4, lines 4, 8, 11; *ad hor ad hor* of *Canzone,* 10; *humil* and *hebbi* of Sonn 6, lines 3 and 5. Other Latin forms are *Gratia* and *inanti* of Sonn 2, line 13, and *turbida* and *loco* of Sonn 5, lines 9 and 12.

3–8   Ben è colui d'gni valore scarco
     Qual tuo spirto gentil non innamora,
     Che dolcemente mostra si di fuora,
     De'suoi atti soavi giamai parco,
     E i don, che son d'amor saette er arco,
     Là onde l'alta tua virtù s'infiora.[2]

He is indeed destitute of all worth who is not enamored by thy noble spirit, which sweetly reveals itself never begrudging its gracious ways, and by the gifts which are the bow and arrows of love there where thy lofty power blooms.

The construction is: *Qual tuo spirto gentil non innamora…e i don, che…* *Spirto* is the subject of *innamora,* and *i don* is an additional subject of the same verb, even though the verb is in the singular.

Cf. Ciro di Pers, Son. *Oblia la fronte,* 9–11. (*Lirici marinisti,* ed. Croce, Bari, 1910, p. 367)

     Non può far d'aurei fregi il manto adorno,
     non le nevi mentite e gli ostri finti
     ricorrer dietro un sol passato giorno.

[2] In quotations preceding these notes, variants from the edition of 1645 are sometimes adopted. Other alterations will always be mentioned. In this quotation a comma has been placed after *fuora* of line 5, and apostrophe after *De* of line 6; an apostrophe after *don* of line 7 has been removed, and an accent has been placed on *Là* of line 8. The valuable annotations of Mr John Purves in *The Poetical Works of John Milton,* ed. by Helen Darbishire (Oxford, 1955), vol. 2, have not been neglected.

The gold-embroidered cloak cannot, nor can the painted flush and whitened flesh, cause to return again one single day.

Bart. Carlo Piccolomini, Canz. *È dunque vero*, 2, 1–6 (Giolito I, 130)

> Com'esser può che'l volto almo e sereno
> Che pur dianzi splendea più ch'altro, e i lumi
> Onde si volge e vera gloria il mondo,
>
> .   .   .   .
>
> Hor sia di nebbia indegna e d'horror pieno
> Giacendo afflitto?

How can it be that the calm and kindly face which just a while ago shone more than any other, and the lights which guide the world to true glory...be now filled with unworthy mist and gloom, lying afflicted?

For other examples see Gaspara Stampa, Son. *Io assomiglio*, 2–3 (*Lirici italiani* ecc. ed. Firmiani, Milan, 1934, p. 94) Nicolò Amanio, Son. *Già mi fu un tempo*, 1–2 (Frati, p. 94). A famous example in Latin is Horace, *C.* 1. 3, 1–5. To make *E i don* depend on *parco*, together with *De'suoi atti soavi*, as most translators have done, is inadmissible. Olivero in *Saggi di letteratura inglese* (Bari, 1913, p. 12) suggests omitting the *E* before *i don*, but that would be too drastic an emendation, changing the meaning of the whole sentence, besides being unnecessary.

3–4 *colui...Qual*—He who.

For *Qual* used as a relative pronoun without the article see Nicolò Amanio, Son. *Quelle pallide, angeliche viole*,...*Qual*...*Donast 'a me* (Frati, p. 92). Also F. M. Molza, Son. *O te, qual Dea dobbiam chiamarti homai* (Giolito, 2. 12).

5 *mostra si*—shows itself.

The separation of *mostra* and *si* is (like *scosso mi* in Son. 5. 10) probably a printer's error, although the author may be responsible. Such separations are frequent in old editions like that of Giolito, e.g. *tesser mi ti*, 2, 112. Others are *aspettar la*, *far se*, as well as *sì come*, *in darno*, *da i*, *co i*, *da gliocchi*. They make no difference to the sound or to the meaning.

6 *atti soavi*—gracious ways.

Atti means *ways*, including *looks* and *movements*. See Della Casa, Canz. *Amor i piango*, 3, 14, and *Come fuggir*, 4, 3. Petrarch, Son *Padre del ciel*, 4, *Solo e pensoso*, 7, and the comment and references of Chiòrboli.

7–8 E i don, che son d'amor saette ed arco
Là onde l'alta tua virtù s'infiora.

And the gifts (the beauty and other endowments of the lady, *i celesti e rari doni—Ch'a in se madonna*, Petrarch, Son. *Amor io fallo*, 12–13) which are the bow and arrows of Love (i.e. which enamor men) there where thy lofty virtue blooms (i.e. in her eyes, *Tanta negli occhi bei for di misura—Par che Amore e dolcezza e gracia piova*. Petrarch, Son. *Le stelle, il cielo*, 7–8).

8 *Là onde* = *Là dove*, There where.

Cf. Petrarch, Son. *Occhi piangete*, 6. Claudio Trivulzio, Son. *Dinanzi al novo Sol*, 7 (*Lirici marinisti*, ed. Croce, Bari, 1910, p. 207).

9 Quando tu vaga parli, o lieta canti.

Cf. Petrarch, Son. *In qual parte del ciel*, 13–14: *come dolce ella sospira,—E come dolce parla, e dolce ride*. Della Casa, Son. *Doglia che vaga donna*, 7: 'Colà've dolce parli, o dolce rida.'

10 *Che mover possa . . . che* = *così che*, so that.

Cf. Petrarch, Son. *La donna che il mio cor*, 10. Tasso, Canz. *Santa Pietà*, IV, 6. Milton, *L'Allegro*, 145: 'That Orpheus' self may heave his head . . .'

11–12 Guardi ciascun a gli occhi ed a gli orecchi
       L'entrata, chi di te si truova indegno;
Let each and everyone who feels himself unworthy of thee, guard the entrance to his eyes and ears.
The construction is: *Chi di te si truova indegno guardi ciascun l'entrata agli occhi ed agli orecchi*. *Chi* is an indefinite pronoun meaning *whoever*. Although singular, it conveys a plural meaning.

12 *L'entrata . . .*

Placed at the beginning of verse 12, this word completes the sentence begun in verse 11; a device practiced by Della Casa and recommended by Tasso to produce an unusual rhythm. See Prince, 27 and 21.

13–14 Gratia sola di su gli vaglia, inanti
       che'l disio amoroso al cuor s'invecchi.
May Grace from above alone avail him, before the amorous desire becomes inveterate in his heart.
Amorous desire, evoked by the lady's beauty, is at war, throughout the verse of the Petrarchists, with the spiritual love inspired by her good influence. When it becomes inveterate the former is almost unconquerable. Cf. Petrarch, Canz. *I'vo pensando*, 7, 17–18: *Un piacer per usanza in me sì forte—Ch'a pattegiar n'ardisce con la morte*. Desire so strong in me from habit that it dares to bargain even with death. Cf. also Son. *Due gran nemiche*.

Sonnet 3

The poet compares his attempt to sing in Italian verse to that of a shepherdess who is trying to grow a plant imported from a foreign and more fertile soil. Neither of the two experimenters is unskilled: she is an expert gardner (*avvezza*) and his tongue is nimble (*lingua snella*), but the task is difficult. He would not have attempted it if Love had not insisted, but who has ever been able to resist Love? He only wishes that his heart were as amenable to the commands of Heaven.

NOTES

1–5   Cf. Dante, *Convivio*, 3, 3, 4, a passage marked in Milton's copy in the New York Public Library, according to Sister Margaret Theresa in *Thought* 22 (1947), 486. See Kelley above, p. 369. See also Francesco Coppetta dei Beccuti, Son. *Porta il buon villanel*, in *Lirici italiani del cinquecento*, ed. Fimiani, Milan, 1934, 57. Smart (147) quotes PL 11, 273–9.

6–7   Così[3] Amore meco insù la lingua snella
   Desta il fior nuovo di strania favella,
So Love in me quickens upon my nimble tongue the strange flower of a foreign speech.

Florio's dictionary gives *nimble* for *snello*. Cf. Petrarch, *Trionfo della fama*, 3, 20: ...*quant'à eloquenzia e frutti e fiori*, how many fruits and flowers has eloquence; and Giovanni Canale, Son. *La tua linguia immortal*, 9: ...*nell'orar fiorita*, blooming with eloquence. *Lirici marinisti*, ed. Croce (Bari, 1910), 474.

8   *vezzosamente altera*—graciously proud.

Cf. Petrarch, Son. *Soleasi nel mio cor star bella e viva,—Come alta donna in loco umile e basso*. Alive and beautiful she used to dwell in my heart, like a noble lady in a low and humble place. Cf. Son. *Nodi ad arte negletti*, 3: *Altiera fronte umil*. Giolito, 2, p. 131,

9   *Canto*
The first word of this verse, completing the sentence begun in the previous verse, cf. note on Sonn 2, 12.

10   E'l bel Tamigi cangio col bel Arno
And exchange the fair Thames for the fair Arno.

Cf. Petrarch, Son. *Quella per cui con Sorga ò cangiato Arno,*...She for whose sake I have exchanged the Arno for the Sorgue. See the note of Smart, 147.

[3] *Così* is without an accent in the texts.

The Petrarchists often use the names of rivers for cities and countries; Milton
uses them here for languages.

11   *a l'altrui peso*—from the distress of others.

Not the same as *alle spese altrui*, at the expense of others. Cf. El 7. 27–8: *Et
miser exemplo sapuisses tutius'inquit*; = *Nunc mea quid possit dextera testis eris.*

13–14   Deh! foss'il mio cuor lento e'l duro seno
   A chi pianta dal ciel si[4] buon terreno.
'Ah! were but my slow heart and hard bosom as good a soil to Him who plants
from heaven.' Smart.

Livingston (*Works* 1, 2, 433), preferred to read *duro'l seno* instead of *'l duro
seno* and translated (1, 1, 31): 'Oh that my heart were less fertile, my breast
more stony, toward one who findeth such fecund soil for the seed she soweth
from Heaven.' Understood in this way, the poet wishes his heart were hard and
resistant to the influence of the lady; he wishes he could resist the power of love.
Livingston may have had in mind the conclusion of the preceding Sonnet 2,
which warns against the danger of an inveterate passion, and perhaps even
more the conventional repentance of the Petrarchists for a youth wasted in the
service of worldly love—the repentance of Petrarch's introductory sonnet *Voi
ch'ascoltate*. Also the poet has just said, in verses 11–12 ,that he has learned from
the sorrows of others that love is irresistible, so the results of love are admittedly
sad. There is evidently much to be said for Livingston's thoughtful interpretation which turns the poet's own lady into another expert gardener similar to the
pastorella of verse 2. On the other hand it is hard to think that the presumed
error in the text could have escaped Milton's attention; it is easier to believe
that *Chi pianta dal ciel* is God; and the conventional recognition of the
inferiority of worldly love in the last two lines is as suitable as that at the end of
Sonnet 2, without any emendation of the text.

The editors are indebted to Professor A. Bartlett Giamatti of Yale for the
following remarks on the last lines of this sonnet:

'I think, with Mr Shaw, that Smart's straightforward reading is the correct
one. However, I notice here an echo of another who was likened to good earth,
in whom greater desires might be planted. For Beatrice says of Dante:

> Ma tanto più maligno e più silvestro
> Si fa 'l terren col mal seme e non colto,
> Quant'elli ha più del buon vigor terrestro.
>
> (*Purg.* 30. 118–20)

---

[4] There is no accent on *sì* in the texts.

The more rank and wild a man's inner self, the better and richer soil he is for that inner cultivation necessary for salvation. This is the point of Dante's self-cultivation in the garden of Eden. However, what is interesting in comparing Dante's lines with Milton's—aside from the congruences in imagery and indeed the similarity in language —is that both poets see themselves as arid or ruined earth (souls) which can respond to the efforts and presences of certain ladies (Matelda and Beatrice in Dante; *l'avezza giovinetta pastorella* in Milton, v. 2). Dante knows that by bringing his inner landscape into harmony with Eden, he will achieve Heaven; Milton wishes that, as his Italian flourishes under her inspiration like a small plant in a strange country, and expresses his love—so might he prove, worthless soil that his breast is, an equally receptive garden for the love of God. Milton's last two lines are distinct, and at a higher remove, so to speak, from the first twelve; but they recapitulate the imagery of the beginning of the simile and give the poem a conventional, yet novel twist. Though the parallel between Milton and Dante may seem far-fetched, the similarities in diction, imagery, and theme strike me forcibly and illustrate certain convictions of mine regarding Dante and Milton.'

Canzone

The subject is like that of Sonn 3, the difficulty of writing Italian verse, but here it is especially the daring of the attempt. The poet is more than ever aware how daring it is when he undertakes a *stanza di canzone*, but he takes pride in it. He might have chosen a simple form of stanza, but he prefers one that is complicated. This form is not unlike that of the stanzas of Della Casa's Canz. *Amor i'piango*, which also have fifteen verses, but Milton's has an additional rhyme.

His young friends gather round him and laugh at him. They remind him that he has already earned the beginnings of fame at home and abroad in English and in Latin, the language familiar to all educated men. Why should he assume a burden too great for his shoulders by writing in a strange and unknown tongue (*lingua ignota e strana*)? The answer is that fame is not his object; his lady has told him that Italian is the language of love.

Canzone

NOTES

1   *Ridonsi donne*—Ladies laugh.

Intransitive reflexive verbs of the kind which are not real reflexives, since they use the pronoun only to intensify the meaning of the verb, are as common in old Italian verse as they are rare in the modern language: e.g. *viversi, morirsi, tacersi, cadersi, discendersi*, etc. *Osarsi* in verse 4: *Come t'osi?* is another.

2   *M'accostandosi attorno*—Gathering around me.

The position of the conjunctive personal pronoun before the present participle is surprising, for, although the Italian poets who were Milton's models felt free to place conjunctive pronouns and adverbial particles before or after any part of the verb, in practice they placed them after the present participle, except sometimes in negative phrases, such as *non mi parendo*, or *non lo vedendo*. Giovanni Florio says: 'Note withall that none of these Particles should be used before any Infinitive Mood, Gerond or Participle (an error wherein Englishmen fall very often).' (*Queen Anna's New World of Words*, etc., London, 1611, 630.) This so-called *error* occurs in Italian authors as late as the nineteenth century. See Guerrazzi, *Isabella Orsini* (Florence, 1910), chapter 3, 56: *Si accorgendo*, and 76, *le stendendo*.

5-6   Dinne, se la tua speme sia mai vana,
     E de'[5] pensieri lo miglior t'arrivi.

Tell us, so may thy hope be never vain and the best of thy wishes come true.

This form of adjuration or appeal, with *se* followed by the subjunctive, is frequent in Italian verse from the thirteenth to the sixteenth century: e.g. Dante, *Inf.* 10, 82-3; Tasso, Son. *Come ne l'ocean*, 12-14; Jacopo Marmitta, Son. *Se l'onesto desio*, in *Opere di Mons. Giovanni della Casa* (Venice, 1572, 1, 120). For bibliography of recent discussion as to the origin of this *se*—whether from Lat. *si, sic, or sit*—see *Italica*, 15 (1938), 152-5; 17 (1940), 16-17.

6   *pensieri*—wishes.

Pensieri may mean either *cure* or *speranze*—anxieties or hopes, as Leopardi says in his note on Petrarch's Son. *Quand'io mi volgo*, 2, and see Chiòrboli's note. Hope has already been expressed by *speme* in the previous line. Smart's translation, 'wishes' seems best.

[5] The apostrophe after *de* in verse 6 is omitted in the texts.

7–9   Così[6] mi van burlando, 'Altri rivi,
      Altri lidi ti aspettan ed altre onde
      Nelle cui verdi sponde.

Thus they banter me, 'Other streams, other shores await thee, and other waters upon whose green edges.

rivi means streams or rivers; *lidi* means sea-shores; *onde* and *sponde* may belong to either sea or river.

Notice the marked pause in verse 7 between 'burlando' and 'Altri', caused by the diaeresis of the syllables *do* and *Al*. This 'asprezza' as Tasso called it, was intended to provide distinction from smooth and less significant verse. See Prince, 27.

10–11   Spuntati ad hor a la tua chioma
      L'immortal guiderdon d'eterne frondi.[7]

There sprouts for thee from time to time the immortal guerdon of perennial fronds for thy hair.

The *tua* of *la tua chioma* may seem a superfluous repetition of the *ti* of *spuntati*, but the construction is not *spuntati…a la tua chioma* but *spuntati… l'immortal guiderdon d'eterne frondi a la tua chioma*.

ad hor ad hor, from time to time. See Petrarch, Son. *Quando fra l'altre*, 1, Son. *Quando'l voler*, 3, and the notes of Leopardi. Also Canz. *Ne la stagion*, 2, 11, and Canz. *Perchè la vita è breve*, 6, 1, and the notes of Chiòrboli.

Sonnet 4

A conventional announcement of a surrender to the wiles of Cupid by one who has hitherto been impervious to them. Compare the more elaborate announcement in Elegia Septima. Unconventional is the preference for the foreign beauty of the black-eyed lady over the golden-haired, rosy-cheeked British type, and the information that the lady speaks more than one language. Then, in the last two lines come a grotesque conceit.

---

[6] The accent on *Così*, the quotation mark before *Altri*, the capital A of *Altri*, and the comma after *rivi*, all in verse 1, are not in the texts.

[7] The comma after the first 'ad hor', in the editions, is evidently a mistake, and the sense requires some kind of stop after 'frondi' of line 11.

Sonnet 4

NOTES

1 Diodati, e te'l dirò con maraviglia...
Diodati—and I shall tell it thee with wonder...(Smart)

For similar parentheses see Petrarch, Son. *Ben sapev'io*, 5, and Canz. *Ben mi credea*, 5. 9.

2 *spreggiar*—to despise.

Spreggiare and *preggio*, worth (Della Casa, p. 209), unusual forms even in old Italian, got their *gg* by analogy to the many words which, in Folk Latin, had a simple intervocalic *y* sound derived from various sources. E.g. *peggiore, peggio, leggenda, legge, suggello, raggio, poggio*.

4 *Già*[8] *caddi*—Have now fallen.

5–6 Nè treccie d'oro, nè guancia vermiglia
   M'abbaglian sì.[9]
Neither golden tresses nor rosy cheeks dazzle me so.

The poet is abandoning the British type of beauty, the supremacy of which he had vaunted in *El.* 1, 51–72, for a foreign black-eyed type.

6–7 sotto nova idea
   Pellegrina bellezza.
Strange beauty copied from a rare idea.

An allusion to Plato's doctrine of *ideas*. Smart quotes from Petrarch, Son. *In qual parte*, 1–4. See also Bernardino Tomitano, *Donna del mondo*, st. 3, in Giolito, 2, 41.

In qual parte del ciel la cura eterna
   Tolse l'idea di voi, l'essempio adorno?
From what part of heaven did the Eternal Providence take the idea of you, the ornate copy?

8 *Portamenti alti honesti*—Fine manners and modest.

Cf. Sonnet 3, 8, *vezzosamente altera*—graciously proud; Petrarch, Son. *Qua donna*, 6, *giunta onestà con leggiadria*—modesty and charm combined; Agnolo Firenzuola, Canz. *Amor da cui conosco*, 3, *Dove porge onestà ciò ch'io desio...* (*Lirici italiani del cinquecento* ed. Fimiani, Milan, 1934, p. 49).

11–12 E'l cantar che di mezzo l'hemispero
   Traviar ben può la faticosa Luna.

---

[8] The accent on *Già* is omitted in the texts.
[9] The accents on *nè* are omitted in the texts.

And her singing which may well send the toiling moon astray from her path in the midst of the sky.

Smart (p. 151) mentions 'the labouring moon' of *P.L.* 2, 665 and quotes Virgil, *Ecl.* 8, 69, 'Carmina vel coelo possunt deducere Lunam.'

13–14   E degli occhi suoi avventa sì gran fuoco
          Che l'incerar gli orecchi mi fia poco.[10]

And from her eyes there darts such fierce fire that to stop my ears with wax will avail me little.

It is no use trying to defend his ears against the charm of her singing—like the sailors of Ulysses—because the fire from her eyes would melt the wax. This is a *concetto* of the kind that is frequent in the verses of Serafino Aquilana and Tebaldeo, the use of a metaphor in a material sense. Della Casa, in his sonnet *Vago augelletto*, warns his lady's pet parrot that the fire from the lady's eyes may burn its feathers, and Serafino, in his *O felice libretto*, wonders why the little book in which his lady is writing does not catch fire. Petrarch's lines (Canz. *Ben mi credea*, 7, 3–5) which may nevertheless have suggested these of Milton's, are without any such deformity:

> ...chè dovea torcer li occhi
> Dal troppo lume, e di serene al suono
> Chiuder li orecchi...

...for I ought to have turned my eyes away from the excessive light, and closed my ears against the sirens' song.

Sonnet 5

This is the only one of the six poems that deals with the suffering of the lover. None of the others would lead one to suspect that he is convulsed with sighs during the day and weeps all night regularly (*tutte le notte mie*) until dawn. But the pathetic pathological condition of the lover is such a favourite subject with the Italian sonneteers that it could hardly be omitted.

The burning light from the lady's eyes draws from his aching heart a hot and turbulent vapour which fills his breast and shakes it. Some of it

---

[10] The texts have *auventa* for *avventa*, but it must be a typographical error for, although *u* is constantly used for *v* in early Italian editions, it does not occur anywhere else in these poems. *Sì* in the same verse 13 is without accent in the texts.

escapes in sighs which freeze in the uncompromising cold of the lady's presence; and some of it finds a way to his eyes, where it condenses into tears at night until the rosy dawn brings a glimmer of hope.

Cf. Girolamo Muzio, Canz. *Donne Gentili* (Giolito, I, p. 302):

> Chiaccio di tema, e foco di desiri,
> Pioggia di pianto, e vento di sospiri.

Smart compares appropriately Petrarchan verses of Ronsard.

NOTES

1–2   Per certo i bei vostr'occhi, Donna mia,
　　　Esser non può che non sian lo mio sole,...[11]
Assuredly, my lady, your beautiful eyes can be naught else but a Sun to me.

The lady's eyes are the poet's sun in quantities of Italian poems, e.g. Petrarch, Canz. *Quando il soave*, 6, 2–3; Bembo, Son. *Se mai ti piacque*, 14; Della Casa, Son. *Già non potrete*, 6.

The inverted order of the sentence in these two verses is characteristic of the manner of Della Casa and Bembo. See Prince, 22–4. A typical example is in Niccolò Amanio's Canz. *Dunque se i miei desiri*, 20–22. (Frati, 89): *Ch'io non posso di quella—Onde mia morte viene,—Luce fugir'il foco.*

5   ...*un caldo vapor*—a hot vapor.
Cf. Petrarch, Son. *Ite caldi sospiri*, 1; *Valle che*, 5; *Al cader*, 10.

5   (*nè senti'pria*)[12]—(nor have I felt [the like] before)...

Sentences beginning with *nor* (Lat. *nec* = *and...not*) without a preceding negative, sometimes parenthetical or eliptical, are frequent in Milton's verse (e.g. *PL* 4, 224, 1014; 5, 548). They are common enough in old Italian verse too, cf. Petrarch, Son. *L'ardente modo*, 3–4, and Canz. *Sì è debile il filo*, 75–6; Della Casa, Son. *Danno* (*nè di tentarlo*), 1; Luigi Alamanni, Son. *Mentre io seguo*, 2 (Giolito, 2, 51v.); Cesare Caporali, Son. *Armata di quel fuoco*, 9 (Frati, 72).

The absence of an object for the verb is, no doubt, a Latinism.

[11] The commas after *Donna mia* and *mio sole* and the accent on *può* are not in the texts. The *fian* of the 1673 edition instead of *sian* is probably a typographical error, which, however, occurs now and then in early Italian printed editions of poems. See Blanc, *Grammatik der Italienische Sprache*, Halle, 1844, p. 387.

[12] The accent on *nè* is not in the texts, nor is the apostrophe after *senti'*. The edition of 1645 has *sentì* with an accent instead of an apostrophe.

8–10   *Parte rinchiusa...*[13]

> *...e poi n'uscendo poco...*

Part of it compressed...then a little escaping...

Cf. Michelangelo, Madr. *Come può essere*, 9–12. *Che cosa è questo, Amore,— Ch'al core entra per gli occhi—Per poco spazio dentro par che cresca?—E s'avvien che trabocchi?*—What is this, Love, that enters the heart through the eyes, and seems to swell the more the less space it finds? And what if it overflows?

10 *Scosso mi il petto*—Having shaken my breast.

For the separation of *Scosso* and *mi* see the note on Sonn 2, 5. Smart seems to find the phrase obscure and proposes to read *Sotto il mio petto* instead, but no emendation is necessary.

11 *...o s'aghiaccia, o s'ingiela*—either is chilled or freezes.

Cf. Petrarch, Canz. *Perchè la vita è breve*, 3, 4–5: *Ma la paura...che'l sangue vago per le vene agghiaccia*—But fear, which chills the blood flowing through the veins. Francesco Coccio, Son. *Veloce mio pensier*, 8, *gelata paura*. (Giolito, 1, 355.)

Sonnet 6

Dante had said that 'the magnanimous man always exalts himself in his own heart' just as 'the pusillanimous man always considers himself of less worth than he is' (*Conv.* 1, 11). Milton was not pusillanimous. He had a high opinion of himself and often praised himself in his defensive writings, never without some good reason, which Dante said was necessary to excuse self-praise. In this sonnet the artistically presumed reason is his need to ingratiate himself with the lady he loves, and the best he can say for himself is required. He is praising his character, not his talent or attainments, and no one can mistake the sincerity of his earnestness or the happiness of its expression, completely freed, in the manner of Della Casa, from the separation of quatrains and tercets. The truth of what he is saying was confirmed later when the great world did roar and the storm struck, and by the manner in which he faced rather than endured his blindness. The last two verses return gracefully to the conventional subject of the poem.

---

[13] The comma after *rinchiusa*, in the editions, is unsuitable to the sense.

NOTES

2   Poi che fuggir me stesso in dubbio sono
Since I am in doubt how to escape from myself

fuggir me stesso is taken from Petrarch, Son. *O cameretta*, 9–10. Son. *Non d'altra*, 204. See also Canz. *Di pensier in pensier*, 3, 9, *obliar me stesso*. For Petrarch it meant escape from the storm of fears and hopes, desires and disappointments, caused by his love, to the calming and ennobling influence of the virtuous Laura. Cf. Michelangelo, Madr. *Un uomo in una donna, Deh fate che a me stesso più non torni*—Pray let me never return to myself. For Milton it is a merely conventional expression meaning escape from the condition described in the preceding artificial sonnet.

For the absence of a word meaning *how*, or a preposition before *fuggir* cf. Della Casa, Son. *Le chiome d'or*, 4: *E ben avrà vigor cenere farmi*—And it may well be fierce enough to turn me to ashes. Also Son. *Già nel mio duol*, 4, and Canz. *Errai gran tempo*, 5, 16.

3   Madonna a voi del mio cuor l'humil dono
     Farò divoto;...
Lady, I will devoutly make the humble gift of my heart to you.

By this formal presentation he ensures the happiness of his heart and relieves himself of all anxiety concerning it.

4   *Farò divoto* completes the sense of the previous verse, the device noted in Sonn 2, 12, and Sonn 4, 4.

8   S'arma di sè, e d'intero diamante,[14]
It (his heart) arms itself with itself (that is with self-confidence) and complete diamant.

Livingston (*Works* I, 2, 433) prefers to read *s'arma di fe*, and translates (*Works* I, part I): 'it girdeth itself with the impenetrable adamant of self-confidence', but *sè* does not need to be altered, and *fe* might be taken to mean religious faith, which is not meant here. See Tasso, *G. L.* 7. 98: *Quei di fine arme di se stesso armato*.

For *intero diamante* cf. *Apology, Works*, 3, 313–14: 'arming in compleat diamond'.

13–14   Sol troverete in tal parte men duro
         Ove Amor mise l'insanabil ago.
Only there will you find it less hard, where Love placed his incurable sting (Smart).

[14] An accent has been put on *sè* of line 8.

men duro may be the object of *troverete*, so that a literal translation would be: 'you will find less hardness,' but the object may be an *it* which has been omitted in the Latin manner, as in Sonn 5, 5 *nè senti'pria*.

The word 'sting' as a translation for *ago* (used by a number of translators) has the advantage of representing both the pain and the instrument of the wound. *Ago* (needle) is often used for the sting of an insect. (Cf. Dante, *Purg.* 32, 133). It is used poetically for Cupid's dart (Petrocchi, *Dizionario, strale d'amore*) as in the sonnet of Tasso *Rose, che l'arte* mentioned by Keightley. See Purves in *Milton's Poetical Works*, ed. Darbishire, 2, 320.

For the adjective (*insanabil*) applied to the instrument instead of the wound cf. Alessandro Guarini (Frati, 283, 114): *L'artiglio irreparabile del tempo.*

Hanford appropriately quotes *PL* 8, 531–3:
> . . .in all enjoyments else
> Superior and unmoved, here only weak
> Against the charm of beauty's powerful glance.

(In *U. of Michigan Publications, Lang. and Lit.* 1 (1925), 121.)

Index of Names and Titles

✿

Smart, John S. *The Sonnets of Milton.* Glasgow, 1921.

Della Casa, Giovanni. *Opere italiane e latine*, vol. I. Venice, 1752.

Giolito De Ferrari, Gabriel, ed. *Rime diverse di molti eccellentiss. auttori ecc.* Libro primo Venice, 1549; Libro secondo, 1548. In one volume. Abbreviation: Giolito.

Prince, F. T. *The Italian Element in Milton's Verse.* Oxford, 1954.

Frati, L., ed. *Rime inedite del cinquecento.* Bologna, 1918.